BAR REVIEW

A Thomson Company

Upper Level Review

Table of Contents

celebrating over

30 YEARS

of preparing law students for the bar exam

BAR REVIEW

Constitutional Law

celebrating over

30YEARS

of preparing law students for the bar exam

CONSTITUTIONAL LAW

TABLE OF CONTENTS

PART ONE: POWERS OF THE FEDERAL GOVERNMENT

I. THE JUDICIAL POWER

A. ARTICLE III

The federal government is a government of limited powers, which means that for federal action to be legitimate, it must be authorized. The Constitution is the instrument that authorizes the federal government to act. Thus, whenever a question involves action by an entity of the federal government, the action will be valid only if it is authorized by the Constitution. The Constitution authorizes a federal court system in Article III, which provides that federal courts shall have judicial power over all "*cases and controversies*":

1. Arising under the Constitution, laws, or treaties of the United States;

2. Of admiralty and maritime jurisdiction;

3. In which the United States is a party;

4. Between two or more states;

5. Between a state and citizens of another state;

6. Between citizens of different states;

7. Between citizens of the same state claiming lands under grants of different states; and

8. Between a state or citizens thereof and foreign states, citizens, or subjects.

B. POWER OF JUDICIAL REVIEW

1. Review of Other Branches of Federal Government

The Constitution does not explicitly state that the Supreme Court may determine the constitutionality of acts of other branches of government. However, judicial review of other branches of the federal government was established in *Marbury v. Madison,* 5 U.S. 137 (1803) (per Marshall, C.J.); the Constitution is "law" and it is the province and duty of the judiciary to declare what the law is.

a. Separation of Powers and Finality of Court Decisions

The Constitution separates governmental powers among the branches of government. This separation of powers doctrine prohibits the legislature from interfering with the courts' final judgments.

Example: The Supreme Court inferred a limitations period under an ambiguous federal securities law. Because new Supreme Court rulings generally apply to all pending cases, the limitations period imposed by the Court resulted in the dismissal of many pending cases as time-barred. Congress amended the securities law to provide (i) a different limitations period and (ii) a special motion for reinstating the cases dismissed as time-barred by the Supreme Court's ruling. The Supreme Court held that the statute providing for the reinstatement of the dismissed cases violated the separation of powers doctrine under the Constitution. [Plaut v. Spendthrift Farm, Inc., 514 U.S. 211 (1995)]

2. Federal Review of State Acts

Federal review of state acts (executive, legislative, or judicial) was established by the Marshall Court in a series of decisions. Clear basis exists here in the Supremacy Clause of Article VI, which states that the Constitution, Laws, and Treaties of the United States take precedence over state laws and that the judges of the state courts must follow federal law, anything in the constitution or laws of any state to the contrary notwithstanding. [Fletcher v. Peck, 10 U.S. 87 (1810)]

C. FEDERAL COURTS

Only the actions of Article III courts are the subject of our outline, but you should know that there are two types of federal courts.

1. Article III Courts

Article III courts are those established by Congress pursuant to the provisions of Article III, Section 1. Although Congress has plenary power to delineate the jurisdictional limits, both original and appellate, of these courts, it is bound by the standards of judicial power set forth in Article III as to subject matter, parties, and the requirement of "case or controversy." Thus, Congress cannot require these courts to render advisory opinions or perform administrative or nonjudicial functions.

2. Article I Courts

Congress has created certain other courts, however, by way of implementing its various legislative powers; *e.g.*, United States Tax Court, courts of the District of Columbia. Judges of such Article I courts do not have life tenure or protection from salary decrease as do Article III court judges. Article I courts are sometimes vested with ***administrative as well as judicial*** functions, and the congressional power to create such "hybrid" courts has been sustained by the Supreme Court. [Glidden v. Zdanok, 370 U.S. 530 (1962)]

a. Limitation

Congress may not take cases of the type traditionally heard by Article III courts and assign jurisdiction over them to Article I courts. [Northern Pipeline Construction Co. v. Marathon Pipeline Co., 458 U.S. 50 (1982)—broad grant of jurisdiction to bankruptcy courts, including jurisdiction over contract claims, violates Article III]

D. JURISDICTION OF THE SUPREME COURT

1. Original (Trial) Jurisdiction

Under Article III, Section 2, the Supreme Court has original jurisdiction "in all cases affecting Ambassadors, other public Ministers and Consuls, and those in which a State shall be a Party." This provision is self-executing: Congress may ***neither restrict nor enlarge*** the Supreme Court's original jurisdiction, but Congress may give concurrent jurisdiction to lower federal courts and has done so regarding all cases except those between states.

2. Appellate Jurisdiction

Article III, Section 2 further provides that "in all other Cases before mentioned [*i.e.,* arising under the Constitution, Act of Congress, or treaty], the Supreme Court shall have appellate jurisdiction, both as to Law and Fact, with such Exceptions, and under such Regulations as the Congress shall make."

a.   Statutory Application of Appellate Jurisdiction

Congress has provided two methods for invoking Supreme Court appellate jurisdiction: *appeal* (where jurisdiction is mandatory), and *certiorari* (where jurisdiction is within the Court's discretion). Very few cases fall within the Court's mandatory appeal jurisdiction; thus, appellate jurisdiction is almost completely discretionary.

1)   Writ of Certiorari (Discretionary)

The Supreme Court has complete discretion to hear cases that come to it by writ of certiorari. A case will be heard if four justices agree to hear it. The following cases may be heard by certiorari:

a)   Cases from the *highest state courts* where (i) the constitutionality of a federal statute, federal treaty, or state statute is called into question; or (ii) a state statute allegedly violates federal law [28 U.S.C. §1257]; and

b)   All cases from *federal courts of appeals* [28 U.S.C. §1254].

2)   Appeal (Mandatory)

The Supreme Court must hear those few cases that come to it by appeal. Appeal is available only as to decisions made by three-judge federal district court panels that grant or deny injunctive relief. [28 U.S.C. §1253]

b.   Limitations on Statutory Regulation

Ex parte McCardle, 74 U.S. 506 (1868), has been read as giving Congress full power to regulate and limit the Supreme Court's appellate jurisdiction. However, *possible* limitations on such congressional power have been suggested:

1)   Congress may eliminate certain avenues for Supreme Court review as long as it does not eliminate all avenues. For example, in *McCardle,* two statutes had allowed the Supreme Court to grant habeas corpus to federal prisoners. The Supreme Court upheld the constitutionality of the repeal of one of the statutes because the other statute remained as an avenue for Supreme Court habeas corpus review.

2)   Although Congress may eliminate Supreme Court review of certain cases within the federal judicial power, it must permit jurisdiction to remain in *some* lower federal court.

3)   If Congress were to deny *all* Supreme Court review of an alleged violation of constitutional rights—or go even further and deny a hearing before any federal judge on such a claim—this would violate due process of law.

E.   CONSTITUTIONAL AND SELF-IMPOSED LIMITATIONS ON EXERCISE OF FEDERAL JURISDICTION—POLICY OF "STRICT NECESSITY"

Even if a federal court has jurisdiction over the subject matter of a case, it still might refuse to hear the case. Whether the court will hear the case (*i.e.,* whether the case is justiciable) depends on whether a "case or controversy" is involved, and on whether other limitations on jurisdiction are present.

1. No Advisory Opinions

The Supreme Court's interpretation of the "case and controversy" requirement in Article III bars rendition of "advisory" opinions (although not a declaratory judgment if the "controversy" is genuine). Thus, federal courts will not render decisions in *moot* cases, *collusive* suits, or cases involving challenges to governmental legislation or policy whose enforcement is neither actual nor threatened.

2. Ripeness—Immediate Threat of Harm

A plaintiff generally is not entitled to review of a state law before it is enforced (*i.e.,* may not obtain a declaratory judgment). Thus, a federal court will not hear a case unless the plaintiff has been harmed or there is an immediate threat of harm.

3. Mootness

A federal court will not hear a case that has become moot; a *real, live controversy* must exist *at all stages of review*, not merely when the complaint is filed. [*See, e.g.,* De Funis v. Odegaard, 416 U.S. 312 (1974)—dismissing as moot a white law student's challenge to state's affirmative action program, since the student, although originally passed over for minority applicants with allegedly poorer records, had been admitted to law school while litigation was pending, was about to graduate by the time the case reached the Supreme Court, and would receive the same law degree whether or not the affirmative action program was invalidated]

a. Exception—Capable of Repetition But Evading Review

Where there is a reasonable expectation that the same complaining party will be subjected to the same action again and would again be unable to resolve the issue because of the short duration of the action (*i.e.,* where the controversy is capable of repetition yet evading review), the controversy will not be deemed moot. [*See* Weinstein v. Bradford, 423 U.S. 147 (1975)]

Examples: 1) Issue concerns events of short duration (*e.g.,* pregnancy, elections, divorce actions); and

2) Defendant voluntarily stops the offending practice, but is free to resume it.

b. Class Actions

A class representative may continue to pursue a class action even though the representative's controversy has become moot, as long as the claims of others in the class are still viable. [United States Parole Commission v. Geraghty, 445 U.S. 388 (1980)]

c. Distinguish Ripeness

Ripeness and mootness are related concepts in that the court will not hear a case unless there is a live controversy. Ripeness bars consideration of claims *before* they have been developed; mootness bars their consideration *after* they have been resolved.

4. Standing

The Supreme Court will not decide a constitutional challenge to a government action unless the person who is challenging the government action has "standing" to raise the constitutional issue. A person has standing only if she can demonstrate a concrete stake in the outcome of the controversy.

a. Components

A plaintiff will be able to show a sufficient stake in the controversy only if she can show an *injury in fact*—caused by the government—that will be *remedied* by a decision in her favor (*i.e.,* causation and redressability).

1) Injury

To have standing, a person must be able to assert that she is injured by a government action or that the government has made a clear threat to cause injury to her if she fails to comply with a government law, regulation, or order. Some *specific injury* must be alleged, and it *must be more* than the merely theoretical injury that all persons suffer by seeing their government engage in unconstitutional actions.

Example: A Communist Party member would have standing to challenge a statute making it a crime to be a member of the Communist Party because the member's freedom of association is directly infringed, but a non-Party member would have no standing.

a) Injury Need Not Be Economic

The injury does not always have to be economic. In some cases the Court has found that an individual is harmed because the alleged illegal act or unconstitutional action has an impact on the person's well-being.

Example: Law students were allowed to challenge Interstate Commerce Commission rate-setting policy on the ground that such policies discouraged recycling and thereby diminished the quality of each student's physical environment. If the ICC rate-setting policy violated congressional statutes, the elimination of those rate-setting policies would have an impact on the students' physical environment. [United States v. SCRAP, 412 U.S. 669 (1973)]

2) Causation

There must be a causal connection between the injury and the conduct complained of—*i.e.,* the injury must be traceable to the challenged conduct of the defendant and not be attributable to some independent third party not before the court.

Example: Plaintiffs claiming that a municipality's zoning policies prevented low income persons from finding housing in the municipality were denied standing because they failed to show a substantial probability that they would be able to afford housing in the municipality even absent the zoning policies. [Warth v. Seldin, 422 U.S. 490 (1975)]

3) Redressability

In determining whether a litigant has a sufficient injury to establish standing, courts ask whether a ruling favorable to the litigant would eliminate the harm to him. If a court order declaring a government action to be illegal or unconstitutional (and ending that government action) would not eliminate the harm to the litigant, then that individual does not have the type of specific injury that would grant him standing to challenge the government action.

Examples: 1) The Supreme Court held that mothers do not have standing to challenge the government's refusal to enforce criminal laws that would require the fathers of their children to pay child support. The enforcement of the criminal laws against a father who is guilty of nonsupport would not necessarily result in the father's providing support to the mothers and their children.

2) Indigents have no standing to challenge an Internal Revenue Service policy that allows hospitals to receive favorable tax treatment even though they refuse to provide free or subsidized care for indigents. The indigents could not demonstrate that a different IRS policy would cause hospitals to provide them with free care.

b.   Common Standing Issues

1)   Congressional Conferral of Standing
Congress has no power to eliminate the case or controversy requirement, because the requirement is based in the Constitution. [*See* United Food & Commercial Workers Union Local 751 v. Brown Group, Inc., 517 U.S. 544 (1996)]

Example: Congress passes a law prohibiting kite flying on Sundays. The law provides that *anyone* who disagrees with it may challenge the law in the Federal District Court for the District of Columbia. This jurisdictional grant violates the case or controversy requirement since it purports to grant standing to persons who have not suffered an "injury in fact." Of course, one arrested for flying a kite on Sundays would have standing.

Compare: Congress passes a law requiring political committees to disclose to voters certain information and providing that *anyone* who believes the law has been violated may file a complaint with the Federal Election Commission ("FEC"). The law further provides that any complainant aggrieved by the FEC's dismissal of such a complaint may seek judicial review in district court. This statute is sufficient to give any voter standing. *Rationale:* Although the injury from a failure to disclose is widely shared, it is sufficiently concrete—the law gives voters a right to information, and any voter denied such information has suffered an injury. [Federal Election Commission v. Akins, 524 U.S. 11 (1998)]

2)   Standing to Enforce Government Statutes—Zone of Interests
In some instances a plaintiff may bring suit to force government actors to conform their conduct to the requirements of a specific federal statute. Even in such cases, the person must have an "injury in fact." Often, the Court asks whether the injury caused to the individual or group seeking to enforce the federal statute is within the "zone of interests" that Congress meant to protect with the statute. If Congress intended the statute to protect such persons, and intended to allow private persons to bring federal court actions to enforce the statute, the courts are likely to be lenient in granting standing to those persons.

Example: Persons who sold data processing services to private businesses had standing to challenge a ruling by the Comptroller of Currency that allowed national banks to make data processing services available to other banks and bank customers. These plaintiffs had an injury in fact because the Comptroller's ruling would hurt their future profits. The plaintiffs were determined to be within the "zone of interests" protected by the federal statutes limiting the authority of the Comptroller and national banks.

3)   Standing to Assert Rights of Others

To have standing, the claimant must have suffered or may presently suffer a direct impairment of his *own* constitutional rights. A plaintiff may, however, *assert third-party rights* where he himself has suffered injury and:

a)   *Third parties find it difficult to assert their own rights* (the NAACP was permitted to assert the freedom of association rights of its members in attacking a state law requiring disclosure of membership lists because its members could not file suit without disclosing their identities) [NAACP v. Alabama, 357 U.S. 449 (1958)]; or

b)   *The injury suffered by the plaintiff adversely affects his relationship with third parties*, resulting in an indirect violation of their rights (a vendor of beer was granted standing to assert the constitutional rights of males under 21 in attacking a state law prohibiting sale of beer to them but not to females under 21) [Craig v. Boren, 429 U.S. 190 (1976)].

4)   Standing of Organizations

An organization (unincorporated association, corporation, union, etc.) has standing to challenge government action that causes injury to *the organization itself*. An organization also has standing to challenge government actions that cause an injury in fact to *its members if* the organization can demonstrate the following three facts:

(i)   There must be an injury in fact to the members of the organization that would give individual members a right to sue on their own behalf;

(ii)   The injury to the members must be related to the organization's purpose; *and*

(iii) Neither the nature of the claim nor the relief requested requires participation of the individual members in the lawsuit.

Example: The All Dentist Association ("ADA") is composed entirely of dentists; its purpose is to promote the professional well-being of dentists. Assume that most ADA members make between $100,000 and $200,000 per year. The ADA would not have standing to challenge a change in the federal income tax rates that will disadvantage all persons making between $100,000 and $200,000 on the basis that the statute deprives all persons (in the income category) of property without due process, because that claim is not related to the organization's purpose—the representation of dentists as such. But the ADA probably could bring a lawsuit challenging a state regulation of dental practices if the regulation injures ADA members, as long as the injury to ADA members does not vary.

Note: Only the first prong of the above three-part test is constitutionally required. Thus, Congress can adopt a statute giving organizations standing even though the nature of the claim asserted or the relief sought would require participation of the individual members in the lawsuit. [United Food & Commercial Workers Union Local 751 v. Brown Group, Inc., *supra*]

5) No Citizenship Standing

As stated above, if an injury is too generalized, there can be no standing. Thus, people have no standing merely "as citizens" to claim that government action violates federal law or the Constitution. Congress cannot change this rule by adopting a statute that would allow persons to have standing merely as citizens (where they otherwise have no direct, personal claim) to bring suit to force the government to observe the Constitution or federal laws. [Lujan v. Defenders of Wildlife, 504 U.S. 555 (1992)]

6) Taxpayer Standing

a) Generally No Standing to Litigate Government Expenditures

A taxpayer, of course, has standing to litigate her tax bill (*e.g.,* whether she really owes X dollars). However, people generally do not have standing as taxpayers to challenge the way tax dollars are spent by the state or federal government, because their interest is too remote.

b) Exception—Measures Under Taxing and Spending Power that Violate Establishment Clause

There is an exception to the general rule: A federal taxpayer has standing to challenge federal appropriation and spending measures if she can establish that the challenged measure:

(i) Was enacted under Congress's taxing and spending power (*see* II.A.2., 3., *infra*); and

(ii) Exceeds some specific limitation on the power.

To date, the only limit that the Supreme Court has found on the taxing power is the Establishment Clause. (*See* XXII.D., *infra.*)

Note: The measure challenged must arise under the taxing and spending power. Thus, there was no standing to challenge a federal government transfer of surplus property under the Property Clause that allegedly violated the Establishment Clause. [Valley Forge Christian College v. Americans United for Separation of Church and State, 454 U.S. 464 (1982)]

7) Legislators' Standing

Legislators may have standing to challenge the constitutionality of government action if they have a sufficient "personal stake" in the dispute and suffer sufficient "concrete injury." [Raines v. Byrd, 521 U.S. 811 (1997)]

Example: A state's lieutenant governor cast the deciding vote to break a tie in the state senate. Legislators who had voted against the prevailing position had standing to challenge the right of the lieutenant governor to vote because his vote completely nullified theirs and caused the specific legislative enactment to go into effect. [Coleman v. Miller, 307 U.S. 433 (1939)]

Compare: Members of Congress had *no* standing to challenge the Line Item Veto Act authorizing the President to cancel (veto) certain spending and tax law measures that are part of a bill that he signs into law. *Rationale:* Rather than causing a "personal" and "concrete" injury, the challenged statute caused only a type of "institutional" injury to all members of Congress equally. [Raines v. Byrd, *supra*]

5. Adequate and Independent State Grounds

The Supreme Court will hear a case from a state court only if the state court judgment turned on federal grounds. The Court will refuse jurisdiction if it finds *adequate and independent* nonfederal grounds to support the state decision.

a. "Adequate"

The nonfederal grounds must be "adequate" in that they are fully dispositive of the case, so that even if the federal grounds are wrongly decided, it would not affect the outcome of the case. Where that is the case, the Supreme Court's review of the federal law grounds for the state court's decision would have no effect on the judgment rendered by the state court, so that the Supreme Court, in effect, would be rendering an advisory opinion.

b. "Independent"

The nonfederal grounds must also be "independent": If the state court's interpretation of its state provision was based on federal case law interpreting an identical federal provision, the state law grounds for the decision are not independent.

c. Where Basis Is Unclear

If it is unclear whether the state court decision turned on federal or state law, the Supreme Court may dismiss the case or remand it to the state court for clarification. However, the Court will usually assume that there is no adequate state ground unless the state court expressly stated that its decision rests on state law. [*See* Michigan v. Long, 463 U.S. 1032 (1983)]

6. Abstention

a. Unsettled State Law

When a federal constitutional claim is premised on an *unsettled question of state law*, the federal court should stay its hand ("abstain" temporarily), so as to give state courts a chance to settle the underlying state law question and thus potentially avoid the needless resolution of a federal constitutional issue. [Railroad Commission of Texas v. Pullman, 312 U.S. 496 (1941)]

b. Pending State Proceedings
Generally, federal courts will *not enjoin pending state criminal proceedings*. [Younger v. Harris, 401 U.S. 37 (1971)]

1) Pending
State court proceedings are pending if begun before the federal court begins proceedings on the merits. Hence, order of filing charges is irrelevant. "Proceedings of substance" must occur first in federal court before an injunction will issue. [Hicks v. Miranda, 422 U.S. 332 (1975)]

2) Civil and Administrative Proceedings
Federal courts should abstain from enjoining pending state administrative or civil proceedings when those proceedings involve an important state interest.

Examples: 1) A federal court should not enjoin a pending state civil action to remove a child from the child's parents due to alleged child abuse.

         2) A federal court should not enjoin: (i) a state court order holding a person or corporation in contempt for failing to pay a civil judgment; or (ii) a state court judgment that permits a plaintiff to execute a lien against a defendant's property. [Judice v. Vail, 430 U.S. 327 (1977); Pennzoil Co. v. Texaco, Inc., 481 U.S. 1 (1987)]

3) Exception
An order enjoining state proceedings will be issued in cases of *proven harassment* or *prosecutions taken in bad faith* (without hope of a valid conviction).

7. Political Questions
The Court will not decide political questions.

a. Definition
Political questions are:

(i)   Those issues committed by the Constitution to another branch of government; or

(ii)   Those inherently incapable of resolution and enforcement by the judicial process.

Examples: Political questions include:

         1) What constitutes a "republican form of government" guaranteed to the states by Article IV, Section 4 [Pacific States Telephone & Telegraph Co. v. Oregon, 223 U.S. 118 (1912)];

         2) Questions regarding the conduct of foreign relations; or issues as to when hostilities have stopped;

         3) Questions relating to which group of delegates should be seated at the Democratic National Convention [O'Brien v. Brown, 409 U.S. 1 (1972)]; and

4) The procedures used by the Senate to "try" impeachments. Thus, the Court refused to rule on the constitutionality of the Senate's delegation of the duty to take evidence and testimony to a committee of senators prior to the Senate deciding whether to vote for conviction on an impeachment of a federal judge [Nixon v. United States, 506 U.S. 224 (1993)].

b. **Compare—"Nonpolitical Controversies"**

1) **Legislative Apportionment**
Legislative apportionment was considered to be "political" until *Baker v. Carr,* 369 U.S. 186 (1962). The numerous court decisions requiring "one person-one vote" make clear that this is no longer true. [Reynolds v. Sims, 377 U.S. 533 (1964)]

2) **Congressional Membership**
The Constitution prescribes the minimum requirements of membership in both houses and further provides that each house shall be the judge of election returns and the qualifications of its members. Generally, the question of which of two candidates is entitled to be seated in the Senate is political. But an *arbitrary exclusion of a delegate is reviewable.* [Powell v. McCormack, 395 U.S. 486 (1969)]

3) **Presidential Papers and Communications**
These are generally considered to be privileged and protected against disclosure in the exercise of the executive power. But where these documents are necessary to the continuation of criminal proceedings, the question of production is *justiciable and not political.* [United States v. Nixon, 418 U.S. 683 (1974)]

4) **"Origination Clause" Cases**
The "Origination Clause" [Art. 1, §7] provides that bills for raising revenue must originate in the House of Representatives. The determination of whether a federal statute is one for raising revenue (as opposed to a statute with an incidental effect of producing such income, which may originate in the Senate) is *not* a political question. [United States v. Munoz-Flores, 495 U.S. 385 (1990)—federal statute requiring monetary assessment to be imposed on persons convicted of some federal misdemeanors is not a revenue measure]

8. **Eleventh Amendment Limits on Federal Courts**
The Eleventh Amendment is a jurisdictional bar that modifies the judicial power by prohibiting a federal court from hearing a private party's or foreign government's claims against a state government. [*See* Hans v. Louisiana, 134 U.S. 1 (1890)]

a. **What Is Barred?**
The Eleventh Amendment's jurisdictional bar extends to the following:

1) Actions against state governments *for damages*;

2) Actions against state governments for injunctive or declaratory relief *where the state is named as a party*;

3) Actions against state government officers where the effect of the suit will be that *retroactive damages* will be paid from the state treasury or where the action is the functional equivalent of a *quiet title action* that would divest the state of ownership of land; and

4) Actions against state government officers *for violating state law*.

b. What Is Not Barred?

1) Actions Against Local Governments
The Eleventh Amendment protects only state governments. Local governments (*e.g.,* cities or counties) are not protected.

2) Actions by the United States Government or Other State Governments
Actions by the United States Government or other state governments are not barred.

Note: Native American tribes are treated as other private parties, and so they are barred from bringing an action against a state government in federal court. [Blatchford v. Native Village of Noatak, 501 U.S. 775 (1991)]

3) Actions in State Courts
The Eleventh Amendment applies to federal court suits only. Hence, a California resident could sue Nevada in California state court. [Nevada v. Hall, 440 U.S. 410 (1979)]

c. Exceptions to Eleventh Amendment

1) Certain Actions Against State Officers
The Supreme Court allows the following actions to be brought against *state officials* despite the Eleventh Amendment:

a) Actions Against State Officers for Injunctions
A federal court may enjoin a state officer to refrain from future actions that violate federal law or to take prospective actions to comply with constitutional mandates. [*Ex parte* Young, 209 U.S. 123 (1908)]

b) Actions Against State Officers for Monetary Damages from Officer
A federal court may hear an action for damages against a state officer for violations of *federal law if* the monetary damages are to be paid out of the officer's own pocket. *Rationale:* By acting outside the scope of federal law, the officer is stripped of his representative capacity—the action is not one against a state, but rather is against an individual.

c) Actions Against State Officers for Prospective Payments from State
A federal court may hear an action for damages against a state officer where the effect of the action will be to force the state to pay money in the future to comply with the court order. [*Ex parte* Young, *supra*] However, federal court jurisdiction is barred if the action will result in retroactive damages to be paid from the state treasury. [Edelman v. Jordan, 415 U.S. 651 (1984)]

Example: P sues the State Commissioner of the Department of Public Welfare for failing to comply with federal welfare regulations. The federal court can order future compliance with the federal regulations, even if this will result in costing the state a large amount of money in the future. However, the federal court cannot award back payments of amounts previously improperly withheld, because the order would require payment from the state treasury for retroactive relief. [Edelman v. Jordan, *supra*]

2)   State Consents

A state may consent to suit in federal court. However, no consent will be found unless the state clearly waives its Eleventh Amendment immunity. A state may only waive its Eleventh Amendment immunity *expressly and unequivocally* (or by voluntarily invoking a federal court's jurisdiction). A state will *not* be held to have impliedly or constructively waived its immunity simply because Congress provides that a state will be subject to private suit if it engages in certain federally regulated conduct (such as infringing a federally granted patent) and the state voluntarily elects to engage in that conduct. [College Savings Bank v. Florida Prepaid Postsecondary Education Expense Board, 527 U.S. 666 (1999), *overruling* Parden v. Terminal Railway, 377 U.S. 184 (1964)]

3)   Congressional Removal of Immunity Under the Fourteenth Amendment

Congress can remove the states' Eleventh Amendment immunity under its power to *prevent discrimination under the Fourteenth Amendment.* For example, the Equal Pay Act—based on the Fourteenth Amendment—can serve as a basis for federal suits against a state by its employees. [Fitzpatrick v. Bitzer, 427 U.S. 445 (1976)]

a)   Compare—Article I Powers

Unlike its power under the Fourteenth Amendment, Congress's legislative powers under Article I (*see* II., *infra*) do *not* include the power to abrogate state immunity under the Eleventh Amendment. [Seminole Tribe of Florida v. Florida, 517 U.S. 114 (1996), *overruling* Pennsylvania v. Union Gas Co., 491 U.S. 1 (1989)—Congress has no power to abrogate state immunity under the Commerce Clause; Florida Prepaid Postsecondary Education Expense Board v. College Savings Bank, 527 U.S. 627 (1999)—Congress has no power to abrogate state immunity under the Patent Clause]

d.   Summary

For most bar exam questions, a key principle to remember is this: The Eleventh Amendment will prohibit a federal court from hearing a claim for damages against a state government (although not against state officers) unless:

1)   The state has consented to allow the lawsuit in federal court;

2)   The plaintiff is the United States or another state; or

3)   Congress has clearly granted federal courts the authority to hear a specific type of damage action under the Fourteenth Amendment (*e.g.*, under a civil rights statute).

e. **Federal Causes of Action in State Court**
Under its legislative power, Congress has attempted to create a private cause of action against states in their own courts (specifically, an action for damages for violating overtime provisions under the federal Fair Labor Standards Act). Such suits violate principles of sovereign immunity unless the state consents to the suit. [Alden v. Maine, 527 U.S. 706 (1999)]

II. LEGISLATIVE POWER

A. **ENUMERATED AND IMPLIED POWERS**
The Constitution grants Congress a number of specific powers, many of which are enumerated in Article I, Section 8. It also grants Congress auxiliary power under the Necessary and Proper Clause.

1. **Necessary and Proper "Power"**
The Necessary and Proper Clause grants Congress the power to make all laws necessary and proper (*i.e.,* appropriate) for carrying into execution *any* power granted to *any* branch of the federal government.
Example: Congress has the power to charter banks since that power is appropriate to executing Congress's enumerated powers to tax, borrow money, regulate commerce, etc. [McCulloch v. Maryland, 17 U.S. 316 (1819)]

Note: The Necessary and Proper Clause is not itself a basis of power; it merely gives Congress power to execute specifically granted powers. Thus, if a bar exam question asks what is the best source of power for a particular act of Congress, the answer should not be the Necessary and Proper Clause, standing alone.

a. **Limitation**
Congress cannot adopt a law that is expressly prohibited by another provision of the Constitution.

2. **Taxing Power**
Congress has the power to lay and collect taxes, imposts, and excises, but they must be uniform throughout the United States. [Art. I, §8] Capitation or other direct taxes must be laid in proportion to the census [Art. I, §9, cl. 4], and direct taxes must be apportioned among the states [Art. I, §2, cl. 3].

a. **Uniformity**
Requirement of uniformity in the levy of indirect taxes (generally, this means any kind of "privilege" tax, including duties and excises) has been interpreted by the Court to mean *geographical uniformity* only—*i.e.,* identical taxation of the taxed Article in every state where it is found. [Fernandez v. Wiener, 326 U.S. 340 (1945)]

b. **Direct Taxes—Must Be Apportioned**
A "direct" tax (imposed directly on property or on the person) has seldom been employed by Congress because of the cumbersome *apportionment requirement*; taxes on income from real or personal property were initially held "direct" by the Court, but the

resulting need for apportioning such taxes was obviated by the Sixteenth Amendment (income tax amendment).

c. Export Taxes Not Permitted
Neither Congress nor the state can tax exports to foreign countries.

d. Taxes Are Generally Valid
Absent a specific restriction such as those above, be very hesitant to rule against a tax measure on the exam. A tax measure will be upheld if it bears some *reasonable relationship to revenue production* or if Congress has the *power to regulate* the taxed activity.
Example: Special excise tax levied on dealers in illegal narcotics is valid because it raises revenue. [United States v. Doremus, 249 U.S. 86 (1919)]

3. Spending Power
Congress may spend to "provide for the common defense and general welfare." [Art. I, §8] This spending may be for *any public purpose*—not merely the accomplishment of other enumerated powers. However, nonspending regulations are not authorized. Remember that the Bill of Rights still applies to this power; *i.e.,* the federal government could not condition welfare payments on an agreement not to criticize government policies.

a. Regulation Through Spending
Note that Congress can use its spending power to "regulate" areas, even where it otherwise has no power to regulate the area, by requiring entities that accept government money to act in a certain manner (*i.e.,* attaching "strings" to government grants). (*See* VI.A.2.b., *infra*.)

4. Commerce Power
Article I, Section 8, Clause 3 empowers Congress to "regulate commerce with foreign nations and among the several states, and with the Indian tribes."

a. Definition of Commerce

1) Includes Basically All Activity Affecting Two or More States
Chief Justice Marshall in *Gibbons v. Ogden*, 22 U.S. 1 (1824), defined commerce as "every species of commercial intercourse . . . which concerns more states than one" and included within the concept virtually every form of activity involving or affecting two or more states.

2) Includes Transportation or Traffic
The Court has consistently regarded transportation or traffic as commerce whether or not a commercial activity is involved.
Example: Interstate transportation of liquor for personal consumption, women for immoral purposes (not necessarily prostitution), and interstate transportation of stolen motor vehicles are all interstate commerce.

a) Vehicular Transportation Not Required
Any *transmission across state lines*, such as electricity, gas, telegraph,

telephone, TV, radio, and mail transmission (including educational materials and sale of insurance), will constitute interstate commerce.

b. **"Substantial Economic Effect"**

The Supreme Court has sustained congressional power to regulate any activity, local or interstate, that either in itself *or in combination with other activities* has a *"substantial economic effect upon,"* or *"effect on movement in,"* interstate commerce.

Example: The classic case is the Court's holding that Congress can control a farmer's *production* of wheat *for home consumption.* [Wickard v. Filburn, 317 U.S. 111 (1942)] *Rationale:* Cumulative effect of many instances of such production could be felt on the supply and demand of the interstate commodity market.

1) **Power Not Unlimited**

The Supreme Court has recently made clear that the power of Congress to regulate commerce, although very broad, does have limits so as not to obliterate the distinction between what is national and what is local. To be within Congress's power under the Commerce Clause, a federal law must either:

(i) *Regulate the channels* of interstate commerce;

(ii) *Regulate the instrumentalities* of interstate commerce and persons and things in interstate commerce; or

(iii) *Regulate activities that have a substantial effect* on interstate commerce.

If Congress attempts to regulate noneconomic (*i.e.,* noncommercial) *intrastate* activity, the federal government must prove to the Court that the activity in fact *affects interstate* commerce. It is unlikely that the Court will allow Congress to use its commerce power to regulate a noneconomic activity occurring in a single state, particularly if the activity has historically been regulated by local law. [*See* United States v. Lopez, 514 U.S. 549 (1995)—federal statute barring possession of a gun in a school zone is invalid; United States v. Morrison, 529 U.S. 598 (2000)—federal civil remedy for victims of gender-motivated violence is invalid]

5. **War and Related Powers**

Article I, Section 8 gives Congress the power to declare war, raise and support armies, provide for and maintain a navy, make rules for the government and regulation of the armed forces, and organize, arm, discipline, and call up the militia. Of course, several other congressional powers may have direct or indirect application to military purposes: tax and spending power, commerce power, Senate's treaty consent power, maritime power, investigatory power, etc.

a. **Economic Regulation**

1) **During War**

Regulatory power of Congress, especially in economic matters and mobilization of troops, in support of war effort is *pervasive* (although theoretically limited by the Bill of Rights); thus, the Court has sustained national price and rent control, as well as conscription and regulation of civilian/military production and services.

2) Postwar

To a considerable extent, this pervasive regulatory power may be validly extended into post-wartime periods both to *remedy wartime disruptions* [*e.g.,* Woods v. Miller, 333 U.S. 138 (1948)—rent controls] and to cope with *"cold war" exigencies*. Legislation in the field of veterans' rights and limitations thereon may be extended indefinitely as long as veterans or their relatives may survive.

b.   Military Courts and Tribunals

The constitutional basis of courts of military justice (trial and review of offenses by military personnel, including courts-martial and reviewing agencies and tribunals) is not Article III, but rather Article I, Section 8, Clause 14 (congressional power to make rules for government and regulation of armed forces), buttressed by the Necessary and Proper Clause.

1)   Judicial Review

The regular federal (or state) courts have *no general power of review* over court-martial proceedings. However, in habeas corpus cases, the Article III courts, including the Supreme Court, may make a limited inquiry into the military court's jurisdiction of the person and offense or the validity of the court's legislative creation.

2)   Court-Martial of Enemy Civilians and Soldiers Permitted

Military courts may try enemy civilians as well as enemy military personnel, at least during wartime, with only the basic jurisdictional review by the Article III courts.

3)   Court-Martial of American Soldiers Permitted

Military courts have jurisdiction over *all* offenses (not just service connected offenses) committed by persons who are members of the armed services both when charged and at the time of the offense. [Solorio v. United States, 483 U.S. 435 (1987), *overruling* O'Callahan v. Parker, 395 U.S. 258 (1969)]

4)   Court-Martial of American Civilians Generally Prohibited

The Supreme Court has denied Congress the power to authorize the court-martial trial of American civilians as long as actual warfare has not forced courts to shut down, even though martial law has been declared [*Ex parte* Milligan, 71 U.S. 2 (1866)]; even though the civilians accused may have been members of the armed forces when committing the alleged offense [Toth v. Quarles, 350 U.S. 11 (1955)] or are dependents of military personnel accompanying the latter overseas [Reid v. Covert, 354 U.S. 1 (1957)] or are civilian employees of the military forces at overseas bases and installations; such trials by court-martial violate the Fifth and Sixth Amendments, particularly the right to trial by jury.

c.   Curfew and Exclusion of Civilians from Sensitive Areas

Both of these powers have been upheld (as jointly exercised by Congress and the President) as implied war powers during World War II, even as to exclusion and confinement elsewhere of United States citizens (of Japanese ancestry). [Korematsu v. United States, 319 U.S. 432 (1944)] However, to avoid violation of due process under the Fifth Amendment, the area of exclusion must be very sensitive militarily; *i.e.,* there must be a reasonable belief that the excluded persons, if allowed to remain, would pose a high risk of assistance to the enemy (by way of invasion, sabotage, or espionage).

d. Calling Forth the Militia

By statute, Congress has authorized the President to order members of National Guard units into federal service in circumstances that do not involve a national emergency (*e.g.,* for training outside of the United States). This statute is constitutional under the Militia Clauses [Art. I, §8, cl. 15, 16], and the President need not obtain the consent of the governor of a unit's home state to call it into such service. [Perpich v. Department of Defense, 496 U.S. 334 (1990)]

6. Investigatory Power

The power to investigate to secure information as a basis for potential legislation or other official action (such as impeachment or trying impeachments) is a well-established implied power. It is a *very broad power*, in that an investigation need not be directed toward enactment of particular legislation, but the following limitations on its use do exist.

a. Authorized Investigation

The investigatory inquiry must be expressly or impliedly authorized by the congressional house concerned, *i.e.,* by statute or resolution creating or directing the investigating committee or subcommittee.

b. Witnesses' Rights

1) Fifth Amendment

The privilege against compulsory self-incrimination (the Fifth Amendment) is available to witnesses, whether formal or informal, unless a statutory immunity coextensive with the constitutional immunity is granted.

2) Relevance

Written or oral information elicited by the investigative body must be "pertinent" to the subject of the inquiry.

3) Procedural Due Process

Witnesses are generally entitled to procedural due process, such as presence of counsel and right of cross-examination; but it is not yet clear whether such rights are constitutionally required or whether some of them are required merely by house rule or statute.

c. Enforcement of Investigatory Powers

Congress can hold a subpoenaed witness in contempt for refusing to appear or answer before Congress.

7. Property Power

Congress has the power to "dispose of and make all needful rules and regulations respecting the territory or other property belonging to the United States." [Art. IV, §3] Many other congressional powers (war, commerce, postal, fiscal, etc.) obviously would be unworkable if the ancillary *power to acquire and dispose of property of all kinds*—real, personal, and intangible—were not also implied from the main grants.

Example: The Property Clause empowers Congress to even protect wildlife wandering onto federally owned lands. [Kleppe v. New Mexico, 426 U.S. 529 (1976)]

a. **No Limits on Disposition of Property**

There is no express limitation on Congress's power to dispose of property owned by the United States. The power extends to all species of property, such as leasehold interests and electrical energy, as well as ordinary realty and personalty. Moreover, disposal may involve direct competition with private enterprise and has never been invalidated on that ground.

b. **Eminent Domain**

Acquisition of property for a public purpose by eminent domain is indirectly recognized by the Fifth Amendment: ". . . nor shall private property be taken for public use, without just compensation." Federal taking must be for the purpose of *effectuating an enumerated power* under some other provision of the Constitution.

8. **No Federal Police Power**

Congress has no general police power (*i.e.,* power to legislate for the health, welfare, morals, etc., of the citizens). Thus, on the bar exam the validity of a federal statute cannot rely on "the police power." However, Congress can exercise police power-type powers as to the District of Columbia pursuant to its power to legislate over the capitol [Art. I, §8, cl. 17] and over all United States possessions (*e.g.,* territories, military bases, Indian reservations) pursuant to the property power.

9. **Bankruptcy Power**

Article I, Section 8, Clause 4 empowers Congress "to establish uniform laws on the subject of bankruptcies throughout the United States." This power has been interpreted by the Supreme Court as nonexclusive; *i.e.,* state legislation in the field is superseded only to the extent that it conflicts with federal legislation therein.

10. **Postal Power**

Article I, Section 8, Clause 7 empowers Congress "to establish post offices and post roads."

a. **Exclusive**

The postal power has been interpreted as granting Congress a postal monopoly. Neither private business nor the states may compete with the Federal Postal Service absent Congress's consent. [Air Courier Conference of America v. American Postal Workers Union, 498 U.S. 517 (1991)]

b. **Scope of Power**

Congress may validly classify and place *reasonable restrictions* on use of the mails, *but may not deprive* any citizen or group of citizens of the general mail "privilege" or regulate the mail in such a way as to abridge freedom of speech or press (except under valid standards, such as "obscenity") or violate the ban of the Fourth Amendment against unreasonable search and seizure.

11. **Power Over Citizenship**

Article I, Section 8, Clause 4 empowers Congress "to establish a uniform rule of naturalization."

a. **Exclusion of Aliens**

Congress's power to exclude aliens is broad.

1) **Nonresident Aliens**

Aliens have no right to enter the United States and ***can be refused entry*** because of their political beliefs. [Kleindienst v. Mandel, 408 U.S. 753 (1972)]

2) **Resident Aliens**

Resident aliens are entitled to ***notice and hearing*** before they can be deported.

b. **Naturalization and Denaturalization—Exclusive Control of Congress**

Congress has exclusive power over naturalization and denaturalization. The Supreme Court has held that this grant gives Congress plenary power over aliens (*see* XVIII.D.2.a., *infra*).

1) **No Loss of Citizenship Without Consent**

Under the Fourteenth Amendment, Congress may not take away the citizenship of any citizen—native-born or naturalized—without his consent.

Example: The Court held unconstitutional a statute that provided for loss of citizenship upon voting in a foreign election. [Afroyim v. Rusk, 387 U.S. 253 (1967)]

a) **Proof of Intent**

A citizen's intent to relinquish citizenship may be expressed by words or conduct—and Congress may provide that such intent may be proven by a preponderance of the evidence. [Vance v. Terrazas, 444 U.S. 252 (1980)]

2) **Rights of Children of Citizens**

A person born in another country to United States citizen parents does not have a constitutional right to become a United States citizen. Congress can grant citizenship to children born abroad conditioned on their return to live in the United States within a specified period of time or for a specified number of years. Such a child who fails to return to the United States loses his grant of citizenship because he has failed to meet the statutory condition precedent to his final grant of citizenship.

12. Admiralty Power

Although congressional power to legislate in maritime matters is not expressed in the Constitution, the Supreme Court has implied it from the exclusive jurisdiction given the federal courts in this field by Article III, Section 2, supported by the Necessary and Proper Clause of Article I, Section 8.

a. **Exclusive Power**

The congressional power is plenary and exclusive, except to the extent that Congress may leave (and has left) some maritime matters to state jurisdiction.

b. **Navigable Waterways**

The federal admiralty power attaches to all navigable waterways—actually or potentially navigable—and to small tributaries that affect navigable waterways. The federal maritime power is not limited to tidewaters or interstate waters.

13. **Power to Coin Money and Fix Weights and Measures**
Congress has the power to coin money and fix the standard of weights and measures under Article I, Section 8, Clause 5.

14. **Patent/Copyright Power**
Congress has the power to control the issuance of patents and copyrights under Article I, Section 8, Clause 8.

B. DELEGATION OF LEGISLATIVE POWER

1. **Broad Delegation Allowed**
Congress has broad discretion to delegate its legislative power to executive officers and/or administrative agencies [Schechter Poultry Corp. v. United States, 295 U.S. 495 (1935)], and even delegation of rulemaking power to the courts has been upheld [Mistretta v. United States, 488 U.S. 361 (1989)].

Example: Congress can delegate the power to establish sentencing guidelines for criminal cases to a sentencing commission located in the federal courts and made up, in part, of federal judges, as long as the tasks delegated do not undermine the integrity of the judiciary or usurp the powers of the other branches. [Mistretta v. United States, *supra*]

2. **Limitations on Delegation**

   a. **Power Cannot Be Uniquely Confined to Congress**
   To be delegable, the power must not be uniquely confined to Congress; *e.g.,* the power to declare war cannot be delegated, nor the power to impeach.

   b. **Clear Standard**
   It is said that delegation will be upheld only if it includes intelligible standards for the delegate to follow. However, as a practical matter almost anything will pass as an "intelligible standard" (*e.g.,* "upholding public interest, convenience, or necessity").

   c. **Separation of Powers Limitations**
   While Congress has broad power to delegate, the separation of powers doctrine restricts Congress from keeping certain controls over certain delegates. For example, Congress cannot give itself the power to remove an officer of the executive branch by any means other than impeachment (*e.g.,* if Congress delegates rulemaking power to an executive branch agency (*e.g.,* the FCC), it may not retain the power to fire the agency head). (*See* III.B.1.b.2)a), *infra.*) Similarly, Congress cannot give a government employee who is subject to removal by Congress (other than by impeachment) purely executive powers. (*See* III.B.1.b.2)b), *infra.*)

   Example: A federal statute transferred the authority to control two D.C. area airports from the federal government to a local authority. However, the statute reserved to a review board a veto power over the local authority's decisions. The review board was comprised of nine members of Congress. The statute violates the separation of powers doctrine in one of two ways: (i) If the review board's power is considered to be legislative, the statute created an unconstitutional legislative veto (*see* D., *infra*). (ii) If the review board's power is considered to be executive, the separation of powers doctrine prohibits members of Congress from exercising it. [Metropolitan Washington Airports Authority v. Citizens for Abatement of Aircraft Noise, 501 U.S. 252 (1991)]

d. **Important Liberty Interests**

If the delegate interferes with the exercise of a fundamental liberty or right, the burden falls upon the delegate to show that she has the power to prevent the exercise of the right and her decision was in furtherance of that particular policy.

Example: In *Kent v. Dulles,* 357 U.S. 116 (1958), the secretary of state was required to issue a passport to a communist because he could not show that Congress gave him the power to encroach upon the fundamental right to travel simply because the applicant was a communist.

e. **Criminal vs. Civil Punishment**

The legislature may delegate its authority to enact regulations, the violation of which are crimes, but prosecution for such violations must be left to the executive and judicial branches. [*See* United States v. Grimaud, 220 U.S. 506 (1911)] However, agencies may enact and impose civil penalties (*i.e.,* fines labeled as civil fines) without prosecution in court. [Helvering v. Mitchell, 303 U.S. 391 (1938)]

C. THE SPEECH OR DEBATE CLAUSE—SPECIAL IMMUNITY FOR FEDERAL LEGISLATORS

Article I, Section 6 provides that "For any speech or debate in either House [members of Congress] shall not be questioned in any other place."

1. Persons Covered

The immunity extends to aides who engage in acts that would be immune if performed by a legislator. [Gravel v. United States, 408 U.S. 606 (1972)]

Note: The Speech or Debate Clause does **not extend to state legislators** who are prosecuted for violation of federal law. [United States v. Gillock, 445 U.S. 360 (1980)]

2. Scope of Immunity

Conduct that occurs in the regular course of the legislative process and the motivation behind that conduct are immune from prosecution.

a. **Bribes Excluded**

Taking of a bribe is not an act in the regular course of the legislative process and is therefore actionable. [United States v. Brewster, 408 U.S. 501 (1972)]

b. **Speeches Outside Congress**

Speeches and publications made outside Congress are not protected.

c. **Defamatory Statements**

Republication in a press release or newsletter of a defamatory statement originally made in Congress is not immune. [Hutchinson v. Proxmire, 443 U.S. 111 (1979)]

D. CONGRESSIONAL "VETO" OF EXECUTIVE ACTIONS INVALID

A legislative veto is an attempt by Congress to overturn an executive agency action *without* bicameralism (*i.e.,* passage by both houses of Congress) or presentment (*i.e.,* giving the bill to the President for his signature or veto). Legislative vetoes of executive actions are invalid. [Immigration & Naturalization Service v. Chadha, 462 U.S. 919 (1983)] The legislative veto usually arises where Congress delegates discretionary power to the President or an executive agency. In an attempt to control the delegation, Congress requires the President or agency to present any action taken under the discretionary power to certain members of Congress for approval. If they disapprove, they veto the action and that is the final decision on the action. This is unconstitutional because to be valid, legislative action (the veto) must be approved by both houses and presented to the President for his approval (*see* III.B.3., *infra*). In *Chadha,* the Court also noted that the legislative veto violates the implied separation of powers requirements of the Constitution.

Examples: 1) Congress granted to the Immigration & Naturalization Service ("INS") the power to deport or suspend from deportation illegal aliens. INS decisions to suspend deportations had to be submitted to Congress. Either house could pass a resolution overriding the decision. This legislative veto provision is unconstitutional. [Immigration & Naturalization Service v. Chadha, *supra*]

2) By statute, Congress grants to the President the power to send military troops into combat, without Congress's prior approval, whenever the United States or its territories are attacked. The statute, however, reserves in Congress the power to force the President to withdraw the troops. The statute does not provide for presidential veto of Congress's decision to withdraw. The decision in *Chadha* suggests that this statute is unconstitutional.

III. THE EXECUTIVE POWER

A. VESTED IN PRESIDENT
The entire "executive power" is vested in the President by Article II, Section 1 of the Constitution. Various executive functions may be and are delegated within the "executive branch" by the President or by Congress.

B. DOMESTIC POWERS

1. Appointment and Removal of Officers

a. Appointment
Under Article II, Section 2, the President is empowered "with the advice and consent of the Senate" to appoint "all *ambassadors*, other *public ministers* and consuls, *judges of the Supreme Court*, and all *other officers of the United States*, whose appointments are not herein otherwise provided for . . . but the Congress may by law vest the appointment of such inferior officers, as they think proper, in the President alone, in the courts of law, or in the heads of departments."

1) Appointment of "Independent Counsel" (Special Prosecutor)
Under the Ethics in Government Act of 1978, a special prosecutor (*i.e.,* a prosecutor appointed by the federal court upon the attorney general's recommendation that alleged government employee misconduct be investigated) is an "inferior

officer," since the prosecutor has limited duties (to investigate and prosecute a narrow range of persons and subjects). Therefore, the Appointment Clause of Article II, Section 2 allows Congress to vest the power to appoint a special prosecutor in the judiciary. Moreover, the Ethics in Government Act scheme does not give executive powers to the judiciary, since the Act gives the executive branch control of the decision to investigate and the power to dismiss the independent counsel for good cause. [Morrison v. Olson, 487 U.S. 654 (1988)]

2)   No Appointments by Congress

Although Congress may appoint its own officers to carry on *internal legislative tasks* (*i.e.,* its staff), it may not appoint members of a body with administrative or enforcement powers; such persons are "officers of the United States" and must, pursuant to Article II, Section 2, be appointed by the President with senatorial confirmation unless Congress has vested their appointment in the President alone, in federal courts, or in heads of departments. [Buckley v. Valeo, 424 U.S. 1 (1976)]

b.   Removal

As to removal of appointees, the *Constitution is silent* except for ensuring tenure of all Article III judges "during good behavior."

1)   By President

Under the Court's decisions, the President probably can remove high level, purely executive officers (*e.g.,* Cabinet members) at will, without any interference from Congress. However, after *Morrison v. Olson, supra,* it appears that Congress may provide statutory limitations (*e.g.,* removal for good cause) on the President's power to remove all other executive appointees.

2)   By Congress

a)   Limitation on Removal Power

Congress cannot give itself the power to remove an officer charged with the execution of laws except through impeachment. A congressional attempt through legislation to remove from government employment specifically named government employees is likely to be held invalid as a bill of attainder.

b)   Limitation on Powers of Removable Officers

Congress cannot give a government employee who is subject to removal from office by Congress any powers that are truly executive in nature. For this reason, Congress could not give to the Comptroller General (who could be removed from office not only by impeachment but also by a joint resolution of Congress) the function of establishing the amount of automatic budget reductions that would be required if Congress failed to make budget reductions necessary to insure that the federal budget deficit did not exceed a legislatively established maximum amount. [Bowsher v. Synar, 478 U.S. 714 (1986)]

2.   Pardons

The President is empowered by Article II, Section 2, "to grant reprieves and pardons for offenses against the United States, *except in cases of impeachment*." This power has been held to apply before, during, or after trial, and to extend to the offense of criminal contempt, but not to civil contempt, inasmuch as the latter involves the rights of third parties. The pardon power *cannot be limited by Congress*, and includes power to commute a sentence on any conditions the President chooses, as long as they are not independently unconstitutional. [Schick v. Reed, 419 U.S. 256 (1974)]

3. **Veto Power**

    a. **Congress May Override Veto by Two-Thirds Vote**
        Every act of Congress must be approved by the President before taking effect, unless passed over his disapproval by two-thirds vote of *each house*. [Art. I, §7]

    b. **President Has Ten Days to Veto**
        The President has 10 days (excepting Sundays) to exercise his veto power. If he fails to act within that time:

        (i)   The bill becomes law if Congress is still in session; or

        (ii) The bill is automatically vetoed if Congress is not in session (a "*pocket veto*"). [Pocket Veto Case, 279 U.S. 655 (1929)]

        Note: Brief recesses during an annual session create no pocket veto opportunity. [Wright v. United States, 302 U.S. 583 (1938)]

    c. **Line Item Veto Unconstitutional**
        The veto power allows the President only to approve or reject a bill in toto; he cannot cancel part (through a line item veto) and approve other parts. *Rationale:* The President's veto power does not authorize him to amend or repeal laws passed by Congress. [Clinton v. City of New York, 524 U.S. 417 (1998)]

4. **Power as Chief Executive**
    The President's power over internal (*i.e.*, within the United States) affairs as the chief executive is unclear. Clearly the President has some power to direct subordinate executive officers, and there is a long history of presidents issuing executive orders. Perhaps the best guide for determining the validity of presidential actions regarding internal affairs can be based on Justice Jackson's opinion in *Youngstown Sheet & Tube v. Sawyer*, 343 U.S. 579 (1952):

    (i)   Where the President acts with the express or implied authority of Congress, his authority is at its maximum and his actions likely are valid;

    (ii) Where the President acts where Congress is silent, his action will be upheld as long as the act does not take over the powers of another branch of the government or prevent another branch from carrying out its tasks [*see, e.g.*, United States v. Nixon, 418 U.S. 683 (1974)—President's invocation of executive privilege was invalidated because it kept federal courts from having evidence they needed to conduct a fair criminal trial];

    (iii) Where the President acts against the express will of Congress, he has little authority and his action likely is invalid.

a. No Power to Impound

It follows from the above that the President has no power to refuse to spend appropriated funds when Congress has expressly mandated that they be spent. [Kendall v. United States, 37 U.S. 524 (1838)]

C. POWER OVER EXTERNAL AFFAIRS

1. War

Although lacking the power to declare or initiate a "formal" war, the President has extensive military powers (essentially an external field, although applicable to civil war as well and to many domestic affairs caught up in military necessities).

a. Actual Hostilities

The President may act militarily under his power as *commander in chief* of the armed forces and militia (when federalized), under Article II, Section 2, in actual hostilities against the United States without a congressional declaration of war. But *Congress* may limit the President under its power to enact a *military appropriation every two years*. (A military appropriation may not be for more than two years.)

b. Military Government

This power includes the establishment of military governments in occupied territories, including military tribunals.

2. Foreign Relations

The President's power to represent and act for the United States in day-to-day foreign relations is paramount. He has the power to appoint and receive ambassadors and make treaties (with the advice and consent of the Senate), and to enter into executive agreements. His power is broad even as to foreign affairs that require congressional consent. No significant judicial control has been exercised over this power.

3. Treaty Power

The treaty power is granted to the President "by and with the advice and consent of the Senate, provided *two-thirds of the Senators* present concur." [Art. II, §2, cl. 2]

a. Supreme Law

All treaties "which shall be made under the authority of the United States" are the "supreme law of the land" (along with the Constitution itself and laws of the United States made in pursuance thereof) under Article VI, Paragraph 2. Thus, it is clear that any state action or law in conflict with a United States treaty is invalid (regardless of whether it is a state law or a state constitutional provision).

1) Self-Executing

No treaty has this supremacy status, however, unless it is expressly or impliedly self-executing, *i.e.,* without necessity for congressional implementation.

2) Non-Self-Executing Treaties

Some treaties require the signatory nations to *pass legislation* to effectuate their ends. This serves as an independent source of congressional power. (Thus, the implementing statute need not be connected to commerce power, etc.)

3) **Conflict with Congressional Acts**
   Valid treaties are clearly on a "supremacy parity" with acts of Congress; assuming that an act of Congress is within its powers, a conflict between such act and a valid treaty is resolved by order of adoption—*the last in time prevails*.

4) **Conflict with Constitution**
   Treaties are not co-equal with the Constitution. For example, no treaty (or executive agreement) could confer on Congress authority to act in a manner inconsistent with any specific provision of the Constitution. [Reid v. Covert, 354 U.S. 1 (1957)] However, a treaty *can broaden* the scope of Congress's affirmative authority—as was the case in *Missouri v. Holland*, 252 U.S. 416 (1920), sustaining the Migratory Bird Act after a treaty with Canada, despite an earlier decision that the Commerce Clause alone did not suffice to support the act.

b. **Other Limitations**
   Other substantive limitations on the treaty power have not been judicially established; but in one case the Court expressed in dictum the view that a treaty could not upset the basic structure of the United States's federalism, or wield a power barred to the national government by the Constitution, or cede any part of a state to a foreign nation without the state's consent. The Court has *never held a treaty unconstitutional* (*Reid v. Covert, supra,* invalidated an executive agreement for violating the Fifth Amendment), but it is conceivable that the treaty power extends only to subjects plausibly bearing on our relations with other countries.

4. **Executive Agreements**
   The President's power to enter into agreements (*i.e.,* executive agreements) with the heads of foreign countries is not expressly provided for in the Constitution; nevertheless, the power has become institutionalized. Executive agreements can probably be on any subject as long as they do not violate the Constitution. They are very similar to treaties, except that they do not require the consent of the Senate.

   a. **Conflicts with Other Governmental Action**
      Executive agreements that are not consented to by the Senate are not the "supreme law of the land." Thus, conflicting federal statutes and treaties will prevail over an executive agreement, regardless of which was adopted first. However, executive agreements prevail over conflicting state laws.

   b. **Example—Power to Settle Claims of United States Citizens**
      The President, with the implicit approval of Congress, has power to settle claims of United States citizens against foreign governments through an executive agreement. [Dames & Moore v. Regan, 453 U.S. 654 (1981)]

D. EXECUTIVE PRIVILEGE/IMMUNITY

1. **Executive Privilege**
   The executive privilege is not a constitutional power, but an inherent privilege necessary to protect the confidentiality of presidential communications.

   a. **Extent of the Privilege**
      Presidential *documents and conversations* are *presumptively privileged*, but the

privilege must yield to the need for such materials as evidence in a criminal case to which they are relevant and otherwise admissible. This determination must be made by the trial judge after hearing the evidence.

1) National Security Secrets
Military, diplomatic, or sensitive national security secrets are given great deference by the courts.

2) Criminal Proceedings
In criminal proceedings, presidential communiques will be available to the prosecution, where a need for such information is demonstrated. [United States v. Nixon, 418 U.S. 683 (1974)]

3) Screening Papers and Recordings of Former President
A federal statute requiring the Administrator of General Services to screen the presidential papers is valid, notwithstanding the privilege. [Nixon v. Administrator of General Services, 433 U.S. 425 (1977)]

4) Screening by Judge in Chambers
The court will determine in an in-camera inspection which communications are protected and which are subject to disclosure.

2. Executive Immunity

a. Absolute Immunity for President
The President has *absolute immunity from civil damages* based on any action that the President took within his *official responsibilities* (even if the action was only arguably within the "outer perimeter" of presidential responsibility). [Nixon v. Fitzgerald, 457 U.S. 731 (1982)] However, the President has *no* immunity from private suits in federal courts based on *conduct that allegedly occurred before taking office*. [Clinton v. Jones, 520 U.S. 681 (1997)] *Rationale:* The immunity is intended only to enable the President to perform his *designated functions* without fear of personal liability.

b. Immunity May Extend to Presidential Aides
Presidential aides share in this immunity only if they are exercising discretionary authority for the President in "sensitive" areas of national concern, such as foreign affairs. Other aides are entitled only to a qualified immunity (a "good faith" defense). [Harlow v. Fitzgerald, 457 U.S. 800 (1982)]

Example: The Attorney General does not share the President's absolute immunity for authorizing a warrantless wiretap on "national security" grounds. The Attorney General would have a defense to a lawsuit regarding such a wiretap if it was shown that he was able to act in good faith because his actions were not violating clearly established or well-settled statutory or constitutional rights. [Mitchell v. Forsyth, 472 U.S. 511 (1985)]

E. IMPEACHMENT

1. Persons Subject to Impeachment
The President, Vice President, and all civil officers of the United States are subject to impeachment.

2. Grounds

The grounds for impeachment are treason, bribery, high crimes, and misdemeanors.

3. Impeachment by the House

A *majority vote* in the House is necessary to invoke the charges of impeachment.

4. Conviction by the Senate

A *two-thirds vote* in the Senate is necessary to convict.

PART TWO: THE FEDERAL SYSTEM

IV. RELATIVE SPHERES OF FEDERAL AND STATE POWER

A. EXCLUSIVE FEDERAL POWERS

1. Power of States Expressly Limited

Some powers are exclusively federal because of express constitutional limitation on or prohibition of the states' exercise thereof—such as the treaty power, coinage of money, and duty on imports.

2. Inherent Federal Powers

Others are exclusively federal in view of their nature—such as declaration of war, federal citizenship, naturalization, and borrowing money on the credit of the United States. Any state exercise of these powers would basically subvert the federal system. On the exam, *do not* allow states to take actions that might touch upon *foreign relations*.

Example: In *Zschernig v. Miller,* 389 U.S. 429 (1968), the Court held invalid state statutes that sought to withhold the proceeds of local decedents' estates from heirs living in nations that (i) discriminate against Americans in their probate laws, (ii) impede the transmission of funds to the United States, or (iii) confiscate property inherited by their citizens. The Court concluded that such laws are so potentially disruptive of a nationally conducted foreign policy that they are invalid notwithstanding the traditional commitment of probate law to the states.

B. EXCLUSIVE STATE POWERS

Whereas the federal government has only those powers granted to it by the Constitution, the state governments are governments of "unlimited" powers, having all powers not prohibited to them by the Constitution. This is recognized by the Tenth Amendment, which provides that all powers not delegated to the federal government by the Constitution are reserved to the states (or to the people). However, given the expansive interpretation of federal powers (*e.g.,* the commerce power; *see* II.A.4., *supra*), little state power is exclusive.

C. CONCURRENT FEDERAL AND STATE POWER—SUPREMACY CLAUSE

Most governmental power is concurrent, belonging to both the states and the federal government. Thus, it is possible for states and the federal government to pass legislation on the same subject matter. When this occurs, the Supremacy Clause provides that the federal law is supreme, and the conflicting state law is rendered void.

1. **Actual Conflict Between State and Federal Laws**

   A valid act of Congress or federal regulation supersedes any state or local action that actually conflicts with the federal rule—whether by commanding conduct inconsistent with that required by the federal rule, or by forbidding conduct that the federal rule is designed to foster.

2. **State Prevents Achievement of Federal Objective**

   The conflict need not relate to conduct; it is sufficient if the state or local law interferes with achievement of a federal objective. This is true even if the state or local law was enacted for some valid purpose and not merely to frustrate the federal law.

   Example: A purpose of the federal bankruptcy laws is to give bankrupts a fresh start, free of their old debts. A state law providing for suspension of the driver's license of persons who have failed to pay off auto accident judgments, regardless of the judgment debtor's discharge in bankruptcy, interferes with the federal objective and will fail. [Perez v. Campbell, 402 U.S. 637 (1971)]

3. **Preemption**

   A state or local law may fail under the Supremacy Clause, even if it does not conflict with federally regulated conduct or objectives, if it appears that Congress intended to "occupy" the entire field, thus precluding *any* state or local regulation. If the federal law does not explicitly indicate whether state law shall be preempted, the courts will consider a number of factors, including the following:

   a. **Comprehensiveness**

      The more a federal scheme leaves uncovered, the less likely a finding of implied preemption.

   b. **Agency to Administer**

      When a federal statute creates an agency (like the NLRB) to enforce the law, all matters arguably in the agency's jurisdiction are ordinarily deemed preempted; such matters must hence be regulated by the federal agency or not at all.

D. ABSENCE OF FEDERAL AND STATE POWERS

Some powers are denied to both Congress and the states. For example, the Supreme Court has held that the Qualifications Clauses [Art. I, §2, cl. 2; §3, cl. 3], setting the qualifications to serve in Congress, are exclusive and cannot be altered by Congress or the states. [United States Term Limits, Inc. v. Thornton, 514 U.S. 779 (1995)—state-imposed term limit for members of Congress invalidated; *and see* Cook v. Gralike, 121 S. Ct. 1029 (2001)—state law instructing each member of its congressional delegation to support a constitutional amendment for term limits, and providing that failure to do so be noted on the ballot, was held invalid because it imposes a substantive qualification rather than regulates the "manner" in which elections are held]

E. INTERSTATE COMPACT CLAUSE

The Constitution provides that states may enter into agreements or compacts with other states upon the consent of Congress. [Art. I, §10, cl. 3] However, not all agreements between states are "compacts" requiring congressional consent. The Compact Clause reaches only interstate agreements that *increase the political power* of the states at the expense of federal supremacy (*e.g.,* an agreement whereby one state cedes territory to another state). [*See* United States Steel Corp. v. Multistate Tax Commission, 434 U.S. 552 (1978)—congressional consent not required for multistate tax compact because the compact does not give member states any powers they could not exercise in its absence] The Supreme Court has the power to interpret such compacts—the member states do not have final authority over interpretation. [West Virginia *ex rel.* Dyer v. Sims, 341 U.S. 22 (1951)]

F. FULL FAITH AND CREDIT CLAUSE

The Full Faith and Credit Clause provides that "full faith and credit shall be given in each state to the public acts, records, and judicial proceedings of every other state." By virtue of the Clause, if a judgment is entitled to full faith and credit, it must be recognized in sister states (*i.e.,* a party who loses a case in New York generally may not relitigate it in New Jersey; the New Jersey courts are bound by the New York ruling). However, not every decision is entitled to full faith and credit. There are three requirements:

1. The court that rendered the judgment must have had *jurisdiction over the parties and the subject matter*;

2. The judgment must have been *on the merits*; *i.e.,* on the substance of the plaintiff's claim rather than on a procedural issue, such as improper venue or running of the statute of limitations; and

3. The judgment must be *final*.

V. INTERSOVEREIGN LITIGATION

A. SUITS BY THE UNITED STATES AGAINST A STATE

1. State Need Not Consent
The United States may sue a state without its consent.

2. Original Jurisdiction in Supreme Court
Congress has restated the scope of original jurisdiction in 28 U.S.C. section 1251. The Supreme Court has *nonexclusive* original jurisdiction in all controversies between the United States and a state. This means that the Supreme Court may take original jurisdiction of such a case if it so chooses or it can allow the case to be heard originally in a lower federal court. The jurisdictional system complies with Article III.

B. SUITS BY STATE AGAINST UNITED STATES—UNITED STATES MUST CONSENT
Public policy forbids a state from suing the United States without its consent. Congress can pass legislation that permits the United States to be sued by a state in given situations.

C. FEDERAL OFFICER AS DEFENDANT

1. Limitation
Suits against a federal officer are *deemed to be brought against the United States* itself *if* the judgment sought would be satisfied out of the public treasury or would interfere with public administration and therefore are not permitted.

2. Specific Relief Against the Individual Officer

Specific relief against an officer as an individual will be granted if the officer acted ultra vires:

    a.   Beyond his statutory powers; or

    b.   The valid power was exercised in an unconstitutional manner.

D. SUITS BY ONE STATE AGAINST ANOTHER

One state may sue another state without the latter's consent. The Supreme Court has *exclusive original jurisdiction*.

E. SUITS AGAINST A STATE IN ANOTHER STATE'S COURT

One state may be subject to the jurisdiction of another state's court. In *Nevada v. Hall,* 440 U.S. 410 (1979), the Court allowed a citizen of California to sue the state of Nevada in California state court. Sovereign immunity does not extend beyond the borders of the state.

VI. INTERGOVERNMENTAL TAX AND REGULATION IMMUNITIES

A. FEDERAL TAXATION AND REGULATION OF STATE OR LOCAL GOVERNMENTS

The Tenth Amendment provides that powers not delegated to the United States by the Constitution, nor prohibited to the states, are reserved to the states. This reservation of power is often cited as a restriction on Congress's power to regulate the states.

1. Tax or Regulation Applying to State and Private Entities—Valid

The Supreme Court will not likely strike down on Tenth Amendment grounds a tax or regulation that subjects states or local governments to regulations or taxes that apply to *both* the public sector and the private sector. It has held that in such cases, the states' interests are best protected by the states' representation in Congress. [Garcia v. San Antonio Metropolitan Transit Authority, 469 U.S. 528 (1985)]

Example: Congress can require state and local governments to follow the provisions of the Federal Fair Labor and Standards Act requiring minimum wages for all employees. [Garcia v. San Antonio Metropolitan Transit Authority, *supra*]

2. Tax or Regulation that Applies Only to States

However, the Tenth Amendment does limit Congress's power to regulate the states alone by requiring the states to act in a particular way. Congress may not compel states to enact or enforce a regulatory program. [New York v. United States, 504 U.S. 144 (1992)—federal statute requiring states to either regulate radioactive waste or take title to it is beyond Congress's power] Similarly, if Congress passes a tax that does not apply to private businesses but merely taxes state government entities, there is a possibility that the Court would use the Tenth Amendment to prohibit the tax.

a. Exception—Civil Rights

Congress *may* use its power under the Fourteenth and Fifteenth Amendments to restrict state activities that it determines would violate the civil liberties of persons within the state.

Examples: 1) Congress may invalidate state laws establishing a literacy test as a prerequisite to voting in state elections. [Oregon v. Mitchell, 400 U.S. 112 (1970)]

2) Congress may restrict changes in state voting laws that have the effect of diminishing the voting power of racial minorities even though the change in state law was not purposeful racial discrimination that would violate Section 1 of the Fifteenth Amendment. [Rome v. United States, 446 U.S. 156 (1980)]

b.   Exception—Spending Power Conditions
Congress may also "regulate" states through the spending power by imposing explicit conditions on the grant of money to state or local governments. Such conditions will not violate the Tenth Amendment merely because Congress lacked the power to directly regulate the activity that is the subject of the spending program.

Example: A federal law that would withhold 5% of the federal highway funds otherwise allocable to a state if the state did not set a 21 years minimum age for the drinking of alcohol has been upheld. [South Dakota v. Dole, 483 U.S. 203 (1987)]

3.   Commandeering State Officials
The Supreme Court has held that the Tenth Amendment prohibits Congress from adopting a statute that "commandeers" state officials by *requiring states to regulate their own citizens*. [Printz v. United States, 521 U.S. 898 (1997)—striking portions of a federal gun law that required state law enforcement officers to collect from gun dealers reports regarding prospective handgun purchasers and to conduct background checks on them] However, the Court has allowed Congress to *regulate the states by prohibiting them from performing certain acts*. [*See* Reno v. Condon, 528 U.S. 141 (2000)—upholding federal act that bars states (as well as private resellers) from disclosing personal information required on drivers' license applications]

B.   STATE TAXATION AND REGULATION OF FEDERAL GOVERNMENT

1.   No Direct Tax on Federal Instrumentalities
A state tax levied directly against the property or operation of the federal government without the consent of Congress is invalid.

2.   Nondiscriminatory, Indirect Taxes
Nondiscriminatory, indirect taxes on the federal government or its property are permissible if they *do not unreasonably burden* federal government.

Examples: 1) State income taxes on salaries of federal employees are valid. However, a state tax that imposes a higher tax on federal employees (or retired federal employees) than on state or local government employees (or retired employees) would violate the principle of intergovernmental tax immunity, unless Congress had approved this discriminatory tax. [Davis v. Michigan Department of Treasury, 489 U.S. 803 (1989)]

2) Private contractors, acting as purchasing agents for the federal government, cannot be compelled to pay state sales or use taxes on materials purchased on behalf of the federal government. State sales or use taxes are valid

where the contractor is working for the federal government on a "cost-plus" basis. These extra costs are not characterized as direct taxes.

3. State Regulation of Federal Government

The states have no power to regulate the activities of the federal government unless Congress consents to the regulation. Thus, instrumentalities and agents of the federal government are immune from state regulations relating to performance of their federal functions.

Examples: 1) A state may not require a post office employee to obtain a state driver's license in order to drive a mail truck. [Johnson v. Maryland, 254 U.S. 51 (1920)]

2) A state may not require a contractor to obtain a state license to build facilities on an Air Force base, located within the state, pursuant to a government contract. [Leslie Miller, Inc. v. Arkansas, 352 U.S. 187 (1956)]

VII.   PRIVILEGES AND IMMUNITIES CLAUSES

A.   INTRODUCTION

There are two Privileges and Immunities Clauses: the Fourteenth Amendment Privileges and Immunities Clause and the Interstate Privileges and Immunities Clause of Article IV. The Fourteenth Amendment clause protects attributes of United States citizenship and is rarely applicable. The Article IV provision prevents some discrimination by states against nonresidents, and is usually more relevant on the bar exam.

B.   ARTICLE IV—PRIVILEGES OF STATE CITIZENSHIP

Article IV, Section 2, the Interstate Privileges and Immunities Clause, provides that "[t]he Citizens of each state shall be entitled to all Privileges and Immunities of citizens in the several states." Thus, it prohibits discrimination by a state against nonresidents.

1. Corporations and Aliens Not Protected

Corporations and aliens are *not citizens* of a state for purposes of the Privileges and Immunities Clause.

2. Only "Fundamental Rights" Protected

The Interstate Privileges and Immunities Clause does not prohibit all discrimination by a state in favor of its own citizens, but only when the denial concerns "fundamental rights"— *i.e.,* those involving important *commercial activities* (such as pursuit of a livelihood) or *civil liberties*. For example, the following have been struck down:

a.   *Statute charging nonresident commercial fishermen substantially more for commercial fishing license* than resident commercial fishermen ($2,500 vs. $25) [Toomer v. Witsell, 334 U.S. 385 (1948); *cf.* Baldwin v. Montana Fish & Game Commission, 436 U.S. 371 (1978)—vast difference between resident and nonresident *recreational* hunting license constitutional since no essential commercial activity involved];

b.   *Statute giving resident creditors priority* over nonresident creditors as to assets of foreign corporations in receivership proceedings [Blake v. McClung, 172 U.S. 239 (1898)];

c. **Statute or court rule requiring state residency to be licensed** to practice law within the state [Supreme Court of Virginia v. Friedman, 487 U.S. 59 (1988)];

d. **State income tax only on nonresidents** who earn money within the state [Austin v. New Hampshire, 420 U.S. 656 (1975)]; and

e. **State law requiring private sector employers to give hiring preference to residents** absent a closely related substantial justification (*see* below) [Hicklin v. Orbeck, 437 U.S. 518 (1978)], but states **may** require a person to be a resident to hold **government employment** [McCarthy v. Philadelphia Civil Service Commission, 424 U.S. 645 (1976) (per curiam)].

3. **Substantial Justification Exception**
A state law discriminating against nonresidents may be valid if the state has a substantial justification for the different treatment. In effect, it must show that nonresidents either cause or are part of the problem it is attempting to solve, and that there are **no less restrictive means** to solve the problem.

Example: The Court held that a city ordinance requiring 40% of employees of contractors and subcontractors working on city construction projects to be city residents was an apparent violation of the Article IV Privileges and Immunities Clause because it gave a preference in private sector employment to city residents. However, the Court found that it could not make a final determination as to **whether the preference was justified** in this case because the record from the lower courts did not allow it to evaluate the city's argument that the preference was necessary **to counteract grave economic and social ills** in urban environments caused by spiraling unemployment and declines in the population base of such cities. [United Building & Construction Trades Council v. Mayor of Camden, 465 U.S. 208 (1984)]

4. **Note—Relationship to Commerce Clause**
Although the Article IV Privileges and Immunities Clause and the Commerce Clause may apply different standards and produce different results, they tend to mutually reinforce each other. Consequently, they both have to be considered in analyzing bar exam questions.

C. FOURTEENTH AMENDMENT—PRIVILEGES OF NATIONAL CITIZENSHIP
The Fourteenth Amendment Privileges and Immunities Clause prohibits states from denying their citizens the privileges and immunities of national citizenship, such as the right to petition Congress for redress of grievances, the right to vote for federal officers, the right to enter public lands, the right to interstate travel, and any other right flowing from the distinct relation of a citizen to the United States Government.

1. **Corporations Not Protected**
Corporations are **not citizens** of the United States and are **not protected**.

2. **Bill of Rights Not Included**
The *Slaughterhouse Cases,* 83 U.S. 36 (1873), held that the fundamental rights protected against federal abuse (first 10 amendments) are **not privileges and immunities of national citizenship** within the meaning of the Fourteenth Amendment; nor are such other basic rights as the right to live, work, and eat. Thus, the guarantees of the Bill of Rights are

protected from state action only by the Due Process and Equal Protection Clauses of the Fourteenth Amendment.

3. **Right to Travel and the Privileges and Immunities Clause**
The right to travel, which is protected by the Fourteenth Amendment, includes the right of newly arrived citizens to enjoy the same privileges and immunities as are enjoyed by other citizens of the state.
Example: A California statute limiting the welfare benefits of first year residents was held unconstitutional under the Fourteenth Amendment Privileges and Immunities Clause. The statute provided that citizens who had lived in California for less than one year could receive only the benefits they would have received in their prior state of residence. The Court noted that the right to travel includes the right to be treated equally in a new state of residence. [Saenz v. Roe, 526 U.S. 489 (1999)]

PART THREE: STATE REGULATION OR TAXATION OF COMMERCE

VIII. REGULATION OF FOREIGN COMMERCE

A. LIES EXCLUSIVELY WITH CONGRESS
For all practical purposes, the power to regulate foreign commerce lies exclusively with Congress. "Foreign" commerce has been held to include traffic on the high seas, even though both terminal ports are within the United States. [Japan Line, Ltd. v. County of Los Angeles, 441 U.S. 434 (1979)]

B. MINOR EXCEPTIONS WHERE STATE REGULATION PERMITTED
The Supreme Court, however, has recognized a few minor exceptions; thus, the states are free to regulate local aspects of port pilotage and navigation of ships in foreign commerce (*e.g.,* aspects such as safety of handling); and in one case the Court permitted state regulation of excursion boat traffic between Detroit and a Canadian island (state barred racial discrimination among boat passengers) since no Canadians or Canadian products or services were involved. [Bob-Lo Excursion Co. v. Michigan, 333 U.S. 28 (1948)]

IX. REGULATION OF INTERSTATE COMMERCE

A. REGULATION OF COMMERCE BY CONGRESS
As already seen, Congress's power over interstate commerce is "plenary" and pervasive. However, the power is *nonexclusive*—it is shared with the states to some degree.

1. **Power of Congress to Supersede or Preempt State Regulation**
Recall that the Supremacy Clause makes federal law supreme. (*See* IV.C., *supra.*) Thus, if a state law regulating commerce conflicts with a federal law, the state law will be void. Moreover, if Congress desires, it may preempt an entire area of regulation, thus preventing states from making any laws concerning the area preempted. (*See* IV.C.3., *supra.*)

2. **Power of Congress to Permit or Prohibit State Regulation**
Although Congress's commerce power is nonexclusive, the states' power to regulate interstate commerce is restricted by the negative implications of the Commerce Clause, even absent federal legislation—the states generally may *not* discriminate against interstate commerce. (*See* below.) Nevertheless, Congress is not so restricted; it may allow the states to adopt legislation that would otherwise violate the Commerce Clause.

Example: A state imposed a 3% tax on out-of-state insurance companies for all premiums received from insuring residents of the state. No similar tax was placed on in-state insurance companies. Although such a tax would ordinarily be held invalid under the Commerce Clause—because it discriminates against interstate commerce—the tax here was upheld because Congress had adopted an act permitting the states to regulate insurance in any manner, as long as the state regulation did not conflict with a federal statute specifically regulating insurance. [Prudential Insurance Co. v. Benjamin, 328 U.S. 408 (1946); *and see* Northeast Bancorp, Inc. v. Board of Governors, 472 U.S. 159 (1985)]

Note: As indicated above, Congress may also prohibit the states from adopting legislation that would otherwise be permitted under the Commerce Clause.

a. **Limitation**
While Congress may permit states to adopt regulations that would otherwise violate the Commerce Clause, such consent will not obviate other constitutional objections to the regulation. Thus, Congress may not give states the power to restrict civil liberties. (*See* X.A.1.b.2)a), *infra.*)

B. **STATE REGULATION OF COMMERCE IN THE ABSENCE OF CONGRESSIONAL ACTION**
If Congress has not enacted laws regarding the subject, a state or local government may regulate local aspects of interstate commerce if the regulation:

(i) Does *not discriminate* against out-of-state competition to benefit local economic interests; and

(ii) Is *not unduly burdensome* (*i.e.,* the incidental burden on interstate commerce does not outweigh the legitimate local benefits produced by the regulation).

If either test is not met, the regulation will be held void for violating the Commerce Clause (sometimes called the "*Dormant Commerce Clause*" or "*Negative Commerce Clause*" under such circumstances).

1. **Discriminatory Regulations**

a. **Generally Invalid**
State or local regulations that discriminate against interstate commerce to protect local economic interests are almost always invalid.

b. **Examples**

1) **Regulations Protecting Local Businesses**

Laws designed to protect local businesses against interstate competition generally will be invalidated.

Examples: 1) A state cannot place a surcharge on out-of-state milk to make that milk as (or more) expensive as milk produced in the state.

2) A state cannot exempt local businesses or products from taxation or regulation that it seeks to apply to out-of-state businesses or products that come into the state.

3) A law requiring all locally produced solid waste to be processed at a local waste processing business was held to violate the Commerce Clause because it was a trade barrier against competition from out-of-state waste processors. [C&A Carbone, Inc. v. Town of Clarkstown, 511 U.S. 383 (1994)]

2) **Regulations Requiring Local Operations**

If a state law requires a business to perform specific business operations in the state to engage in other business activity within the state, the law will normally be held invalid as an attempt to discriminate against other states where the business operations could be performed more efficiently.

Example: If a state required all businesses that produce melons in the state and all businesses that purchase melons from local producers to wrap or package the melons in the state (before the melons were exported from the state), the law would be invalid as an attempt to force businesses to locate their packaging operations in the state.

3) **Regulations Limiting Access to In-State Products**

A state law that makes it difficult or impossible for out-of-state purchasers to have access to in-state products (other than products owned by the state itself) is likely to be held invalid.

Examples: 1) A state cannot prohibit in-state owners of "ground water" from selling and exporting the water they own to persons in other states.

2) A state cannot require in-state companies to sell products at a lower price to in-state residents than to out-of-state residents.

4) **Regulations Prohibiting Out-of-State Wastes**

A state may not prohibit private landfill or waste disposal facilities from accepting out-of-state garbage or waste or surcharge such waste [Philadelphia v. New Jersey, 437 U.S. 617 (1978); Chemical Waste Management v. Hunt, 504 U.S. 334 (1992)] unless Congress authorizes such discrimination [New York v. United States, VI.A.2., *supra*—federal statute allowing states to impose surcharge on certain out-of-state nuclear wastes upheld]. This rule applies even to hazardous wastes. [Oregon Waste Systems, Inc. v. Department of Environmental Quality, 511 U.S. 93 (1994)]

c.   **Exceptions**

1) **Necessary to Important State Interest**

A discriminatory state or local law may be valid if it furthers an important, non-economic state interest (*e.g.,* health or safety) and there are *no reasonable alternatives* available.

Example: A state could prohibit the importation of live baitfish (such as minnows) into the state because the state could demonstrate that it had no other way of effectively avoiding the possibility that such baitfish might bring certain parasites into the state or, in other ways, have a detrimental effect on the state's wild fish population. [Maine v. Taylor, 476 U.S. 1138 (1986)] However, a state could not prohibit the export of live baitfish to out-of-state purchasers because the sale of such fish to out-of-state purchasers would not impair any interest of the state, except the interest of protecting local purchasers of baitfish from competition by out-of-state purchasers. [Hughes v. Oklahoma, 441 U.S. 322 (1979)]

2) **State as Market Participant**

The Commerce Clause does not prevent a state from preferring its own citizens when the state is acting as a market participant (*e.g.,* buying or selling products, hiring labor, giving subsidies).

Examples: 1) A state may purchase scrap automobiles from its citizens at a higher-than-market rate and refuse to pay nonresidents the same amount. [Hughes v. Alexandria Scrap Corp., 426 U.S. 794 (1976)]

2) Under the market participant exception to the Commerce Clause, a city may require that all construction *projects funded by the city* be performed by contractors using a workforce composed of at least 50% bona fide residents of the city. [White v. Massachusetts Council of Construction Employers, 460 U.S. 204 (1983)]

a) **Limitation—Interstate Privileges and Immunities Clause**

While a state or local government does not violate the *Commerce Clause* by preferring its own citizens while acting as a market participant, there is no market participant exception to the Interstate Privileges and Immunities Clause. Thus, a regulation that interferes with private sector employment, such as the one in example 2), above, may violate the Privileges and Immunities Clause unless the regulating entity can show a substantial justification for the regulation. (*See* VII.B.3., *supra.*)

b) **Limitation—"Downstream" Restrictions**

While a state may choose to sell only to state residents, it may not attach conditions to a sale that would discriminate against interstate commerce.

Example: Alaska violated the Commerce Clause when it imposed a contractual requirement on purchasers of state-owned timber that the timber be processed in Alaska before being shipped out of state. [South-Central Timber Development, Inc. v. Wunnicke, 467 U.S. 82 (1984)—plurality opinion]

2. **Nondiscriminatory Laws—Balancing Test**
Sometimes a nondiscriminatory state or local law that regulates commerce may impose a burden on interstate commerce; *e.g.,* a state law regulating the size of trucks within that state may burden interstate commerce because interstate trucking operations will be subject to the law when their trucks enter the state. A nondiscriminatory law will be invalidated only if the burden on interstate commerce outweighs the promotion of legitimate (not discriminatory) local interests. This is a case-by-case balancing test. Thus, some regulations of trucks will be upheld, because they do not impose an undue burden on interstate commerce, whereas other truck regulations will be invalidated, because they would make it extremely difficult for interstate trucking operators to have their trucks travel into or through the state.

a. **Less Restrictive Alternatives**
In determining whether a nondiscriminatory state regulation of interstate commerce violates the Commerce Clause, a court will sometimes consider whether less restrictive alternatives are available.
Example: Although it is legitimate for a city to pass laws designed to ensure that milk products sold within the city are safe, a city cannot require those businesses that wish to sell milk in the city to have the milk processed (purified and placed in bottles) at a processing site close to the city. *Rationale:* The city has a variety of alternatives that impose less burden on interstate commerce.

b. **Absence of Conflict with Other States**
Although this factor has not been held by the Supreme Court to be a separate test, state and local laws regulating commerce are more likely to be upheld when there is little chance that states would have conflicting regulations of the same subject matter.
Example: A state could validly apply a state law prohibiting racial or gender discrimination in the hiring of personnel to an airline doing business in the state because the law was not discriminatory against out-of-state businesses, it promoted a legitimate interest, and no other state could validly require or permit racial or gender discrimination by airlines.

C. **TWENTY-FIRST AMENDMENT—STATE CONTROL OVER INTOXICATING LIQUOR**

1. **Intrastate Regulations**
The Twenty-First Amendment, which repealed prohibition, gives state governments wide latitude over the importation of liquor and the conditions under which liquor is sold or used within the state. However, state liquor regulations that constitute only an economic preference for local liquor manufacturers may violate the Commerce Clause. The Commerce Clause prohibits both outright economic favoritism for local businesses and attempts to regulate out-of-state transactions in order to guarantee the competitive position of in-state businesses.
Examples: 1) A state sales tax on liquor produced in other states that does not tax sales of locally produced alcoholic beverages violates the Commerce Clause.

2) A state law that requires out-of-state distillers or sellers of alcoholic beverages to affirm that the price the distiller/seller is charging liquor retailers

or wholesalers in the state is no greater than the price the distiller/seller is charging in other states violates the Commerce Clause. Such a price affirmation law directly interferes with and burdens interstate commerce. The Twenty-First Amendment does not authorize this type of state interference with commerce. [Brown-Forman Distillers Corp. v. New York State Liquor Authority, 476 U.S. 573 (1986); Healy v. The Beer Institute, Inc., 491 U.S. 324 (1989)]

2. Interstate Regulations

Transitory liquor (liquor bound for out-of-state destinations) is subject to the Commerce Clause. Thus, a state prohibition on transporting liquor through the state would probably be held unconstitutional as violating the Commerce Clause.

3. Conflicts Between State Liquor Laws and Individual Rights

a. General Rule—Individual Rights Paramount

Individual rights guaranteed by the Bill of Rights and the Fourteenth Amendment outweigh state liquor control laws.

b. "Excessive Drinkers"

"Excessive drinkers" are entitled to procedural due process before the state can post their names in liquor stores. [Wisconsin v. Constantineau, 400 U.S. 433 (1971)]

c. Equal Protection Clause

The Equal Protection Clause prohibits different age minimums based on sex in the sale of liquor. A state cannot permit 18-year-old females to buy beer and prohibit 18- to 21-year-old males from doing so. [Craig v. Boren, 429 U.S. 190 (1976)]

4. Federal Power

The Twenty-First Amendment does not prohibit Congress from controlling economic transactions involving alcoholic beverages under the federal commerce power. Thus, federal antitrust law can prohibit a practice of liquor dealers that has the effect of fixing minimum prices. [324 Liquor Corp. v. Duffy, 479 U.S. 335 (1987)] Similarly, as mentioned above, Congress may, without violating the Twenty-First Amendment, "regulate" liquor distribution by imposing conditions on the grant of federal funds given under the spending power. [South Dakota v. Dole, VI.A.2.b., *supra*]

D. BAR EXAM APPROACH

Whenever a bar exam question involves a state regulation that affects the free flow of interstate commerce, you should proceed as follows:

First, see if the question refers to *any federal legislation* that might be held either to: (i) *supersede* the state regulation or *preempt* the field, or (ii) *authorize* state regulation otherwise impermissible.

Second, if neither of these possibilities is dispositive of the question, ask if the state legislation either *discriminates* against interstate or out-of-state commerce or places an *undue burden* on the free flow of interstate commerce. If the legislation is discriminatory, it will be invalid unless (i) it furthers an important state interest *and* there are no reasonable nondiscriminatory alternatives, or (ii) the state is a market participant. If the legislation does not discriminate but burdens interstate commerce, it will be invalid if the burden on commerce outweighs the state's interest. Consider whether there are less restrictive alternatives.

X. POWER OF STATES TO TAX INTERSTATE COMMERCE

A. GENERAL CONSIDERATIONS

The same general considerations applicable to state regulation of commerce (*supra*) apply to taxation. Pursuant to the Commerce Clause, Congress has complete power to authorize or forbid state taxation affecting interstate commerce. If Congress has not acted, look to see whether the tax *discriminates* against interstate commerce. If it does, it is invalid. If it does not, assess whether the burden on interstate commerce outweighs the benefit to the state. Three tests must be met: (i) there must be a *substantial nexus* between the taxpayer and the state; (ii) the tax must be *fairly apportioned*; and (iii) there must be a *fair relationship* between the tax and the services or benefits provided by the state.

1. Discriminatory Taxes

Unless authorized by Congress, state taxes that discriminate against interstate commerce violate the Commerce Clause. Such taxes may also be held to violate the Interstate Privileges and Immunities Clause (*see* VII.B., *supra*) if they also discriminate against nonresidents of the state [Austin v. New Hampshire, 420 U.S. 656 (1975)], as well as the Equal Protection Clause if the discrimination is not rationally related to a legitimate state purpose [WHYY, Inc. v. Borough of Glassboro, 393 U.S. 117 (1968)—denial of tax exemption solely because taxpayer was incorporated in another state is invalid].

a. Finding Discrimination

1) Tax Singles Out Interstate Commerce

If a state tax singles out interstate commerce for taxation, the Court ordinarily will not "save" the tax by finding other state taxes imposed only on local commerce (which might arguably eliminate the "apparent" discrimination against interstate commerce).

Example: The Supreme Court invalidated an Ohio statute that gave a tax credit against the Ohio motor vehicle fuel sales tax (paid by fuel dealers) for each gallon of ethanol sold as a component of gasohol if, but only if, the ethanol was produced in Ohio or in a state that granted a similar tax advantage to ethanol produced in Ohio. The Supreme Court found that this tax credit system constituted discrimination against interstate commerce. [New Energy Co. of Indiana v. Limbach, 486 U.S. 269 (1988)]

Note: However, state taxes that single out interstate commerce are considered *nondiscriminatory* if the particular statutory section or scheme *also* imposes the same type of tax on *local* commerce (*e.g.,* sales and use taxes, discussed *infra*).

2) Tax with In-State Subsidy
A seemingly uniform tax may be ruled to be discriminatory if the proceeds from the tax are "earmarked" for subsidies to in-state businesses.

Example: A state imposed a tax on all milk dealers, but the tax law provided that revenue from the tax would be put into a fund that would be used to pay subsidies to in-state dairy farmers. This assessment-subsidy system violates the Commerce Clause because it operates identically to a tax placed only on sales of milk produced outside the state. [West Lynn Creamery, Inc. v. Healy, 512 U.S. 186 (1994)]

b. Choosing the Proper Clause
While a state or local tax that discriminates against interstate commerce generally violates the Commerce Clause, the Clause is not always the strongest argument against the tax.

1) Interstate Privileges and Immunities Clause
If a state or local tax discriminates against a *natural person who is a nonresident*, the Article IV Interstate Privileges and Immunities Clause is the strongest argument against the tax's validity, because it is more direct than a Commerce Clause argument.

2) Equal Protection

a) Where Congress Approves the Discrimination
Although the Supreme Court normally uses the Commerce Clause to invalidate discriminatory legislation, it may also find that such discrimination violates the Equal Protection Clause. This is important where Congress has given the states the power to do something that would otherwise violate the Commerce Clause: Congress can give states the power to take actions that otherwise would violate the Commerce Clause, but it *cannot* approve state actions that would violate equal protection. Thus, if Congress has approved a type of state tax that discriminates against out-of-state businesses, that state tax will not be in violation of the Commerce Clause, but it might be found to be a violation of equal protection.

Example: In *Metropolitan Life Insurance Co. v. Ward,* 470 U.S. 869 (1985), the Court invalidated a state tax on insurance companies that imposed a higher tax on out-of-state insurance companies than was paid by in-state companies. The Court found that federal statutes exempted state regulation of insurance businesses from Commerce Clause restrictions but found that the tax violated equal protection because it did not relate to a legitimate interest of government (*i.e.,* the state does not have a legitimate interest in discriminating against out-of-state businesses simply to protect local economic interests from competition).

b) Taxes Based on Suspect Classifications or Infringing on Fundamental Rights

The Court may use equal protection analysis rather than Commerce Clause analysis to strike state taxes that are imposed on the basis of a *suspect classification* or that burden a *fundamental right*. A state tax system giving tax exemptions only to long-time residents of the state and denying a similar tax exemption to newer residents will be held to violate the Equal Protection Clause.

Example: The Court invalidated a state property tax provision that gave an exemption from the property tax only to those Vietnam era veterans who had been residents of the state before May 1976. [Hooper v. Bernalillo County Assessor, 472 U.S. 612 (1985)]

2. Nondiscriminatory Taxes

The Court reviews nondiscriminatory state and local taxes affecting interstate commerce and balances the state need to obtain the revenue against the burden the tax imposes on the free flow of commerce—an approach similar to the one used for examining nondiscriminatory regulations to see whether they impose an undue burden on interstate commerce (*see* IX.B.2., *supra*).

a. Factors

The Court generally considers three factors in determining whether the nondiscriminatory tax is valid:

1) Substantial Nexus

A state tax will be valid under the Commerce Clause only if there is a substantial nexus between the activity or property taxed and the taxing state.

Example: A state in which a sale is made may force the seller to pay a sales tax if the seller has some significant contact with the state (*e.g.,* carries on business in the state). However, the state may not force the seller to pay a sales tax if its only contact with the state is the receipt of orders from sales representatives that may be accepted or rejected by the seller.

a) More than "Minimum Contacts" Under Due Process Clause

The substantial nexus requirement is not necessarily satisfied by establishing the "minimum contacts" between the taxed party and the state necessary to satisfy the Due Process Clause. Minimum contacts only requires there to be sufficient contacts with the forum such that it is reasonable for the taxed party to expect to be subject to the taxing state's jurisdiction. Substantial nexus requires significant or substantial activity within the taxing state. Thus, substantial nexus is not (necessarily) established by showing minimum contacts.

Example: If an interstate seller solicits sales in a state by mail only with orders shipped to the state by mail or common carrier, minimum contacts are present. However, the substantial nexus required by the Commerce Clause is not present—the mere mailing of catalogs to the state and shipment by mail or common carrier is not significant activity within the state. [Quill Corp. v. North Dakota, 504 U.S. 298 (1992)]

2) Fair Apportionment

A state or local tax affecting interstate commerce will be valid under the Commerce Clause only if it is fairly apportioned according to a rational formula (*i.e.,* the tax should be based on the extent of the taxable activity or property in the state). Otherwise the activity or property would be subject to cumulative tax burdens.

Examples: 1) State A imposes a 1% tax on gross receipts of all businesses within the state. Harvester is located in State A but makes a number of sales out-of-state. The tax is invalid as to Harvester's out-of-state sales since it potentially subjects those sales to cumulative burdens—the tax by the seller's state and a similar tax by the buyer's state—without apportioning the tax.

2) Chooch is a resident of State A. It owns railroad cars used in interstate commerce. The cars are in State A three months each year and State B three months each year. For a State B property tax on the railroad cars to be valid, it must fairly apportion the tax, so that the cars will not be subjected to a similar tax by State A, thus cumulating Chooch's tax burden.

Note: The taxpayer has the burden of proving an unfair apportionment.

a) Equal Protection Clause

If a tax is not fairly apportioned, it may also violate the Equal Protection Clause. Equal protection requires state or local government tax classifications to have a rational relationship to a legitimate government interest. The state may divide property into different classifications, and impose different levels of tax on each classification, if the classification system meets the rational relationship test. [Lehnhausen v. Lake Shore Auto Parts Co., 410 U.S. 356 (1973)—state personal property tax only on property owned by corporations is valid]

Example: If a government tax assessment system results in identical pieces of property being valued and taxed at different rates for no reason other than the government assessor's refusal to adopt a more evenhanded valuation system, the resulting difference in the taxes imposed on the similar pieces of property will violate the Equal Protection Clause. [Allegheny Pittsburgh Coal Co. v. County Commission, 488 U.S. 336 (1989)]

3) Fair Relationship

A state or local tax affecting interstate commerce will be valid under the Commerce Clause only if the tax is fairly related to the services or benefits provided by the state.

Example: A state may levy a tax on passengers enplaning at a state airport if the tax is related to the benefits that the passengers receive from the state (*e.g.,* the airport facilities). [*See* Evansville-Vanderburg Airport Authority District v. Delta Airlines, Inc., 405 U.S. 707 (1972)]

B. USE TAX
Use taxes are taxes imposed on the users of goods purchased out of state.

1. Permissible in Buyer's State
Use taxes are not considered to discriminate against interstate commerce even though they single out interstate commerce for taxation (*i.e.,* they are imposed only on goods purchased outside the state), as long as the use tax rate is not higher than the sales tax rate. *Rationale:* The purpose of such a tax is to *equalize* the tax on in-state and out-of-state goods rather than to give in-state goods an advantage. [*See* Henneford v. Silas Mason Co., 300 U.S. 577 (1937)]

2. Credit for Sales Tax Paid in Seller's State
It has been argued that if the sale is consummated outside the state and is subjected *there* to a *sales tax*, a use tax by the buyer's state must give a credit for the sales tax already paid in the seller's state; *i.e., if no credit* is given, the transaction is subjected to *two taxes* (a multiple burden) simply because the transaction involved interstate commerce.

3. State May Force Seller to Collect Use Tax
Often, states force the user to come forward and pay the state the use tax owed. However, a state may force the nonresident, interstate seller to *collect* the use tax from the local buyer and remit it to the state *if* the seller has the substantial nexus required by the Commerce Clause. The substantial nexus requirement can be met if the seller engages in some *significant activity* in the buyer's state, *e.g.,* maintains offices there.

a. Drummers Sufficient
The use of "drummers" (*i.e.,* persons who solicit orders locally, but who must submit all orders to the out-of-state seller's offices for approval and shipment) in the buyer's state *is* significant activity and can subject the out-of-state seller to the duty of collecting a use tax for the buyer's state. [General Trading Co. v. Iowa Tax Commission, 322 U.S. 335 (1944)]

Note: The use of "drummers" is *not* sufficient to force an out-of-state seller to collect a sales tax for the buyer's state. (*See* C.2.b., *infra.*)

b. Mail Solicitation Insufficient
If the interstate seller solicits sales by mail, with orders to be shipped by mail or common carrier, the interstate seller lacks the substantial nexus required by the Commerce Clause, and thus the buyer's state may *not* impose a duty on the interstate seller to collect a use tax on sales to local residents. [Quill Corp. v. North Dakota, A.2.a.1)a), *supra*]

C. SALES TAXES
Sales taxes are taxes imposed on the seller of goods for sales consummated within the state. They

generally do not discriminate against interstate commerce; rather the issue usually involves whether there is a substantial nexus (*see* A.2.a.1), *supra*) between the taxpayer and the taxing state, or whether the tax is properly apportioned.

1. Sales Tax by Seller's State

a. Sale Consummated Within the State
If the sale is consummated within the state (*i.e.,* buyer takes possession within the state), there is a substantial nexus between the taxing state and the taxpayer; thus, the tax is valid under the Commerce Clause—even if the buyer immediately takes the goods outside the state for use. [International Harvester Co. v. Department of Treasury, 322 U.S. 340 (1944)] Also, there is no need to apportion the sales tax, even if the sale includes services to be performed in another state. [Oklahoma Tax Commission v. Jefferson Lines, Inc., 517 U.S. 1 (1995)—sale of bus ticket for transportation beginning in one state and ending in another]

b. Sale Made to a Buyer Outside the State
If the sale is made to a buyer outside the state (*i.e.,* goods delivered there by the seller or a common carrier), the tax will not be invalid for lack of a substantial nexus, because the relationship between the seller and the state is sufficient. However, all such laws to date have been found to violate the Commerce Clause because they were not fairly apportioned (*i.e.,* they did not provide for apportionment when the transaction could be taxed by other states, such as the buyer's state). [*See* J.D. Adams Manufacturing Co. v. Storen, 304 U.S. 307 (1938)]

2. Sales Tax by Buyer's State

a. Tax Permitted If Seller Has Substantial Contacts
If the interstate seller has ***substantial contacts*** with the consumer state (*e.g.,* office, salesroom, property, etc.), the substantial nexus requirement is satisfied and the Commerce Clause does not prohibit a sales tax by the consumer state—even though the goods are delivered from outside the state. [McGoldrick v. Berwind-White Coal Mining Co., 309 U.S. 33 (1940)]

b. "Drummers" Insufficient
However, if the only contact between the interstate seller and the consumer state consists of "drummers," the Commerce Clause ***prohibits any sales tax*** by the consumer state—because there is no substantial nexus. [McLeod v. J.E. Dilworth Co., 322 U.S. 327 (1944)] Note, however, that the buyer's state could force the seller to collect a use tax. (*See* B.3., *supra*.)

c. Tax on Telephone Calls
A state may impose a tax on the amount paid for a telephone call (in lieu of a sales or use tax on the transaction) if: (i) one of the parties to the telephone call (the caller or the recipient of the call) was in the taxing state; (ii) the call is charged to an address billed within the taxing state or paid within the taxing state; and (iii) the state tax minimizes the chance of a single call being subject to multiple state taxes by granting some form of credit against its tax for taxes paid to another state. [Goldberg v. Sweet, 488 U.S. 252 (1989)]

D. AD VALOREM PROPERTY TAXES

Ad valorem property taxes are taxes based on a percentage of the assessed value of the property in question. Such taxes are generally valid. However, a Commerce Clause issue arises when the property taxed moves in interstate commerce. Goods in transit are *totally exempt* from taxation. Once the goods come to a halt in a state (*i.e.,* obtain a *taxable situs*), they may be taxed. Then, the issue usually revolves around whether the tax imposes an undue cumulative burden (*i.e.,* apportionment).

1. No Tax on Commodities in the Course of Interstate Commerce

Commodities in the course of interstate commerce are *entirely exempt* from local taxation—since each state could otherwise exact a toll as the goods passed through, imposing an intolerable burden on interstate commerce. [Standard Oil v. Peck, 342 U.S. 382 (1952)] Thus, states may not levy an ad valorem property tax on commodities being shipped in interstate commerce, even if the goods happen to be in the state on tax day.

a. When Is Property "in the Course of" Interstate Commerce?

Only property "in the course of" interstate commerce is immune from local property taxation.

1) When Does Interstate Transportation Begin?

Interstate transportation begins when (i) the cargo is delivered to an interstate carrier (the shipper thereby relinquishing further control), *or* (ii) the cargo actually starts its interstate journey. Goods merely being prepared for transit are *not* in the course of interstate commerce.

a) Severance Taxes Are Permissible

A nondiscriminatory state tax on *extraction of minerals* from the state, measured by a percentage of the value of the minerals, is valid even though most of the minerals are *sold in interstate commerce*. [Commonwealth Edison Co. v. Montana, 453 U.S. 609 (1981)]

2) Effect of a "Break" in Transit

Once started, a shipment remains in the course of interstate commerce unless actually diverted. Breaks in the continuity of transit will not destroy the interstate character of the shipment, unless the break was *intended to end or suspend* (rather than temporarily interrupt) the shipment.

3) When Does Interstate Shipment End?

The interstate shipment usually ends when it *reaches its destination*, and thereafter the goods are *subject to local tax*. However, a few cases have held that goods are still in transit where further acts are necessary after arrival to make an effective delivery. [York v. Colley, 247 U.S. 21 (1917)—shipment of complex industrial machinery, which vendor had to erect and install before effective delivery to purchaser] But there are limits to this doctrine. Thus, the Court has refused to find goods still in transit after the arrival of machinery that was simple to install and could be assembled by the purchaser as well as the vendor. [Browning v. City of Waycross, 233 U.S. 16 (1914)]

b.   **No Apportionment Required**
The validity of state taxes on goods in interstate commerce is strictly a Commerce Clause question; *i.e.*, either the goods are "in the course of" interstate commerce and exempt from tax or they are not. There is no need for apportionment.

2.   **Tax on Instrumentalities Used to Transport Goods Interstate**
The validity of ad valorem property taxes on instrumentalities of commerce (airplanes, railroad cars, etc.) depends on (i) whether the instrumentality has acquired a *"taxable situs"* in the taxing state (*i.e.*, whether there are *sufficient "contacts" with the taxing state* to justify the tax), and (ii) since the physical situs of the instrumentalities may change from state to state during the year, whether the *value* of the instrumentality has been properly *apportioned according to the amount of "contacts"* with each taxing state. (The taxable situs ("nexus") is required by the Due Process Clause to establish the state's power to tax at all, and apportionment is required by the Commerce Clause to prevent an intolerable burden on interstate commerce.)

a.   **Taxable Situs ("Nexus")**

1)   **Property Receiving Benefits or Protection from Taxing State**
In general, an instrumentality has a taxable situs in a state if it receives *benefits or protection* from the state. [Braniff Airways v. Nebraska Board of Equalization and Assessment, 347 U.S. 490 (1954)—airplanes have taxable situs in non-domiciliary state where airline company owned no property but made 18 regularly scheduled flights per day from rented depot space, even though same aircraft did not land every day]

2)   **May Be More than One Taxable Situs**
An instrumentality may have more than one taxable situs, upon each of which states can impose a tax subject to the required apportionment (*infra*).

3)   **Exception for Ships in International Waters—"Home-Port Doctrine"**
An exception to the general rule prohibits taxation of ships sailing international waters by any state other than that in which the owner of the ship (or the ship itself) is domiciled. The domiciliary state may tax the ship at *full value*.

Note: The "home-port doctrine" was developed prior to the concept of apportioned taxation, and its validity today is questionable. It has been expressly *repudiated* as to ships sailing inland or on interstate waters. [Ott v. Mississippi Valley Barge Line Co., 336 U.S. 169 (1949)]

b.   **Apportionment Requirement**
Where an instrumentality has only one situs, the domiciliary state can tax at full value. Where the instrumentality has more than one taxable situs, a tax apportioned on the value of the instrumentality will be upheld if it fairly approximates the average physical presence of the instrumentality within the taxing state. [Union Tank Line Co. v. Wright, 249 U.S. 275 (1919)]

1)   **Proper Apportionment**
The following methods have been upheld:

(i) Using the proportion of *miles traveled* within the taxing state to the total number of miles traveled by the instrumentalities in the entire operation. [Ott v. Mississippi Valley Barge Line Co., *supra*]

(ii) Computing the *average number of instrumentalities* (tank cars) *physically present* in the taxing state on any one day during the tax year and taxing that portion at full value—*i.e.,* as if in the state all year. [Johnson Oil Refining Co. v. Oklahoma, 290 U.S. 158 (1933)]

Note: Since different states may use different apportionment formulas to tax the same property, there may still be some double taxation of the same instrumentalities. However, the double taxation should be minimal if proper apportionment formulas have been used.

2) Improper Apportionment

The apportionment formula used must be *rational*, both on its face and as applied to property values connected with the taxing state. A state is not permitted to use imprecise formulas resulting in totally unrealistic assessments, since this would violate both the Due Process and Commerce Clauses. However, the taxpayer has a heavy burden of showing "gross overreaching." [Norfolk & Western Railroad v. Missouri Tax Commission, 390 U.S. 317 (1968)]

3) Domiciliary State Can Tax Full Value Unless Taxpayer Proves Taxable Situs Elsewhere

The taxpayer's domiciliary state can tax the full value of instrumentalities used in interstate commerce unless the taxpayer can prove that a defined part thereof has acquired a taxable "situs" elsewhere. [Northwest Airlines, Inc. v. Minnesota, 322 U.S. 292 (1944)]

a) Taxpayer's Required Proof

In this regard, mere proof that some determinable fraction of the instrumentalities was absent from the domiciliary state for part of the tax year is not enough. The taxpayer must prove either (i) that the instrumentalities were *permanently* located in some other state, or (ii) that they were *habitually employed* in interstate commerce in some other state or states, thus acquiring a "taxable situs" outside the domiciliary state. But the taxpayer need not prove that the instrumentalities are actually being taxed by a nondomiciliary state. [Central Railroad v. Pennsylvania, 370 U.S. 607 (1962)]

c. Tax on Value of Entire Interstate Enterprise

As an alternative to taxing each separate piece of property, a state may tax the value of an interstate business as a whole. Again, however, such a tax will be upheld only if the value of the total business is *apportioned* so as to reflect fairly that portion of the business property attributable to the taxing state. [Nashville, Chattanooga & St. Louis Railway v. Browning, 310 U.S. 362 (1940)—apportionment of value of railroad by local track mileage as compared to its total track]

E. PRIVILEGE, LICENSE, FRANCHISE, OR OCCUPATION TAXES

These taxes (cumulatively known as "doing business" taxes) may be measured by a flat amount or by a proportional rate based on revenue derived from the taxing state.

1. **General Rule—Such Taxes Are Permitted**

   States generally can impose such taxes—on companies engaged exclusively in interstate commerce, as well as on interstate companies engaged in local commerce—for the privilege of doing business within the state. However, the tax must meet the basic requirements—the activity taxed must have a *substantial nexus to the taxing state*; and the tax must be *fairly apportioned*, must *not discriminate* against interstate commerce, and must *fairly relate to services provided* by the state. [Complete Auto Transit, Inc. v. Brady, 430 U.S. 274 (1977)—*overruling* Spector Motor Service v. O'Connor, 340 U.S. 602 (1951)]

   Examples: 1) A privilege tax for doing business, based on the gross income derived from transporting goods within the state, can be applied to a trucking company that delivers goods coming from outside the state. [Complete Auto Transit, Inc. v. Brady, *supra*]

   2) An occupation tax on all businesses, based on gross income derived within the state, can be applied to a stevedoring company operating within the state that loads and unloads ships carrying goods in interstate commerce. [Department of Revenue v. Association of Washington Stevedoring Cos., 435 U.S. 734 (1978)—*overruling* Joseph v. Carter & Weekes Stevedoring Co., 330 U.S. 442 (1947)]

   a. **Taxpayer Has Burden of Proof**

      The taxpayer has the burden of showing that the state's apportionment formula is unfair. However, a state tax that discriminates against interstate commerce will be held invalid regardless of whether the taxpayer can show that an actual, unfair multiple burden is imposed on his business.

2. **Flat License Taxes on "Drummers" Prohibited**

   Flat license fees may not be levied upon "drummers" (solicitors) who seek local orders to be filled from goods shipped interstate, even if the same fee is levied on those selling intrastate goods. [Nippert v. Richmond, 327 U.S. 416 (1946)] Otherwise each municipality visited by the drummer could impose such a tax (resulting in a tremendous cumulative burden), while the local retail merchant would be subject to only one local tax—thereby constituting an unreasonable burden upon interstate commerce.

   a. **Compare—License Tax on Peddler Selling and Delivering Wares Within State**

      However, the state *may* impose a license tax on a peddler (itinerant salesperson) who *actually sells and delivers* her wares within a state (regardless of the fact that the goods are shipped into the state by interstate commerce), provided the tax rates are *nondiscriminatory*. [Dunbar Stanley Studios v. Alabama, 393 U.S. 537 (1969)]

3. **Taxes on Interstate Carriers**

   a. **In General**

      Interstate carriers (such as trucking companies) can be made to pay taxes that compensate the state for the use of its roads and the cost of administering traffic regulations. If a tax is fairly related to the use of the roads it is valid even though the proceeds are used for purposes unrelated to road use or road maintenance. However, a tax must not discriminate against interstate commerce or interstate carriers.

b. **Flat Taxes**

A "flat tax" on an interstate carrier is one that establishes a single fee to use the roads of the state (such as a fixed fee or a fee based on the size of the vehicle); it is not related to the amount of time that a vehicle spends in the state. Such a tax will violate the Commerce Clause whenever it has the effect of discriminating against out-of-state carriers by exposing a multistate carrier to a higher tax burden than would be borne by a solely in-state carrier. The Supreme Court has indicated that flat taxes on trucks may be inherently discriminatory unless either: (i) the state grants out-of-state carriers a credit against the flat tax for license fees (or similar taxes) paid to other states (so that the interstate carrier is not subject to multiple or discriminatory tax burdens); or (ii) the particular flat tax is nondiscriminatory and a reasonable charge for the use of the roads, and administrative difficulties make the collection of a more carefully apportioned tax (based on actual road use) impracticable. [American Trucking Associations, Inc. v. Scheiner, 483 U.S. 266 (1987)]

4. **Taxes on Interstate Passengers**

A $1 state or municipal tax, imposed on enplaning commercial airline passengers to help defray airport construction costs, does not violate the Commerce Clause (or the Equal Protection Clause, or the "right to travel"). As long as (i) the amount of the tax is based on some *fair approximation of use* and is not excessive in comparison with the government benefit conferred, and (ii) the tax *does not discriminate* against interstate commerce, it is valid even though some other formula might better reflect the relative use of airports by individual users. [Evansville-Vanderburg Airport Authority District v. Delta Airlines, Inc., 405 U.S. 707 (1972)]

F. **NET INCOME TAXES**

States may impose fairly apportioned, nondiscriminatory net income taxes on interstate firms that conduct business within their borders. [Northwestern States Portland Cement Co. v. Minnesota, 358 U.S. 450 (1959)]

1. **Adequate Contacts**

In *Portland Cement,* the taxpayer had several sales representatives and a rented office in the taxing state, and the Court found this a sufficient "nexus" for the tax. (*Note:* Congress subsequently enacted 15 U.S.C. sections 381-384, *prohibiting* state net income taxes, irrespective of fair apportionment, on out-of-state businesses whose only contacts with the taxing state are salespeople.)

2. **Fair Apportionment**

a. **Three-Factor Formula**

The state in *Portland Cement* used a "three-factor" apportionment formula (ratio of property, payroll, and sales within state to taxpayer's total property, payroll, and sales). The taxpayer could not show that this was unfair, given state protection and services for the taxpayer's local activities; and there was no showing of "multiple burden."

b. **Single-Factor Formula**

A "single-factor" formula (ratio of sales within state to taxpayer's total sales) has also been *upheld* as "presumptively valid"—the taxpayer being unable to prove by "clear and cogent evidence" that it "led to a grossly distorted result." The fact that some income may be subject to overlapping taxes because other states (even a majority) use a different formula (the "three-factor" formula) does not prove that the single-factor formula is arbitrary. [Moorman Manufacturing Co. v. Bair, 437 U.S. 267 (1978)]

3. **Income Includible in Tax Base**
Income from separate corporate divisions or from subsidiary corporations operating in other states or foreign countries may be included in the tax base—unless the taxpayer proves that the divisions or subsidiaries were not part of its "single unitary business."

Examples: 1) The Court has applied the *unitary business tax* principle to allow California to include both *domestic and foreign subsidiary income* in the tax base of a corporation for purposes of applying the state income tax to the domestic corporation.

2) A substantial flow of value from the foreign subsidiary to the domestic parent company and a substantial degree of mutual interdependence justified including the foreign subsidiary income in the domestic parent corporation's tax base. [Container Corp. of America v. Franchise Tax Board, 463 U.S. 159 (1983)]

G. VALUE ADDED TAX
A value added tax is a tax on the value added at each stage of production or distribution. A state may impose such a tax on value added to products by businesses in the state. Like other state taxes, to be valid the tax must: (i) not discriminate against interstate commerce; (ii) tax an activity with a substantial nexus to the state; (iii) be fairly apportioned; and (iv) be fairly related to the services provided by the state.

1. **Apportionment**
The state is not required to measure precisely the value added to each product by each business in the state. It may use an apportionment formula to fairly determine the share of value added to the business's products attributable to its in-state activities. Thus, a three-part test based on the business's property, payroll, and sales, as is used for apportioning state income taxes (*see* F.2.a., *supra*), is proper. [Trinova Corp. v. Michigan Department of Treasury, 498 U.S. 358 (1991)]

H. TAXES ON FOREIGN CORPORATIONS

1. **State May Impose Tax as a Condition of Doing Business**
A state may impose a tax or fee as a condition of allowing a foreign corporation (one incorporated in another state) to do business in the state. [Atlantic Refining Co. v. Virginia, 302 U.S. 22 (1937)]

2. **State Cannot Discriminate Against Foreign Corporation Once Admitted to Do Business**
Once a foreign corporation *is* admitted to do business, the state cannot impose discriminatory rates as to business done locally. This would constitute an unreasonable burden on interstate commerce and deprive the corporation of the equal protection to which it is entitled. [Western Union v. Kansas, 216 U.S. 1 (1910)] Under the *Equal Protection Clause*, a state may *not* impose more onerous taxes or other burdens on foreign corporations than on

domestic corporations unless the discrimination is *rationally* related to a *legitimate* state purpose. [Western & Southern Life Insurance Co. v. State Board of Equalization, 451 U.S. 648 (1981)]

XI. POWER OF STATES TO TAX FOREIGN COMMERCE

A. IMPORT-EXPORT CLAUSE

Article I, Section 10, Clause 2 provides: "No state shall, without the Consent of the Congress, lay any Imposts or Duties on Imports or Exports, except what may be absolutely necessary for executing its inspection Laws . . . ."

1. State Taxation of "Imports" Prohibited Absent Congressional Consent

The Import-Export Clause prohibits the states from imposing any tax on imported goods as such or on commercial activity connected with imported goods *as such* (*i.e.*, taxes discriminating against imports), except with congressional consent. [Brown v. Maryland, 25 U.S. 419 (1827)]

a. Nondiscriminatory Ad Valorem Property Taxes on Goods in State—Permissible

A nondiscriminatory ad valorem property tax on all goods located in the state (including imported goods) is not prohibited. [Michelin Tire Corp. v. Wages, 423 U.S. 276 (1976)] *Rationale:* Such taxes merely apportion the cost of state services among all beneficiaries, and imports must bear their fair share.

Example: It is permissible for a state to impose a nondiscriminatory property tax on imported goods stored under bond in a warehouse and destined for domestic manufacture and sale. [R.J. Reynolds Tobacco Co. v. Durham County, 479 U.S. 130 (1986)]

1) Goods in Transit

a) Property Tax

The Court has left as an *open question* whether a nondiscriminatory property tax may be imposed on imported goods still in transit.

b) Occupation Tax

But a nondiscriminatory occupation tax on all businesses operating within the state may be applied to a company that *services* imported (or exported) goods, even when the goods are still in transit. [Department of Revenue v. Association of Washington Stevedoring Cos., *supra*]

2. Inspection Fees for Imports and Exports

Such fees are permitted if "absolutely necessary," and are presumed reasonable (and upheld) unless the fees are so excessive that the state purpose is deemed to be revenue-raising rather than reimbursement of inspection costs. [Red "C" Oil Manufacturing Co. v. Board of Agriculture, 222 U.S. 380 (1912)]

3. State Taxation of "Exports" Prohibited

The Import-Export Clause prohibits the states from imposing any tax on goods after they have entered the "export stream."

a. **"Export Stream" Defined**
Commodities sold to foreign purchasers enter the "export stream" (and hence are exempt from tax) only after it is *certain* that they are headed for their foreign destination and will not be diverted to domestic use.

B. COMMERCE CLAUSE

The Commerce Clause gives Congress the exclusive power to regulate foreign commerce and thus inherently limits a state's power to tax that commerce. Therefore, a state tax applied to foreign commerce must meet all of the Commerce Clause tests that apply to state taxation of interstate commerce. (*See* X.A., *supra.*) And even if a state tax meets those tests, the tax is invalid if it would (i) create a substantial risk of international multiple taxation or (ii) prevent the federal government from "speaking with one voice" regarding international trade or foreign affairs issues. [Barclays Bank PLC v. Franchise Tax Board, 512 U.S. 298 (1994)]

1. **Instrumentalities of Foreign Commerce**
A state may *not* impose an ad valorem property tax on instrumentalities that are *foreign owned* and used *exclusively in international commerce*. This is true even if the property has a situs in the taxing state and the tax is nondiscriminatory and fairly apportioned. [Japan Line, Ltd. v. County of Los Angeles, 441 U.S. 434 (1979)] In the absence of congressional authorization, there are stricter limits on state taxation of foreign commerce than of interstate commerce because there is greater need for federal uniformity and a lesser opportunity for the court to prevent multiple taxation.

2. **Compare—Domestically Owned Instrumentalities of Foreign Commerce**
A state may impose a fairly apportioned sales tax on a lease of domestically owned cargo containers that will be used in foreign commerce. Such a tax does not interfere with the federal interest in international commerce or present a substantial possibility of international multiple taxation. [Itel Containers International Corp. v. Huddleston, 507 U.S. 60 (1993)]

3. **Income Tax—Apportioned Share of Unitary Business Income**
A state may apply its income tax to a share of a multinational corporation's unitary (total) business income attributable to its activity in the state. The state tax must meet the same nexus (contacts), fair apportionment, and nondiscrimination requirements that are applied to determine whether the state can tax the unitary business of a multistate business. [Container Corp. of America v. Franchise Board, 463 U.S. 159 (1983); Barclays Bank PLC v. Franchise Tax Board, *supra*]

PART FOUR: INDIVIDUAL GUARANTEES
AGAINST GOVERNMENTAL OR PRIVATE ACTION

XII. LIMITATIONS ON POWER AND STATE ACTION REQUIREMENT

A. CONSTITUTIONAL RESTRICTIONS ON POWER OVER INDIVIDUALS

The Constitution provides individuals with a number of rights that restrict the power of the government (*e.g.*, the right to speak freely). Some rights/restrictions are applicable only to the federal government, some are applicable only to state and local governments, and some are applicable to all governmental bodies. A few even apply to private action. Several constitutional provisions also give Congress the power to adopt legislation to protect individual rights.

1. **Bill of Rights**

    The Bill of Rights (first 10 Amendments to the Constitution) is the most important source of limitations on the federal government's power. By its terms, the Bill is not applicable to the states, although most of its safeguards have been held to be applicable to the states through the Fourteenth Amendment Due Process Clause.

    a. **Rights Applicable to States**

    The Supreme Court has stated that only those safeguards in the Bill of Rights that are "essential to liberty" are applicable to the states through the Fourteenth Amendment. Included in this concept are: *all the First Amendment* guarantees (speech, press, assembly, right to petition, free exercise, and nonestablishment of religion); the *Fourth Amendment* (unreasonable search and seizure); some *elements of the Fifth Amendment* (privilege against self-incrimination; compensation for taking of private property for public use); the *Sixth Amendment* (speedy and public trial by impartial jury, notice and right of confrontation, compulsory process, and right to legal counsel in all serious criminal proceedings); and the *Eighth Amendment* (cruel and unusual punishment, excessive bail, and excessive fine provisions are *assumed* to be incorporated but there is no precise ruling).

    b. **Rights Not Applicable to States**

    The Supreme Court has refused to "incorporate" (make applicable to the states) the following:

    (i) *Second Amendment*—arms;

    (ii) *Grand Jury Clause* of the Fifth Amendment;

    (iii) *Seventh Amendment*—jury in civil cases; and

    (iv) It is not clear whether the *Ninth Amendment* (regarding the existence of unenumerated individual rights) applies to the states, but in any event, the Ninth Amendment has not been the primary basis for Supreme Court invalidation of a federal, state, or local law.

    There has never been a Supreme Court decision on the Third Amendment (quartering of soldiers). The *Tenth Amendment*, by its terms, limits the federal government's power over states, and so is inapplicable to the states.

2. **Thirteenth Amendment**

    The Thirteenth Amendment provides that slavery shall not exist in the United States.

    a. **No Requirement of State Action**

    The amendment contains no language limiting its effect to governmental action (*e.g.,* "no *state* shall . . . "); thus, it is applicable even to *private action*.

    b. **Congressional Power**

    The enabling clause of the amendment gives Congress the power to adopt appropriate legislation, and the Supreme Court apparently will uphold legislation proscribing almost any private racially discriminatory act that can be characterized as a "badge or incident of slavery."

Examples: The Supreme Court has upheld legislation:

1) Prohibiting private parties from refusing to rent or sell housing to a person because of race [Jones v. Alfred H. Mayer Co., 392 U.S. 409 (1968)];

2) Prohibiting private, nonsectarian schools from refusing to admit nonwhite children [Runyon v. McCrary, 427 U.S. 160 (1967)]; and

3) Prohibiting a private employer from discriminating in hiring on the basis of race [Patterson v. McLean Credit Union, 491 U.S. 164 (1989)].

Note: The above are examples of where Congress used its power to adopt statutes prohibiting "badges of slavery"; the proscribed activities would not necessarily be held to violate the Thirteenth Amendment absent the legislation.

3. Fourteenth Amendment

The Fourteenth Amendment *prohibits states* (not the federal government or private persons) from depriving any person of life, liberty, or property without due process and equal protection of the law. As discussed above, this amendment is a most important source of limitations on the states' power over individuals, since through the Due Process Clause, most of the protections of the Bill of Rights are applicable to the states.

Note: The meaning of due process and equal protection will be discussed later in this outline.

a. Requirement of State Action

The Fourteenth Amendment applies only if there is action by a state or local government, government officer, or private individual whose behavior meets the requirements for state action (*see* B., below).

b. Scope of Congressional Power

Section 5 of the Fourteenth Amendment is an enabling clause giving Congress the power to adopt *appropriate legislation* to enforce the rights and guarantees provided by the Fourteenth Amendment. Under Section 5, Congress may *not* expand existing constitutional rights or create new ones—it may only enact laws to prevent or remedy violations of rights already recognized by the courts. To adopt a valid law, Congress must point to a history or pattern of state violation of such rights and adopt legislation that is *congruent and proportional* (*i.e.*, narrowly tailored) to solving the identified violation.

Examples: 1) The Americans With Disabilities Act ("ADA") includes provisions that, among other things, prohibit states from discriminating against disabled persons in hiring practices and requires states to make reasonable accommodations for disabled employees. Under the Fourteenth Amendment Equal Protection Clause, the Court has recognized a right of disabled people to be free from irrational state discrimination. In adopting the ADA, Congress did not identify a history or pattern of irrational employment practices by the states. Even if there were such a pattern, the provisions here were not congruent and proportional to remedying irrational discrimination; they are overinclusive, because they prohibit states from making employment decisions that are constitutional under the rational basis test. [Board of Trustees of University of Alabama v. Garrett, 121 S. Ct. 955 (2001)]

2) Under similar reasoning, the Supreme Court has held that Congress has no power under Section 5 to broadly restrict age discrimination by state employers. [Kimel v. Florida Board of Regents, 528 U.S. 62 (2000)—the federal law is not congruent and proportional because it would forbid many employment decisions based on age that have a "rational basis," which the Court has held is the standard for judgment under the Equal Protection Clause for age-based discrimination]

3) The Supreme Court held that there is no violation of the First Amendment, applicable to the states through the Fourteenth Amendment, where a state law incidentally burdens a religious practice. [Employment Division v. Smith, XXII.C.3., *infra*] In response, Congress adopted a statute, purportedly under Section 5, providing that a state may not burden religious practices absent a compelling interest. The statute was held unconstitutional because it sought to expand substantive First Amendment rights beyond those recognized by the Supreme Court. [City of Boerne v. Flores, 521 U.S. 507 (1997)]

4. Fifteenth Amendment
The Fifteenth Amendment is a limitation on both the *states and the federal government*. It prohibits them from denying any citizen the right to vote on account of race or color. As indicated above, the amendment contains an enabling clause that allows Congress to adopt legislation protecting the right to vote from discrimination.

5. Commerce Clause
The Supreme Court has allowed Congress to use the Commerce Clause to limit the power of individuals over other individuals—by adopting legislation barring private racial discrimination in activities "connected with" interstate commerce. Recall that under the affectation doctrine, almost any activity can be said to be connected with interstate commerce. (*See* II.A.4.a.1), *supra*.)

a. Civil Rights Act
Provisions of the Civil Rights Act of 1964 *barring discrimination in places of public accommodation* are proper and valid exercises of commerce power.

b. Extent of Commerce Power
The reach of the commerce power is broad. Any business which is *open to interstate travelers* or *uses products shipped in interstate commerce* is covered. [Daniel v. Paul, 395 U.S. 298 (1969)—private resort held to be a public place of accommodation encompassed within the Act because drinks and entertainment facilities had been purchased and shipped through interstate commerce]

6. Rights of National Citizenship

The Supreme Court has also allowed Congress to limit the power of private individuals to infringe upon others' rights of national citizenship (*e.g.,* the right of interstate travel, the right to assemble to petition Congress for redress), without pointing to any specific constitutional source for the power. [Griffin v. Breckenridge, 403 U.S. 88 (1971)]

B. STATE ACTION REQUIREMENT

As indicated above, the Constitution generally prohibits only governmental infringement of constitutional rights. Thus, to find some action unconstitutional, it is generally necessary to attribute the action to the state, which includes government agencies and officials acting under the color of state law. However, this does not mean that the act must be directly by a government actor; "state action" can be found in the actions of seemingly private individuals who (i) perform exclusive public functions, or (ii) have significant state involvement in their activities.

1. Exclusive Public Functions

The Supreme Court has found that certain activities are so ***traditionally*** the ***exclusive*** prerogative of the state that they constitute state action even when undertaken by a private individual or organization. To date, only running a town and running an election for public office have been found to be such exclusive public functions.

Examples: 1) The owner of a "company town" with ***all*** of the attributes of a public town (*e.g.,* homes, sidewalks, streets, police and fire protection, etc.) cannot deny a person's First Amendment right to distribute religious literature in the town, since the company town is equivalent to a town. [Marsh v. Alabama, 326 U.S. 501 (1946)] However, the owner of a shopping mall can deny people their First Amendment right to picket, since a mall does not have all of the attributes of a town. [Hudgens v. NLRB, 424 U.S. 507 (1976)]

2) Running elections is an exclusive public function, so if a private organization runs a preprimary that has a substantial effect on who is ultimately elected, its actions will be state action. [Terry v. Adams, 345 U.S. 461 (1953)—county political group whose candidate almost always runs unopposed in primary and general election cannot discriminate]

a. Must Be Traditional *and* Exclusive Function

To be state action, the activity must be ***both*** a ***traditional*** and ***exclusive*** government function. Thus, the Court has held that a warehouseman authorized by statute to sell goods stored with him for unpaid charges is not exercising state action when he makes the sale, because while resolution of private disputes is a traditional public function, it is not exclusive—the bailor had state law remedies to check abuses by the warehouseman. [Flagg Brothers v. Brooks, 436 U.S. 149 (1978)] State action exists, and due process guarantees apply, ***only if*** the creditor uses judicial or executive agencies to secure properties in the possession of the debtor.

2. Significant State Involvement—Facilitating Private Action

"State action" also exists whenever a state ***affirmatively*** facilitates, encourages, or authorizes acts of discrimination by its citizens. Note, however, that there must be some sort of affirmative act by the state approving the private action; it is not enough that the state permits the conduct to occur.

a. Instances of Significant State Involvement

1) Official Encouragement
Purportedly private action will be given state action status if the action is encouraged or sanctioned by the state.

a) Judicial Approval
State court enforcement of *restrictive covenants prohibiting sale or lease of property to blacks* constitutes state action even in civil proceedings between private parties. [Shelley v. Kraemer, 334 U.S. 1 (1948)]

(1) Peremptory Challenges
The use of peremptory challenges, even by a private party, constitutes state action both because jury selection is a traditional public function and because there is overt, significant participation by the government (the judge) in the jury selection process. Thus, private litigants and defendants are prohibited from using peremptory challenges in a discriminatory manner. [*See* Edmonson v. Leesville Concrete, 500 U.S. 614 (1992); Georgia v. McCollum, 505 U.S. 42 (1992)]

b) Official Acts
State action may be found in the absence of an unconstitutional statute or ordinance if it appears that the state sanctions constitutional violations by its own officers.

(1) Discriminatory Law Enforcement
The Court reversed a conviction of sit-in demonstrators where no statute or ordinance required segregation but the mayor and police had announced publicly that they would invoke trespass and breach of the peace laws to enforce a local custom of racial separation in eating places. [Lombard v. Louisiana, 373 U.S. 267 (1963)]

(2) Apparent Legal Authority
Even if a state forbids officers from acting in a certain way (*e.g.,* depriving constitutional rights), the forbidden action may still constitute state action if the state puts the actor in a position to commit the unconstitutional act.

Example: A sheriff beat a prisoner to death in an effort to secure a confession. Both the state and the sheriff were held liable. The actions of the sheriff involved "state action" because the sheriff *acted under "the color of state law—* the state in effect cloaked him with the apparent legal authority." [Screws v. United States, 325 U.S. 91 (1945)]

(3) Public Defenders
A public defender does *not act for the state* when he represents an indigent client. Negligence or malpractice by the public defender is not a denial of due process because his actions are not "state actions." [Polk County v. Dodson, 454 U.S. 312 (1982)]

2) State Authorization

In *Reitman v. Mulkey,* 387 U.S. 369 (1967), the Court invalidated a state constitutional provision that *repealed* all existing *state laws banning discrimination* in the sale or lease of property and prohibited reenactment of such laws in the future because such laws "authorize" private discrimination.

3) The State as Lessor for a Racially Discriminatory Lessee

In *Burton v. Wilmington Parking Authority,* 365 U.S. 715 (1961), Delaware was held responsible under the Fourteenth Amendment Equal Protection Clause for the exclusion of blacks from a coffee shop which was located in a public building. The shop was constructed by and leased from the state. The *maintenance* of the facility was *paid for with public funds* and Delaware was able to charge a higher rent because it allowed the restaurant owner to cater to the prejudices of its white customers.

4) Administration of Private Discriminatory Trust by Public Officials

State action exists where city personnel maintain a park, "open to all except blacks," under a private trust. [Evans v. Newton, 382 U.S. 296 (1966)]

5) Entwinement of State and Private Entities

The fact that a state entity helps formulate and adopts the rules of a private entity, and chooses to follow the order of the private entity pursuant to those rules, does not convert the private entity's action into state action. However, a state may be so entwined with a private organization that the organization's actions will be considered state action. [Brentwood Academy v. Tennessee Secondary School Athletic Association, 121 S. Ct. 924 (2001)]

Example: The National Collegiate Athletic Association ("NCAA") is a voluntary association of public and private universities that establishes rules for its members regarding collegiate sports. Pursuant to its rules, the NCAA urged a member college to suspend its coach for recruiting violations. The coach cannot successfully sue the NCAA for violating his constitutional rights because there is no state action. [National Collegiate Athletic Association v. Tarkanian, 488 U.S. 179 (1988)]

Compare: An association that regulates high school sports within a single state: (i) to which most public high schools belong; (ii) whose governing body is made up mostly of public school officials; (iii) whose meetings are held during regular school hours; (iv) whose employees may join the state retirement system; and (v) which is funded by gate receipts from the regulated sports is so entwined with the state that its action can be considered state action. [Brentwood Academy v. Tennessee Secondary School Athletic Association, *supra*]

b. Instances of Insignificant State Involvement

1) Heavily Regulated Businesses and/or Granting of a Monopoly to a Utility

a) **Electric Company**

State action will not be found merely because the state has granted a monopoly to a business or heavily regulates it.

Example: In *Jackson v. Metropolitan Edison,* 419 U.S. 345 (1974), *no state action* was found where an electric company terminated the user's service without notice and hearing. The state had not directed or ordered the termination and the fact that the company was heavily regulated and the state commission had approved private utility regulations authorizing such termination was not enough.

b) **Nursing Home**

A nursing home operated by a private corporation did *not exercise state action* when it discharged Medicaid patients, even though its operation was extensively regulated by the government. [Blum v. Yaretsky, 457 U.S. 991 (1982)]

c) **School**

A school operated by a private corporation did *not* exercise state action when it discharged teachers (allegedly in violation of their First Amendment rights) even though the school had contracts with the state to educate or care for many of its students and it received almost all of its operating funds from the government. [Rendell-Baker v. Kohn, 457 U.S. 830 (1982)]

2) **Licensing and Provision of Essential Services**

Granting a liquor license and providing essential services (police, fire, water, power, etc.) to a *private club* that imposes racial restrictions on its members and guests are *not* sufficient to constitute state action. [Moose Lodge v. Irvis, 407 U.S. 163 (1972)]

3) **Congressional Grant of Corporate Charter and Exclusive Name**

Congressional grant of a corporate charter and exclusive use of a name is not sufficient to constitute state action. [San Francisco Arts & Athletics, Inc. v. United States Olympic Committee, 483 U.S. 522 (1987)—congressional charter and grant of exclusive name "Olympic" does not clothe United States Olympic Committee with state action]

4) **No Government Duty to Protect Individuals from Harm by Private Persons**

The mere refusal of government agents to protect a victim from harm by a private person will not result in a finding that the harm was attributable to "state action," at least when state law does not give the victim a right to government protection. [DeShaney v. Winnebago County Department of Social Services, 489 U.S. 189 (1989)—government not responsible for harm inflicted on a child by his father, even though government social worker had reason to believe the child was being abused and did nothing to protect the child] However, if government employees enter into an agreement or conspiracy with private persons to cause harm to a victim, the victim's injuries are the result of state action; the private persons, as well as the government employees with whom they conspired, will have violated the victim's constitutional rights. [Screws v. United States, 325 U.S. 91 (1945); Dennis v. Sparks, 449 U.S. 24 (1980)]

C. TIPS FOR BAR EXAM

1. State Must Be "Significantly Involved" in Private Entity
The state must be "significantly involved" in the private entity. Merely granting a license or providing essential services is insufficient.

2. No Constitutional Mandate to Outlaw Discrimination
States are not constitutionally required to outlaw discrimination. The Constitution forbids only their encouraging or authorizing it.

XIII. RETROACTIVE LEGISLATION

A. CONTRACT CLAUSE—IMPAIRMENT OF CONTRACT
The Contract Clause prohibits *states* from enacting any law that *retroactively* impairs contract rights. It does not affect contracts not yet entered into.

1. Not Applicable to Federal Government
There is no comparable clause applicable to the federal government, although a flagrant contract impairment would be forbidden by the Due Process Clause of the Fifth Amendment.

2. Only Applicable to State Legislation
The provision applies only to state *legislation*, not court decisions. [*See* Tidal Oil v. Flanagan, 263 U.S. 444 (1924)]

3. Basic Impairment Rules

a. Private Contracts
The Contract Clause prevents only *substantial impairments* of contract (*i.e.,* destruction of most or all of a party's rights under a contract). However, not all substantial impairments are invalid. In determining whether legislation is valid under the Contract Clause, use a three-part test:

(i) Does the legislation substantially impair a party's rights under an existing contract? If it does not, the legislation is valid under the Contract Clause. If it does, it will be valid *only if* it:

(ii) Serves an important and legitimate public interest; and

(iii) Is a reasonable and narrowly tailored means of promoting that interest.

Examples: 1) A Minnesota statute that imposed a moratorium on mortgage foreclosures during a severe depression did not violate the Contract Clause. [Home Building & Loan Association v. Blaisdell, 290 U.S. 398 (1934)]

2) A state statute that restricted underground coal mining to protect a variety of public and private uses of surface land (and buildings) and that left the owners of subsurface mining rights with some reasonable value in, or return from, their investment does not violate the Contract Clause. [Keystone Bituminous Coal Association v. DeBenedictis, 480 U.S. 470 (1987)]

b. Public Contracts—Stricter Scrutiny

Public contracts (*i.e.,* those in which the state or political subdivision is a party) are tested by the same basic test detailed above, however, they will likely receive stricter scrutiny, especially if the legislation reduces the contractual burdens on the state. When applying the three-part test, note the following:

1) There is no substantial impairment if the state has reserved the power to *revoke, alter, or amend* either in the contract itself or in a statute or law the terms of which should be considered to be incorporated into the contract [Dartmouth College v. Woodward, 17 U.S. 518 (1819)];

2) In determining whether the law serves as a legitimate public interest, note that the state cannot be obligated by contract to refrain from exercising its police powers necessary to protect the health and safety of its residents; and

3) To be narrowly tailored, the law should not constitute an unnecessarily broad repudiation of contract obligations.

4. Important Decisions

a. Covenant to Private Bondholders Violated

In the past few decades, the Supreme Court allowed states to statutorily modify many contracts for a public purpose, including the termination of redemption rights to state lands when oil was discovered there. However, the Court subsequently invalidated such an action. In *United States Trust Co. v. New Jersey,* 431 U.S. 1 (1977), the Court held that New York and New Jersey violated the Contract Clause by enacting legislation to allow the Port Authority to use port income to subsidize rail passenger transportation in violation of a previous statutory covenant to private bondholders. The state had agreed to certain terms that the bondholders might have relied upon—the public interest in improved rail service could be pursued without violating their contract rights.

b. State Pension Reform Legislation Violated

In *Allied Structural Steel Co. v. Spannaus,* 438 U.S. 234 (1978), the Court invalidated state pension reform legislation which increased the obligation of companies under preexisting pension plans to employees who previously had terminated their work for the company or who previously had retired from employment with the company. Because the legislation constituted a substantial impairment of contract by changing the compensation for work already completed and because it was not necessary to remedy an important social problem in the nature of an emergency, it was held to be a violation of the Contract Clause.

c.   **Regulation of Future Pricing Conduct Permissible**
In *Exxon Corp. v. Eagerton,* 462 U.S. 176 (1983), the Court upheld a state law that increased the state severance tax on oil and gas taken from property in the state and prohibited oil or gas producers from "passing on" that tax increase to their customers. This statute was not a Contract Clause violation even though it effectively limited price increases under preexisting contracts. The law regulated future pricing conduct (conduct after the effective date of the legislation); it was not merely a repeal or impairment of preexisting contracts.

B.   EX POST FACTO LAWS

1.   **Two Ex Post Facto Clauses**
Neither the state nor the federal government may pass an ex post facto law. [Art. I, §9—federal prohibition; Art. I, §10—state prohibition] An ex post facto law is *legislation* that *retroactively* alters the *criminal law* (not civil regulations such as denial of professional licenses) as to offenses or punishments in a *substantially prejudicial* manner. Thus, within the definition are the following:

a.   **Create New Crime**
Statutes that make criminally punishable an act that was not a crime when it was committed.

b.   **Increase Punishment**
Statutes that increase the severity of punishment for a crime after its commission.
Example: Florida has sentencing guidelines that restrict judicial discretion by creating a presumptive sentence for certain types of crimes. On the day D committed a "sexual battery," the guidelines created a presumptive 3½-4½ year sentence for that crime. The guidelines were subsequently modified to provide for a 5½-7 year presumptive sentence. The Ex Post Facto Clause prohibits imposition of the new guidelines on D since the guidelines establish a higher presumptive sentence than existed on the date D committed the crime. [Miller v. Florida, 482 U.S. 423 (1987)]

c.   **Reduce Required Evidence**
Statutes that reduce the quantum of evidence or burden of proof required for conviction below what was required at the time of commission.
Example: A law that raises the age of a sexual abuse victim whose testimony need not be corroborated for a conviction *is* an ex post facto law. [Carmell v. Texas, 529 U.S. 513 (2000)]

2.   **Procedural Changes that Do Not Affect Substantive Elements Are Not Ex Post Facto**
Mere procedural changes in state law will not necessarily trigger the Ex Post Facto Clause. A modified law can be applied to a crime committed before the law's modification if the defendant had notice of the possible penalty and the modified law does not increase the burden on the defendant.
Example: Florida had a death penalty statute that was invalidated by the Supreme Court because the statute restricted discretion in sentencing. Before a new statute was enacted, D committed a murder. Florida then passed a new death penalty provision that complied with Supreme Court criteria. The new

provision was applied at D's trial, and he was sentenced to death. This was not a prohibited ex post facto law, since the earlier statute (though unconstitutional) gave D notice of the possible penalty and the new provision made it *less likely* that the death penalty would be imposed in a given case. [Dobbert v. Florida, 432 U.S. 282 (1977)]

3. **Indirect "Application" to Courts**

Although the Ex Post Facto Clauses prohibit only retroactive *legislation*, the Supreme Court has held that due process prohibits courts from retroactively interpreting criminal law in an unexpected and indefensible way. [Rogers v. Tennessee, 121 S. Ct. 1693 (2001)—state supreme court's abolition of common law "year and a day rule" (which prohibits prosecution for murder if the victim dies more than a year after an attack) was not unexpected and indefensible because medical science has undermined the rule's usefulness and the rule has already been abolished in most jurisdictions]

C. BILLS OF ATTAINDER

A bill of attainder is a legislative act that *inflicts punishment without a judicial trial* upon individuals who are designated either by name or in terms of past conduct. Past conduct acts to define who those particular persons are.

1. **Two Clauses**

Both the *federal and state governments* are prohibited from passing bills of attainder.

2. **Two Requirements Preclude Finding of Bill of Attainder**

These provisions *require both judicial machinery* for trial and punishment of crime and *definition of criminal conduct in such general terms* as not to ensnare within the definition a single individual or small group for punishment because of past behavior.

Example: The Court found a provision in the Landrum-Griffin Act, making it a crime for a member of the Communist Party to act as an officer or employee of a labor union, to be legislative punishment for a party membership, and hence a bill of attainder. [United States v. Brown, 381 U.S. 437 (1965)]

3. ***Nixon* Case**

In *Nixon v. Administrator of General Services,* 433 U.S. 425 (1977), Congress passed legislation to authorize government control of the presidential papers and tape recordings of former President Nixon. The Supreme Court held that this was *not a bill of attainder*. The circumstances of the Nixon resignation made him a unique "class of one" as to the need to control his papers. The act was held "*nonpunitive*" and in pursuance of *important public policy*.

4. **Draft Registration Case**

In *Selective Service System v. Minnesota Public Interest Research Group,* 468 U.S. 841 (1984), the Court upheld a federal statute denying financial aid for higher education to male students between the ages of 18 and 26 who had failed to register for the draft. The law required applicants for the aid to file a statement with their institutions of higher learning certifying their compliance. Failure to register within 30 days of one's 18th birthday was a felony, but the regulations allowed men who failed to register in a timely manner to qualify for aid by registering late. The Court found that this was *not a bill of attainder*. The law reasonably *promoted nonpunitive goals* and was *not a legislative punishment* taken on the basis of any irreversible act, since aid was awarded to those who registered late. The Court also found that the statute did not violate the Fifth Amendment privilege against self-incrimination.

D. DUE PROCESS CONSIDERATIONS

Under the Due Process Clauses of the Fifth and Fourteenth Amendments, retroactive legislation or other governmental action may be, but is not necessarily, a violation of the Constitution. The question of whether a retroactive law (that does not violate the Contracts, Ex Post Facto, or Bill of Attainder Clauses) violates due process is a **substantive due process** issue. If the law does not relate to a fundamental civil right, the retroactive law should be upheld if it is rationally related to a legitimate government interest.

Examples: 1) A retroactive tax law will be upheld as long as the retroactive aspects of the law are rationally related to legitimate government interests. [United States v. Carlton, 512 U.S. 26 (1994)—upholding retroactive modification of the estate tax]

2) Retroactive legislation affecting **merely a remedy** does not violate due process (*e.g.,* repealing or extending a statute of limitations), unless it would oust an already vested property interest. [Chase Securities Corp. v. Donaldson, 325 U.S. 304 (1945)—permissible to revive a previously dead cause of action]

3) Employers may be compelled to compensate former employees for work-connected diseases even if the employment terminated before the compensation statute was passed. [Usery v. Elkhorn Mining Co., 428 U.S. 1 (1976)]

XIV. PROCEDURAL DUE PROCESS

A. BASIC PRINCIPLE

The Due Process Clauses of the Fifth Amendment (applicable to the federal government) and the Fourteenth Amendment (applicable to the states) provide that the government shall not take a person's life, liberty, or property without due process of law. Due process contemplates fair process/procedure, which requires at least an opportunity to present objections to the proposed action to a fair, neutral decisionmaker (not necessarily a judge).

1. When Is Individualized Adjudication Required?

There is a right to procedural due process only when the government acts to deprive an **individual** of life, liberty, or property (*see* below). There is no right to individualized adjudication when the government acts generally, even if the action will result in burdening individuals' life, liberty, or property interests.

Example: A state legislature need not provide individuals with an opportunity for a hearing when adopting the general requirements for obtaining a driver's license (*e.g.,* age, residence, ability, etc.), but it must provide individualized process to determine whether a particular person meets the requirements.

2. Intentional Deprivation vs. Negligent Deprivation

Fair process is required for **intentional** acts of the government or its employees. If an injury is caused to a person through the mere **negligence** of a government employee, there is no violation of the Due Process Clause. [Daniels v. Williams, 474 U.S. 327 (1986); Davidson v. Cannon, 474 U.S. 344 (1986)]

a. "Deprivation"

A "deprivation" of life, liberty, or property requires more than a mere denial of certain kinds of remedies. Only when the government affords *no* remedy or *inadequate* remedies may a deprivation of life, liberty, or property result. [Florida Prepaid Postsecondary Education Expense Board v. College Savings Bank, 527 U.S. 627 (1999)]

3. Protection vs. Creation

The due process provisions do not create property or liberty interests; their purpose is to provide *procedural safeguards against arbitrary deprivation*. Hence, the Fourteenth Amendment Due Process Clause does not, for example, give out-of-state attorneys the right to appear in state courts without meeting a state's bar admission requirements. [Leis v. Flynt, 439 U.S. 438 (1979)]

B. IS LIFE, LIBERTY, OR PROPERTY BEING TAKEN?

Older Supreme Court cases indicated that due process protects "rights," but not "privileges." This approach is no longer followed; rather the Court will determine whether a *legitimate* liberty or property interest is being taken.

1. Liberty

The term "liberty" is not specifically defined. It includes more than just freedom from bodily restraints (*e.g.,* it includes the right to contract and to engage in gainful employment). A deprivation of liberty occurs if a person:

(i) Loses significant freedom of action; *or*

(ii) Is denied a freedom provided by the Constitution or a statute.

Examples of liberty interests include:

a. Commitment to Mental Institution

1) Adults

Adults are entitled to an *adversary hearing* before they are indefinitely committed to a mental institution against their will. The state must prove the basis for commitment by "clear and convincing" evidence. However, after a person has been acquitted of criminal charges on the basis of an insanity defense, the acquitted defendant can be committed if a court finds by a "preponderance of the evidence" that the person should be committed to a mental health care facility. [Jones v. United States, 463 U.S. 354 (1983)]

2) Minor Children

Minor children have a substantial liberty interest in not being confined unnecessarily for medical treatment. Thus, they are entitled to a *screening by a "neutral factfinder"* before commitment to a mental institution. Mere parental consent to commitment is not enough. [Parham v. J.R., 442 U.S. 584 (1979)]

b. Injury to Reputation

Injury to reputation in itself is not a deprivation of liberty or property. [Paul v. Davis, 424 U.S. 693 (1976)] However, if governmental acts (such as a statement of reasons given for termination of public employment) so injure a person's reputation that he will have *lost significant employment or associational opportunities*, there is a loss of liberty.

   c. **Exercise of Fundamental Constitutional Rights**
The Due Process Clause protects a person's freedom to engage in activities that involve fundamental constitutional rights, such as the right to speak and associate, the right to travel, and the right to vote.

     1) **Application—Government Employee's Freedom of Speech**
A public employee may not be discharged for engaging in constitutionally protected speech. If a government employee is discharged for her speech or writing, a hearing must be held to determine whether the speech was protected. If so, the employee cannot be fired. [*See* Girhan v. Western Line Consolidated School District, 439 U.S. 410 (1979)—Court held that teacher could not be fired for privately communicating her grievances about working conditions or opinions concerning public issues to her employer]

2. Property
"Property" includes more than personal belongings and realty, chattels, or money, but an abstract need or desire for (or a unilateral expectation of) the benefit is not enough. There must be a *legitimate claim* or "*entitlement*" to the benefit under state or federal law. [Board of Regents v. Roth, 408 U.S. 564 (1972); Leis v. Flynt, *supra*] Examples of property interests include:

   a. **Public Education**
There is a property interest in public education when school attendance is required. Thus, a significant suspension (*e.g.*, 10 days) requires procedural due process. [Goss v. Lopez, 419 U.S. 565 (1975)]

   b. **Welfare Benefits**
One has a property interest in welfare benefits if she has previously been determined to meet the statutory criteria. [Goldberg v. Kelly, 397 U.S. 254 (1970)]

   c. **Continued Public Employment**
If there is a state statute or ordinance that creates a public employment contract, or there is some clear practice or mutual understanding that an employee can be terminated only for "cause," then there is a property interest [Arnett v. Kennedy, 416 U.S. 134 (1974)]; but if the employee holds his position only at the "will" of the employer, there is no property interest in continued employment [Bishop v. Wood, 426 U.S. 341 (1976)].

C. WHAT TYPE OF PROCESS IS REQUIRED?
While all intentional governmental deprivations of life, liberty, or property require fair process, what constitutes fair process in terms of the timing and scope of the hearing varies according to the circumstances of the deprivation. The Court will weigh:

(i) The importance of the *individual interest* involved;

(ii) The value of specific *procedural safeguards* to that interest; and

(iii) The *governmental interest* in fiscal and administrative efficiency.

[Mathews v. Eldridge, 424 U.S. 319 (1976)] In all situations, the Court will probably require *fair procedures* and an *unbiased decisionmaker*. Normally, the person whose interest is being deprived should also receive *notice* of the government's action and have an *opportunity to respond before* termination of the interest. However, the court may allow a post-termination hearing in situations where a pre-termination hearing is highly impracticable. The Court has made the following rulings with regard to specific types of deprivations:

1. Welfare Benefits

Due process requires an *evidentiary hearing prior to termination* of welfare benefits. It need not be a judicial or quasi-judicial trial if there is adequate post-termination review; but the recipient must have timely and adequate *notice* of the reasons for the proposed termination, the right to confront adverse witnesses, and the right to present his own arguments and evidence orally. Counsel need not be provided, but must be permitted. Finally, the decision must be based solely on evidence adduced at the hearing and must be rendered by an impartial decisionmaker (thus disqualifying any participant in the termination proposal under review). [Goldberg v. Kelly, *supra*]

2. Disability Benefits

No prior evidentiary hearing is required for termination of disability benefits, as long as there is *prior notice* to the recipient, an opportunity to respond in writing, and a *subsequent evidentiary hearing* (with retroactive payment if the recipient prevails). *Rationale*: Disability benefits (unlike welfare benefits) are not based on financial need and hence are not vital. [Mathews v. Eldridge, *supra*]

3. Public Employment

A public employee who is subject to removal only for "cause" (and who, therefore, has a property interest in his job) generally must be given *notice* of charges against him that are to be the basis for his job termination, and a *pre-termination opportunity to respond* to those charges. The employee does not have to be given a full, formal hearing before his termination, as long as there is a fair system of pre-termination notice, an opportunity to respond (to the person making the termination decision), and a *subsequent evidentiary hearing* regarding the termination (with reinstatement if the employee prevails). [Cleveland Board of Education v. Loudermill, 470 U.S. 532 (1985)] *But note:* If there is a *significant reason* for not keeping the employee on the job, he may be suspended without pay and without an opportunity to respond as long as there is a prompt post-suspension hearing with reinstatement and back pay if the employee prevails. [Gilbert v. Homar, 520 U.S. 924 (1997)—police officer suspended after being arrested and formally charged with a felony]

4. Public Education—Disciplinary Suspension

Although no formal evidentiary hearing is required before a student may be temporarily suspended (for 10 days or less), due process usually requires *notice* of the charges and an *opportunity to explain*. However, if the student's presence poses a danger to persons or property, or threatens to disrupt the academic process, such notice and hearing may *follow* removal as soon as practicable. [Goss v. Lopez, *supra*]

a. **Corporal Punishment in Public School**

This may involve constitutionally protected "liberty." However, the traditional common law tort remedies for excessive punishment satisfy procedural due process, and a prior hearing is not required. [Ingraham v. Wright, 430 U.S. 651 (1977)]

5. **Public Education—Academic Dismissal**

No prior evidentiary hearing is required when a student is dismissed for "academic" deficiencies rather than for "disciplinary" reasons. Due process is satisfied if the student is adequately informed of the deficiency and given an opportunity to respond. [Board of Curators v. Horowitz, 435 U.S. 78 (1978)]

6. **Creditors' Remedies**

Pretrial remedies, such as attachment of property or garnishment of wages, that are merely designed to provide a plaintiff with some guarantee that there will be assets to satisfy a judgment against the defendant if the plaintiff eventually wins the case *should not be issued by a court without notice* to the defendant and a *hearing prior to the issuance* of the order. A court may issue a temporary order of this type if there are exigent circumstances that justify the order and the defendant is given a hearing after the order is issued but prior to trial. [Sniadach v. Family Finance Corp., 395 U.S. 337 (1969); Connecticut v. Doehr, 501 U.S. 1 (1991)] However, laws authorizing creditors to garnish assets, or a conditional seller to seize or sequester property, will be upheld *without prior notice* to the debtor *if*:

a. The creditor posts a security bond;

b. The application is made to a judge, is not conclusory, and documents narrowly confined facts susceptible of summary disposition; *and*

c. Provision is made for an early hearing at which the creditor must show probable cause.

7. **Driver's License**

The state generally must afford a *prior hearing* before a driver's license is suspended or terminated. [Bell v. Burson, 402 U.S. 535 (1971)] However, a post-suspension hearing satisfies due process where a statute mandates suspension of a driver's license for refusing to take a breathalyzer test upon arrest for drunk driving. [Mackey v. Montrym, 443 U.S. 1 (1979)]

8. **Parental Status Litigation and Hearing**

a. **Termination of Parental Status**

Due process does *not require the appointment of counsel* for indigent parents in every case in which the state seeks to terminate parental status (*i.e.,* take children from their parents), *but* only when "fundamental fairness" requires the appointment. [Lassiter v. Department of Social Services, 452 U.S. 18 (1981)] To terminate parental rights, the state must prove its allegations of parental neglect or misconduct by "clear and convincing evidence." [Santosky v. Kramer, 455 U.S. 745 (1982)]

b. **Paternity Actions**

A state may allow paternity to be established in a support proceeding brought by a mother or child by a *preponderance of evidence*—no greater burden of proof is required by the Due Process Clause. [Rivera v. Minnich, 483 U.S. 574 (1987)] However, due process requires the state to *pay for blood tests* that might exculpate an indigent defendant in a paternity action if the *state is responsible for the lawsuit* (the suit is brought by a state agency or the state requires the mother to bring the civil paternity suit). [Little v. Streater, 452 U.S. 1 (1981)]

c. **Hearings for Men Who Seek to Establish Paternity**

1) **Unmarried Father Living with Mother**
    If the father of an illegitimate child is a part of a "family unit" that includes the child, the relationship between the father and child will be protected by due process. [Stanley v. Illinois, 405 U.S. 645 (1972)—state cannot take child from father after mother dies, unless state has a fair process to determine whether the parental relationship should be severed]

2) **Father Who Never Tried to Establish Paternity**
    The father of an illegitimate child who has never attempted to establish a legal or personal relationship with the child has no right to notice prior to the adoption of the child by other persons. [Lehr v. Robertson, 463 U.S. 248 (1983)]

3) **Mother Married to Another Man**
    The Supreme Court has upheld a statute that presumed that a child born during wedlock was the husband's child where the statute allowed an alleged biological father to have a hearing regarding visitation rights, but the Court did not rule on whether a biological father could be denied visitation under these circumstances without a hearing. [Michael H. v. Gerald D., 491 U.S. 110 (1989)]

9. **Treatment of Patients in Mental Health Care Facilities**
Persons who have been involuntarily committed to a state mental health care facility have a *liberty interest* in reasonably *safe conditions and treatment*. Patients have a due process right to determination by a "professional" in the health care field as to the proper treatment of the patient. [Youngberg v. Romeo, 457 U.S. 307 (1982)]

10. **Notice of Adversary Proceedings**
When the government seeks to use a judicial or administrative process to take or terminate property interests, it *must give notice* to those persons whose property interests may be taken by that process. The form of notice must be reasonably designed to insure that those persons will in fact be notified of the proceedings.
Example: Personal notice or notice by mail must be given to both mortgagor and mortgagee before a "tax sale" of property for unpaid taxes. [Mennonite Board of Missions v. Adams, 462 U.S. 791 (1983)]

11. **Limitation of Attorneys' Fees for Veterans Benefit Hearings**
Persons applying for veterans benefits for service related disabilities apparently have little due process right to be represented by an attorney at hearings before a Veterans Administration Board. The Supreme Court has upheld a statute that limited payments to attorneys in such cases to $10. [Walters v. National Association of Radiation Survivors, 468 U.S. 1323 (1985)]

12. **Civil Forfeitures**

Procedural due process limits the government's ability to seize property allegedly subject to forfeiture (which most often occurs when the government claims that the property was connected to, or was the product of, criminal activity). Absent exceptional circumstances, the government must provide the owner of *real property* notice and an opportunity for some type of hearing *prior* to seizing real property. [United States v. James Daniel Good Real Property, 510 U.S. 43 (1993)] However, the government might be able to seize *personal property prior* to providing the owner a hearing, since personal property can be hidden or destroyed. [Calero-Toledo v. Pearson Yacht Leasing Co., 416 U.S. 663 (1974)]

13. **Punitive Damages**

Substantive due process might require that punitive damages be reasonable under the circumstances of the case. There must be a *fair process for awarding* punitive damages, and the states may not eliminate all judicial review of the amount of punitive damages awarded—there must be a *fair opportunity to appeal* punitive damage awards to an appellate court. [Honda Motor Corp., Ltd. v. Oberg, 512 U.S. 415 (1994)]

D. DUE PROCESS RIGHTS ARE SUBJECT TO WAIVER

Due process rights are subject to waiver. However, the Supreme Court has not clearly defined the standard for determining whether someone has validly waived the right to a hearing before governmental deprivation of liberty or property. Presumably, any such waiver must be *voluntary*. Additionally, it is possible that a waiver will be valid only if it is made *knowingly* (with an understanding of the nature of the rights being waived).

E. ACCESS TO COURTS—INDIGENT PLAINTIFFS

There may often be a fee for government services, including a fee for use of courts (*e.g.*, a filing fee). Whether the government must waive such fees for indigents depends on the nature of the rights involved.

1. **Fundamental Rights—Waiver Required**

The Supreme Court has required a waiver of government fees when the imposition of a fee would deny a fundamental right to the indigent. (Fundamental rights are examined in the substantive due process and equal protection sections of this outline.)

Examples: 1) The government cannot deny an indigent the right to marry or divorce because of the indigent's inability to pay a marriage license fee or a divorce court filing fee.

2) The government must waive even a reasonable filing fee for candidates for electoral office if it can be shown that the candidate cannot afford to pay the filing fee. The right to be a candidate is connected to the fundamental right of individuals to vote for candidates of their choice.

3) The government may not require an indigent to pay the cost of a transcript in order to appeal from termination of her parental rights. [M.L.B. v. S.L.J., 519 U.S. 102 (1997)]

2. **Nonfundamental Rights—Waiver Not Required**

When there is no fundamental right regulated by the imposition of a fee, the government can refuse to grant the service to those persons who cannot pay the required fee.

Examples: 1) The federal government can refuse to grant access to bankruptcy courts to persons who cannot pay a filing fee. There is no fundamental right to receive a bankruptcy discharge from debts.

2) A state can limit judicial review of welfare termination hearings to those persons who pay a $25 fee.

XV.   THE "TAKING" CLAUSE

A.   IN GENERAL
The Fifth Amendment prohibits governmental taking of private property "for public use without just compensation." The prohibition is applicable to the states through the Fourteenth Amendment [Chicago Burlington & Quincy Railroad v. Chicago, 166 U.S. 226 (1897)], and taking questions often arise in connection with states' exercise of their police power (*i.e.,* the power to legislate for the health, welfare, safety, etc., of the people).

1.   Not a Grant of Power
The Fifth Amendment is not a grant of power, but rather is a limitation on power (*i.e.,* a taking must be for a public purpose and compensation must be paid). The power for a taking must arise out of some other source (*e.g.,* the police power).

2.   Scope of Taking
The concept of a governmental taking probably originally contemplated only physical appropriations of property. Today, however, the term also encompasses some governmental action that significantly damages property or impairs its use (*e.g.,* frequent flyovers by airplanes near airport [United States v. Causby, 328 U.S. 256 (1946)]). Moreover, even intangibles may be the subject of a taking. [*See* Ruckelshaus v. Monsanto Co., 467 U.S. 986 (1984)—government requirement that trade secret be disclosed may be a taking where government takes and discloses the secret in such a way that it diminishes the secret's economic value and interferes with reasonable, investment-backed expectations of its holders]

3.   Scope of Property
Whether an item is property is determined by state law, but in any case, there is no constitutional requirement that an item have positive economic or market value to constitute property; *i.e.,* "worthless" property is still property. [*See* Phillips v. Washington Legal Foundation, 524 U.S. 156 (1998)—even if interest attributable to a particular client in an attorney's trust fund account is economically worthless to the client—because the costs of accounting and crediting the interest would eat up all the interest earned—the interest still is the client's property and so is subject to the Takings Clause]

B.   "PUBLIC USE" LIMITATION LIBERALLY CONSTRUED
The Court will not review underlying policy decisions, such as general desirability for a particular public use or the extent to which property must be taken therefor. A use will be held to be "public" as long as it is rationally related to a legitimate public purpose, *e.g.,* health, welfare, safety, moral, social, economic, political, or aesthetic ends. The government may even authorize a taking by private enterprise, as long as the taking will redound to the public advantage (*e.g.,* railroads and public utilities).

Example: The Supreme Court upheld a state program under which the fee simple interest in land would be condemned and the fee owner paid a *fair market value* for that property interest, which the state would then transfer for value to tenants on the land. The state's asserted interest in ending social problems caused by "land oligopoly" was sufficient public use. [Hawaii Housing Authority v. Midkiff, 467 U.S. 229 (1984)]

C. "TAKING" VS. "REGULATION"

While the government must fairly compensate an owner when her property is taken for public use, it need not pay compensation for mere regulation of property. Thus, whether government action amounts to a taking or is merely regulation is a crucial issue. The question is one of degree; there is no clear cut formula for determining whether there has been a taking. The following guidelines have emerged.

1. Actual Appropriation or Physical Invasion

A taking will almost always be found if there is an actual appropriation or destruction of a person's property or a permanent physical invasion by the government or by authorization of law.

Examples: A taking was found in the following situations:

1) Ordinance requiring landlords to allow installation of cable TV in their rental units but limiting to $1 the fee landlords could charge for this access. [Loretto v. Teleprompter Manhattan CATV Corp., 455 U.S. 904 (1982)]

2) Statute *abolishing* rights of descent and devise of property (although government has broad authority to regulate this area). [Hodel v. Irving, 481 U.S. 704 (1987)]

3) Requirement that public be given free access to a privately developed waterway. [Kaiser Aetna v. United States, 444 U.S. 164 (1980)]

a. Exception—Emergencies

A taking is less likely to be found in emergency situations, even where there is destruction or actual occupation of private property.

Examples: 1) No compensation was required when the state ordered the destruction of cedar trees that threatened to spread disease to apple orchards. [Miller v. Schoene, 276 U.S. 272 (1928)]

2) No compensation was required when federal troops destroyed oil facilities to prevent them from falling into enemy hands. [United States v. Caltex, Inc., 344 U.S. 149 (1952)]

2. Use Restrictions

a. Denial of *All* Economic Value of Land—Taking

If a government regulation denies a landowner *all* economic use of his land, the regulation is equivalent to a physical appropriation and is thus a taking unless principles of nuisance or property law that existed when the owner acquired the land make the use prohibitable. [Lucas v. South Carolina Coastal Council, 505 U.S. 1003 (1992)—state's zoning ordinance, adopted after owner purchased lots, amounted to a taking because the ordinance prohibited owner from erecting any permanent structures on his lots]

b. Decreasing Economic Value—Balancing Test
Regulations that merely decrease the value of property (*e.g.,* prohibit its most beneficial use) do not necessarily result in a taking, *as long as they leave an economically viable use for the property*. The Court balances:

(i)   The social goals sought to be promoted;

(ii) The diminution in value to the owner; *and*

(iii) The owner's reasonable expectations regarding use of the property.

Generally, the regulation will be found to be a taking only if it *unjustly* reduces the economic value of the property (*e.g.,* greatly reduces property value and only slightly promotes public welfare).

Examples: The Supreme Court has considered two cases where statutes prohibited coal companies from mining under property, even though the mining company had previously entered into contract for, or received a deed for, subsurface mineral rights. If the statutory prohibition is designed to protect only the economic interests of a *limited group* of building owners and the reduction in the value of the mining company's mineral rights is *almost 100%*, a court might be authorized in finding that the prohibition of subsurface mining constitutes a taking of property for which compensation is due. [Pennsylvania Coal Co. v. Mahon, 260 U.S. 393 (1922)] If the statute promotes a *public purpose* because a danger of subsidence threatens a variety of public and nonpublic buildings, and *diminution in the value of the mining company's rights is not extreme*, the statute restricting the mining activities may be a permissible regulation for which no compensation is due. [Keystone Bituminous Coal Association v. DeBenedictis, XIII.A.3.a., *supra*]

1) Zoning Ordinances
The Court has long held that governments may adopt zoning ordinances that regulate the way real property may be used, pursuant to the police power (*e.g.,* limiting development in a particular area to single family homes, restricting buildings to a particular height, etc.). Such regulations do not amount to a taking—even if they deny an owner the highest and best use of her property—as long as they "substantially advance legitimate state interests" and do not "extinguish a fundamental attribute of ownership." [Agins v. Tiburon, 447 U.S. 255 (1980)—ordinance permitting only five houses on five-acre tract upheld]

Example: The Court upheld a "landmark" zoning ordinance that prohibited altering the external appearance of Grand Central Station. It found historic preservation to be an important government interest and that certain rights granted to the landmark owners mitigated their loss. [Penn Central Transportation Co. v. New York, 438 U.S. 104 (1978)]

2) Building/Development Permits—Transfer of Occupation Rights
Municipalities often attempt to condition building or development permits on a landowner's (i) conveying title to part, or all, of the property to the government or (ii) granting the public access to the property (*e.g.*, an easement across the property). Such conditions constitute an uncompensated taking unless (i) the government can show that the condition relates to a legitimate government interest and (ii) the adverse impact of the proposed building/development on the area is roughly proportional to the loss caused to the property owner from the forced transfer of occupation rights. [Nollan v. California Coastal Commission, 483 U.S. 825 (1987); Dolan v. City of Tigard, 512 U.S. 374 (1994)]

Example: City agreed to approve a permit to expand plaintiff's retail store and pave a parking lot on the condition that plaintiff dedicate land for (i) a public greenway and (ii) a bike path. The Supreme Court found that City did not show a sufficient relationship between the dedications and the impact that the expansion would have on the area. [Dolan v. City of Tigard, *supra*]

3) Utility Rate Regulation
There is no taking where the government sets rates that utility companies can charge, as long as the rates are not set so low that they are unjust and confiscatory. [Duquesne Light Co. v. Barash, 488 U.S. 299 (1989)]

3. Remedy
If a property owner challenges a regulation and the court determines that there was a taking, the government will be required to either:

(i) *Pay the property owner compensation* for the taking (*see* below); or

(ii) *Terminate the regulation and pay the owner for damages* that occurred while the regulation was in effect (*i.e.*, temporary taking damages).

[First English Evangelical Church v. County of Los Angeles, 482 U.S. 304 (1987)]

a. Who May Sue
The right to claim a "taking" is *not* limited to persons who held title to the property at the time a challenged use restriction was imposed. A person who purchases property after a regulation is in place still may bring a taking claim. [Palazzolo v. Rhode Island, 121 S. Ct. 2448 (2001)]

D. "JUST COMPENSATION"
The owner is entitled to the *reasonable value* of her property *at the time of the taking*—fair market value. The test is ordinarily a *loss to the owner*, not a gain to the taker. Due process guarantees notice and hearing, administrative or judicial, on the amount of compensation, but the hearing need not precede the taking.

XVI. INTRODUCTION TO SUBSTANTIVE DUE PROCESS AND EQUAL PROTECTION

A. RELATIONSHIP BETWEEN SUBSTANTIVE DUE PROCESS AND EQUAL PROTECTION

The Due Process Clauses and the Equal Protection Clause guarantee the fairness of laws—substantive due process guarantees that laws will be reasonable and not arbitrary, and equal protection guarantees that similarly situated persons will be treated alike. Both guarantees require the Court to review the *substance of the law* rather than the procedures employed.

1. Substantive Due Process

Generally where a law limits the liberty of *all* persons to engage in some activity, it is a due process question.

2. Equal Protection

Where a law treats a person or class of persons differently from others, it is an equal protection question. [*See* Village of Willowbrook v. Grace, 528 U.S. 562 (2000)—equal protection claims may be brought by a class with as few as one member]

3. Examples

If a law prohibits all persons from purchasing contraceptive devices, there is a due process issue; if the law prohibits only purchases by unmarried persons, there is an equal protection issue. A state's refusal to have any publicly funded schools raises a due process issue; a state law that establishes separate schools for children of different races raises an equal protection issue.

4. Note—Clauses Not Necessarily Mutually Exclusive

Since both clauses protect against unfairness, both may be appropriate challenges to the same governmental act, and a discussion of both may be appropriate in an essay answer. On the MBE, however, the examiners will probably not include both as alternatives in the same question. The above approaches can be used as a rough guideline of when each clause applies.

B. WHAT STANDARD OF REVIEW WILL THE COURT APPLY?

The Court employs one of three tests in reviewing laws under these clauses, depending on the circumstances.

1. Strict Scrutiny (Maximum Scrutiny)

The Court uses the strict scrutiny standard when a suspect classification or fundamental right (these terms will be discussed *infra*) is involved. Under the strict scrutiny standard, a law will be upheld only if it is *necessary* to achieve a *compelling* or *overriding* government purpose. The Court will always consider whether less burdensome means for accomplishing the legislative goal are available. Most governmental action examined under this test fails.

a. Burden of Proof on Government

When the strict scrutiny standard is applied, the *government* will have the burden of proving that the law is necessary. The Court will not allow a loose fitting law (*i.e.*, if a law reaches more people or conduct than is necessary (overinclusive) or does not reach all of the people or conduct sought to be regulated (underinclusive), it will likely be struck down).

2. **Intermediate Scrutiny**

The Court uses intermediate scrutiny when a classification based on gender or legitimacy is involved. Under the intermediate scrutiny standard, a law will be upheld if it is *substantially* related to an *important* government purpose.

    a. **Burden of Proof Probably on Government**

    It is unclear who has the burden of proof when the Court uses the intermediate standard, but in most cases, it appears to be the government.

3. **Rational Basis (Minimal Scrutiny)**

The rational basis standard is used whenever the other two standards are not applicable (*i.e.*, most legislation). Under the rational basis standard, a law will be upheld if it is *rationally related to a legitimate* interest. It is difficult to fail this test; so most governmental action examined under this standard is upheld unless it is *arbitrary* or *irrational*.

    a. **Burden of Proof on Challenger**

    Under the rational basis standard, laws are presumed valid. Therefore, the challenger has the burden of proof. This is a very difficult burden to meet, given the deference the Court gives to legislatures under the rational basis standard. (*See* below.)

    b. **Deference to Legislature**

    Under the rational basis standard, the Court will usually defer to a legislature's decision that a law is rational. Loose fitting laws are permissible here: The law need not be the best law that could have been written to achieve the legislative goal. Indeed, it need not go far at all toward a conceivable legislative goal; the Court will uphold a law taking a "first step" toward any legitimate goal, even if the Court thinks the law is unwise.

      Example: City decided that advertisements on motor vehicles are traffic hazards; so it banned such advertisements except for those on vehicles advertising the owner's own product. Even though the excepted advertisements were no less distracting than the banned ones, the Court upheld the "first step" law. [Railway Express Agency v. New York, 336 U.S. 106 (1949)]

XVII. SUBSTANTIVE DUE PROCESS

A. **CONSTITUTIONAL SOURCE—TWO CLAUSES**

There are two separate clauses protecting substantive due process:

(i) The Due Process Clause of the Fifth Amendment (applies to the federal government); and

(ii) The Due Process Clause of the Fourteenth Amendment (applies to state and local governments).

As indicated above, *the same tests* are employed under each clause.

B. APPLICABLE STANDARDS

1. **Fundamental Right—Strict Scrutiny**
   Where a law limits a fundamental right, strict scrutiny will be applied, and the law (or other governmental action) will be upheld only if it is necessary to promote a *compelling or overriding interest*. Fundamental rights include:

   a. Right to travel;

   b. Privacy;

   c. Voting; and

   d. All First Amendment rights.

2. **All Other Cases—Mere Rationality**
   In all other cases, the mere rationality test is applied, and the law will be upheld if it is *rationally related to any conceivable legitimate end of government*. Examples include the following:

   a. **Business and Labor Regulations**
      The Court will sustain all varieties of business regulation; *e.g.,* "blue sky" laws, bank controls, insurance regulation, price and wage controls, unfair competition and trade practice controls, etc.

   b. **Taxation**
      Taxation is also invariably *sustained*. However, discriminatory taxes might still be invalidated.

   c. **Lifestyle**
      There is, as yet, *no recognized right* to lead a certain lifestyle. Thus, the Supreme Court will uphold laws: prohibiting drugs ("hard" or "soft"), requiring motorcyclists to wear helmets, or requiring police officers to wear short hair. [Kelley v. Johnson, 425 U.S. 238 (1976)]

   d. **Zoning**
      Regulation of the ownership or use of property has also been liberally tolerated by the Court.

      1) **Statutes Forbidding Nuisances or Promoting Community's Preferred Lifestyle**
         Statutes forbidding certain uses as nuisances have been sustained, as have all kinds of statutes designed to promote the public's enjoyment of space and safety or to promote a community's preferred lifestyle and character. For example, the Supreme Court held that a Long Island suburb could zone out all groups of three or more persons unrelated by blood, adoption, or marriage. [Village of Belle Terre v. Boraas, 416 U.S. 1 (1974)]

      2) **Cannot Prohibit Traditionally Related Families from Living Together**
         However, you should know that the Supreme Court held that zoning regulations

that prohibit members of traditional families from living together (*i.e.,* zoning excluding cousins or grandchildren) violate due process. [Moore v. City of East Cleveland, 431 U.S. 494 (1977)]

e. **Punitive Damages**
The Supreme Court has held that punitive damages—even large punitive awards—do not necessarily violate substantive due process. [Pacific Mutual Life Insurance Co. v. Haslip, 499 U.S. 1 (1991)—upholding punitive damages 200 times greater than compensatory damages] However, "grossly excessive" damages—those that are unreasonably high to vindicate the state's interest in punishment—are invalid. [TXO Production Corp. v. Alliance Resources Corp., 509 U.S. 443 (1993)] Although there is no bright line marking the limits on punitive awards, a person must receive fair notice of their possible magnitude. The Court has indicated that it will look to the following factors: (i) the degree of reprehensibility of the defendant's conduct, (ii) the disparity between the actual or potential harm suffered by the plaintiff and the punitive award, and (iii) the difference between the punitive damages awarded and the criminal and civil penalties authorized for comparable misconduct. [BMW of North America, Inc. v. Gore, 517 U.S. 559 (1996)]

f. **High Speed Chases**
A high speed police chase that results in a death violates due process only when the chase is arbitrary (or irrational) in the constitutional sense. Only a chase that shocks the conscience of the court (*i.e.,* where the police intend to cause harm) will be found to be sufficiently arbitrary to be unconstitutional. [County of Sacramento v. Lewis, 523 U.S. 833 (1998)—no due process violation where officers chased motorcycle that sped by the officers for no apparent reason and a passenger on the motorcycle fell off and was killed when struck by an officer's car]

g. **Compare—Vagueness Doctrine**
Under the Due Process Clause of the Fourteenth Amendment, a law can be held unconstitutional if it fails to provide minimal guidelines to govern law enforcement officers so as to encourage arbitrary and discriminatory enforcement. [Kolender v. Lawson, 461 U.S. 352 (1983); City of Chicago v. Morales, 527 U.S. 41 (1999)—holding unconstitutional on vagueness grounds an ordinance that allowed officers to disperse suspected gang members when they were "loitering," which was defined as remaining in any one place with no *apparent purpose*]

C. A FEW IRREBUTTABLE PRESUMPTIONS MAY BE INVALID

If the government "presumes facts" against a person so that she is not qualified for some important benefit or right, the irrebuttable presumption may be unconstitutional. Although the Court often characterizes this as a due process question, it is more accurately an equal protection question because the government is creating an arbitrary classification. In any case, if the presumption affects a fundamental right (*e.g.,* right to travel) or a suspect or quasi-suspect classification (*e.g.,* gender), it will likely be invalid under strict scrutiny or intermediate scrutiny analysis, because the administrative convenience created by the presumption is not an important enough interest to justify the burden on the right or class. If some other classification or right is involved, the presumption will likely be upheld under the rational basis standard.

Examples: 1) A state may not presume a teacher incapable of continuous service in the classroom merely because she is four or five months pregnant or has a child under age three. [Cleveland Board of Education v. LaFleur, 414 U.S. 632 (1974)]

2) The government may presume that a marriage entered into within nine months of a wage earner's death was simply to secure Social Security benefits. [Weinberger v. Salfi, 422 U.S. 749 (1975)]

XVIII. EQUAL PROTECTION

A. CONSTITUTIONAL SOURCE

The Equal Protection Clause of the Fourteenth Amendment has *no counterpart in the Constitution applicable to the federal government*; it is limited to state action. Nevertheless, it is clear that grossly unreasonable discrimination by the federal government violates the *Due Process Clause of the Fifth Amendment*. [Bolling v. Sharpe, 347 U.S. 497 (1954)—racial discrimination in the public schools of the District of Columbia held a violation of due process] Thus, there are really two equal protection guarantees. The Court applies the same standards under either constitutional provision.

B. APPLICABLE STANDARDS

As indicated above, the Court will apply one of three standards when examining governmental action involving classifications of persons. If a *suspect classification or fundamental right* is involved, the strict scrutiny standard will be applied and the action will be struck down unless the government proves that it is necessary to achieve a compelling interest. If a *quasi-suspect classification* is involved, the Court will likely require the government to prove that the action is substantially related to an important government interest. If *any other classification* is involved, the action will be upheld unless the challenger proves that the action is not rationally related to a legitimate government interest.

C. PROVING DISCRIMINATORY CLASSIFICATION

The mere fact that legislation or governmental action has a discriminatory effect is not sufficient to trigger strict scrutiny or intermediate scrutiny. There must be *intent* to discriminate on the part of the government. Intent can be shown in three ways: (i) facial discrimination; (ii) discriminatory application; or (iii) discriminatory motive.

1. Facial Discrimination

A law may include a classification on its face. This type of law, by its own terms, makes an explicit distinction between classes of persons (perhaps by race or gender; *e.g.,* all white males 21 or older may serve as jurors [*see* Strauder v. West Virginia, 100 U.S. 303 (1880)]). In such cases the courts merely have to apply the appropriate standard of review for that classification. (The standards for racial classifications and gender classifications are described below.)

a. Facial Discrimination Absent Racial Language

In a few cases the Supreme Court has held that a law used a racial classification "on its face" even though the language of the law did not include racial language. In these cases, the Supreme Court found that the law could not be explained except in racial terms.

Example: The Court found that a state law establishing districts for the election of Representatives to the United States Congress should be deemed to use a racial classification on its face because one bizarrely shaped district could not be explained except in terms of establishing a district where minority race voters would control the outcome of the election. The Court did not rule on the question of whether this racial classification was narrowly tailored to a compelling interest, such as remedying proven past discrimination, because that question had not been addressed in the lower courts. [Shaw v. Reno, 509 U.S. 630 (1993)]

Note: If a legislative districting map could be explained in terms other than race, the Court would not find that the law constituted racial discrimination on its face. In such a case, the persons attacking legislative districts as being based on racial classification would have to show that district lines were drawn for a racially discriminatory purpose. [Hunt v. Cromartie, 121 S. Ct. 1452 (2001)—"Hunt II"]

2. Discriminatory Application

In some instances, a law that appears to be neutral on its face will be applied in a different manner to different classes of persons. If the persons challenging the governmental action can prove that the government officials applying the law had a discriminatory purpose (and used discriminatory standards based on traits such as race or gender), the law will be invalidated.

Examples: 1) A law prohibited operating a laundry in wooden buildings, but gave a government agency discretion to grant exemptions. It was shown that most such laundries were owned by people of Chinese descent, but the agency granted exemptions only to non-Asian applicants. The law was deemed to involve racial or national origin classification and was invalidated as applied. [Yick Wo v. Hopkins, 118 U.S. 356 (1886)]

2) Laws allow attorneys to move to strike potential jurors from a jury either for cause or without cause (a peremptory strike). In either case, there is an equal protection violation when it is proved that an attorney excluded a person from a jury on account of the person's race or sex. [*See* Batson v. Kentucky, 476 U.S. 79 (1986); J.E.B. v. Alabama *ex rel.* T.B., 511 U.S. 127 (1994)] Note that because striking potential jurors from a jury significantly involves the state, even attorneys representing private parties are prohibited from discriminatory strikes. (*See* XII.B.2.a.1)a)(1), *supra.*)

3. Discriminatory Motive

Sometimes a government action will appear to be neutral on its face and in its application, but will have disproportionate impact on a particular class of persons (such as a racial minority or women). Such a law will be found to involve a classification (and be subject to the level of scrutiny appropriate to that classification) only if a court finds that the law-making body enacted or maintained the law for a *discriminatory purpose*. In such cases, the court should admit into evidence statistical proof that the law has a disproportionate impact on one class of persons. However, mere statistical evidence will rarely be sufficient in itself to prove that the government had a discriminatory purpose in passing a law. Statistical evidence may be combined with other evidence of legislative or administrative intent to show that a law or regulation is the product of a discriminatory purpose.

Examples: 1) A police department used a written test as criteria for hiring police officers. Members of identifiable racial minorities consistently got low scores on the test, although there was no proof that the test was written or otherwise employed for the purpose of disadvantaging minority applicants. Because of the absence of nonstatistical proof of discriminatory purpose, there was no equal protection violation. [Washington v. Davis, 426 U.S. 229 (1976)]

2) A state law gave a preference in the hiring and promotion of civil service employees to persons who were honorably discharged from the United States military. The foreseeable and actual impact of this law was to disadvantage the female population of job applicants, because the majority of veterans are men. Because there was no proof (other than the statistical impact of the law) that the legislature enacted the law for the purpose of hurting women (as opposed to the purpose of aiding veterans), the law was upheld.

3) A statistical study showing that black defendants in capital cases are much more likely to receive the death penalty than are white defendants in a state will not in itself establish that a particular black defendant was denied equal protection by being sentenced to death for murder in that state. The statistical study is insufficient to prove purposeful discrimination. [McCleskey v. Kemp, 481 U.S. 279 (1987)]

D. SUSPECT CLASSIFICATIONS

1. Race and National Origin

If governmental action classifies persons based on exercise of a fundamental right or involves a suspect classification (race, national origin, or alienage), strict scrutiny is applied. The result is invalidation of almost every case where the classification would burden a person because of her status as a member of a racial or national origin minority. The only explicit race discrimination upheld despite strict scrutiny was the wartime incarceration of United States citizens of Japanese ancestry on the West Coast. [Korematsu v. United States, 323 U.S. 214 (1944)—found to be necessary to achieve compelling interest of national security]

Example: A state could not deny custody of a child from a previous marriage to a white mother merely because her new husband was black, where the mother was otherwise found to be an appropriate parent. Racial prejudice against mixed race couples does not justify taking a child from his mother. [Palmore v. Sidoti, 466 U.S. 429 (1984)]

a. School Integration

Recall that only intentional discrimination will be found to create discriminatory classifications calling for strict scrutiny (*see* C., *supra*); thus, only intentional segregation in schools will be invalidated under equal protection.

Example: No equal protection violation was found where a school system established attendance zones in a racially neutral manner, but racial imbalance occurred because of housing patterns. [Keyes v. School District No. 1, 413 U.S. 189 (1973)]

1) **Remedying Intentional School Segregation**

If it is proven that a school board has engaged in the racial districting of schools, the board must take steps to eliminate the effects of that discrimination. If the school board refuses to do so, a court may order the school district to take all appropriate steps to eliminate the discrimination.

a) **Busing**

To remedy past discrimination, a court may order the "busing" of students. A federal court order requiring the transfer or busing of students must be tailored to eliminate proven racial discrimination in the school system.

(1) **Limitation—Interdistrict Busing**

A court may order busing between two independent school districts only if it has been proven that both districts cooperated in the purposeful discriminatory scheme.

(2) **Limitation—Voter Initiatives**

While citizens of a state may vote to prohibit state judges from ordering busing to remedy past discrimination, they may not prohibit the transfer of students to other attendance zones if such transfers are allowed for other reasons. [Washington v. Seattle School District No. 1, 458 U.S. 457 (1982); Crawford v. Board of Education, 458 U.S. 527 (1982)]

b) **Order Limited**

A court may not impose a remedy that goes beyond the purpose of remedying the vestiges of past segregation. Thus, it is impermissible for a court to impose a remedy whose purpose is to attract nonminority students from outside the school district when there is no evidence of past segregation outside the district (*see* a.1)a), *supra*). [Missouri v. Jenkins, 515 U.S. 70 (1995)—state not required to fund salary increases and remedial programs to create magnet schools to attract suburban students to urban schools]

c) **Termination of Order**

When a school district subject to a federal court-ordered integration plan has eliminated "the vestiges of past discrimination," the federal court should terminate its integration decree. [Board of Education v. Dowell, 498 U.S. 237 (1991)] If the district has eliminated discrimination only over certain aspects of school administration (*e.g.,* student assignments), the court *may* withdraw supervision over this aspect even though vestiges of discrimination remain with respect to other aspects. [Freeman v. Pitts, 503 U.S. 467 (1992)]

b. **"Benign" Government Discrimination—Affirmative Action**

Government action—whether by federal, state, or local governmental bodies—that *favors* racial or ethnic minorities is subject to strict scrutiny, as is government action discriminating *against* racial or ethnic minorities. [Adarand Constructors, Inc. v. Pena, 515 U.S. 200 (1995)—*overruling* Metro Broadcasting, Inc. v. Federal Communications Commission, 497 U.S. 547 (1990), which applied intermediate standard to federal discrimination]

Note: Prior to its ruling in *Adarand, supra*, the Supreme Court upheld a federal requirement that 10% of federal grants for public works be set aside for minority businesses. [Fullilove v. Klutznick, 448 U.S. 448 (1980)] In *Adarand*, the Court reserved judgment on whether a *Fullilove*-type program would survive strict scrutiny. Some commentators have suggested that it might, because the Court might give Congress more deference than the states based on Congress's power under the Enabling Clause of the Fourteenth Amendment (*see* XII.A.3., *supra*), but the continued validity of *Fullilove* is, at best, uncertain.

1) **Remedying Past Discrimination**

The government has a compelling interest in remedying past discrimination against a racial or ethnic minority. Thus, if a court finds that a governmental agency has engaged in racial discrimination, it may employ a race conscious remedy tailored to end the discrimination and eliminate its effects. A remedy of this type is permissible under the Equal Protection Clause because it is narrowly tailored to further a compelling interest (the elimination of the illegal or unconstitutional discrimination).

Example: When it has been proven that a public employer engaged in persistent racial discrimination, a court may order relief that establishes a goal for the hiring or promotion of minority persons so as to eliminate the effects of the past discrimination. [United States v. Paradise, 480 U.S. 149 (1987)]

2) **Where There Has Been No Past Discrimination by Government**

Even where a state or local government has not engaged in past discrimination, it may have a compelling interest in affirmative action. However, the governmental action must be *narrowly tailored* to that interest. [City of Richmond v. J.A. Croson Co., 488 U.S. 469 (1989)]

a) **Remedial Justifications**

(1) **Local Private Discrimination**

Remedying past private discrimination *within* the governmental agency's jurisdiction is a compelling interest, but there is no compelling interest in remedying the general effects of societal discrimination. Thus, for a city to give a preference to minority race applicants for city construction contracts, it must identify the past unconstitutional or illegal discrimination against minority-owned construction businesses that it is now attempting to correct. [City of Richmond v. J.A. Croson Co., *supra*]

Example: In *United Jewish Organizations v. Carey,* 430 U.S. 144 (1977), the Court upheld New York's revised voting district plan, based solely on racial statistics, because the revisions were made to insure that minorities that had previously been discriminated against in New York would be represented in the legislature.

(2) **Diversity in Public Education**

The government appears to have a "compelling interest" in promoting racial diversity in public school student bodies and faculties (although a majority of the Justices have not accepted this principle in a majority opinion). However, this interest will not support a program that attempts to achieve or maintain a mathematical balance in student bodies or faculties (*i.e.,* quota systems will not be found to be necessary to promote educational diversity).

Examples: 1) A state university may consider race or ethnic origin when admitting students, in an attempt to have a diverse student body. [University of California Regents v. Bakke, 438 U.S. 265 (1978)]

2) A school board may not fire or lay off white teachers with greater seniority than minority race teachers for the sole purpose of maintaining racial balance in a faculty during a period when teacher layoffs are necessary. [Wygant v. Jackson Board of Education, 476 U.S. 267 (1989)]

c. **Discriminatory Legislative Apportionment**
Race can be considered in drawing up new voting districts, but it *cannot be the predominant factor*. If a plaintiff can show that a redistricting plan was drawn up predominantly on the basis of racial considerations (as opposed to the more traditional factors, such as compactness, contiguity, and community interest), the plan will violate the Equal Protection Clause *unless* the government can show that the plan is *narrowly tailored* to serve a *compelling state interest*. [Miller v. Johnson, 515 U.S. 900 (1995)—while eradicating the effects of past discrimination would be a compelling state interest, the redistricting here was driven by the Justice Department's policy of maximizing the number of districts where racial minority members are the majority, which is not a compelling interest]

d. **Private Affirmative Action**
Private employers, of course, are not restricted by the Equal Protection Clause, since the Clause applies only to the government, and private employers lack state action. Nevertheless, Congress has adopted statutes regulating private discrimination by employers pursuant to its power under the enabling provisions of the Thirteenth and Fourteenth Amendments and the Commerce Clause. Thus, if an exam question asks whether private employer discrimination is valid, the answer generally cannot be based on equal protection.

2. **Alienage Classifications**

a. **Federal Classifications**
The standard for review of federal government classifications based on alienage is not clear, but they never seem to be subject to strict scrutiny. Because of Congress's plenary power over aliens, these classifications are valid if they are *not arbitrary and unreasonable*. Thus, federal Medicare regulations could establish a five-year residency requirement for benefits that eliminated many resident aliens. [Mathews v. Diaz, 426 U.S. 67 (1976)]

b. State and Local Classifications

State/local laws are *subject to strict scrutiny* if based on alienage. A "compelling state interest" must be shown to justify disparate treatment. For example, a state law requiring United States citizenship for welfare benefits, civil service jobs, or a license to practice law will be struck down because there is no compelling interest justifying the requirement.

1) Exception—Participation in Self-Government Process

If a law discriminates against alien participation in the functioning of the state government, the *rational basis* standard is applied.

Examples: 1) A state cannot require a notary public to be a citizen. A notary's responsibilities are essentially clerical and do not fall within the exception for positions related to participation in the governmental process, and there is no compelling government interest justifying such a requirement. [Bernal v. Fainter, 467 U.S. 216 (1984)]

2) A state can validly refuse to hire aliens as police officers and teachers and for all other positions that have a direct effect on the functioning of government. [Ambach v. Norwick, 441 U.S. 68 (1979); Cabell v. Chavez-Salido, 454 U.S. 432 (1982)]

c. Undocumented Aliens

1) Punitive Laws Against "Illegal" Alien Adults

The Supreme Court has *not* held that undocumented ("illegal") aliens are a suspect classification. Thus, a state law that denies benefits to (or imposes burdens on) persons who are in the United States without the permission of the federal government might be upheld under the rational basis test as long as the law was not totally arbitrary.

2) Education Rights of Alien Children

In *Plyler v. Doe,* 457 U.S. 202 (1982), the Court held that a state denied equal protection to undocumented alien children when it denied them state supported primary or secondary education. However, the Supreme Court upheld a state statute that permitted a school district to deny tuition-free education to any child (whether or not he was a United States citizen) who lived apart from his parent or lawful guardian if the child's presence in the school district was for the "primary purpose" of attending school in the district. The state does not have to consider such a child to be a bona fide resident of the school district. [Martinez v. Bynum, 461 U.S. 321 (1983)]

E. QUASI-SUSPECT CLASSIFICATIONS

Classifications based on gender or legitimacy are almost always suspect. When analyzing government action based on such classifications, the Court will apply the intermediate standard and strike the action unless it is *substantially related* to an *important* government interest.

1. Gender

The Court has expressly held that the *government* bears the burden of proof in gender discrimination cases and that an *"exceedingly persuasive justification"* is required in order to show that gender discrimination is substantially related to an important government interest. [United States v. Virginia, 518 U.S. 515 (1996)]

a. **Intentional Discrimination Against Women**
Gender classifications that ***intentionally*** discriminate against women will generally be invalid under the intermediate standard, because the government is unable to show the "exceedingly persuasive justification" that is required.

Examples: 1) A statute giving the husband, as head of the household, the right to unilaterally dispose of property jointly owned with his wife violates equal protection. [Kirchberg v. Feenstra, 450 U.S. 455 (1981)]

2) A statute giving preference to males over females to act as administrator of an estate violates equal protection. [Reed v. Reed, 404 U.S. 71 (1971)—ease in determining who should serve is not an important interest]

Compare: 1) A state law that excluded from state disability insurance benefits "disabilities" arising from normal pregnancy and childbirth was upheld on a holding that it did not constitute a gender classification and so did not constitute intentional discrimination. [Geduldig v. Aiello, 417 U.S. 484 (1974)]

2) A state statute granting a hiring preference to veterans was upheld even though the result would disadvantage women since most veterans are men. The Court found that the purpose of the statute was to help veterans, not to discriminate against women. [Personnel Administrator of Massachusetts v. Feeney, 442 U.S. 256 (1979)]

1) **Government Interest Must Be Genuine**
The "important government interest" advanced to justify categorization on the basis of gender must be ***genuine***—not hypothesized for the purpose of litigation defense. Neither may the government's justification rely on ***overbroad generalizations*** about males and females that will create or perpetuate the legal, social, and economic inferiority of women. [United States v. Virginia, *supra*]

Example: When a state military school's policy of admitting only men was challenged, the state justified the policy claiming that: (i) offering a diversity of educational approaches within the state (*e.g.,* some schools having men only, some having women only, and some having both) yields important educational benefits, and (ii) females ***generally*** would not be able to meet the school's physical requirements and would not do well under the school's adversative approach to education. The Supreme Court found these arguments unavailing. There was no evidence that the single-sex school in question was established or had been maintained with a view toward fostering a diversity of educational opportunities, and there was some evidence that *some* women could meet the school's physical requirements and thrive under the school's adversative approach. [United States v. Virginia, *supra*]

b. **Affirmative Action Benefiting Women**
Classifications benefiting women that are designed to *remedy past discrimination* against women will generally be upheld.
Examples: 1) Social Security and tax exemptions that entitle women to greater benefits to make up for past discrimination in the workplace are valid. [Califano v. Webster, 430 U.S. 313 (1977)]

2) A Navy rule granting female officers longer tenure than males before mandatory discharge for nonproduction is valid to make up for past discrimination against females in the Navy. [Schlesinger v. Ballard, 419 U.S. 498 (1975)]

c. **Intentional Discrimination Against Men**
Intentional discrimination against men generally is invalid. However, a number of laws have been held valid as being substantially related to an important government interest.

1) **Invalid Discrimination**
The following have been held invalid under the Equal Protection Clause:

a) Denial to admit males to a state university or nursing school [Mississippi University for Women v. Hogan, 458 U.S. 718 (1982)];

b) Law that provides that only wives are eligible for alimony [Orr v. Orr, 40 U.S. 268 (1979)];

c) Law that permits unwed mother but not unwed father to stop adoption of offspring [Caban v. Mohammed, 441 U.S. 380 (1979)]; and

d) Law providing a higher minimum drinking age for men than for women [Craig v. Boren, 429 U.S. 190 (1976)].

2) **Valid Discrimination**
The following have been upheld under the Equal Protection Clause despite their discriminatory intent:

a) Law punishing males but not females for statutory rape (sexual intercourse with a minor) [Michael M. v. Superior Court, 450 U.S. 464 (1981)—classification was found to be substantially related to important interest of preventing pregnancy of minors];

b) Male only draft registration [Rostker v. Goldberg, 453 U.S. 57 (1981)—classification was found to be substantially related to important interest of preparing combat troops]; and

c) A law granting automatic United States citizenship to nonmarital children born abroad to American mothers, but requiring American fathers of children born abroad to take specific steps to establish paternity in order to make such children United States citizens. [Nguyen v. Immigration and Naturalization Service, 121 S. Ct. 2053 (2001)—promotes the important governmental interest of avoiding proof of paternity problems, which are more difficult to resolve for fathers]

2. Legitimacy Classifications
Distinctions drawn between legitimate and illegitimate children are also reviewed under the intermediate scrutiny standard. Such classifications "must be *substantially related* to an *important* governmental objective." [Clark v. Jeter, 486 U.S. 456 (1988)]

a. No Punitive Purpose
When the Court examines a classification based on illegitimacy, it gives greater attention to the purpose behind the distinction. It will not uphold discriminatory legislation intended to punish the offspring of illicit relationships.

1) Inheritance from Father
A state statute cannot absolutely exclude illegitimate children from inheriting from their intestate fathers. [Trimble v. Gordon, 430 U.S. 762 (1977)]

Note: However, to promote efficient disposition of property at death (an important government interest), a state can require that the paternity of the father be proved before his death, since the requirement is substantially related to the important interest. [Lalli v. Lalli, 439 U.S. 259 (1978)]

2) Statute of Limitations on Paternity Suits May Be Discriminatory
The Supreme Court struck down a state statute that required illegitimate children to bring paternity suits within six years of their birth while allowing legitimate children to seek support from parents at any time. The Court found that the law was not related to the state interest of preventing stale or fraudulent claims. [Clark v. Jeter, *supra*]

b. Immigration Preference to Legitimate Children—Permissible
Due to the plenary power over immigration, the Court upheld a federal law granting immigration preferences to legitimate children. [Fiallo v. Bell, 430 U.S. 787 (1977)]

F. OTHER CLASSIFICATIONS
All other classifications are reviewed under the rational basis standard and will be upheld unless they bear no rational relationship to any conceivable legitimate government interest. Nevertheless, if the government has no interest in denying a benefit or imposing a burden on a group of persons other than a societal fear or dislike of them, the classification will not meet the standard.

Examples: 1) The Court struck down a zoning ordinance that allowed denial of a special use permit to a group of unrelated, mentally retarded persons who wished to share a residential home or apartment building. Retarded persons are not a suspect or quasi-suspect class and the right to housing is not a fundamental right; thus the Court applied the rational basis standard. It found that the sole reason the permit was denied was the applicants' mental condition and that the government has no legitimate interest in prohibiting mentally retarded persons from living together. [Cleburne v. Cleburne Living Center, Inc., 470 U.S. 1002 (1985)]

2) Several municipalities passed ordinances banning discrimination in housing, employment, etc., based on sexual orientation. In response, the state voters

adopted a state constitutional amendment prohibiting any state or local action protecting the status of persons based on their homosexual, lesbian, or bisexual orientation. *Held:* A state constitutional provision that identifies persons by a single trait and then denies them the right to seek *any* specific protections from the law—no matter how local or widespread the injury—is so unprecedented as to imply animosity toward such persons and is thus not related to any legitimate state interest. [Romer v. Evans, 517 U.S. 620 (1996)]

1. Age Not Suspect

Age is not a suspect class. Thus, government action based on age will be upheld if there is a conceivable rational basis for the classification. [*See, e.g.,* Massachusetts Board of Retirement v. Murgia, 427 U.S. 307 (1976)—police officer can be forced to retire at age 50, even though he is as physically fit as a younger officer; Gregory v. Ashcroft, 501 U.S. 452 (1991)—a state constitution that requires state judges to retire at age 70 does not violate the Equal Protection Clause]

2. Wealth Not Suspect

The Court has never held that wealth alone is a "suspect classification." However, the lack of wealth, or the inability to pay a governmentally required fee, cannot be the sole basis upon which a person is deprived of a *fundamental* constitutional right.

Example: The government will be required to waive a marriage license fee or divorce court fee for a person who cannot afford to pay that fee. Marriage and divorce rights are part of the right of privacy.

a. Abortions

The Supreme Court upheld the governmental refusal to pay for abortions. The Court found that a woman did not have a fundamental constitutional right to obtain abortion services, but only a fundamental right to make her decision to have an abortion without government interference.

b. Education

The Supreme Court has not yet held education to be a fundamental right. The Court has not found that children are denied equal protection when the government provides greater educational opportunities for children who can afford to pay for access to the best state operated schools. In fact, the Court has upheld the use of a property tax to fund local schools where the tax system resulted in children in districts with a high tax base getting a significantly better education than children in tax districts that could not afford significant taxes for education. [San Antonio Independent School District v. Rodriguez, 411 U.S. 1 (1973)] The Court has also upheld a statute that authorizes some school districts in the state to charge user fees for bus transportation to the local public schools. [Kadrmas v. Dickinson Public Schools, 487 U.S. 450 (1988)]

XIX. FUNDAMENTAL RIGHTS

A. INTRODUCTION

Certain fundamental rights are protected under the Constitution. If they are denied to everyone, it is a substantive due process problem. If they are denied to some individuals but not to others, it is an equal protection problem. The applicable standard in either case is strict scrutiny. Thus, to be valid the governmental action must be *necessary* to protect a *compelling interest*.

B. RIGHT OF PRIVACY

Various privacy rights, including marriage, sexual relations, abortion, and childrearing, are fundamental rights. Thus, regulations affecting these rights are reviewed under the *strict scrutiny* standard and will be upheld only if they are *necessary* to a *compelling interest*.

1. Marriage

The right of a male and female to enter into (and, probably, to dissolve) a marriage relationship is a fundamental right. Although not all cases examining marriage regulations clearly use the compelling interest standard, a law prohibiting a class of adults from marrying is likely to be invalidated unless the government can demonstrate that the law is narrowly tailored to promote a compelling or overriding or, at least, important interest.

Note: The Court has indicated that there is a "marital zone of privacy" [*see* Griswold v. Connecticut, 381 U.S. 479 (1965)], so it will likely grant broader protection to private sexual relations between married persons than it does concerning nonmarried persons.

a. Special Test in Prisoners' Rights Cases

A statute or regulation that restricts the constitutional rights of prison inmates will be upheld as long as the statute or regulation "is reasonably related to legitimate penological interests."

Example: Even under this lenient standard, a prison regulation that prohibited an adult prisoner from establishing a legal marriage relationship with another adult unless the prison superintendent approved the marriage was held invalid, because the regulation was not reasonably related to any asserted penological interest. [Turner v. Safley, 482 U.S. 78 (1987)]

2. Use of Contraceptives

A state cannot prohibit distribution of nonmedical contraceptives to adults except through licensed pharmacists, nor prohibit sales of such contraceptives to persons under 16 who do not have approval of a licensed physician. [Carey v. Population Services International, 431 U.S. 678 (1977)]

3. Abortion

The Supreme Court has held that the right of privacy includes the right of a woman to have an abortion under certain circumstances without undue interference from the state. [Roe v. Wade, 410 U.S. 113 (1973)] However, because the Court has held that the states have a compelling interest in protecting the health of both the woman and the fetus that may become a child, it is difficult to apply the normal "strict scrutiny" analysis to abortion regulations (since these two compelling interests may conflict with each other and with the woman's privacy right). Moreover, the Supreme Court has actively been changing the rules regarding abortions and the Justices have not come to agreement on any applicable standard. In the Court's latest announcement, the plurality opinion adopted two rules: a pre-viability rule and a post-viability rule.

a. Pre-Viability Rule—No Undue Burdens

Before viability (*i.e.,* a realistic possibility of maintaining the fetus's life outside the womb), a state may adopt regulations protecting the mother's health and the life of the fetus only if the regulation does not impose an "undue burden" or substantial obstacle to the woman's right to have an abortion. The Court has not specifically defined what will constitute an undue burden, stating that a state can adopt a statute designed to persuade a woman to choose childbirth over abortion as long as the statute is reasonably related to that purpose and does not put a *substantial* obstacle to abortion in the woman's path. A statute will not impose a substantial obstacle or an undue burden simply because it has the incidental effect of making it more difficult or more expensive to obtain an abortion. [Planned Parenthood of Southeastern Pennsylvania v. Casey, 505 U.S. 833 (1992)]

1) **Informed Consent—No Undue Burden**
States can require abortions to be performed by licensed physicians, and it is not an "undue burden" to require the *physician* to provide the woman with truthful information about the nature of the abortion procedure, the health risks of abortion and childbirth, and the probable gestational age of the fetus. [Planned Parenthood of Southeastern Pennsylvania v. Casey, *supra*]

2) **Waiting Period—No Undue Burden**
Requiring a 24-hour waiting period between the time the woman gives her informed consent and the time of the abortion does not amount to an undue burden. [Planned Parenthood of Southeastern Pennsylvania v. Casey, *supra*]

3) **Parental Consent—No Undue Burden**
A state may require a minor to obtain her parents' (one or both) consent to have an abortion (or give notice to them even if their consent is not required) if there is a "bypass procedure" whereby the minor may obtain the abortion (without notice to or consent of her parents) with the consent of a judge. The judge is required to make a prompt decision as to (i) whether the minor is sufficiently mature to make her own abortion decision, and (ii) if she is not sufficiently mature, whether having an abortion without notice to her parents is in her best interests. [Hodgson v. Minnesota, 497 U.S. 417 (1990); Ohio v. Akron Center for Reproductive Health, 497 U.S. 502 (1990); Planned Parenthood of Southeastern Pennsylvania v. Casey, *supra;* Lambert v. Wicklund, 520 U.S. 292 (1997)]

4) **Compare—Spousal Consent Is Undue Burden**
It is an undue burden to require a woman to sign a statement that she has notified her spouse that she is about to undergo an abortion. [Planned Parenthood of Southeastern Pennsylvania v. Casey, *supra*]

5) **"Physician Only" Requirement—No Undue Burden**
A law restricting the performance of abortions to licensed physicians does not impose an undue burden on a woman seeking an abortion. [Mazurek v. Armstrong, 520 U.S. 968 (1997)—*per curiam*]

6) **"Partial-Birth Abortion"**
A state may *not* completely proscribe so-called partial-birth abortion procedures

since they are the *most commonly* used methods for pre-viability, second-trimester abortions. Such a ban would impose an undue burden on a woman's right to choose a pre-viability abortion. [Stenberg v. Carhart, 530 U.S. 793 (2000)] However, a state could bar one type of partial-birth abortion if there are other adequate, safe methods of abortion available *and* the law provides an exception for those instances when the banned procedure is necessary to preserve the life or *health* of the mother. [Stenberg v. Carhart, *supra*]

7) Other Regulations Uncertain
Prior to *Planned Parenthood of Southeastern Pennsylvania v. Casey, supra,* the Supreme Court upheld a requirement that abortions be performed in a clinic or medical facility with all of the basic medical equipment that would be found in a hospital surgery room. The Court also upheld a requirement that tissue from an aborted fetus be sent to a pathologist. These holdings surely are still valid. But the Court struck down certain other regulations (*e.g.,* requiring early term abortions to be approved by another doctor or hospital committee). Whether these regulations would be found to be undue burdens is uncertain.

b. Post-Viability Rule—May Prohibit Abortion Unless Woman's Health Threatened
Once the fetus has become viable, the state's interest in the fetus's life can override the woman's right to choose an abortion, but it does not override the state's interest in the woman's health. Thus, after viability the state can prohibit a woman from obtaining an abortion unless an abortion is necessary to protect the mother's life or health. However, viability is itself a medical question, and a state cannot unduly interfere with the attending physician's judgment as to the reasonable likelihood that the fetus can survive outside the womb. [Colautti v. Franklin, 439 U.S. 379 (1979)]

c. Financing Abortions
Neither federal nor local governments are required to grant medical benefit payments for abortions to indigent women, even if they grant benefits to indigent women for childbirth services. [Maher v. Roe, 432 U.S. 464 (1977); Harris v. McRae, 448 U.S. 297 (1980)] Moreover, a state may prohibit the public funding of abortions by prohibiting the use of public facilities for abortions and prohibiting any public employee acting within the scope of her public employment from performing or assisting in the performance of abortions. [Webster v. Reproductive Health Services, 486 U.S. 592 (1989)] The Court has not addressed the question of whether a state could prohibit public employees from performing abortions at times and places not a part of their public employment.

4. Obscene Reading Material
The right of privacy encompasses the freedom to read obscene material in your home, except for child pornography. [Stanley v. Georgia, 394 U.S. 557 (1969); Osborne v. Ohio, 495 U.S. 103 (1990)] It does not, however, include the right to sell, purchase, receive, or transport obscene material. [Paris Adult Theatre v. Slayton, 413 U.S. 49 (1973)]

5. Keeping Extended Family Together
The right of privacy includes the right of family members—even extended ones—to live together. Thus, a zoning ordinance cannot prohibit extended families from living in a single

household since there is no compelling interest to justify such a rule. [Moore v. City of East Cleveland, 431 U.S. 494 (1977)]

6. Rights of Parents

Parents have a fundamental right to make decisions concerning the care, custody, and control of their children. [Troxel v. Granville, 530 U.S. 57 (2000)]

a. Education

Although the state may prescribe reasonable educational standards, it may *not* require that all children be educated in public schools. [Pierce v. Society of Sisters, 268 U.S. 510 (1925)] Neither may the state forbid education in a language other than English. [Meyer v. Nebraska, 262 U.S. 390 (1923)]

b. Visitation

A state law was found to be overbroad and in violation of parents' rights where it (i) authorized the courts to grant "any person" (including grandparents) a right to visit a child upon finding that this would be in the child's best interests and (ii) did not allow the judge to give significant weight to the parent's offer of meaningful visitation opportunity and the traditional presumption that a fit parent will act in the child's best interests. [Troxel v. Granville, *supra*]

7. Sodomy—No Privacy Right

The right of privacy does not include the right of consenting adults to engage in sodomy. [Bowers v. Hardwick, 478 U.S. 186 (1986)] It should be noted that the Supreme Court did not determine whether a significant prison sentence for private, consensual homosexual acts would violate the Eighth Amendment prohibition of cruel and unusual punishment.

8. Freedom from Collection and Distribution of Personal Data

The right of privacy does not prevent the state from accumulating and computerizing the names and addresses of patients for whom dangerous drugs are prescribed. [Whalen v. Roe, 429 U.S. 589 (1977)] And the state can republish the recording of an official act, such as an arrest. [Paul v. Davis, 424 U.S. 693 (1976)]

C. RIGHT TO VOTE

The right of all United States citizens over 18 years of age to vote is mentioned in the Fourteenth, Fifteenth, Nineteenth, Twenty-Fourth, and Twenty-Sixth Amendments. It extends to all national and state government elections, including primaries. The right is fundamental; thus, restrictions on voting, other than on the basis of age, residency, or citizenship, are *invalid* unless they can pass strict scrutiny.

1. Restrictions on Right to Vote

a. Residency Requirements

Relatively short residency requirements restricting the right to vote (*e.g.,* 30 days) are valid because there is a compelling interest in ensuring that only bona fide residents vote. However, longer residency requirements will probably be held invalid (*e.g.,* one year) because they discriminate against newer residents without a compelling reason, and thus violate the Equal Protection Clause. Such residency requirements might also violate the right to travel interstate. (*See* D.1.b.1), *infra.*) Note also that Congress may override state residency requirements in ***presidential*** elections. [Oregon v. Mitchell, 400 U.S. 112 (1970)]

1) Members of Armed Forces
The right to vote cannot automatically be denied to members of the armed forces stationed at a particular locality. They must be given an opportunity to prove their bona fide residency. [Carrington v. Rash, 380 U.S. 89 (1965)]

2) Compare—Nonresidents
Laws that prohibit nonresidents from voting are generally valid as long as they have a rational basis. [*See* Holt Civic Club v. City of Tuscaloosa, 439 U.S. 60 (1978)—upholding denial of right to vote in city elections to persons outside of city limits, but within the city's police and licensing jurisdiction]

b. Property Ownership
Conditioning the right to vote, to be a candidate, or to hold office on property ownership is usually invalid under the Equal Protection Clause, since property ownership is not necessary to any compelling governmental interest related to voting. [*See, e.g.,* Kramer v. Union Free School District, 395 U.S. 622 (1969)—requirement of owning property or having children in schools to vote in school board elections struck] However, certain special purpose elections (*e.g.,* water storage district elections) can be based on property ownership. (*See* below.)

c. Poll Taxes
Poll taxes are prohibited under the Twenty-Fourth Amendment, and the Supreme Court has held that they also violate equal protection because wealth is not related to the government's interest in having voters vote intelligently. [Harper v. Virginia Board of Elections, 383 U.S. 663 (1966)]

d. Primary Elections

1) State Regulation of Party Primaries
States may exercise some control over primary elections, but such regulation is subject to restrictions under the First Amendment (freedom of political association) and the Fourteenth Amendment (Equal Protection Clause). Thus, to prevent interparty "raiding," the Supreme Court has held that states can require a person to have been registered with a party for a reasonable time before that party's primary election in order to be eligible to vote in the primary. [Rosario v. Rockefeller, 410 U.S. 752 (1973)—11 months registration upheld; Kusper v. Pontikes, 414 U.S. 51 (1973)—23 months not upheld] However, if a political party wishes to open its primary elections to anyone, whether or not registered with the party, the state cannot prohibit this because the state interest here is overridden by the right of political association. [Tashjian v. Republican Party of Connecticut, 479 U.S. 208 (1986)]

2) States May Subsidize Primaries of Major Parties
States may subsidize the primaries of major parties without similarly defraying the costs of mechanisms through which minor parties qualify candidates for the

general election [American Party of Texas v. White, 415 U.S. 767 (1974)—upholding law requiring new or small parties to proceed by petition or convention at their own expense rather than by publicly funded primary], as long as new or small parties are given some effective way to qualify for the general election [Williams v. Rhodes, 393 U.S. 23 (1968)—unduly burdensome petition requirements for new or small parties struck down as not justified].

2. Dilution of Right to Vote

a. One Person, One Vote Principle
The Equal Protection Clause of the Fourteenth Amendment has been interpreted to prohibit state dilution of the right to vote, and Article I has been interpreted to place the same type of restriction on the federal government.

1) Establishing Voting Districts
Whenever a governmental body establishes voting districts for the election of representatives, the number of persons in each district may not vary significantly. This is commonly referred to as the one person, one vote principle.

a) Congressional Elections—Almost Exactly Equal
States establish the districts for congressional elections. However, the Supreme Court requires *almost exact mathematical equality* between the *congressional* districts within a state; thus, deviations of even a few percentage points between the congressional districts within a state may result in the invalidation of the congressional district plan.

(1) Compare—Apportionment Among the States
Congress apportions representatives among the states "according to their respective number." [Art. I, §2] Congress's good faith choice of method in so apportioning the representatives commands far more deference than state districting decisions and is *not* subject to the same precise mathematical standard as state plans. [United States Department of Commerce v. Montana, 503 U.S. 442 (1992)]

b) State and Local Elections—Variance Not Unjustifiably Large
The variance in the number of persons included in districts for the purpose of electing representatives to a *state or local governmental body* must not be unjustifiably large, but the districts need not be within a few percentage points of each other: If a state can show that the deviation from mathematical equality between districts is reasonable and tailored to promote a legitimate state interest, the law establishing the districts may be upheld. [Mahan v. Howell, 410 U.S. 315 (1973)—16% variance in district populations was upheld in light of state's interest in preserving political subdivisions, although 30% variance would be excessive]

c) Scope
The one person, one vote principle applies to almost every election where a person is being elected to perform normal governmental functions. [Hadley

v. Junior College District, 397 U.S. 50 (1970)—trustees for junior college district] However, there are a few exceptions to note:

(1) Exception—Appointed Officials and Officials Elected "At-Large"
The apportionment requirement is inapplicable to appointed officials. Neither is it applicable in at-large systems of election, because in such a system there are no electoral districts to violate the one person, one vote principle. However, if an at-large voting system were established or maintained for the purpose of suppressing the voting power of minority race voters, it would be unconstitutional.

(2) Exception—Special Purpose Government Units (Water Storage Districts)
The government can limit the class of persons who are allowed to vote in an election of persons to serve on a special purpose government unit *if* the government unit has a special impact on the class of enfranchised voters. To date, the Supreme Court has found only "water storage districts" to be so specialized that their governing boards are not subject to the one person, one vote principle. [Salyer Land Co. v. Tulane Water District, 410 U.S. 719 (1973); Ball v. James, 451 U.S. 355 (1981)— apportionment rules do not apply to water district even if the district is major supplier of electricity in the state]

2) Standardless Recount
Counting uncounted ballots in a presidential election without standards to guide ballot examiners in determining the intent of the voter violates the Fourteenth Amendment Equal Protection Clause. [Bush v. Gore, 121 S. Ct. 525 (2000)]

b. Gerrymandering

1) Racial Gerrymandering
As indicated above, race (and presumably other suspect classifications) cannot be the predominate factor in drawing the boundaries of a voting district unless the district plan can pass muster under strict scrutiny. [*See* Miller v. Johnson, XVIII.D.1.c., *supra*] Moreover, a district's bizarre shape can be used to show that race was the predominate factor in drawing the district's boundaries [*see* Shaw v. Reno, XVIII.C.1.a., *supra*], although a bizarre shape is not necessary to such a finding. Note that the person challenging the reapportionment has the burden of proving the race-based motive. [Shaw v. Hunt, 517 U.S. 899 (1996)]

2) Political Gerrymandering
It is also unconstitutional to gerrymander based on political-group membership, but to prove unconstitutional *political* gerrymandering, a plaintiff would have to show that the district lines were drawn to suppress voting power of a political party *and* that (through one or more elections) the districting system consistently diluted the voting power of a particular group of voters. [Davis v. Bandemer, 478 U.S. 109 (1986)]

c. **Multi-Member Districts**

A state is generally free to have some multi-member districts together with some single-member districts, as long as the number of members representing a district is proportional to its population. However, single-member or multi-member districts will be held to violate equal protection (even though they meet the one person, one vote principle) if the district lines were drawn on the basis of unconstitutional criteria, such as to suppress the voting power of racial minorities or an identifiable political group.

3. **Candidates and Campaigns**

a. **Candidate Qualifications**

1) **Fee Must Not Preclude Indigents as Candidates**

States may not charge candidates a fee that results in making it impossible for indigents to run for office. An unreasonably high filing fee (which was not tailored to promote a substantial or overriding state interest) might be held totally invalid so that no candidate would have to pay the fee. A reasonable, valid fee would have to be waived for an indigent candidate who could not pay the fee.

2) **Restrictions on Ability of Person to Be a Candidate**

Restrictions on the ability of persons to be candidates must be examined to see if they violate either the First Amendment right of political association or the Fourteenth Amendment Equal Protection Clause. Such regulations are judged on a sliding scale of scrutiny. (*See* XXI.B., *infra.*)

Example: The Court invalidated a March deadline for filing a nominating petition for independent candidates for a November election where the state allowed the major political parties to name their candidates later in the year. [Anderson v. Celebrezze, 460 U.S. 780 (1983)]

Note: A state may require candidates to show reasonable support (signatures or votes) to qualify to have their names placed on the ballot. [Munro v. Socialist Workers Party, 479 U.S. 189 (1986)—upholding requirement of receipt of at least 1% of the votes cast in the primary election]

3) **Required Resignation of Office Is Permissible**

A state may require state officials to resign their office if they enter an election for another government office. [Clements v. Fashing, 457 U.S. 957 (1982)]

b. **Campaign Funding, Contributions, and Expenditures**

Government *may* allocate more public funds to the two "major" parties than to "minor" parties for political campaigns, and may withhold public funding from candidates who do not accept reciprocal limits on their total campaign expenses; but such expenses cannot otherwise be limited, unlike campaign contributions to political candidates, which may be limited if government chooses. (XXI.B., *infra.*)

4. **Extraordinary Majorities—Referendum Elections**

The government may require a supermajority vote for voter referendums, even though such a requirement might give a minority disproportionate power. [Gordon v. Lance, 403 U.S. 1 (1971)—upholding 60% requirement for referendum approval; Town of Lockport v. Citizens for Community Action, 430 U.S. 259 (1977)—upholding requirement that new county charter be approved by separate majorities of city and noncity voters]

5. **Absentee Ballots**
The state has no duty to provide absentee ballots to persons otherwise unable to vote in some manner. However, if it does provide for absentee ballots, it may not deny the ballots in a discriminatory manner. [*See* McDonald v. Board of Election Officials, 394 U.S. 802 (1969)—striking law that granted absentee ballots to those incarcerated outside of their home county but denied them to those incarcerated within their home county]

6. **Replacement of Incumbent Legislators**
A state may validly give to a political party the right to name an interim appointee to the legislature to fill out the unexpired term of a legislator from that political party who left office. No voter is denied equal protection by this system. [Rodriguez v. Popular Democratic Party, 457 U.S. 1 (1982)]

D. RIGHT TO TRAVEL

1. **Interstate Travel**

   a. **Nature of the Right**
   Individuals have a fundamental right to travel from state to state, which encompasses the right: (i) to leave and enter another state, and (ii) to be treated equally if they become permanent residents of that state. [Saenz v. Roe, VII.C.3., *supra*—striking California law that limited welfare benefits for new residents to what they would have received in their prior state of residence]

   b. **Standard of Review**
   When a state uses a durational residency requirement (a waiting period) for dispensing benefits, that requirement normally should be subject to the "strict scrutiny" test. This means that the government must show that the waiting period requirement is tailored to promote a compelling or overriding interest. However, in some right to travel cases, the Court has not been clear as to whether it is using this strict scrutiny-compelling interest standard of review. The important point to note for the bar exam is that state residency requirements should not be upheld merely because they have some theoretical rational relationship to an arguably legitimate end of government.

      1) **Examples**
      Because of the ad hoc nature of these rulings, we will list four examples of Supreme Court decisions in this area:

         a) A one-year waiting period before a person may receive subsistence welfare payments is *invalid*. Similarly, a law providing that persons residing in the state for less than a year may receive welfare benefits no greater than those paid in the state of prior residence is also invalid. [Saenz v. Roe, *supra*]

         b) A one-year waiting period for state subsidized medical care is *invalid*.

c) A one-year waiting period to get a divorce is **valid**.

d) A state may require a voter to register to vote in a party primary 10 months before the primary election (to avoid interparty "raiding"). However, a 23-month registration period would be **invalid**.

c. Distinctions Between Old and New Residents

Some state laws that have an adverse impact on new residents do not involve a waiting period. For example, a state may attempt to dispense state benefits on the basis of the length of time a person has resided in the state. A state law that distinguishes between residents of the state on the sole basis of their length of residency will serve no legitimate state interest. This type of law should be **stricken** under the rational basis test because it has **no rational relationship** to any legitimate state interest.

Examples: 1) A state statute that dispensed differing amounts of state money to residents of the state based on each resident's length of residence was held invalid.

2) A state statute that grants an annual property tax exemption to a veteran of military service only if he resided in the state before a specific date (May 1976) is invalid.

3) A state law that grants a hiring preference (for civil service employment) to a veteran only if he was a resident of the state prior to joining the armed services is invalid.

2. International Travel

The Supreme Court has not yet declared that the right to international travel is fundamental, although the right appears to be **protected from arbitrary federal interference** by the Due Process Clause of the Fifth Amendment. The Court has held that this right is not violated when the federal government refuses to pay social security benefits to persons who leave the country. The test here is "mere rationality, not strict scrutiny." [Califano v. Aznavorian, 439 U.S. 170 (1978)] Congress may give the executive branch the power to revoke the passport of a person whose conduct in another country presents a danger to United States foreign policy. [Haig v. Agee, 453 U.S. 280 (1981)] The Treasury Department, with congressional authorization, could restrict travel to and from Cuba without violating the Fifth Amendment. [Regan v. Wald, 468 U.S. 222 (1984)]

E. RIGHT TO REFUSE MEDICAL TREATMENT

The Supreme Court had held that the right to refuse medical treatment is a part of an individual's "liberty" that is protected by the Fifth and Fourteenth Amendment Due Process Clauses. However, the Supreme Court has not ruled that this aspect of liberty is a "fundamental right" and **has not** explained which standard of review should be used. Nevertheless, the Court has ruled on the validity of several types of legislation.

1. Vaccination

An individual can be made to submit to vaccination against contagious diseases because of the governmental and societal interest in preventing the spread of disease. [Jacobsen v. Massachusetts, 197 U.S. 11 (1905)]

2. **Refusal of Medical Treatment**
The Supreme Court has assumed (without deciding) that a mentally competent adult has the right to refuse lifesaving medical treatment (including lifesaving nutrition). [Cruzan v. Director, Missouri Department of Health, 497 U.S. 261 (1990)]

a. **Compare—No Right to Assisted Suicide**
There is no general right to commit suicide; thus, a state may ban persons from giving individuals assistance in committing suicide. [Washington v. Glucksberg, 521 U.S. 702 (1997)] It is not irrational to permit competent persons to refuse life-sustaining treatment but prohibit physicians to assist in suicide because there is a logical, rational, and well-established distinction between letting someone die and making someone die. [Vacco v. Quill, 521 U.S. 793 (1997)]

3. **Family or Guardian Decisions for Comatose Adult**
A state may give relatives or the guardian of an individual the power to decide whether to refuse lifesaving medical treatment if the individual is incapable of making or expressing the decision (*e.g.,* if the individual is in a coma), but the state does not have to grant this power. If the state chooses to grant the power, it can condition the power on proof, by clear and convincing evidence, that the comatose adult would have chosen to refuse medical treatment if she were capable of making the decision and expressing herself. [Cruzan v. Director, Missouri Department of Health, *supra*]

PART FIVE: FIRST AMENDMENT FREEDOMS

The First Amendment prohibits Congress from establishing a religion or interfering with the exercise of religion, abridging the freedom of speech or the press, or interfering with the right of the people to assemble. These prohibitions have been made applicable to the states through the Fourteenth Amendment. The freedoms, however, are not absolute, and exam questions often focus on their boundaries. The following material will outline the scope of each freedom.

XX.   FREEDOM OF SPEECH AND ASSEMBLY

A. GENERAL PRINCIPLES
The freedoms of speech and assembly protect the free flow of ideas, a most important function in a democratic society. Thus, whenever the government seeks to regulate these freedoms, the Court will weigh the importance of these rights against the interests or policies sought to be served by the regulation. When analyzing regulations on speech and press, keep the following guidelines in mind:

1. **Content vs. Conduct**
A regulation seeking to forbid communication of specific ideas (*i.e.,* a **content** regulation) is less likely to be upheld than a regulation of the **conduct** incidental to speech.

a. **Content**
It is presumptively unconstitutional for the government to place burdens on speech because of its content. To justify such content-based regulation of speech, the government must show that the regulation (or tax) is **necessary** to serve a **compelling** state

interest and is narrowly drawn to achieve that end. [Simon & Schuster, Inc. v. Members of the New York State Crime Victims Board, 502 U.S. 105 (1991)—striking a law requiring that proceeds to criminals from books and other productions describing their crimes be placed in escrow for five years to pay claims of victims of the crimes]

1) **Exception—Unprotected Categories of Speech**

The Supreme Court has previously determined that certain categories of speech (*e.g.,* obscenity, defamation, and "fighting words"; *see* C., *infra*) generally are proscribable despite the First Amendment. Even in these cases, however, the Court is less likely to uphold a prior restraint (*i.e.,* a regulation prohibiting speech before it occurs) than a punishment for speech that has already occurred.

2) **Content-Neutral Speech Regulations**

While content-based regulation of speech is subject to strict scrutiny, content-neutral speech regulations generally are subject to *intermediate scrutiny*—they will be upheld if the government can show that: (i) they advance *important* interests unrelated to the suppression of speech, and (ii) they *do not burden substantially more speech than necessary* to further those interests. [Turner Broadcasting System, Inc. v. FCC, 512 U.S. 622 (1994)]

b. **Conduct**

The Court has allowed the government more leeway in regulating the conduct related to speech, allowing it to adopt content-neutral, *time, place, and manner* regulations. Regulations involving public forums (*i.e.,* forums historically linked with the exercise of First Amendment freedoms) must be *narrowly tailored* to achieve an *important* government interest (*e.g.,* a prohibition against holding a demonstration in a hospital zone). Regulations involving nonpublic forums must have a reasonable relationship to a legitimate regulatory purpose (*e.g.,* a law prohibiting billboards for purposes of traffic safety).

2. **Reasonableness of Regulation**

a. **Overbroad Regulation Invalid**

Since the purpose of the freedoms of speech and assembly is to encourage the free flow of ideas, a regulation will not be upheld if it is overbroad (*i.e.,* prohibits *substantially* more speech than is necessary). Thus, if a regulation bans a broad range of speech at a particular location or under a particular circumstance, it will likely be held invalid for overbreadth.

Examples: 1) The Supreme Court struck down as overbroad an ordinance that prohibited speech that *"in any manner"* interrupts a police officer in the performance of her duties. [Houston v. Hill, 482 U.S. 451 (1987)]

2) An airport authority rule that bans "*all* First Amendment activities" within the "central terminal area" is invalid as being substantially overbroad. [Board of Airport Commissioners v. Jews for Jesus, 482 U.S. 569 (1987)]

3) A law banning *all* door to door solicitations will be struck as being overbroad [Martin v. City of Struthers, 319 U.S. 141 (1943)], but a law

requiring solicitors to obtain a homeowner's consent to solicit is valid [Breard v. City of Alexandria, 341 U.S. 622 (1951)].

4) A city ordinance that prohibits homeowners from displaying *any sign* on their property except "residence identification" or "for sale" signs is invalid because the ordinance bans virtually all residential signs. [Ladue v. Gilleo, 512 U.S. 43 (1994)]

b.   **Vague Regulations Invalid—Void for Vagueness Doctrine**
If a criminal law or regulation fails to give persons reasonable notice as to what is prohibited, it violates the Due Process Clause. This principle is applied strictly when First Amendment activity is involved to avoid the chilling effect a vague law might have on speech (*i.e.,* if it is unclear what speech is regulated, people might refrain from speech that is permissible for fear that they will be violating the law). Vagueness issues most often arise in relation to content regulations, but the same principles would apply to time, place, and manner restrictions.

Examples: 1) A municipal ordinance that prohibited vagrants was held void for vagueness when it defined vagrants as "rogues and vagabonds . . . lewd, wanton, and lascivious persons . . . persons wandering or straying around from place to place without any lawful purpose or object . . . ." [Papachristou v. City of Jacksonville, 405 U.S. 156 (1972)]

2) A statute that prohibits attorneys representing clients in a pending case from making statements that would have a substantial likelihood of prejudicing a trial, but that also allows attorneys to make public statements regarding the "general nature of the defense" they will present at trial, is void for vagueness, because it does not give fair notice of the types of trial-related statements that are punishable. [Gentile v. State Bar, 501 U.S. 1030 (1991)]

1)   **Funding Speech Activity**
Greater imprecision is allowed when the government acts as a patron in funding speech activity than when enacting criminal statutes or regulatory schemes, because speakers are less likely to steer clear of forbidden areas when only a subsidy is at stake. [National Endowment for the Arts v. Finley, 524 U.S. 569 (1998)—requirement that NEA consider standards of "decency" and "respect for values of American people" is not invalid on its face]

c.   **Cannot Give Officials Unfettered Discretion**
A regulation cannot give officials broad discretion over speech issues; there must be *defined standards* for applying the law. The fear, of course, is that the officials will use their discretionary power to prohibit dissemination of ideas that they do not agree with. This issue usually arises under licensing schemes established to regulate the time, place, and manner of speech. To be valid, such licensing schemes must be related to an important government interest, contain procedural safeguards (*see* D.2., *infra*), and not grant officials unbridled discretion.

Example: County required persons desiring to hold a parade, march, or rally to first obtain a permit from the county administrator. The administrator was empowered to charge up to $1,000 for the permit, but could adjust the fee to meet the necessary expenses of administration and police protection. This scheme is invalid because it gives the administrator unbridled discretion despite the $1,000 limit. It also is unconstitutional because it is a content-based restriction (the administrator theoretically would adjust the costs based on the popularity of the subject at issue—an unpopular subject would require greater police protection). [Forsyth County, Georgia v. Nationalist Movement, 505 U.S. 123 (1992)]

1) Unlimited Discretion—Void on Face

If a statute gives licensing officials unbridled discretion, it is *void on its face*, and speakers need not even apply for a permit. They may exercise their First Amendment rights even if they could have been denied a permit under a valid law, and they may not be punished for violating the licensing statute. [Lovell v. City of Griffin, 303 U.S. 444 (1938)]

Examples: 1) An ordinance vesting officials with the power to grant or deny parade permits based on their judgment as to the effect of the parade on community "welfare" or "morals" is unconstitutional on its face. [Shuttlesworth v. Birmingham, 394 U.S. 147 (1969)] Similarly, ordinances giving officials broad discretion as to who may place magazine racks on public property or who may obtain licenses to solicit door to door are invalid. [City of Lakewood v. Plain Dealer Publishing Co., 486 U.S. 750 (1988); Lovell v. City of Griffin, *supra*]

2) A statute prohibiting excessively loud sound trucks is valid [Kovacs v. Cooper, 336 U.S. 77 (1949)], but an ordinance giving officials discretion as to who may use sound trucks is invalid [Saia v. New York, 334 U.S. 558 (1948)].

2) Statutes Valid on Face

If the licensing statute is valid on its face because it contains adequate standards, a speaker may not ignore the statute, but must seek a permit. If he is denied a permit, even if he believes the denial was incorrect, he must then seek reasonably available administrative or judicial relief. Failure to do so precludes later assertion that his actions were protected by the First Amendment. [Poulos v. New Hampshire, 345 U.S. 395 (1953)]

3. Scope of Speech

a. Includes Freedom Not to Speak

The freedom of speech includes not only the right to speak, but also the right to refrain from speaking or endorsing beliefs with which one does not agree.

Examples: 1) A state *cannot force school children to salute* or say a pledge to the flag. [West Virginia State Board of Education v. Barnette, 319 U.S. 624 (1943)]

2) A motorist *could not be punished* for blocking out the portion of his automobile license plate bearing the motto "Live Free or Die"; as long

as he left the license plate in a condition that served its auto identification purpose, he did not have to display a slogan endorsed by the state. [Wooley v. Maynard, 430 U.S. 705 (1977)]

3) A state may not require private parade organizers to include in their parade groups with messages with which the organizers disagree. [Hurley v. Irish-American Gay, Lesbian & Bisexual Group of Boston, 515 U.S. 557 (1995)]

1) **Mandatory Financial Support**
The government may require a person to pay fees to support a *comprehensive program* that is benefiting the person, even if some of the money is being used to support ideas offensive to the person. However, mandatory financial support will violate the First Amendment if the primary purpose of the program is to require individuals to pay subsidies for speech to which they object. [United States v. United Foods, Inc., 121 S. Ct. 2334 (2001)]

Examples: 1) Public university students can be required to pay a student fee to attend a public university even if the fee is used to support political and ideological speech by student groups whose beliefs are offensive to the student, as long as the program is *viewpoint neutral* (*see* B.2.a.1), *infra*). [Board of Regents of University of Wisconsin v. Southworth, 529 U.S. 217 (2000)]

2) Government employees can be made to pay dues to a union even if they refuse to technically join it, because the government may allow the unions to negotiate benefits for all and impose a reasonable "service charge." However, government employees cannot be required to pay an amount above the service fee that would be used by the union to contribute to political candidates or express social or political views. [Abood v. Detroit Board of Education, 431 U.S. 209 (1977); Lehnert v. Ferris Faculty Association, 500 U.S. 507 (1991)]

3) Attorneys can be required to pay mandatory bar dues, as long as the money is used for activities related to regulating the legal profession. [Keller v. State Bar of California, 496 U.S. 1 (1990)]

Compare: Mushroom handlers objected to paying subsidies that were used solely to generically advertise mushrooms. [United States v. United Foods, Inc., *supra*] The Court differentiated *United Foods* from prior cases because in the prior cases required fees were used to support a comprehensive program that incidentally impacted speech; in *United Foods* the fee was used primarily to fund advertising that the plaintiff objected to.

2) **State Can Require Shopping Center to Permit Persons to Exercise Speech Rights**
Note that the freedom not to speak does not prohibit a state's requiring a large shopping center (that is open to the public) to permit persons to exercise their speech rights on shopping center property—at least as long as the particular

message is not dictated by the state and is not likely to be identified with the owner of the shopping center. [Pruneyard Shopping Center v. Robins, 447 U.S. 74 (1980)]

b.   **Includes Symbolic Conduct**
Speech includes not only verbal communication, but also conduct that is undertaken to communicate an idea. Of course, not all regulation of symbolic conduct is prohibited. The Court will uphold a conduct regulation if: (i) the regulation is within the constitutional power of the government; (ii) it furthers an important governmental interest; (iii) the governmental interest is *unrelated to suppression of speech*; and (iv) the incidental burden on speech is no greater than necessary. [United States v. O'Brien, 391 U.S. 367 (1968)—upholding a prohibition against burning draft cards to protect the government's important interest in facilitating the smooth functioning of the draft system]

Examples: 1) A state may prohibit public nudity, even as applied to nude dancing at bars and places of adult entertainment. Although nude dancing is marginally within the protections of the First Amendment—because it involves the communication of an erotic message—the government has a "substantial" interest in combating crime and other "secondary effects" caused by the presence of adult entertainment establishments that is unrelated to the suppression of free expression. [Barnes v. Glen Theatre, Inc., 501 U.S. 560 (1991); City of Erie v. Pap's A.M., 529 U.S. 277 (2000)—city council made findings regarding secondary effects]

2) To protect the smooth operation of the draft system, the government may selectively prosecute for draft registration violations only those persons who have been brought to the government's attention, *e.g.,* because they sent protest letters or participated in rallies. [Wayte v. United States, 470 U.S. 598 (1985)]

Compare: 1) A prohibition against students wearing armbands to protest the war in Vietnam was struck because it had no regulatory interest other than prohibiting the communicative impact of the conduct. [Tinker v. Des Moines Independent Community School District, 393 U.S. 503 (1969)]

2) A prohibition against mutilating a United States flag (except in cases of proper disposal of a soiled flag) was held invalid as an attempt to restrain speech; the Court found that no imminent breach of the peace was likely to result, and the government has no other interest in prohibiting such burnings. [United States v. Eichman, 496 U.S. 310 (1990)]

4.   **Prison Speech**
A regulation concerning the activities of prison inmates, including *any* First Amendment activities, is governed by a different standard to facilitate prison order: they will be upheld if they are *reasonably related to legitimate penological interests.* [Shaw v. Murphy, 121 S. Ct. 1475 (2001)] Thus, a restriction on *incoming* mail will be upheld if it is rational; a restriction on *outgoing* mail must be narrowly tailored because there is less of a penological interest involved. [*See* Thornburgh v. Abbott, 490 U.S. 401 (1989)]

5. **Funding vs. Regulation**
    In contrast to direct regulation of speech, government *funding* of speech may be based on content-based criteria as long as the criteria are viewpoint neutral (*see* B.2.a.1), *infra*). Congress may selectively fund programs to encourage activities it believes to be in the public interest while denying funding to alternative programs.
    Examples: 1) The government may prohibit organizations receiving government funds for "family planning services" from providing abortion information as part of the federally funded service. The government is not required to subsidize abortion (*see* XIX.B.3.c., *supra*), and this prohibition is merely a viewpoint neutral means of ensuring that government funds are spent only on the family planning services for which they were granted. [Rust v. Sullivan, 500 U.S. 173 (1991)]

    2) The government cannot fund all artists, and choosing among those it will fund and those it will not inevitably must be based on the content of the art. [National Endowment for the Arts v. Finley, 2.b.1), *supra*]

    a. **Government Encouragement of Private Speech**
        In contrast to government funding of speech for the purpose of promoting its own policies (such as the family planning program in *Rust v. Sullivan, supra*), viewpoint restrictions are ordinarily invalid when government funds *private* speech. [Rosenberger v. Rector and Visitors of the University of Virginia, 515 U.S. 819 (1995)—state university exclusion of religious magazine from program financially supporting student publications violates First Amendment]
        Example: A federal statute funding legal assistance to indigents, but forbidding assisting lawyers from challenging the validity of welfare regulations, violates the First Amendment. [Legal Services Corp. v. Velazquez, 121 S. Ct. 1043 (2001)—federal program was designed to promote private (not government) speech, and prohibition would substantially distort traditional role of lawyers]

B. **TIME, PLACE, AND MANNER RESTRICTIONS—REGULATION OF CONDUCT**
    All speech is conveyed through physical action (*e.g.*, talking, writing, distributing pamphlets, etc.), and while the freedom of belief is absolute, the freedom to convey beliefs cannot be. The government may reasonably regulate speech related conduct through *content neutral* time, place, and manner regulations.

1. **Public Forums**
    Certain public property is so historically associated with the exercise of First Amendment rights (*e.g.*, pamphleteering, broadcasting, picketing, etc.) that denial of all access to it for the purpose of exercising such rights is forbidden. *Streets, sidewalks, and parks* fall into this category. [Hague v. CIO, 307 U.S. 496 (1939)] Other public property, although not a "traditional" public forum, may become a *designated public forum* for such time as the state "by policy or by practice" opens it for expressive activity. [Lamb's Chapel v. Center Moriches Union Free School District, 508 U.S. 384 (1993)—school rooms opened for after-school meetings by social, civic, and recreation groups, *see* 2.a.3)b), *infra*] Speech in such public places may be regulated by reasonable time, place, and manner restrictions.

a. **Test**

To be valid, government regulations on speech and assembly in public places must be:

(i) *Content neutral* (*i.e.,* subject matter neutral and viewpoint neutral);

(ii) *Narrowly tailored* to serve a *significant* government interest; and

(iii) Leave open *alternative channels* of communication.

Remember: Even if a regulation meets the above conditions, it might still be struck down on other grounds (*e.g.,* overbreadth, vagueness, unfettered discretion; *see* A.2., *supra*).

1) **Content Neutral**

The regulation cannot be based on the content of the speech, absent substantial justification (*see* C., *infra*).

Examples: 1) The Court held invalid an ordinance allowing peaceful *labor* picketing near schools, but prohibiting all other picketing, since it was a content based restriction. [Chicago Police Department v. Mosely, 408 U.S. 92 (1972)]

2) A law may not forbid only those signs within 500 feet of a foreign embassy that are critical of the foreign government. [Boos v. Barry, 485 U.S. 312 (1988)]

2) **Narrowly Tailored**

The regulation must be narrowly tailored (*i.e.,* it may not burden **substantially** more speech than is necessary to further the significant government interest). However, the regulation need not be the least restrictive means of accomplishing the goal.

Example: A law requiring persons performing at a city's theater to use the city's sound equipment is narrowly tailored to the city's interest in preventing excessive noise. [Ward v. Rock Against Racism, 491 U.S. 781 (1989)]

Note: A regulation that is not narrowly tailored might also fail on overbreadth grounds. (*See* A.2.a., *supra*.)

3) **Significant Interest**

The regulation must further an important government interest. Such interests include: traffic safety, orderly crowd movement, personal privacy, noise control, litter control, aesthetics, etc.

Example: The Court upheld the constitutionality of a state law prohibiting persons within 100 feet of a health care facility from approaching within eight feet of those seeking access to the health care facility for purposes of oral protest, education, or counseling. The Court found that the law was a content-neutral regulation of speech and a reasonable time, place, and manner restriction that served the important interest of preserving access to health care facilities.

[Hill v. Colorado, 530 U.S. 703 (2000)—statute upheld against challenge by petitioners who wished to "counsel" women as they enter abortion clinics]

4) Alternative Channels Open
The law must leave open alternative channels of communication; *i.e.,* other reasonable means for communicating the idea must be available.

b. Examples—Residential Areas

1) Targeted Picketing
The Supreme Court upheld a statute that prevented focused residential picketing (*i.e.,* picketing in front of a single residence). The street/sidewalk involved was a public forum, but the ordinance passed the three-part test: (i) it was content neutral since it regulated the location and manner of picketing rather than its message; (ii) it was narrowly tailored (since it applied only to focused picketing) to the important interest of protecting a homeowner's privacy; and (iii) alternative means of communications were available since the protesters could march *through* the neighborhood in protest. [Frisby v. Schultz, 487 U.S. 474 (1988)]

2) Charitable Solicitations
Charitable solicitations for funds in residential areas are within the protection of the First Amendment. However, they are subject to reasonable regulation.

Example: A state cannot require professional fundraisers (before making an appeal for funds) to disclose to potential donors the percentage of contributions collected over the previous year that were actually turned over to the charity. The disclosure is not necessary to promote the state interest of protecting the public from fraud. However, the state can require a fundraiser to disclose her professional status. [Riley v. National Federation of the Blind of North Carolina, 487 U.S. 781 (1988)] In *Riley,* the Court also invalidated a restriction on the fees that professional fundraisers could charge a charity, because the particular statute was not narrowly tailored to protect either the public or the charities.

c. Injunctions
Injunctions that restrict First Amendment activity in public forums are treated differently from generally applicable ordinances because injunctions present a greater risk of censorship and discriminatory application. The test to be used to determine whether an injunction that restricts speech or protest is constitutional depends on whether the injunction is content neutral.

1) Content Based—Necessary to a Compelling Interest
If the injunction is content based, it will be upheld only if it is necessary to achieve a compelling government interest.

2) Content Neutral—Burdens No More Speech than Necessary
If the injunction is content neutral, it will be upheld only if it burdens no more speech than is necessary to achieve a *significant* government purpose.

Example: Parts of an injunction establishing a 36-foot buffer zone between protesters and abortion clinic entrances were upheld. [Madsen v. Women's Health Center, 512 U.S. 753 (1994)]

Compare: An injunction providing for a "floating buffer zone" of 15 feet between protesters and persons entering and leaving an abortion clinic was held to violate the First Amendment. The floating zone barred all verbal and written communication from a normal conversational distance on public sidewalks, and thus burdened more speech than necessary to ensure ingress and egress from the clinic. [Schneck v. Pro-Choice Network of Western New York, 510 U.S. 357 (1997)]

2. Nonpublic Forums

Most locations other than streets, sidewalks, and parks are *not* public forums, either because they historically have not been linked to speech and assembly or because such activities would be inconsistent with their use; *e.g.,* military bases, school sponsored activities, government workplaces, mailboxes, jails, etc. Speech and assembly in such places can be regulated by reasonable time, place, and manner restrictions.

a. Test

When a nonpublic forum is involved, government regulations on time, place, and manner of speech will be upheld if they are:

(i) *Viewpoint neutral*; and

(ii) *Reasonably related to a legitimate government purpose.*

1) Viewpoint Neutral

Regulations on speech in nonpublic forums need not be content neutral; *i.e.,* the government may allow speech regarding some subjects but not others. However, such regulations must be *viewpoint* neutral; *i.e.,* if the government allows an issue to be presented in a nonpublic forum, it may not limit the presentation to only one view.

Example: A school newspaper is a nonpublic forum; thus, a school board could decide to prohibit articles in school newspapers regarding nuclear power. However, it may not allow an article in favor of nuclear power and prohibit an article against nuclear power.

Similarly, the government may discriminate based on the identity of the speaker in nonpublic forums (*e.g.,* a school board might limit speakers to licensed teachers).

2) Reasonableness

Regulation of speech and assembly in nonpublic forums need only be rationally related to a legitimate governmental objective.

Examples: 1) A city bus is not a public forum. The city, therefore, may constitutionally sell space for signs on the public buses for commercial and public service advertising while refusing to sell space for political or public issue advertising. [Lehman v. Shaker Heights, 418 U.S. 298 (1974)]

2) Public school activities such as newspapers or assemblies are not public forums. Thus, schools can control the content of student speeches or student newspapers for legitimate pedagogical concerns. [*See, e.g.,* Bethel School District No. 403 v. Fraser, 478 U.S. 675 (1986)—student suspended for sexually explicit speech at school assembly] However, a school was forbidden to prohibit the wearing of black armbands in the school (to protest government policies), because that prohibition was designed to suppress communication, *i.e.,* not related to regulatory interest. [Tinker v. Des Moines Independent Community School District, A.3.b., *supra*]

3)   Significant Cases

a)   Military Bases
Military bases are not public forums; thus, on-base speech and assembly may be regulated, even during open houses where the public is invited to visit. [*See* United States v. Albertini, 472 U.S. 675 (1985)] However, if the military leaves its streets open as thoroughfares, they will be treated as public forums. [Flower v. United States, 407 U.S. 197 (1972)]

b)   Schools
Generally, schools are not public forums. Thus, speech in schools may be reasonably regulated. However, if a public school or university allows members of the public and private organizations to use school property for meetings when school programs or classes are not in session, it cannot deny a religious organization permission to use the property for meetings merely because religious topics will be discussed. Such a restriction would be viewpoint discrimination. [Widmar v. Vincent, 454 U.S. 263 (1981); Lamb's Chapel v. Center Moriches Union Free School District, 1., *supra*]

c)   Government Workplace or Charity
Neither a government workplace (including a court building and its grounds) nor a government controlled charity drive constitutes a public forum.

Examples: 1) The government may conduct an annual fundraising drive which includes some charities but excludes others on some ideologically neutral basis (*e.g.,* all charities that lobby). However, it cannot exclude a charity merely because it disagrees with the organization's political views. [Cornelius v. NAACP Legal Defense and Education Fund, Inc., 473 U.S. 788 (1985)]

2) A state may develop a system for meeting with and hearing the views of a select group of its employees (*e.g.,* union representatives) while denying the ability to voice opinions at such restricted meetings to other government employees. [Minnesota State Board v. Knight, 465 U.S. 271 (1984)]

Compare: In a public forum, the government cannot restrict the ability to participate in public speech on the basis of union membership. Thus, the Court has held that a teacher cannot be constitutionally prohibited from speaking at a meeting of the school board that was open to the public. [City of Madison Joint School District No. 8 v. Wisconsin Employment Relations Commission, 429 U.S. 167 (1976)]

d)   Postal Service Property
Sidewalks on postal service property are not public forums. [United States v. Kokinda, 497 U.S. 720 (1990)]

e)   Signs on Public Property
The Supreme Court has upheld a city ordinance prohibiting posting signs on public property (including sidewalks, crosswalks, street lamp posts, fire hydrants, and telephone poles), even if the sign is temporary in nature and could be removed without damage to the public property. [Members of City Council v. Taxpayers for Vincent, 466 U.S. 789 (1984)]

f)   Airport Terminals
Airport terminals operated by a public authority are *not* public forums. Thus, it is reasonable to ban *solicitation* within airport terminals, since it presents a risk of fraud to hurrying passengers. [International Society of Krishna Consciousness v. Lee, 505 U.S. 672 (1992)] However, it is *not* reasonable to ban *leafletting* within multipurpose terminals having qualities similar to a shopping mall [Lee v. International Society of Krishna Consciousness, 505 U.S. 830 (1992)]; although such leafletting can still be subject to reasonable time, place, and manner regulations (*see* B.1.a., *supra*).

g)   Candidate Debates on Public Television
A public television station debate for congressional candidates from major parties or who have strong popular support is not a "public forum" because such debates are not open to a class of speakers (*e.g.*, all candidates), but rather to selected members of the class. Exclusion of candidates not from a major party and lacking popular support is permissible because these criteria are (i) viewpoint neutral and (ii) reasonable in light of the logistics for an educationally valuable debate. [Arkansas Educational Television Commission v. Forbes, 523 U.S. 666 (1998)]

3.   Private Forums
The government may reasonably regulate access to private forums.

a.   The Home
A home is a private place. The government may adopt reasonable regulations limiting access to homes for First Amendment purposes—pursuant to its interest in protecting the homeowner's privacy. Recall, however, that if a regulation is overbroad, it might still be struck down for violating the First Amendment, even if it is related to a legitimate government interest.

> *Examples:* An ordinance requiring a private homeowner's consent before commercial solicitation is valid [Breard v. City of Alexandria, A.2.a., *supra*]; but an ordinance prohibiting all door to door solicitation is overbroad, since an unwilling homeowner could post a "no solicitors" sign [Martin v. City of Struthers, A.2.a., *supra*].

    b. Mailboxes
A letter/mailbox at a business or residence is *not* a public forum. Thus, the government may prohibit the placing of unstamped items in post boxes to promote efficient mail service. [United States Postal Service v. Council of Greenburgh Civic Association, 453 U.S. 114 (1981)]

    c. Shopping Malls
A shopping mall is a private forum; thus, mall owners may limit speech activities within their malls. [Hudgens v. NLRB, 424 U.S. 507 (1976)] However, a state may require malls to allow certain speech activities without violating the owners' right to not speak. (*See* A.3.a.2), *supra*.)

C. UNPROTECTED SPEECH—REGULATION OR PUNISHMENT BECAUSE OF CONTENT

Restrictions on the content of speech must be narrowly tailored to achieve a compelling government interest. As indicated above, very few restrictions on the content of speech are tolerated. The Court allows them only to prevent grave injury. The following is a list of the only reasons for which the Court has allowed content based restrictions on speech (*i.e.,* the following are categories of unprotected speech):

(i)   It creates a *clear and present danger* of imminent lawless action.

(ii) It constitutes *"fighting words"* as defined by a narrow, precise statute.

(iii) The speech, film, etc., is *obscene*. (This category includes "child pornography.")

(iv) The speech constitutes *defamation*, which may be the subject of a civil "penalty" through a tort action brought by the injured party in conformity with the rules set out *infra*.

(v) The speech violates regulations against *false or deceptive advertising—commercial speech is protected* by the First Amendment and it cannot be proscribed simply to help certain private interests.

(vi) The government can demonstrate a *"compelling interest"* in limitation of the First Amendment activity.

Recall that even if a regulation falls within one of the above categories, it will not necessarily be held valid; it might still be held to be void for vagueness or overbreadth. (*See* A.2., *supra*.)

1. Clear and Present Danger of Imminent Lawlessness
A state cannot forbid advocating the use of force or of law violation unless such advocacy (i) *is directed to producing or inciting imminent lawless action,* and (ii) *is likely to produce or incite such action*. [Brandenberg v. Ohio, 395 U.S. 444 (1969)]

Example: The "clear and present danger" test has been applied to hold that a state may not punish as contempt out-of-court utterances critical of a judge, absent special circumstances showing an extremely high likelihood of serious interference with the administration of justice. [*See* Wood v. Georgia, 370 U.S. 375 (1962)]

a. Allows for Sanctions Against Speech

The test allows for sanctions against speech causing demonstrable danger to important government interests. Disclosure of United States intelligence operations and personnel is "clearly not protected" speech. [Haig v. Agee, 453 U.S. 280 (1981)]

b. Compelling Justification Test

A similar test—one of "compelling justification"—was employed to hold unconstitutional the Georgia legislature's refusal to seat Julian Bond, an elected black representative, where Bond's speeches, critical of United States policy on Vietnam and the draft, led the legislature to doubt his fitness and his ability to take the oath of office in good faith. [Bond v. Floyd, 385 U.S. 116 (1966)]

2. Fighting Words

a. States May Ban Words Likely to Incite Physical Retaliation

States are free to ban the use of "fighting words," *i.e.,* those personally abusive epithets that, when addressed to the ordinary citizen, are inherently likely to incite immediate physical retaliation. [Chaplinsky v. New Hampshire, 315 U.S. 568 (1942)] *Chaplinsky* has, however, been narrowly read. Thus, in *Cohen v. California,* 403 U.S. 15 (1971), the Court held that the state may not punish the defendant for wearing a jacket bearing the words "Fuck the Draft," pointing out that "while the four-letter word displayed by Cohen in relation to the draft is commonly employed in a personally provocative fashion, in this instance, it was clearly not directed to the person of the hearer."

b. Statutes Regulating Fighting Words Tend to Be Overbroad or Vague

While this classification of punishable speech continues to exist *in theory*, the Court rarely upholds punishments for the use of such words. Statutes that attempt to punish fighting words will tend to be overbroad or vague; the statute will define the punishable speech as "opprobrious words," "annoying conduct," or "abusive language." Such statutes will fail, as their imprecise terms could be applied to protected (nonfighting words) speech. Such a statute could not be used to punish a person for saying to a police officer, "White son of a bitch, I'll kill you." [Gooding v. Wilson, 405 U.S. 518 (1972); Lewis v. City of New Orleans, 415 U.S. 130 (1974)]

c. Statutes Cannot Be Content-Based—Limits Hate Crime Legislation

Although the general class of "fighting words" is proscribable under the First Amendment, the Supreme Court will not tolerate in fighting words statutes restrictions that are designed to punish only certain viewpoints (*i.e.,* proscribing fighting words only if they convey a particular message). [R.A.V. v. City of St. Paul, 505 U.S. 377 (1992)— ordinance that applies only to those fighting words that insult or provoke violence on the basis of race, religion, or gender is invalid]

1) **Compare—Punishing Racially Motivated Conduct**
The First Amendment does not protect conduct simply because it happens to be motivated by a person's views or beliefs. Thus, a state can increase a convicted defendant's sentence for aggravated battery based on the fact that the defendant selected the victim of his crime because of the victim's race. [Wisconsin v. Mitchell, 508 U.S. 476 (1993)] However, punishment may not be increased merely because of the defendant's abstract beliefs. [Dawson v. Delaware, 503 U.S. 159 (1992)—unconstitutional to increase defendant's sentence merely because it was proved that he belongs to an organization that advocates racism]

3. **Obscenity**
Obscenity is *not protected* speech. [Roth v. United States, 354 U.S. 476 (1957)] The Court has defined "obscenity" as a description or depiction of sexual conduct that, taken *as a whole*, by the *average person*, applying *contemporary community standards*:

(i) Appeals to the *prurient interest* in sex;

(ii) Portrays sex in a *patently offensive* way; and

(iii) Does not have serious literary, artistic, political, or scientific value—using a national, reasonable person standard, rather than the contemporary community standard. [Miller v. California, 413 U.S. 15 (1973); Pope v. Illinois, 481 U.S. 497 (1987)]

a. **Elements**

1) **Appeal to Prurient Interest**
The dominant theme of the material considered as a *whole* must appeal to the prurient interest in sex of the average person. The Supreme Court has found this to include that which appeals to *shameful or morbid interests* in sex, but not that which incites *lust* (insofar as lust may include a *normal* interest in sex). [Brockett v. Spokane Arcades, Inc., 472 U.S. 491 (1985)] For exam purposes, it is probably sufficient merely to know the standard (since its application is a fact determination).

a) **Average Person**
Both sensitive and insensitive adults may be included in determining contemporary community standards, but children may not be considered part of the relevant audience.

b) **Material Designed for Deviant Group**
Where the allegedly obscene material is designed for and primarily disseminated to a clearly defined deviant sexual group (*e.g.,* sadists), rather than to the public at large, the prurient appeal requirement is satisfied if the *dominant theme* of the material, taken as a whole, *appeals to the prurient interest of that group*. [Mishkin v. New York, 383 U.S. 502 (1966)]

2) **Patently Offensive**

a) **Community Standard**
The material must be patently offensive in affronting contemporary community standards regarding the description or portrayal of sexual matters.

b) National Standard Not Required

A statewide standard is permissible but not mandatory. A juror may draw on knowledge of the community or vicinity from which he comes, and the court may either direct the jury to apply "community standards" without specifying what "community," or to define the standard in more precise geographic terms. [Hamling v. United States, 418 U.S. 87 (1974); Jenkins v. Georgia, 418 U.S. 153 (1974)]

3) Lacking in Serious Social Value

The fact that the material may have some redeeming social value will not necessarily immunize it from a finding of obscenity. It must have serious literary, artistic, political, or scientific value, using a national standard. [Pope v. Illinois, *supra*]

4) Standard May Be Different for Minors

The state can adopt a specific definition of obscenity applying to materials sold to minors, even though the material might not be obscene in terms of an adult audience. [Ginsberg v. New York, 390 U.S. 629 (1968)] However, government may not prohibit the sale or distribution of material to adults merely because it is inappropriate for children.

Example: Because of the present lack of "gateway" technology that would permit speakers on the Internet to block their communications, a federal statute's bar on transmitting "indecent" or "patently offensive" messages to minors effectively amounts to a total ban and thus violates the First Amendment right of adults to receive such materials. [Reno v. American Civil Liberties Union, 521 U.S. 844 (1997)]

a) School Libraries

The Supreme Court has held that a school board decision to remove books from a school library may be reviewed by a court to determine if the rationale for the removal violated First Amendment principles. However, there was no majority opinion that addressed the issue of what standards of review should be used in such a case. [Board of Education v. Pico, 457 U.S. 853 (1982)]

b. Question of Fact and Law

1) Jury Question

The determination of whether material is obscene is a question of fact for the jury. Of course, the judge can grant a directed verdict if the evidence is such that a reasonable, unprejudiced jury could not find that all parts of the test have been met.

2) Independent Review by Appellate Court

Appellate courts will conduct an independent review of constitutional claims, when necessary, to assure that the proscribed materials "depict or describe patently offensive 'hard core' sexual conduct." [Jenkins v. Georgia, *supra*]

3) Evidence of Pandering
In close cases, evidence of "pandering"—commercial exploitation for the sake of prurient appeal—by the defendant may be probative on whether the material is obscene. Such evidence may be found in the defendant's advertising, his instructions to authors and illustrators of the material, or his intended audience. In effect, this simply accepts the purveyor's own estimation of the material as relevant. [Ginzburg v. United States, 383 U.S. 463 (1966)]

4) Evidence—Similar Published Materials Not Automatically Admissible
The state need not produce expert testimony. Evidence that similar materials are available on community newsstands, or that the publication has acquired a second-class mailing privilege, does not necessarily show that the material is not obscene and hence is not automatically admissible. Nor is there any automatic right to have other materials held not to be obscene admitted into evidence. [Hamling v. United States, *supra*]

c. Statutes Must Not Be Vague

1) Sweeping Language
Attempts to define obscenity broadly have encountered difficulties before the Court.

Examples: 1) A statute banning publication of news or stories of "bloodshed or lust so massed as to become vehicle for inciting crime" is unconstitutionally vague and uncertain. [Winters v. New York, 333 U.S. 507 (1948)]

2) The Court held invalid a statute prohibiting the sale of any book "tending to the corruption of the morals of youth." [Butler v. Michigan, 352 U.S. 380 (1957)]

2) Construction May Save Vague Statute
A state statute will be upheld if it meets the tests as construed by the courts of the state. Thus, a seemingly vague obscenity statute may be saved by a state supreme court opinion that limits it to a proscription of depictions of specific types of sexual conduct. [Ward v. Illinois, 430 U.S. 983 (1977)]

d. Zoning
A zoning ordinance prohibiting the location of theaters that show adult, sexually oriented movies from areas close to residential zones and restricting such theaters to a limited area of the city is permissible if it is designed to promote legitimate local (zoning) interests and it does not prohibit all such entertainment in the community. [City of Renton v. Playtime Theaters, Inc., 475 U.S. 41 (1986)]

e. Liquor Regulation
The Twenty-First Amendment grants states more than the usual regulatory authority with respect to intoxicating beverages. Therefore, regulations prohibiting explicit live sexual entertainment and films in establishments licensed to sell liquor by the drink, even though proscribing some forms of visual presentation that would not be obscene under *Miller,* do not violate the First Amendment as long as they are not "irrational."

f.   Display

The Court has suggested that the state **may regulate** the display of certain material, to prevent it from being so obtrusive that an unwilling viewer cannot avoid exposure to it. [Redup v. New York, 386 U.S. 767 (1967)]

g.   Separate Test for Child Pornography

The government may prohibit the sale or distribution of **visual** depictions of sexual conduct involving children below a specified age even though the material could not be found obscene (under the tests described above) if it did not involve children. [New York v. Ferber, 456 U.S. 942 (1982)]

h.   Private Possession of Obscenity

Private possession of obscenity at home cannot be made a crime because of the constitutional right of personal privacy. [Stanley v. Georgia, 394 U.S. 557 (1969)] However, the protection does not extend beyond the home. Thus, importation, distribution, and exhibition of obscene materials can be prohibited.

1)   Exception—Child Pornography

The state may make private possession of child pornography a crime, even private possession for personal viewing in a residence. [Osborne v. Ohio, 495 U.S. 103 (1990)]

4.   Defamatory Speech

When a person is sued for making a defamatory statement, the First Amendment places restrictions on the ability of the government (through its tort law and courts) to grant a recovery where the person suing is a **public official or public figure**, or where the defamatory statement involves an issue of **public concern**. In these cases the plaintiff must prove not only the elements of defamation required by state law, but also that the statement was **false** and that the person making the statement was at **fault** to some degree in not ascertaining the truth of the statement.

a.   Falsity

At common law, a defamatory statement was presumed to be false; to avoid liability for an otherwise defamatory statement on the ground that it was true, the defendant had to assert truth as an affirmative defense. The Supreme Court has rejected this presumption in all public figure or public concern cases. In these cases, the plaintiff must prove by clear and convincing evidence that the statement was false. [Philadelphia Newspapers, Inc. v. Hepps, 475 U.S. 767 (1986)]

1)   Requirement of Factual Statement

To be defamatory, the false statement must be viewed by a reasonable person as a statement of fact, rather than as a statement of opinion or a parody. Furthermore, a public figure cannot circumvent the First Amendment restrictions by using a different tort theory to collect damages for a published statement about him that is not a false statement of fact.

Example: Even though a publisher may have intended to cause psychological distress to a public figure by publishing statements about him that were derogatory, the public figure cannot receive a judgment for "emotional distress" damages if a reasonable person who read or viewed the publication would not understand it to contain a statement of fact about that public figure. [Hustler Magazine Inc. v. Falwell, 485 U.S. 46 (1988)]

Note: The fact that a publisher labels a statement as "opinion" will not provide First Amendment protection if the statement would reasonably be understood to be a statement of fact. [Milkovich v. Lorain Journal Co., 497 U.S. 1 (1990)]

b. Fault

At common law, a defendant who had no reason to know that the statement he was making was false and defamatory could still be liable for defamation. Now, however, a plaintiff in a public figure or public concern case must prove fault on the part of the defendant. The degree of fault required is higher when the plaintiff is a public official or public figure than when the plaintiff is a private person suing on a matter of public concern.

1) Public Official or Public Figure—Malice Required

A public official may not recover for defamatory words relating to his official conduct or a matter of public concern without clear and convincing evidence that the statement was made with "malice" (defined below). [New York Times v. Sullivan, 376 U.S. 254 (1964)] This rule has since been extended to public figure plaintiffs. (Note that while the Supreme Court has not specifically held that all statements regarding public officials or public figures necessarily involve matters of public concern, a case to the contrary should be rare.)

a) Malice Defined

Malice was defined by the Supreme Court in *New York Times v. Sullivan* as:

(i) *Knowledge* that the statement was false, *or*

(ii) *Reckless disregard* as to its truth or falsity.

The plaintiff must show that the defendant was subjectively aware that the statement he published was false or that he subjectively *entertained serious doubts* as to its truthfulness.

(1) Malice in False Quotation Cases

Proof that a defamation plaintiff was inaccurately quoted does not, by itself, prove actual malice, even if the quotation was intentionally altered by the defendant. If the published "quotation" is substantially accurate, the plaintiff may not collect damages. To show malice, the public figure plaintiff must prove that the defendant's alteration of the quotation materially changed the meaning of the actual statements made by the plaintiff. [Masson v. New Yorker Magazine, Inc., 501 U.S. 496 (1991)]

(2) Permitted Inquiries by Plaintiff

In attempting to prove knowing or reckless disregard of the truth, the plaintiff may inquire into the state of mind of those who edit, produce, or publish (*i.e.,* conversations with editorial colleagues). [Herbert v. Lando, 441 U.S. 153 (1979)]

(3) Petition Clause Does Not Protect Defamatory Statement Made with Malice

The First Amendment guarantees individuals the right to "petition government for a redress of grievances." However, this right to petition the government does not grant absolute immunity to persons who make defamatory statements about public officials or public figures in their communications with government officials. The defamed individual may prevail by meeting the *New York Times* requirements. [McDonald v. Smith, 472 U.S. 479 (1985)]

b) Two Ways to Become a Public Figure

(1) General Fame or Notoriety

A person may be a public figure for all purposes and all contexts if he achieves "*general fame or notoriety* in the community and pervasive involvement in the affairs of society," although "a citizen's participation in community and professional affairs" does not render him a public figure for all purposes.

(2) Involvement in Particular Controversy

A person may "*voluntarily inject* himself or be drawn into a particular controversy to influence the resolution of the issues involved" and thereby become a public figure for a limited range of issues. [Gertz v. Robert Welch, Inc., 418 U.S. 323 (1974)]

Note that *Gertz* appears to allow for the possibility of a person's being an involuntary public figure for a limited range of issues, although such a case would be "exceedingly rare."

c) Examples of Persons Not Deemed Public Figures

(1) Spouse of Wealthy Person

Marriage to an extremely wealthy person and divorcing such a person does not amount to voluntarily entering the public arena, even though press conferences are held by the plaintiff, because going to court is the only way she could dissolve her marriage. [Time, Inc. v. Firestone, 424 U.S. 448 (1976)]

(2) Person Engaging in Criminal Conduct

A person who engages in *criminal conduct* does not automatically become a public figure even when the defamatory statements relate solely to his conviction. [Wolston v. Reader's Digest Association, 443 U.S. 157 (1979)]

(3)   Scientist in Federally Funded Program
A behavioral scientist engaged in *federally funded* animal research studies is not a public figure because he applies for federal grants and *publishes* in professional journals. [Hutchinson v. Proxmire, 443 U.S. 111 (1979)]

2)   Private Individual Suing on Matter of Public Concern—At Least Negligence Required
When a private individual is defamed, there is less of a need to protect freedom of speech and press and more of a need to protect private individuals from injury from defamation because they do not have as effective opportunities for rebuttal as public figures. Accordingly, defamation actions brought by private individuals are subject to constitutional limitations only when the defamatory statement involves a matter of public concern. And even in those cases, the limitations are not as great as those established for public officials and public figures. [Gertz v. Robert Welch, Inc., *supra*] When the defamatory statement involves a matter of public concern, *Gertz* imposes two restrictions on private plaintiffs: (i) it prohibits liability without fault, and (ii) it restricts the recovery of presumed or punitive damages.

a)   No Liability Without Proof of at Least Negligence
The plaintiff must show that the defendant was negligent in failing to ascertain the truth of the statement. If plaintiff establishes negligence but not malice, which is a higher degree of fault, he also has to provide competent evidence of "actual" damages. (This changes the common law rule that damages would be presumed by law for injury to reputation and did not need to be proved by plaintiff.) Actual damages may be awarded not only for economic losses but also for injury to plaintiff's reputation in the community and for personal humiliation and distress.

b)   Presumed or Punitive Damages Allowed Only If Malice Established
If plaintiff establishes that the defendant made the statement with malice, the actual damage requirement is extinguished. Plaintiff can recover whatever damages are permitted under state law (usually presumed damages and even punitive damages in appropriate cases). In other words, there is no constitutional protection for statements made with malice, even though a matter of public concern is involved.

c)   What Is a Matter of Public Concern?
The courts decide on a case-by-case basis whether the defamatory statement involves a matter of public concern, looking at the content, form, and context of the publication. [Dun & Bradstreet, Inc. v. Greenmoss Builders, Inc., 472 U.S. 749 (1985)]
Example: In *Dun & Bradstreet,* the Court determined that a credit agency's erroneous report of plaintiff's bankruptcy, distributed to five subscribers, was speech solely in the private interest of the speaker and its specific business audience. Therefore, because a matter of public concern was not involved, the First Amendment restrictions did not apply and

the state court award of presumed and punitive damages was upheld.

3) Private Individual Suing on Matter Not of Public Concern

The Supreme Court has not imposed constitutional restrictions on defamation actions brought by private individuals that do not involve a matter of public concern. Hence, presumed and punitive damages can be recovered even if malice is not established.

c. Procedural Issues

1) Federal Summary Judgment Standard

When ruling on a motion for summary judgment in a federal court defamation action in a case involving an issue of public concern, a judge must apply the clear and convincing evidence standard (*i.e.,* the judge should grant the motion **unless** it appears that the plaintiff could meet his burdens of proving falsity and actual malice at trial by clear and convincing evidence). However, the Supreme Court has not clearly held that state courts must follow this practice under similar circumstances.

2) Judicial Review

An appellate court must review a defamation case by conducting an independent review of the record to determine if the finder of fact (the jury) could have found that the malice standard was met in the case. [Harte-Hanks Communications, Inc. v. Connaughton, 491 U.S. 657 (1989)]

d. Recovery for Depiction in a False Light

To recover damages for depiction in a false light (as opposed to a defamatory injury to reputation) arising out of comments directed at activities of public interest, an individual must establish *falsity* and *actual malice* whether or not he qualifies as a public figure under *Time, Inc. v. Hill,* 385 U.S. 374 (1967). However, it is *assumed* that the Court would now modify this to mirror the *Gertz* negligence rule for private plaintiffs.

e. True Privacy Actions

1) Publishing True Fact of Public Record

A newspaper or broadcaster cannot be sued for publishing a true fact once it is lawfully obtained from the public record or otherwise released to the public. [Cox Broadcasting Corp. v. Cohn, 420 U.S. 469 (1975)—rape victim's name already in court records open to the public; The Florida Star v. B.J.F., 491 U.S. 524 (1989)—rape victim's name inadvertently given to the press by police]

2) Publishing Name of Juvenile Charged with Crime

A state cannot require judicial approval before the media can print the name of a juvenile charged with murder where the name of the juvenile was obtained through legal means (reporter heard name of defendant over police frequency radio and questioned witnesses to the crime). [Smith v. Daily Mail Publishing Co., 442 U.S. 97 (1979)]

    3)   Publishing Information on Judge's Competency
A state cannot make it a crime to publish information, released in a confidential proceeding, concerning the competency of members of the state judiciary. [Landmark Communications v. Virginia, 435 U.S. 829 (1978)]

f.   Commercial Privacy—Disclosing a Private Performance Can Violate "Right to Publicity"
In *Zacchini v. Scripps-Howard Broadcasting Co.,* 433 U.S. 562 (1977), the Court held that state law could award damages to an entertainer who attempted to restrict the showing of his act to those who paid admission, when a television station broadcast his entire act. Here the "human cannonball" had his entire 15-second act broadcast over his objection.

g.   Copyright Infringement
The First Amendment does not require an exception to copyright protection for material written by a former President or other public figures. Magazines have no right to publish such copyrighted material beyond the statutory fair use exception. [Harper & Row Publishers v. Nation Enterprises, 471 U.S. 539 (1985)]

5.   Some Commercial Speech
False advertising is not protected by the First Amendment, although commercial speech in general does have some First Amendment protection. In determining whether a regulation on commercial speech is valid, the Supreme Court asserts that it uses a four-step process. However, it may be easiest to think about this as an initial question followed by a three-step inquiry. *First,* determine whether the commercial speech concerns a lawful activity and is not misleading or fraudulent. Speech proposing an unlawful transaction (*e.g.,* "I will sell you this pound of heroin for X dollars") and fraudulent speech may be outlawed. If the speech regulated concerns a *lawful activity* and is *not misleading or fraudulent*, the regulation will be valid only if it:

(i)   Serves a *"substantial"* government interest;

(ii)   *"Directly advances"* the asserted interest; and

(iii) Is *narrowly tailored* to serve the substantial interest. This part of the test does *not* require that the "least restrictive means" be used. Rather, there must be a *reasonable fit* between the legislation's end and the means chosen. [Board of Trustees of State University of New York v. Fox, 492 U.S. 469 (1989)]

[Central Hudson Gas v. Public Service Commission, 447 U.S. 557 (1980)]
Examples: 1) Under the above rules, the Court has stricken statutes prohibiting truthful advertisements for: (i) legal abortions; (ii) contraceptives; and (iii) drug prices.

               2) A city could not prohibit the use of newsracks on sidewalks for the distribution for commercial publications (such as free publications advertising products or real estate for sale) if the city allowed sidewalk newsracks for the distribution of newspapers. This city law failed the commercial speech test because there was no "reasonable fit" between the category of commercial

speech and any substantial interest. Commercial newsracks did not cause any physical or aesthetic harm different from that caused by newspaper newsracks. [Cincinnati v. Discovery Network, Inc., 507 U.S. 410 (1993)] Similarly, a law prohibiting beer bottle labels from displaying alcohol content was held invalid because, although the government has a substantial interest in preventing "strength wars," the government did not show that the label prohibition advanced this interest in a material way. [Rubin v. Coors Brewing Co., 514 U.S. 476 (1995)]

3) A law prohibiting advertising of smokeless tobacco and cigars within 1,000 feet of a school or playground, which amounted to a complete ban in many areas, was held invalid. Even though such a ban directly advances the substantial government interest in preventing underage use of those products, its geographic reach demonstrates a *"lack of tailoring,"* thus unduly affecting use of tobacco products by adults (which is a legal activity). [Lorillard Tobacco Co. v. Reilly, 121 S. Ct. 2404 (2001)]

a. Liquor Price Regulation

The Court has stricken a ban prohibiting *all* advertisement of liquor prices. [44 Liquormart, Inc. v. Rhode Island, 517 U.S. 484 (1996)] In *44 Liquormart,* five Justices in separate opinions found that a complete ban on truthful, nonmisleading commercial speech in order to protect the public (*i.e.,* people will drink less if liquor prices are not advertised because the advertising ban makes it difficult to comparison shop, which keeps the price of liquor artificially high) will rarely be upheld. Note also that the *Twenty-First Amendment*—giving states power to regulate liquor commerce within their borders—*does not give states power to override First Amendment protections.*

Note: After *44 Liquormart,* it seems unlikely that the government can *completely ban* truthful advertising of any lawful product or service.

b. Commercial Sign Regulation

It is unclear whether billboards may be totally banned from a city. However, they can be regulated for purposes of traffic safety and aesthetics.

1) Blockbusting

A town could not prohibit the use of outdoor "for sale" signs by owners of private homes as a way of reducing the effect of "blockbusting" real estate agents. [Linmark Associates v. Willingboro Township, 431 U.S. 85 (1977)]

c. Attorney Advertising

The Court applies the general three-part *Central Hudson Gas* commercial speech standard to attorney advertisement. Thus, the Court has struck down absolute bans against attorney advertising. [Bates v. State Bar of Arizona, 433 U.S. 350 (1977)—ban against advertising nature and price of attorneys' professional services; Peel v. Illinois Attorney Registration & Disciplinary Commission, 496 U.S. 91 (1990)—ban against advertising status as "certified" or a "specialist" by or of a legitimate attorney organization] However, the Court has upheld prohibitions against in-person solicitation for pecuniary gain [Ohralik v. Ohio State Bar, 436 U.S. 447 (1978)—state interest in protecting lay persons from fraud and overreaching is substantial, and prohibition here is narrowly tailored and directly advances that interest] and sending mail solicitations to accident victims and their relatives within 30 days following an accident [Florida Bar v. Went For It, Inc., 515 U.S. 618 (1995)—state interest in protecting lawyers' reputation is substantial, and ban here is narrowly tailored and directly advances that interest].

d. **Certified Public Accountants' Services**
A state may not ban uninvited in-person or telephone soliciting, and advertising for business, by certified public accountants ("CPAs"). The Court held that the ban on CPA solicitation was not reasonably tailored to protecting consumers because the state failed to demonstrate that this type of solicitation by CPAs presented potential danger to consumers (as would in-person solicitation by attorneys). [Edenfield v. Fane, 507 U.S. 761 (1993)] Similarly, a CPA cannot be prevented from truthfully indicating that she is a "certified financial planner" and an attorney, because these terms are neither false nor misleading. [Ibanez v. Florida Department of Business and Professional Regulation, 512 U.S. 136 (1994)]

D. PRIOR RESTRAINTS
A prior restraint is any governmental action that would prevent a communication from reaching the public (*e.g.,* a licensing system, a prohibition against using mails, an injunction, etc.). Prior restraints are not favored in our political system; the Court would rather allow speech and then punish it if it was unprotected. However, the Court will uphold prior restraints if some special harm would otherwise result. As with other restrictions on speech, a prior restraint must be narrowly tailored to achieve some compelling or, at least, significant governmental interest. The Court has also required that certain procedural safeguards be included in any system of prior restraint.

1. **Sufficiency of Governmental Interest**
The Supreme Court has not adopted a brightline standard for determining when a prior restraint is justified, but it has said that the government's burden is heavy. For exam purposes, you should ask whether there is some ***special societal harm*** that justifies the restraint.

a. **National Security**
National security is certainly a sufficient harm justifying prior restraint. Thus, a newspaper could be prohibited from publishing troop movements in times of war. [Near v. Minnesota, 283 U.S. 697 (1931)] However, the harm must be more than theoretical. Thus, the Court refused to enjoin publication of *The Pentagon Papers* on the basis that publication might possibly have a detrimental effect on the Vietnam War. [New York Times v. United States, 403 U.S. 713 (1971)]

b. **Preserving Fair Trial**
Preserving a fair trial for an accused might be a sufficient basis for prior restraint. However, the restraint will be upheld only if it is the only sure way of preserving a fair trial. [Nebraska Press Association v. Stewart, 427 U.S. 539 (1976)]

1) **Compare—Grand Jury Prior Restraint**
A state law prohibiting a grand jury witness from ever disclosing the testimony he gave to the grand jury (even after the grand jury term had ended) violates the First

Amendment. Such a law is not narrowly tailored to a compelling interest, since any such interest that the government may have in protecting the grand jury process can be protected by a nonpermanent prohibition. [Butterworth v. Smith, 494 U.S. 624 (1990)]

c. **Contractual Agreements**

The Supreme Court has held that prior restraint is permissible where the parties have contractually agreed to the restraint. [Snepp v. United States, 444 U.S. 507 (1980)—CIA agent contractually agreed to give agency a prepublication review of any item related to his employment]

d. **Military Circumstances**

The Supreme Court has held that the interests of maintaining discipline among troops and efficiency of operations on a military base justify a requirement that persons on a military base obtain the commander's permission before circulating petitions.

e. **Obscenity**

The Court has held in a number of cases that the government's interest in preventing the dissemination of obscenity is sufficient to justify a system of prior restraint.

2. **Procedural Safeguards**

The Supreme Court has held that no system of prior restraint will be upheld unless it provides the persons whose speech is being restrained certain procedural safeguards. The safeguards arose in the context of movie censorship for obscenity, but the court has held that similar safeguards must be provided in all prior restraint cases:

(i) The standards must be "*narrowly drawn, reasonable, and definite,*" so as to include only prohibitable speech (*e.g.,* improper to permanently enjoin witness from disclosing grand jury testimony; government interest can be protected by nonpermanent injunction [Butterworth v. Smith, *supra*]);

(ii) If the restraining body wishes to restrain dissemination of an item, it must *promptly seek an injunction* (*e.g.,* improper to allow 50 days before seeking injunction [Tietel Film Corp. v. Cusack, 390 U.S. 676 (1968)]); and

(iii) There must be a *prompt and final judicial determination* of the validity of the restraint (*e.g.,* improper to leave an injunction in place pending an appeal that could take up to a year; government must either lift the injunction or expedite the appeal [National Socialist Party v. Village of Skokie, 432 U.S. 43 (1977)]).

A number of other cases, especially in the area of movie censorship, also provide that the *government bears the burden* of proving that the speech involved is unprotected. [Freedman v. Maryland, 380 U.S. 51 (1965)]

a. **Example—Denial of Use of Mails**

A federal statute authorized the Postmaster General (i) to deny use of the mails and postal money orders for materials found to be obscene in an administrative hearing, and (ii) to obtain a court order, upon a showing of probable cause, to detain incoming mail pending completion of the administrative hearing. The Court found that this denial of use of the mails violated the First Amendment: The procedures did not require the government to initiate proceedings to obtain a final judicial determination of obscenity, failed to assure prompt judicial review, and failed to limit any restraint in advance of a final judicial determination to preserving the status quo for "the shortest fixed period compatible with sound judicial resolution." [Blount v. Rizzi, 400 U.S. 410 (1971)]

b. **"Informal" Blacklists**
"Informal" sanctions by a state agency that have the *effect* of a prior restraint without adequate procedural and judicial safeguards are unconstitutional.

Example: In *Bantam Books, Inc. v. Sullivan*, 372 U.S. 58 (1963), a state juvenile delinquency commission made "informal" recommendations to book distributors as to which publications were objectionable for sale to youths; and the recommendations were followed by threats of court action, visits from police, etc. Distributors were given no notice or hearing before their publications were listed as objectionable. The Court held that compliance with the commission's directives by distributors was not voluntary and represented unconstitutional censorship.

c. **Adversary Hearing Usually Required**
An adversary hearing, upon notice to all interested parties, is usually essential to any injunction procedure—especially when *political* speech is involved and timing is important. [Carroll v. Princess Anne Co., 393 U.S. 175 (1969)—invalidating an ex parte court order restraining members of a political party from holding rallies that would tend to "disturb or endanger" local residents]

3. **Obscenity Cases**
Much of the case law in the area of prior restraint has arisen in connection with banning obscenity.

a. **Seizure of Books and Films**
As with any seizure by the government, seizures of books and films may be made only upon probable cause that they contain obscenity or are otherwise unlawful. (*See* Criminal Procedure outline.)

1) **Single Seizures**
Seizures of a single book or film (to preserve it as evidence) may be made only with a warrant issued by a neutral and detached magistrate. And even here, a prompt post-seizure determination of obscenity must be available. If other copies of a seized film are not available to the exhibitor, he must be allowed to make a copy so that he may continue showing the film until a final determination has been made. [Heller v. New York, 413 U.S. 483 (1973)] Of course, if the materials are available for sale to the general public, an officer may enter into the establishment and purchase the book or film to use it as evidence in a later prosecution without obtaining a warrant. [Maryland v. Macon, 472 U.S. 463 (1985)]

2) **Large Scale Seizures**
"Large scale" seizures of allegedly obscene books and films—"to destroy them or block their distribution or exhibition"—must be *preceded* by a *full adversary hearing* and a judicial determination of obscenity. [Fort Wayne Books, Inc. v. Indiana, 489 U.S. 46 (1989)]

3) **Forfeiture of Business**

The First Amendment does not prohibit forfeiture of a defendant's adult entertainment business after the defendant has been found guilty of violating the Racketeer Influenced and Corrupt Organizations Act and criminal obscenity laws, even though the business assets included nonobscene books and magazines, where the entire business was found to be part of the defendant's racketeering activity. [Alexander v. United States, 509 U.S. 544 (1993)]

b. **Injunction**

After seizing material, the government may enjoin its further publication only after it is determined to be obscene in a *full judicial hearing*. [Kingsley Books, Inc. v. Brown, 354 U.S. 346 (1957)]

c. **Movie Censorship**

The Court has noted that movies are different from other forms of expression, and that time delays incident to censorship are less burdensome for movies than for other forms of expression. Thus, the Court allows governments to establish censorship boards to screen movies *before* they are released in the community, as long as the procedural safeguards mentioned above are followed. The censor bears the burden of proving that the movie is unprotected speech.

E. FREEDOM OF THE PRESS

As a general rule, the press has no greater freedom to speak than does the public. However, a number of issues have arisen in the freedom of press context.

1. **Publication of Truthful Information**

Generally, the press has a right to publish information about a matter of public concern, and this right can be restricted only by a sanction that is narrowly tailored to further a state interest of the highest order. The right applies even if the information has been unlawfully obtained in the first instance, as long as (i) the speech relates to a matter of public concern, (ii) the publisher did not obtain it unlawfully nor know who did, and (iii) the original speaker's privacy expectations are low. [Bartnicki v. Vopper, 121 S. Ct. 1753 (2001)]

Example: During heated collective bargaining negotiations between a teachers' union and a school board, an unknown person intercepted a cell phone call between a union negotiator and the union's president. The tape was forwarded to a radio commentator, who played it on the radio. The commentator was sued for damages under civil liability provisions of state and federal wiretap laws that prohibited intentional disclosure of the contents of an electronically transmitted conversation when one has reason to know that the conversation was intercepted unlawfully. The Supreme Court held that the statute violated the First Amendment as applied under these circumstances. [Bartnicki v. Vopper, *supra*]

2. **Access to Trials**

The First Amendment guarantees the public and press a right to attend criminal trials. But the right may be outweighed by an overriding interest articulated in findings by the trial judge. [Richmond Newspapers v. Virginia, 448 U.S. 555 (1980)—no majority opinion] The right probably applies to civil trials, although the Supreme Court has not conclusively resolved that issue.

a. **Access to Voir Dire Examination**

The First Amendment guarantee of public and press access to criminal trials also includes access to proceedings involving the voir dire examination of potential jurors. In *Press-Enterprise Co. v. Superior Court,* 464 U.S. 501 (1984), the Court found that a trial court could not constitutionally close voir dire examination of potential jurors without consideration of alternatives to closure even though, in some circumstances, there may be a compelling interest in restricting access to such proceedings to protect the privacy of potential jurors or the fairness of the trial.

b. **Access to Other Pretrial Proceedings**

Pretrial proceedings are presumptively subject to a First Amendment right of access for the press and public. Thus, a law requiring that all preliminary hearings be closed to the press and public violates the First Amendment. [El Vocero de Puerto Rico (Caribbean International News Corp.) v. Puerto Rico, 508 U.S. 147 (1993)—per curiam] If the prosecution and defense counsel seek to have a judge close pretrial proceedings, the judge would have to make specific findings on the record demonstrating (i) that closure was essential to preserve "higher" or "overriding" values, and (ii) that the closure order was narrowly tailored to serve the higher or overriding value. [Press-Enterprise Co. v. Superior Court, 478 U.S. 1 (1986)]

If the prosecution seeks to have a pretrial hearing or trial closed to the public and the defendant objects to the closure, there will be a Sixth Amendment violation if the judge excludes the public and the press from the hearing or trial without a clear finding that a closure order was necessary to protect an overriding interest.

c. **Compelling Interest in Protecting Children**

The government has a compelling interest in protecting children who are victims of sex offenses. Portions of trials wherein such children testify may be closed to the public and press, but only if the trial court makes a finding that such closure is necessary to protect the child in the individual case. A state statute, however, violates the First Amendment if it requires closure of the trial during testimony of a child victim of a sex offense without a finding of necessity by the trial judge. [Globe Newspaper Co. v. Superior Court, 457 U.S. 596 (1982)]

d. **Protective Order in Publishing Information Gained in Pretrial Discovery**

The Supreme Court has upheld a state trial court "protective order" prohibiting a newspaper defendant in a defamation suit from publishing, disseminating, or using information gained through pretrial discovery from the plaintiff in any way except where necessary for preparation for trial. [*See* Seattle Times Co. v. Rhinehart, 467 U.S. 20 (1984)]

3. **Requiring Members of the Press to Testify Before Grand Juries**

In *Branzburg v. Hayes,* 408 U.S. 665 (1972), the Court held that requiring a journalist to appear and testify before state or federal grand juries *does not abridge freedom of speech or press*, despite the claim that such a requirement would so deter the flow of news from confidential sources as to place an unconstitutionally heavy burden on the First Amendment interest in the free flow of information to the public. The Court's opinion refused to create—and even rejected—a conditional privilege not to reveal confidential sources to a grand jury conducting a good faith inquiry. This position was affirmed in *New York Times v. Jascalevich,* 439 U.S. 1331 (1978).

4. Interviewing Prisoners

Although the First Amendment protects prisoners, and especially those corresponding with them by mail, from a sweeping program of censorship [Procunier v. Martinez, 416 U.S. 396 (1974)], it does not permit journalists to insist upon either interviewing specified prisoners of their choice [Pell v. Procunier, 417 U.S. 817 (1974)] or inspecting prison grounds [Houchins v. KQED, Inc., 438 U.S. 1 (1978)].

5. Business Regulations or Taxes

Press and broadcasting companies can be subject to general business regulations (*e.g.,* antitrust laws) or taxes (*e.g.,* federal or state income taxes). Thus, a tax or regulation applicable to both press and non-press businesses will be upheld, even if it has a special impact on a portion of the press or broadcast media, as long as it is not an attempt to interfere with First Amendment activities. However, no tax or regulation impacting on the press or subpart of the press may be based on the content of the publication absent a compelling justification.

Examples: 1) State tax on publisher's use of more than $100,000 of paper and ink products annually violates the First Amendment. [Minneapolis Star & Tribune v. Minnesota Commissioner of Revenue, 460 U.S. 575 (1983)]

2) State sales tax or "receipts tax" on the sale of general interest magazines that exempts newspapers and religious, professional, trade, and sports journals from the tax violates the First Amendment. [Arkansas Writers' Project, Inc. v. Ragland, 481 U.S. 221 (1987)]

3) A state sales tax that exempted the sales of newspapers and magazines from the tax but did not give a similar exemption to the sale of broadcast services (cable or subscription television) did not violate the First Amendment. The tax was not based on the content of broadcasts and did not target a small category of publishers. The tax was applicable to all cable or satellite television sales. (There is no comparable sale of "free T.V." such as network broadcasts.) [Leathers v. Medlock, 499 U.S. 439 (1991)]

6. Monetary Damages for Failure to Keep Identity Confidential

When a reporter or publisher promises a "source person" to keep his identity confidential and then publishes the source person's name, state contract law or promissory estoppel law may allow the source person to recover from the reporter or publisher any damages caused by the publication of his identity. [Cohen v. Cowles Media Co., 501 U.S. 663 (1991)]

7. Broadcasting Regulations

Radio and television broadcasting may be more closely regulated than the press. *Rationale:* Due to the limited number of frequencies available, broadcasters have a special privilege—and, consequently, a special responsibility to give suitable time to matters of public interest and to present a suitable range of programs. The paramount right is the ***right of viewers and listeners*** to receive information of public concern, rather than the right of broadcasters to broadcast what they please.

a. Fairness Doctrine

Accordingly, the Court has upheld, under a regulatory "fairness doctrine" (which is no longer enforced), FCC orders requiring a radio station to offer free broadcasting time (i) to opponents of political candidates or views endorsed by the station, and (ii) to any person who has been personally attacked in the course of a broadcast, for a reply to the attack. [Red Lion Broadcasting Co. v. FCC, 395 U.S. 367 (1969)]

1)   Compare—Grant of Equal Newspaper Space
A statute granting political candidates a right to equal space to reply to criticism by the newspaper *violates* First Amendment freedom of the press. Decisions respecting size and content of newspaper are forbidden to government. [Miami Herald Publishing Co. v. Tornillo, 418 U.S. 241 (1974)]

b.   Newspaper Ownership of Radio or TV Station
Similarly, to promote the diversity of information received by the public, the FCC may forbid ownership of a radio or television station by a daily newspaper located in the same community. [FCC v. National Citizens Committee, 436 U.S. 765 (1978)]

c.   Prohibiting Indecent Speech
Because of a broadcast's ability to invade the privacy of the home, the First Amendment does not forbid imposing civil sanctions on a broadcaster for airing a full monologue (in contrast to isolated use of a few such words) of "patently offensive sexual and excretory speech," even though it is not "obscene"—at least at those times when children are likely to be listening. [FCC v. Pacifica Foundation, 438 U.S. 726 (1978)]

d.   Political Advertisements
The First Amendment does *not* require broadcasters to accept political advertisements. Congress and the FCC, in seeking to assure balanced coverage of public issues, could appropriately conclude that licensed broadcasters subject to the "fairness doctrine" should generally determine what should be broadcast, rather than having affluent persons monopolize air time. [CBS, Inc. v. Democratic National Committee, 412 U.S. 94 (1973)] However, *under a statutory right of access*, the FCC may require licensed broadcasters to sell reasonable amounts of time to legally qualified candidates for federal office. [CBS, Inc. v. FCC, 453 U.S. 367 (1981)]

e.   Elimination of Editorial Speech from Stations Receiving Public Grants
Congress violated the First Amendment when it forbade any noncommercial educational station receiving a grant from the Corporation for Public Broadcasting from engaging in "editorializing." [FCC v. League of Women Voters, 468 U.S. 364 (1984)] This was the *suppression of speech* because of its content; the elimination of editorial speech from stations receiving public grants of this type was not narrowly tailored to promote an overriding government purpose regarding the regulation of broadcasting in general or noncommercial broadcasters in particular. Congress could deny persons receiving the federal funds the right to use those funds for editorial activities, but it could not condition the receipt of those funds upon a promise not to engage in any such speech.

8.   Cable Television Regulation
While generally regulations of newspapers are subject to strict scrutiny, and regulations of the broadcast media are subject to less critical review, regulations of cable television transmissions are subject to review by a standard somewhere between these two. *Rationale:* The physical connection to a viewer's television set makes the cable subscriber a more captive audience than a newspaper reader and distinguishes cable from newspapers, which cannot

prevent access to competing newspapers. On the other hand, unlike broadcast media, which is limited to a small number of frequencies (*see* 6., *supra*), there is no practical limitation on the number of cable channels; thus, the government's interest in protecting viewers' rights is weaker with regard to cable. [Turner Broadcasting System v. FCC, A.1.a.2), *supra*]

Example: A law requiring cable operators to carry local stations is subject to "intermediate scrutiny" since it is content-neutral (*see* A.1.a.2), *supra*). Since a "must carry" provision directly serves the important interest of preserving economic viability of local broadcasters and promotes the dissemination of information to noncable viewers, it is constitutional. [Turner Broadcasting System v. FCC, *supra*]

a. Compare—Content-Based Cable Broadcast Regulations

A content-based cable broadcast regulation will be upheld only if it passes muster under the strict scrutiny test. [United States v. Playboy Entertainment Group, Inc., 529 U.S. 803 (2000)—law requiring cable operators to limit "sexually oriented" programs to after 10 p.m. is invalid because of the less restrictive alternative of enabling each household to block undesired channels]

9. Internet Regulation

The strict standard of First Amendment scrutiny, rather than the more relaxed standard applicable to broadcast regulation, applies to regulation of the Internet. *Rationale*: In contrast to broadcasting, there is no scarcity of frequencies (*see* 7., *supra*) on the Internet and little likelihood that the Internet will unexpectedly invade the privacy of the home (*see* 7.c., *supra*). [Reno v. American Civil Liberties Union, C.3.a.4), *supra*]

XXI. FREEDOM OF ASSOCIATION AND BELIEF

A. NATURE OF THE RIGHT

Although the First Amendment does not mention a right of freedom of association, the right to join together with other persons for expressive or political activity is protected by the First Amendment. However, the right to associate for expressive purposes is *not absolute*. Infringements on the right may be justified by *compelling state interests*, unrelated to the suppression of ideas, that cannot be achieved through means significantly less restrictive of associational freedoms.

Example: A state's interest in ending invidious discrimination justifies prohibiting private clubs that are large and basically unselective in their membership, or that are often used for business contacts, from discriminating on the basis of race, creed, color, national origin, or sex—at least when it is not shown that this would impede the individual members' ability to engage in First Amendment activity. [New York State Club Association, Inc. v. New York City, 487 U.S. 1 (1988); Board of Directors of Rotary Club International v. Rotary Club of Duarte, 481 U.S. 537 (1987); Roberts v. United States Jaycees, 468 U.S. 609 (1984)]

Compare: 1) A state antidiscrimination law may not bar the Boy Scouts from excluding an openly gay assistant scoutmaster from membership. Forced inclusion would *significantly burden* the right of expressive association of the Boy Scouts, since one of the *sincerely held* purposes of the Scouts is to instill certain moral values in young people, including the value that "homosexual conduct is not morally straight." [Boy Scouts of America v. Dale, 530 U.S. 640 (2000)]

2) A city ordinance that restricted admission to certain dance halls to persons between the ages of 14 and 18 was constitutional; it did not have to be justified with a compelling interest because the associational activity of meeting in a dance hall is not an activity within the protection of the First Amendment. [Dallas v. Stanglin, 490 U.S. 19 (1989)]

B. ELECTORAL PROCESS

Laws regulating the electoral process might impact on First Amendment rights of speech, assembly, and association. The Supreme Court uses a balancing test in determining whether a regulation of the electoral process is valid: if the restriction on First Amendment activities is severe, it will be upheld only if it is narrowly tailored to achieve a compelling interest, but if the restriction is reasonable and nondiscriminatory, it generally will be upheld on the basis of the states' important regulatory interests. [Burdick v. Takushi, 504 U.S. 428 (1992)—upholding prohibition against write-in candidates]

1. Ballot Regulation

a. Signature Requirements

The Court has found that the interest of running an efficient election supports a requirement that candidates obtain a reasonable number of signatures to get on the ballot [Munro v. Socialist Workers Party, 479 U.S. 189 (1986)—1%], but the Court struck down a severe ballot restriction requiring new political parties to collect twice as many signatures to run for county office as for state office [Norman v. Reed, 502 U.S. 279 (1992)].

b. Primary Voting Regulations

A state may enforce a party rule requiring that a person be registered as a member of the party within a reasonable amount of time prior to a primary to be able to vote. [Rosario v. Rockefeller, 410 U.S. 752 (1973)] However, such a state law is invalid if it is contrary to the party's rules (*e.g.*, the party would allow unregistered independent voters to vote). [Tashjan v. Republican Party of Connecticut, 479 U.S. 208 (1986)]

c. Single Party Limitation

A state law that prohibits an individual from appearing on the ballot as the candidate of more than one party does *not* impose a severe burden on the association rights of political parties. The state's interest in ballot integrity and political stability are "sufficiently weighty" to justify the law. [Timmons v. Twin Cities Area New Party, 520 U.S. 35 (1997)]

2. Party Regulation

The state has less interest in governing party activities than in governing elections in general. Thus, the Court has held invalid a statute prohibiting the governing committee of a political party from endorsing or opposing candidates in primary elections. [Eu v. San Francisco County Democratic Central Committee, 489 U.S. 214 (1989); *and see* California

Democratic Party v. Jones, 530 U.S. 567 (2000)—state cannot require political parties to allow nonparty members to vote in the party's primary election] Similarly, it has held invalid state regulations concerning the selection of delegates to a national party convention and the selection of candidates at such elections. [Cousins v. Wigoda, 419 U.S. 477 (1975); Democratic Party v. LaFolette, 450 U.S. 107 (1981)]

3. Limits on Contributions

a. To Political Candidate

Laws limiting the amount of money that a person or group may contribute to a political candidate are *valid*, since the government has a sufficiently important interest in stopping the fact (or appearance) of corruption that may result from large contributions. Moreover, such laws do not substantially restrict freedom of expression or freedom of association (as long as the contributor may spend his money directly to discuss candidates and issues). [Buckley v. Valeo, 424 U.S. 1 (1976)]

b. To Ballot Referendum Committee

The government may *not* limit contributions to a political committee that supports or opposes a ballot referendum (as opposed to one that supports a political candidate). Such a limitation on contributions to influence referendum elections violates the freedoms of speech and association. [Citizens Against Rent Control v. Berkeley, 454 U.S. 290 (1982)]

c. Disclosure of Contributors or Recipients of Money

The government may require a political party or committee to disclose the names of contributors or recipients of money to or from the party or committee. However, if the party or committee can show a "reasonable probability" that disclosure will cause harm to the party, committee, or private individuals, they have a First Amendment right to refuse to make such disclosures. [Brown v. Socialist Workers '74 Campaign Committee, 454 U.S. 1122 (1982)]

4. Limits on Expenditures

Laws limiting the amount that an individual or group (including a candidate) may spend on a political campaign are *invalid*. Such laws impose "direct and substantial restraints" on political speech and do not satisfy the "exacting scrutiny applicable to limitations on core First Amendment rights of political expression." Government may not restrict the speech of wealthy persons to enhance the voice of others. [Buckley v. Valeo, *supra*]

Examples: 1) The Supreme Court invalidated a state statute that prohibited paying individuals to circulate initiative or referendum petitions. The prohibition against the use of paid circulators was not necessary to the promotion of any state interest that might override the freedom to engage in political speech. [Meyer v. Grant, 486 U.S. 414 (1988)]

2) The federal government *cannot* make it a crime for a "political committee" to expend more than $1,000 to further the nomination or election of a presidential candidate who is receiving federal financing. [Federal Election Commission v. National Conservative Political Action Committee, 470 U.S. 480 (1985)]

a.   **Corporations**

   1)   **Limiting Contributions to Political Candidates—Permissible**
      Laws limiting the amount that a corporation or unincorporated association may contribute to a political candidate have been upheld. [California Medical Association v. Federal Election Commission, 453 U.S. 182 (1981)] Corporations or unions can be prohibited from making contributions to political candidates from funds that are not contributed by corporate or union members but, instead, solicited from nonmembers. [Federal Election Commission v. National Right to Work Committee, 456 U.S. 914 (1982)]

      a)   **Exception—Ideological Corporations**
         Although contributions to political candidates by ordinary corporations may be limited, contributions by *ideological corporations* (*i.e.,* voluntary political associations that have incorporated; *e.g.,* a corporation formed to oppose abortion) may not be limited. [Federal Election Commission v. Massachusetts Citizens for Life, Inc., 479 U.S. 238 (1986)] To be exempt from the independent campaign expenditure limitations placed on corporations, a nonprofit corporation must: (i) be formed to promote ideas and not business activity; (ii) not have shareholders who have a claim on its assets; and (iii) not be tied to business interests or business corporations. Thus, even though a "Chamber of Commerce" is a nonprofit corporation, its campaign spending can be limited in the same way as other corporations. [Austin v. Michigan Chamber of Commerce, 494 U.S. 652 (1990)]

   2)   **Expenditures to Influence Vote on Referendum—Permissible**
      The Court has left open the broad question of whether corporations have the full measure of rights that individuals have under the First Amendment. But laws prohibiting corporate expenditures to influence the vote on a *referendum* violate the First Amendment. Such speech is "indispensable to decisionmaking in a democracy."

      Examples: 1) A law limiting corporate expenditures to referenda that "materially affect" corporate business or property was held invalid. [First National Bank v. Bellotti, 435 U.S. 765 (1978)]

      2) A law forbidding a corporation from using bill inserts to express its views on controversial issues of public policy also violates the First Amendment. [Consolidated Edison Co. v. Public Service Commission, 447 U.S. 530 (1980)]

b.   **"Coordinated" Expenditures**
   If political parties, like others, make expenditures "in cooperation, consultation, or concert" with a candidate, the expenditures are treated like "contributions" and may be limited accordingly. *Rationale*: The opposite rule would induce individuals to circumvent contribution limits by simply giving money to the party with the understanding that it should go to the candidate, thus furthering corruption or its appearance. [Federal Election Commission v. Colorado Republican Federal Campaign Committee, 121 S. Ct. 2351 (2001)]

5. **Compare—Regulations of Core Political Speech**

Regulation of "core political speech" must be distinguished from regulation of the process surrounding elections. Regulation of "core political speech" will be upheld only if it passes muster under strict scrutiny. [McIntyre v. Ohio Elections Commission, 514 U.S. 334 (1995)—prohibition against anonymous campaign literature invalid]

a. **Prohibiting Any Election Day Campaigning**

A state law prohibiting *any* campaigning on election day has been held *invalid* as applied to a newspaper urging people to vote in a certain way. The right to comment on political issues is one of the most essential elements of free speech, and such conduct by newspapers would pose little danger to conducting elections. [Mills v. Alabama, 384 U.S. 214 (1966)]

1) **Compare—Hundred-Foot Limit**

A law prohibiting campaign activity within 100 feet of a polling place is *valid*. Even though the law is content-based and concerns an essential element of free speech, it is *necessary* to serve the *compelling* interest of preventing voter intimidation and election fraud. [Burson v. Freeman, 504 U.S. 191 (1992)]

b. **Prohibiting Anonymous Campaign Literature**

Laws prohibiting distribution of anonymous campaign literature involve core political speech and have been stricken because they were not narrowly tailored to a compelling state interest. [McIntyre v. Ohio Elections Commission, *supra*; Buckley v. American Constitutional Law Foundation, 525 U.S. 182 (1999)]

C. **BAR MEMBERSHIP AND PUBLIC EMPLOYMENT**

The government often requires persons who accept government jobs to submit to loyalty oaths and refrain from certain conduct (*e.g.,* campaigning). Such regulations often impact upon the freedom of speech and association.

1. **Restraints on Conduct**

If a government employer seeks to fire an employee for speech-related conduct, one of two tests will apply depending on whether the speech involved a matter of public concern. If a matter of public concern is involved, courts must carefully balance the employee's rights as a citizen to comment on a matter of public concern against the government's interest as an employer in efficient performance of public service. If the speech did not involve a matter of public concern, the courts should give a wide degree of deference to the government employer's judgment concerning whether the speech was disruptive.

Examples: 1) A teacher cannot be fired for writing a letter to a newspaper attacking school board policies. [Pickering v. Board of Education, 391 U.S. 563 (1968)]

2) The Court held invalid the firing of a clerical employee from a constable's office for expressing her disappointment that an assassination attempt on President Reagan did not succeed, because in context the statement could not be understood to be an actual threat or an action that would interfere with the running of the office; rather, the Court viewed it as a commentary on the public issue of the President's policies. [Rankin v. McPherson, 483 U.S. 378 (1987)]

Compare: The Court upheld the firing of an attorney for circulating in the office a petition regarding transfer policies. [Connick v. Myers, 461 U.S. 138 (1983)]

a.   Independent Contractors Have Similar Rights

With regard to government projects, an independent contractor has speech rights similar to those of a government employee—the contractor cannot be discharged or have a contract not renewed merely because the government disagrees with something the contractor says. [*See* Board of County Commissioners v. Umbehr, 518 U.S. 668 (1996); *and see* O'Hare Truck Service Inc. v. City of Northlake, 518 U.S. 712 (1996)]

b.   Participation in Political Campaigns

A provision of the Hatch Act making it unlawful for employees in the federal executive branch to take an active part in political campaigns has been sustained. The rationale is twofold: to further nonpartisanship in administration and to protect employees from being coerced to work for the election of their employers. [United Public Workers v. Mitchell, 330 U.S. 75 (1947)]

c.   Bans on Receiving Honoraria

A provision of the Ethics in Government Act banning government employees from accepting an honorarium for making speeches, writing articles, or making appearances was held to violate the First Amendment when applied to "rank and file" employees. Such a rule deters speech within a broad category of expression by a massive number of potential speakers and thus can be justified only if the government can show that the employees' and their potential audiences' rights are outweighed by the necessary impact the speech would have on actual operation of the government. The government failed to cite any evidence of misconduct related to honoraria by the rank and file employees, and so failed to meet the burden here. [United States v. National Treasury Employees Union, 513 U.S. 454 (1995)]

d.   Patronage

The First Amendment freedoms of political belief and association forbid the hiring, promotion, transfer, firing, or recall of a public employee because of political party affiliation unless the hiring authority demonstrates that party affiliation is an appropriate requirement for the effective performance of the public office involved, *e.g.,* "policymaking" or "confidential" nature of work. [Rutan v. Republican Party of Illinois, 497 U.S. 62 (1990)]

e.   Bill of Attainder

Legislative punishment without judicial trial by discharging a public employee for political activity is invalid as a bill of attainder. [United States v. Lovett, 328 U.S. 303 (1946)]

f.   Must Not Be Vague

A standard for conduct may not be vague.

Example: A statute providing for removal of public school teachers for "treasonable or seditious" utterances is void for vagueness. [Keyishian v. Board of Regents, 385 U.S. 589 (1967)]

2. Loyalty Oaths

It is permissible for the federal government to require employees and other public officers to take loyalty oaths. However, such oaths will not be upheld if they are overbroad (*i.e.*, prohibit constitutionally protected activities) or are vague so that they have a chilling effect on First Amendment activities.

a. Overbreadth

1) Knowledge of Organization's Aim Required

Public employment cannot be denied to persons who are simply members of the Communist Party because only knowing membership with "specific intent to further unlawful aims" is unprotected by the First Amendment. [Keyishian v. Board of Regents, *supra*]

2) Advocacy of Doctrine Protected

A political party may not be denied a place on the ballot for refusing to take a loyalty oath that it does not advocate violent overthrow of the government as an abstract doctrine. The First Amendment forbids "statutes regulating advocacy that are not limited to advocacy of action." [Communist Party v. Whitcomb, 414 U.S. 441 (1974)]

b. Vagueness

1) Oaths Upheld

Compare the following oaths that have been upheld:

a) To Support the Constitution

An oath that required public employees and bar applicants to "support the Constitution of the United States" and the state constitution has been upheld. [Connell v. Higgenbotham, 403 U.S. 207 (1971)]

b) To Oppose the Overthrow of the Government

An oath required of all state employees "to oppose the overthrow of the government . . . by force, violence, or by an illegal or unconstitutional method" has also been upheld. The Court read this oath as akin to those requiring the taker simply to "support" the Constitution, "to commit themselves to live by the constitutional processes of our system." Moreover, the oath provided fair notice, because its violation could be punished only by a prosecution for perjury, which required proof of knowing falsity. [Cole v. Richardson, 405 U.S. 676 (1972)]

2) Oath Not Upheld

A loyalty oath for public employees that they "promote respect for the flag and . . . reverence for law and order" is void for vagueness, since a refusal to salute the flag on religious grounds might be found in breach thereof. [Baggett v. Bullitt, 377 U.S. 360 (1964)]

3. Disclosure of Associations

Forcing disclosure of First Amendment activities as a condition of public employment, bar membership, or other public benefits may have a chilling effect. Thus, the state cannot force every prospective government employee to disclose *every* organizational membership. Such a broad disclosure has ***insufficient relation*** to loyalty and professional competence, and the state has available ***less drastic means*** to achieve its purpose. [Shelton v. Tucker, 364 U.S. 479 (1960)] The state may inquire only into those activities that are relevant to the position. If the candidate fails to answer relevant questions, employment may be denied. [Konigsberg v. State Bar of California, 366 U.S. 36 (1961)]

a. **Fifth Amendment Limitation**

If the job candidate refuses to answer on a claim of the privilege against self-incrimination, denial of the job violates the Fifth and Fourteenth Amendments. [Spevack v. Klein, 385 U.S. 511 (1967)] However, if individuals are ordered by appropriate authorities to answer questions "specifically, directly, and narrowly relating to their official duties," and they refuse to do so by claiming the privilege against self-incrimination, they may be denied the job or discharged without violating the Fifth Amendment, if they were given immunity from the use of their answers or the fruits thereof in a criminal prosecution. [Lefkowitz v. Turley, 414 U.S. 70 (1973); Gardner v. Broderick, 392 U.S. 273 (1968)]

4. **Practice of Law**

Regulation of the legal profession may conflict with the freedom of association rights of certain groups since it may impair their ability to band together to advise each other and utilize counsel in their common interest.

a. **Countervailing State Interest Required**

To overcome a group's right to exercise its First Amendment rights, the state must show a substantial interest, such as evidence of objectionable practices occurring or an actual or clearly threatened conflict of interest between lawyer and client.

Examples: 1) NAACP encouraged, instructed, and offered to represent parents of black children to litigate against school segregation. This was held to be protected political expression. The state's ban on solicitation of legal business was inapplicable because the NAACP sought no monetary gain. [NAACP v. Button, 371 U.S. 415 (1963)]

2) Railroad labor union recommended specific lawyer to pursue rights of members injured on the job, and also obtained fee from lawyer for performing investigative services. This was held protected. [Brotherhood of Railroad Trainmen v. Virginia, 377 U.S. 1 (1964)]

D. **SOCIAL ISSUE BOYCOTTS**

A state may not impose civil or criminal liability on those persons who engage in a nonviolent boycott of commercial enterprises to influence governmental and private decisions on social issues. Imposition of liability in such circumstances would violate the freedoms of speech and association. [NAACP v. Claiborne Hardware Co., 458 U.S. 886 (1982)] However, courts may regulate or punish labor organizations that engage in "secondary boycotts." [International Longshoreman's Association v. Allied International, Inc., 456 U.S. 212 (1982)]

1. **Compare—Economic Boycotts**

Economic boycotts can be restricted.

Example: A group of attorneys in the District of Columbia agreed not to represent indigent criminal defendants until the District raised the compensation for such cases. The Federal Trade Commission charged the attorneys with conspiracy to fix prices. The Supreme Court held that the attorneys had no First Amendment right to engage in the boycott because it involved economic, rather than social, issues. Further, the FTC found that the boycott could be a *per se* violation of federal law. [FTC v. Superior Court Trial Lawyers Association, 493 U.S. 411 (1990)]

E. TAX EXEMPT ORGANIZATIONS LIMITED IN LOBBYING ACTIVITIES

Tax exempt charitable organizations (ones to which contributions are tax deductible) are prohibited by the Internal Revenue Code from "substantial" lobbying activities. This prohibition is permissible even though certain military veterans' organizations are eligible for tax exempt status despite their lobbying activities. The Congress does not have to subsidize First Amendment activity, but it may choose to give a special subsidy to military veterans' organizations. [Regan v. Taxation With Representation of Washington, 461 U.S. 540 (1983)]

XXII. FREEDOM OF RELIGION

A. CONSTITUTIONAL PROVISION

The First Amendment provides "Congress shall make no law respecting an establishment of religion, or prohibiting the free exercise thereof."

B. APPLICABILITY TO THE STATES

Both the Establishment and Free Exercise Clauses of the First Amendment apply to the states under the Fourteenth Amendment.

C. FREE EXERCISE CLAUSE

1. No Punishment of Beliefs

The Free Exercise Clause prohibits the government from punishing (denying benefits to, or imposing burdens on) someone on the basis of the person's *religious beliefs*. It is sometimes said that the government can engage in such activity only if it is necessary to achieve a compelling interest; sometimes the rule is stated as a total prohibition of such government actions. In any case, the Supreme Court has never found an interest that was so "compelling" that it would justify punishing a religious belief.

a. What Constitutes Religious Belief?

The Supreme Court has not defined what constitutes a religious belief. However, it has made clear that religious belief does not require recognition of a supreme being [Torcaso v. Watkins, 367 U.S. 488 (1961)], and need not arise from a traditional, or even an organized, religion [*see* Frazee v. Illinois Department of Employment Security, 489 U.S. 829 (1989)]. One possible definition is that the "belief must occupy a place in the believer's life parallel to that occupied by orthodox religious beliefs." [United States v. Seeger, 380 U.S. 163 (1965)—interpreting statutory, rather than constitutional, provision] In any case, the Court has never held an asserted religious belief to be not religious for First Amendment purposes.

1) Courts May Not Find Religious Beliefs to Be False
The courts may not declare a religious belief to be "false." For example, if a person says he talked to God and that God said the person should solicit money, he cannot be found guilty of fraud on the basis that God never made such a statement. However, the court may determine whether the person is sincerely asserting a belief in the divine statement. [United States v. Ballard, 322 U.S. 78 (1944), *as described in* Employment Division v. Smith, 494 U.S. 872 (1990)]

b. Religious Oaths for Governmental Jobs Prohibited
The *federal* government may not require any federal office holder or employee to take an oath based on a religious belief as a condition for receiving the federal office or job, because such a requirement is prohibited by Article VI of the Constitution. State and local governments are prohibited from requiring such oaths by the Free Exercise Clause. [Toccaso v. Watkins, 367 U.S. 488 (1961)]

c. States May Not Exclude Clerics from Public Office
A state may not exclude clerics (persons who hold an office or official position in a religious organization) from being elected to the state legislature, or from other governmental positions, because that exclusion would impose a disability on these persons based upon the nature of their religious views and their religious status. [McDaniel v. Paty, 435 U.S. 618 (1978)]

2. No Punishment of Religious Conduct Solely Because It Is Religious
The Supreme Court has stated that the Free Exercise Clause prohibits the government from punishing conduct merely because it is religious or displays religious belief (*e.g.*, the state cannot ban the use of peyote only when used in religious ceremonies). [Employment Division v. Smith, *supra*—dicta] A law that is designed to suppress actions only because the actions are religiously motivated is not a neutral law of general applicability. Such a law will be invalid unless it is necessary to promote a compelling interest.

Example: A city law that prohibited the precise type of animal slaughter used in the ritual of a particular religious sect violated the Free Exercise Clause because the Court found that the law was designed solely to exclude the religious sect from the city. The law was not a neutral law of general applicability; nor was the law necessary to promote a compelling interest. [Church of the Lukumi Babalu Aye, Inc. v. Hialeah, 508 U.S. 520 (1993)]

3. States Can Regulate General Conduct—Criminal Laws and Other Regulations
Of course, states may prohibit or regulate conduct in general, and this is true even if the prohibition or regulation happens to interfere with a person's religious practices. The Free Exercise Clause cannot be used to challenge a law of general applicability unless it can be shown that the law was motivated by a desire to interfere with religion. [Employment Division v. Smith, *supra*]

a. Generally No Exemptions Required
The Free Exercise Clause does not require exemptions from criminal laws or other

governmental regulations for a person whose religious beliefs prevent him from conforming his behavior to the requirements of the law. In other words, a law that regulates the conduct of all persons can be applied to prohibit the conduct of a person despite the fact that his religious beliefs prevent him from complying with the law.

b.   Examples

The Supreme Court has held that no religious exemption was required from the following religiously neutral regulations, even though certain groups objected because the regulation interfered with conduct inspired by sincerely held religious beliefs:

1)   Prohibition against *use of peyote* [Employment Division v. Smith, *supra*—challenged by person whose religious beliefs require use of peyote during religious ceremony];

2)   *Denial of tax exempt status to schools that discriminate* on the basis of race [Bob Jones University v. United States, 461 U.S. 574 (1983)—challenged by religious school whose tenets require certain separations of races];

3)   Requirement that employers comply with *federal minimum wage laws* [Tony and Susan Alamo Foundation v. Secretary of Labor, 471 U.S. 290 (1985)—challenged by employer that argued minimum wages interfere with members' religious desires to work without compensation];

4)   Requirement that employers pay *Social Security taxes* [United States v. Lee, 455 U.S. 252 (1982)—challenged by person whose religious beliefs prohibited payment and receipt of Social Security type payments]; and

5)   *Sales and use taxes* [Jimmy Swaggart Ministries v. Board of Equalization of California, 493 U.S. 378 (1990)—challenged as applied to sales of goods and literature by religious group].

4.   Unemployment Compensation Cases—Some Exemptions Required

Many state unemployment compensation programs make payments only to persons who are involuntarily unemployed (*i.e.,* were fired or laid off rather than resigned), and who are available for work (*i.e.,* willing to accept offered employment). Here, however, unlike other areas of regulation, the Supreme Court has held that the states must grant religious exemptions. Thus, if a person resigns from a job or refuses to accept a job because it conflicts with her religious beliefs, the state must pay her unemployment compensation if she is otherwise entitled.

Examples: 1) A state cannot deny unemployment compensation merely because the applicant quit a job rather than work on a "holy day" on which religious beliefs forbid work. [Sherbert v. Verner, 374 U.S. 398 (1963)]

2) A state cannot deny unemployment compensation merely because the applicant quit his job rather than work on production of military equipment after his factory converted from nonmilitary to military production. [Thomas v. Review Board, 450 U.S. 707 (1981)]

a. Need Not Belong to Formal Religious Organization

A person does not have to be a member of a formal religious organization to receive the above exemptions from unemployment compensation requirements. All that is required is that the person *sincerely hold* religious beliefs that prevent him from working on a certain day or on military products. [Frazee v. Illinois Department of Employment Security, 1.a., *supra*]

b. Limitation—Criminal Prohibitions

The unemployment compensation cases do not give individuals a right to disregard criminal laws due to their religious beliefs. Thus, unemployment compensation laws may disqualify persons fired for "misconduct" (which includes any violation of criminal law).

Example: A person was fired from his job as a counselor at a private drug abuse clinic when it was discovered that he used peyote (at times when he was not at work) for religious reasons. All use of peyote was illegal in the state (even if the use was part of a religious ceremony). The Supreme Court held that unemployment compensation could properly be denied here. [Employment Division v. Smith, *supra*]

5. Right of Amish Not to Educate Children

The Supreme Court has required an exemption for the Amish from a neutral law that required school attendance until age 16, because a fundamental tenet of Amish religion forbids secondary education. The Court found that the Amish are productive and law-abiding, and ruled that the right to educate one's children (*see* XIX.B.6., *supra*) and the Free Exercise Clause outweighed the state's interest here. [Wisconsin v. Yoder, 406 U.S. 205 (1972)]

6. Special Rule for Prison Regulations

A prison regulation restricting inmates' constitutional rights (including First Amendment rights) will be upheld if the regulation is "reasonably related to legitimate penological interests." Applying this standard, the Supreme Court has upheld a prison regulation regarding the work duties of inmates that precluded Islamic inmates from attending a religious service held on Friday afternoons. [O'Lone v. Estate of Shabazz, 482 U.S. 342 (1987)]

D. ESTABLISHMENT CLAUSE

The Establishment Clause prohibits laws respecting the establishment of religion.

1. Sect Preference

If a law or government program includes a preference for some religious sects over others, the law will be held invalid unless it is *narrowly tailored* to promote a *compelling interest*.

Example: A state law created a public school district whose boundaries were intentionally set to match the boundaries of a particular Jewish neighborhood (so that several handicapped students would not have to be sent outside their neighborhood to attend special education classes that the state required and which the students' private school could not adequately provide). The Supreme Court found the law unconstitutional. [Board of Education v. Grumet, 512 U.S. 687 (1994)]

2. No Sect Preference

Where there is no "sect preference," the compelling interest test is not used; instead the governmental program will be valid under the Establishment Clause if it:

(i) Has *secular purpose*;

(ii) Has a *primary effect* that neither advances nor inhibits religion; *and*

(iii) Does not produce *excessive government entanglement* with religion.

The Establishment Clause cases can be grouped into three categories: (i) a limited group of cases unconnected to financial aid or education; (ii) cases involving financial aid to religiously affiliated institutions; and (iii) cases concerning religious activities in public schools. The details regarding the Supreme Court rulings are given below.

a. Cases Unconnected to Financial Aid or Education

In cases unconnected to financial aid or education, a good rule of thumb is that a law favoring or burdening religion or a specific religious group in particular will be invalid, but a law favoring or burdening a larger segment of society that happens to include religious groups will be upheld.

Example: The government may not delegate governmental power to religious organizations because such action would involve excessive governmental entanglement. [Larkin v. Grendel's Den, Inc., 456 U.S. 913 (1982)—statute gave church-affiliated schools power to veto nearby liquor licenses]

Compare: The IRS may deny tax exemptions claimed for religious donations when the sums were paid to the church *in exchange for services* (*e.g.*, classes) since this is a general rule that applies to all charities. [Hernandez v. Commissioner of Internal Revenue, 490 U.S. 680 (1989)]

1) State Legislature Can Employ a Chaplain

Despite the principle of separation of church and state, the Court has held that a state legislature could employ a chaplain and begin each legislative day with a prayer. [Marsh v. Chambers, 463 U.S. 783 (1983)] This decision was based on the history of legislative prayer in America; it does not modify the "Religious Activities in Public Schools" rulings examined below.

2) Some Holiday Displays Are Permissible

If the *government* maintains a holiday-Christmastime display that does not appear to endorse religion, the display will survive review under the three-part Establishment Clause test. If a government's holiday display includes religious symbols (*e.g.*, a nativity scene or a menorah) as well as other holiday decorations (*e.g.*, a Christmas tree or a Santa Claus figure), the courts will hold that the display: (i) has a secular purpose (based on the history of government recognition of holidays); (ii) has a primary nonreligious effect (it does not endorse religion); and (iii) does not create excessive entanglement between government and religion. If the display includes only the religious symbols (*e.g.*, only a nativity scene), it will violate the Establishment Clause because it has a religious effect (it "endorses" religion). [County of Allegheny v. A.C.L.U., 492 U.S. 573 (1989)]

3) Absolute Right Not to Work on a Sabbath Impermissible

The state may not force employers to grant all employees an absolute right to refrain from working on their sabbath, since the primary effect of such a law is to advance religion. [Estate of Thornton v. Caldor, 472 U.S. 703 (1985)] However, a state may require employers to make reasonable efforts to accommodate employee religious practices.

4) Exemptions from Antidiscrimination Laws

The federal government may exempt religious organizations from the federal statutory prohibition against discrimination in employment on the basis of religion, at least regarding their nonprofit activities. Thus, a janitor can be discharged from his employment at a gymnasium owned by a religious organization (which was open to the public and run as a nonprofit facility) because he was not a member of that religious organization. [Corporation of the Presiding Bishop of the Church of Jesus Christ of Latter-Day Saints v. Amos, 483 U.S. 327 (1987)]

b. Cases Involving Financial Benefits to Church-Related Institutions

A statute authorizing governmental aid to a religiously affiliated institution (hospital, school, etc.) must be tested under the general test detailed above (secular purpose, primary effect, and excessive entanglement). However, the Supreme Court applies these tests with greater strictness when the government aid is going to a religiously affiliated grade school or high school (or their students) than it does when the aid is going to another type of religiously affiliated institution (such as a college or hospital).

1) Aid to Colleges, Hospitals, Etc.

The Court will uphold a government grant of aid to the secular activity of a religiously affiliated hospital or college (such as grant to build a new hospital ward or a laboratory-classroom building) as long as the government program requires that the aid be used only for *nonreligious purposes*, and the recipient so agrees in good faith. [Tilton v. Richardson, 403 U.S. 672 (1971); Bradfield v. Roberts, 175 U.S. 291 (1899)]

Example: The Adolescent Family Life Act—which provides for grants of government funds to a variety of public and private (including religiously affiliated) agencies to provide counseling and educational services to young people regarding sexual activity—has been upheld. The Act has a secular purpose (dealing with problems of teenage pregnancy). The Act does not on its face advance religion because a religiously affiliated organization could contractually be required to use the funds for nonreligious counseling. And the Act does not give rise to excessive entanglement because there is no reason to assume that a significant percentage of the funds would be granted to pervasively sectarian institutions. [Bowen v. Kendrick, 487 U.S. 589 (1988)]

a) Recipient Based Aid

The government may give aid in the form of financial assistance to a defined class of persons as long as the class is defined without reference to religion or religious criteria. Such a program is valid even if persons who receive the financial assistance are thereby enabled to attend a religiously affiliated college.

Example: The Supreme Court upheld a state program that made education subsidy payments directly to a blind or disabled student even though a student used his aid to study at a Christian college for the purpose of becoming a pastor or missionary. The class of persons who received the aid was defined without reference to any religious criteria; only an incidental benefit would go to the religiously affiliated college or vocational training institution. The aid program thus passed review under the purpose, effect, and entanglement tests. [Witters v. Washington Department of Services, 474 U.S. 481 (1986)]

2) Aid to Religiously Affiliated Grade Schools or High Schools

Programs of aid to these institutions are subject to the same three-part test as are all other laws under the Establishment Clause. All government programs examined by the Supreme Court which provide aid for religiously affiliated grade schools or high schools have been found to have a "secular purpose." However, if significant aid is given to the religious school, or if the aid significantly improves the ability of students to go to religious schools, the program may be deemed to have a primary effect that advances religion. If the government program has detailed administrative or legislative regulations that are designed to ensure that the aid does not result in a primary effect of advancing religion, the law may be stricken as giving rise to an excessive entanglement between government and religion.

a) Aid Upheld

The Supreme Court has upheld state programs that:

(1) Provide state-approved *textbooks* to *all* students [Board of Education v. Allen, 392 U.S. 236 (1968)] (but note that the state may not loan textbooks to students attending schools that discriminate on the basis of race, since this would violate the Fourteenth Amendment [Norwood v. Harrison, 413 U.S. 455 (1973)]);

(2) Lend religiously neutral instructional materials (*e.g.*, library books, computers) to parochial schools as well as to public and other nonprofit private schools, where the program did not define recipients by reference to religion and the *challenger did not prove* that the neutral aid was used for religious indoctrination. [Mitchell v. Helms, 530 U.S. 793 (2000), *overruling* Meek v. Pittenger, 421 U.S. 349 (1975)];

(3) Provide *transportation to and from school* to *all* students [Everson v. Board of Education, 330 U.S. 1 (1947)];

(4) Reimburse private schools for the expenses of *compiling state required data*, such as student attendance records, or administering and grading

standardized state educational achievement tests [Committee for Public Education and Religious Liberty v. Regan, 444 U.S. 646 (1980)];

(5) Provide government employees to perform *diagnostic tests* for health and learning problems at private schools [Wolman v. Walter, 443 U.S. 229 (1977)];

(6) Provide *"auxiliary services"* (*e.g.*, remedial education, guidance, or job counseling) to all disadvantaged children at their school, including children at parochial schools [Agostini v. Felton, 521 U.S. 203 (1997)]; and

(7) *Recipient-based aid* to a class of students defined *without reference to religion* may be upheld. Thus, the Court held that the Establishment Clause would not prevent a public school district from paying for a sign language interpreter for a deaf student at a religious high school under a religiously neutral program of aid to all handicapped school children in both public and private schools [Zobrest v. Catalina Foothills School District, 509 U.S. 1 (1993)].

b) Aid Invalidated
The Supreme Court has struck down the following state programs, either because they had a primary effect that advanced religion or because they involved excessive entanglement between government and religion:

(1) Programs paying for *field trip transportation* for private school students (goes too far; primary effect aids religion) [Wolman v. Walter, *supra*];

(2) Programs paying a portion of private school *teachers' salaries* (for their secular classes), since the primary effect would be to advance religion and a system to ensure that the money/teachers not be used for religious purposes would involve excessive entanglements. [Grand Rapids School District v. Ball, 473 U.S. 373 (1985); Lemon v. Kurtzman, 403 U.S. 602 (1971)]; and

(3) Programs reimbursing private schools for *writing achievement tests* (this would have the primary effect of advancing religion since the schools could write tests advancing their religious mission) [Levitt v. Community for Public Education, 413 U.S. 472 (1973)].

3) Tuition Tax Deductions or Credits
A state may not use a system of statutory grants, tax credits, or tax deductions to reimburse parents or students for tuition paid *only to religiously affiliated schools*. However, a tax deduction to all students or parents based upon the actual expenditures for attending any public or private school (including religious schools) has been upheld. [Mueller v. Allen, 463 U.S. 388 (1983)]

It would appear that a valid tax deduction statute must allow a deduction for: (i) expenditures for public as well as private schools; and (ii) some expenditures other than tuition (such as expenditures for school supplies or books) so that public school students or their parents may benefit from the deduction.

4) **Tax Exemption for Religious, Charitable, or Educational Property**
An exemption from property taxation for "real or personal property used exclusively for religious, educational, or charitable purposes" does not violate the Establishment Clause. Neither the purpose nor the effect of such an exemption is the advancement or the inhibition of religion; and it constitutes neither sponsorship nor hostility, nor excessive government entanglement with religion. The "government does not transfer part of its revenue to churches but simply abstains from demanding that the church support the state . . . ." [Walz v. Tax Commission, 397 U.S. 664 (1970)]

5) **Tax Exemption Available Only to Religions**
Although religious schools or religious associations may be included in tax exemptions available to a variety of secular and religious organizations, a tax exemption that is available only for religious organizations or religious activities violates the Establishment Clause. [Texas Monthly, Inc. v. Bullock, 489 U.S. 1 (1989)—an exemption from the sales and use tax for religious magazines or books (but no other publications) violates the Establishment Clause]

c. **Religious Activities in Public Schools**

1) **Prayer and Bible Reading**
Prayer and Bible reading in school are invalid as establishments of religion. [Engel v. Vitale, 370 U.S. 421 (1962); Abington School District v. Schempp, 374 U.S. 203 (1963)] It does not matter whether participation is voluntary or involuntary, and neither does it matter that the prayer period is designated as a period of silent prayer or meditation. [Wallace v. Jaffree, 472 U.S. 38 (1985)] This rule extends to prohibit public school officials from having clerics give invocation and benediction prayers at graduation ceremonies. [Lee v. Weisman, 505 U.S. 577 (1992)] Similarly, a school policy authorizing students to elect whether to have a student invocation before varsity games, to select a student to deliver it, and to decide its content *violates* the Establishment Clause. Unlike student speeches at an open public forum (*see* 4)b), below), this policy's purpose is to encourage religious messages. [Santa Fe Independent School District v. Doe, 530 U.S. 290 (2000)]

2) **Posting Ten Commandments in Classroom Is Invalid**
Posting the Ten Commandments on the walls of public school classrooms plainly serves a religious purpose and is invalid despite the legislature's statement that it was for a secular purpose. [Stone v. Graham, 449 U.S. 39 (1980)]

3) **Released-Time Programs**

a) **In Public School Building**
Programs in which regular classes end an hour early one day a week and religious instruction is given in public school classrooms to students who request it are invalid. [McCollum v. Board of Education, 333 U.S. 203 (1948)]

b) **Nonpublic Building Used**
Programs in which participating children go to religious classes conducted at religious centers away from the public school do not violate the Establishment Clause. [Zorach v. Clauson, 343 U.S. 306 (1952)]

4) **Accommodation of Religious Students—On Campus Meetings**
As discussed at XX.B.2.a.3)b), *supra*, under the Free Speech Clause, if a public school allows members of the public and private organizations to use school property when classes are not in session, it cannot deny a religious organization permission to use the property for meetings merely because religious topics will be discussed. Such an "equal access rule" does not violate the Establishment Clause because the primary purpose of such programs is secular (to accommodate all interests), people are not likely to assume that the government endorses the religious ideas discussed, and there is no excessive government entanglement, at least where the meetings are not run by school personnel. [Good News Club v. Milford Central School, 121 S. Ct. 2093 (2001)]

5) **Curriculum Controls**
A government statute or regulation that modifies a public school curriculum will violate the Establishment Clause if it fails the secular purpose test, primary effect test, or excessive government entanglement test.

Example: A state statute that prohibited the teaching of human biological evolution in the state's public schools was held to violate the Establishment Clause because the Supreme Court found that the legislature had a religious purpose for enacting the statute. [Epperson v. Arkansas, 393 U.S. 97 (1968)] Similarly, the Court invalidated a state statute that prohibited instruction regarding "evolution science" (the theory of human biological evolution) in the public schools unless that instruction was accompanied by instruction regarding "creation science" because the Court found that the legislature enacted this statute for the purpose of promoting religion. [Edwards v. Aguillard, 482 U.S. 578 (1987)]

BAR REVIEW

Corporations

CORPORATIONS

TABLE OF CONTENTS

PART ONE—CHARACTERISTICS AND FORMATION OF CORPORATIONS

I. CORPORATION VS. OTHER BUSINESS ENTITIES

A. INTRODUCTION

The corporation is a form of business ownership that has advantages and disadvantages over other forms of business ownership. There are even a number of forms of corporations, each with its own advantages and disadvantages. Thus, the first issue to be addressed in corporate law is how the corporate form differs from other business entities and how the various corporate forms differ from each other.

B. GENERAL CHARACTERISTICS OF A CORPORATION

A corporation is a legal entity distinct from its owners. Creation of such an entity generally requires filing certain documents with the state, and running a corporation generally requires more formality than is required to run most other types of business entities. Corporations generally have the following characteristics:

1. Limited Liability for Owners, Directors, and Officers

The owners of a corporation (called "shareholders") generally are not personally liable for the obligations of the corporation; neither are the corporation's directors or officers. Generally only the corporation itself can be held liable for corporate obligations. The owners risk only the investment that they make in the business to purchase their ownership interests ("shares"). Thus, if a person wants to set up a business entity that protects his personal assets from the possibility of being seized to satisfy obligations of the business, a corporation would be a good business form to consider.

2. Centralized Management

Generally, the right to manage a corporation is not spread out among the shareholders, but rather is centralized in a board of directors, who usually delegate day-to-day management duties to officers. Thus, if a person wants to avoid conflicts with co-owners of a business regarding management of the business, a corporation may be a good form of business to choose.

Note: Although the general rule is that a corporation is run by managers, shareholders can enter into agreements vesting management power in themselves rather than in a board.

3. Free Transferability of Ownership

Generally, ownership of a corporation is freely transferable; a shareholder can sell his shares to whomever he wants, whenever he wants, at whatever price he wants in most circumstances. Thus, if a person wants to set up a business entity that will enable him to easily bring in new investors in exchange for ownership interests, the corporate form is worth considering.

Note: Transferability of shares can be restricted by agreement of the shareholders. Such restriction is popular in close corporations so that current owners have some control over who may join their business in the future. Restrictions may also be necessary to assure eligibility of S corporation status. (*See* below.)

4. Continuity of Life

A corporation may exist perpetually and generally is not affected by changes in ownership (*i.e.*, sale of shares). Thus, if a person wants to create a business entity that can exist apart from and beyond its current owners, the corporate form is worth considering.

5. Taxation

a. C Corporation

Generally, a corporation is taxed as an entity distinct from its owners; *i.e.*, it must pay income taxes on any profits that it makes, and generally shareholders do not have to pay income tax on the corporation's profits until the profits are distributed. (Under the tax laws, such a corporation is known as a "C corporation.") The corporate tax rate generally is lower than the personal tax rate, and so this arrangement can be advantageous to persons who want to delay the realization of income. However, this advantage comes at a price—double taxation—because when the corporation does make distributions to shareholders, the distributions are treated as taxable income to the shareholders even though the corporation has already paid taxes on its profits.

b. S Corporation

The tax laws permit certain corporations to elect to be taxed like partnerships and yet retain the other advantages (above) of the corporate form. Such corporations are called "S corporations" under the tax laws. Partnerships and S corporations are not subject to double taxation—profits and losses flow directly through to the owners. This may be advantageous when losses are expected for the first few years that the business will be operating, since it allows the owners to offset the losses against their current incomes. It also may result in lower overall taxes on profits because there is no double taxation. However, there are a number of restrictions on S corporations (*e.g.*, stock can be held by no more than 75 persons, generally shareholders must be individuals, there can be only one class of stock, etc.).

C. COMPARISON WITH SOLE PROPRIETORSHIP

A sole proprietorship is a form of business in which one person owns all of the assets of the business. The sole proprietorship generally does not exist as an entity apart from its owner, and thus little formality is required to form it. However, since a sole proprietorship is not an entity distinct from its owner, its owner is personally liable for the business's obligations and the business "entity" cannot continue beyond the life of the owner. Management is centralized (since there is only one owner), and the owner is free to transfer his interest in the sole proprietorship at will. All profits and losses from the business flow through directly to the owner. Thus, if a person is interested in setting up a business with only one owner, desires little formality, is willing to risk personal assets, and wants to avoid double taxation, the sole proprietorship is worth considering as a business form.

D. COMPARISON WITH PARTNERSHIP

A partnership is similar to a sole proprietorship except that there are at least two owners of a partnership. Little formality is required to form a partnership (just an intention to run as co-owners a business for profit). Partnerships may have a few entity characteristics (*e.g.*, property may be held in the name of the partnership, suits can be maintained in the name of the partnership), but generally partnerships are not treated as legal entities. Partners are personally liable for obligations of the partnership; management generally is not centralized, but rather is spread among the partners; ownership interests of partners cannot be transferred without the consent of the other partners; and a partnership generally does not continue beyond the lives of its owners (although the partners can agree to allow remaining partners to continue the partnership business after a partner leaves). Finally, as indicated above, profits and losses of a partnership flow through directly to the partners. Thus, if a person is interested in forming a business with more than one owner, does not want to bother with a lot of formality, does not mind sharing management rights with co-owners, does not mind putting personal assets at risk, etc., a partnership might be an appropriate entity to form.

E. COMPARISON WITH LIMITED PARTNERSHIP

A limited partnership is a partnership that provides for limited liability of some investors (called "limited partners"), but otherwise is similar to other partnerships. A limited partnership can be formed only by compliance with the limited partnership statute. There must be at least one general partner, who has full personal liability for partnership debts and has most management rights. Thus, this form of business entity offers limited liability to most investors, centralized management (*i.e.*, management by the general partner(s) rather than by all owners), and the flow-through tax advantages of a partnership, without the 75-investor limit of an S corporation.

F. COMPARISON WITH LIMITED LIABILITY PARTNERSHIP

A limited liability partnership ("LLP") is a relatively new form of business entity that provides for the limited liability of all of its members; there is not a general partner who stands liable for the actions of the partnership. Formation requires filing a "statement of qualification" with the secretary of state. Otherwise, the entity is similar to other partnerships.

G. COMPARISON WITH LIMITED LIABILITY COMPANY

The limited liability company ("LLC") is a relatively new form of business entity designed to offer the limited liability of a corporation and the flow-through tax advantages of a partnership. Like a corporation, it may be formed only by filing appropriate documents with the state, but otherwise it is a very flexible business form: owners may choose centralized management or owner management, free transferability of ownership or restricted transferability, etc. (For more detail, *see* XI., *infra*.)

H. CONSTITUTIONAL CHARACTERISTICS OF A CORPORATION

1. "Person"

Corporations are entitled to due process of law and equal protection of the law. A corporation is entitled to raise the attorney-client privilege, but cannot invoke the privilege against self-incrimination. Generally, unless the context of the statute or constitutional provision requires application only to *natural* persons, a corporation is entitled to the protection and rights afforded thereby.

2. "Citizen"

a. Constitutional References to "Citizens"

A corporation is *not* a citizen for purposes of the Privileges and Immunities Clause of the Constitution. Therefore, state-imposed restrictions on a foreign corporation's activities are valid if they are a reasonable exercise of the state's police power. A foreign corporation is one conducting business in a particular state but not incorporated under that state's laws.

    b. **Federal Diversity Jurisdiction**
By federal statute a corporation is deemed to be a citizen of any state by which it has been incorporated **and** of the state where it has its principal place of business. [28 U.S.C. §1332]

        1) **Principal Place of Business**
Where the corporation has its principal place of business is a question of fact, using the tests of "corporate nerve center" (location of executive offices) or "corporate operations" (location of major business activity).

        2) **Multiple Incorporation**
If a corporation has incorporated in more than one state, the preferable rule is that it is deemed to be a citizen of every state of incorporation.

3. **"Resident"**
A corporation may be a resident of the state where it is incorporated, where it is doing business, and perhaps where it is merely qualified to do business.

4. **"Domicile"**
A corporation's domicile is the state of its incorporation. Like residence, however, a corporation may have multiple domiciles for some purposes, particularly for state taxation if the corporation has its principal place of business outside the state of its incorporation.

II. FORMATION AND STATUS OF THE CORPORATION

A. **CREATED UNDER STATUTE**
Corporations are created by complying with state corporate law. A majority of states have laws based on the Revised Model Business Corporation Act ("RMBCA"), and therefore this outline is based on that act. However, some states have varied from certain RMBCA provisions, and those variations will be discussed as well.

B. **FORMATION TERMINOLOGY**
A corporation formed in accordance with all applicable laws is a de jure corporation and its owners generally will not be personally liable for the corporation's obligations. However, if all applicable laws have not been followed, a business may still be treated as a corporation under the de facto corporation doctrine if there was a good faith attempt to incorporate. Even if no attempt to incorporate was made, under some circumstances, a business may be treated as a corporation for the purposes of a particular transaction under an estoppel theory.

C. **FORMATION OF A DE JURE CORPORATION**
To form a de jure corporation under the RMBCA, incorporators (*i.e.*, the persons who undertake to form a corporation) must file a document called the "articles of incorporation" with the state and must pay whatever fees the state directs.

1. **Incorporator Defined**
An incorporator is simply a person who signs the articles of incorporation. Under the RMBCA, only one incorporator is necessary, but there may be more than one. [RMBCA

§2.01] In most states, incorporators may be either natural persons or artificial entities, such as a corporation.

2. Contents of Articles

The articles are required to set out certain basic information about the corporation and may contain any other provision that the incorporators deem appropriate.

a. Mandatory Provisions

The articles must set out:

(i) The *name of the corporation,* which must include the word "corporation," "incorporated," "company," "limited," or the like (or an abbreviation of such words) and generally may not be similar to the name of another business entity qualified to do business in the state, unless the other business consents;

(ii) The *number of shares* the corporation is authorized to issue;

(iii) The street address of the corporation's *initial registered office* and the *name of the corporation's initial registered agent* at that office upon whom legal process may be served (the office must be within the state of incorporation, and the agent must be a resident of the state); and

(iv) The *name and address of each incorporator.*

[RMBCA §2.02(a)]

b. Optional Provisions

The articles may set forth any other provision not inconsistent with law regarding managing the business and regulating the affairs of the corporation. However, it should be noted that the RMBCA includes a number of features that a corporation need not adopt, but if they are adopted they must be provided for in the articles. For example, a corporation may choose to limit directors' liability for damages in certain circumstances, but if a corporation wants to so limit liability, it may do so only by including the limitation in the articles. A number of these conditionally mandatory provisions will be discussed later in this outline.

1) Business Purposes

Traditionally, the articles had to include a statement of the business purposes of the corporation, and the corporation was limited to activities pursuing the stated purposes. Over time, statutes became more lenient and allowed a broad purpose statement, such as "to conduct any lawful business." The RMBCA has gone even further and *presumes* that a corporation is formed for *any lawful business* unless the articles provide a more restricted business purpose.

a) Ultra Vires Acts

Generally, a corporation is allowed to undertake any action necessary or convenient to carry out its business or affairs. If a corporation includes a narrow purpose statement in its articles of incorporation, it may *not* undertake activities unrelated to achieving the stated business purpose (*e.g.,* if the articles state that the corporation's purpose is to operate restaurants, the corporation may not undertake to run a mink farm). If a corporation undertakes activities beyond the scope of its stated purpose, it is said to be acting "ultra vires."

(1) Effect

At common law, if a corporation acted ultra vires, the action was void; no one could enforce the action. Modern laws and the RMBCA have changed this dramatically. Typically, an ultra vires act is enforceable, and the ultra vires nature of an act may be raised in only three circumstances:

(i) A *shareholder* may sue the corporation to enjoin a proposed ultra vires act;

(ii) The *corporation* may sue an officer or director for damages arising from the commission of an ultra vires act authorized by the officer or director; and

(iii) The *state* may bring an action against the corporation to have it dissolved for committing an ultra vires act.

[RMBCA §3.04(b)] Note that if an officer or director is found liable for committing an ultra vires act, the officer or director may be held ***personally*** liable for damages. Note also that an ultra vires act will be enjoined only if it is equitable to do so. This generally means that an act involving an innocent third party (*i.e.*, one who did not know that the action was ultra vires) will not be enjoined.

Example: Mary Ann and Ginger incorporate a business called Castaway Foods, Inc. ("CF"). CF's articles include a purpose clause stating that the corporation was formed for the purpose of baking and selling coconut cream pies. The business is successful, and a few years later, in an attempt to expand business, Mary Ann enters into a contract with "Skipper" Jonas Grumby to purchase his tour boat. When Mary Ann tells Ginger about the deal, Ginger is furious and brings an action to enjoin the purchase. The court will grant the injunction only if Skipper knew that the transaction was beyond CF's purpose clause.

(2) Charitable Donations

At one time, charitable donations were thought to be outside the scope of any business purpose, but most states and the RMBCA now allow corporations to make charitable donations. [RMBCA §3.02(13)]

(3) Loans

Formerly, some courts held that corporations did not have the power to make loans to employees, officers, or directors. Today, most states and the RMBCA allow such loans. [RMBCA §3.02(11)]

2) Initial Directors
The articles may provide the names and addresses of the persons who will serve as the corporation's initial directors until new directors are elected.

3. Corporate Existence Begins on Filing by the State
The articles must be submitted to the state (in most states, to the secretary of state or the corporation commission) along with any required filing fees. If the state finds that the articles comply with the requirements of law and that all required fees have been paid, it will file the articles. [RMBCA §2.03] This filing of the articles by the state is conclusive proof of the beginning of the corporate existence.

4. Additional Procedures to Make De Jure Corporation Operative
After the articles are filed, the initial directors will hold an organizational meeting to adopt bylaws, elect officers, and transact other business. If the articles do not name the initial directors, the incorporators call the organizational meeting.

a. Bylaws
Bylaws may contain any provision for managing the corporation that is not inconsistent with law or the articles of incorporation. [RMBCA §2.06] Bylaws are adopted by the directors, but can usually be modified or repealed by *either* the directors *or* the shareholders. However, the articles of incorporation may reserve this power exclusively to the shareholders. Even without such a reservation, the shareholders may provide that a particular bylaw adopted or amended by them may not be repealed or amended by the directors. [RMBCA §10.20]

1) Compare—Articles
As will be discussed at IX.B., *infra*, amendment of the articles usually requires a vote of *both* the directors *and* the shareholders. Thus it is less difficult to change a corporate rule contained in the bylaws than it is to change a rule contained in the articles. This is an important planning tool. If future flexibility is desired with regard to a particular aspect of corporate management, the aspect should be addressed in the bylaws rather than the articles.

D. RECOGNITION OF CORPORATENESS WHEN CORPORATION IS DEFECTIVE
As discussed above, one of the main reasons to incorporate is to avoid personal liability for obligations of a business enterprise. This veil of protection generally is available when a de jure corporation is formed (*i.e.*, when all the steps required by statute for incorporation have been followed). The veil of protection may also be available in some circumstances even when all of the steps necessary under the incorporation statute have not been followed—under the de facto corporation or corporation by estoppel doctrines.

1. De Facto Corporation
A de facto corporation has all the rights and powers of a de jure corporation at common law, but it remains subject to direct attack in a *quo warranto* proceeding by the state.

a. **Common Law Requirements**

Traditionally, the requirements for establishing a de facto corporation are:

1) **Statute for Valid Incorporation Available**

There must be a corporate law under which the organization could have been legally incorporated, such as the RMBCA.

2) **Colorable Compliance and Good Faith**

There must be colorable compliance with the incorporation laws. "Colorable" compliance means a *good faith attempt to comply* with the state law.

3) **Exercise of Corporate Privileges**

Finally, the corporation must act like a corporation, *i.e.,* conduct the business in its corporate name and exercise corporate privileges.

b. **Limitation on De Facto Doctrine**

Under prior law, the de facto doctrine was thought to be eliminated, but the RMBCA seems to recognize the doctrine in some circumstances. The Act provides that persons who purport to act as or on behalf of a corporation *knowing* that there was no incorporation are liable for all liabilities created in so acting. [RMBCA §2.04] It follows under the common law maxim *expressio unius est exclusio alterius* (expression of one thing is the exclusion of another), that persons who do not know that there was no incorporation will not be liable (*i.e.*, the de facto corporation doctrine probably is available for such persons).

Examples: 1) Andrea and Bart agree to form AbbeyCorp. They properly draw up the necessary papers and Bart tells Andrea that he will file them the next day. Bart forgets to file the papers and forgets to tell Andrea of his failure. The following week, Andrea enters into a contract with a supplier on behalf of AbbeyCorp. Andrea probably can avoid personal liability on the contract under the de facto corporation doctrine.

2) Same facts as above, but the day after Andrea and Bart draw up the articles, Bart mails them to the secretary of state, and a few days after Andrea entered into the contract with the supplier, Andrea and Bart receive a letter from the secretary of state indicating that the articles were not filed because they were missing the incorporators' signatures. Andrea probably can avoid personal liability on the contract under the de facto corporation doctrine.

2. **Corporation by Estoppel**

A business might also be treated as a corporation despite the lack of de jure status under the corporation by estoppel doctrine. Under the doctrine, persons who treat an entity as a corporation will be estopped from later claiming that the entity was not a corporation. The doctrine can be applied either to an outsider seeking to avoid liability on a contract with the purported corporation, or to a purported corporation seeking to avoid liability on a contract with an outsider.

Examples: 1) Suppose X, an outsider, deals with the entity as though it were a valid corporation. Upon discovering a defect in formation, X seeks to hold the shareholders personally liable. A shareholder without prior knowledge of the defect may successfully assert that X is estopped to deny the corporation's existence, since X always treated the corporation as though it were properly formed.

2) Z, an improperly formed corporation, contracts to buy supplies from W. If Z tries to avoid the contract on the basis of its formation defects so that the "shareholders" can purchase goods elsewhere, Z would be treated as a corporation by estoppel.

3. Application of De Facto and Estoppel Doctrines
When an organization is considered to be a de facto corporation, it is treated as if it were de jure, except in a direct attack by the state. That is, its shareholders enjoy limited liability and it has perpetual life, ability to buy and sell property, etc. Estoppel, on the other hand, is applied on a case-by-case basis between two parties to equitably resolve a dispute.

a. Contracts
In contract cases, both doctrines are easily applied. When the parties have previously dealt on a corporate basis, or have assumed there to be a valid corporation, corporate status is generally upheld.

b. Torts
The de facto doctrine has been applied in tort cases [*see* Kardo Co. v. Adams, 231 F. 950 (6th Cir. 1916)], but normally there is little room for an estoppel argument when a tort claim is involved, because recognition of corporateness has no relevance to the commission of the tort (*i.e.,* the plaintiff did not allow herself to be injured in reliance on the fact that the defendant was acting as a corporation). Thus, parties with tort claims are generally free to sue the shareholders of an improperly formed corporation.

c. Liability of Associates
Generally, when the court finds no corporate status, the associates will be held liable as partners. However, courts are prone to hold "*active*" associates (those participating in the particular transaction involved) personally liable, and absolve inactive associates from personal liability. The RMBCA imposes *joint and several liability* for all liabilities created by persons who purport to act as or on behalf of a corporation *with knowledge that no corporation exists*. [RMBCA §2.04]

4. Limitation of Doctrines
Because the incorporation process is very simple, a number of states refuse to recognize either or both the de facto corporation doctrine and/or the doctrine of incorporation by estoppel.

E. DISREGARD OF CORPORATE ENTITY (PIERCING THE CORPORATE VEIL)
In some circumstances, even though a corporation has been validly formed, the courts will hold the shareholders, officers, or directors *personally liable* for corporate obligations because the corporation is abusing the legislative privilege of conducting business in the corporate form. This is frequently called "piercing the corporate veil." This doctrine counterbalances the de facto corporation and corporation by estoppel doctrines, for here a *valid corporate existence is ignored* in equity to serve the ends of justice.

1. Elements Justifying Piercing the Corporate Veil

As a general rule, a de jure corporation will be treated as a legal entity until sufficient reason to the contrary appears. Each case is different, but there are three recurring situations in which the veil is often pierced: (i) when corporate formalities are ignored; (ii) when the corporation is inadequately capitalized at the outset; and (iii) to prevent fraud.

a. Alter Ego (Ignoring Corporate Formalities)

If a corporation is the "alter ego," "agent," or "instrumentality" of a sole proprietor or of another corporation, its separate identity may be disregarded.

1) Individual Shareholders

If the shareholders treat the assets of the corporation as their own, use corporate funds to pay their private debts, fail to keep separate corporate books, and fail to observe corporate formalities (such as holding meetings, issuing stock, and conducting business by resolution), courts often find that the corporate entity is a mere "alter ego" of the shareholders. However, sloppy administration alone may not be sufficient to warrant piercing the corporate veil. The operation of the corporation must result in some *basic injustice* so that equity would require that the individual shareholders respond to the damage they have caused.

Note: As will be discussed later, the RMBCA allows the shareholders to vest power to run the corporation in themselves, rather than in a board of directors. Their doing so is *not* a ground for disregarding the corporate veil, even if it results in a failure to keep corporate records. [RMBCA §7.32; *and see* V.C.3., *infra*]

2) Parent-Subsidiary Corporations

A subsidiary or affiliated corporation will not be deemed to be a separate corporate entity if the formalities of separate corporate procedures for each corporation are not observed. For example, both corporations must be held out to the public as separate entities; separate meetings of directors and officers should be held; identical or substantially overlapping directors and officers should be avoided; and corporate policies should be significantly different.

3) Affiliated Corporations

If one person owns most or all of the stock in several corporations, a question may arise as to whether one of the corporations, although not formally related to the other, should be held responsible for the other's liabilities. Dominating stock ownership alone is not enough in such a case, unless the majority shareholder dominates finances, policies, and practices of both corporations so that both are a business conduit for the principal shareholder.

b. Inadequate Capitalization

It is generally accepted that shareholders will be personally liable for their corporation's obligations if *at incorporation* they fail to provide adequate capitalization. The shareholders must "put at the risk of the business *unencumbered capital reasonably adequate for its prospective liabilities.*" Undercapitalization cannot be proved merely by showing that the corporation is now insolvent. However, if insolvency occurs soon after incorporation, it may be a primary indicator of undercapitalization.

1) One-Person or Close Corporation
No absolute test for adequate capitalization has been formed. In any case, the corporation should have enough capital "to pay debts when they become due." The scope of the contemplated operations of the corporation, and the potential liability foreseeable from the operations, are factors to consider.

2) Parent-Subsidiary Corporations
A parent corporation's inadequate capitalization of a subsidiary corporation may constitute constructive fraud on all persons who deal with that subsidiary. One additional test should be applied in the parent-subsidiary situation: whether the subsidiary may reasonably expect to achieve independent financial stability from its operation.

c. Avoidance of Existing Obligations, Fraud, or Evasion of Statutory Provisions
The corporate entity will be disregarded any time it is necessary to prevent fraud or to prevent an individual shareholder from using the corporate entity to avoid his *existing* personal obligations.

1) Avoiding Liability
The mere fact that an individual chooses to adopt the corporate form of business to avoid personal liability is not, of itself, a reason to pierce the corporate veil.

2) Fraud
The corporate veil will be pierced whenever the avoidance of personal liability through the formation of a corporation operates as a fraud on creditors or other outsiders.
Example: If A is bound by a covenant not to compete with B, he cannot avoid the covenant by forming a corporation and having it compete with B.

2. Who Is Liable?
When the corporate entity is ignored and the shield of limited liability is pierced, the persons composing the corporate entity may be held personally liable.

a. Active-Inactive Tests
Normally, only the persons who were active in the management or operation of the business will be held personally liable. In other words, passive investors who acted in good faith will not be held liable for corporate obligations.

b. Theories of Liability

1) Joint and Several
When shareholders are held liable, they will be held liable for the entire amount of the claim (even if it exceeds the amount that would have been considered "adequate capitalization"). Liability for obligations of the corporation is extended to the shareholders as joint and several liability.

2) Property Cases
If a corporation has conveyed its assets to a shareholder in fraud of creditors, upon

piercing the corporate veil the assets may be reached on principles of fraudulent conveyance.

3. Types of Liability

a. Tort

A tort victim is often a successful plaintiff under the theory of piercing the corporate veil, since he usually has not been involved with the corporation in a transactional sense, and should not be forced to sue an insolvent corporate shell for his damages.

b. Contract

Courts are reluctant to pierce the corporate veil in contract cases, since the contracting party has an opportunity to investigate the financial condition of the corporation and, in the absence of misrepresentation or fraud, has a less equitable claim for relief. When the creditor deals at arm's length with the corporation, the court will most likely effect the reasonable expectation of the parties and force the creditor to look only to the corporation for satisfaction of the contract.

c. Bankruptcy and Subordination of Claims

When the corporation is insolvent and some of the shareholders have claims as "creditors," the shareholders' claims may be subordinated to those of the other creditors *if equity so requires* (*e.g.,* because of fraud). This is an application of "piercing the corporate veil" by refusing to recognize the shareholders as creditors of a separate legal entity—the corporation.

In the subordination situation, called the "Deep Rock" doctrine from the case that first applied it, a court has discretion to subordinate the shareholder's claim to any class of creditors, including subordinating the claim even as to unsecured creditors.

4. Who May "Pierce"?

a. Creditors

The creditors of a corporation are the most likely persons to pierce the corporate veil, and the cases involving disregard of corporateness primarily involve creditors.

b. Shareholders

Generally, those who choose to conduct business in the corporate form may not disregard the corporate entity at their will to serve their own purposes. Courts virtually never pierce the corporate veil at the request of the shareholder.

III. CAPITAL STRUCTURE

A. TYPES OF CORPORATE SECURITIES

Corporate capital comes from the issuance of many types of "securities." The word "security" is used generically to describe many obligations, including equity obligations (*e.g.,* shares of stock) and debt obligations (*e.g.,* bonds).

1. **Debt Securities**
    A debt security represents a creditor-debtor relationship with the corporation, whereby the corporation has borrowed funds from an "outside creditor" and promises to repay the creditor. A debt security holder has *no ownership interest* in the corporation.

2. **Equity Securities**
    An equity security is an instrument representing an investment in the corporation whereby its holder becomes a part *owner of the business*. Equity securities are shares of the corporation, and the investor is called a shareholder.

B. DEBT SECURITIES

A debt obligation usually has a stated maturity date and a provision for interest. Debt obligations may be secured (a "mortgage bond") or unsecured (a "debenture"), and may be payable either to the holder of the bond (a "coupon" or "bearer" bond) or to the owner registered in the corporation's records (a "registered bond"). A debt obligation may also have special features; *e.g.*, it may provide that it is convertible into equity securities at the option of the holder, or it might provide that the corporation may redeem the obligation at a specified price before maturity of the obligation.

C. EQUITY SECURITIES (SHARES)

1. **Terminology**
    The shares that are described in a corporation's articles are called the *"authorized shares."* The corporation may not sell more shares than are authorized. Shares that have been sold to investors are *"issued and outstanding."* Shares that are reacquired by the corporation are no longer issued and outstanding, and so revert to being "authorized shares" (formerly reacquired shares became "treasury shares"). [*See* RMBCA §6.03] Shares may be "certificated" (*i.e.*, represented by share certificates) or "uncertificated" (*i.e.*, not represented by certificates, but described in a written statement of information). [RMBCA §§6.25, 6.26]

2. **Classification of Shares**
    As stated above, equity securities represent an ownership interest in the corporation. A corporation may choose to issue only one type of shares, giving each shareholder an equal ownership right (in which case the shares are generally called *"common shares"*), or it may divide shares into *classes*, or *series within a class*, having varying rights, as long as one or more classes together have unlimited voting rights and one or more classes together have a right to receive the corporation's net assets on dissolution. [RMBCA §6.01]

    a. **Classes and Series Must Be Described in Articles**
        If shares are to be divided into classes, the articles must (i) prescribe the number of shares of each class, (ii) prescribe a distinguishing designation for each class (*e.g.*, "Class A preferred," "Class B preferred," etc.), and (iii) either describe the rights, preferences, and limitations of each class or provide that the rights, preferences, and limitations of any class or series within a class shall be determined by the board of directors prior to issuance. [RMBCA §§6.01, 6.02]

        1) **Authorized Rights, Preferences, and Limitations**
            The RMBCA specifies the types of rights, preferences, and limitations that may be used to vary classes and series. The articles may authorize shares that:

> (i) Have special, conditional, or limited *voting rights*, or no right to vote;
>
> (ii) Can be *redeemed or converted* for cash, indebtedness, securities, or other property (the redemption or conversion can take place at the option of the corporation or the shareholder, or on the occurrence of a designated event);
>
> (iii) Entitle the holders to *distributions, including dividends*; or
>
> (iv) Have *preference over any other class of shares with respect to distributions*, including on dissolution of the corporation.
>
> [RMBCA §6.01(c)]

3. Fractional Shares

A corporation may: (i) issue certificates representing fractions of a share or pay in money the fair value of fractions of a share as determined by the board; (ii) arrange for the disposition of fractional shares by those entitled to the fractional shares; or (iii) issue scrip that entitles the holder to a full share on surrendering enough scrip to equal a full share. [RMBCA §6.04(a)]

a. Rights of Holders of Fractional Shares and Scrip

A certificate representing fractions of a share entitles the holder to exercise the rights of a shareholder. In contrast, the holder of scrip may not exercise any rights of a shareholder unless otherwise provided in the scrip. [RMBCA §6.04(c)]

4. Subscription Agreements

A subscription is an offer to purchase shares from a corporation. Subscriptions can be made to existing corporations or to corporations to be formed.

a. Acceptance and Revocation

A subscription does not become a contract until it is accepted by the corporation. Nevertheless, under the RMBCA, a *preincorporation* subscription is irrevocable by the subscriber for *six months* from the date of the subscription unless otherwise provided in the terms of the subscription or unless all subscribers consent to revocation. [RMBCA §6.20(a)]

b. Payment

Unless otherwise provided in the subscription agreement, subscriptions for shares are payable on demand by the board of directors.

1) Discrimination Not Allowed

The board of directors may not discriminate among subscribers in calling for payment of subscriptions. Any demand for payment must be uniform as to all shares of the same class or as to all shares of the same series. [RMBCA §6.20(b)]

2) Penalties for Failure to Pay

If a subscriber fails to pay under a subscription agreement, the corporation may collect the amount owed as it would any other debt. Alternatively, the subscription agreement may set forth other penalties for failure to pay. However, the corporation may not effect a rescission or forfeiture unless the subscriber fails to cure the default within 20 days after the corporation sends *written notice* of default to the subscriber. Note that rescission is the corporation's (not the subscriber's) option. A subscriber may not escape her liability by voluntarily rescinding. Also, the board of directors may release, settle, or compromise any subscription or dispute arising from a subscription, unless otherwise provided in the subscription agreement. [RMBCA §6.20(d)]

5. Consideration for Shares

The RMBCA prescribes rules regarding the types and amount of consideration that may be received in exchange for stock issued by the corporation.

a. Forms of Consideration

Traditionally, states limited the type of consideration that could be received by a corporation issuing stock (stock could be issued only in exchange for cash, property, or services already rendered). The RMBCA has virtually abandoned such limitations and allows stock to be issued in exchange for *any tangible or intangible property or benefit to the corporation.* [RMBCA §6.21(b)] However, a number of states have not gone as far as the RMBCA and still prohibit corporations from issuing stock in exchange for promissory notes or future services. The best approach for the exam is to recite the RMBCA rule but then mention the possible limitation.

b. Amount of Consideration

1) Traditional Par Value Approach

Traditionally, the articles of incorporation would indicate whether the corporation's shares were to be issued with a stated par value or with no par value. Stock with a par value could not be issued by the corporation for less than the par value (although this rule did not apply to stock repurchased by the corporation and held as treasury shares). Furthermore, the money received from the issuance of par value stock had to go into a special account—called stated capital. The stated capital account could not be reduced below the aggregate par value of all the stock that had been issued. The idea was to guaranty creditors that the corporation would be capitalized at a certain level.

2) RMBCA Approach

The RMBCA has totally eliminated the concept of par value and allows corporate directors to issue stock for whatever consideration they deem adequate. The RMBCA also provides that the board of directors' *good faith determination* as to the adequacy of the consideration received is *conclusive* as to whether the stock exchanged for the consideration is validly issued, fully paid, and nonassessable. [RMBCA §6.21]

Example: Roger and Tony form Genie Carpets, Inc. ("Genie") to manufacture faux Persian rugs. Genie's articles authorize the issuance of 1,000 shares of stock. The corporation issued its first 500 shares at a price of $1,000 each. Bellows approached Roger and Tony and offered to sell to the corporation his carpet manufacturing facility in exchange for 500 shares of Genie stock. Although a six-month-old appraisal found the property to be worth $400,000, other factors made Roger and Tony believe the property to be worth more, so they agreed to the transaction. One of Genie's shareholders thinks the facility was not sufficient consideration and brings suit to have the issuance to Bellows declared invalid. The suit will fail. The board's good faith determination of value is conclusive as to whether the stock exchanged for the consideration is validly issued, fully paid, and nonassessable.

a) Watered Stock

Historically, if par value stock was issued for less than its par value, the original purchaser and the directors who authorized the sale would be liable for the difference (known as "water") between the par value and the amount received. Since the RMBCA provides that stock is validly issued, fully paid, and nonassessable when the corporation receives the consideration for which the board authorized the issuance, there can be no watered stock problem under the RMBCA.

b) Exam Approach

It should be noted that the concept of par value is not completely dead. Although most states that have adopted the RMBCA have eliminated the traditional par value accounting classifications and restrictions, a number retained the concept of par value with respect to the minimum price at which stock can be issued. Thus, the best approach for exam purposes is to recite the RMBCA rule, but note that a court might hold that directors may not sell stock for less than any par value stated in the articles and are personally liable for damages caused to the corporation if they issue stock for less than the stated par value.

c. Unpaid Stock

A shareholder is liable to pay the corporation the full consideration for which her shares were authorized to be issued. [RMBCA §6.22] If the shareholder fails to pay the full consideration, the shares are referred to as "unpaid stock." If the corporation is insolvent, a trustee in bankruptcy can enforce the corporation's claim for unpaid stock.

6. Federal Law

Certain aspects regarding the issuance of corporate securities are governed by the federal Securities Act of 1933 ("SA"). Although the Act appears to be outside the scope of most bar exams, a brief discussion of it follows.

a. Registration and Prospectus Requirements

In general, the 1933 Act requires issuers of stock to register the issuance with the Securities Exchange Commission ("SEC"). The registration statement must include all information that a reasonable investor would consider important in deciding whether to invest (e.g., balance sheet, profit and loss statement, director compensation, plans for expansion, etc.). The Act also requires the issuer to provide each investor with a prospectus summarizing the information in the registration statement.

b. Exemptions

Registration is expensive and time consuming, but there are a number of exemptions from the registration requirement. For example, securities issued by banks, governments, or charitable organizations are generally exempt. Similarly, issuances of securities offered and sold only to persons residing in a single state are exempt. Issuances of less than $1 million are exempt, as are issuances made to sophisticated investors and no more than 35 "unaccredited" (*i.e.,* inexperienced) investors. [*See* SA §§3, 4(2); SA Rules 504, 505, 506]

c. Civil Liability
Under the Act, *anyone* who signs a registration statement (including lawyers, accountants, and corporate officers) is liable for any damages caused by a false statement in the registration statement unless the person can prove that he reasonably believed the statement to be true after making a *reasonable investigation* or that the plaintiff knew of the false statement. [SA §11] Somewhat similar liability attaches when a security is sold without registering or providing a prospectus as required. [SA §12]

PART TWO—INTRACORPORATE PARTIES

IV. PROMOTERS

A. PROMOTERS PROCURE CAPITAL AND OTHER COMMITMENTS
The first step in forming a corporation is the procurement of commitments for capital and other instrumentalities that will be used by the corporation after formation. This is done by promoters. Generally, promoters enter into contracts with third parties who are interested in becoming shareholders of the corporation once it is formed (*i.e.,* "stock subscriptions"). Promoters might also enter into contracts with others for goods or services to be provided to the corporation once it is formed. Usually, the promoters will go on to serve as incorporators, but this is not necessary.

B. PROMOTERS' RELATIONSHIP WITH EACH OTHER
Absent an agreement indicating a contrary relationship, promoters are considered to be joint venturers, and they occupy a *fiduciary relationship to each other*. As fiduciaries, promoters are prohibited from secretly pursuing personal gain at the expense of their fellow promoters or the corporation to be formed.

Example: Arnie and Barb have agreed to form a corporation to engage in a real estate business. Arnie tells Barb that he can acquire a piece of land suitable for subdividing for $100,000. Arnie acquires the land for $70,000 and pockets the difference. Arnie is liable to Barb for breach of a fiduciary duty, since the promotion began when Arnie and Barb agreed to form the corporation.

C. PROMOTERS' RELATIONSHIP WITH CORPORATION
Upon incorporation, the promoters owe fiduciary duties to the corporation and to those persons investing in it. The promoters' duty in this respect is one of fair disclosure and good faith. Promoters are not permitted to retain a secret profit resulting from transactions with, or on behalf of, the corporation. Promoters' liabilities will arise under one of three theories: (i) breach of fiduciary duty; (ii) fraud or misrepresentation; or (iii) obtaining unpaid stock.

1. Breach of Fiduciary Duty Arising from Sale to Corporation
A promoter who profits on the sale of property to the corporation may be liable to the

corporation for the profit, or may be forced to rescind the sale, unless the promoter has disclosed all of the material facts of the transaction.

a. Independent Board of Directors
If the transaction is disclosed to an independent board of directors (not under the control of the promoter) and approved, there is no breach of a fiduciary duty.

b. Disclosure to Subscribers or Shareholders
If the board of directors is not completely independent, the promoter's transaction must be approved by the shareholders or subscribers to the stock of the corporation. The promoter is insulated from a breach of fiduciary duty if the subscribers knew of the transaction at the time they subscribed or, after full disclosure, unanimously ratified the transaction. Disclosure must be to all shareholders, not merely to the controlling shareholders. In addition, disclosure must include those *persons contemplated as part of the initial financing scheme*. [Old Dominion Copper Mining & Smelting Co. v. Bigelow, 203 Mass. 159 (1909)]

Example: Alex, Becky, and Chloe decide to form a corporation with 200,000 shares of authorized common stock. They plan to sell 50,000 shares to the public. Prior to formation they obtain subscriptions to 20,000 shares. Alex, Becky, and Chloe contribute property in exchange for 150,000 shares and they "profit" on the transaction. They obtain approval of the transaction from the subscribers for the 20,000 shares. The remaining 30,000 shares are sold within three weeks after formation of the corporation, but the promoters do not disclose their profit to the new shareholders. Under the *Bigelow* rule, the promoters are liable to the corporation because the transaction was not approved by all shareholders who were contemplated as part of the original promotion plan.

c. Promoters' Purchase of All the Stock
If the promoters purchase all the stock of the corporation themselves, with no intention to resell the stock to outsiders, but subsequently do sell their individual shares to outsiders, they *cannot be liable* for breach of a fiduciary duty with respect to their promoter transactions, since at the time they purchased the stock there was no one from whom the profit was kept secret.

2. Fraud
Promoters may always be held liable if plaintiffs can show that they were defrauded by the promoters' fraudulent misrepresentations or fraudulent failure to disclose all material facts. The basis of this liability can be either common law fraud or the state and federal securities acts.

3. Federal Securities Law
The failure to disclose material facts or any material misrepresentations of a fact in connection with the purchase or sale of securities may violate rule 10b-5 of the Securities Exchange Act. (*See* XIII.A., *infra.*)

D. PROMOTERS' RELATIONSHIP WITH THIRD PARTIES—PREINCORPORATION AGREEMENTS

1. Promoter's Liability

The RMBCA provides that if a person acts on behalf of a corporation, knowing that there has been no incorporation, the person is jointly and severally liable for any obligations incurred. [RMBCA §2.04] Thus, as a general rule, if a promoter enters into an agreement with a third party to benefit a planned, but as of yet, unformed corporation, the promoter is personally liable on the agreement.

Example: Fred and Barney agree to pool their money to form a corporation ("Dyno, Inc.") to run a rock quarry. Fred approaches Mr. Slate, explains his plans, and enters into a contract to purchase a small quarry from Slate for $100,000—$50,000 to be paid at closing and an additional $50,000 to be paid six months later. The contract provides that the closing will not be held for 45 days so that Fred and Barney will have time to incorporate Dyno, Inc. before the closing. Fred signs the contract, "Fred, on behalf of Dyno Inc." Subsequently, Fred and Barney have a falling out, and Dyno, Inc. is never formed. Fred probably will be found to be personally liable on the contract with Mr. Slate since he entered the contract knowing that Dyno, Inc. had not yet been formed.

a. Liability Continues After Formation Absent Novation

A promoter's liability on preincorporation agreements continues after the corporation is formed, even if the corporation adopts the contract and benefits from it. The promoter's liability can be *extinguished only if there is a novation*—an agreement among the parties releasing the promoter and substituting the corporation. To clearly establish a novation, the third party should expressly release the promoter after the corporation has adopted the contract, although some cases have implied a novation from the conduct of the third party and the corporation.

Example: Same facts as in the example in 1., above, but Fred and Barney do not have a falling out, Dyno, Inc. is formed, and a few days later the parties close on the quarry. At the closing, title to the quarry is transferred to Dyno, Inc. Despite Dyno, Inc.'s adoption of the purchase contract, Fred remains personally liable for the remainder of the purchase price unless the parties agreed to a novation at the closing.

b. Exception—Agreement Expressly Relieves Promoter of Liability

If the agreement between the parties expressly indicates that the promoter is not to be bound, there is no contract. Such an arrangement may be construed as a revocable offer to the proposed corporation. The promoter has no rights or liabilities under such an arrangement.

c. Promoter Indemnification

When a promoter is liable on a preincorporation contract and the corporation thereafter adopts the contract but no novation is agreed upon, the promoter may have the right of indemnification from the corporation if he is subsequently held liable on the contract.

2. Corporation's Liability

a. General Rule—No Liability Prior to Incorporation

Since the corporate entity does not exist prior to incorporation, it is not bound on contracts entered into by the promoter in the corporate name. A promoter cannot act as an agent of the corporation prior to incorporation, since an agent cannot bind a nonexistent principal.

b. Adoption

The corporation may become bound on promoter contracts by adopting them. The effect of an adoption is to make the corporation a party to the contract at the time it adopts, although adoption of the contract by the corporation does not of itself relieve the promoter of his liability. The liability of the corporation runs from the date of adoption, not from the making of the original contract. Adoption may be express (*e.g.*, by board of directors' resolution) or implied (*e.g.*, by acquiescence or conduct normally constituting estoppel).

V. SHAREHOLDERS

A. SHAREHOLDER CONTROL OVER MANAGEMENT

1. Direct Control

At common law, shareholders have no right to directly control the day-to-day management of their corporation. Instead, the right to manage is vested in the board of directors, who usually delegate their day-to-day management duties to officers. This is still the general rule under the RMBCA. However, the RMBCA also allows a departure from the general rule: Shareholders may enter into agreements concerning management of the corporation, including an agreement to vest the powers that the board would ordinarily have in one or more shareholders. The requirements for such agreements are discussed at C.3., *infra*.

2. Indirect Control

Even absent a shareholder agreement vesting direct control of the corporation in shareholders, shareholders have indirect control over their corporation through their power to elect directors, amend the bylaws, and approve fundamental changes to the corporation.

a. Shareholders Elect and May Remove Directors

Shareholders have the right to elect directors. [RMBCA §8.03(d)] The shareholders may also remove a director, *with or without cause*, at any time. [RMBCA §8.08]

b. Shareholders May Modify Bylaws

As discussed above (II.C.4.a., *supra*), shareholders have the power to adopt, amend, or repeal bylaws.

c. Shareholders Must Approve Fundamental Corporate Changes

Changes to the fundamental structure of a corporation cannot be made without the approval of the shareholders. Shareholder approval is required in cases of merger, sale of corporate assets outside the ordinary course of business, dissolution, and for other extraordinary corporate matters. Similarly, amendments to the articles of incorporation may require shareholder approval. (*See* IX., *infra*.)

B. SHAREHOLDERS' MEETINGS AND VOTING POWER

1. **Convening Meetings**

   a. **Annual Meetings**
      Corporations must hold annual meetings, the primary purpose of which is the election of directors. [RMBCA §7.01] If a meeting is not held within the earlier of six months after the end of the corporation's fiscal year or 15 months after the last annual meeting, the court in the county where the corporation's principal office is located may order an annual meeting to be held on the application of any shareholder entitled to participate in an annual meeting. [RMBCA §7.03(a)]

   b. **Special Meeting**
      The board of directors, or those persons authorized to do so by the articles or bylaws, may call special meetings during the year to conduct business that requires shareholder approval. A special meeting may also be called by the holders of at least 10% of all the votes entitled to be cast at the meeting. [RMBCA §7.02]

2. **Place of the Meeting**
   Shareholders meetings may be held *anywhere* within or outside the state, at the place stated in or fixed in accordance with the bylaws. If no place is so stated or fixed, annual meetings are held at the corporation's principal office. [RMBCA §§7.01(b), 7.02(c)]

3. **Notice**
   Generally, written notice of the shareholders' meetings—special or annual—must be sent to the shareholders entitled to vote at the meeting. [RMBCA §7.05]

   a. **Time Within Which Notice Must Be Sent**
      Under the RMBCA, the notice must be delivered not less than 10 days or more than 60 days before the meeting. [RMBCA §7.05(a)]

   b. **Contents of Notice**
      The notice must state the place, day, and hour of the meeting. For special meetings, the purpose(s) for which the meeting is called must also be stated in the notice. [RMBCA §7.05(a)]

   c. **Notice May Be Waived**
      Action taken at a meeting can be set aside if notice was improper. However, a shareholder will be held to have waived any defects in notice if the shareholder (i) waives notice in a *signed writing* either before or after the meeting or (ii) *attends the meeting* and does not object to notice at the beginning of the meeting (or, if the defect is that the notice did not identify a special purpose, when the purpose is first brought up). [RMBCA §7.06]

4. **Eligibility to Vote**

   a. **Record Date**
      A corporation's bylaws may fix, or provide the manner of fixing, a *record date* to determine which shareholders are entitled to notice of a meeting, to vote, or to take any other action. If the bylaws do not so provide, the board may specify a date as the record

date. The record date may not be more than **70 days** before the meeting or action requiring a determination of shareholders. [RMBCA §7.07]

1) If Record Date Not Set
If there is no fixed record date, the record date will be the day before the first notice of the meeting is delivered to the shareholders. [RMBCA §7.05(d)]

b. Shareholders' List for Meeting
After a record date for a meeting has been fixed, the corporation must prepare an alphabetical list of all shareholders entitled to notice of a shareholders' meeting. The list must show each shareholder's address and the number of shares held by each shareholder. [RMBCA §7.20(a)]

1) List Available for Inspection
Beginning two business days after notice of the meeting for which the list was prepared is given, and continuing through the meeting, the shareholders' list must be made available for inspection by any shareholder or her agent at the corporation's principal office or at another place identified in the notice. The shareholder may, by written demand, inspect and copy the list during regular business hours. [RMBCA §7.20(b)]

a) Refusal to Allow Inspection
If the corporation refuses to allow inspection of the list, the court in the county where the corporation's principal office (or if none, its registered office) is located may, on application by the shareholder, order the inspection or copying at the corporation's expense. The court may postpone the meeting for which the list was prepared until completion of the inspection or copying, but a refusal or failure to prepare or make available the shareholders' list otherwise does **not** affect the validity of actions taken at the meeting. [RMBCA §7.20(d), (e)]

c. Voting Entitlement of Shares
Unless otherwise provided in the articles, each outstanding share, regardless of class, is entitled to one vote on a matter to be voted on at a shareholders' meeting. Shares held by one corporation in a second corporation generally may be voted like any other outstanding shares, unless the second corporation owns a majority of shares entitled to vote for directors of the first corporation (*e.g.*, a subsidiary holding shares of its parent usually cannot vote those shares). [RMBCA §7.21(a), (b)] Note that shares held by the corporation in a fiduciary capacity (*e.g.*, under an employee stock ownership plan) can be voted by the corporation. [RMBCA §7.21(c)]

d. Corporation's Acceptance of Votes
If the name signed on a vote, consent, waiver, or proxy appointment corresponds to that of a shareholder, the corporation is entitled to accept the vote, consent, etc., if the corporation is acting in good faith. The corporation may also accept signatures from representatives (*e.g.,* an executor, an officer of an entity that holds the shares, a guardian of the owner of the shares, etc.). However, if the corporate officer authorized to tabulate votes has a good faith, reasonable doubt about the validity of a signature or

about the signatory's authority to sign for the shareholder, the corporation may reject the vote, consent, waiver, or proxy appointment. [RMBCA §7.24]

5. Proxies

A shareholder may vote his shares either in person or by proxy executed in writing by the shareholder or his attorney-in-fact. [RMBCA §7.22]

a. Duration of Proxy

A proxy is valid for only 11 months unless it provides otherwise.

b. Revocability of Proxy

An appointment of a proxy is revocable by a shareholder unless the appointment form *conspicuously states that it is irrevocable* and the appointment is *coupled with an interest*. Appointments coupled with an interest include the appointment of any of the following:

(i) A *pledgee*;

(ii) A *person who purchased* or agreed to purchase the shares;

(iii) A *creditor* of the corporation who extended credit to the corporation under terms requiring the appointment;

(iv) An *employee* of the corporation whose employment contract requires the appointment; or

(v) A *party to a voting agreement*.

[RMBCA §7.22(d)]

1) Death or Incapacity of Shareholder

Death or incapacity of a shareholder appointing a proxy does *not* affect the right of the corporation to accept the authority of the proxy unless the corporate officer authorized to tabulate votes receives *written notice* of the death or incapacity prior to the time the proxy exercises her authority under the appointment. [RMBCA §7.22(e)]

c. Statutory Proxy Control

Proxies are subject to federal control under the Securities Exchange Act of 1934. Section 14 of the Act regulates the shareholder voting machinery for corporations subject to the registration requirements of section 12 and the reporting requirements of section 13. Generally, these rules require a proxy statement describing the matter being submitted to a vote of the security holders together with the proper form of proxy on which the holders can vote for or against each matter being submitted.

1) Basic Requirements

The rules governing proxy solicitation basically require that:

a) There must be full and fair disclosure of all *material* facts with regard to any management-submitted proposal upon which the shareholders are to vote;

b) Material misstatements, omissions, and fraud in connection with the solicitation of proxies are prohibited; and

c) Management must include certain shareholder proposals on issues other than the election of directors and allow proponents to explain their position.

2) Key Issue—Materiality

In determining whether the proxy rules have been violated, courts will focus on whether the statement of fact or omission was material. Whether a statement of fact or omission is material depends on the likelihood that a reasonable shareholder would consider it important in deciding how to vote.

3) Shareholder Proposals

The federal proxy rules generally provide that a shareholder proposal that is proper for consideration under state law must be included in the management's proxy statement along with a brief statement explaining the shareholder's reason for supporting the proposal's adoption if the proposal is submitted to the corporation in a timely fashion. To preclude exclusion from management's proxy materials, the shareholder submitting the proposal must be a beneficial owner of the security that would be entitled to vote on the proposal at a shareholders' meeting and must have continuously held, for at least one year prior to the date the proposal is submitted, the lesser of 1% or $2,000 in market value of the security. The proponent must continue to hold such securities through the date of the meeting.

Example: Making a recommendation to the board of directors that they increase the number of directors would be a proper action for shareholders; but a proposal to require an increase in the dividends would not be a proper action, since that decision is a matter entirely within the board's discretion.

6. Mechanics of Voting

a. Quorum

A quorum must attend a meeting before a vote may validly be taken. A *majority of the votes entitled to be cast* on the matter by a particular voting group (*see* below) will constitute a quorum unless the articles provide *greater* quorum requirements. Once a share is represented at a meeting, it is deemed present for quorum purposes for the remainder of the meeting; thus, a shareholder cannot prevent a vote by leaving before the vote is taken. [RMBCA §§7.25, 7.27]

1) Voting by Group

The articles may, and the RMBCA does, require approval by certain groups of shares separately under some circumstances. For example, an amendment to the articles must be approved by a share group when the share group will be significantly affected if the amendment is approved. (*See* IX.B.2.a., *infra.*)

b. Voting—In General

Generally, each outstanding share is entitled to one vote unless the articles provide otherwise. [RMBCA §7.21] (The articles may provide that a certain class or classes shall have more than one vote—weighted voting—or no vote. [RMBCA §§6.01, 6.02]) If a quorum exists, an action will be deemed approved by the shareholders (or appropriate shareholder group) if the *votes cast in favor of the action exceed the votes cast against the action*, unless the articles provide for a greater voting requirement. [RMBCA §§7.25, 7.27]

c. Director Elections

Unless the articles provide otherwise, directors are elected by a *plurality* of the votes cast at a meeting at which there is a quorum. In other words, as long as a quorum is present, the candidates receiving the most votes—even if not a majority—win.

1) Cumulative Voting Optional

Instead of the normal one share, one vote paradigm, the articles may provide for *cumulative voting* in the election of directors. [RMBCA §7.28] Cumulative voting is a device that gives minority shareholders a better chance to elect a director to the board than the shareholders would have using the ordinary voting procedure described above. In cumulative voting, each share may cast as many votes as there are board vacancies to be filled. Thus, if three directors are to be elected, each voting share is entitled to cast three votes. The votes may be cast for a single candidate, or they may be divided among the candidates in any manner that the shareholder desires.

Example: Tammy owns 300 voting shares of Circle X stock. Nine directors are to be elected at the next annual meeting. Tammy is entitled to cast 2,700 votes (300 shares x 9 vacancies). She may cast all 2,700 votes for one candidate or divide her 2,700 votes in any manner she desires.

a) Notice Required for Cumulative Voting

Even if the articles provide for cumulative voting, shares may not be cumulatively voted unless the notice for the meeting in question conspicuously states that cumulative voting is authorized or at least one shareholder in the class possessing the right to vote cumulatively notifies the corporation of her intent to vote cumulatively at least 48 hours before the meeting. [RMBCA §7.28(d)]

b) Devices to Avoid Cumulative Voting

To protect minority shareholders, cumulative voting was and still is required in a number of states. When cumulative voting was largely mandatory, a number of devices were developed to avoid its effects (*e.g.*, reducing the size of the board, staggering the election of directors, giving certain classes of shares the sole right to elect certain directors, electing directors on separate ballots, etc.). If the devices were employed for proper corporate purposes, they were upheld, but if no proper purpose was found, the devices were held to have been improperly imposed.

Example: A corporation may decide to stagger the election of directors (*see* VI.C.3.a., *infra*) in order to ensure continuity on the board, even though reducing the number of directors to be elected each year makes it more difficult for minority shareholders to elect a director.

Compare: A corporation with cumulative voting probably would be prohibited from electing directors on separate ballots, since a simple majority would then be able to elect each director, thus negating the effect of cumulative voting.

2) Classification of the Board

The articles may grant certain classes of shares the right to elect a certain director or number of directors. Only shareholders of that class may vote to fill the specified position(s). [RMBCA §8.04]

d. Class Voting on Article Amendments

Whenever an amendment to the articles of incorporation affects only one class of shares (Class A common, preferred, etc.), that class generally has the right to vote on the amendment *even if the class would not otherwise be permitted to vote* at a shareholders' meeting. Typical situations where class voting may occur include:

(i) A *change in the designation, preferences, rights* (including preemptive and dividend rights), *or aggregate number of shares of a class;*

(ii) An *exchange, reclassification, or cancellation of some of the shares* of the class or a change of the shares of the class into a different class; and

(iii) The *creation of a new class having superior rights* to the shares of this particular class.

[RMBCA §10.04] Generally, it may be said that class voting should be used if a proposed amendment has any effect—adverse or advantageous—on holders of the class.

7. Shareholders May Act Without Meeting by Unanimous Written Consent

Shareholders may take action without a meeting by the unanimous written consent of all shareholders entitled to vote on the action. [RMBCA §7.04]

C. SHAREHOLDER AGREEMENTS

Shareholders may enter into several types of agreements in an effort to protect their voting power, proportionate stock ownership, or other special interests in the corporation. Although most shareholder agreements are encountered in the close corporation (where stock is held by a few individuals and is not actively traded), most of these agreements can be used in any corporation.

1. Voting Trusts

To ensure that a group of shares will be voted a particular way in the future, one or more shareholders may create a voting trust by (i) entering into a signed agreement setting forth the trust's terms and (ii) transferring legal ownership of their shares to the trustee. The trust may contain any lawful provision not inconsistent with the trust purposes, and the trustee must vote the shares in accordance with the trust. A copy of the trust agreement and the names and addresses of the beneficial owners of the trust must be given to the corporation. The trust is not valid for more than 10 years unless it is extended by agreement of the parties. [RMBCA §7.30]

2. **Voting Agreements**
Rather than creating a trust, shareholders may enter into a written and signed agreement that provides for the manner in which they will vote their shares. Unless the voting agreement provides otherwise, it will be *specifically enforceable*. Unlike a voting trust, such an agreement need not be filed with the corporation and is not subject to any time limit. [RMBCA §7.31]

3. **Shareholder Agreements**
The shareholders may enter into an agreement among themselves regarding almost *any aspect of the exercise of corporate powers or management*. For example, an agreement may:

(i) *Eliminate* the board of directors or *restrict* the discretion or powers of the board;

(ii) *Govern the authorization or making of distributions*;

(iii) *Establish who shall be directors or officers*, as well as their terms and conditions of office, or the manner of selection or removal; or

(iv) *Transfer* to one or more shareholders or other persons the *authority to exercise the corporate powers* or to manage the business and affairs of the corporation.

[RMBCA §7.32(a)]

a. **Statutory Requirements**
To be valid, the agreement must either (i) be set forth in the *articles or bylaws*, and be approved by all persons who are shareholders at the time of the agreement or (ii) be set forth in a *written agreement signed by all persons who are shareholders* at the time of the agreement, and be filed with the corporation. Unless otherwise provided, the agreement is valid for 10 years. The agreement is subject to amendment or termination only by *all* persons who are shareholders at the time of the amendment, unless the agreement provides otherwise. [RMBCA §7.32(b)]

b. **Enforceability**
Any party to the agreement may enforce it against any other party. One who purchases shares without knowledge of the agreement is entitled to rescind the purchase. [RMBCA §7.32(c)]

c. **Termination of Agreement's Effectiveness**
The agreement ceases to be effective when shares of the corporation are listed on a national securities exchange or are regularly traded in a market maintained by a member of a national or affiliated securities association. [RMBCA §7.32(d)]

d. **Agreement Does Not Impose Personal Liability on Shareholders**
Even if the agreement treats the corporation as a partnership or results in failure to

observe corporate formalities, the agreement does not constitute a ground for imposing personal liability on any shareholder for the acts or debts of the corporation. [RMBCA §7.32(f)]

4. Restrictions on Transfer of Shares

Another way shareholders may control the destiny of their corporation is by imposing restrictions on transfers of outstanding shares. The articles, the bylaws, an agreement among shareholders, or an agreement between shareholders and the corporation may impose restrictions on the transfer of the corporation's shares for *any reasonable purpose* (*e.g.*, to preserve the corporation's eligibility for S corporation status or for a securities law exemption). [RMBCA §6.27]

a. Permissible Restrictions

The RMBCA permits restrictions that:

(i) Obligate the shareholder to *first offer* the corporation or other persons an opportunity to acquire the restricted shares;

(ii) Obligate *the corporation or other persons to acquire* the restricted shares;

(iii) Require the corporation, the holders of any class of its shares, or another person to *approve the transfer* of the restricted shares, if the requirement is not manifestly unreasonable; or

(iv) *Prohibit transfer* of the restricted shares to designated persons or classes, if the prohibition is not manifestly unreasonable.

[RMBCA §6.27(d)]

b. Enforceability

A permitted stock transfer restriction is enforceable against the holder of the stock or a transferee of the holder only if (i) the restriction's existence is *noted conspicuously on the certificate* (or is contained in the information statement, if the shares are uncertificated) or (ii) the holder or transferee *had knowledge* of the restriction. [RMBCA §6.27(b)]

5. Agreements Affecting Action by Directors

The board has the authority to exercise corporate powers and to manage the business and affairs of the corporation. However, limitations may be imposed on this authority by the articles or by a shareholders' agreement, as discussed above. [RMBCA §8.01]

D. SHAREHOLDERS' INSPECTION RIGHTS

At common law, shareholders had a qualified right to inspect corporate books and records: They could inspect upon request if they had a *proper purpose* for the inspection. Proper purposes include purposes such as waging a proxy battle, investigating possible director or management misconduct, seeking support for a shareholder initiative, etc. Improper purposes are purposes aimed primarily at personally benefiting the inspecting shareholder, such as to obtain the names and addresses of the shareholders in order to create a commercial mailing list to sell to third parties.

1. **RMBCA Approach—In General**

The RMBCA generally continues the common law approach. Under the RMBCA, a shareholder may inspect the corporation's books, papers, accounting records, shareholder records, etc. To exercise this right, the shareholder must give *five days' written notice* of his request, stating a *proper purpose* for the inspection. The shareholder need not personally conduct the inspection; he may send an attorney, accountant, or other agent. [RMBCA §16.02] Some states limit inspection to shareholders who: (i) hold at least 5% of the corporation's outstanding shares, or (ii) have held any lesser number of shares for at least six months.

   a. **Unqualified Right**

   The RMBCA also includes an exception to the general rule. It provides that any shareholder may inspect the following records *regardless of purpose*: (i) the corporation's articles and bylaws, (ii) board resolutions regarding classification of shares, (iii) minutes of shareholders' meetings from the past three years, (iv) communications sent by the corporation to shareholders over the past three years, (v) a list of the names and business addresses of the corporation's current directors and officers, and (vi) a copy of the corporation's most recent annual report.

   b. **Right May Not Be Limited**

   The right of inspection may not be abolished or limited by the articles or bylaws. [RMBCA §16.02(d)]

   c. **Inspection by Court Order**

   If a corporation does not allow a required inspection, a court may order that the inspection and copying take place. Where a court so orders, it must also order the corporation to pay the shareholder's costs incurred in obtaining the order, unless the corporation proves that its refusal to allow inspection was in good faith. [RMBCA §16.04]

E. PREEMPTIVE RIGHTS

When the corporation proposes to issue additional shares of stock, the current shareholders often want to purchase some of the new shares in order to maintain their proportional voting strength. The common law granted shareholders such a right, known as the "preemptive right." Under the RMBCA, a shareholder *does not have any preemptive rights unless* the articles of incorporation so provide. [RMBCA §6.30(a)]

1. **Waiver**

A shareholder may waive her preemptive right. A waiver evidenced by a writing is irrevocable *even if it is not supported by consideration*. [RMBCA §6.30(b)(2)]

2. **Limitations**

Even if the articles provide for preemptive rights, the rights *do not* apply to:

   (i) Shares *issued as compensation* to directors, officers, agents, or employees of the corporation;

(ii) Shares *authorized in the articles that are issued within six months* after incorporation;

(iii) Shares *issued for consideration other than money* (*i.e.,* shares issued in exchange for property or services); or

(iv) Shares *without general voting rights but having a distribution preference*.

[RMBCA §6.30(b)(3), (4)] Moreover, holders of nonpreferential voting shares have no preemptive rights in any class of preferred shares unless the preferred shares are convertible into shares without preferential rights. [RMBCA §6.30(b)(5)]

3. Sales to Outsiders

Shares subject to preemptive rights that are not acquired by shareholders can be issued to anyone else for up to one year following their offer to the shareholders, as long as they are sold for no less than the price at which they were offered to the shareholders. Sales for less than the price offered to the shareholders or after one year are subject to the shareholders' preemptive rights. [RMBCA §6.30(b)(6)]

F. SHAREHOLDER SUITS

Shareholders enjoy a dual personality. They are entitled to enforce their own claims against the corporation, officers, directors, or majority shareholders by *direct* action. Shareholders are also the guardians of the corporation's causes of action, provided no one else in the corporation will assert them. In this sense, shareholders may sue *derivatively* to enforce the corporate cause of action, as long as they meet the requirements specified by law and they have made necessary demands on the corporation or the directors to enforce the cause of action. In either capacity, direct or derivative action, the shareholder may sue for herself and for others similarly situated.

1. Direct Actions

a. Nature of Action

A breach of a fiduciary duty *owed to the shareholder* by an officer or director of a corporation is a proper subject for a shareholder's direct action against that officer or that director. However, be careful to distinguish breaches of duty owed to a shareholder from duties owed to the corporation. If the duty is owed to the corporation rather than to an individual shareholder, the cause of action is derivative rather than direct. The basic tests are: (i) who suffers the most immediate and direct damage? and (ii) to whom did the defendant's duty run?

b. Recovery

In a shareholder direct action, any recovery is for the benefit of the individual shareholder, or, if the action was a class action, for the benefit of the class.

2. Derivative Actions

a. Nature of Action

The derivative action is often described as a "representative" action, since the shareholders are enforcing the rights of another—*i.e.,* the corporation. Recovery in a derivative action generally goes to the corporation rather to the shareholder bringing the action.

b. **Standing—Ownership at Time of Wrong**
To commence or maintain a derivative proceeding, a shareholder must have been a shareholder of the corporation *at the time of the act or omission* complained of, or must have become a shareholder through *transfer by operation of law* from one who was a shareholder at that time. Also, the shareholder must fairly and adequately represent the interests of the corporation. [RMBCA §7.41]

c. **Demand Requirements**
The shareholder must make a *written demand* on the corporation to take suitable action. A derivative proceeding may not be commenced until 90 days after the date of demand, unless: (i) the shareholder has earlier been notified that the corporation has rejected the demand; or (ii) irreparable injury to the corporation would result by waiting for the 90 days to pass. [RMBCA §7.42]

1) **If Demand Futile**
Under older law, demand was excused if it would be futile (*e.g.*, where a shareholder is seeking damages from the entire board for breach of duty, they are unlikely to approve the action). However, it has been argued that this exception does not apply under the RMBCA for two reasons: (i) the RMBCA does not provide for the exception; and (ii) even though it may seem futile to ask the directors to sue themselves, the demand gives the directors an opportunity to resolve the issue through means other than litigation.

d. **Corporation Named as Defendant**
In a derivative action, the corporation is named as a party defendant. Although the cause of action asserted belongs to the corporation (so the corporation is the real plaintiff in interest), the failure of the corporation to assert its own claim justifies aligning it as a defendant.

e. **Dismissal If Not in Corporation's Best Interests**
If a majority of the directors (but at least two) who have no personal interest in the controversy found *in good faith after reasonable inquiry* that the suit is not in the corporation's best interests, but the shareholder brings the suit anyway, the suit may be dismissed on the corporation's motion. [RMBCA §7.44] Good business reasons for the directors' refusal might be the fact that there is no likelihood of prevailing, or that the damage to the corporation from litigating would outweigh any possible recovery.

1) **Burden of Proof**
To avoid dismissal, in most cases the *shareholder* bringing the suit has the burden of proving to the court that the decision was *not* made in good faith after reasonable inquiry. However, if a majority of the directors had a personal interest in the controversy, the *corporation* will have the burden of showing that the decision was made in good faith after reasonable inquiry. [RMBCA §7.44(e)]

f. **Discontinuance or Settlement Requires Court Approval**
A derivative proceeding may be discontinued or settled only with court approval. [RMBCA §7.45]

g. Court May Order Payment of Expenses

Upon termination of a derivative action, the court may order the corporation to pay the plaintiff's reasonable expenses (including attorneys' fees) incurred in the proceeding if it finds that the action has resulted in a substantial benefit to the corporation. If the court finds that the action was commenced or maintained without reasonable cause or for an improper purpose, it may order the plaintiff to pay reasonable expenses of the defendant. [RMBCA §7.46]

G. DISTRIBUTIONS

1. Types of Distributions

Distributions of the corporation's assets to shareholders may take a number of forms: Dividends can be paid to shareholders in the form of cash or indebtedness while the corporation is operating. Shares can be redeemed from shareholders where there is a redemption right (*i.e.,* a built-in right of the corporation to repurchase the shares in a forced sale at a particular price) or repurchased (a voluntary sale by a current shareholder and purchase by the corporation). Finally, liquidating distributions can be paid to the shareholders when the corporation is dissolved. [RMBCA §1.40(6)]

2. Rights to Distributions

At least one class of stock must have a right to receive the corporation's net assets on dissolution. [RMBCA §6.01(b)] Beyond this rule, the articles may provide for distributions in any manner.

a. Declaration Generally Solely Within Board's Discretion

Even if the articles authorize distributions, the decision whether or not to declare distributions generally is *solely within the directors' discretion* (recall, however, that a shareholder agreement can change this rule; *see* C.3., *supra*), subject to any limitations in the articles and statutory solvency requirements (*see* below). The shareholders have no general right to compel a distribution; it would take a very strong case in equity to induce a court to interfere with the directors' discretion.

1) Limitations

a) Solvency Requirements

A distribution is not permitted if, after giving it effect, either:

(i) The corporation would *not be able to pay its debts as they become due* in the usual course of business (*i.e.,* the corporation is insolvent in the bankruptcy sense); or

(ii) The corporation's *total assets would be less than the sum of its total liabilities plus* (unless the articles permit otherwise) the amount that would be needed, if the corporation were to be dissolved at the time of the distribution, *to satisfy the preferential rights* on dissolution of shareholders whose preferential rights are superior to those receiving the distribution (*i.e.,* the corporation is insolvent in the balance sheet sense).

[RMBCA §6.40(c)]

b) Restrictions in the Articles

The articles may restrict the board's right to declare dividends. For example, to assure repayment, a creditor might be able to have the corporation include in its articles a provision prohibiting payment of any distributions unless the corporation earns a certain amount of profits.

c) Share Dividends

Distributions of a corporation's own shares (*i.e.,* "share dividends" or "stock dividends") to its shareholders are excluded from the definition of "distribution" under the RMBCA. [RMBCA §1.40(6)] Therefore, the above solvency rules are inapplicable to share dividends. However, shares of one class or series may not be issued as a share dividend in respect to shares of another class or series unless one of the following occurs: (i) the articles so authorize; (ii) a majority of the votes entitled to be cast by the class or series to be issued approves the issuance; or (iii) there are no outstanding shares of the class or series to be issued. [RMBCA §6.23]

2) Historical Note—Par Value and Capital Accounts

Under traditional corporate laws, distributions were also prohibited unless there was sufficient money in a particular account or accounts. Generally, dividends could be paid only from accounts containing "surplus," such as an account containing retained earnings; dividends could not be paid out of the "stated capital account," which had to contain at least the aggregate par value of all outstanding par value shares. These limitations no longer apply in most states.

b. Contractual Rights in Regard to Distributions

1) Limitations and Preferences

As discussed previously, a corporation need not give each shareholder an equal right to receive distributions. Shares may be divided into classes with varying rights (*e.g.,* some classes may be redeemable, others not; some may have no right to receive distributions, others could have preferences; etc.). The following are common preference terms with which you should be familiar:

a) (Noncumulative) Preferred Shares

Shares that have a preference usually are entitled to a fixed amount of money (*e.g.,* $5 each year if the preference is a dividend preference, $5 on dissolution if the preference is a liquidation preference) before distributions can be made with respect to nonpreferred shares. Note that the right is not absolute; the directors must still declare a dividend before the preferred shareholder has any right to receive it. Unless the dividend is cumulative (*see infra*), the right to a dividend preference for a particular year is extinguished if a dividend is not declared for that year.

b) Cumulative Preferred Shares

Cumulative preferred shares are like noncumulative preferred shares, but if a dividend is not declared in a particular year, the right to receive the preference accumulates and must be paid before nonpreferred shares may be paid any dividend.

Example: NavaCorp has 1,000 shares of $5 cumulative preferred stock outstanding. The directors did not declare a dividend in 1999 or 2000. If the directors want to declare a dividend in 2001, they will have to pay the cumulative preferred shareholders $15,000 (1,000 shares x $5 x 3 years) before any payment can be made to shares without a preference.

c) Cumulative If Earned Shares

If shares are "cumulative if earned," dividends for any one year cumulate only if the corporation's total earnings for that year exceed the total amount of the preferred dividends that would have to be paid out for that year.

d) Participating Shares

Generally, preferred shares are entitled only to their stated preference. However, preferred shares may be designated as "participating," in which case they have a right to receive whatever the nonpreferred shares receive in addition to the preference.

2) Rights After Declaration—Same as a General Creditor

As established above, shareholders have no general right to receive distributions. However, once a distribution is lawfully declared, the shareholders generally are treated as creditors of the corporation, and their claim to the distribution is equal in priority to claims of other unsecured creditors. [RMBCA §6.40(f)] Note, however, that a distribution can be enjoined or revoked if it was declared in violation of the solvency limitations, the articles, or a superior preference right.

c. Who May Receive—Shareholder of Record on Record Date

Once declared, dividends are payable to the persons named as shareholders in the corporate records on a particular date—known as the record date. If shares have been sold prior to the record date but have not been transferred on the corporation's books, the corporation pays the record owner (*i.e.,* the seller), and the beneficial owner (*i.e.,* the purchaser) must look to the seller for payment.

3. Liability for Unlawful Distributions

A director who votes for or assents to a distribution that violates the above rules is personally liable to the corporation for the amount of the distribution that *exceeds what could have been properly distributed*. A director will be deemed to have assented to the declaration of a distribution if she was present at the meeting at which the declaration was made and failed to dissent either during the meeting or by 5 p.m. on the business day next following the meeting. [RMBCA §8.33]

a. Good Faith Defense

A director is not liable for distributions approved in good faith (i) based on financial statements prepared according to reasonable accounting practices, or on a fair valuation or other method that is reasonable under the circumstances [RMBCA §6.40(d)] or (ii) by relying on information from officers, employees, legal counsel, accountants, etc. or a committee of the board of which the director is not a member [RMBCA §8.30(b)].

b. Contribution
A director who is held liable for an unlawful distribution is entitled to contribution from (i) *every other director* who could be held liable for the distribution and (ii) *each shareholder*, for the amount she accepted knowing that the distribution was improper. [RMBCA §8.33(b)]

H. SHAREHOLDERS' LIABILITIES

1. General Rule—No Fiduciary Duty
Generally, shareholders may act in their own personal interests and owe no fiduciary duty to the corporation or their fellow shareholders except as outlined above concerning shareholder liability for:

1) Unpaid stock;

2) A pierced corporate veil; and

3) Absence of de facto corporation when the shareholder knew that there was no incorporation.

2. Liability Pursuant to Shareholder Agreement
As discussed above, shareholders may enter into agreements that vest some or all of the right to manage the corporation in one or more shareholders. When such agreements exist, the shareholder(s) in whom the management power is vested have the liabilities that a director ordinarily would have with respect to that power. [RMBCA §7.32(e)]

3. Close Corporations
Shareholders in a close corporation (*i.e.,* a corporation owned by a few persons) owe each other the same duty of loyalty and utmost good faith that is owed by partners to each other. [Donahue v. Rodd Electrotype Co., 328 N.E.2d 505 (Mass. 1975)]

4. Limitations on Controlling Shareholders
Certain common law limitations have emerged with regard to the sale by controlling shareholders (an individual or group) of a controlling interest. A controlling shareholder must refrain from using his control to obtain a special advantage or to cause the corporation to take action that unfairly prejudices the minority shareholders. [Pepper v. Litton, 308 U.S. 295 (1939)]

Examples: 1) Controlling shareholders who sell the controlling interest to individuals who subsequently loot the company to the detriment of the minority shareholders will be liable for damages, unless reasonable measures were taken to investigate the character and reputation of the buyer.

2) Majority shareholders were held liable to minority shareholders where the 85% majority shareholders transferred their shares to a holding company and then made a public offering of the holding company shares, because the result was that the minority shareholders were left holding shares that had no appreciable market value. [Jones v. H.F. Ahmanson & Co., 1 Cal. 3d 93 (1969)]

a. Sale at a Premium
No case has specifically held that controlling shareholders were liable simply for

selling a controlling interest at a price unavailable to the other shareholders, *i.e.,* a price that includes a premium attributable solely to the right to control the corporation. However, in *Perlman v. Feldman,* 219 F.2d 173 (2d Cir. 1955), the controlling shareholders were held liable for the sale of their shares at a premium, where the court found that the premium really was paid for the right to allocate scarce materials during wartime. This wartime right of allocation was considered a corporate asset, and the rule has always been that shareholders who *illegally* sell corporate assets for their own benefit will be forced to disgorge their profit.

b. Controlling Shareholder Under Securities Laws

Controlling shareholders generally are treated as "insiders" under the Securities Exchange Act and may be liable under the securities laws for trading on inside information. (*See* XIII.A., *infra.*) Shareholders owning 10% or more of a class of a corporation's stock may be liable for making short swing profits. (*See* XIII.B., *infra.*)

VI. DIRECTORS

A. GENERAL POWERS

Unless the articles or a shareholder agreement provides otherwise, the board of directors of the corporation has general responsibility for the management of the business and the affairs of the corporation. [RMBCA §8.01]

B. QUALIFICATIONS

The articles of incorporation or bylaws may prescribe qualifications for directors. A director need not be a resident of the state or a shareholder of the corporation unless so required by the articles or bylaws. [RMBCA §8.02]

C. NUMBER, ELECTION, AND TERMS OF OFFICE

1. Number of Directors—One or More as Set in Articles or Bylaws

The board of directors may consist of one or more individuals, as the articles or bylaws provide. In lieu of a set number of directors, the articles or bylaws may provide a variable range for the size of the board by fixing a minimum and maximum number of directors. If a variable range is established, the number may be fixed or changed from time to time, within the specified minimum and maximum, by the shareholders or the board. [RMBCA §8.03]

2. Election of Directors

The directors are elected at the first annual meeting of the shareholders, and at each annual meeting thereafter unless the directors' terms are staggered. [RMBCA §8.03(d)]

3. Terms of Directors

Directors' terms expire at the annual shareholders' meeting following their election, except for directors with staggered terms. [RMBCA §8.05(a), (b)] Even if a director's term expires, she remains in office until her successor is elected and qualifies. [RMBCA §8.05(e)]

a. Staggering Director Terms

If there are at least nine directors, the articles may divide the directors into two or three groups (as close to equal in size as is possible) to serve staggered two- or three-year terms. Thus, only one-half or one-third of the board is elected each year. [RMBCA §8.06] Such staggering of terms ensures some continuity in the board, but it also lessens the effect of cumulative voting since fewer directors are elected at each annual meeting.

4. Resignation of Director

A director may resign at any time by delivering written notice to the board, its chairperson, or the corporation. The resignation takes effect when notice is delivered, unless the notice specifies a later effective date or event. [RMBCA §8.07]

5. Vacancies May Be Filled by Directors or Shareholders

Absent a contrary provision in the articles, a vacancy on the board may be filled by either the shareholders or the board. If the directors remaining in office constitute fewer than a quorum, they may fill the vacancy by the affirmative vote of a majority of all the directors remaining in office. [RMBCA §8.10(a)]

a. Where Director Elected by Voting Group

If the vacant office was held by a director elected by a voting group of shareholders, only holders of shares of that voting group may vote to fill the vacancy if it is filled by shareholders. [RMBCA §8.10(b)]

D. REMOVAL OF DIRECTORS

Directors may be removed *with or without cause* by the shareholders, unless the articles provide that removal may be only for cause. [RMBCA §8.08]

1. Cumulative Voting Limitation

If less than the entire board is to be removed, a director elected by cumulative voting may not be removed if the votes cast against her removal would have been sufficient to elect her if cumulatively voted at an election of the board.

2. Where Director Elected by Voting Group

If a director is elected by a voting group of shareholders, only shareholders of that group may vote to remove the director.

E. DIRECTORS' MEETING

The board may hold regular or special meetings either within or outside the state. Unless otherwise provided in the articles or bylaws, the board may permit any or all directors to participate in a regular or special meeting by, or conduct the meeting through, the use of any means of communication by which *all directors participating may simultaneously hear each other* (*e.g.*, a conference call). [RMBCA §8.20]

1. Initial Meeting

After incorporation, the board must hold an organizational meeting, called by a majority of directors. The directors complete the organization of the corporation at this meeting by appointing officers, adopting bylaws, and carrying on any other business brought up at the meeting. [RMBCA §2.05]

2. Notice of Meetings

Regular board meetings may be held **without notice**. Special meetings require at least **two days' notice** of the date, time, and place of the meeting, but a purpose need not be included in the notice. [RMBCA §8.22]

a. Notice May Be Waived

A director may waive notice by a signed writing, filed with the minutes or corporate records. Attendance at or participation in a meeting waives notice unless the director, at the beginning of the meeting or promptly on her arrival, objects to holding the meeting or transacting business at the meeting, and does not thereafter vote for or assent to action taken at the meeting. [RMBCA §8.23]

3. Quorum

A majority of the board of directors constitutes a quorum for the meeting unless a higher or lower number is required by the articles of incorporation or the bylaws, but a quorum may be **no fewer than one-third** of the board members. [RMBCA §8.24]

a. Breaking Quorum

A quorum must be present **at the time the vote is taken** for the vote to constitute valid action. Thus, even if a quorum is present at the beginning of a meeting, a group of minority directors may break quorum by leaving a meeting before a vote is taken. This is not true of shareholders at shareholders' meetings. Once a shareholder is present for a shareholders' meeting, he is deemed present even if he leaves.

4. Approval of Action

If a quorum is present, resolutions will be deemed approved if approved by a **majority of directors present** unless the articles or bylaws require the vote of a greater number. [RMBCA §8.24(c)]

a. Right to Dissent

A director who is present at a board meeting when corporate action is taken is deemed to have assented to the action taken unless:

(i) **The director objects at the beginning of the meeting** or promptly on her arrival to holding it or transacting business at the meeting;

(ii) **The director's dissent or abstention** from the action taken is **entered in the minutes** of the meeting; **or**

(iii) **The director delivers written notice** of her dissent or abstention to the presiding officer of the meeting before its adjournment.

[RMBCA §8.24(d)]

b. Action May Be Taken Without Meeting by Unanimous Written Consent

Action required or permitted to be taken at a directors' meeting may be taken without a meeting if the action is taken by **all directors**. Each director must sign a **written consent** that describes the action taken and is included in the minutes or filed with the corporate records. [RMBCA §8.21]

F. MAY DELEGATE AUTHORITY TO COMMITTEES OR OFFICERS

The board of directors is not expected to participate in the daily business affairs of the corporation. Rather, they usually delegate management functions for daily business affairs to executive committees or to officers.

1. Executive Committees

The board may create one or more committees, each made up of *two or more members* of the board. [RMBCA §8.25]

a. Selection

Creation of a committee and appointment of its members must be approved by the greater of (i) a majority of all directors in office when the action is taken or (ii) the number of directors required to take action under statutory voting requirements. [RMBCA §8.25(b)]

b. Powers

Subject to the following limitations, each committee may exercise the authority granted to it by the board. However, a committee may *not* do any of the following:

(i) Authorize *distributions*;

(ii) Approve or *submit to shareholders* any action that requires shareholder approval;

(iii) *Fill vacancies* on the board or a committee;

(iv) *Amend articles* of incorporation;

(v) *Adopt, amend, or repeal bylaws*;

(vi) *Approve a plan of merger* not requiring shareholder approval;

(vii) *Authorize reacquisition of shares*, except according to a formula or method prescribed by the board; or

(viii) *Authorize the issuance, sale, or contract for sale of shares,* or determine the relative rights and preferences of a class or series (however, the board may authorize a committee or an executive officer of the corporation to do so within limits set forth by the board).

[RMBCA §8.25(d), (e)]

2. Officers

The officers have whatever duties the board prescribes. The board remains responsible for supervision of the officers despite the delegation of duty.

G. DIRECTORS' RIGHT TO INSPECT

Directors have a right to inspect corporate books. [RMBCA §16.05]

H. DE FACTO DIRECTORS

Directors who have not been properly elected, either by a failure to call a proper shareholders' meeting, an error in the balloting, or a failure to satisfy bylaw qualifications, are de facto directors. De facto directors bind the corporation in their performance of normal director activities.

I. DIRECTORS' DUTIES AND LIABILITIES

The directors' management duties are typical fiduciary duties, including the duty of due care, the duty of loyalty, and the duty to protect the interests of the other intracorporate parties.

1. Personal Liability of Directors May Be Limited

The articles of incorporation can limit or eliminate directors' personal liability for money damages to the corporation or shareholders for action taken or failure to take action as a director. However, no provision can limit or eliminate liability for (i) the amount of a financial benefit received by the director to which she is not entitled, (ii) an intentionally inflicted harm on the corporation or its shareholders, (iii) unlawful corporate distributions, or (iv) an intentional violation of criminal law. [RMBCA §2.02(b)(5)]

2. Duty of Care

Directors are vested with the duty to manage the corporation to the best of their ability; they are not insurers of corporate success, but rather are merely required to discharge their duties:

(i)   In *good faith*;

(ii) *With the care that an ordinarily prudent person in a like position* would exercise under similar circumstances; and

(iii) In a manner the directors *reasonably believe to be in the best interests of the corporation*.

[RMBCA §8.30(a)] Directors who meet this standard of conduct will not be liable for corporate decisions that, in hindsight, turn out to be poor or erroneous. At common law, this was known as the "*business judgment rule*."

a. Burden on Challenger

The person challenging the directors' action has the burden of proving that the statutory standard was not met. [RMBCA §8.30(d)]

b. Director May Rely on Reports or Other Information

In discharging her duties, a director is entitled to rely on information, opinions, reports, or statements (including financial statements), if prepared or presented by any of the following:

(i)   *Corporate officers or employees* whom the director reasonably believes to be reliable and competent;

(ii) *Legal counsel, accountants, or other persons* as to matters the director reasonably believes are within such person's professional competence; or

(iii) A *committee* of the board of which the director is not a member, if the director reasonably believes the committee merits confidence.

[RMBCA §8.30(b)]

3. Duty of Loyalty (Common Law)

A director owes a duty of loyalty to her corporation and will not be permitted to profit at the expense of the corporation. The problems in this area involve the director's dealings with the corporation and her potential conflict of interest; her dealings with third parties and her usurpation of a corporate opportunity; and her dealings with shareholders, which may raise insider trading issues.

a. Conflicting Interest Transactions

If a director has a personal interest in a transaction in which her corporation is a party, a conflict of interest arises.

1) What Constitutes a Conflicting Interest Transaction

A director has a conflicting interest with respect to a transaction or proposed transaction if the director knows that she or a related person (*e.g.,* a spouse, parent, child, grandchild, etc.):

(i) *Is a party* to the transaction;

(ii) *Has a beneficial financial interest* in, or is so closely linked to, the transaction that the interest would reasonably be expected to influence the director's judgment if she were to vote on the transaction; or

(iii) Is a *director, general partner, agent, or employee* of another entity with whom the corporation is transacting business and the transaction is of such importance to the corporation that it would in the normal course of business be brought before the board (the so-called interlocking directorate problem).

[RMBCA §8.60]

2) Standards for Upholding Conflicting Interest Transaction

A conflicting interest transaction will not be enjoined or give rise to an award of damages due to the director's interest in the transaction if:

(i) The transaction was approved by a *majority of the directors* (but at least two) *without a conflicting interest* after all material facts have been disclosed to the board;

(ii) The transaction was approved by *a majority of the votes entitled to be cast by shareholders without a conflicting interest* in the transaction after all material facts have been disclosed to the shareholders (notice of the meeting must describe the conflicting interest transaction); or

(iii) The transaction, judged according to circumstances at the time of commitment, was *fair to the corporation*.

[RMBCA §§8.61-8.63]

a) Interested Director's Presence at Meeting Irrelevant

The presence of the interested director(s) at the meeting at which the directors or shareholders voted to approve the conflicting interest transaction does not affect the action. [RMBCA §§8.62(c), 8.63(c)]

b) Special Quorum Requirements

Because the director with a conflicting interest has no right to vote whether to approve the transaction, quorum requirements are changed for purposes of the vote on the transaction. *For purposes of a directors' meeting*, a majority of the directors without a conflicting interest, but not less than two, constitutes a quorum for purposes of the vote on the transaction. [RMBCA §8.62(c)] *For purposes of a shareholders' meeting*, a quorum consists of a majority of the votes entitled to be cast, not including shares owned or controlled directly or beneficially by the director with the conflicting interest. [RMBCA §8.63(c)]

c) Factors to Be Considered in Determining Fairness

In determining whether a transaction is fair, courts traditionally look to factors such as adequacy of the consideration, corporate need to enter into the transaction, financial position of the corporation, and available alternatives.

d) Statutory Interpretation

It has been argued that the RMBCA's conflicting interest statute is not quite as absolute as it seems. For example, a transaction approved by the board or shareholders might still be set aside if the party challenging the transaction can prove that it constitutes a waste of corporate assets. On the other hand, a transaction approved by *all* of the shareholders probably cannot be set aside, because the shareholders would be estopped from complaining.

e) Remedies

Possible remedies for an improper conflicting interest transaction include enjoining the transaction, setting aside the transaction, damages, and similar remedies. [*See* RMBCA §8.61(b)]

3) Directors May Set Own Compensation

Despite the apparent conflict of interest, unless the articles or bylaws provide otherwise, the board may set director compensation. [RMBCA §8.11] Of course, setting an unreasonable compensation will breach the directors' fiduciary duties.

b. Corporate Opportunity Doctrine

The directors' fiduciary duties prohibit them from diverting a business opportunity from their corporation to themselves without first giving their corporation an opportunity to act. This is sometimes known as a "usurpation of a corporate opportunity" problem.

1) Corporation Must Have Interest or Expectancy

A usurpation problem will not arise from every business opportunity that comes to the directors. Directors are prohibited from taking advantage of business opportunities only if their corporation would have an *interest or expectancy* in the business opportunity.

Example: Saguaro Corp. packages cactus seeds to sell to tourists. Business is good, and the corporation needs to expand its packaging facility. Rick, a Saguaro director, learns that the owner of a lot adjacent to Saguaro's factory might be interested in selling the lot. Rick approaches the owner, who agrees to sell the lot to Rick. Because Saguaro Corp. has an interest in expanding, the lot is a corporate opportunity, and Rick must give the corporation a chance to purchase the lot before he may do so.

a) Scope of Interest

A corporation's interest does not extend to every conceivable business opportunity, but neither does the opportunity have to be necessary to the corporation's current business. The closer the opportunity is to the corporation's *line of business*, the more likely a court will find it to be a corporate opportunity.

b) Lack of Financial Ability Probably Not a Defense

The corporation's lack of financial ability to take advantage of the opportunity probably is not a defense. The director should still present the opportunity to the corporation and allow the corporation to decide whether it can take advantage of the opportunity.

2) Board Generally Decides

Because the board generally makes decisions concerning management of the corporation, it is the board that must decide whether to accept an opportunity or to reject it; generally, shareholders need not be consulted.

3) Remedies

If a director does not give the corporation an opportunity to act, but rather usurps the opportunity, the corporation can recover the profits that the director made from the transaction or may force the director to convey the opportunity to the corporation, under a constructive trust theory, for whatever consideration the director purchased the opportunity.

c. Competing Business

Directors are permitted to engage in unrelated businesses, but a clear conflict of interest may arise if the director's personal business is in direct competition with the corporation.

d. Common Law Insider Trading—Special Circumstances Rule

Federal statutes control most insider trading litigation. However, the statutes do not destroy common law actions for insider trading, and common law concepts appear occasionally in bar exam questions. Traditionally at common law, a director owes fiduciary duties only to the corporation and not to individual shareholders. Therefore, a director was free to buy and sell corporate shares without disclosing to the prospective seller or buyer any inside knowledge that the director had. However, this rule gave insiders an unfair advantage, and eventually state courts developed the *special circumstances rule*. Under the rule, if special circumstances exist which may have a significant impact on the value of the stock being traded (*e.g.*, the director knows of an upcoming extraordinary dividend or a planned merger), those circumstances may give rise to a fiduciary duty to disclose them to the person with whom the director is dealing, and a failure to completely disclose will result in the breach of that duty.

VII. OFFICERS

A. IN GENERAL
The RMBCA does not require a corporation to have any specific officers, but rather provides that a corporation shall have the officers described in its bylaws or appointed by the board pursuant to the bylaws. An officer may appoint other officers or assistant officers if so authorized by the bylaws or the board. One person may simultaneously hold more than one office. [RMBCA §8.40]

B. DUTIES
Officers' duties are determined by the bylaws or, to the extent consistent with the bylaws, by the board or an officer so authorized by the board. [RMBCA §8.41]

C. POWERS
The officers are agents of the corporation and receive their power to manage from the directors. The ordinary rules of agency determine the authority and powers of the officers and agents. Authority may be actual or apparent. If authority exists, actions taken by an officer or agent (such as entering into contracts) bind the corporation.

1. Actual Authority
An officer's actual authority includes not only the authority expressly granted to the officer by the directors, the bylaws, the articles, and statutes, but also any authority that may be implied by the express grant. Appointment to the following offices implies the following powers absent an express provision otherwise:

a. President
There is a presumption that the president has implied authority to enter into contracts and otherwise act on behalf of the corporation in the ordinary course of corporate affairs.

b. Vice President
The vice president has implied authority to act when the president is unavailable because of death, illness, or other incapacity.

c. Secretary
The secretary has implied authority to keep the corporate records.

d. Treasurer
The treasurer has implied authority to receive and keep corporate funds.

2. Apparent Authority
When the corporation "holds out" an officer as possessing certain authority, thereby inducing others reasonably to believe that the authority exists, the officer has apparent authority to act and to bind the corporation even though actual authority to do so has not been granted.

D. STANDARD OF CONDUCT

Officers' standard of conduct is similar to the standard for directors: If an officer has any discretionary authority with respect to any duties, the officer must carry out her duties *in good faith*, *with the care an ordinarily prudent person in a like position* would exercise under similar circumstances, and in a manner she *reasonably believes to be in the best interests of the corporation*. [RMBCA §8.42(a)]

E. RESIGNATION AND REMOVAL

Despite any contractual term to the contrary, an officer has the power to resign at any time by delivering notice to the corporation, and the corporation has the power to remove an officer at any time, *with or without cause*. If the resignation or removal constitutes a breach of contract, the nonbreaching party's rights to damages are not affected by the resignation or removal, but note that mere appointment to office itself does not create any contractual right to remain in office. [RMBCA §§8.43, 8.44]

VIII. INDEMNIFICATION OF DIRECTORS, OFFICERS, AND EMPLOYEES

A. IN GENERAL

If a person is made a party to a legal proceeding because of his status as a director, officer, employee, or agent of the corporation, depending on the circumstances, the corporation may be required to indemnify the person, may have discretion to indemnify the person, or may be prohibited from indemnifying the person.

1. Mandatory Indemnification

Unless limited by the articles, a corporation *must* indemnify a director or officer who *prevailed* in defending the proceeding against the officer or director for reasonable expenses, including attorneys' fees incurred in connection with the proceeding. [RMBCA §§8.52, 8.56(c)]

B. DISCRETIONARY INDEMNIFICATION

A corporation *may* indemnify a director for reasonable expenses incurred in *unsuccessfully defending* a suit brought against the director on account of the director's position if:

(i) The director acted in *good faith*; and

(ii) Believed that her conduct was:

    i. In the *best interests of the corporation* (when the conduct at issue was within the director's official capacity);

    ii. *Not opposed to the best interests of the corporation* (when the conduct at issue was not within the director's official capacity); or

    iii. *Not unlawful* (in criminal proceedings).

[RMBCA §8.51]

1. **Exceptions**

A corporation does not have discretion to indemnify a director who is unsuccessful in defending (i) a direct or derivative action when the *director is found liable to the corporation* or (ii) an action charging that the director received an *improper benefit*. [RMBCA §8.51(d)]

2. **Who Makes Determination**

Generally, the determination whether to indemnify is to be made by a disinterested majority of the board, or if there is not a disinterested quorum, by majority of a disinterested committee or by legal counsel. The shareholders may also make the determination (the shares of the director seeking indemnification are not counted). [RMBCA §8.55(b)]

3. **Officers**

Officers generally may be indemnified to the same extent as a director. [RMBCA §8.56]

C. **COURT-ORDERED INDEMNIFICATION**

A court may order indemnification whenever it is appropriate. [RMBCA §8.54]

D. **ADVANCES**

A corporation may advance expenses to a director defending an action as long as the director furnishes the corporation with a statement that she believes she met the appropriate standard of conduct and that she will repay the advance if she is later found to have not met the appropriate standard. [RMBCA §8.53]

E. **LIABILITY INSURANCE**

A corporation may purchase liability insurance to indemnify directors for actions against them even if the directors would not have been entitled to indemnification under the above standards. [RMBCA §8.55]

F. **AGENTS AND EMPLOYEES**

The RMBCA does not limit a corporation's power to indemnify, advance expenses to, or maintain insurance on an agent or employee. [RMBCA §8.58(e)]

PART THREE—CHANGES IN STRUCTURE

IX. FUNDAMENTAL CHANGES IN CORPORATE STRUCTURE

A. **INTRODUCTION**

The RMBCA permits corporations to undertake fundamental changes to their structure, but because it would be unfair to force a person to remain an owner of a fundamentally changed corporation, the Act provides special procedures that allow shareholders to vote whether to adopt a fundamental change, and in some cases provides dissenting shareholders a right to have the corporation purchase their shares after a fundamental change has been approved.

1. **Types of Fundamental Corporate Changes**
   The RMBCA provides special procedures for the following corporate changes: most amendments of the articles, mergers, share exchanges, dispositions of substantially all property outside the usual and regular course of business, and dissolution.

2. **General Procedure for Fundamental Change**
   The basic procedure for adopting a fundamental corporate change is the same for all fundamental changes:

   a. *A majority of the board of directors adopts a resolution* recommending the fundamental change;

   b. *Notice* of the proposed change is sent to *all shareholders* (whether or not entitled to vote). The notice must (i) describe the change and inform the shareholders that a vote will be taken on the matter at a shareholders' meeting, and (ii) be given not less than 10 or more than 60 days before the meeting;

   c. The change is *approved by a majority of all votes entitled to be cast and by a majority of any voting group entitled to vote as a group*; and

   d. The change is formalized in *articles* (*e.g.*, articles of amendment, articles of merger, etc.), which are *filed* with the state.

B. **AMENDMENTS OF THE ARTICLES OF INCORPORATION**
   A corporation may amend its articles at any time to add or change a provision that is required or permitted or to delete a provision that is not required. [RMBCA §10.01] Certain "housekeeping" amendments can be made without shareholder approval, but most require approval by the shareholders.

   1. **Amendments that Board Can Make Without Shareholder Approval**
      The board of directors may make any amendment to the articles before any shares are issued. [RMBCA §10.05] Once shares have been issued, the board may make the following amendments without approval by the shareholders:

      (i) To *extend the corporation's duration* if the corporation was formed when the law required a limited duration;

      (ii) To *delete the names and/or addresses of the initial directors* or registered agent or office;

      (iii) To *change the authorized number of shares* to implement a share split, as long as there is *only one class* of shares outstanding;

      (iv) To *change the company name* by substituting a *different word or abbreviation* than the one currently *indicating the corporation's corporate status* (*e.g.*, "Co." in place of "Inc.") or changing a geographical attribute (*e.g.*, "X Corp. of Arizona" in place of "X Corp."); and

(v)   Any other change *permitted by the RMBCA without shareholder approval*.

[RMBCA §10.02]

2.   Amendments by Board and Shareholders

Any amendment to the articles other than those listed above requires implementation of the general fundamental change procedure as discussed *supra* (*i.e.*, resolution of the board, notice to the shareholders, approval by the shareholders, and filing articles of amendment with the state). [RMBCA §10.03(a)]

a.   Vote Required

In addition to the shareholder vote that is ordinarily required to pass fundamental corporate changes, an amendment must also be approved by a majority of the votes of any voting group that would have dissenters' rights with respect to the amendment. [RMBCA §10.03(e)(1)] Dissenters' rights arise if the amendment will do one of the following:

(i)   *Change the aggregate number of authorized shares* of the class;

(ii)   *Change shares of the class into a different number* of shares (*e.g.*, a stock split);

(iii)   *Exchange or reclassify shares of the class* into shares of another class or of another class into shares of this class;

(iv)   *Change the rights or preferences* of the shares of the class, including limiting or denying existing preemptive rights;

(v)   *Change the rights of another class, or create another class*, so that the changed or new class has *rights or preferences equal or superior* to rights and preferences of this class; or

(vi)   *Cancel rights to distributions* that have accumulated but have not yet been declared for the shares of the class.

[RMBCA §10.04]

C.   MERGER AND SHARE EXCHANGE

The RMBCA provides that the basic procedure for fundamental corporate changes must be followed to approve a merger or share exchange. A merger involves the blending of one or more corporations into another corporation, and the latter corporation survives while the merging corporations cease to exist following the merger. A share exchange involves one corporation purchasing all of the outstanding shares of one or more classes or series of another corporation.

1.   Not All Shareholders Need Approve

Mergers and share exchanges vary a little from the basic fundamental change procedure in that not all shareholders have a right to approve these procedures under all circumstances.

a. Merger

1) No Significant Change to Surviving Corporation
Approval by shareholders of the *surviving* corporation on a plan of merger is *not* required if *all* the following conditions exist:

(i) The articles of incorporation of the surviving corporation will *not differ* from the articles before the merger;

(ii) Each shareholder of the survivor whose shares were outstanding immediately prior to the effective date of the merger will hold the *same number of shares*, with identical preferences, limitations, and rights;

(iii) The number of *voting shares* outstanding immediately after the merger, plus the number of voting shares issuable as a result of the merger, will not exceed by more than *20%* the total number of voting shares of the surviving corporation outstanding immediately prior to the merger; and

(iv) The number of *participating shares* (*i.e.,* shares entitled to dividends when declared) outstanding immediately after the merger, plus the number of participating shares issuable as a result of the merger will not exceed by more than *20%* the total number of participating shares outstanding immediately before the merger.

[RMBCA §11.03(g)]

2) Short Form Merger of Subsidiary
A parent corporation owning at least 90% of the outstanding shares of each class of a subsidiary corporation may merge the subsidiary into itself *without the approval of the shareholders of either* the parent or the subsidiary. [RMBCA §11.04] This is known as a "short form merger." The parent must mail a copy of the plan of merger to each shareholder of the subsidiary who does not waive the mailing requirement in writing. Articles of merger may not be delivered to the state for filing until at least 30 days after the plan was mailed to the shareholders.

b. Share Exchange
In a share exchange, only the shareholders of the corporation whose shares will be *acquired* in the share exchange need approve; a share exchange is *not* a fundamental corporate change for the acquiring corporation. [RMBCA §11.03(a)] Notice requirements are the same as for amendment of the articles.

2. Effect

a. Merger
Where there is a merger, every other corporation that is a party to the merger merges into the surviving corporation, and the separate existence of every corporation except the survivor ends. All property owned by the separate entities, and all obligations of the separate entities, become the property and obligations of the surviving corporation. A proceeding pending against a party to the merger may continue as if the merger did not occur, or the surviving corporation may be substituted.

b. Share Exchange

When a share exchange takes effect, the shares of each acquired corporation are exchanged as provided in the plan, and the former holders of the shares are entitled only to the exchange rights provided in the plan. The corporations remain separate.

D. DISPOSITION OF PROPERTY OUTSIDE THE USUAL AND REGULAR COURSE OF BUSINESS

A sale, lease, exchange, or other disposition of *all or substantially all* of a corporation's property outside of the usual and regular course of business is a fundamental corporate change *for the corporation disposing of the property*. Thus, the corporation disposing of the property must follow the fundamental change procedure. [RMBCA §12.02(a)] Note that the corporation *purchasing* the property is not undergoing a fundamental corporate change, and so approval from that corporation's shareholders is not required.

1. Compare—Dispositions Within Usual and Regular Course of Business

A disposition of a corporation's property within the usual and regular course of business is not a fundamental change and need not be approved by the shareholders. [RMBCA §12.01(a)(1)]

2. Compare—Mortgages, Pledges, Etc.

The fundamental change procedure need not be followed to approve the grant of a mortgage, pledge, or similar security interest, even if the security interest is in all or substantially all of a corporation's assets, and even if the grant is not within the usual and regular course of the corporation's business. [RMBCA §12.01(a)(2)]

3. Effect on Purchaser

Generally, the purchaser of another corporation's property does not become liable for the seller's obligations; the seller remains solely liable. However, if the disposition of property is really a disguised merger, a court might treat it as a merger under the de facto merger doctrine and hold the purchaser liable for the seller's obligations just as if a merger had occurred.

a. Factors Contributing to De Facto Merger

Courts adopting the de facto merger doctrine have stressed a number of factors that can cause an ostensible sale of assets or stock to be recharacterized as a merger:

1) The fact that the acquiring corporation *used its own stock as consideration* rather than cash or promissory notes;

2) The fact that the *acquired corporation was required to dissolve*;

3) In the case of an acquisition of stock, the fact that the *acquired corporation was merged* into the acquiring corporation after its stock had been acquired; and

4) The fact that the *smaller corporation was buying the assets of the larger* corporation (rather than the converse).

E. PROTECTION AGAINST AND LIMITATIONS ON FUNDAMENTAL CHANGES

1. Dissenting Shareholders' Appraisal Remedy

Shareholders who are dissatisfied with the terms of a fundamental corporate change generally are permitted to compel the corporation to buy their shares at a fair value by following a special statutory procedure. Generally, absent fraud, misrepresentation, or improper procedure, a shareholder entitled to appraisal rights may not challenge a completed corporate action for which appraisal rights are available (*i.e.*, the appraisal right generally is a shareholder's exclusive remedy for completed corporate action). [RMBCA §13.02(d)]

a. Who May Dissent?

1) Merger
Any shareholder *entitled to vote* on a plan of merger and *shareholders of the subsidiary* in a short form merger have the right to dissent. [RMBCA §13.02(a)(2)]

2) Share Exchange
Shareholders of the corporation whose shares are being *acquired* in a share exchange have the right to dissent. [RMBCA §13.02(a)(2)]

3) Disposition of Property
A shareholder who is *entitled to vote* on a disposition of all or substantially all the corporation's property outside the usual and regular course of business is entitled to dissent. This does not include a sale pursuant to court order, or a cash sale pursuant to a plan by which the net sale proceeds will be distributed to the shareholders within one year of the date of sale. [RMBCA §13.02(a)(3)]

4) Amendment of Articles
A shareholder has a right to dissent from an amendment of the articles that *materially and adversely affects the shareholder's rights* (*e.g.*, changes preferential redemption or preemptive rights, limits voting rights, or reduces the shareholder's shares to fractional shares to be purchased by the corporation), unless there is a court order for reorganization. [RMBCA §13.02(a)(4)]

b. Procedure

1) Corporation Must Give Shareholders Notice
If a proposed corporate action will create dissenters' rights, the notice of the shareholders' meeting at which a vote on the action will be taken must state that the shareholders will be entitled to exercise their dissenting rights. [RMBCA §13.20(a)] If the action may be taken without a vote of the shareholders (*e.g.*, in a short form merger), they must be given notice that the action was taken and of their right to dissent. [RMBCA §13.20(b)]

2) Shareholder Must Give Notice of Intent to Demand Payment
If the shareholder will be entitled to vote and wishes to exercise her dissenting rights, she must, *before a vote is taken*, deliver *written notice of her intent to demand payment* for her shares if the proposed action is taken. Also, she cannot vote in favor of the proposed action. Failure to satisfy these requirements means that the shareholder is not entitled to payment for her shares. [RMBCA §13.21(a)]

3) Corporation Must Give Dissenters Notice
If the proposed action is approved at the shareholders' meeting, the corporation *must notify, within 10 days* after the vote, all shareholders who filed an intent to demand payment. The notice must tell the shareholders when and where they

must submit their shares and state the other terms of the repurchase. The corporation cannot set the time for receiving the payment demands less than 30 or more than 60 days after the date the corporation's notice is delivered. [RMBCA §13.22]

4) Shareholders Must Demand Payment
A shareholder who is sent a dissenter's notice must then ***demand payment*** in accordance with the notice given by the corporation. [RMBCA §13.23]

5) Corporation Must Pay
When the proposed action is taken, the corporation must pay the dissenters the ***amount the corporation estimates as the fair value*** of the shares, plus accrued interest. Along with the payment, the corporation must send the corporation's balance sheet and income statement, and an explanation of how fair value and interest were determined. [RMBCA §13.25]

6) Notice of Dissatisfaction
If the shareholder is dissatisfied with the corporation's determination of value, the shareholder has 30 days in which to send the corporation her ***own estimate of value*** and demand payment of that amount (or the difference between her estimate and the amount sent by the corporation). [RMBCA §13.28]

7) Court Action
If the corporation does not want to pay what the shareholder demanded, ***the corporation*** must file an action in court within 60 days after receiving the shareholder's demand, requesting the court to determine the fair value of the shares. If the corporation fails to file suit within 60 days, it will be required to pay the shareholder the amount the shareholder demanded. [RMBCA §13.30]

2. Tender Offers and Corporate Control Transactions
It is common for one corporation to try to take over another corporation. The federal Williams Act and state control share acquisition statutes have been devised to help protect shareholders of the company being acquired.

a. Federal Regulation of Tender Offers—The Williams Act
A tender offer is an offer to shareholders (the offerees) of a corporation (the target) asking them to tender their shares in exchange for either cash or securities. The tender offer is usually made by another corporation (the bidder), but the bidder may also be an individual or a group. Tender offers have replaced proxy fights as the primary method of gaining control over a target corporation. Tender offers are regulated in a number of respects by the Williams Act, which added sections 13(d), 14(d), and 14(e) to the Securities Exchange Act of 1934.

1) Regulation of the Bidder
What constitutes a tender offer within the meaning of the Williams Act is not settled. For bar exam purposes, a tender offer will usually include most of the following elements:

(i)   A ***widespread solicitation of public shareholders***;

(ii) For a *substantial percentage* of the target's stock;

(iii) At a *premium price* (above the prevailing market price);

(iv) *Contingent* on the tender of a fixed number of shares.

Open market purchases made anonymously generally are not considered to be tender offers within the meaning of the Act.

a) Disclosure Required

Section 14(d) requires any person who makes a tender offer for a class of registered securities which would result in the person owning more than *5%* of a class of securities of the target to file a schedule 14D containing extensive disclosure of the identity of the bidder, past dealings between the bidder and the target, the bidder's source of funds, the bidder's plans concerning the target, the bidder's financial statements (if the bidder is not an individual), and the arrangements, if any, made between the bidder and those holding important positions with the target.

Note: Anyone who *obtains* more than 5% of any class of registered equity securities must file a somewhat similar (schedule 13D) disclosure.

b) Regulation of Terms of Tender Offer

Under section 14(d) and rules 14d and 14e:

(1) A tender offer *must be held open for at least 20 days*;

(2) A tender offer *must be open to all security holders of the class* of securities subject to the tender offer;

(3) Shareholders *must be permitted to withdraw tendered shares* while the offer remains open;

(4) If the offer is oversubscribed, the bidder *must purchase on a pro rata basis* from among the shares deposited during the first 10 days or such other period as the bidder designates; and

(5) If the tender offer price is increased, the *higher price must be paid to all tendering shareholders.*

2) Regulation of the Target

Rule 14e-2 requires the management of the target corporation, within 10 business days from the date the tender offer is first published, to give its shareholders a statement disclosing that the target either: (i) recommends acceptance or rejection of the tender; (ii) expresses no opinion and is remaining neutral toward the tender offer; or (iii) is unable to take a position with respect to the tender offer. In any case, the statement must also include the reasons for the position taken.

3) General Antifraud Provisions

The Williams Act also contains a broad antifraud provision prohibiting any false or misleading statements or omissions in connection with a tender offer, by either the offeror, the target (*i.e.,* the incumbent management in attempting to oppose the tender offer), or any other person.

a) Shareholders of Target Have Standing for Civil Damage Action

The shareholders of the target corporation, as the primary beneficiaries of the Williams Act, have standing under the Act to bring a civil action for ***damages*** or an injunction for violation of the Act. An unsuccessful bidder does ***not*** have standing to assert a claim for damages against a successful competing bidder or the target for violation of the Act [Piper v. Chris-Craft Industries, Inc., 430 U.S. 1 (1977)], although the bidder might have standing to seek an injunction against any false statements.

b) SEC May Seek Injunction

The SEC clearly has standing to seek to enjoin false or misleading statements under the Williams Act.

b. State Regulation—Control Share Acquisition Statutes

A number of states have also sought to protect shareholders from takeovers, particularly hostile takeovers. Although state regulations vary, of states adopting such legislation, control share acquisition statutes are the most popular. Under a control share acquisition statute, if a designated stock ownership threshold (*e.g.,* 20% of the shares in a class) is crossed by an acquiring shareholder, he loses the right to vote the acquired shares until the right to vote is restored by a vote of a majority of the shares held by disinterested shareholders. Since this could leave a takeover bidder powerless to control the management of the target corporation, it can prevent hostile takeovers.

Example: A state statute has three thresholds: 20%, 33%, and 50%. If a purchase of shares takes the purchaser across one of these lines, voting power in the control shares can be restored only with approval of the target's disinterested shareholders.

1) Limitation on Scope

The first generation of control share acquisition statutes were very broad, attempting to reach all tender offers made to target shareholders who were residents of the state and all target corporations doing business in the state. The Supreme Court held that such broad statutes were unconstitutional, both because they imposed an undue burden on interstate commerce and because they conflicted with the Williams Act and so violated the Supremacy Clause. [*See, e.g.,* Edgar v. MITE Corp., 457 U.S. 624 (1982)] However, the Court has upheld narrow statutes. To be valid, the statute should be applicable only to ***corporations or transactions significantly connected to the state***, such as a corporation whose principal place of business is the regulating state and which has a significant number of shareholders (*e.g.,* 1,000 shareholders, 10% of the target class, etc.) in the regulating state.

X. DISSOLUTION AND LIQUIDATION

A. INTRODUCTION
Dissolution is the termination of the corporate existence. To dissolve the corporation, some act must be taken, which may be voluntary by the corporation or its aggregate members, or may be involuntary through judicial proceedings.

B. VOLUNTARY DISSOLUTION
Dissolution by corporate action without judicial proceedings is termed voluntary dissolution and may be accomplished in the following ways:

1. Dissolution by Incorporators or Initial Directors

A majority of the incorporators or initial directors may dissolve the corporation if *shares have not yet been issued or business has not yet been commenced* by delivering articles of dissolution to the state. All corporate debts must be paid before dissolution, and if shares have been issued, any assets remaining after winding up must be distributed to the shareholders. [RMBCA §14.01]

2. Dissolution by Corporate Act

The corporation may dissolve voluntarily by an act of the corporation, involving both board of directors and shareholder approval. The standard procedure for *fundamental corporate change* is followed. [RMBCA §14.02]

3. Effect of Dissolution

A corporation that has been dissolved continues its corporate existence, but is not allowed to carry on any business except that which is appropriate to *wind up and liquidate its affairs*. Permissible activities include collection of assets, disposal of property that will not be distributed in kind to shareholders, discharging liabilities, and distributing remaining property among shareholders according to their interests. Dissolution does not transfer title to the corporation's property, change quorum or voting requirements, suspend proceedings pending against or by the corporation, or prevent commencement of a proceeding by or against the corporation. [RMBCA §14.05]

a. Barring Claims Against the Corporation

A claim can be asserted against a dissolved corporation—even if the claim does not arise until after dissolution—to the extent of the corporation's undistributed assets. If the assets have been distributed to the shareholders, a claim can be asserted against each shareholder for his pro rata share of the claim, to the extent of the assets distributed to him. To provide some finality for liquidating distributions, the RMBCA provides special procedures that a corporation may follow in order to bar claims against the corporation sooner than they might be barred under the statute of limitations for the claims.

1) Known Claims Against Dissolved Corporation—120 Days

To bar known claims against the corporation, the corporation must notify its known claimants in writing of the dissolution. The notice must describe the procedure for asserting a claim and set a deadline not less than 120 days from the effective date of notice by which the claim must be received. A claim is barred if a claimant who receives notice fails to deliver the claim by the deadline, or if a claimant whose claim has been rejected does not commence a proceeding to enforce the claim within 90 days from the effective date of the rejection. [RMBCA §14.06]

2) Unknown Claims Against Dissolved Corporation—Five Years

To bar claims not known to the corporation, the corporation must publish notice of its dissolution in a newspaper in the county where the corporation's principal place of business is located. The notice must describe the procedure for asserting a claim and state that a claim will be barred unless a proceeding to enforce it is commenced within five years after notice is published. [RMBCA §14.07]

4. Revocation of Voluntary Dissolution

A corporation may revoke a voluntary dissolution by using the same procedure that was used to approve the dissolution. The revocation relates back to and takes effect as of the effective date of the dissolution, so that the corporation may resume carrying on its business as if there had never been a dissolution. [RMBCA §14.04]

C. ADMINISTRATIVE DISSOLUTION

1. Grounds for Administrative Dissolution

The state may bring an action to administratively dissolve a corporation for any of the following reasons:

(i) *Failure to pay any fees or penalties* imposed by law within 60 days after their due date;

(ii) *Failure to deliver the annual report* to the state within 60 days after it is due;

(iii) *Failure to maintain a registered agent in the state* for 60 days or more;

(iv) *Failure to notify the state of a change in registered agent* within 60 days; or

(v) *Expiration of the period of corporate duration* set forth in the articles of incorporation.

[RMBCA §14.20]

2. Procedure and Effect

If grounds for dissolution exist as set forth above, the state must serve the corporation with written notice. If the corporation does not correct the grounds for dissolution or show that the grounds do not exist within *60* days after service of notice, the state effectuates the dissolution by signing a certificate of dissolution. [RMBCA §14.21]

3. Reinstatement May Be Retroactive for up to Two Years

A corporation that is administratively dissolved may apply for reinstatement within two years after the effective date of dissolution. The application must state that the grounds for dissolution did not exist or that they have been eliminated. *Reinstatement relates back* to the date of dissolution and the corporation may resume carrying on business as if the dissolution had never occurred. [RMBCA §14.22]

D. JUDICIAL DISSOLUTION

1. Action by Attorney General
The attorney general may seek judicial dissolution of a corporation on the ground that the corporation *fraudulently obtained its articles* of incorporation or that the corporation is *exceeding or abusing its authority*. [RMBCA §14.30(a)]

2. Action by Shareholders
Shareholders may seek judicial dissolution on any of the following grounds:

(i) The *directors are deadlocked* in the management of corporate affairs, the shareholders are unable to break the deadlock, and *irreparable injury* to the corporation is threatened or corporate affairs cannot be conducted to the advantage of the shareholders because of the deadlock;

(ii) The directors have acted or will act in a manner that is *illegal, oppressive, or fraudulent*;

(iii) The *shareholders are deadlocked* in voting power and have *failed to elect one or more directors* for a period that includes at least two consecutive annual meeting dates; or

(iv) *Corporate assets are being wasted or misapplied to noncorporate purposes.*

[RMBCA §14.30(b)]

a. Election to Purchase in Lieu of Dissolution
If the proceeding to dissolve is by the shareholders and the corporation has no shares listed on a national securities exchange or regularly traded in a market maintained by one or more members of a national or affiliated securities association, the corporation (or one or more shareholders) may elect to purchase the shares owned by the petitioning shareholder at their fair value. The petitioning shareholder may not dispose of her shares without court permission until the repurchase is completed. [RMBCA §14.34]

3. Action by Creditors
Creditors may seek judicial dissolution if: (i) the creditor's claim has been reduced to judgment, execution of the judgment has been returned unsatisfied, and *the corporation is insolvent*; or (ii) the corporation has admitted in writing that the creditor's claim is due and owing and *the corporation is insolvent*. [RMBCA §14.30(c)]

4. Action by Corporation—Court Supervision of Voluntary Dissolution
A court may dissolve a corporation in an action by the corporation to have its voluntary dissolution continued under court supervision. [RMBCA §14.30(d)]

PART FOUR—LIMITED LIABILITY COMPANIES AND FOREIGN CORPORATIONS

XI. LIMITED LIABILITY COMPANIES

A. INTRODUCTION
A majority of states have adopted statutes providing for the creation of Limited Liability Companies ("LLCs").

B.   PURPOSE

An LLC is an entity eligible to be taxed like a partnership while offering its owners (called "members") the limited liability that shareholders of a corporation enjoy. Under current tax laws, unless an LLC requests to be taxed as a corporation, it will receive partnership tax treatment (*i.e.*, the LLC will not be treated as a taxable entity; profits and losses flow through the LLC to its owners).

1.   Compare—S Corporations and Limited Partnerships

If a person is seeking a business format that offers limited personal liability and an opportunity to control the business, an LLC may be better than a Subchapter S corporation (a corporation that elects to be taxed as a partnership under the Tax Code) in that an LLC is not subject to the limitations of Subchapter S (*e.g.*, S corporations are limited to 75 or fewer shareholders). Similarly, an LLC may be better than a limited partnership because limited partnership acts require that there be at least one general partner, who is personally liable for the partnership's obligations; the LLC statutes do not require that a member (*i.e.*, shareholder) of the LLC be personally liable.

2.   Controlling Law—Statute vs. Operating Agreement

Although LLCs are governed by statute, the statute provides that LLC members may adopt *operating agreements* to control most aspects of the LLC's business and management. These agreements will control unless contrary to law.

3.   Distinct Entity

An LLC is treated as an entity distinct from its members. It may hold property in its own name, sue or be sued, etc.

C.   FORMATION

An LLC is formed by filing articles of organization with the secretary of state.

1.   Contents of Articles

The articles of an LLC must include the following:

a.   A statement that the entity is an LLC;

b.   The name of the LLC, which must include an indication that it is an LLC;

c.   The street address of the LLC's registered office and name of its registered agent; and

d.   The names of all of the members.

2.   Management

Management of the LLC is presumed to be by all members. Other management arrangements can be made (*e.g.*, management by only some of the members or by outside managers), but they must be specified in the articles. If management is by the members: (i) a majority vote is required to approve most decisions and (ii) each member is an agent of the LLC (*i.e.,* the LLC may be bound by the acts of any member).

D.   LIABILITY OF MEMBERS

As indicated above, members are *not* personally liable for the LLC's obligations.

E. SHARING OF PROFITS AND LOSSES
Profits and losses of an LLC are allocated *on the basis of contributions*.

F. TRANSFERS OF INTEREST
An assignment of a member's interest in an LLC transfers only the member's right to receive profits and losses. Management rights are not transferred. One can become a member (*i.e.*, management rights can be transferred) only with the consent of *all* members.

G. DISSOLUTION
Disassociation (*e.g.*, death, retirement, resignation, bankruptcy, incompetence, etc.) of an LLC member generally causes dissolution of the LLC.

XII. FOREIGN CORPORATIONS

A. POWER TO EXCLUDE
"A state has unlimited power to exclude or regulate foreign corporations other than those engaged in interstate commerce, since corporations are not citizens within the meaning of the Privileges and Immunities Clause." [Paul v. Virginia, 75 U.S. 168 (1869)]

B. ADMISSION
Usually, a foreign corporation may not transact business within a state until it has obtained a "certificate of authority" from the secretary of state.

1. Contents of Application for Certificate of Authority
The application must include the same basic information as is contained in the articles of a domestic corporation.

2. Issuance of Certificate
On finding compliance with law and payment of fees, the secretary will issue a certificate of authority.

C. STATE POWER OVER INTERNAL AFFAIRS OF FOREIGN CORPORATIONS
A foreign corporation may not be denied a certificate of authority because the laws of its state of incorporation governing its organization and internal affairs differ from the host jurisdiction.

D. EFFECT OF TRANSACTING BUSINESS WITHOUT CERTIFICATE

1. Cannot Bring Suit
Until a foreign corporation has obtained a certificate of authority to do business, a common penalty is refusal to allow access to state courts. The corporation may defend suits. However, it usually may obtain the certificate at any time, even after suit has been commenced.

2. No Effect on Contracts
Failure to obtain a certificate does not usually impair the validity of any contract or corporate act, although a minority of jurisdictions render contracts of an unauthorized foreign corporation void or voidable.

E. WITHDRAWAL

An authorized foreign corporation may, at any time, file an application for withdrawal which, when accepted by the secretary, terminates its authority to do business in the state. The corporation usually must consent to service of process on the secretary with respect to any proceeding based on a cause of action arising in the state while it was authorized to do business there.

PART FIVE—SECURITIES REGULATION

XIII. RULE 10b-5 AND SECTION 16(b)

A. RULE 10b-5

Under rule 10b-5, it is unlawful for any person, directly or indirectly, by the use of any means or instrumentality of interstate commerce or the mails, or of any facility of any national securities exchange to:

(i) Employ any device, scheme, or artifice *to defraud*;

(ii) *Make any untrue statement of a material fact or omit to state a material fact* necessary in order to make the statements made, in light of the circumstances under which they were made, not misleading; or

(iii) Engage in any act, practice, or course of business that *operates or would operate as a fraud or a deceit* upon any person, in connection with the purchase or sale of any security.

A violation of the rule can result in a private suit for damages, an SEC suit for injunctive relief, or criminal prosecution.

1. General Elements of Cause of Action

A private plaintiff must show the following elements to recover damages under rule 10b-5:

a. Fraudulent Conduct

The plaintiff must show that the defendant engaged in some fraudulent conduct. This can take a number of forms, *e.g.*, making a material misstatement or making a material omission.

1) Materiality

A statement or omission will be considered material if there is a *substantial likelihood that a reasonable investor would consider it important* in making her investment decision.

Example: Several insiders bought stock in their mining company on the basis of inside information regarding a substantial mineral find. When the information was publicly released, the price of the stock soared. The mineral find was a material fact. [SEC v. Texas Gulf Sulphur Co., 401 F.2d 833 (2d Cir. 1968)]

2) Scienter

To be fraudulent and actionable under rule 10b-5, the conduct complained of must have been undertaken with an ***intent to deceive, manipulate, or defraud***. The Supreme Court has held that this standard includes cases where a misstatement was made knowingly, but has reserved the issue whether misstatements that are made recklessly are proscribed (the circuit courts have uniformly held recklessness to be sufficient).

b. In Connection with the Purchase or Sale of a Security by Plaintiff
If the plaintiff is a private person, the fraudulent conduct must be connected to the purchase or sale of a security by the plaintiff. This includes transactions such as exchanges of stock for assets, mergers, contracts to sell, etc. It excludes potential purchasers who did not buy (because of the fraud) and people who already own shares and refrain from selling (because of the fraud). [*See* Blue Chip Stamps v. Manor Drug Stores, 421 U.S. 723 (1975)]

1) Nontrading Defendants Can Be Held Liable
Note that the focus here is on a sale or purchase ***by the plaintiff***; the defendant need not have purchased or sold any securities. Thus, a nontrading defendant, such as a company that intentionally publishes a misleading press release, can be held liable to a person who purchased or sold securities on the market on the basis of the press release.

2) Private Plaintiff May Not Maintain Suit Based on Aiding and Abetting
An action brought by a ***private plaintiff*** pursuant to section 10(b) of the 1934 Act may not be based on a defendant's status as an "aider and abettor" of other defendants' fraud [Central Bank of Denver, N.A. v. First Interstate Bank of Denver, N.A., 511 U.S. 164 (1994)]; but the ***government*** may base an action on aiding and abetting [1934 Act §20(f)].

c. In Interstate Commerce
The fraudulent conduct must involve the use of some means of interstate commerce; something as simple as use of the telephone or the mail will suffice.

d. Reliance
Generally, it is said that reliance is an element of a rule 10b-5 cause of action. However, in a nondisclosure case reliance is presumed; *i.e.,* the plaintiff need not prove reliance on the undisclosed information. Similarly, in a misrepresentation action on securities sold in a well-defined market (*e.g.,* national stock exchange), reliance on any public misrepresentations may be presumed based on the ***fraud on the market theory***: An investor who buys or sells stock at the price set by the market does so in reliance on the integrity of that stock, which in turn is based on publicly available information. [Basic, Inc. v. Levinson, 485 U.S. 224 (1988)] Thus, it appears that only in the case of face-to-face misrepresentation (*i.e.,* stock not sold on an exchange) will the plaintiff have to prove reliance.

1) Rebuttal of Presumption
The presumption of reliance may be rebutted (*e.g.,* by showing that the plaintiff would have acted the same way even with full disclosure, that the price was not affected by the misrepresentation, or that the plaintiff did not trade in reliance on the integrity of the market).

e.   Damages
A private plaintiff must show that the defendant's fraud caused the plaintiff damages.

2.   Insider Trading

While it may not be obvious, rule 10b-5's greatest impact is to prohibit most instances of trading securities on the basis of inside information (*i.e.*, information not disclosed to the public that an investor would think is important when deciding whether or not to invest in a security). Early insider trading cases focused on the duty of the trader to *disclose or abstain* from trading. Now, it is clear that a person violates rule 10b-5 if he breaches a *duty of trust and confidence* owed to: (i) the issuer, (ii) shareholders of the issuer, or (iii) in the case of misappropriators (*see* below), another person who is the source of the material nonpublic information. [*See* Rule 10b5-1(a)]

a.   Who May Be Liable

1)   "Insiders"
Anyone who breaches a duty not to use inside information for personal benefit can be held liable under rule 10b-5. Typical securities insiders, such as directors, officers, controlling shareholders, and employees of the issuer are deemed to owe a duty of trust and confidence to their corporation which is breached by trading on inside information. Constructive insiders, such as a securities issuer's CPAs, attorneys, and bankers performing services for securities issuers, also owe such a duty.

Example: On Monday, Dee, the president of a publicly held mining company, is told by company geologists that they just discovered a huge cache of gold on company property. Dee contacts the company's outside attorney, Alex, to discuss how she should go about disclosing the information. Dee and Alex decide that it would be best to announce the information to the public on Friday. The announcement will probably cause the price of the company's stock to skyrocket. Neither the geologists, Dee, nor Alex may purchase company stock before the information is made public, unless they disclose the information to the seller.

2)   Tippers and Tippees
Where an insider gives a tip of inside information to someone else who trades on the basis of the inside information, the tipper can be liable under rule 10b-5 if the tip was made for *any improper purpose* (*e.g.*, in exchange for money or a kickback, as a gift, for a family member's benefit, for reputational benefit, etc.). The tippee can be held liable derivatively if the tipper breached a duty *and* the tippee knew that the tipper was breaching the duty.

Example: Same facts as in a., above. If Dee meets her brother Bob in a restaurant and tells him about the gold find, and Bob purchases company stock before the announcement, Dee can be held liable as a tipper and Bob can be held liable derivatively as a tippee. But if a stranger, Steve, overhears Dee explain that the company has just discovered gold and purchases stock before the public announcement is made, Steve would not be liable under rule 10b-5.

3) Misappropriators

Under the misappropriation doctrine, *the government* can prosecute a person under rule 10b-5 for trading on market information (*i.e.*, information about the supply of or demand for stock of a particular company) in breach of a duty of trust and confidence *owed to the source of the information*; the duty need not be owed to the issuer or shareholders of the issuer. [United States v. O'Hagan, 521 U.S. 642 (1997)] Rule 10b5-2 provides a nonexclusive list of circumstances under which a person will be deemed to owe a duty of trust and confidence in a misappropriation case:

(i) When the person *agrees to maintain information in confidence*;

(ii) When the person communicating the information and the person with whom it is communicated have a *history of sharing confidences* so that the recipient of the information should know that the person communicating the information expects the recipient to maintain confidentiality; or

(iii) When the person *receives the information from a spouse, child, parent, or sibling* (unless the recipient can prove that he had no reason to know that the information was confidential).

[Rule 10b5-2]

Example: Alex works as an attorney at a law firm. BigCorp retains Alex's firm in connection with a tender offer it is planning to make. Alex does not work on the tender offer in any way, but he comes across information about it while in the firm's photocopy room. If Alex trades in securities related to the tender offer, he can be held liable under rule 10b-5 in an action by the government, because by trading on the information, he breaches a duty of trust and confidence that he owes to the firm. [*See* United States v. O'Hagan, *supra*]

3. Remedies

a. In General

The federal courts have exclusive jurisdiction over claims arising under rule 10b-5. To remedy a rule 10b-5 violation, *individual* plaintiffs can sue for damages or rescission. *Damages* are based on the difference between the price paid (or received) by the plaintiff, and the average share price in the 90-day period after corrective information is disseminated. [1934 Act §21D(e)] *Rescission* is available in lieu of damages. Note that *punitive damages* are *not* available under rule 10b-5, but might be under appropriate state-law claims for fraud.

b. Insider Trading Sanctions Act and Insider Trading and Securities Fraud Enforcement Act

The Insider Trading Sanctions Act [1934 Act §21A] provides an important weapon against insider trading. It authorizes the SEC to sue persons who illegally trade on the securities exchanges while in possession of material, nonpublic information (and their tippees), as well as persons who violate the Act by communicating such information, for a *civil penalty* equal to three times the profit gained or loss avoided by the defendant's unlawful purchase, sale, or communication. This treble-damages penalty is important, because it means a defendant may lose more than his ill-gotten profits, thereby creating a powerful disincentive to insider trading.

1) Private Right of Action—Insider Trading and Securities Fraud Enforcement Act

The Act creates a private remedy against one who illegally trades while in possession of material, nonpublic information on behalf of any person who contemporaneously traded the same class of securities. Damages are limited, however, to the *profit gained or loss avoided* by the defendant in the subject transactions. [1934 Act §20A(1), (2)]

2) Criminal Penalties

The penalties above are in addition to all other existing sanctions, including jail terms of up to 10 years, and criminal fines of up to $1 million for individuals and $2.5 million for corporations.

B. SECTION 16(b)

Section 16(b) of the Securities Exchange Act of 1934 provides that any profit realized by a director, officer, or shareholder owning 10% or more of the outstanding shares of the corporation from any purchase and sale, or sale and purchase, of any equity security of his corporation within a period of *less than six months* must be returned to the corporation. The section applies to publicly held corporations whose shares are *traded on a national exchange or* that have *at least 500 shareholders* in any outstanding class and *at least $10 million in assets*.

1. Strict Liability Imposed

The purpose of section 16(b) is to prevent unfair use of inside information and internal manipulation of price. This is accomplished by imposing strict liability for covered transactions whether or not there is any material fact that should or could have been disclosed—no proof of use of inside information is required.

2. Elements of Cause of Action

a. Purchase and Sale or Sale and Purchase Within Six Months

Section 16(b) applies only to profits from purchases and sales made within a six-month period. In most instances, it is easy to define a purchase or sale. However, there are some areas of corporate stock transactions—such as reclassification, conversion, and exercise of stock options—where the time and event of purchase or sale is uncertain. The test normally applied to determine whether there is a purchase or sale is whether "this is the kind of transaction in which abuse of inside information is likely to occur."

b. Equity Security

Section 16(b) applies only to purchases and sales of equity securities. An equity security is any security other than a pure debt instrument, including options, warrants, preferred stock, common stock, etc.

c. Officer, Director, or Ten Percent Shareholder

Section 16(b) applies only to purchases and sales made by officers, directors, or 10% shareholders.

1) **Deputization of Director**

Ordinarily, it is easy to identify the officers, directors, and 10% shareholders of a corporation. In some instances, however, a person may "deputize" another person to act as his representative on the board. In these cases, securities transactions of the principal will come within section 16(b).

2) **Timing Issues**

a) **Officers or Directors**

Purchases or sales made by persons *before* becoming an officer or director generally are excluded from the scope of section 16(b), because a person generally does not have access to the inside information sought to be protected from abuse under section 16(b) before becoming an officer or director. On the other hand, purchases and sales made within six months after ceasing to be an officer or director can come within section 16(b).

b) **Ten Percent Shareholder**

A person is a 10% shareholder if he directly or indirectly owns 10% of any class of equity security of the corporation at the time immediately before *both* the purchase and the sale. Thus, the purchase that brings a shareholder over the 10% threshold is not within the scope of section 16(b).

3. **Profit Realized**

The profit recoverable under section 16(b), known as "short swing profits," includes not only traditional profits, but also losses avoided. "Profit" is determined by matching the ***highest sales price against the lowest purchase price*** during any six-month period. Remember that use of inside information is not material to this recovery.

Example: Don Director purchases 100 shares of his company's stock at $9 on February 1. He sells 100 shares on August 1 at $7 per share. He then buys 100 shares at $1 per share on November 15. Despite the fact that the stock he purchased in February was sold at a loss of $2 per share in August, and he now holds shares with a basis of $1, he will be liable for a profit under section 16(b). The August sale will be matched with the November purchase, resulting in a "profit" of $6 per share, and causing him to be liable in the amount of $600.

BAR REVIEW

Criminal Procedure

celebrating over

30 YEARS

*of preparing
law students
for the bar exam*

CRIMINAL PROCEDURE

TABLE OF CONTENTS

I. CONSTITUTIONAL RESTRAINTS ON CRIMINAL PROCEDURE

A. INTRODUCTION

The development of numerous constitutional limitations upon the manner in which a criminal suspect may be arrested, convicted, and punished has rendered much of criminal procedure an inquiry into constitutional law.

B. INCORPORATION OF BILL OF RIGHTS INTO DUE PROCESS

The first eight amendments to the United States Constitution apply by their terms only to the federal government. However, the Supreme Court has incorporated many of these rights into the due process requirement binding on the states by virtue of the Fourteenth Amendment. Those portions of the Bill of Rights "fundamental to our concept of ordered liberty" have been so incorporated. [Duncan v. Louisiana, 391 U.S. 145 (1968)]

C. CONSTITUTIONAL REQUIREMENTS BINDING ON STATES

The following rights have been held binding on the states under the due process provisions of the Fourteenth Amendment:

1. The Fourth Amendment *prohibition against unreasonable searches and seizures* [Wolf v. Colorado, 338 U.S. 25 (1949)], and the *exclusionary rule* requiring that the result of a violation of this prohibition not be used as evidence against the defendant [Mapp v. Ohio, 367 U.S. 643 (1961)];

2. The Fifth Amendment *privilege against compulsory self-incrimination* [Malloy v. Hogan, 378 U.S. 1 (1964)];

3. The Fifth Amendment *prohibition against double jeopardy* [Benton v. Maryland, 395 U.S. 784 (1969)];

4. The Sixth Amendment right to a *speedy trial* [Klopfer v. North Carolina, 386 U.S. 213 (1967)];

5. The Sixth Amendment right to a *public trial* [*In re* Oliver, 333 U.S. 257 (1948)];

6. The Sixth Amendment right to *trial by jury* [Duncan v. Louisiana, 391 U.S. 145 (1968)];

7. The Sixth Amendment right to *confront witnesses* [Pointer v. Texas, 380 U.S. 400 (1965)];

8. The Sixth Amendment right to *compulsory process* for obtaining witnesses [Washington v. Texas, 388 U.S. 14 (1967)];

9. The Sixth Amendment right to *assistance of counsel* in felony cases [Gideon v. Wainwright, 372 U.S. 335 (1963)], and in misdemeanor cases in which imprisonment is imposed [Argersinger v. Hamlin, 407 U.S. 25 (1972)]; and

10. The Eighth Amendment *prohibition against cruel and unusual punishment* [Robinson v. California, 370 U.S. 660 (1962)].

D. CONSTITUTIONAL RIGHTS NOT BINDING ON STATES

Two provisions of the Bill of Rights have not been held binding on the states.

1. **Right to Indictment**

   The right to indictment by a grand jury for capital and infamous crimes has been held not to be binding on the states. [Hurtado v. California, 110 U.S. 516 (1884)]

2. **Prohibition Against Excessive Bail**

   It has not yet been determined whether the Eighth Amendment prohibition against excessive bail creates a right to bail (or whether it simply prohibits excessive bail where the right to bail exists) and whether it is binding on the states. However, most state constitutions create a right to bail and prohibit excessive bail.

II. EXCLUSIONARY RULE

A. IN GENERAL

The exclusionary rule is a judge-made doctrine that prohibits the introduction at a criminal trial, of evidence obtained in violation of a defendant's Fourth, Fifth, or Sixth Amendment rights.

1. **Rationale**

   The main purpose of the exclusionary rule is to deter the government (primarily the police) from violating a person's constitutional rights: If the government cannot use evidence obtained in violation of a person's rights, it will be less likely to act in contravention of those rights. The rule also serves as one remedy for deprivation of constitutional rights (other remedies include civil suits, injunctions, etc.).

2. **Scope of the Rule**

   a. **Fruit of the Poisonous Tree**

      Generally, not only must ***illegally obtained evidence*** be excluded, but also ***all evidence obtained or derived*** from exploitation of that evidence. The courts deem such evidence the tainted fruit of the poisonous tree. [Nardone v. United States, 308 U.S. 338 (1939); Wong Sun v. United States, 371 U.S. 471 (1963)]

Example:	D was arrested ***without probable cause*** and brought to the police station. The police read D his *Miranda* warnings three times and permitted D to see two friends. After being at the station for six hours, D confessed. The confession must be excluded because it is the direct result of the unlawful arrest—if D had not been arrested illegally, he would not have been in custody and would not have confessed. [Taylor v. Alabama, 457 U.S. 687 (1982)]
Compare:	Police ***have probable cause*** to arrest D. They go to D's home and improperly arrest him without a warrant, in violation of the Fourth Amendment (*see* III.B.2.b.3), *infra*). D confesses at home, and the police then take him to the station. D confesses again at the station. The home confession must be excluded from evidence since it is the fruit of the illegal arrest, but the station house confession is admissible because it is not a fruit of the unlawful arrest. Because the police had probable cause to arrest D, they did not gain anything from the unlawful arrest—they could have lawfully arrested D the moment he stepped outside of his home and then brought him to the station for his confession. Thus,

the station house confession was not an exploitation of the police misconduct; *i.e.,* it was not a fruit of the fact that D was arrested at home as opposed to somewhere else. [New York v. Harris, 495 U.S. 14 (1990)]

b.   Exception—Breaking the Causal Chain
Under the fruit of the poisonous tree doctrine, the exclusionary rule can be very broadly applied. Recently, however, the Court has begun to narrow the scope of the rule by balancing its purpose (deterrence of government misconduct) against its costs (exclusion of probative evidence). The Court generally will not apply the rule when it will not likely deter government misconduct. Thus, if there is a weak link between the government misconduct and the evidence (*i.e.,* it is not likely that the misconduct caused the evidence to be obtained), the Court will probably not exclude the evidence.

1)   Independent Source
Evidence is admissible if the prosecution can show that it was obtained from a source independent of the original illegality.

Example: Police illegally search a warehouse and discover marijuana, but do not seize it. The police later return to the warehouse with a valid warrant based on information totally unrelated to the illegal search. If police seize the marijuana pursuant to the warrant, the marijuana is admissible. [Murray v. United States, 487 U.S. 533 (1988)]

2)   Intervening Act of Free Will
An intervening act of free will by the defendant will break the causal chain between the evidence and the original illegality and thus remove the taint. [Wong Sun v. United States, *supra*]

Example: The defendant was released on his own recognizance after an illegal arrest but later returned to the station to confess. This voluntary act of free will removed any taint from the confession. [Wong Sun v. United States, *supra*]

Compare: The reading of *Miranda* warnings, even when coupled with the passage of six hours and consultation with friends, was not sufficient to break the causal chain under the facts of *Taylor v. Alabama* (*see* 2.a., above).

3)   Inevitable Discovery
If the prosecution can show that the police would have discovered the evidence whether or not they had acted unconstitutionally, the evidence will be admissible. [Nix v. Williams, 467 U.S. 431 (1984)]

4)   Live Witness Testimony
It is difficult for a defendant to have live witness testimony excluded as the fruit of illegal police conduct, because a more direct link between the unconstitutional police conduct and the testimony is required than for exclusion of other evidence. The factors a court must consider in determining whether a sufficiently direct link exists include the extent to which the witness is freely willing to testify and the extent to which excluding the witness's testimony would deter future illegal conduct. [United States v. Ceccolini, 435 U.S. 268 (1978)]

5) In-Court Identification

The defendant *may not exclude* the witness's in-court identification on the ground that it is the fruit of an unlawful detention. [United States v. Crews, 445 U.S. 463 (1980)]

B. LIMITATIONS ON THE RULE

1. Inapplicable to Grand Juries

A grand jury witness may not refuse to answer questions on the ground that they are based on evidence obtained from an unlawful search and seizure [United States v. Calandra, 414 U.S. 338 (1974)], unless the evidence was obtained in violation of the federal wiretapping statute [Gelbard v. United States, 408 U.S. 41 (1972)].

2. Inapplicable to Civil Proceedings

The exclusionary rule does not forbid one sovereign from using in civil proceedings evidence that was illegally seized by the agent of another sovereign. [United States v. Janis, 428 U.S. 433 (1976)] Moreover, the Supreme Court would probably allow the sovereign that illegally obtained evidence to use it in a civil proceeding. The exclusionary rule does apply, however, to a proceeding for forfeiture of an article used in violation of the criminal law, when forfeiture is clearly a penalty for the criminal offense. [One 1958 Plymouth Sedan v. Pennsylvania, 380 U.S. 693 (1965)]

Example: Evidence that is inadmissible in a state criminal trial because it was illegally seized by the police may be used by the IRS. [United States v. Janis, *supra*]

3. Inapplicable to Internal Agency Rules

The exclusionary rule applies only if there is a violation of the Constitution or federal law; it does not apply to a violation of only internal agency rules. [United States v. Caceres, 440 U.S. 741 (1979)]

4. Inapplicable in Parole Revocation Proceedings

The exclusionary rule does not apply in parole revocation proceedings. [Pennsylvania v. Scott, 524 U.S. 357 (1998)]

5. Good Faith Reliance on Existing Law, Defective Search Warrant, or Clerical Error

The exclusionary rule does not apply when the police act in good faith based on case law later changed by another judicial opinion [United States v. Peltier, 422 U.S. 531 (1975)] or on a facially valid statute or ordinance as it then exists, even if the law is declared unconstitutional or the law is changed by court decision [Michigan v. DeFillippo, 443 U.S. 31 (1979); Illinois v. Krull, 480 U.S. 340 (1987)]; or when they act in reliance in good faith on a defective search warrant [United States v. Leon, 468 U.S. 897 (1984); Massachusetts v. Sheppard, 468 U.S. 981 (1984)]. Similarly, the exclusionary rule does not apply to evidence obtained during an arrest made on the basis of a computer report that, due to clerical errors not made by the police, indicated that there was an arrest warrant outstanding against the defendant. [Arizona v. Evans, 514 U.S. 1 (1995)] *Rationale:* One of the main purposes of the exclusionary rule is to deter improper police conduct, and this purpose cannot be served where police are acting in good faith.

a. Exceptions to Good Faith Reliance on Search Warrant

The Court in *Leon* and *Sheppard* suggested four exceptions to the good faith defense for reliance on a defective search warrant. A police officer cannot rely on a defective search warrant in good faith if:

1) The affidavit underlying the warrant is so lacking in probable cause that no reasonable police officer would have relied on it;

2) The warrant is defective on its face (*e.g.*, it fails to state with particularity the place to be searched or the things to be seized);

3) The police officer or government official obtaining the warrant lied to or misled the magistrate; or

4) The magistrate has "wholly abandoned his judicial role."

6. Use of Excluded Evidence for Impeachment Purposes
Some illegally obtained evidence that is inadmissible in the state's case in chief may nevertheless be used to impeach the defendant's credibility if he takes the stand at trial.

a. Voluntary Confessions in Violation of *Miranda*
An otherwise voluntary confession taken in violation of the *Miranda v. Arizona* requirements is admissible at trial for impeachment purposes. [Harris v. New York, 401 U.S. 222 (1971); Oregon v. Hass, 420 U.S. 714 (1975)] However, a truly involuntary confession is not admissible for any purpose. [Mincey v. Arizona, 437 U.S. 385 (1978)]

b. Fruit of Illegal Searches
The prosecution may use evidence obtained from an illegal search that is inadmissible in its direct case to impeach the defendant's statements made in response to proper cross-examination reasonably suggested by the defendant's direct examination [United States v. Havens, 446 U.S. 620 (1980)], but such illegally obtained evidence cannot be used to impeach the trial testimony of witnesses other than the defendant [James v. Illinois, 493 U.S. 307 (1990)].

7. *Miranda* Violations
The Supreme Court has suggested that fruits derived from statements obtained in violation of *Miranda* (*see* IV.D.1., *infra*) might be admissible despite the exclusionary rule. [Oregon v. Elstad, *infra*, IV.D.4.b.]

C. HARMLESS ERROR TEST
A conviction will not necessarily be overturned merely because improperly obtained evidence was admitted at trial; the harmless error test applies, so a conviction can be upheld if the conviction would have resulted despite the improper evidence. On appeal, the government bears the burden of showing *beyond a reasonable doubt* that the admission was harmless. [Chapman v. California, 386 U.S. 18 (1967); Milton v. Wainwright, 407 U.S. 371 (1972)] In a habeas corpus proceeding, if a petitioner claims a constitutional error, the petitioner must be released if the error had *substantial and injurious effect or influence* in determining the jury's verdict. [Brecht v. Abrahamson, 507 U.S. 619 (1993)] If the judge is in "grave doubt" as to the harm (*e.g.*, where

the record is evenly balanced as to harmlessness), the petition must be granted. [O'Neal v. McAninch, 513 U.S. 432 (1995)]

D. ENFORCING THE EXCLUSIONARY RULE

1. Right to Hearing on Motion to Suppress
The defendant is entitled to have the admissibility of evidence or a confession decided as a matter of law by a judge out of the hearing of the jury. [Jackson v. Denno, 378 U.S. 368 (1964)] It is permissible to let the jury reconsider the "admissibility" of the evidence if the judge finds it admissible, but there is no constitutional right to such a dual evaluation. [Lego v. Twomey, 404 U.S. 477 (1972)] And the defendant is not constitutionally entitled to have a specific finding of fact on each factual question. [LaValee v. Delle Rose, 410 U.S. 690 (1973)]

2. Burden of Proof
The government bears the burden of establishing admissibility by a preponderance of the evidence. [Lego v. Twomey, *supra*]

3. Defendant's Right to Testify
The defendant has the right to testify at the suppression hearing without his testimony being admitted against him at trial on the issue of guilt. [Simmons v. United States, 390 U.S. 377 (1968)]

III. FOURTH AMENDMENT

A. IN GENERAL
The Fourth Amendment provides that people should be free in their persons from ***unreasonable*** searches and seizures.

1. Search
A search can be defined as a governmental intrusion into an area where a person has a reasonable and justifiable expectation of privacy.

2. Seizure
A seizure can be defined as the exercise of control by the government over a person or thing.

3. Reasonableness
What is reasonable under the Fourth Amendment depends on the circumstances. For example, certain searches and seizures are considered to be reasonable only if the government has first obtained a warrant authorizing the action, while other searches and seizures are reasonable without a warrant. The material that follows specifically outlines the requirements for searches and seizures under the Fourth Amendment.

B. ARRESTS AND OTHER DETENTIONS
Governmental detentions of persons, including arrests, certainly constitute seizures of the person,

so they must be reasonable to comply with the Fourth Amendment. Whether a seizure of the person is reasonable depends on the scope of the seizure (*e.g.,* is it an arrest or merely an investigatory stop?) and the strength of the suspicion prompting the seizure (*e.g.,* an arrest requires probable cause while an investigatory detention can be based on reasonable suspicion).

1. **What Constitutes a Seizure of the Person?**

Generally, it is obvious when police arrest or seize a person. When it is not readily apparent, the Supreme Court has indicated that a seizure occurs only when a reasonable person would believe that she is not free to leave. [Michigan v. Chesternut, 486 U.S. 567 (1988)—police pursuit of suspect generally not a seizure] This requires a *physical application of force* by the officer or a *submission* to the officer's show of force. It is not enough that the officer merely ordered the person to stop. [California v. Hodari D., 499 U.S. 621 (1991)]

Example: Officers boarded a bus shortly before its departure and asked individuals for identification and consent to search their luggage. The mere fact that people felt they were not free to leave because they feared that the bus would depart does not make this a seizure of the person. The test is whether under the totality of the circumstances, a reasonable person would feel that he was not free to decline the officers' requests or otherwise terminate the encounter. [Florida v. Bostick, 501 U.S. 429 (1991)]

2. **Arrests**

An arrest occurs when the police take a person into custody against her will for purposes of criminal prosecution or interrogation.

a. **Probable Cause Requirement**

An arrest must be based on probable cause. Probable cause to arrest is present when at the time of arrest, the officer has within her knowledge reasonably trustworthy facts and circumstances sufficient to warrant a reasonably prudent person to believe that the suspect has committed or is committing a crime. [Beck v. Ohio, 379 U.S. 89 (1964)]

b. **Warrant Generally Not Required**

In contrast to the rule for searches, police generally need not obtain a warrant before arresting a person in a *public place*, even if they have time to get a warrant. [United States v. Watson, 423 U.S. 411 (1976)]

1) **Felony**

A police officer may arrest a person without a warrant when she has *reasonable grounds to believe* that a felony has been committed and that the person before her committed it.

2) **Misdemeanor**

An officer may make a warrantless arrest for a misdemeanor *committed in her presence*. A crime is committed in the officer's "presence" if she is aware of it through any of her senses.

Note: The police may make a warrantless misdemeanor arrest even if the crime for which the arrest is made cannot be punished by incarceration. [Atwater v. Lago Vista, 121 S. Ct. 1536 (2001)]

3) Exception—Home Arrests Require Warrant

The police must have an arrest warrant to effect a nonemergency arrest of an individual in her own home. [Payton v. New York, 445 U.S. 573 (1980)] All warrantless searches of homes are presumed unreasonable. The burden is on the government to demonstrate sufficient exigent circumstances to overcome this presumption. [Welsh v. Wisconsin, 466 U.S. 740 (1984)]

a) Homes of Third Parties

Absent exigent circumstances, the police executing an arrest warrant may not search for the subject of the warrant in the home of a third party without first obtaining a separate search warrant for the home. [Steagald v. United States, 451 U.S. 204 (1981)]

c. Effect of Invalid Arrest

An unlawful arrest, *by itself*, has no impact on a subsequent criminal prosecution. Thus, if the police improperly arrest a person (*e.g.,* at his home without a warrant), they may detain him if they have probable cause to do so [*see* New York v. Harris, 495 U.S. 14 (1990)], and the invalid arrest is not a defense to the offense charged [Frisbie v. Collins, 342 U.S. 519 (1952)]. Of course, evidence that is a fruit of the unlawful arrest may not be used against the defendant at trial because of the exclusionary rule.

3. Other Detentions

a. Investigatory Detentions (Stop and Frisk)

Police have the authority to briefly detain a person for investigative purposes even if they lack probable cause to arrest. To make such a stop, police must have a *reasonable suspicion* supported by *articulable facts* of criminal activity or involvement in a completed crime. [Terry v. Ohio, 392 U.S. 1 (1968)] *Note:* If the police also have reasonable suspicion to believe that the detainee is armed and dangerous, they may also conduct a frisk (a limited search) to ensure that the detainee has no weapons (*see* C.5.e., *infra*).

1) Reasonable Suspicion Defined

The Court has not specifically defined "reasonable suspicion." It requires something more than a vague suspicion (*e.g.,* it is not enough that the detainee was in a crime-filled area [Brown v. Texas, 443 U.S. 47 (1979)]), but full probable cause is not required. Whether the standard is met is judged under the totality of the circumstances. [United States v. Sokolow, 490 U.S. 1 (1989)]

Examples: 1) Reasonable suspicion justifying a stop is present when: (i) a suspect who is standing on a corner in a high crime area (ii) flees after noticing the presence of the police. Neither factor standing alone is enough to justify a stop, but together they are sufficiently suspicious. [Illinois v. Wardlow, 528 U.S. 119 (2000)]

2) Police had reasonable suspicion—and therefore there was no Fourth Amendment violation—where they detained Defendant at an airport while dogs sniffed his bags for drugs based on the following facts known by the police: (i) Defendant paid for airline

tickets in cash with small bills; (ii) Defendant traveled under a name that did not match the name for the phone number he gave; (iii) Defendant traveled to a drug source city (Miami) and stayed for only 48 hours, while his flight time was 20 hours; (iv) Defendant appeared nervous; and (v) Defendant refused to check his bags. [United States v. Sokolow, *supra*] *Note:* The fact that these suspicious circumstances are part of a drug courier profile used by the police neither helps nor hurts the totality of the circumstances inquiry.

2) Source of Suspicion

Like probable cause, reasonable suspicion need not arise from a police officer's personal knowledge. The suspicion can be based on a flyer, a police bulletin, or a report from an informant. [United States v. Hensley, 469 U.S. 221 (1985)]

a) Informant's Tips

Where the source of suspicion of criminal activity is an informant's tip, the tip must be accompanied by indicia of reliability sufficient to make the officer's suspicion reasonable.

Example: Police received an anonymous tip asserting that a woman was carrying cocaine and predicting that she would leave a specified apartment at a specified time, get into a specified car, and drive to a specified motel. After observing that the informant had accurately predicted the suspect's movements, it was reasonable for the police to think that the informant had inside knowledge that the suspect indeed had cocaine, thus justifying a *Terry* stop. [Alabama v. White, 496 U.S. 325 (1990)]

Compare: Police received an anonymous tip that a young black man in a plaid shirt standing at a particular bus stop was carrying a gun. When police arrived at the bus stop, they found a young black man there wearing a plaid shirt. They searched the man and found an illegal gun. Here there was not sufficient indicia of reliability in the tip to provide reasonable suspicion. The fact that the informant knows a person is standing at a bus stop does not show knowledge of any inside information; any passerby could observe the suspect's presence. Unlike the tip in *White,* the tip here did not provide predictive information and left police with no way to test the informant's knowledge and credibility. [Florida v. J.L., 529 U.S. 266 (2000)]

3) Duration and Scope

To be valid under *Terry,* the investigatory stop must be relatively brief and in any event no longer than is necessary to conduct a limited investigation to verify the officer's suspicions.

4) Development of Probable Cause

If during an investigatory detention, the officer develops probable cause, the detention becomes an arrest, and the officer can proceed on that basis. He can, for example, conduct a full search incident to that arrest.

5) What Constitutes a Stop?

If an officer merely approaches a person but does not detain her, no arrest or investigatory detention occurs. Not even reasonable suspicion is necessary in such cases. A seizure or stop occurs only if a reasonable person would believe she is not free to leave. (*See* B.1., *supra.*)

6) Property Seizures on Reasonable Suspicion

Police may briefly seize items upon reasonable suspicion that they are or contain contraband or evidence, but such seizures must be limited. [United States v. Place, 462 U.S. 696 (1983)—90-minute detention of luggage reasonably suspected to contain drugs unconstitutional]

b. Automobile Stops

Stopping a car is a seizure for Fourth Amendment purposes. Thus, generally, police may not stop a car unless they have at least reasonable suspicion to believe that a law has been violated. However, in certain cases where special law enforcement needs are involved, the Court allows police to set up roadblocks to stop cars without individualized suspicion that the driver has violated some law. To be valid, it appears that such roadblocks must: (i) stop cars on the basis of some neutral, articulable standard (*e.g.*, every car or every third car); and (ii) be designed to serve purposes closely related to a particular problem related to automobiles and their mobility. [*See* Delaware v. Prouse, 440 U.S. 648 (1979); *and see* Indianapolis v. Edmond, 531 U.S. 32 (2000)]

Examples: 1) Because of the gravity of the drunk driving problem and the magnitude of the states' interest in getting drunk drivers off the roads, police may set up roadblocks to check the sobriety of all drivers passing by. [Michigan Department of State Police v. Sitz, 496 U.S. 444 (1990)]

2) Because of the difficulty of discerning whether an automobile is transporting illegal aliens, police may set up roadblocks near the border to stop every car to check the citizenship of its occupants. [United States v. Martinez-Fuerte, 428 U.S. 543 (1976); *and see* United States v. Villamonte-Marquez, 462 U.S. 579 (1983)—suspicionless boarding of boat in channel leading to open sea justified on similar grounds]

Compare: The police may not set up roadblocks to check cars for illegal drugs. The nature of such a checkpoint is to detect evidence of ordinary criminal wrongdoing unrelated to use of cars or highway safety. If suspicionless stops were allowed under these circumstances, all suspicionless seizures would be justified. [Indianapolis v. Edmond, *supra*]

1) Police May Order Occupants Out

Provided that a police officer has lawfully stopped a vehicle, in the interest of officer safety, the officer may order the occupants (*i.e.*, the vehicle's driver *and* passengers) to get out. [Pennsylvania v. Mimms, 434 U.S. 106 (1978); Maryland v. Wilson, 519 U.S. 408 (1997)]

2) Pretextual Stops

If an officer has probable cause to believe that a traffic law has been violated, the officer may stop the suspect's car, even if the officer's ulterior motive is to investigate whether some *other law*—for which the officer lacks reasonable suspicion—is being violated. [Whren v. United States, 517 U.S. 806 (1996)—police in a high drug area stopped D's car after observing D wait a long time at an intersection, abruptly turn without signaling, and speed off at an unreasonable speed; *and see* Arkansas v. Sullivan, 121 S. Ct. 1876 (2001)]

c. **Detention to Obtain a Warrant**
If the police have probable cause to believe that a suspect has hidden drugs in his house, they may, for a reasonable time, prevent him from going into the house unaccompanied so that they can prevent him from destroying the drugs while they obtain a search warrant. [Illinois v. McArthur, 531 U.S. 326 (2001)—police kept suspect from reentering his trailer alone for two hours while an officer obtained a warrant]

d. **Occupants of Premises Being Searched May Be Detained**
Pursuant to the execution of a *valid warrant* to search for contraband, the police may detain occupants of the premises while a proper search is conducted. [Michigan v. Summers, 452 U.S. 692 (1981)]

e. **Station House Detention**
Police officers must have *full probable cause* for arrest to bring a suspect to the station for questioning [Dunaway v. New York, 442 U.S. 200 (1969)] or for fingerprinting [Hayes v. Florida, 470 U.S. 811 (1985)]. The Supreme Court has suggested that under some limited circumstances it might be permissible to require a person to go to the police station for investigatory purposes without probable cause for arrest [Davis v. Mississippi, 394 U.S. 721 (1969)], but the Court has never found such circumstances to exist.

4. **Stop and Identify Statutes**
A criminal statute requiring persons who loiter or wander on the streets to provide a "credible and reliable" identification when stopped by police is *unconstitutionally vague* for failure to clarify what will satisfy the identification requirement. [Kolender v. Lawson, 461 U.S. 352 (1983)]

5. **Grand Jury Appearance**
For all practical purposes, seizure of a person (by subpoena) for a grand jury appearance is *not within the Fourth Amendment's protection*. Even if, in addition to testifying, the person is to be asked to give handwriting or voice exemplars, there is no need for the subpoena to be based on probable cause or even objective suspicion. In other words, a person compelled to appear cannot assert that it was unreasonable to compel the appearance. However, the Supreme Court has suggested that it is conceivable that such a subpoena could be unreasonable if it was extremely broad and sweeping or if it was being used for harassment purposes. [United States v. Dionisio, 410 U.S. 1 (1973); United States v. Mara, 410 U.S. 19 (1973)]

6. **Deadly Force**
There is a Fourth Amendment "seizure" when a police officer uses deadly force to apprehend a suspect. An officer may not use deadly force unless the officer has *probable cause* to believe that the suspect poses a significant threat of death or serious physical injury to the officer or others. [Tennessee v. Garner, 471 U.S. 1 (1985)] On the other hand, a mere *attempt*

to arrest that results in the death of a suspect is not necessarily a seizure governed by the Fourth Amendment. For example, the Court has held that there was no seizure where an officer in a car pursued two suspects riding a motorcycle at high speeds and ran over and killed one of the suspects who had fallen. [Sacramento v. Lewis, 523 U.S. 833 (1998)—the Due Process Clause (not the Fourth Amendment) is applicable and would be violated only if the chase "shocked the conscience" of the Court, *see* D., *infra*]

C. EVIDENTIARY SEARCH AND SEIZURE

Like arrests, evidentiary searches and seizures must be reasonable to be valid under the Fourth Amendment. Reasonableness here usually means that the police must have obtained a warrant before conducting the search, but there are six circumstances where a warrant is not required (*see* 5., *infra*).

1. General Approach

A useful analytical model of the law of search and seizure requires answers to the following questions:

    a. Does the defendant have a *Fourth Amendment right*?

        1) Was there *governmental conduct*?

        2) Did the defendant have a *reasonable expectation of privacy*?

    b. If so, did the police have a *valid warrant*?

    c. If the police did not have a valid warrant, did they make a *valid warrantless search* and seizure?

2. Governmental Conduct Required

The Fourth Amendment generally protects only against governmental conduct and not against searches by private persons. Government agents here include only the *publicly paid police* and those *citizens acting at their direction* or behest; private security guards are not government agents unless deputized as officers of the public police.

Example: A private freight carrier opened a package and resealed it; police later re-opened the package. The Supreme Court found that this was not a "search" under the Fourth Amendment because the police found nothing more than the private carrier had found. Moreover, the warrantless field test of a substance found in the package to determine whether it was cocaine was not a Fourth Amendment "seizure," even though the testing went beyond the scope of the original private search. [United States v. Jacobsen, 466 U.S. 109 (1984)]

3. Reasonable Expectation of Privacy

To have a Fourth Amendment right, a person must have a reasonable expectation of privacy with respect to the place searched or the item seized.

a. Standing

It is not enough merely that *someone* has an expectation of privacy in the place searched or the item seized. The Supreme Court has imposed a standing requirement so that a person can complain about an evidentiary search or seizure only if it violates his *own* reasonable expectations of privacy. [Rakas v. Illinois, 439 U.S. 128 (1978)] Whether a person has a legitimate expectation of privacy generally is based on the *totality of the circumstances*, considering factors such as ownership of the place searched and location of the item seized. [Rawlings v. Kentucky, 448 U.S. 98 (1980)] The Court has held that a person has a legitimate expectation of privacy anytime:

(i)   She owned or had a right to possession of the place searched;

(ii) The place searched was in fact her home, whether or not she owned or had a right to possession of it; or

(iii) She was an overnight guest of the owner of the place searched [Minnesota v. Olson, 495 U.S. 91 (1990)].

1)   **Search of Third-Party Premises**
     Standing does not exist merely because a person will be harmed by introduction of evidence seized during an illegal search of a third person's property.

> *Example:*   A police officer peered through the closed window blind of Lessee's apartment and observed Lessee and defendants bagging cocaine. When defendants left the apartment, the officer followed them to their car and arrested them. The car and apartment were searched, and cocaine and a weapon were found. At trial, defendants moved to suppress all evidence, claiming that the officer's peeking through the window blind constituted an illegal search. It was determined that defendants had spent little time in Lessee's apartment and had come there solely to conduct a business transaction (*i.e.,* bagging the cocaine). *Held:* The defendants did not have a sufficient expectation of privacy in the apartment. They were there only for a few hours and were not overnight guests. Moreover, they were there for business purposes rather than social purposes, and there is a lesser expectation of privacy in commercial settings. Therefore, the defendants had no Fourth Amendment protections in the apartment and cannot challenge the search. [Minnesota v. Carter, 525 U.S. 83 (1999)]

2)   **No Automatic Standing to Object to Seizure of Evidence in Possessory Offense**
     Formerly, a defendant had automatic standing to object to the legality of a search and seizure anytime the evidence obtained was introduced against her in a possessory offense. (This allowed a defendant to challenge the search without specifically admitting possession of the items.) Because a defendant at a suppression hearing may now assert a legitimate expectation of privacy in the items without his testimony being used against him at trial [*see* Simmons v. United States, *supra*, II.D.3.], the automatic standing rule has been abolished as unnecessary [United States v. Salvucci, 448 U.S. 83 (1980)].

3)   **No Automatic Standing for Co-Conspirator**
     That a co-conspirator may be aggrieved by the introduction of damaging evidence does not give the co-conspirator automatic standing to challenge the seizure of the

evidence; the co-conspirator must show that her own expectation of privacy was violated. [United States v. Padilla, 508 U.S. 77 (1993)]

b.   Things Held Out to the Public

1)   Generally—No Expectation of Privacy

A person does not have a reasonable expectation of privacy in objects held out to the public, such as the sound of one's voice [United States v. Dionisio, *supra*, B.5.]; one's handwriting [United States v. Mara, *supra*, B.5.]; paint on the outside of a car [Cardwell v. Lewis, 417 U.S. 583 (1974)]; the smell of one's luggage (*e.g.,* drug sniffs by narcotics dogs) [United States v. Place, 462 U.S. 696 (1983)]; account records held by the bank [United States v. Miller, 425 U.S. 435 (1976)]; an automobile's movement on public roads and arrival at a private residence, even if detection of such movement requires the use of an electronic beeper placed on the automobile by the police [United States v. Knotts, 460 U.S. 276 (1983)]; or magazines offered for sale [Maryland v. Macon, 472 U.S. 463 (1985)].

a)   Compare—Feel of Luggage

Although the Supreme Court has held that one does not have a reasonable expectation of privacy in the smell of one's luggage, one does have a reasonable expectation of privacy in luggage against physically invasive inspections. Squeezing luggage to discern its contents constitutes a search. [Bond v. United States, 529 U.S. 334 (2000)]

Example: After completing an immigration status check of passengers on a bus, Officer began walking toward the front of the bus and squeezing soft-sided luggage in the overhead compartment. Upon feeling what felt like a brick in Defendant's bag, Officer searched the bag and found a "brick" of methamphetamine. The Court held that while travelers might expect their luggage to be lightly touched or moved from time-to-time, they do not expect their luggage to be subjected to an exploratory squeeze. Therefore, Officer's conduct constitutes a search under the Fourth Amendment. [Bond v. United States, *supra*]

2)   "Open Fields" Doctrine

Furthermore, under the "open fields" doctrine, areas outside the "curtilage" (dwelling house and outbuildings) are subject to police entry and search—these areas are "held out to the public" and are unprotected by the Fourth Amendment. (The court will consider the building's proximity to the dwelling, whether it is within the same enclosure—such as a fence—that surrounds the house, whether the building is used for activities of the home, and the steps taken by the resident to protect the building from the view of passersby.) [Oliver v. United States, 466 U.S. 170 (1984)] Even a building such as a barn may be considered to be outside the curtilage and therefore outside the protection of the Fourth Amendment. [United States v. Dunn, 480 U.S. 294 (1987)] In addition, the Fourth Amendment does not prohibit the warrantless search and seizure of garbage left for collection outside the curtilage of a home. [California v. Greenwood, 486 U.S. 35 (1988)]

3) **Fly-Overs**

The police may, within the Fourth Amendment, fly over a field to observe with the naked eye things therein. [California v. Ciraolo, 476 U.S. 207 (1986)] Even a low (400 feet) fly-over by a helicopter to view inside a partially covered greenhouse is permissible. [Florida v. Riley, 488 U.S. 445 (1989)—plurality decision based on flight being permissible under FAA regulations] The police may also take aerial photographs of a particular site. [Dow Chemical Co. v. United States, 476 U.S. 227 (1986)]

a) **Compare—Technologically Enhanced Searches of Homes**

The Supreme Court has held that because of the strong expectation of privacy within one's home, obtaining by sense enhancing technology any information regarding the interior of a home that could not otherwise have been obtained without physical intrusion constitutes a search, at least where the technology in question is not in general public use. [Kyllo v. United States, 121 S. Ct. 2038 (2001)—use of thermal imager on defendant's home from outside the curtilage to detect the presence of high intensity lamps commonly used to grow marijuana constitutes a search]

4) **Vehicle Identification Numbers**

A police officer may constitutionally reach into an automobile to move papers to observe the auto's vehicle identification number. [New York v. Class, 475 U.S. 106 (1986)]

4. **Searches Conducted Pursuant to a Warrant**

To be reasonable under the Fourth Amendment, most searches must be pursuant to a warrant. The warrant requirement serves as a check against unfettered police discretion by requiring police to apply to a neutral magistrate for permission to conduct a search. A search conducted without a warrant will be invalid (and evidence discovered during the search must be excluded from evidence) unless it is within one of the six categories of permissible warrantless searches (*see* 5., *infra*).

a. **Requirements of a Warrant**

To be valid, a warrant must:

1) Be issued by a *neutral and detached magistrate*;

2) Be *based on probable cause* established from facts submitted to the magistrate by a government agent upon oath or affirmation; and

3) *Particularly describe* the place to be searched and the items to be seized.

b. **Showing of Probable Cause**

A warrant will be issued only if there is probable cause to believe that seizable evidence will be found on the premises or person to be searched. [Carroll v. United States, 267 U.S. 132 (1925)] The officers requesting the warrant must submit to the magistrate an affidavit containing sufficient facts and circumstances to enable the magistrate to make an independent evaluation of probable cause (*i.e.,* the officers cannot merely present their conclusion that probable cause exists). [United States v. Ventresca, 380 U.S. 102 (1965)]

1) Use of Informers—Totality of Circumstances Test

If the officers' affidavit of probable cause is based on information obtained from informers, its sufficiency is determined by the *totality of the circumstances*. [Illinois v. Gates, 462 U.S. 213 (1983)] The affidavit need not contain any particular fact about the informer, as long as it includes enough information to allow the magistrate to make a common sense evaluation of probable cause (*i.e.,* that the information is trustworthy).

a) Reliability, Credibility, and Basis of Knowledge

Formerly, the affidavit had to include information regarding the reliability and credibility of the informer (*e.g.,* she has given information five times in the past and it has been accurate) and her basis for the knowledge (*e.g.,* she purchased cocaine from the house to be searched). These are still relevant factors, but are no longer prerequisites.

b) Informer's Identity

Generally, the informer's identity need *not* be revealed to obtain a search warrant [McCray v. Illinois, 386 U.S. 300 (1967)] (although if the informer is a material witness to the crime, her identity may have to be revealed at or before trial).

c) Going "Behind the Face" of the Affidavit

When a defendant attacks the validity of a search warrant, the Fourth Amendment permits her to contest the validity of some of the assertions in the affidavit upon which the warrant was issued. The defendant may go "behind the face" of the affidavit.

(1) Three Requirements to Invalidate Search Warrant

A search warrant issued on the basis of an affidavit that, on its face, is sufficient to establish probable cause will be invalid if the defendant establishes *all three* of the following:

(i) A *false statement* was included in the affidavit by the affiant (*i.e.,* the police officer applying for the warrant);

(ii) The affiant *intentionally or recklessly* included that false statement (*i.e.,* the officer either knew it was false or included it knowing that there was a substantial risk that it was false); and

(iii) The false statement was *material* to the finding of probable cause (*i.e.,* without the false statement, the remainder of the affidavit could not support a finding of probable cause). Thus, the mere fact that an affiant intentionally included a false statement in the affidavit apparently will not automatically render the warrant invalid under Fourth Amendment standards.

[Franks v. Delaware, 438 U.S. 154 (1978)]

(2) Evidence May Be Admissible Even Though Warrant Not Supported by Probable Cause

A finding that the warrant was invalid because it was not supported by probable cause will not entitle a defendant to exclude the evidence obtained under the warrant. Evidence obtained by police in *reasonable reliance* on a facially valid warrant may be used by the prosecution, despite an ultimate finding that the warrant was not supported by probable cause. [United States v. Leon, 468 U.S. 897 (1984); *and see* Massachusetts v. Sheppard, 468 U.S. 981 (1984)—technical defect in warrant insufficient basis for overturning murder conviction]

c. Warrant Must Be Precise on Its Face

The warrant must describe with reasonable precision the place to be searched and the items to be seized. This requirement will be strictly enforced where the warrant authorizes the seizure of books and similar items potentially protected by the First Amendment. [Stanford v. Texas, 379 U.S. 476 (1965)]

Examples: 1) A warrant authorizes the search of premises at 416 Oak Street for heroin. The structure at 416 Oak Street is a duplex. Is the warrant sufficiently precise? No. In a multi-unit dwelling, the warrant must specify which unit is to be searched. *But note:* If police reasonably believe there is only one apartment on the floor of a building, the warrant is not invalid if they discover, during the course of their search, that there are in fact two apartments on the floor. Indeed, any evidence police seize from the wrong apartment prior to the discovery of the error will be admissible. [Maryland v. Garrison, 480 U.S. 79 (1987)]

2) A was believed to have committed criminal fraud in regard to certain complex land transactions. A search warrant was issued authorizing the search for and seizure of numerous described documents and "other fruit, instrumentalities and evidence of the crime at this time unknown." Was the warrant sufficiently precise? Yes, given the complex nature of the crime and the difficulty of predicting precisely what form evidence of guilt would take. [Andresen v. Maryland, 427 U.S. 463 (1976)]

d. Search of Third-Party Premises Permissible

The Fourth Amendment does not bar searches of premises belonging to persons not suspected of crime, as long as there is *probable cause* to believe evidence of someone's guilt (or something else subject to seizure) will be found. Thus, a warrant can issue for the search of the offices of a newspaper if there is probable cause to believe evidence of someone's guilt of an offense will be found. [Zurcher v. Stanford Daily, 436 U.S. 547 (1978)]

e. Neutral and Detached Magistrate Requirement

The magistrate who issues the warrant must be neutral and detached from the often competitive business of law enforcement.

Examples: 1) The state attorney general is not neutral and detached. [Coolidge v. New Hampshire, 403 U.S. 443 (1971)]

2) A clerk of court may issue warrants for violations of city ordinances. [Shadwick v. City of Tampa, 407 U.S. 345 (1972)]

3) A magistrate who receives no salary other than compensation for each warrant issued is not neutral and detached. [Connally v. Georgia, 429 U.S. 245 (1977)]

4) A magistrate who participates in the search to determine its scope is not neutral and detached. [Lo-Ji Sales, Inc. v. New York, 442 U.S. 319 (1979)]

f. Execution of a Warrant

1) Must Be Executed by the Police

Only the police (and not private citizens) may execute a warrant. Moreover, when executing a warrant *in a home*, the police may not be accompanied by a member of the media or any other third party unless the third party is there to aid in executing the warrant (*e.g.*, to identify stolen property that might be found in the home). [Wilson v. Layne, 526 U.S. 603 (1999)—unreasonable to allow newspaper reporter and photographer to accompany police during execution of an arrest warrant in plaintiff's home] *Rationale:* To be reasonable, police action pursuant to a warrant must be related to the objectives of the warrant. The presence of reporters or other third parties not aiding in the execution of the warrant renders the search unreasonable. Note that while the First Amendment prohibition against abridging freedom of the press is an important right, it does not supersede the very important Fourth Amendment right of persons to be free of unreasonable searches.

2) Execution Without Unreasonable Delay

The warrant should be executed without unreasonable delay because probable cause may disappear.

3) Announcement Requirement

Generally, an officer executing a search warrant must knock and announce her authority and purpose and be refused admittance before using force to enter the place to be searched. However, no announcement need be made if the officer has reasonable suspicion, based on facts, that knocking and announcing would be *dangerous or futile* or that it would *inhibit the investigation*, *e.g.*, because it would lead to the destruction of evidence. [Richards v. Wisconsin, 520 U.S. 385 (1997)] Whether a "no knock" entry is justified must be made on a case-by-case basis; a blanket exception for warrants involving drug investigations is impermissible. [Richards v. Wisconsin, *supra*] *Note:* The fact that property damage will result from a no knock entry does not require a different standard—reasonable suspicion is sufficient. [United States v. Ramirez, 523 U.S. 65 (1998)]

4) Seizure of Unspecified Property

When executing a warrant, the police generally may seize any contraband or fruits or instrumentalities of crime that they discover, whether or not specified in the warrant.

5)   Search of Persons Found on the Premises

A search warrant does not authorize the police to search persons found on the premises who are not named in the warrant. [Ybarra v. Illinois, 444 U.S. 85 (1979)] If the police have probable cause to arrest a person discovered on the premises to be searched, however, they may search her *incident to the arrest*.

6)   Detention of the Occupants

A warrant to search for contraband founded on probable cause implicitly carries with it the limited authority to detain occupants of the premises while a proper search is conducted. [Michigan v. Summers, *supra*, B.3.d.]

5.   Exceptions to Warrant Requirement

There are *six exceptions* to the warrant requirement; *i.e.,* six circumstances where a warrantless search is reasonable and therefore is valid under the Fourth Amendment. To be valid, a warrantless search must meet all the requirements of at least one exception.

a.   Search Incident to a Lawful Arrest

The police may conduct a warrantless search incident to a lawful arrest.

1)   Lawful Arrest Requirement

If an arrest is unlawful, then any search incident to that arrest is also unlawful.

2)   Any Arrest Sufficient

The police may conduct a search incident to arrest whenever they arrest a person. Although the rationale for the search is to protect the arresting officer and to preserve evidence, the police need not actually fear for their safety or believe that they will find evidence of a crime as long as the suspect is placed under arrest. [United States v. Robinson, 414 U.S. 218 (1973)]

a)   Issuance of Traffic Citation—Insufficient Basis

For traffic violations, if the suspect is not arrested, there can be no search incident to arrest, even if state law gives the officer the option of arresting a suspect or issuing a citation. [Knowles v. Iowa, 525 U.S. 113 (1999)—a nonconsensual automobile search conducted after the suspect was issued a citation for driving 43 m.p.h. in a 25 m.p.h. zone was illegal, and contraband found during search was excluded from evidence] *Rationale:* When a citation is issued, there is less of a threat to the officer's safety than there is during an arrest, and the only evidence that needs to be preserved in such a case (*e.g.,* evidence of the suspect's speeding or other illegal conduct) has already been found.

3)   Geographic Scope

Incident to a lawful arrest, the police may search the person and areas into which he might reach to obtain weapons or destroy evidence (his *"wingspan"*). [Chimel v. California, 395 U.S. 752 (1969)] The arrestee's wingspan follows him as he moves. Thus, if the arrestee is allowed to enter his home, police may follow and search areas within the arrestee's wingspan in the home. [Washington v. Chrisman, 455 U.S. 1 (1982)] The police may also make a *protective sweep* of the area beyond the defendant's wingspan if they believe accomplices may be present. [Maryland v. Buie, 494 U.S. 325 (1990)]

a) Automobiles

A police officer may conduct a warrantless search of the **passenger compartment** of an automobile (including containers) after arresting the occupants. The entire passenger compartment is within the arrestee's "wingspan," but not the trunk. [New York v. Belton, 453 U.S. 454 (1981)]

4) Contemporaneousness Requirement

A search incident to an arrest must be contemporaneous in time and place with the arrest. [Preston v. United States, 376 U.S. 364 (1964); United States v. Chadwick, 433 U.S. 1 (1977)]

5) Search Incident to Incarceration

The police may search an arrestee's personal belongings before incarcerating him after a valid arrest. [Illinois v. Lafayette, 459 U.S. 986 (1983)] Similarly, the police may search an entire vehicle—including closed containers within the vehicle—that has been impounded. [Colorado v. Bertine, 479 U.S. 367 (1987)]

b. "Automobile" Exception

If the police have probable cause to believe that a vehicle such as an automobile contains contraband or fruits, instrumentalities, or evidence of a crime, they may search the vehicle without a warrant. [Carroll v. United States, 267 U.S. 132 (1925)] *Rationale:* Automobiles and similar vehicles are mobile and so will not likely be available for search by the time an officer returns with a warrant. Moreover, the Supreme Court has declared that people have a lesser expectation of privacy in their vehicles than in their homes.

Note: Similarly, if the police have probable cause to believe that the car itself is contraband, it may be seized from a public place without a warrant. [Florida v. White, 526 U.S. 559 (1999)]

Example: On three occasions, the police observed Defendant selling cocaine from his car, giving the police probable cause to believe that Defendant's car was used to transport cocaine. Under state law, a car used to transport cocaine is considered to be contraband subject to forfeiture. Several months later, the police arrested Defendant on unrelated drug charges while he was at work and seized his car from the parking lot without a warrant based on their prior observations. While inventorying the contents of the car, the police found cocaine and brought the present drug charges against Defendant. The cocaine was admissible into evidence. Even though the police did not have probable cause to believe that the car contained cocaine when it was seized, they did have probable cause to believe that it was contraband and therefore seizable, and inventory searches of seized items are proper (*see* 6.b., *infra*). [Florida v. White, *supra*]

1) Scope of Search

If the police have full probable cause to search a vehicle, they can search the *entire vehicle* (including the trunk) and all containers within the vehicle that *might contain the object* for which they are searching. [United States v. Ross, 456 U.S. 798 (1982)] Thus, if the police have probable cause to believe that drugs are within the vehicle, they can search almost any container, but if they have probable cause to believe that an illegal alien is hiding inside the vehicle, they must limit their search to areas where a person could hide.

a) Passenger's Belongings

The search is not limited to the driver's belongings and may extend to packages belonging to a passenger. [Wyoming v. Houghten, 526 U.S. 295 (1999)—search of passenger's purse upheld where officer noticed driver had syringe in his pocket] *Rationale:* Like a driver, a passenger has a reduced expectation of privacy in a car.

b) Limited Probable Cause—Containers Placed in Vehicle

If the police only have probable cause to search a container (recently) placed in a vehicle, they may search that container, but the search may not extend to other parts of the car. [California v. Acevedo, 500 U.S. 565 (1991)]

Example: Assume police have probable cause to believe that a briefcase that D is carrying contains illegal drugs. Unless they arrest D, they may not make a warrantless search of the briefcase because no exception to the warrant requirement applies. They follow D, and he places the briefcase in a car. They may then approach D and search the briefcase even though they could not search it before it was placed in the car. They may not search the rest of the car, however, because D has not had an opportunity to move the drugs elsewhere in the car. Presumably, if some time passes and D has an opportunity to move the drugs, the police will have probable cause to search the entire car.

2) Motor Homes

The automobile exception extends to any vehicle that has the attributes of mobility and a lesser expectation of privacy similar to a car. For example, the Supreme Court has held that it extends to motor homes if they are not at a fixed site. [California v. Carney, 471 U.S. 386 (1985)]

3) Contemporaneousness Not Required

If the police are justified in making a warrantless search of a vehicle under this exception at the time of stopping, they may tow the vehicle to the station and search it later. [Chambers v. Maroney, 399 U.S. 42 (1970)]

Example: A vehicle search, based on probable cause, conducted three days after the vehicle was impounded is permissible. [United States v. Johns, 469 U.S. 478 (1985)]

c. Plain View

The police may make a warrantless seizure when they:

(i) Are *legitimately on the premises*;

    (ii)   Discover *evidence, fruits or instrumentalities* of crime, or *contraband*;

    (iii)   See such evidence *in plain view*; and

    (iv)   *Have probable cause* to believe (*i.e.,* it must be immediately apparent) that the item *is* evidence, contraband, or a fruit or instrumentality of crime.

[Coolidge v. New Hampshire, *supra*, 4.e.; Arizona v. Hicks, 480 U.S. 321 (1987)]

Examples: 1) Police may seize *unspecified property* while executing a search warrant.

2) Police may seize from a lawfully stopped automobile an opaque balloon that, based on knowledge and experience, the police have probable cause to believe contains narcotics, even though the connection with the contraband would not be obvious to the average person. [Texas v. Brown, 460 U.S. 730 (1983)]

Compare: While investigating a shooting in an apartment, Officer spotted two sets of expensive stereo equipment which he had reasonable suspicion (but not probable cause) to believe were stolen. Officer moved some of the components to check their serial numbers. Such movement constituted an invalid search because of the lack of probable cause. [Arizona v. Hicks, *supra*]

1)   Inadvertence Not Required

Formerly, the plain view exception applied only if the evidence was inadvertently discovered, but inadvertence is no longer a requirement. [Horton v. California, 496 U.S. 128 (1990)]

Example: Police have probable cause to believe that the weapons and proceeds from an armed robbery are at D's home. If they obtain a warrant only to search for the proceeds, they still may seize the weapons if they are found in plain view during the search.

d.   Consent

The police may conduct a valid warrantless search if they have a *voluntary and intelligent* consent to do so. Knowledge of the right to withhold consent, while a factor to be considered, is not a prerequisite to establishing a voluntary and intelligent consent. [Schneckloth v. Bustamonte, 412 U.S. 218 (1973)]

Example: After Deputy stopped Defendant for speeding, gave him a verbal warning, and returned his license, Deputy asked Defendant if he was carrying any drugs in the car. Defendant answered "no" and consented to a search of his car which uncovered drugs. Defendant argued that his consent was invalid because he had not been told that he was free to go after his license was returned. The Supreme Court, applying the principles of *Schneckloth*, found that no such warning was necessary. Voluntariness is to be determined from all of the circumstances, and knowledge of the right to refuse consent is just one factor to be considered in determining voluntariness. [Ohio v. Robinette, 519 U.S. 33 (1996)]

Note: An officer's false announcement that she has a warrant negates the possibility of consent. [Bumper v. North Carolina, 391 U.S. 543 (1968)]

1) Authority to Consent

Any person with an *apparent equal right to use or occupy* the property may consent to a search, and any evidence found may be used against the other owners or occupants. [Frazier v. Cupp, 394 U.S. 731 (1969); United States v. Matlock, 415 U.S. 164 (1973)] The search is valid even if it turns out that the person consenting to the search did not actually have such right, as long as the police reasonably believed that the person had authority to consent. [Illinois v. Rodriguez, 497 U.S. 177 (1990)]

2) Scope of Search

The scope of the search is limited by the *scope of the consent*. However, consent extends to all areas to which a reasonable person under the circumstances would believe it extends.

Example: Police stopped D for a traffic violation, told him that they suspected him of carrying drugs, and asked for permission to search the car. D consented. The officers found a bag containing cocaine. At trial, D argued that his consent did not extend to any closed container (the bag). The Supreme Court held that since D knew the police were searching for drugs and did not place any restriction on his consent, it was reasonable for the police to believe that the consent extended to all areas where drugs might be found. [Florida v. Jimeno, 500 U.S. 248 (1991)]

e. Stop and Frisk

1) Standards

As noted above (*see* B.3.a., *supra*), a police officer may *stop* a person without probable cause for arrest if she has an articulable and *reasonable suspicion* of criminal activity. In such circumstances, if the officer also *reasonably believes* that the person may be *armed and presently dangerous*, she may conduct a protective *frisk*. [Terry v. Ohio, 392 U.S. 1 (1968); United States v. Cortez, 449 U.S. 411 (1981)]

2) Scope of the Intrusion

a) Patdown of Outer Clothing

The scope of the frisk is generally limited to a patdown of the outer clothing for concealed instruments of assault. [Terry v. Ohio, *supra*] However, an officer may reach directly into an area of the suspect's clothing, such as his belt, without a preliminary frisk, when she has specific information that a weapon is hidden there, even if the information comes from an informant's tip lacking sufficient reliability to support a warrant. [Adams v. Williams, 407 U.S. 143 (1972)]

b) Passenger Compartment of Automobile

The Supreme Court has expanded *Terry v. Ohio, supra,* to include the warrantless search of the passenger compartment of an automobile by police officers who have *detained* but *not arrested* the occupant, provided the search is *limited to those areas in which a weapon may be placed* or hidden and the officers possess a reasonable belief that the occupant is dangerous. [Michigan v. Long, 463 U.S. 1032 (1983)]

c) Time Limit

There is no rigid time limit for the length of an investigative stop. The Court will consider the purpose of the stop, the reasonableness of the time in effectuating the purpose, and the reasonableness of the means of investigation to determine whether a stop was too long. [United States v. Sharpe, 470 U.S. 675 (1985)]

3) Admissibility of Evidence

If a police officer conducts a patdown within the bounds of *Terry*, the officer may reach into the suspect's clothing and seize any item that the officer reasonably believes, based on its *"plain feel,"* is a *weapon or contraband*. [Terry v. Ohio, *supra*; Minnesota v. Dickerson, 508 U.S. 366 (1993)—excluding from evidence cocaine that officer found during valid patdown because officer had to manipulate package to discern that it likely was drugs] Properly seized items are admissible as evidence against the suspect.

4) Ordering a Driver Out of the Car Permissible

Once a vehicle has been properly stopped for a traffic violation, a police officer may order the driver out of the automobile even without a suspicion of criminal activity. If the officer then reasonably believes that the driver may be armed and dangerous, she may conduct a frisk. [Pennsylvania v. Mimms, 434 U.S. 106 (1978)]

5) Stop and Identify Statutes

The Supreme Court has suggested, and state courts have held, that the failure to identify oneself when stopped and asked for identification by a police officer does not create probable cause for arrest. [Brown v. Texas, 443 U.S. 47 (1979); Michigan v. DeFillippo, *supra*, II.B.5.]

f. Hot Pursuit, Evanescent Evidence, and Other Emergencies

1) No General Emergency Exception

The Supreme Court has made clear that there is no general "emergency" exception, as the need to check occupational safety violations [Marshall v. Barlow's, Inc., 436 U.S. 307 (1978)], the need to investigate a fire after it has been extinguished and its cause determined [Michigan v. Tyler, 436 U.S. 499 (1978)], and the need to search a murder scene [Mincey v. Arizona, *supra*, II.B.6.a.] do not justify warrantless searches.

2) Hot Pursuit Exception

Police officers in hot pursuit of a *fleeing felon* may make a warrantless search and seizure. The scope of the search may be as broad as may reasonably be necessary to prevent the suspect from resisting or escaping. [Warden v. Hayden, 387 U.S. 294 (1967)] When the police have probable cause and attempt to make a warrantless arrest in a "public place," they may pursue the suspect into private dwellings. [United States v. Santana, 427 U.S. 38 (1976)]

3) Evanescent Evidence Exception
The police may seize without a warrant evidence likely to disappear before a warrant can be obtained, such as a blood sample containing alcohol [Schmerber v. California, 384 U.S. 757 (1966)] or fingernail scrapings [Cupp v. Murphy, 412 U.S. 291 (1973)].

4) Other Emergencies Where Warrant Not Required
Certain other emergencies, such as *contaminated food or drugs* [North American Cold Storage v. City of Chicago, 211 U.S. 306 (1908)], *children in trouble* [State v. Hunt, 406 P.2d 208 (Ariz. 1965)], and *burning fires* [Michigan v. Tyler, *supra*] may justify warrantless searches and seizures.

6. Administrative Inspections and Searches

a. Warrant Required for Searches of Private Residences and Businesses
Inspectors must have a warrant for searches of private residences and commercial buildings. [Camara v. Municipal Court, 387 U.S. 523 (1967); Michigan v. Clifford, 464 U.S. 287 (1984)—warrantless administrative search of fire-damaged residence by officials seeking to determine origin of fire violated owners' Fourth Amendment rights; owners retained reasonable expectation of privacy in the damaged structure, and the warrantless search was unconstitutional] However, the same standard of probable cause as is required for other searches is not required for a valid administrative inspection warrant. A showing of a general and *neutral enforcement plan* will justify issuance of the warrant, which is designed to guard against selective enforcement. [Marshall v. Barlow's, Inc., *supra*]

1) Exceptions Permitting Warrantless Searches

a) Contaminated Food
A warrant is not required for the seizure of spoiled or contaminated food. [North American Cold Storage v. City of Chicago, *supra*]

b) Highly Regulated Industries
A warrant is not required for searches of businesses in highly regulated industries, because of the urgent public interest and the theory that the business has impliedly consented to warrantless searches by entering into a highly regulated industry. Such industries include liquor [Colonnade Catering Corp. v. United States, 397 U.S. 72 (1970)], guns [United States v. Biswell, 406 U.S. 311 (1972)], strip mining [Donovan v. Dewey, 452 U.S. 594 (1981)], and automobile junkyards [New York v. Burger, 479 U.S. 812 (1987)], but not car leasing [G.M. Leasing Corp. v. United States, 429 U.S. 338 (1977)] or general manufacturing [Marshall v. Barlow's, Inc., *supra*].

b. Inventory Searches

The police may search an arrestee's personal belongings in order to inventory them before incarcerating the arrestee. [Illinois v. Lafayette, *supra,* 5.a.5)] Similarly, the police may search an entire vehicle—including closed containers within the vehicle—that has been impounded. [Colorado v. Bertine, *supra,* 5.a.5)]

c. Search of Airline Passengers

Courts have generally upheld searches of airline passengers prior to boarding. This seems to be regarded as somewhat akin to a consent or administrative search. One court, however, has held that a passenger must be permitted to avoid such a search by agreeing not to board the aircraft.

d. Public School Searches

A warrant or probable cause is not required for searches conducted by public school officials; only *reasonable grounds* for the search are necessary. This exception is justified due to the nature of the school environment. [New Jersey v. T.L.O., 469 U.S. 325 (1985)] The Court has also upheld a school district rule that required student athletes to submit to random drug testing throughout the athletic season. [Veronia School District v. Acton, 515 U.S. 646 (1995)]

e. Probationers' Homes

The Fourth Amendment is not violated by a statute authorizing warrantless searches of a probationer's home when there are reasonable grounds to believe contraband is present. Probation systems present "special needs" that justify departures from the usual Fourth Amendment warrant requirement. [Griffin v. Wisconsin, 479 U.S. 1053 (1987)]

f. Government Employees' Desks and Files

A warrantless search of a government employee's desk and file cabinets is permissible under the Fourth Amendment if it is reasonable in scope and if it is justified at its inception by a noninvestigatory, work-related need or a reasonable suspicion of work-related misconduct. [O'Connor v. Ortega, 480 U.S. 709 (1987)]

g. Drug Testing

Although government-required drug testing constitutes a search, the Supreme Court has upheld such testing without a warrant, probable cause, or even individualized suspicion when justified by *"special needs"* beyond the general interest of law enforcement.

Examples:　　1) The government can require railroad employees who are involved in accidents to be tested for drugs after the accidents. [Skinner v. Railway Labor Executives' Association, 489 U.S. 602 (1989)]

2) The government can require persons seeking Customs positions connected to drug interdiction to be tested for drugs. There is a special need for such testing because persons so employed will have ready access to large quantities of drugs. [National Treasury Employees Union v. Von Raab, 489 U.S. 656 (1989)]

Compare: 1) Special needs do not justify a warrantless and nonconsensual urinalysis test to determine whether a pregnant woman has been using cocaine, where the main purpose of the testing is to generate evidence that may be used by law enforcement personnel to coerce women into drug programs. [Ferguson v. Charleston, 121 S. Ct. 1281 (2001)]

2) The government may not require candidates for state offices to certify that they have taken a drug test within 30 days prior to qualifying for nomination or election—there is no special need for such testing. [Chandler v. Miller, 520 U.S. 305 (1997)]

7.   Searches in Foreign Countries and at the Border

a.   Searches in Foreign Countries
The Fourth Amendment does *not* apply to searches and seizures by United States officials in foreign countries and involving an alien, at least where the alien does not have a substantial connection to the United States. Thus, for example, the Fourth Amendment was held not to bar the use of evidence obtained in a warrantless search of an alien's home in Mexico. [United States v. Verdugo-Urquidez, 494 U.S. 259 (1990)]

b.   Searches at the Border or Its Functional Equivalent
Neither citizens nor noncitizens have any Fourth Amendment rights at the border or its functional equivalent as part of the concept of national sovereignty. A functional equivalent of the border might be a point near the border where several routes all leading to the border merge.

c.   Roving Patrols

1)   Stops
Roving patrols inside the United States border may stop an automobile for questioning of the occupants if the officer *reasonably suspects* that the automobile may contain illegal aliens, but the apparent Mexican ancestry of the occupants alone cannot create a reasonable suspicion. [United States v. Brignoni-Ponce, 422 U.S. 873 (1975)]

2)   Searches
A roving patrol inside the border may not conduct a warrantless search unless the requirements of one of the *exceptions* to the warrant requirement, such as the "automobile" exception (probable cause) or consent, are met. [Almeida-Sanchez v. United States, 413 U.S. 266 (1973)]

d.   Fixed Checkpoints
Border officials may stop an automobile at a fixed checkpoint inside the border for questioning of the occupants even *without a reasonable suspicion* that the automobile contains illegal aliens, but they must have probable cause or consent for a search. [United States v. Martinez-Fuerte, *supra*, B.3.b.2)]

e.   Opening International Mail
Permissible border searches include the opening of international mail, which postal

regulations authorize when postal authorities have **reasonable cause** to suspect that the mail contains **contraband**, although the regulations prohibit the authorities from reading any correspondence inside. [United States v. Ramsey, 431 U.S. 606 (1977)]

1) Reopening

Once customs agents lawfully open a container and identify its contents as illegal, their **subsequent reopening** of the container after it has been resealed and delivered to defendant is not a search within the meaning of the Fourth Amendment, unless there is a substantial likelihood that the container's contents have been changed during any gap in surveillance. [Illinois v. Andreas, 463 U.S. 765 (1983)]

f. I.N.S. Enforcement Actions

The I.N.S. may do a "factory survey" of the entire work force in a factory, to determine citizenship of each employee, without raising Fourth Amendment issues. The "factory survey" is not "detention" or a "seizure" under the Fourth Amendment. [Immigration & Naturalization Service v. Delgado, 466 U.S. 210 (1984)] Furthermore, evidence illegally obtained, in violation of the Fourth Amendment, may be used in a civil deportation hearing. [Immigration & Naturalization Service v. Lopez-Mendoza, 468 U.S. 1032 (1984)]

g. Detentions

If the officials have a "reasonable suspicion" that a traveler is smuggling contraband in her stomach, they may detain her for a time reasonable under the circumstances. *Rationale:* Stopping such smuggling is important, yet very difficult; stomach smuggling gives no external signs that would enable officials to meet a "probable cause" standard in order to conduct a search. [United States v. Montoya de Hernandez, 473 U.S. 531 (1985)—16-hour detention upheld until traveler, who refused an X-ray, had a bowel movement]

8. Wiretapping and Eavesdropping

a. Fourth Amendment Requirements

Wiretapping and any other form of electronic surveillance that violates a reasonable expectation of privacy constitute a search under the Fourth Amendment. [Katz v. United States, 389 U.S. 347 (1967)] In *Berger v. New York*, 388 U.S. 41 (1967), the Supreme Court indicated that for a valid **warrant** authorizing a wiretap to be issued, the following **requirements** must be met:

1) A showing of **probable cause** to believe that a **specific crime** has been or is being committed must be made;

2) The **suspected persons** whose conversations are to be overheard must be **named**;

3) The warrant must **describe with particularity** the conversations that can be overheard;

4) The wiretap must be limited to a **short period of time** (although extensions may be obtained upon an adequate showing);

5) *Provisions* must be made for the *termination* of the wiretap when the desired information has been obtained; and

6) A *return* must be made to the court, showing what conversations have been intercepted.

b. Exceptions

1) **"Unreliable Ear"**
A speaker assumes the risk that the person to whom she is talking is unreliable. If the person turns out to be an informer wired for sound or taping the conversation, the speaker has no basis in the Fourth Amendment to object to the transmitting or recording of the conversation as a warrantless search. [United States v. White, 401 U.S. 745 (1971)]

2) **"Uninvited Ear"**
A speaker has no Fourth Amendment claim if she makes no attempt to keep the conversation private. [Katz v. United States, *supra*]

c. Judicial Approval Required for Domestic Security Surveillance
A neutral and detached magistrate must make the determination that a warrant should issue authorizing electronic surveillance, including internal security surveillance of domestic organizations. The President may not authorize such surveillance without prior judicial approval. [United States v. United States District Court, 407 U.S. 297 (1972)]

d. Federal Statute
Title III of the Omnibus Crime Control and Safe Streets Act regulates interception of private "wire, oral or electronic communications." [18 U.S.C. §§2510-2520] All electronic communication surveillance (*e.g.,* phone taps, bugs, etc.) must comply with the requirements of this federal statute, which exhibits a legislative decision to require more than the constitutional minimum in this especially sensitive area.

e. Pen Registers
A pen register records only the numbers dialed from a certain phone. The Fourth Amendment does not require prior judicial approval for installation and use of pen registers. [Smith v. Maryland, 442 U.S. 735 (1979)] Neither does Title III govern pen registers, since Title III applies only when the *contents* of electronic communications are intercepted. However, by statute [18 U.S.C. §§3121 *et seq.*], police must obtain a court order finding pen register information to be relevant to an ongoing criminal investigation before utilizing a pen register. Note, however, that information obtained in violation of the statute would not necessarily be excluded from evidence in a criminal trial; the statute merely provides a criminal penalty.

f. Covert Entry to Install a Bug Permissible
Law enforcement officers do not need prior express judicial authorization for a covert entry to install equipment for electronic surveillance, which has been approved in compliance with Title III. [Dalia v. United States, 441 U.S. 238 (1979)]

D. METHODS OF OBTAINING EVIDENCE THAT SHOCK THE CONSCIENCE

Due process of law requires that state criminal prosecutions be conducted in a manner that does not offend the "sense of justice" inherent in due process. Evidence obtained in a manner offending that sense is *inadmissible*, even if it does not run afoul of one of the specific prohibitions against particular types of misconduct.

1. Searches of the Body

Intrusions into the human body implicate a person's most deep-rooted expectations of privacy. Thus, Fourth Amendment requirements apply. Ultimately, the "reasonableness" of searches into the body depends on weighing society's need for the evidence against the magnitude of the intrusion on the individual (including the threat to health, safety, and dignitary interests). [Winston v. Lee, 470 U.S. 753 (1985)]

a. Blood Tests

Taking a blood sample (*e.g.,* from a person suspected of drunk driving) by commonplace medical procedures "involves virtually no risk, trauma, or pain" and is thus a *reasonable* intrusion. [Schmerber v. California, *supra,* C.5.f.3)]

b. Compare—Surgery

But a surgical procedure under a general anesthetic (to remove a bullet needed as evidence) involves significant risks to health and a severe intrusion on privacy, and thus is *unreasonable*—at least when there is substantial other evidence. [Winston v. Lee, *supra*]

2. Shocking Inducement

If a crime is induced by official actions that themselves shock the conscience, any conviction therefrom offends due process.

Example: D appears before a state legislative commission. Members of the commission clearly indicate that the privilege against self-incrimination is available to D, although in fact D could be convicted for failure to answer. Can D's conviction for refusal to answer be upheld? No, because the crime was induced by methods that shock the conscience. [Raley v. Ohio, 360 U.S. 423 (1959)]

IV. CONFESSIONS

A. INTRODUCTION

The admissibility of a defendant's confession or incriminating admission involves analysis under the Fourth, Fifth, Sixth, and Fourteenth Amendments. We have already discussed Fourth Amendment search and seizure limitations. The Fifth Amendment gives defendants rights against testimonial self-incrimination. The Sixth Amendment gives defendants rights regarding the assistance of counsel. The Fourteenth Amendment protects against involuntary confessions.

B. FOURTEENTH AMENDMENT—VOLUNTARINESS

For confessions to be admissible, the Due Process Clause of the Fourteenth Amendment requires that they be voluntary. Voluntariness is assessed by looking at the totality of the circumstances, including the suspect's age, education, and mental and physical condition, along with the setting, duration, and manner of police interrogation. [Spano v. New York, 360 U.S. 315 (1959)]

Examples: 1) A confession will be involuntary where it was obtained by physically beating the defendant. [Brown v. Mississippi, 297 U.S. 278 (1936)]

2) D was being held for questioning. O, a young officer who was a friend of D, told D that if he did not obtain a confession, he would lose his job, which would be disastrous to his wife and children. D confessed, but the Court found the confession involuntary. [Leyra v. Denno, 347 U.S. 556 (1954)]

1. Must Be Official Compulsion
Only official compulsion will render a confession involuntary for purposes of the Fourteenth Amendment. A confession is not involuntary merely because it is the product of mental disease that prevents the confession from being of the defendant's free will. [Colorado v. Connelly, 479 U.S. 157 (1986)]

2. Harmless Error Test Applies
A conviction will not necessarily be overturned if an involuntary confession was erroneously admitted into evidence. The harmless error test applies, and the conviction will not be overturned if the government can show that there was other overwhelming evidence of guilt. [Arizona v. Fulminante, 499 U.S. 279 (1991)]

3. Can "Appeal" to Jury
A finding of voluntariness by the trial court does not preclude the defendant from introducing evidence to the jury of the circumstances of the confession in order to cast doubt on its credibility. [Crane v. Kentucky, 476 U.S. 683 (1986)]

C. SIXTH AMENDMENT RIGHT TO COUNSEL APPROACH

The Sixth Amendment provides that in all criminal prosecutions, the defendant has a right to the assistance of counsel. The right protects defendants from having to face a complicated legal system without competent help. It applies at all *critical stages* of a criminal prosecution (*see* VII.C.1., *infra*) and is violated when the police obtain a confession from a defendant without first obtaining a waiver of the defendant's right to have counsel present. Since *Miranda,* below, the Sixth Amendment right has been limited to cases where *adversary judicial proceedings* have begun (*e.g.,* formal charges have been filed). [Massiah v. United States, 377 U.S. 201 (1964)] Thus, the right does not apply in precharge custodial interrogations.

Examples: 1) The Sixth Amendment right to counsel is violated when an undisclosed, paid government informant is placed in the defendant's cell, after defendant has been indicted, and deliberately elicits statements from the defendant regarding the crime for which the defendant was indicted. [United States v. Henry, 447 U.S. 264 (1980)] However, it is not a violation merely to place an informant in a defendant's cell—the informant must take some action, beyond mere listening, designed deliberately to elicit incriminating remarks. [Kuhlman v. Wilson, 477 U.S. 436 (1986)]

2) The right to counsel is violated when police arrange to record conversations between an indicted defendant and his co-defendant. [Maine v. Moulton, 474 U.S. 159 (1985)]

1. Offense Specific
The Sixth Amendment right to counsel is "offense specific." Thus, if a defendant makes a

Sixth Amendment request for counsel for one charge, he must make another request if he is subsequently charged with a separate, unrelated crime if he desires counsel for the second charge. Similarly, even though a defendant's Sixth Amendment right to counsel has attached regarding one charge, he may be questioned without counsel concerning an unrelated charge. [Illinois v. Perkins, 496 U.S. 292 (1990)]

Example: D was in jail on a battery charge. Because the police suspected D of an unrelated murder, they placed an undercover officer in D's cell. The officer elicited damaging confessions from D regarding the murder. The interrogation did not violate the Sixth Amendment since D had not been charged with the murder. [Illinois v. Perkins, *supra*] Neither did the interrogation violate D's Fifth Amendment right to counsel under *Miranda*. (*See* D.2.a., *infra*.)

a.   **Test for "Different Offenses"**

The test for determining whether offenses are different under the Sixth Amendment is the *Blockburger* test (*see* XIII.C.1., *infra*). Under the test, two crimes are considered different offenses if each requires proof of an additional element that the other crime does not require. [Texas v. Cobb, 121 S. Ct. 1335 (2001)]

D.   **FIFTH AMENDMENT PRIVILEGE AGAINST COMPELLED SELF-INCRIMINA-TION—*MIRANDA***

The Fifth Amendment, applicable to the states through the Fourteenth Amendment, provides that no person "shall be compelled to be a witness against himself. . . ." This has been interpreted to mean that a person shall not be compelled to give self-incriminating testimony. The scope of what is considered to be "testimony" under the amendment will be discussed later (*see* XIV., *infra*). This section explains the applicability of the amendment to confessions.

1.   **The Warnings**

In *Miranda v. Arizona*, 384 U.S. 436 (1966), the Fifth Amendment privilege against compelled self-incrimination became the basis for ruling upon the admissibility of a confession. The *Miranda* warnings and a valid waiver are ***prerequisites to the admissibility*** of any statement made by the accused during custodial interrogation. A person in custody must, prior to interrogation, be clearly informed that:

(i)   He has the right to remain silent;

(ii)   Anything he says can be used against him in court;

(iii)   He has the right to the presence of an attorney; and

(iv)   If he cannot afford an attorney, one will be appointed for him if he so desires.

Note: The Supreme Court has held that the holding of *Miranda* was based on the ***requirements*** of the Fifth Amendment as made applicable to the states through the Fourteenth Amendment, and therefore Congress cannot eliminate the *Miranda* requirements by statute. [Dickerson v. United States, 530 U.S. 428 (2000)—invalidating a statute that purportedly eliminated *Miranda*'s requirements that persons in custody and being interrogated be informed of the right to remain silent and the right to counsel]

a. **Need Not Be Verbatim**

Miranda requires that all suspects be informed of their rights without considering any prior awareness of those rights. The warnings need not be given verbatim, as long as the substance of the warning is there. [Duckworth v. Eagan, 492 U.S. 195 (1989)—upholding warning that included statement, "We [the police] have no way of giving you a lawyer, but one will be appointed for you, if you wish, if and when you go to court"] The failure to advise a suspect of his right to appointed counsel may be found to be harmless error. [Michigan v. Tucker, 417 U.S. 433 (1974); California v. Prysock, 453 U.S. 355 (1981)]

b. **Rewarning Not Needed After Break**

There is generally no need to repeat the warnings merely because of a break in the interrogation, **unless** the time lapse has been so long that a failure to do so would seem like an attempt to take advantage of the suspect's ignorance of his rights.

2. **When Required**

Anyone in police custody and accused of a crime, no matter how minor a crime, must be given *Miranda* warnings **prior to interrogation** by the police. [Berkemer v. McCarty, 468 U.S. 420 (1984)]

a. **Governmental Conduct**

Miranda generally applies only to interrogation by the publicly paid police. It does not apply where interrogation is by an informant who the defendant does not know is working for the police. [Illinois v. Perkins, *supra*—*Miranda* warnings need not be given before questioning by a cellmate covertly working for the police] *Rationale:* The warnings are intended to offset the coercive nature of police-dominated interrogation, and if the defendant does not know that he is being interrogated by the police, there is no coercive atmosphere to offset.

b. **Custody Requirement**

Whether a person is in custody depends on whether the person's freedom of action is denied in a significant way. The more a setting resembles a traditional arrest (*i.e.,* the more constrained the defendant feels), the more likely the Court will consider it to be custody. If the detention is voluntary, it does not constitute custody. [*See* Berkemer v. McCarty, *supra*; Oregon v. Mathiason, 429 U.S. 492 (1977)] If the detention is long and is involuntary (*e.g.,* defendant is in jail on another charge), it will likely be held to constitute custody. [*See* Mathas v. United States, 391 U.S. 1 (1968)]

Example: D is in custody when he is awakened in his own room in the middle of the night by four officers surrounding his bed, who then begin to question him. [Orozco v. Texas, 394 U.S. 324 (1969)]

1) **Test Is Objective**

The initial determination of whether a person is in custody depends on the **objective** circumstances of the interrogation, not on the subjective views harbored by either the interrogating officers or the person being interrogated. Thus, for example, an officer's belief that the person being questioned is not a suspect cannot bear on the custody issue unless that view is somehow manifested. [Stansbury v. California, 511 U.S. 318 (1994)]

2) Traffic Stops Generally Not Custodial

Although a routine traffic stop curtails a motorist's freedom of movement, such a stop is presumptively temporary and brief, and the motorist knows that he typically will soon be on his way; therefore, the motorist should not feel unduly coerced. Thus, *Miranda* warnings normally need not be given during a traffic stop.

Example: Officer stopped Defendant for weaving in and out of traffic. When Officer noticed Defendant had trouble standing, he performed a field sobriety test, which Defendant failed. Without giving *Miranda* warnings, Officer then asked Defendant if he had been drinking, and Defendant admitted to recent drinking and drug use. The admission is admissible. [Berkemer v. McCarty, *supra*]

c. Interrogation Requirement

"Interrogation" refers not only to express questioning, but also to any words or actions on the part of the police that the police should know are reasonably likely to elicit an incriminating response from the suspect. [Rhode Island v. Innis, 446 U.S. 291 (1980)] However, *Miranda* does not apply to **spontaneous statements** not made in response to interrogation, although officers must give the warnings before any follow-up questioning. Neither does *Miranda* apply to routine booking questions (*e.g.,* name, address, age, etc.), even when the booking process is being taped and may be used as evidence. [Pennsylvania v. Muniz, 496 U.S. 582 (1990)—defendant failed sobriety test and had trouble answering booking questions]

Examples: 1) Police comments about the danger a gun would present to handicapped children, which resulted in a robbery suspect's leading them to a weapon, did not constitute interrogation when the officers were not aware that the suspect was peculiarly susceptible to an appeal to his conscience. [Rhode Island v. Innis, *supra*]

2) Allowing a suspect's wife to talk to the suspect in the presence of an officer who is taping the conversation with the spouses' knowledge does not constitute interrogation. [Arizona v. Mauro, 481 U.S. 520 (1987)]

1) Break in Interrogation—Questioning by Different Police Agencies

When a second police agency continues to question a suspect at a point when the first police department terminates its questioning, the impact of an earlier denial of rights by the first department carries over into the questioning by the second agency. [Westover v. United States, 384 U.S. 436 (1966)]

d. Waiver

A suspect may waive his *Miranda* rights. To be valid, the government must show, by a preponderance of the evidence, that the waiver was **knowing, voluntary, and intelligent.** The Court will look to the totality of the circumstances. Note that the suspect need not be informed of all subjects of an interrogation to effect a valid waiver. [Colorado v. Spring, 479 U.S. 564 (1987)]

1) Silence

Waiver will not be presumed from the mere silence of the accused after the warnings are given or from the fact that a confession was eventually obtained. Again, the court will look at the totality of the circumstances. [*See* Fare v. Michael C., 442 U.S. 707 (1979)] The accused's refusal to sign a written waiver when requested to do so is not conclusive as to the absence of a waiver. [North Carolina v. Butler, 441 U.S. 369 (1979)]

2) **Request for Attorney**
A request for an attorney must be specific; a request by the accused to see his probation officer, for example, is not tantamount to a request for an attorney, so that waiver of the right to counsel may still be found. [Fare v. Michael C., *supra*] In addition, a limited request for counsel accompanied by a willingness to speak without counsel is a valid waiver of the right to have counsel present during interrogation. [Connecticut v. Barrett, 479 U.S. 523 (1987)]

3) **Police Deception of Defendant's Lawyer**
If the *Miranda* warnings are given, a voluntary confession will be admissible even if the police lie to the defendant's lawyer about their intent to question the defendant or fail to inform the defendant that his lawyer is attempting to see him, as long as adversary judicial proceedings have not commenced. [Moran v. Burbine, 475 U.S. 412 (1986)]

e. **Types of Statements**
Miranda applies to both inculpatory statements and statements alleged to be merely "exculpatory."
Example: The suspect's "exculpatory" statement, when confronted with another suspect, that "I didn't shoot Manuel, you did it," led to the first suspect's conviction for murder. [Escobedo v. Illinois, 378 U.S. 478 (1964)]

f. **State-Ordered Psychiatric Examination**
The Fifth Amendment privilege against self-incrimination forbids admission of evidence based on a psychiatric interview of defendant who was not warned of his right to remain silent. [Estelle v. Smith, 451 U.S. 454 (1981)] The admission of such evidence may, however, constitute harmless error. [Satterwhite v. Texas, 486 U.S. 249 (1988)]

g. **Limits on *Miranda***
Miranda suggested that every encounter between police and citizen was inherently coercive. Hence, interrogation would result in compelled testimony for Fifth Amendment purposes. However, the Supreme Court has been narrowing the scope of *Miranda's* application.
Example: Admission of rape and murder by a probationer to his probation officer was not compelled or involuntary, despite the probationer's obligation to periodically report and be "truthful in all matters." [Minnesota v. Murphy, 465 U.S. 420 (1984)]

h. **Inapplicable at Grand Jury Hearing**
The *Miranda* requirements *do not apply* to a witness testifying before a grand jury, even if the witness is under the compulsion of a subpoena. Such a witness who has not been charged or indicted does not have the right to have counsel present during the

questioning, but he may consult with an attorney outside the grand jury room. A witness who gives false testimony before a grand jury may be convicted of perjury even though he was not given the *Miranda* warnings. [United States v. Mandujano, 425 U.S. 564 (1976); United States v. Wong, 431 U.S. 174 (1977)]

3. Right to Terminate Interrogation

The accused may terminate police interrogation by invoking either the right to remain silent or the right to counsel. The effect of each differs.

a. Right to Remain Silent

At any time prior to or during interrogation, the accused may indicate that he wishes to remain silent. If the accused so indicates, all *questioning related to the particular crime must stop.*

1) Police May Resume Questioning If They "Scrupulously Honor" Request

The police may reinitiate questioning after the defendant has invoked the right to remain silent, as long as they "scrupulously honor" the defendant's request. This means, at the very least, that the police may not badger the defendant into talking and must wait a significant time before reinitiating questioning.

Example: In the Supreme Court's only opinion directly on point, it allowed police to reinitiate questioning where: (i) the police *immediately ceased questioning* upon Defendant's request and did not resume questioning for several hours; (ii) Defendant was *rewarned* of his rights; and (iii) questioning was *limited to a crime that was not the subject of the earlier questioning*. [Michigan v. Mosely, 423 U.S. 96 (1975)]

b. Right to Counsel

At any time prior to or during interrogation, the accused may also invoke a *Miranda* (*i.e.,* "Fifth Amendment") right to counsel. If the accused invokes this right, *all questioning must cease* until the accused is provided with an attorney or initiates further questioning himself. [Edwards v. Arizona, 451 U.S. 477 (1981)]

1) Police May Not Resume Questioning About Any Crime

Once the accused invokes his right to counsel under *Miranda,* all questioning must cease; the police may not even question the accused about a totally unrelated crime, as they can where the accused merely invokes the right to remain silent. [*See* Arizona v. Roberson, 486 U.S. 675 (1988)] *Rationale:* The right to counsel under *Miranda* is a prophylactic right designed by the Court to prevent the police from badgering an accused into talking without the aid of counsel, and this purpose can be accomplished only if *all* questioning ceases. [*See* McNeil v. Wisconsin, 501 U.S. 171 (1991)]

a) Compare—Accused May Initiate Resumption of Questioning

The accused may waive his right to counsel (*see* D.2.d.2), *supra*) after invoking the right, and thus initiate resumption of questioning.

Example: Accused cut off interrogation by asking for an attorney, but then asked the interrogating officer, "What is going to happen to me now?" The officer explained that the accused did not have to talk, and the accused said he understood. The officer then described the charge against the accused and gave him fresh *Miranda* warnings. The accused then confessed after taking a polygraph test. The Court upheld admission of the confession into evidence, finding that the accused had validly waived his rights. [Oregon v. Bradshaw, 462 U.S. 1039 (1983)]

b) Scope of Right—Custodial Interrogation

The Fifth Amendment right to counsel under *Miranda* applies whenever there is custodial interrogation.

c) Compare—Sixth Amendment Right "Offense Specific"

Recall that the Sixth Amendment right to counsel (*see* C., *supra*) attaches only after formal proceedings have begun. Moreover, whereas invocation of the Fifth Amendment right prevents all questioning, the Sixth Amendment right is "offense specific." (*See* C.1., *supra*.)

2) Request Must Be Unambiguous and Specific

A Fifth Amendment request for counsel can be invoked only by an *unambiguous* request for counsel *in dealing with the custodial interrogation*. [McNeil v. Wisconsin, *supra*; Davis v. United States, 512 U.S. 452 (1994)] The request must be sufficiently clear that a reasonable police officer in the same situation would understand the statement to be a request for counsel.

Examples:
1) The statement by the suspect being interrogated "Maybe I should talk to a lawyer" is not an unambiguous request for counsel under the Fifth Amendment, and so does not prevent further questioning.

2) D was arrested and charged with robbery. At his initial appearance, he requested the aid of counsel. After D's appearance, the police came to D's cell, gave him *Miranda* warnings, and questioned D about a crime unrelated to the robbery. D made incriminating statements. D's Fifth Amendment right to counsel was not violated because D did not request counsel in dealing with the interrogation. His post-charge request for counsel at his initial appearance was a *Sixth Amendment* request for counsel, which is offense specific (*see* C.1., *supra*).

3) Ambiguities Relevant Only If Part of Request

Once the accused has expressed an unequivocal desire to receive counsel, no subsequent questions or responses may be used to cast doubt on the request and all questioning of the accused must cease. Where the request is ambiguous, police may ask clarifying questions, but are not required to do so; rather, they may continue to interrogate the suspect until an unambiguous request is received. [Davis v. United States, *supra*] Note that if the defendant agrees to answer questions orally, but requests the presence of counsel before making any written statements, the defendant's oral statements are admissible. The defendant's agreement to talk constitutes a voluntary and knowing waiver of the right to counsel. [Connecticut v. Barrett, *supra,* 2.d.2)]

4) Counsel Must Be Present at Interrogation

Mere consultation with counsel prior to questioning does not satisfy the right to counsel—the police cannot resume questioning the accused in the absence of counsel. [Minnick v. Mississippi, 498 U.S. 146 (1991)] Of course, counsel need not be present if the defendant waives the right to counsel by initiating the exchange. (*See* 3.b.1)a), *supra.*)

Example: The accused answered a few questions during interrogation, but then requested an attorney. He was allowed to meet with his attorney three times. Subsequently, in the absence of counsel, police resumed interrogating the accused, and he made incriminating statements. The Court held that the statements must be excluded from evidence. [Minnick v. Mississippi, *supra*]

5) Statements Obtained in Violation May Be Used to Impeach

As indicated above, if the accused requests counsel, all questioning must cease unless counsel is present or the accused initiates a resumption of questioning. If *the police* initiate further questioning, the defendant's statements cannot be used by the prosecution in its case in chief, but they can be used to *impeach the defendant's* trial testimony, as long as the court finds that the defendant voluntarily and intelligently waived his right to counsel. [Michigan v. Harvey, 494 U.S. 344 (1990)] Note, however, that such illegally obtained evidence cannot be used to impeach trial testimony of witnesses other than the defendant. [James v. Illinois, 493 U.S. 307 (1990)]

4. Effect of Violation

Generally, evidence obtained in violation of *Miranda* is inadmissible at trial.

a. Use of Confession for Impeachment

A confession obtained in violation of the defendant's *Miranda* rights, but otherwise voluntary, may be used to *impeach the defendant's testimony* if he takes the stand at trial, even though such a confession is inadmissible in the state's case in chief as evidence of guilt. [Harris v. New York, 401 U.S. 222 (1971); Oregon v. Hass, 420 U.S. 714 (1975)] However, a truly involuntary confession is *inadmissible* for any purpose. [Mincey v. Arizona, *supra,* III.C.5.f.1)]

1) Silence

The prosecutor may not use the defendant's silence after receiving *Miranda* warnings to counter the defendant's insanity defense. [Wainwright v. Greenfield, 474 U.S. 284 (1986)]

2) May Be Harmless Error

A single question by the prosecutor about the defendant's silence may constitute harmless error when followed by an objection sustained by the judge and an instruction to jurors to disregard the question. [Greer v. Miller, 483 U.S. 756 (1987)]

b. Subsequent Valid Confession Admissible

An invalid confession obtained while the suspect was in custody but before the *Miranda* warnings were given will not render inadmissible a ***subsequent valid confession*** obtained after the warnings were given. The subsequent confession will be admissible evidence. [Oregon v. Elstad, 470 U.S. 298 (1985)] The Court in *Elstad* also suggested—but did *not* clearly hold—that "fruits" derived from statements obtained in violation of *Miranda* (physical evidence such as contraband, weapons, etc.) may be admissible, reasoning that failure to give the *Miranda* warnings is a prophylaxis and not itself a violation of the Fifth Amendment.

5. Public Safety Exception to *Miranda*

If ***police interrogation*** is reasonably prompted by ***concern for public safety***, responses to the questions may be used in court, even though the accused is in custody and *Miranda* warnings are not given. The scope of this exception is unclear, but may be limited to the facts of the case in which the Supreme Court announced the new rule. In that case, the suspect was handcuffed, then asked where he had hidden his gun. The arrest and questioning were virtually contemporaneous, and police were reasonably concerned that the gun might be found and cause injury to an innocent person. [New York v. Quarles, 467 U.S. 649 (1984)]

V. PRETRIAL IDENTIFICATION

A. IN GENERAL

The purpose of all the rules concerning pretrial identification is to ensure that when the witness identifies the person at trial, she is identifying the person who committed the crime and not merely the person whom she has previously seen at the police station.

B. SUBSTANTIVE BASES FOR ATTACK

1. Sixth Amendment Right to Counsel

a. When Right Exists

A suspect has a right to the presence of an attorney at any ***post-charge lineup or showup***. [Moore v. Illinois, 434 U.S. 220 (1977); United States v. Wade, 388 U.S. 218 (1967)] At a lineup, the witness is asked to pick the perpetrator of the crime from a group of persons, while a showup is a one-to-one confrontation between the witness and the suspect for the purpose of identification.

b. Role of Counsel at a Lineup

The right is simply to have an attorney present during the lineup so that the lawyer can observe any suggestive aspects of the lineup and bring them out on cross-examination of the witness. There is no right to have the lawyer help set up the lineup, to demand changes in the way it is conducted, etc.

c. Photo Identification

The accused does *not* have the right to counsel at photo identifications. [United States

v. Ash, 413 U.S. 300 (1973)] However, as in the case of lineups, the accused may have a due process claim regarding the photo identification. (*See 2., infra.*)

d. Physical Evidence

The accused does *not* have the right to counsel when the police take physical evidence such as handwriting exemplars or fingerprints from her.

2. Due Process Standard

A defendant can attack an identification as denying due process when the identification is *unnecessarily suggestive* and there is a *substantial likelihood of misidentification*. It is clear that both parts of this standard must be met for the defendant to win, and that to meet this difficult test, the identification must be shown to have been extremely suggestive.

Examples: 1) A showup at a hospital did not deny the defendant due process when such a procedure was necessary due to the need of an immediate identification, the inability of the identifying victim to come to the police station, and the possibility that the victim might die. [Stovall v. Denno, 388 U.S. 293 (1967)]

2) A photo identification with only six snapshots did not violate due process where the procedure was necessary because perpetrators of a serious felony (robbery) were at large, and the police had to determine if they were on the right track, and the Court found little danger of misidentification. [Simmons v. United States, 390 U.S. 377 (1968)]

3) No substantial likelihood of misidentification was found in the showing of a single photograph to a police officer two days after the crime. [Manson v. Brathwaite, 432 U.S. 98 (1977)]

4) A fundamentally unfair procedure, such as when the perpetrator of the crime is known to be black and the suspect is the only black in the lineup, would violate the due process standard.

C. THE REMEDY

The remedy for an unconstitutional identification is *exclusion* of the in-court identification (unless it has an independent source). This remedy is so severe that relief is rarely granted.

1. Independent Source

A witness may make an in-court identification despite the existence of an unconstitutional pretrial identification if the in-court identification has an independent source. The factors a court will weigh in determining an independent source include the opportunity to observe the defendant at the time of the crime, the ease with which the witness can identify the defendant, and the existence or absence of prior misidentifications.

2. Hearing

The admissibility of identification evidence should be determined at a suppression hearing in the absence of the jury, but exclusion of the jury is not constitutionally required. [Watkins v. Sowders, 449 U.S. 341 (1981)] The government bears the burden of proof as to the presence of counsel or a waiver by the accused, or as to an independent source for the in-court identification, while the defendant must prove an alleged due process violation.

D. NO RIGHT TO LINEUP

The defendant is not entitled to any particular kind of identification procedure. The defendant may not demand a lineup.

E. NO SELF-INCRIMINATION ISSUE

Since a lineup does not involve compulsion to give evidence *"testimonial"* in nature, a suspect has no basis in the Fifth Amendment privilege against compelled self-incrimination to refuse to participate in one. [United States v. Wade, *supra,* B.1.a.]

VI. PRETRIAL PROCEDURES

A. PRELIMINARY HEARING TO DETERMINE PROBABLE CAUSE TO DETAIN (*"GERSTEIN* HEARINGS")

A defendant has a Fourth Amendment right to be released from detention if there is no probable cause to hold him. Thus, a defendant has a right to a determination of probable cause. A preliminary hearing is a hearing held after arrest but before trial to determine whether probable cause for detention exists. The hearing is an informal, ex parte, nonadversarial proceeding.

1. When Right Applies

If probable cause has already been determined (*e.g.,* the arrest is pursuant to a grand jury indictment or an arrest warrant), a preliminary hearing need not be held. If no probable cause determination has been made, a defendant has a right to a preliminary hearing to determine probable cause if *"significant pretrial constraints on the defendant's liberty"* exist. Thus, the right applies if the defendant is released only upon the posting of bail or if he is held in jail in lieu of bail. It does not apply if the defendant is released merely upon the condition that he appear for trial.

Note: The fact that the defendant has been released does not preclude a finding of a significant constraint on liberty, since many conditions can be attached to liberty.

2. Timing

The hearing must be held within a reasonable time, and the Court has determined that 48 hours is presumptively reasonable. [Riverside County v. McLaughlin, 500 U.S. 44 (1991)]

3. Remedy

There is *no real remedy* for the defendant for the mere denial of this hearing, because an unlawful detention, without more, has no effect on the subsequent prosecution. However, if evidence is discovered as a result of the unlawful detention, it will be suppressed under the exclusionary rule.

B. PRETRIAL DETENTION

1. Initial Appearance

Soon after the defendant is arrested, she must be brought before a magistrate who will advise her of her rights, set bail, and appoint counsel if necessary. The initial appearance may be combined with the *Gerstein* hearing, but will be held whether or not a *Gerstein* hearing is necessary. For misdemeanors, this appearance will be the trial.

2. Bail
Most state constitutions or statutes create a right to be released on appropriate bail (either on personal recognizance or on a cash bond).

a. Due Process Concerns
Since denial of release on bail deprives a person of liberty, such denials must comply with the Due Process Clause. In upholding the Federal Bail Reform Act (which permits a court to detain an arrestee if the judge determines that no condition of release would ensure the arrestee's appearance or the safety of any person or the community), the Court held that denial of bail does not violate substantive due process (by imposing punishment before a defendant is found guilty), because the denial of bail is not punishment but a regulatory solution to the problem of persons committing crimes while out on bail. The Court also held that the federal act does not violate procedural due process because it provides detainees with a right to a hearing on the issue, expedited review, etc. [United States v. Salerno, 479 U.S. 1026 (1987)] Similar state statutes would likely be upheld, but a state statute that arbitrarily denies bail (*e.g.,* by not allowing the detainee to present evidence or denying release to a whole class of detainees) would probably violate the Due Process Clause.

b. Right to Be Free from Excessive Bail
Where the right to release exists, state constitutions and state statutes—and perhaps the Eighth Amendment as well—prohibit "excessive" bail. This has traditionally been interpreted to require that bail be set no higher than is necessary to ensure the defendant's appearance at trial.

c. Bail Issues Are Immediately Appealable
In most jurisdictions and under federal law, a refusal to grant bail or the setting of excessive bail may be appealed immediately, as an exception to the final judgment rule for appeals. If not immediately appealable, the denial of bail can be reached by an immediate petition for a writ of habeas corpus. Once the defendant is convicted, an appeal of a pretrial bail decision is moot. [Murphy v. Hunt, 455 U.S. 478 (1982)]

d. Defendant Incompetent to Stand Trial
As to deprivation of pretrial liberty by commitment of one who is not competent to stand trial, the standards for commitment and subsequent release must be essentially identical with those for the commitment of persons not charged with crime; otherwise, there is a denial of equal protection. [Jackson v. Indiana, 406 U.S. 715 (1972)]

3. Pretrial Detention Practices
Pretrial detention practices that are reasonably related to the interest of maintaining jail security, such as double-bunking, prohibiting inmates from receiving from the outside food and personal items or books not mailed directly from the publisher, routine inspections while the detainees remain outside their rooms, and body cavity searches following contact visits, do not violate due process or the Fourth Amendment and without more do not constitute punishment. [Bell v. Wolfish, 441 U.S. 520 (1979)]

C. PRELIMINARY HEARING TO DETERMINE PROBABLE CAUSE TO PROSECUTE
A later preliminary hearing may be held to determine whether probable cause to prosecute exists.

The accused has the *right to counsel* at this hearing [Coleman v. Alabama, 399 U.S. 1 (1970)], and both the prosecutor and the accused may present evidence for the record. The accused may waive the hearing. Either side may use this hearing to preserve testimony of a witness unavailable at trial (*e.g.,* the witness testifies at the preliminary hearing and dies before trial) provided there was some opportunity to cross-examine the witness at the preliminary hearing. [Ohio v. Roberts, 448 U.S. 56 (1980)]

D. GRAND JURIES
The Fifth Amendment right to indictment by grand jury has not been incorporated into the Fourteenth Amendment, but some state constitutions require grand jury indictment.

1. Charging Grand Juries
Most states east of the Mississippi and the federal system use the grand jury as a regular part of the charging process. The charging grand jury *determines probable cause to prosecute* by returning the bill of indictment submitted by the prosecutor as a "true bill." Western states generally charge by filing an information, a written accusation of crime prepared and presented by the prosecutor. Informations also are used when the defendant waives her right to grand jury indictment.

2. Special or Investigative Grand Juries
Special or investigative grand juries are used almost everywhere. This type of grand jury investigates, on its own motion, crime in the particular jurisdiction, and can initiate a criminal case by bringing an indictment.

3. Grand Jury Proceedings

a. Secrecy and Defendant's Lack of Access
Grand jury proceedings are conducted in secret. In most jurisdictions, a defendant has no right to notice that a grand jury is considering an indictment against her, to be present and confront witnesses at the proceeding, or to introduce evidence before the grand jury.

b. Particularized Need Required for Prosecutor's Access to Grand Jury Materials
The "particularized need" standard generally required under Rule 6(e) of the Federal Rules of Criminal Procedure in order to obtain access to grand jury materials must be shown by state attorneys general [Illinois v. Abbott, 460 U.S. 557 (1983)], as well as Justice Department attorneys [United States v. Sells Engineering, Inc., 463 U.S. 418 (1983)]. The disclosure of such materials to the Internal Revenue Service for the purpose of assessing tax liability, rather than for litigation, is not permitted. [United States v. Baggot, 463 U.S. 476 (1983)]

c. Subpoena Powers of Grand Jury
The grand jury may use its subpoena power to investigate the matters before it or to initiate criminal investigations of its own. Rather than returning an indictment, grand juries sometimes issue a report.

1) Government Need Not Prove Relevance
A grand jury subpoena may be quashed only if the opposing party can prove that

there is no reasonable possibility that the material sought will be relevant to the grand jury investigation. The government has no initial burden of proving that the material is relevant. [United States v. R. Enterprises, Inc., 498 U.S. 292 (1991)]

2) Defamatory Reports
If the defendant or any other person believes that she has been defamed by a grand jury report, she may make a motion to seal the report.

d. No Right to Counsel or *Miranda* Warnings
A witness subpoenaed to testify before a grand jury does not have the right to receive the *Miranda* warnings, and the witness may be convicted of perjury despite the lack of warnings if she testifies falsely. A grand jury witness does not have the right to have an attorney present, but she may consult with an attorney outside the grand jury room. [United States v. Mandujano, *supra*, IV.D.2.h.; United States v. Wong, *supra*, IV.D.2.h.]

e. No Right to "Potential Defendant" Warnings
A witness who is under investigation and may well become a defendant is not entitled to a warning that she is a "potential defendant" when called to testify before the grand jury. [United States v. Washington, 431 U.S. 181 (1977)]

f. No Right to Have Evidence Excluded
A grand jury may base its indictment on evidence that would not be admissible at trial [Costello v. United States, 350 U.S. 359 (1956)], and a grand jury witness may not refuse to answer questions on the grounds that they are based upon unconstitutionally obtained evidence [United States v. Calandra, 414 U.S. 338 (1974)]. Nor may an indicted defendant have the indictment quashed on the grounds that it is based upon illegally obtained evidence.

g. No Right to Challenge Subpoena on Fourth Amendment Grounds
A suspect-witness (or any witness, for that matter) subpoenaed before a grand jury cannot attack the subpoena on the ground that the grand jury lacked "probable cause"—or any reason at all—to call her for questioning. No such attack can be made even if the subpoena also requires the witness to provide a handwriting exemplar, a voice sample, or otherwise cooperate with law enforcement officials in a manner not violating the self-incrimination privilege.

h. Exclusion of Minorities
Minorities may not be excluded from grand jury service. A conviction resulting from an indictment issued by a grand jury from which members of a minority group have been excluded will be reversed without regard to the harmlessness of the error. [Vasquez v. Hillery, 474 U.S. 254 (1986)] Note that the defendant and the excluded members need not be of the same race. [Campbell v. Louisiana, 423 U.S. 392 (1998)]

i. Dismissal Seldom Required for Procedural Defect
An indicted defendant is seldom entitled to dismissal of an indictment upon a showing that procedural error occurred during the grand jury proceedings. Generally, she is entitled to dismissal only upon a showing that the error substantially influenced the

grand jury's decision to indict. [Bank of Nova Scotia v. United States, 487 U.S. 250 (1988)—defendant failed to show that prosecutorial misconduct before grand jury substantially influenced its decision to indict]

j.   Exculpatory Evidence
An indictment may not be dismissed by a federal court for a prosecutor's failure to present exculpatory evidence to the grand jury unless the prosecutor's conduct violates a preexisting constitutional, legislative, or procedural rule. [United States v. Williams, 504 U.S. 36 (1992)]

E.   SPEEDY TRIAL

1.   Societal Interest
The Sixth Amendment right to a speedy trial is an unusual one in that the interests of society and the defendant coincide.

2.   Constitutional Standard
A determination of whether the defendant's right to a speedy trial has been violated will be made by an evaluation of the totality of the circumstances. The following factors should be considered:

(i)   Length of the delay;

(ii)   Reason for the delay;

(iii)   Whether the defendant asserted his right; and

(iv)   Prejudice to the defendant.

[Barker v. Wingo, 407 U.S. 514 (1972)]
Example: A defendant who was arrested 8½ years after his federal indictment due solely to the government's neglect and who promptly asserted his right to a speedy trial claim was *presumptively prejudiced* so that an actual showing of prejudice was not necessary. [Doggett v. United States, 505 U.S. 647 (1992)]

3.   Remedy—Dismissal
The remedy for a violation of the constitutional right to a speedy trial is dismissal with prejudice. [Strunk v. United States, 412 U.S. 434 (1973)]

4.   When Right Attaches
The right to a speedy trial does not attach until the defendant has been *arrested or charged*. It is very difficult to get relief for a pre-arrest delay under this standard, because the defendant must show prejudice from a delay, and good faith investigative delays do not violate due process. [United States v. Lovasco, 431 U.S. 783 (1977)]

A defendant is not entitled to speedy trial relief for the period between the dismissal of charges and later refiling. [United States v. MacDonald, 456 U.S. 1 (1982)] The only limitation on pre-arrest delay (other than general due process requirements) seems to be the statute of limitations for the particular crime.

a. Knowledge of Charges Unnecessary

The Speedy Trial Clause attaches even if the defendant does not know about the charges against him and is thus not restrained in any way. [Doggett v. United States, *supra*]

5. Special Problems

Two situations create special speedy trial problems:

a. Detainees

A defendant incarcerated in one jurisdiction who has a charge pending in another jurisdiction has a right to have the second jurisdiction exert reasonable efforts to obtain his presence for trial of these pending charges. Failure to exert such efforts violates his right to speedy trial. [Smith v. Hooey, 393 U.S. 374 (1969)]

b. Indefinite Suspension of Charges

It is a violation of the right to speedy trial to permit the prosecution to indefinitely suspend charges, such as permitting the government to dismiss "without prejudice," which permits reinstatement of the prosecution *at any time*. [Klopfer v. North Carolina, 386 U.S. 213 (1967)—nolle prosequi that indefinitely suspended the statute of limitations violated speedy trial requirements]

F. PROSECUTORIAL DUTY TO DISCLOSE EXCULPATORY INFORMATION AND NOTICE OF DEFENSES

1. Prosecutor's Duty to Disclose Exculpatory Evidence

The government has a duty to disclose material, exculpatory evidence to the defendant. [Brady v. Maryland, 373 U.S. 83 (1963)] Failure to disclose such evidence—whether willful *or inadvertent*—violates the Due Process Clause and is grounds for reversing a conviction if the defendant can prove that:

(i) The evidence at issue is *favorable to the defendant* because it impeaches or is exculpatory; and

(ii) *Prejudice has resulted* (*i.e.*, there is a *reasonable probability* that the result of the case would have been different if the undisclosed evidence had been presented at trial).

[Strickler v. Green, 527 U.S. 263 (1999); United States v. Bagley, 473 U.S. 667 (1985)] *Note:* If the prosecution can show that the verdict is strongly supported by other evidence, sufficient prejudice will not be found.

a. Exception—Reports on Sexually Abused Minors

A defendant may not automatically obtain investigative reports made by a state agency in charge of investigating sexually abused minors because of the confidentiality of the minors' records. Such reports can be obtained only if they are *favorable* to the defendant and are *material* to guilt or punishment. [Pennsylvania v. Ritchie, 480 U.S. 39 (1987)]

b. Probably Must Be Relevant to Merits

The duty to disclose appears to extend only to evidence relevant to the prosecution's case in chief. Material going to a defense not on the merits probably need not be disclosed. [*See* United States v. Armstrong, 517 U.S. 456 (1996)—material relevant to defendant's claim that he was selected for prosecution because of his race need not be disclosed]

2. Notice of Alibi and Intent to Present Insanity Defense

a. Reciprocity Required

The prosecution may demand to know whether the defendant is going to plead insanity or raise an alibi as a defense. If the defendant is going to raise an alibi, he must list his witnesses. In return, the prosecution is required to list the witnesses it will call to rebut the defendant's defense. [Williams v. Florida, 399 U.S. 78 (1970); Wardius v. Oregon, 412 U.S. 470 (1973)]

b. Commenting on Failure to Present the Alibi

The prosecutor may not comment at trial on the defendant's failure to produce a witness named as supporting the alibi or on the failure to present the alibi itself. But the prosecutor may use the notice of an alibi to *impeach* a defendant who takes the stand and testifies to a different alibi.

G. COMPETENCY TO STAND TRIAL

1. Competency and Insanity Distinguished

Competency to stand trial must be carefully distinguished from the insanity defense, although both rest on a defendant's abnormality. Insanity is a defense to the criminal charge; a defendant acquitted by reason of insanity may not be retried and convicted, although she may be hospitalized under some circumstances. *Incompetency* to stand trial depends on a defendant's mental condition at the *time of trial*, unlike *insanity*, which turns upon a defendant's mental condition at the *time of the crime*. Incompetency is not a defense but rather a bar to trial. A defendant who is incompetent to stand trial cannot be tried. But if she later regains her competency, she can then be tried and—unless she has a defense—convicted. Note that a defendant who is competent to stand trial is competent to plead guilty.

2. Due Process Standard

Due process of law, as well as the state law of most jurisdictions, prohibits the trial of a defendant who is incompetent to stand trial. A defendant is incompetent to stand trial under the due process standard if, because of her present mental condition, she either:

(i) Lacks a rational as well as a factual *understanding of the charges and proceedings*; or

(ii) Lacks sufficient present *ability to consult with her lawyer* with a reasonable degree of understanding.

[Dusky v. United States, 362 U.S. 402 (1960)]

3. Trial Judge's Duty to Raise Competency Issue

If evidence of a defendant's incompetency appears to the trial judge, the judge has a constitutional obligation to conduct further inquiry and determine whether in fact the defendant is incompetent. If a defendant is tried and convicted but it later appears she was incompetent to stand trial, the judge's failure to raise the issue or to request a determination of competency does not constitute a "waiver." [Pate v. Robinson, 383 U.S. 375 (1966)]

Example: During preliminary proceedings at X's trial for robbery, X, while in open court, speaks irrationally and repeatedly interrupts the proceedings by shouting to a nonexistent dog in the courtroom. What, if anything, must the trial judge do before proceeding to trial? The facts here clearly require the trial judge to investigate and determine X's competency to stand trial. The judge must hold a hearing and determine whether X is mentally ill and, if so, whether she can consult with her lawyer and understand the charges and proceedings. This must be done even if neither X nor her lawyer raises the issue.

4. Burden Can Be Placed on Defendant

A state can require a criminal defendant to prove that he is not competent to stand trial by a preponderance of the evidence; this does not violate due process. [Medina v. California, 505 U.S. 437 (1992)] However, requiring a defendant to prove incompetence by *clear and convincing evidence* violates due process. [Cooper v. Oklahoma, 517 U.S. 348 (1996)]

5. Detention of Defendant

a. Based on Incompetency

A defendant who has been found incompetent may be detained in a mental hospital for a brief period of time for evaluation and treatment. But she cannot be hospitalized indefinitely or for a long period of time simply because she has been found incompetent. This can be done only if independent "civil commitment" proceedings are begun and result in her commitment. [Jackson v. Indiana, 406 U.S. 715 (1972)]

b. Based on Insanity

A defendant who has made a successful insanity defense can be confined in a mental hospital for a term longer than the maximum period of incarceration for the offense. The insanity acquittee is not entitled to any separate civil commitment hearing at the expiration of the maximum sentence. [Jones v. United States, 463 U.S. 354 (1983)] However, a defendant acquitted by reason of insanity who is determined to have recovered sanity cannot be indefinitely committed in a mental facility merely because he is unable to prove himself not dangerous to others. [Foucha v. Louisiana, 504 U.S. 71 (1992)]

H. PRETRIAL PUBLICITY AND THE RIGHT TO A FAIR TRIAL

Excessive pretrial publicity prejudicial to the defendant may require change of venue or retrial.

Examples: 1) Defendant sought and was improperly denied a change of venue on the ground of local prejudice. His trial by a jury that was familiar with the material facts and had formed an opinion as to his guilt before the trial began (on the basis of unfavorable newspaper publicity) denied him due process. [Irvin v. Dowd, 366 U.S. 717 (1961)] However, due process will be satisfied if the judge asks the venirepersons whether they were exposed to pretrial publicity, and if so, whether it would affect their impartiality and ability to hear the case with an open mind. The judge does not have to ask about the specific source or content of the pretrial information. [Mu'Min v. Virginia, 500 U.S. 415 (1991)]

2) A new trial is required where defendant sought and was denied a change of venue after a televised interview in which defendant admitted that he had perpetrated the crimes with which he was charged, and the jury was drawn from the people who had seen the interview. [Rideau v. Louisiana, 373 U.S. 723 (1963)—jurors' claims that they could be neutral were inherently implausible]

3) Defendant's request for a change of venue because of pretrial publicity was denied because state law did not permit a change of venue in misdemeanor cases. *Held:* The law violates the right to trial by an impartial jury; a defendant must be given the opportunity to show that a change of venue is required in his case. [Groppi v. Wisconsin, 400 U.S. 505 (1971)]

VII. TRIAL

A. BASIC RIGHT TO A FAIR TRIAL

1. Right to Public Trial
The Sixth and Fourteenth Amendments guarantee the right to a public trial. [*In re* Oliver, 333 U.S. 257 (1948); Herring v. New York, 422 U.S. 853 (1975)] However, the extent of this right varies according to the stage of the proceeding involved.

a. Preliminary Probable Cause Hearing
Preliminary hearings to determine whether there is probable cause on which to prosecute are presumptively open to the public and the press. [Press Enterprise Co. v. Superior Court, 478 U.S. 1 (1986)]

b. Suppression Hearings
The Sixth Amendment right to a public trial extends to *pretrial suppression hearings*. Such hearings may not be closed to the public unless:

(i) The party seeking closure shows an *overriding interest* likely to be prejudiced by a public hearing;

(ii) The closure is *no broader than necessary* to protect such an interest;

(iii) *Reasonable alternatives* to closure have been considered; and

(iv) *Adequate findings* to support closure are entered by the trial court.

[Waller v. Georgia, 467 U.S. 39 (1984)]

c. Trial
The press and the public have a right under the First Amendment to attend the trial itself, even when the defense and prosecution agree to close it. A judge may not exclude the press and the public from a criminal trial without first finding that closure is necessary for a fair trial. [Richmond Newspapers, Inc. v. Virginia, 448 U.S. 555 (1980)]

1) Televising Permissible

The state may constitutionally permit televising criminal proceedings over the defendant's objection. [Chandler v. Florida, 449 U.S. 560 (1981)]

2. Right to an Unbiased Judge

Due process is violated if the judge is shown to have **actual malice** against the defendant or to have had a **financial interest** in having the trial result in a verdict of guilty.

Example: D is tried before a "mayor's court" presided over by a judge who is also the mayor of the town. Half of the town's income comes from fines imposed in the court after convictions. Is the trial permissible? No. The judge has too great a financial interest in the outcome to meet due process standards. [Ward v. City of Monroeville, 409 U.S. 57 (1972)]

3. Must Judge Be a Lawyer?

A defendant in a minor misdemeanor prosecution has no right to have the trial judge be a lawyer, if upon conviction he has a right to trial de novo in a court with a lawyer-judge. [North v. Russell, 427 U.S. 328 (1976)] It is likely, however, that in serious crime cases the Supreme Court will require that the judge be law-trained.

4. Right to Be Free of Trial Disruption

Due process is violated if the trial is conducted in a manner or atmosphere making it unlikely that the jury gave the evidence reasonable consideration. Televising and broadcasting parts of a trial, for example, may interfere with courtroom proceedings and influence the jury by emphasizing the notoriety of the trial to such an extent that it infringes the defendant's right to a fair trial. [Estes v. Texas, 381 U.S. 532 (1965)]

5. Trial in Prison Clothing

It is unconstitutional for the state to **compel** the defendant to stand trial in prison clothing. If the defendant does not wish to be tried in prison clothing, he must make a timely objection. [Estelle v. Williams, 425 U.S. 501 (1976)]

6. Right to Have Jury Free from Unfair Influences

If the jury is exposed to influences favorable to the prosecution, due process is violated.

Example: During X's trial, two sheriffs, who were also prosecution witnesses, were in constant and intimate association with the jurors, eating with them, running errands for them, etc. Did the trial violate due process standards? Yes, since this association must have influenced the jurors' assessment of the credibility of the witnesses. [Turner v. Louisiana, 379 U.S. 466 (1965)]

7. No Right to Preservation of Potentially Exculpatory Evidence

Defendants have no right to have the police preserve all evidence for trial, at least where it is not certain that the evidence would have been exculpatory. Due process is violated, however, if the police **in bad faith** destroy evidence potentially useful to the defense at trial. [Arizona v. Youngblood, 488 U.S. 51 (1988)—no due process violation where police failed to preserve seminal fluid on sodomy victim's clothing; California v. Trombetta, 467 U.S. 479 (1984)—same result where police failed to preserve samples of defendant's breath]

B. RIGHT TO TRIAL BY JURY

The Sixth Amendment right to trial by jury applies to the states. [Duncan v. Louisiana, 391 U.S.

145 (1968)] The cases after *Duncan,* while zealously guarding the jury trial right, have permitted the states great latitude in the details of jury use and conduct because of (i) the view that many of the details of the jury were historical accidents, (ii) the belief that the jury will act rationally, and (iii) the cost.

1. Right to Jury Trial Only for "Serious" Offenses

There is no constitutional right to jury trial for petty offenses, but only for serious offenses. Also, there is no right to jury trial in juvenile delinquency proceedings. [McKeiver v. Pennsylvania, 403 U.S. 528 (1971)]

a. What Constitutes a Serious Offense?

For purposes of the right to jury trial, an offense is serious if *imprisonment for more than six months* is authorized. If imprisonment of less than six months is authorized, the offense is presumptively petty, and there is no right to a jury trial. [Blanton v. City of North Las Vegas, 489 U.S. 538 (1989)] The presumption may be overcome by showing additional penalties, but a possibility of a $5,000 fine and five years' probation is not sufficient to overcome the presumption that the crime is petty. [United States v. Nachtigal, 507 U.S. 1 (1993)]

1) Aggregation of Petty Offenses

The right to a jury trial does not arise when in a single proceeding, sentences for multiple petty offenses are imposed which result in an aggregate prison sentence of more than six months. [Lewis v. United States, 518 U.S. 322 (1996)]

b. Contempt

1) Civil Contempt—No Jury Trial Right

If a penalty is imposed for purposes of compelling future compliance with a court order and the witness can avoid further penalty by complying with the order (*e.g.,* judge sentences witness to prison until she is willing to testify), the proceeding is one of "civil" contempt and no jury trial is required.

2) Criminal Contempt—Six Months Rule

When there is no statutorily authorized penalty for a crime, such as criminal contempt, the actual sentence governs the right to jury trial. Cumulative penalties totaling more than six months cannot be imposed in a *post-verdict contempt adjudication* without affording the defendant the right to a jury trial. [Codispoti v. Pennsylvania, 418 U.S. 506 (1974)]

3) Summary Contempt Punishment During Trial

If the judge summarily imposes punishment for contempt during trial, the penalties may aggregate more than six months without a jury trial. [Codispoti v. Pennsylvania, *supra*]

4) Appellate Modification Sufficient

An appellate court may reduce the sentence imposed for contempt to six months or less and thereby protect the conviction and sentence imposed without a jury from constitutional attack. [Taylor v. Hayes, 418 U.S. 488 (1974)]

5) Probation

A judge may place a contemnor on probation for a term of up to five years without affording him the right to jury trial as long as revocation of probation would not result in imprisonment for more than six months. [Frank v. United States, 395 U.S. 147 (1969)]

2. Number and Unanimity of Jurors

a. No Right to Jury of Twelve

There is no constitutional right to a jury of 12, but there must be *at least six* jurors to satisfy the right to jury trial under the Sixth and Fourteenth Amendments. [Ballew v. Georgia, 435 U.S. 223 (1978)]

b. No Absolute Right to Unanimity

There is no right to a unanimous verdict. The Supreme Court has upheld convictions based upon 11-1, 10-2, and 9-3 votes [Apodaca v. Oregon, 406 U.S. 404 (1972); Johnson v. Louisiana, 406 U.S. 356 (1972)], but probably would not approve an 8-4 vote for conviction. Six-person juries must be unanimous. [Burch v. Louisiana, 441 U.S. 130 (1979); Brown v. Louisiana, 447 U.S. 323 (1980)]

3. Right to Venire Selected from Representative Cross-Section of Community

A defendant has a right to have the venire from which the jury is selected be from a representative cross-section of the community. A defendant can complain of an exclusion of a significant segment of the community from the venire, even if he is not a member of that excluded segment. [Taylor v. Louisiana, 419 U.S. 522 (1975); Holland v. Illinois, 493 U.S. 474 (1990)]

a. Showing of Exclusion of Significant Group Sufficient

To make out a case for exclusion, the defendant need only show the underrepresentation of a distinct and numerically significant group. [Taylor v. Louisiana, *supra*]

b. No Right to Proportional Representation on Particular Jury

The cross-sectional requirement applies only to the venire from which the jury is selected. A defendant does not have the right to proportional representation of all groups on his particular jury. [Holland v. Illinois, *supra*]

c. Use of Peremptory Challenges for Racial and Gender-Based Discrimination

In contrast to striking potential jurors for cause, a prosecutor generally may exercise peremptory challenges for any rational *or irrational* reason. However, the Equal Protection Clause forbids the use of peremptory challenges to exclude potential jurors solely on account of their race or gender. [Batson v. Kentucky, 476 U.S. 79 (1989); J.E.B. v. Alabama, 511 U.S. 127 (1994)]

1) Proving Strike Improper

An equal protection-based attack on peremptory strikes involves three steps: (i) The defendant must show *facts or circumstances that raise an inference* that the exclusion of potential jurors was based on race or gender. (ii) If such a showing is made, the prosecutor must then come forward with a *race-neutral explanation* for the strike. The reason for the strike need not be reasonable, as long as it is race-neutral.

[Purkett v. Elem, 514 U.S. 765 (1995)—explanation that potential jurors were struck because of their long hair and beards was sufficient] (iii) The judge then determines whether the prosecutor's explanation was the genuine reason for striking the juror, or merely a pretext for purposeful discrimination. If the judge believes that the *prosecutor was sincere*, the strike may be upheld. [Purkett v. Elem, *supra*]

Note that the defendant need not be a member of the group excluded. [Powers v. Ohio, 499 U.S. 400 (1991)]

2) Defendants

It is also unconstitutional for a criminal *defendant* or the defendant's attorney to use peremptory challenges in a racially discriminatory manner. [Georgia v. McCollum, 505 U.S. 42 (1992)] The same rule probably applies to a defendant's peremptory strike based on gender.

d. Distinct and Significant Groups

A fair cross-section of the community must include minorities and women, and possibly other distinct and significant groups. A state may neither exclude women from jury duty nor automatically exempt them upon request. [Duren v. Missouri, 439 U.S. 357 (1979)]

4. Right to Impartial Jury

a. Right to Questioning on Racial Bias

A defendant is entitled to questioning on voir dire specifically directed to racial prejudice whenever race is inextricably bound up in the case. [Ham v. South Carolina, 409 U.S. 524 (1973)] In *noncapital* cases, the mere fact that the victim is white and the defendant is black is not enough to permit such questioning. [Ristaino v. Ross, 424 U.S. 589 (1976); Rosales-Lopez v. United States, 451 U.S. 182 (1982)] However, a *capital* defendant accused of an interracial crime is entitled to have prospective jurors informed of the victim's race and is entitled to voir dire questioning regarding the issue of racial prejudice. [Turner v. Murray, 476 U.S. 28 (1986)]

b. Juror Opposition to Death Penalty

In cases involving capital punishment, a state may not automatically exclude for cause all prospective jurors who express a doubt or scruple about the death penalty. [Witherspoon v. Illinois, 391 U.S. 510 (1968); Adams v. Texas, 448 U.S. 38 (1980)]

1) Standard—Impair or Prevent Performance

The standard for determining when a prospective juror should be excluded for cause is whether the juror's views would *prevent or substantially impair* the performance of his duties in accordance with his instructions and oath. [Wainwright v. Witt, 469 U.S. 412 (1985)] Thus, if a juror's doubts or scruples about the death penalty prevent or substantially impair the performance of his duties, he may be excluded from the jury, and the fact that this may result in a "death qualified" jury does not infringe on a defendant's constitutional rights. [Lockhart v. McCree, 476 U.S. 162 (1986)] However, if a juror has scruples about the death penalty, but could perform her duties and follow instructions, it is error to exclude the juror.

2) Improper Exclusion May Result in Reversal
A death sentence imposed by a jury from which a juror was improperly excluded is subject to automatic reversal. [Gray v. Mississippi, 481 U.S. 648 (1987)]

c. Juror Favoring Death Penalty
If a jury is to decide whether a defendant in a capital case is to be sentenced to death, the defendant must be allowed to ask potential jurors at voir dire if they would automatically give the death penalty upon a guilty verdict. A juror who answers affirmatively should be excluded for cause because such a juror has indicated the same type of inability to follow jury instructions (as to mitigating circumstances) as a juror who has indicated an inability to impose the death penalty under any circumstances (*see supra*). [Morgan v. Illinois, 504 U.S. 719 (1992)]

d. Use of Peremptory Challenge to Maintain Impartial Jury
Peremptory challenges are not constitutionally required. Therefore, if a trial court refuses to exclude a juror for cause whom the court should have excluded, and the defendant uses a peremptory challenge to remove the juror, there is no constitutional violation. [Ross v. Oklahoma, 487 U.S. 81 (1988); United States v. Martinez-Salazar, 528 U.S. 304 (2000)]

5. Inconsistent Verdicts
Inconsistent jury verdicts (*e.g.,* finding defendant guilty of some counts but not guilty on related counts or one defendant guilty and a co-defendant innocent on the same evidence) are not reviewable. A challenge to an inconsistent verdict would be based upon pure speculation because it is impossible to tell on which decision the jury erred. [United States v. Powell, 469 U.S. 57 (1984)]

C. RIGHT TO COUNSEL
A defendant has a right to counsel under the Fifth and Sixth Amendments. The Fifth Amendment right applies at all custodial interrogations (*see* IV.D., *supra*). The Sixth Amendment right applies at all *critical stages* of a prosecution after formal proceedings have begun. If the right to counsel is denied *at trial*, a conviction will automatically be reversed. For nontrial denials, the harmless error test is applied.

1. Stages at Which Applicable
The defendant has the right to be represented by privately retained counsel or to have counsel appointed for him by the state if he is indigent, at the following stages:

(i) Custodial police interrogation [Miranda v. Arizona, *supra*, IV.D.1.];

(ii) Post-indictment interrogation whether custodial or not [Massiah v. United States, *supra*, IV.C.];

(iii) Preliminary hearings to determine probable cause to prosecute [Coleman v. Alabama, *supra*, VI.C.];

(iv) Arraignment [Hamilton v. Alabama, 368 U.S. 52 (1961)];

(v) Post-charge lineups [Moore v. Illinois, *supra*, V.B.1.a.];

(vi) Guilty plea and sentencing [Mempa v. Rhay, 389 U.S. 128 (1967); Moore v. Michigan, 355 U.S. 155 (1957); Townsend v. Burke, 334 U.S. 736 (1948)];

(vii) Felony trials [Gideon v. Wainwright, 372 U.S. 335 (1963)];

(viii) Misdemeanor trials when imprisonment is actually imposed [Scott v. Illinois, 440 U.S. 367 (1979)];

(ix) Overnight recesses during trial [Geders v. United States, 425 U.S. 80 (1976)]; and

(x) Appeals as a matter of right [Douglas v. California, 372 U.S. 353 (1963)].

Note: The Fifth Amendment right to counsel is involved at (i) and (ii), above; the Sixth Amendment right is also involved at (ii) and at all the remaining stages.

2. **Stages at Which Not Applicable**
The defendant does not have a constitutional right to be represented by counsel at the following stages:

a. Blood sampling [Schmerber v. California, *supra*, III.D.1.a.];

b. Taking of handwriting or voice exemplars [Gilbert v. California, 388 U.S. 263 (1967)];

c. Pre-charge or investigative lineups [Kirby v. Illinois, 406 U.S. 682 (1972)];

d. Photo identifications [United States v. Ash, *supra*, V.B.1.c.];

e. Preliminary hearings to determine probable cause to detain [Gerstein v. Pugh, 420 U.S. 103 (1975)];

f. Brief recesses during the defendant's testimony at trial [Perry v. Leeke, 488 U.S. 272 (1989)];

g. Discretionary appeals [Ross v. Moffitt, 417 U.S. 600 (1974)];

h. Parole and probation revocation proceedings [Gagnon v. Scarpelli, 411 U.S. 778 (1973)]; and

i. Post-conviction proceeding (*e.g.,* habeas corpus) [Pennsylvania v. Finley, 481 U.S. 551 (1987)] including petitions by death-row inmates [Murray v. Giarratano, 492 U.S. 1 (1989)].

3. **Waiver of Right to Counsel and Right to Defend Oneself**
A defendant has the absolute right to represent himself *at trial* as long as his waiver of the right to counsel is knowing and intelligent. The court must carefully scrutinize the waiver to ensure that the defendant has a rational and factual understanding of the proceeding against him. However, the defendant need not be found capable of representing himself—the

defendant's ability to represent himself has no bearing on his competence to choose self-representation. [Faretta v. California, 422 U.S. 806 (1975); Godinez v. Moran, 509 U.S. 389 (1993)] A back-up attorney may be appointed and may intervene to a limited extent, as long as the impression of self-representation is not destroyed. [McKaskle v. Wiggins, 465 U.S. 168 (1984)]

Note: On appeal, a defendant has no right to represent himself. [Martinez v. Court of Appeal, 528 U.S. 152 (2000)]

4. Indigence and Recoupment of Cost

As indicated above, if the defendant is indigent, the state will provide an attorney. Indigence involves the present financial inability to hire counsel, but none of the right to counsel cases defines indigence precisely. In any case, judges generally are reluctant to refuse to appoint counsel because of the risk of reversal should the defendant be determined indigent. The state generally provides counsel in close cases of indigence, but it may then seek reimbursement from those convicted defendants who later become able to pay. [Fuller v. Oregon, 417 U.S. 40 (1974)]

5. Effective Assistance of Counsel

The Sixth Amendment right to counsel includes the right to effective counsel. The ineffective assistance claim is the most commonly raised constitutional claim. With this claim, the defendant seeks to secure not malpractice damages, but rather a reversal of his conviction and a new trial.

a. Effective Assistance Presumed

Effective assistance of counsel is *presumed* unless the adversarial process is so undermined by counsel's conduct that the trial cannot be relied upon to have produced a just result. [Strickland v. Washington, 466 U.S. 668 (1984)]

b. Right Extends to First Appeal

Effective assistance of counsel is also guaranteed on a first appeal as of right. [Evitts v. Lucey, 469 U.S. 387 (1985)]

c. Circumstances Constituting Ineffective Assistance

An ineffective assistance claimant must show:

(i) *Deficient performance* by counsel; and that

(ii) But for such deficiency, the *result of the proceeding would have been different* (*e.g.,* defendant would not have been convicted or his sentence would have been shorter).

[Strickland v. Washington, *supra*] Typically, such a claim can be made out only by specifying particular errors of trial counsel, and cannot be based on mere inexperience, lack of time to prepare, gravity of the charges, complexity of defenses, or accessibility of witnesses to counsel. [United States v. Cronic, 466 U.S. 648 (1984)]

Example: Defendant pleaded guilty, was convicted, and was given 60 days to appeal. His attorney neither asked him whether he wanted to appeal nor filed an appeal. Defendant subsequently challenged his conviction, claiming ineffective assistance of counsel. The appellate court held that failure to ask a client whether he wants to appeal is per se ineffective assistance. But the Supreme Court held that the *Strickland* two-pronged test applies. The Court noted that it is not always deficient to fail to ask a client whether he wants to appeal, especially where the client has pleaded guilty. Also, even where the failure is deficient, it does not necessarily affect the ultimate outcome. The defendant must show that but for counsel's deficiency, defendant would have appealed. If the defendant cannot show that he had any valid defenses, this tends to show that the outcome would not have been affected because he probably would not have appealed. [Roe v. Flores-Ortega, 528 U.S. 470 (2000)]

d. Circumstances Not Constituting Ineffective Assistance

Circumstances not constituting ineffective assistance include:

1) Trial Tactics

Courts will not grant relief for any acts or omissions by counsel that they view as trial tactics.

2) Failure to Argue Nonfrivolous Issues

An indigent criminal defendant has no constitutional right to compel his appointed lawyer to argue nonfrivolous issues that the counsel decides, in the exercise of her professional judgment, not to present. [Jones v. Barnes, 463 U.S. 745 (1983)]

3) Rejection of Defendant's Request for a Continuance

The right to counsel is not violated by a trial court's denial of an indigent defendant's request for a continuance in order to permit further investigation when his appointed counsel asserts that she is sufficiently prepared, nor by the court's denial of the indigent defendant's request for a continuance so that he may be represented by the counsel originally assigned to the case, but who was hospitalized at the time of trial. [Morris v. Slappy, 461 U.S. 1 (1983)]

4) Failure to Raise Constitutional Claim that Is Later Invalidated

The failure of a defendant's counsel to raise a federal constitutional claim that was the law at the time of the proceeding but that was later overruled does not prejudice the defendant within the meaning of the Sixth Amendment and does not constitute ineffective assistance of counsel. [Lockhart v. Fretwell, 506 U.S. 364 (1993)]

6. Conflicts of Interest

Joint representation (*i.e.,* a single attorney representing co-defendants) is not per se invalid. However, if an attorney advises the trial court of a resulting conflict of interest at or before trial, and the court refuses to appoint separate counsel, the defendant is entitled to *automatic reversal*. [Holloway v. Arkansas, 435 U.S. 475 (1978); Cuyler v. Sullivan, 446 U.S. 335 (1980)] If the defendant does not object to joint representation in a timely manner, to obtain reversal the defendant must show that the attorney *actively* represented conflicting interests and thereby prejudiced the defendant. [Burger v. Kemp, 483 U.S. 776 (1987)]

a. Conflict with Attorney Is Rarely Ground for Relief

A defendant can rarely obtain relief by claiming a conflict of interest between himself and counsel. Conflicts between a defendant and his attorney are best analyzed as claims of ineffective assistance of counsel. To be successful, the defendant must demonstrate that the conflict with his attorney was so severe that the attorney could not effectively investigate or present the defendant's claims.

b. No Right to Joint Representation

While a defendant ordinarily has the right to counsel of her own choosing, a defendant has no right to be jointly represented with her co-defendants. Trial courts have the authority to limit joint representation to avoid potential and actual conflicts of interest. Even when all of the defendants waive any claim to conflicts of interest, the trial court can still prohibit the joint representation. [Wheat v. United States, 486 U.S. 153 (1988)]

7. Right to Support Services for Defense

Where a defendant has made a preliminary showing that he is likely to be able to use the insanity defense, the state must provide a psychiatrist for the preparation of the defense. Where a state presents evidence that the defendant is likely to be dangerous in the future, the defendant is entitled to psychiatric examination and testimony in the sentencing proceeding. [Ake v. Oklahoma, 470 U.S. 68 (1985)]

8. Seizure of Funds Constitutional

The right to counsel does not forbid the seizure—under the federal drug forfeiture statute [21 U.S.C. §853]—of drug money and property obtained with drug money, even when such money and property were going to be used by the defendant to pay his attorney of choice. [Caplin & Drysdale, Chartered v. United States, 491 U.S. 617 (1989)]

9. Right Limited While Testifying

A defendant has a general right to consult with his attorney during the course of trial; however, he has no right to consult with his attorney while he is testifying. Whether a defendant has a right to consult with his attorney during breaks in his testimony depends on the character of the break. Generally, the longer the break, the more likely the Court will find the right. [*Compare* Geders v. United States, *supra*, C.1.—defendant must be allowed to talk with attorney during overnight break in defendant's testimony because ordinary trial tactics can be, and usually are, discussed during such breaks—*with* Perry v. Leeke, 488 U.S. 272 (1989)—sequestration during 15-minute break between defendant's direct testimony and cross-examination permissible because cross-examination of uncounseled witness more likely to lead to truth]

D. RIGHT TO CONFRONT WITNESSES

The Sixth Amendment grants to the defendant in a criminal prosecution the right to confront adverse witnesses. This right, held applicable to the states in *Pointer v. Texas*, 380 U.S. 400 (1965), seeks to ensure that:

(i) The fact finder and the defendant *observe the demeanor* of the testifying witness; and

(ii) The defendant has the opportunity to *cross-examine* any witness testifying against him.

The defendant is entitled to a face-to-face encounter with the witness, but absence of face-to-face confrontation between the defendant and the accuser does not violate the Sixth Amendment when preventing such confrontation serves an important public purpose (such as insulating a child witness from trauma) and the reliability of the witness's testimony is otherwise assured. [Maryland v. Craig, 497 U.S. 836 (1990)]

1. Right Not Absolute

a. Disruptive Defendant
A defendant has no absolute right to confront witnesses, as a judge may remove a disruptive defendant. [Illinois v. Allen, 397 U.S. 337 (1970)]

b. Voluntarily Leaving Courtroom
A defendant has not been deprived of his right of confrontation if he voluntarily leaves the courtroom during the trial, and the trial continues in his absence. [Taylor v. United States, 414 U.S. 17 (1974)]

c. Government May Discourage Attendance
Government action that has an effect of discouraging a defendant's attendance at trial will not necessarily violate the right to attend and confront witnesses.

Example: Defendant attended his trial and testified in his own defense as the last witness. On summation, the prosecutor commented to the jury that they should consider that by choosing to testify last, defendant had an opportunity to listen to all of the other witnesses and adjust his testimony accordingly. After he was convicted, defendant claimed that the prosecutor's summation was unconstitutional because it used defendant's constitutionally protected right to attend trial as a tool to impeach his credibility and so would have the effect of discouraging attendance. The Supreme Court held that the right to attend may be burdened and upheld the conviction. [Portuondo v. Agard, 529 U.S. 61 (2000)]

2. Introduction of Co-Defendant's Confession
A right of confrontation problem develops with the introduction of a co-defendant's confession because of the inability of the nonconfessing defendant to compel the confessing co-defendant to take the stand for cross-examination at their joint trial.

a. General Rule—Confession Implicating Co-Defendant Prohibited
If two persons are tried together and one has given a confession that implicates the other, the right of confrontation prohibits the use of that statement, even with instructions to the jury to consider it only as going to the guilt of the "confessing" defendant. [Bruton v. United States, 391 U.S. 123 (1968)] A co-defendant's confession is inadmissible even when it interlocks with the defendant's own confession, which is admitted. [Cruz v. New York, 481 U.S. 186 (1987)]

b. Exceptions
Such a statement may be admitted if:

1) All portions referring to the other defendant can be eliminated. *Note:* It is not sufficient merely to insert a blank or some other substitution for the name of the

other defendant; the redaction must not indicate the defendant's involvement. [*Compare* Richardson v. Marsh, 481 U.S. 200 (1987)—after redaction, confession indicated that defendant and a third party (who was not a co-defendant) participated in the crime and contained no indication of co-defendant's involvement, *with* Gray v. Maryland, 523 U.S. 185 (1998)—redaction "me, deleted, deleted, and a few other guys killed" the victim held to clearly refer to co-defendant];

2) The confessing defendant takes the stand and subjects himself to cross-examination with respect to the truth or falsity of what the statement asserts. This rule applies even if he denies having ever made the confession. [Nelson v. O'Neil, 402 U.S. 622 (1973)] In effect, an opportunity at trial to cross-examine the hearsay declarant with respect to the underlying facts makes the declaration nonhearsay for purposes of the Confrontation Clause; or

3) The confession of the nontestifying co-defendant is being used to rebut the defendant's claim that his confession was obtained coercively. The jury must be instructed as to the purpose of the admission. [Tennessee v. Street, 471 U.S. 409 (1985)]

3. Use of Prior Judicial Proceeding Hearsay

"Hearsay" (evidence of a person's statements other than those made at the trial) may be admissible despite the Confrontation Clause. However, if the hearsay consists of *statements made at a prior judicial proceeding,* two facts must be shown before the hearsay statement will be admitted [Ohio v. Roberts, 448 U.S. 56 (1980), *as modified by* United States v. Inadi, 475 U.S. 387 (1986)]:

(i) The prosecution has made a *good faith effort* to obtain the in-court testimony of the witness and has failed (*i.e.*, the witness is unavailable); and

(ii) The defendant has had an *opportunity to cross-examine* the person as to the testimony or has otherwise had an opportunity to test its accuracy.

[Barber v. Page, 390 U.S. 719 (1968)]

Example: Witness against D testified at a preliminary hearing that D sold him drugs. D was represented by counsel at the time. At trial, witness took the stand and testified that he could no longer remember—because of drugs—what had happened. Prosecution then offered testimony of witness at the preliminary hearing. Did admission of this violate D's right of confrontation? No. Prosecution had tried and failed to produce in-court testimony. D had adequate opportunity to test accuracy of evidence at either of two points: cross-examination at the preliminary hearing or cross-examination of witness at trial. [California v. Green, 399 U.S. 149 (1970)]

a. Limited to Prior Judicial Proceedings

The unavailability analysis of *Ohio v. Roberts, supra,* is a necessary part of the Confrontation Clause inquiry only when the challenged out-of-court statements were made in a prior judicial proceeding. The Confrontation Clause does not require a declarant to be produced at trial or shown to be "unavailable" as a prerequisite to introduction of out-of-court statements that qualify under the hearsay exceptions for "spontaneous statements" or statements made in the course of securing medical treatment. [White v. Illinois, 502 U.S. 346 (1992)]

E.   BURDEN OF PROOF AND SUFFICIENCY OF EVIDENCE

1.   Burden of Proof

a.   Proof Beyond a Reasonable Doubt

The Due Process Clause requires in all criminal cases that the state prove guilt beyond a reasonable doubt. [*In re* Winship, 397 U.S. 358 (1970)] The prosecution must have the burden of proving the elements of the crime charged. Thus, the Supreme Court has held that if "malice aforethought" is an element of murder, the state may not require the defendant to prove that he committed the homicide in the heat of passion, on the rationale that this would require the defendant to disprove the element of malice aforethought. [Mullaney v. Wilbur, 421 U.S. 684 (1975)] However, a state may impose the burden of proof upon the defendant in regard to an *affirmative defense* such as insanity [Leland v. Oregon, 343 U.S. 790 (1952)] or self-defense [Martin v. Ohio, 480 U.S. 228 (1987)].

Example: Under state law, in a prosecution for second degree murder, the state must prove intentional causing of death. A defendant is entitled to acquittal of second degree murder and conviction of manslaughter if he proves by a preponderance of the evidence that he acted under the influence of "an extreme emotional disturbance." May the burden of proving that be placed on the defendant? Yes, because it does not affect the state's obligation to prove all elements of the crime of second degree murder. [Patterson v. New York, 432 U.S. 197 (1977)]

b.   Presumption of Innocence

Although not mentioned in the Constitution, the presumption of innocence is a basic component of a fair trial. A defendant does not have an absolute right to a jury instruction on the presumption of innocence, but the trial judge should evaluate the totality of the circumstances, including (i) the other jury instructions, (ii) the arguments of counsel, and (iii) whether the weight of the evidence was overwhelming, to determine whether such an instruction is necessary for a fair trial. [Kentucky v. Whorton, 441 U.S. 786 (1979)]

2.   Presumptions

A permissive presumption allows, but does not require, the jury to infer an element of an offense from proof by the prosecutor of the basic fact, while the jury must accept a mandatory presumption even if it is the sole evidence of the elemental fact.

a.   Permissive Presumptions—Rational Relation Standard

A permissive presumption must comport with the standard that there be a rational connection between the basic facts that the prosecution proved and the ultimate fact presumed, and that the latter is more likely than not to flow from the former. [Ulster County Court v. Allen, 442 U.S. 140 (1979)]

b. Mandatory Presumptions Unconstitutional

A mandatory presumption or a presumption that shifts the burden of proof to the defendant violates the Fourteenth Amendment's requirement that the state prove every element of a crime beyond a reasonable doubt. [Sandstrom v. Montana, 442 U.S. 510 (1979)]

Examples: 1) A mandatory presumption was created by jury instructions in a "malice murder" trial which stated that the "acts of a person of sound mind and discretion are presumed to be the product of a person's will, but the presumption may be rebutted," and a "person of sound mind and discretion is presumed to intend the natural and probable consequences of his acts, but the presumption may be rebutted." These instructions are unconstitutional because they would lead a reasonable juror to conclude that the state's burden of proof on intent to kill may be inferred from proof of the defendant's acts unless the defendant proves otherwise. [Francis v. Franklin, 471 U.S. 307 (1985)]

2) In a criminal contempt proceeding for failure to pay child support, the state may not presume that the defendant was able to pay the amount due. One of the elements of contempt is the ability to comply with the court's order. Thus, the state may not presume ability to pay, but rather ability to pay must be proved beyond a reasonable doubt. [Hicks v. Feiock, 485 U.S. 624 (1988)]

3. Sufficiency of Evidence

The requirement of proof beyond a reasonable doubt in the Due Process Clause means that the sufficiency of the evidence supporting a criminal conviction in state court is, to some extent, a federal constitutional issue. Due process is violated if, viewing all the evidence in the light most favorable to the prosecution, no rational judge or jury would have found the defendant guilty of the crime of which he was convicted. [Jackson v. Virginia, 443 U.S. 307 (1979)]

4. Prior Act Evidence

Under the Due Process Clause, as a general constitutional rule, prior act evidence is admissible for various purposes if it is probative and relevant. Thus in a criminal trial evidence of prior bodily injury was admissible to show that a child victim had sustained repeated and/or serious injuries by nonaccidental means (the "battered child syndrome") to infer that the victim's death was not accidental, even though there was no direct evidence linking the prior injuries to the defendant. [Estelle v. McGuire, 502 U.S. 62 (1991)]

5. Right to Present Defensive Evidence

Due process requires an opportunity to establish innocence.

Example: The arbitrary exclusion of a class of defense witnesses violates both due process and the right to compel the production of witnesses on one's own behalf.

a. Application—Exclusionary Rules of Evidence

Even exclusionary rules of evidence that are valid on their face may combine to deprive a defendant of a fair opportunity to rebut the prosecution's case.

Examples: 1) Given the right to an acquittal if there is reasonable doubt on any element of a criminal charge, a defendant is denied a fair trial when the state's hearsay rule prevents him from showing that another person has confessed to the crime for which he is being tried, and where the state's rule against impeaching one's own witness prevents the defendant from even using the prior confession to cast doubt on the credibility of the confessor's unexpectedly damning testimony. [Chambers v. Mississippi, 410 U.S. 284 (1973)]

2) A state's per se rule excluding hypnotically refreshed testimony unconstitutionally infringes on a defendant's right to present testimony on his own behalf. A per se rule excludes even testimony that may be reliable. [Rock v. Arkansas, 479 U.S. 1079 (1987)]

b.   Exclusion as Sanction
A trial court may, however, exclude defense evidence as a sanction for the defendant's violation of discovery rules or procedures. For example, if the defendant's attorney fails to give advance notice that a witness will testify, the trial court may prohibit that witness from testifying. [Taylor v. Illinois, 484 U.S. 400 (1988)]

VIII.   GUILTY PLEAS AND PLEA BARGAINING

A.   GUILTY PLEA WAIVES RIGHT TO JURY TRIAL
A guilty plea is a waiver of the Sixth Amendment right to jury trial. Between 70% and 95% of all criminal cases are settled by guilty pleas.

B.   BASIC TRENDS

1.   Intelligent Choice Among Alternatives
The Court from 1970 to the present has indicated an unwillingness to disturb a guilty plea it views as an intelligent choice among the defendant's alternatives on the advice of counsel.

2.   Contract View
There is a trend toward the contract view of plea negotiation and bargaining. In this view, the plea agreement should be revealed in the record of the taking of the plea and its terms enforced against both the prosecutor and the defendant. [Ricketts v. Adamson, 483 U.S. 1 (1987)]

C.   TAKING THE PLEA

1.   Advising the Defendant of the Charge, the Potential Penalty, and Her Rights
The judge must advise the defendant personally (not the defense counsel) [McCarthy v. United States, 394 U.S. 459 (1969)], informing her:

a.   Of the nature of the charge to which the plea is offered (the judge need not touch upon all elements of the offense, but the record must show that he explained to the defendant the crucial elements, such as the intent element of murder) [Henderson v. Morgan, 426 U.S. 637 (1976)];

b. Of the maximum possible penalty and of any mandatory minimum, but the failure to explain a special parole term is not fatal [United States v. Timmreck, 441 U.S. 780 (1979)]; and

c. That she has a right not to plead guilty, and that if she does, she waives her right to trial.

2. Requirement of Adequate Record

Boykin v. Alabama, 395 U.S. 238 (1969), requires that a record be made of the taking of all guilty pleas. The record must show that the above information was explained to the defendant, indicating that the plea was *voluntary and intelligent*.

a. Unfairly Informed Defendant Not Bound

If counsel makes unfair representations to the defendant concerning the result of the defendant's pleading guilty, and the defendant can prove this, the defendant is not bound by her record answer, obtained at the plea taking, that her counsel made no such representations. [Blackledge v. Allison, 431 U.S. 63 (1977)]

b. Not Applicable in Some Recidivist Proceedings

The requirement of a record and transcript to show that a guilty plea was voluntary and intelligent is not applicable to recidivist proceedings where the state introduces prior guilty pleas without having transcripts of those earlier guilty plea proceedings. [Parke v. Raley, 506 U.S. 20 (1993)]

3. Remedy

The remedy for a failure to meet the standards for taking a plea is withdrawal of the plea and *pleading anew*.

4. Factual Basis for Plea Not Constitutionally Required

There is no general requirement that the record contain evidence of the defendant's guilt or other factual basis for the plea. (*But see* D.1., below.)

D. COLLATERAL ATTACKS ON GUILTY PLEAS AFTER SENTENCE

Those pleas that are seen as an intelligent choice among the defendant's alternatives are immune from collateral attack.

Examples: 1) A plea is not involuntary merely because it was induced by a fear of the death penalty, which could be imposed only after a jury trial. Fear of the death penalty is like fear of any other penalty, which is the reason defendants plead guilty. [Brady v. United States, 397 U.S. 742 (1970)]

2) Fear of a coerced confession in the hands of the state will not support a collateral attack, and the defendant will be bound to his choice to plead guilty. If the defendant thought the confession was coerced, he should have made a motion to suppress; if he did not, the court will think it was because he believed he could not win. [McMann v. Richardson, 397 U.S. 759 (1970)]

3) Unconstitutional, systematic, racial exclusion in the indicting grand jury will not entitle the defendant to collateral relief. Here, also the Court views the choice not to object and to plead guilty as the result of the defendant's informed decision

as to what course would be in his best interest. [Tollett v. Henderson, 411 U.S. 258 (1973)]

1. Plea Offered by Defendant Who Denies Guilt

When a defendant pleads guilty despite protesting his innocence, the plea will be seen as an intelligent choice by the defendant, and withdrawal of the plea will not be permitted when there is other strong evidence of guilt in the record. Admission of guilt is not a constitutional requisite to imposition of criminal penalty. [North Carolina v. Alford, 400 U.S. 25 (1970)]

2. Bases for an Attack on a Guilty Plea After Sentence

a. Plea Involuntary
Failure to meet the constitutional standards for taking a guilty plea will support a post-sentence attack on the plea.

b. Lack of Jurisdiction
The defendant may withdraw his plea if the court lacked jurisdiction to take the plea, or if prosecution for the offense for which the plea was offered is barred by double jeopardy. [Menna v. New York, 423 U.S. 61 (1975)]

c. Ineffective Assistance of Counsel
Ineffective assistance of counsel undercuts the assumption of an intelligent choice among the defendant's alternatives on the advice of counsel, and so will support a post-sentence attack on a guilty plea.

d. Failure to Keep the Plea Bargain
See E.1., below.

E. PLEA BARGAINING

1. Enforcement of the Bargain

A defendant who enters into a plea bargain has a right to have that bargain kept. The plea bargain will be *enforced against the prosecutor and the defendant*, *but not against the judge*, who does not have to accept the plea.

a. Prosecution
If the prosecution does not keep the bargain, the court should decide whether the circumstances require specific performance of the plea agreement or whether the defendant should be granted an opportunity to withdraw her guilty plea. [Santobello v. New York, 404 U.S. 257 (1971)] However, if the prosecutor withdraws a proposed plea bargain and the accused subsequently pleads guilty on other terms, the original offer cannot be specifically enforced despite the accused's attempt to "accept" the offer. [Mabry v. Johnson, 467 U.S. 504 (1984)]

b. Defendant
If the defendant does not live up to the plea agreement, his plea and sentence can be vacated.

Example: D agrees to testify against a co-defendant in exchange for a reduction in charges from first to second degree murder. If D fails to testify, the prosecution can have D's plea and sentence vacated and reinstate the first degree murder charge. [Ricketts v. Adamson, B.2., *supra*]

2. Power of the State to Threaten More Serious Charge

Consistent with the contract theory of plea negotiation, the state has the power to drive a hard bargain. A guilty plea is not involuntary merely because it was entered in response to the prosecution's threat to charge the defendant with a more serious crime if she does not plead guilty. [Bordenkircher v. Hayes, 434 U.S. 357 (1978)]

3. Power to Charge More Serious Offense

The Supreme Court has held that there is no prosecutorial vindictiveness in charging a more serious offense when defendant demands a jury trial. [United States v. Goodwin, 457 U.S. 368 (1982)]

4. Admission of Statements Made in Connection with Plea Bargaining

Under the Federal Rules of Evidence and of Criminal Procedure, statements made by a defendant in the course of unsuccessful plea negotiations are inadmissible at trial. However, such statements can be admitted *if* the defendant has knowingly and voluntarily waived the Federal Rules' exclusionary provisions. [United States v. Mezzanatto, 513 U.S. 196 (1995)]

F. COLLATERAL EFFECTS OF GUILTY PLEAS

1. Conviction May Be Used in Other Proceedings

The Supreme Court has held that evidence of a defendant's conviction, based on a guilty plea in one state, may be introduced at trial in a second state for the purpose of proving a "specification" allowing imposition of the death penalty [Marshall v. Lonberger, 459 U.S. 422 (1983)], and a defendant is "convicted" within the meaning of the firearms disabilities provisions of the 1968 Gun Control Act when the defendant pleads guilty to a state charge punishable by more than one year, even if no formal judgment is entered and the record has been expunged. [Dickerson v. New Banner Institute, 460 U.S. 103 (1983)]

2. Does Not Admit Legality of Search

The Court has decided that a defendant's guilty plea neither admits the legality of the incriminating search nor waives Fourth Amendment claims in a subsequent civil damages action challenging the constitutionality of the incriminating search. [Haring v. Prosise, 462 U.S. 306 (1983)]

IX. CONSTITUTIONAL RIGHTS IN RELATION TO SENTENCING AND PUNISHMENT

A. PROCEDURAL RIGHTS IN SENTENCING

1. Right to Counsel

Sentencing is usually a "critical stage" of a criminal proceeding, thus requiring the assistance of counsel, as substantial rights of the defendant may be affected.

Examples: 1) The absence of counsel during sentencing after a plea of guilty, coupled with the judge's materially untrue assumptions concerning a defendant's criminal record, deprived the defendant of due process. [Townsend v. Burke, 334 U.S. 736 (1984)]

2) The absence of counsel at the time of sentencing where no sentence of imprisonment was imposed, but the defendant was put on probation, deprived the defendant of due process because certain legal rights (*i.e.,* the right to appeal) might be lost by failing to assert them at this time. [Mempa v. Rhay, *supra*, VII.C.1.]

2. Right to Confrontation and Cross-Examination

The *usual* sentence may be based on hearsay and uncross-examined reports. [Williams v. New York, 337 U.S. 241 (1949)]

a. "New" Proceeding

Where a magnified sentence is based on a statute (*e.g.,* one permitting indeterminate sentence) that requires new findings of fact to be made (*e.g.,* that defendant is a habitual criminal, mentally ill, or deficient, etc.), those facts must be found in a context that grants the right to confrontation and cross-examination. [Specht v. Patterson, 386 U.S. 605 (1966)]

b. Capital Sentencing Procedures

It is clear that a defendant in a death penalty case must have more opportunity for confrontation than need be given a defendant in other sentencing proceedings. [Gardner v. Florida, 430 U.S. 349 (1977)—sentence of death based in part upon report not disclosed to defendant invalid]

B. RESENTENCING AFTER SUCCESSFUL APPEAL AND RECONVICTION

1. General Rule—Record Must Show Reasons for Harsher Sentence

If a judge imposes a greater punishment than at the first trial after the defendant has successfully appealed and then is reconvicted, she must set forth in the record the reasons for the harsher sentence based on "objective information concerning identifiable conduct on the part of the defendant occurring after the time of the original sentencing proceedings." [North Carolina v. Pearce, 395 U.S. 711 (1969)] The purpose of this requirement is to ensure that the defendant is not vindictively penalized for exercising his right to appeal.

Note: When a defendant successfully appeals, an exception to the Double Jeopardy Clause permits retrial. (*See* XIII.B.3., *infra.*)

2. Exceptions

a. Reconviction upon Trial De Novo

Some jurisdictions grant the defendant the right to a trial de novo as a matter of course after a trial in an inferior court. A trial de novo involves a fresh determination of guilt or innocence without reference to the lower conviction or fact of appeal. The rationale of *Pearce* does not apply when the defendant receives a greater sentence upon a trial de novo, because the new judge reduces the likelihood of vindictiveness. [Colten v. Kentucky, 407 U.S. 104 (1972)]

b. Jury Sentencing

Pearce does not apply to states that use jury sentencing, unless the second jury was told of the first jury's sentence. [Chaffin v. Stynchcombe, 412 U.S. 17 (1973)]

3. Recharging in a Trial De Novo

The prosecutor may not obtain an indictment for a more serious charge in a trial de novo, because of the possibility of prosecutorial vindictiveness and retaliation for exercising the statutory right to a trial de novo. [Blackledge v. Perry, 417 U.S. 21 (1974)]

C. SUBSTANTIVE RIGHTS IN REGARD TO PUNISHMENT

1. Criminal Penalties Constituting "Cruel and Unusual Punishment"

The Eighth Amendment prohibition against cruel and unusual punishment places several limitations upon criminal punishments.

a. Punishment Grossly Disproportionate to Offense

A penalty that is grossly disproportionate to the seriousness of the offense committed is cruel and unusual.

Examples: 1) D, convicted of falsifying a public record, received a sentence of 20 years' imprisonment at hard labor. Did this violate the Eighth Amendment? Yes, since the penalty was so disproportionate to the offense. [Weems v. United States, 217 U.S. 349 (1910)]

2) A sentence of life imprisonment without the possibility of parole imposed upon a recidivist following conviction of his seventh nonviolent felony, the uttering of a bad check, is significantly disproportionate to the crime and is thus a violation of the Eighth Amendment. The unconstitutional taint is not eliminated by the possibility of commutation which, unlike parole, is granted on an ad hoc, standardless basis. [Solem v. Helm, 463 U.S. 277 (1983)]

Compare: A mandatory life sentence for possession of a certain quantity of cocaine (650 grams—indicating that the defendant was a dealer) is **not** cruel and unusual, even though the statute did not allow consideration of mitigating factors (*compare* death penalty cases, below). [Harmelin v. Michigan, 501 U.S. 957 (1991)]

b. Proportionality—No Right to Comparison of Penalties in Similar Cases

The Eighth Amendment does not require state appellate courts to compare the death sentence imposed in a case under appeal with other penalties imposed in similar cases. [Pulley v. Harris, 465 U.S. 37 (1984)]

c. Death Penalty

1) For Murder

The death penalty is not inherently cruel and unusual punishment, but the Eighth Amendment requires that it be imposed only under a *statutory scheme* that gives the judge or jury reasonable *discretion*, full *information* concerning defendants, and *guidance* in making the decision. [Furman v. Georgia, 408 U.S. 238 (1972); Gregg v. Georgia, 428 U.S. 153 (1976)]

a)   **Discretion**

A jury must be allowed discretion to consider mitigating circumstances in death penalty cases. Thus, a statute cannot make the death penalty mandatory upon conviction of first degree murder [Woodson v. North Carolina, 428 U.S. 280 (1976)], or for the killing of a police officer or firefighter [Roberts v. Louisiana, 431 U.S. 633 (1977)], or for a killing by an inmate who is serving a life sentence [Sumner v. Shuman, 483 U.S. 66 (1987)]. Moreover, it is not sufficient to allow the jury to consider only some mitigating circumstances; they must be allowed to consider any aspect of the defendant's character or any circumstance of his crime as a factor in mitigation. [Penry v. Lynaugh, 492 U.S. 302 (1989)—death sentence reversed because jury was not allowed to consider defendant's mental retardation and abused childhood in mitigation] In addition, a death sentence must be reversed if the jurors may have been confused by jury instructions regarding their right to consider mitigating circumstances. [Mills v. Maryland, 486 U.S. 367 (1988)]

Examples: 1) A statute requires the jury to impose the death penalty if a defendant is convicted of specific crimes with aggravation, but also requires the trial judge to hear evidence of aggravating and mitigating circumstances before sentencing the defendant. The statute is constitutional. [Baldwin v. Alabama, 472 U.S. 372 (1985)]

2) A statute that instructs jurors to impose the death penalty if they find it probable that the defendant would commit criminal acts in the future, considering all aggravating or mitigating evidence presented at trial, was upheld against an argument that the instruction foreclosed consideration of the defendant's youth. The court found that consideration of future dangerousness leaves open ample room for considering youth as a mitigating factor since "the signature qualities of youth are transient." [Johnson v. Texas, 509 U.S. 350 (1993)]

(1)   **Judge May Impose Death Against Advisory Jury Opinion**

A trial judge may impose the death penalty even though an advisory jury has recommended a life sentence. [Spaziano v. Florida, 468 U.S. 447 (1984)] Moreover, a state is not required to define the weight that the judge must accord to an advisory jury's recommendation. [Harris v. Alabama, 513 U.S. 504 (1995)]

(2)   **Evidence Required for Mitigation Instruction**

Nothing in the Constitution requires state courts to give mitigating circumstance instructions where the jury has heard no evidence on mitigating circumstances. [Delo v. Lashley, 507 U.S. 272 (1993)]

b)   **Information**

(1) Instructions on Lesser Included Offenses

A defendant is not entitled to a jury instruction on every possible lesser included offense supported by the facts in a capital case [Schad v. Arizona, 501 U.S. 624 (1991)], but a statute cannot prohibit instructions on **all** lesser included offenses [Beck v. Alabama, 447 U.S. 625 (1980)]. *Rationale:* If the jurors are not instructed on any lesser included offense and believe that the defendant is guilty of a crime other than murder, they might impose the death penalty rather than let the defendant go unpunished. But if the jury is given instructions on a lesser included offense (*e.g.*, second degree murder), they will not have to make an all or nothing choice, and so a resulting death penalty will stand.

(2) Victim Impact Statements

A "victim impact statement" (*i.e.*, an assessment of how the crime affected the victim's family) may be considered during the sentencing phase of a capital case. *Rationale:* The defendant has long been allowed to present mitigating factors, so the jury must be allowed to counterbalance the impact on the victim's family in order to "assess meaningfully the defendant's moral culpability and blameworthiness." [Payne v. Tennessee, 501 U.S. 808 (1991)]

c) Guidance

A statute providing for the death penalty may not be vague.

Example: A statute that permits imposition of the death penalty when a murder is "outrageously or wantonly vile, horrible, or inhuman in that it involved torture, depravity of mind, or an aggravated battery to the victim" is unconstitutionally vague. [Godfrey v. Georgia, 446 U.S. 420 (1980); Maynard v. Cartwright, 486 U.S. 356 (1988)]

Compare: A statute that imposes the death penalty where the murderer displayed "utter disregard for human life" provides sufficiently clear and objective standards for imposition of the death penalty where the state supreme court had construed the statute to apply only where the killing was committed by a "cold-blooded, pitiless slayer." [Arave v. Creech, 507 U.S. 463 (1993)]

d) Prior Crimes

Most states provide that prior crimes by the defendant, particularly those involving force or violence, are aggravating factors that either make the defendant eligible for the death penalty or are weighed by the jurors in reaching their decision on whether to impose the death penalty. If a death sentence is based in any part on a defendant's prior conviction, the sentence must be reversed if the prior conviction is invalidated. [Johnson v. Mississippi, 486 U.S. 578 (1988)]

e) Standard of Review

Where a death sentence has been affected by a vague or otherwise unconstitutional factor, the death sentence can still be upheld, but only if all aggravating and mitigating factors involved are reweighed by all of the judges to whom the sentence is appealed and death is still found to be appropriate. [Richmond v. Lewis, 506 U.S. 40 (1993)]

2) For Rape
The Eighth Amendment prohibits imposition of the death penalty for the crime of raping an adult woman, because the penalty is disproportionate to the offense. [Coker v. Georgia, 433 U.S. 584 (1977)]

3) For Felony Murder
The death penalty may not be imposed for felony murder where the defendant, as an accomplice, "did not take or attempt or intend to take life, or intend that lethal force be employed." [Enmund v. Florida, 458 U.S. 782 (1982)] However, the death penalty may be imposed on a felony murderer who neither killed nor intended to kill where he participated in a major way in a felony that resulted in murder, and acted with *reckless indifference to the value of human life*. [Tison v. Arizona, 481 U.S. 137 (1987)—defendants helped prisoner escape and provided him with weapons]

4) Jury Responsibility for Verdict
It is unconstitutional to diminish the jury's sense of responsibility of its role in determining a death sentence. [Caldwell v. Mississippi, 527 U.S. 373 (1985)—prosecutor's comment to the jury that its verdict is reviewable and that the verdict is not the final decision is sufficient to diminish the jury's sense of responsibility]

a) Compare—Instruction Regarding Failure to Agree
Even at the defendant's request, the court need not instruct the jury of the consequences of its failure to agree on a verdict. [Jones v. United States, 527 U.S. 373 (1999)—Eighth Amendment was not violated where court denied defendant's request that jury be instructed that judge would impose sentence if jury could not unanimously agree]

5) Racial Discrimination
Statistical evidence that black defendants who kill white victims are more likely to receive the death penalty does not establish that the penalty was imposed as a result of unconstitutional discrimination. [McCleskey v. Kemp, 481 U.S. 279 (1987)]

6) Sanity Requirement
The Eighth Amendment prohibits states from inflicting the death penalty upon a prisoner who is insane (*i.e.*, one who was sane at the time the crime was committed and was properly sentenced to death, but is insane at the time of execution) [Ford v. Wainwright, 477 U.S. 399 (1986)], but the Court has indicated that the Eighth Amendment does not prohibit execution of a murderer who is mentally retarded but competent to stand trial and not insane [Penry v. Lynaugh, *supra*, 1)a)—death penalty reversed on other grounds].

7) For Minors

It is not cruel and unusual to impose the death penalty on murderers who were 16 or older at the time they committed murder because there is no national consensus forbidding such executions. [Stanford v. Kentucky, 492 U.S. 361 (1989)] However, execution of murderers who were younger than 16 at the time of their crime might be forbidden. [Thompson v. Oklahoma, 487 U.S. 815 (1988)—four Justices finding it cruel and unusual, one Justice finding it necessary to have a statute specifically authorizing such executions]

d. "Status" Crimes

A statute that makes it a crime to have a given "status" violates the Eighth Amendment because it punishes a mere propensity to engage in dangerous behavior. But it is no violation of the amendment to make specific activity related to a certain status criminal.

Example: A statute makes it criminal to "be a common drunkard" and to appear in public in an intoxicated condition. May a chronic alcoholic be convicted of both of these? No. He may not be convicted of being a common drunkard, because this is a prohibited status crime. But he may be convicted of appearing in public while intoxicated, because this crime prohibits the act of "appearing." [Powell v. Texas, 392 U.S. 514 (1968)]

2. Recidivist Statutes

A mandatory life sentence imposed pursuant to a recidivist statute does *not* constitute cruel and unusual punishment, even though the three felonies that formed the predicate for the sentence were nonviolent, property-related offenses. [Rummel v. Estelle, 445 U.S. 263 (1980)] (There is an apparent conflict with *Solem v. Helm, supra,* C.1.a. While *Solem* is inconsistent with *Rummel,* the Supreme Court declined to distinguish *Rummel* in reaching its holding in *Solem.*)

3. Punishing the Exercise of Constitutional Rights

A punishment of greater length or severity cannot constitutionally be reserved by statute for those who assert their right to plead innocent and to demand trial by jury. [United States v. Jackson, 390 U.S. 570 (1968)—death penalty available only for federal kidnapping defendants who insist on jury trial; penalty of death in such circumstances cannot be carried out, but guilty pleas induced by such a scheme are not automatically involuntary]

4. Consideration of Defendant's Perjury at Trial

In determining sentence, a trial judge may take into account a belief that the defendant, while testifying at trial on his own behalf, committed perjury. This is important in evaluating the defendant's prospects for rehabilitation and does not impose an improper burden upon a defendant's right to testify. [United States v. Grayson, 438 U.S. 41 (1978)]

5. Imprisonment of Indigents for Nonpayment of Fines Violates Equal Protection Clause

Where the aggregate imprisonment exceeds the maximum period fixed by statute and results directly from an involuntary nonpayment of a fine or court costs, there is an impermissible discrimination and a violation of the Equal Protection Clause. [Williams v. Illinois, 399 U.S. 235 (1970)] It is also a violation of equal protection to limit punishment to payment of a fine for those who are able to pay it, but to convert the fine to imprisonment for those who are unable to pay it. [Tate v. Short, 401 U.S. 395 (1971)—30 days or $30]

a. **Imprisonment of Parolee for Nonpayment of Fine**
A trial court may not revoke a defendant's probation and imprison him for the remainder of the probation term for failure to pay a fine and make restitution without showing that the defendant actually was capable of payment or that there were no alternative forms of punishment available to meet the state's interest in punishment and deterrence. [Bearden v. Georgia, 461 U.S. 660 (1983)]

X. CONSTITUTIONAL PROBLEMS ON APPEAL

A. NO RIGHT TO APPEAL
There is apparently no federal constitutional right to an appeal. Several Supreme Court opinions suggest that all appeals could constitutionally be abolished.

B. EQUAL PROTECTION AND RIGHT TO COUNSEL ON APPEAL

1. First Appeal
If an avenue of post-conviction review (appellate or collateral) is provided, conditions that make the review less accessible to the poor than to the rich violate equal protection. [Griffin v. Illinois, 351 U.S. 12 (1956)—indigent entitled to free transcript on appeal]

Examples: 1) The Equal Protection Clause was violated where a statute requiring the payment of fees for a transcript of a preliminary hearing was applied to deny a free transcript to an indigent. [Roberts v. LaValle, 389 U.S. 40 (1968)]

2) Requiring reimbursement for costs of a trial transcription only of those incarcerated (not from those fined, given suspended sentence, or placed on probation) violates equal protection. [Rinaldi v. Yaeger, 384 U.S. 305 (1966)] But a state can distinguish between convicted and acquitted defendants in this context and require reimbursement only from those convicted. [Fuller v. Oregon, 417 U.S. 40 (1974)]

3) Illinois rule providing for trial transcript on appeal only in felony cases is an unreasonable distinction in violation of equal protection. Even in misdemeanor cases punishable by fine only, a defendant must be afforded as effective an appeal as a defendant who can pay, and where the grounds of the appeal make out a colorable need for a complete transcript, the burden is on the state to show that something less will suffice. [Mayer v. City of Chicago, 404 U.S. 189 (1971)]

a. **Right to Appointed Counsel**
Indigents must be given counsel at state expense during a first appeal granted to all as a matter of right. [Douglas v. California, *supra*, VII.C.1.] Mere failure to request appointment of counsel does not constitute waiver of the right to assistance of counsel on appeal.

b. **Attorney May Withdraw If Appeal Frivolous**
An appellate court can permit withdrawal of counsel who concludes that appeal would

be frivolous. However, before doing so, the state must take steps to *ensure that the defendant's right to counsel is not being denied.*

Examples: 1) It is sufficient to (i) require counsel to file a brief referring to anything in the record that might arguably support an appeal (an *Anders* brief) and (ii) require the appellate court to determine that counsel has correctly concluded that appeal is frivolous. [Anders v. California, 386 U.S. 738 (1967)—striking California procedure that allowed counsel to withdraw upon filing a conclusory letter that simply stated the appeal had no merit]

2) It is sufficient to require counsel to (i) summarize the procedural and factual history of the case but (ii) remain silent on the merits of the case unless the appellate court directs otherwise. [Smith v. Robbins, 528 U.S. 259 (2000)—reasoning that this procedure ensures that a "trained legal eye" will search the record and provide some assistance to the reviewing court]

2. Discretionary Appeals

In a jurisdiction using a two-tier system of appellate courts with discretionary review by the highest court, an indigent defendant need not be provided with counsel during the second, discretionary appeal. Representation also need not be provided for an indigent seeking to invoke the United States Supreme Court's discretionary authority to review criminal convictions. [Ross v. Moffit, 417 U.S. 600 (1974)]

C. NO RIGHT TO SELF-REPRESENTATION

On appeal, a defendant has no right to represent himself. [Martinez v. Court of Appeal, 528 U.S. 152 (2000)]

D. RETRIAL AFTER REVERSAL ON APPEAL

Due process prohibits retrying a defendant whose conviction has been reversed on appeal for any offense more serious than that for which she was convicted at the first trial. This right is violated by *retrial for the more serious offense*, even if at the second trial the defendant is convicted only of an offense no more than that for which she was convicted at the first trial. [Price v. Georgia, 398 U.S. 323 (1970)]

Example: X is charged with murder. She is convicted of manslaughter and her conviction is reversed on appeal. She is again tried for murder and again convicted of manslaughter. May this conviction stand? No, because she could not be retried for anything more serious than manslaughter. This is not harmless error, because the charge of murder in the second trial may have influenced the jury toward conviction of manslaughter.

E. RETROACTIVITY

If the Court announces a new rule of criminal procedure (*i.e.*, one not dictated by precedent) in a case on direct review, the rule must be applied to *all other cases on direct review*. [Griffith v. Kentucky, 479 U.S. 314 (1987)] *Rationale:* It would be unfair to allow the one defendant whose case the Supreme Court happened to choose to hear to benefit from the new rule, while denying the benefit to other similarly situated defendants simply because they were not lucky enough to have their case chosen.

XI. COLLATERAL ATTACK UPON CONVICTIONS

A. AVAILABILITY OF COLLATERAL ATTACK

After appeal is no longer available or has proven unsuccessful, defendants may generally still attack their convictions collaterally, usually by beginning a new and separate civil proceeding involving an application for a writ of habeas corpus. This proceeding focuses on the lawfulness of a detention, naming the person having custody as the respondent.

B. HABEAS CORPUS PROCEEDING

1. No Right to Appointed Counsel
An indigent does not have the right to appointed counsel to perfect her petition for a writ of habeas corpus.

2. Burden of Proof
Because the proceeding for a writ of habeas corpus is civil in nature, the petitioner has the burden of proof by a *preponderance of the evidence* to show an unlawful detention.

3. State May Appeal
The state may appeal the granting of a writ of habeas corpus, and double jeopardy bars neither the appeal nor retrial after the granting of the writ.

4. Requirement of Custody
The state defendant must be "in custody," but it is sufficient if he is out on bail, probation, or parole. [Hensley v. Municipal Court, 411 U.S. 345 (1973)] Generally, the "in custody" requirement is *not* met by a petitioner whose sentence has expired, even if his prior conviction is used to enhance a later one [Maleng v. Cook, 490 U.S. 488 (1989)], but a petitioner who remains in jail on a *consecutive sentence* is in custody, even if the jail time for the crime being challenged has expired [Garlotte v. Fordice, 515 U.S. 39 (1995)].

XII. RIGHTS DURING PUNISHMENT—PROBATION, IMPRISONMENT, PAROLE

A. RIGHT TO COUNSEL AT PAROLE AND PROBATION REVOCATIONS

1. Probation Revocation Involving Resentencing
If revocation of probation also involves the imposition of a new sentence, the defendant is entitled to representation by counsel in all cases in which she is entitled to counsel at trial. [Mempa v. Rhay, *supra*, IX.A.1.]

2. Other Situations
If, after probation revocation, an already imposed sentence of imprisonment springs into application, *or* the case involves parole revocation, the right to counsel is much more limited.

There is a right to be represented by counsel only if, on the facts of the case, such representation is *necessary to a fair hearing*. Generally, it will be necessary if the defendant denies commission of the acts alleged or asserts an argument as to why revocation should not occur that is "complex or otherwise difficult to develop or present." In addition, each defendant must be told of her right to request appointment of counsel, and if a request is refused, the record must contain a succinct statement of the basis for the refusal. [Gagnon v. Scarpelli, 411 U.S. 778 (1973)]

B. PRISONERS' RIGHTS

1. Due Process Rights

Prison regulations and operations may create liberty interests protected by the Due Process Clause, but due process is violated only where the regulations and operations *impose "atypical and significant hardship"* in relation to the ordinary incidents of prison life. [Sandin v. Conner, 515 U.S. 472 (1995)]

2. No Fourth Amendment Protections in Search of Cells

Prisoners have no reasonable expectation of privacy in their cells, or in personal property in their cells, and hence no Fourth Amendment protection therein. [Hudson v. Palmer, 468 U.S. 517 (1984)] Additionally, prisoners have no right to be present when prison officials search their cells. [Block v. Rutherford, 468 U.S. 576 (1984)]

3. Right of Access to Courts

Prison inmates must have reasonable access to courts, and no unreasonable limitations may be put upon their ability to develop and present arguments. Inmates may not be prevented from consulting with other inmates, unless a reasonable substitute (such as a law library) is provided. [Bounds v. Smith, 430 U.S. 817 (1977); Johnson v. Avery, 393 U.S. 483 (1969)] No absolute bar against law students and other paraprofessionals interviewing inmates for lawyers may be imposed. [Procunier v. Martinez, 416 U.S. 396 (1974)]

Note: A prisoner's *Bounds* claim of inadequate prison legal resources must include a showing that the alleged deficiencies in the legal resources have resulted in a hindrance of access to court. [Lewis v. Casey, 518 U.S. 343 (1996)]

4. First Amendment Rights

Prison officials need some discretion to limit prisoners' First Amendment activities (*e.g.*, speech and assembly) in order to run a safe and secure prison. Therefore, prison regulations *reasonably related to penological interests* will be upheld even though they burden First Amendment rights. [Turner v. Safley, 482 U.S. 78 (1987)] For example, prison officials have broad discretion to regulate incoming mail to prevent contraband and even sexually explicit materials from entering the prison. Officials may even open letters from a prisoner's attorney, as long as they do so in the prisoner's presence and the letters are not read. [*See* Thornburgh v. Abbott, 490 U.S. 401 (1989); Wolff v. McDonnell, 418 U.S. 539 (1974)] However, prison officials have less discretion to regulate outgoing mail, since it usually does not have an effect on prison safety. [Procunier v. Martinez, *supra*]

5. Right to Adequate Medical Care

"Deliberate indifference to serious medical needs of prisoners" constitutes cruel and unusual punishment in violation of the Eighth Amendment. However, simple negligent failure to provide care—"medical malpractice"—does not violate the amendment. [Estelle v. Gamble,

429 U.S. 97 (1976)] And while prisoners have a liberty interest in refusing medication, they can be forced to take antipsychotic drugs if an unbiased and qualified decisionmaker finds it necessary to protect the prisoner or others. [Washington v. Harper, 494 U.S. 210 (1990)] However, the forced administration of antipsychotic medication during a defendant's murder trial absent a showing that (i) an essential state interest outweighed possible trial prejudice from the drug's side effects, and (ii) the drug was medically appropriate was held to violate rights guaranteed by the Sixth and Fourteenth Amendments. [Riggins v. Nevada, 504 U.S. 127 (1992)]

C. NO RIGHT TO BE FREE FROM DISABILITIES UPON COMPLETION OF SENTENCE

There is no right to be free from state disenfranchisement upon conviction of a felony, even if this continues after completion of the sentence imposed. [Richardson v. Ramirez, 418 U.S. 24 (1974)]

XIII. DOUBLE JEOPARDY

A. WHEN JEOPARDY ATTACHES

The Fifth Amendment right to be free of double jeopardy for the same offense has been incorporated into the Fourteenth Amendment. [Benton v. Maryland, 395 U.S. 784 (1969)] The general rule is that once jeopardy attaches, the defendant may not be retried for the same offense.

1. Jury Trials

Jeopardy attaches in a jury trial at the *empaneling and swearing* of the jury. [Crist v. Bretz, 437 U.S. 28 (1978)]

2. Bench Trials

In bench trials, jeopardy attaches when the *first witness is sworn*.

3. Juvenile Proceedings

The *commencement* of a juvenile proceeding bars a subsequent criminal trial for the same offense. [Breed v. Jones, 421 U.S. 519 (1975)]

4. Not in Civil Proceedings

Jeopardy generally does not attach in civil proceedings other than juvenile proceedings. [One Lot Emerald Cut Stones & One Ring v. United States, 409 U.S. 232 (1972)]

Example: After the defendant is acquitted of criminal charges of smuggling, the government may still seek forfeiture of the items that the defendant allegedly smuggled into the country. [One Lot Emerald Cut Stones & One Ring v. United States, *supra*]

B. EXCEPTIONS PERMITTING RETRIAL

Certain exceptions permit retrial of a defendant even if jeopardy has attached.

1. Hung Jury

The state may retry a defendant whose first trial ends in a hung jury.

2. Mistrial for Manifest Necessity

A trial may be discontinued and the defendant reprosecuted for the same offense when there is a manifest necessity to abort the original trial [United States v. Perez, 22 U.S. 579 (1824); Illinois v. Somerville, 410 U.S. 458 (1973)] or when the termination occurs at the behest of the defendant on any grounds not constituting an acquittal on the merits [United States v. Scott, 437 U.S. 82 (1978)]. Thus, double jeopardy does not bar two trials but only a retrial after a determination on the merits.

3. Retrial After Successful Appeal

The state may retry a defendant who has successfully appealed a conviction, unless the ground for the reversal was insufficient evidence to support the guilty verdict. [Burks v. United States, 437 U.S. 1 (1978)] On the other hand, retrial is permitted when reversal is based on the *weight*, rather than *sufficiency*, of the evidence [Tibbs v. Florida, 457 U.S. 31 (1982)], or where a case is reversed because of erroneously admitted evidence [Lockhart v. Nelson, 488 U.S. 33 (1988)].

a. Charging and Sentencing on Retrial

Under both the Due Process Clause (*supra*, X.D.) and the Double Jeopardy Clause [*see* Green v. United States, 355 U.S. 184 (1957)], a defendant who successfully appeals a conviction cannot be *tried for a greater offense* than that of which he was convicted. However, the Double Jeopardy Clause generally does *not* prohibit imposition of a *harsher sentence* on conviction after retrial, and such a sentence is valid provided it does not run afoul of the vindictiveness concerns discussed at IX.B.1., *supra*.

1) Death Penalty Cases

Where there is a formalized, separate process for imposing the death penalty (*e.g.*, where guilt is first determined and then the jury is presented with evidence on whether to impose death), if the death penalty was not imposed at the first trial, it cannot be imposed at a second trial. [Bullington v. Missouri, 451 U.S. 430 (1981)] This rule applies only to capital sentencing proceedings. [Monge v. California, 524 U.S. 721 (1998)]

4. Breach of Plea Bargaining

When a defendant breaches a plea bargain agreement, his plea and sentence can be vacated and the original charges can be reinstated. [Ricketts v. Adamson, VIII.E.1.b., *supra*]

C. SAME OFFENSE

1. General Rule—When Two Crimes Do Not Constitute Same Offense

Two crimes do not constitute the same offense if *each crime requires proof of an additional element* that the other crime does not require, even though some of the same facts may be necessary to prove both crimes. [Blockburger v. United States, 284 U.S. 299 (1932)]

Example: D is arrested after the car he is driving strikes and kills a pedestrian. D is tried on the charges of reckless homicide and driving while intoxicated. D can receive separate punishments for both of the offenses because each crime requires proof of an additional element not required by the other: the homicide charge requires proof of a death but not proof of intoxication, while the driving while intoxicated charge requires proof of intoxication but not proof of a death.

a. **Application of** *Blockburger*

Under *Blockburger*, the following do *not* constitute the same offenses:

1) Manslaughter with an automobile and hit-and-run;

2) Reckless driving and drunk driving;

3) Reckless driving and failure to yield the right of way; and

4) Uttering a forged check and obtaining money by false pretenses by using the forged check.

2. **Cumulative Punishments for Offenses Constituting Same Crime**

Imposition of cumulative punishments for two or more statutorily defined offenses, *specifically intended by the legislature to carry separate punishments*, even though constituting the "same" crime under the *Blockburger* test, *supra*, does not violate the prohibition of multiple punishments for the same offense of the Double Jeopardy Clause, when the punishments are *imposed at a single trial*. [Missouri v. Hunter, 459 U.S. 359 (1983)]

Example: D robs a store at gunpoint. D can be sentenced to cumulative punishments for both the robbery and under a "Use a gun, go to jail" statute.

Note: Absent a clear intention, it will be presumed that multiple punishments are not intended for offenses constituting the same crime under *Blockburger*. Also, imposition of multiple punishments is prohibited even if the sentences for the two crimes run concurrently. [Rutledge v. United States, 517 U.S. 292 (1996)]

3. **Lesser Included Offenses**

a. **Retrial for Lesser Included Offense Barred**

Attachment of jeopardy for the greater offense bars retrial for lesser included offenses. [Harris v. Oklahoma, 433 U.S. 682 (1977)]

Example: D is convicted of felony murder based on proof that he and an accomplice shot and killed a store clerk during an armed robbery. D cannot then be tried for the armed robbery because it is a lesser included offense of the felony murder. [Harris v. Oklahoma, *supra*]

b. **Retrial for Greater Offense**

Attachment of jeopardy for a lesser included offense bars retrial for the greater offense [Brown v. Ohio, 432 U.S. 161 (1977)], except that retrial for murder is permitted if the victim dies after attachment of jeopardy for battery [Diaz v. United States, 223 U.S. 442 (1912)]. However, a state may continue to prosecute a charged offense, despite the defendant's guilty plea to lesser included or "allied" offenses stemming from the same incident. [Ohio v. Johnson, 467 U.S. 493 (1984)—defendant charged with murder and manslaughter, and robbery and theft, arising from the same incident, can be prosecuted for murder and robbery after pleading guilty to manslaughter and theft over state's objection]

1) **Exception—New Evidence**

An exception to the double jeopardy bar exists if unlawful conduct that is subsequently used to prove the greater offense (i) has not occurred at the time of the prosecution for the lesser offense, or (ii) has not been discovered despite due diligence. [Garrett v. United States, 471 U.S. 773 (1985)]

4. Conspiracy and Substantive Offense

A prosecution for *conspiracy* is not barred merely because some of the alleged *overt acts* of that conspiracy have already been prosecuted. [United States v. Felix, 503 U.S. 378 (1992)]

5. Prior Act Evidence

The introduction of evidence of a substantive offense as prior act evidence is not equivalent to *prosecution* for that substantive offense, and therefore subsequent prosecution for that conduct is not barred. [United States v. Felix, *supra*]

6. Conduct Used as a Sentence Enhancer

The Double Jeopardy Clause is not violated when a person is indicted for a crime the conduct of which was already used to enhance the defendant's sentence for another crime. [Witte v. United States, 515 U.S. 389 (1995)—defendant indicted for conspiring to import cocaine after the conduct of the conspiracy was used to enhance his earlier sentence when he pleaded guilty to possession of marijuana]

7. Civil Actions

The Double Jeopardy Clause prohibits only repetitive *criminal* prosecutions. Thus, a state generally is free to bring a civil action against a defendant even if the defendant has already been criminally tried for the conduct out of which the civil action arises. Similarly, the government may bring a criminal action even though the defendant has already faced civil trial for the same conduct. However, if there is clear proof from the face of the statutory scheme that its purpose or effect is to impose a criminal penalty, the Double Jeopardy Clause applies. [Hudson v. United States, 522 U.S. 93 (1998)—finding no clear proof of such purpose or effect where a civil statute allowed a government agency to impose a fine and bar defendants from working in banking industry for improperly approving loans]

D. SEPARATE SOVEREIGNS

The constitutional prohibition against double jeopardy *does not apply* to trials by separate sovereigns. Thus, a person may be tried for the same conduct by both a state and the federal government [United States v. Lanza, 260 U.S. 377 (1922)] or by two states [Heath v. Alabama, 474 U.S. 82 (1986)], but not by a state and its municipalities [Waller v. Florida, 397 U.S. 387 (1970)].

E. APPEALS BY PROSECUTION

Even after jeopardy has attached, the prosecution *may appeal any dismissal* on the defendant's motion *not constituting an acquittal on the merits*. [United States v. Scott, 437 U.S. 82 (1978)] Also, the Double Jeopardy Clause does not bar appeals by the prosecution if a *successful appeal would not require a retrial*, such as when the trial judge granted a motion to set aside the jury verdict. [United States v. Wilson, 420 U.S. 332 (1975)]

1. Appeal of Sentence

Government appeal of a sentence, *pursuant* to a congressionally enacted *statute* permitting such review, does not constitute multiple punishment in violation of the Double Jeopardy Clause. [United States v. DiFrancesco, 449 U.S. 117 (1980)]

F. COLLATERAL ESTOPPEL

The notion of collateral estoppel is embodied in the guarantee against double jeopardy. A defendant may not be tried or convicted of a crime if a prior prosecution by that sovereignty resulted in a *factual determination inconsistent with one required for conviction*. However, this doctrine has limited utility because of the general verdict in criminal trials.

Examples: 1) Where three or four armed men robbed six poker players in the home of one of the victims and the defendant was charged in separate counts with robbery of each of the six players and was tried on one count and was acquitted for insufficient evidence in a prosecution in which identity was the single rationally conceivable issue in dispute, he may not thereafter be prosecuted for robbery of a different player. [Ashe v. Swenson, 397 U.S. 436 (1970)] A second trial would not have been barred if there had been dispute at the first trial whether the alleged victim was robbed. The court did not adopt the "same transaction" test proposed by some justices, under which a defendant could not be more than once put in jeopardy for offenses arising out of the "same transactions."

2) Where the ultimate issue of identity of the person who mailed a package with a bomb that killed two persons was decided at the first trial at which defendant was acquitted, the defendant may not thereafter be convicted of the second murder, even if the jury in the first trial (for the first murder) did not have all the relevant evidence before it and the state acted in good faith. [Harris v. Washington, 404 U.S. 55 (1971)]

XIV. PRIVILEGE AGAINST COMPELLED SELF-INCRIMINATION

A. APPLICABLE TO THE STATES

As discussed above (*see* IV.D., *supra*), the Fifth Amendment prohibits the government from compelling self-incriminating testimony. The Fifth Amendment prohibition against compelled self-incrimination was made applicable to the states through the Fourteenth Amendment in *Malloy v. Hogan*, 378 U.S. 1 (1964).

B. WHO MAY ASSERT THE PRIVILEGE

Only *natural persons* may assert the privilege, not corporations or partnerships. [Bellis v. United States, 417 U.S. 85 (1974)] The privilege is personal, and so may be asserted by a defendant, witness, or party only if the answer to the question might tend to incriminate him.

C. WHEN PRIVILEGE MAY BE ASSERTED

A person may refuse to answer a question whenever his response might furnish a link in the chain of evidence needed to prosecute him.

1. Proceedings Where Potentially Incriminating Testimony Sought

A person may assert the privilege in *any* proceeding in which testimony that could tend to incriminate is sought. The privilege must be claimed in civil proceedings to prevent the privilege from being waived for a later criminal prosecution. If the individual responds to the questions instead of claiming the privilege during a civil proceeding, he cannot later bar that evidence from a criminal prosecution on compelled self-incrimination grounds. [United States v. Kordel, 397 U.S. 1 (1970)]

2. **Privilege Not a Defense to Civil Records Requirements**

The government may require that certain records be kept and reported on where the records are relevant to an *administrative purpose*, unrelated to enforcement of criminal laws. Such records acquire a public aspect and are not protected by the Fifth Amendment.

Examples: 1) The government may require people to keep tax records and to report their income on tax forms, since this serves a legitimate administrative purpose. Thus, a person may be prosecuted for failure to file a tax form. However, there is a Fifth Amendment privilege to refuse to answer specific questions on such forms that might be incriminating (*e.g.*, source of income). [United States v. Sullivan, 274 U.S. 259 (1927)] Therefore, if a person chooses to answer incriminating questions on such forms, the answers may be used against him in court, since they were not compelled. [Garner v. United States, 424 U.S. 648 (1976)]

2) A person charged with being an unfit parent in a proceeding to determine whether she should maintain custody of her child may be compelled to produce the child in court. Even though the production might be testimonial in nature (admits control), the state's interest here is civil (protecting the child) rather than punitive in nature. [Baltimore City Department of Social Services v. Bouknight, 493 U.S. 549 (1990)] Note, however, that the state might have to grant immunity to the parent for the production. (*See* H.1., *infra*.)

3) A person may not claim the privilege and fail to comply with a law requiring motorists to stop at the scene of an accident and leave their name and address. [California v. Byers, 402 U.S. 424 (1971)]

a. **Limitation—Criminal Law Enforcement Purpose**

If the registration requirement is directed not at the general public but at a *select group inherently suspect of criminal activities* and the inquiry is in an area permeated with criminal statutes, the person may assert the privilege to avoid prosecution for failure to comply with the requirement. [Albertson v. Subversive Activities Control Board, 382 U.S. 70 (1965)]

Example: The government may not require registration of a sawed-off shotgun [Haynes v. United States, 390 U.S. 85 (1968)], payment of a wagering excise tax [Grosso v. United States, 390 U.S. 62 (1968)], payment of an occupational tax for engaging in the business of accepting wagers [Marchetti v. United States, 390 U.S. 39 (1968)], individual registration as a member of the Communist Party [Albertson v. Subversive Activities Control Board, *supra*], or the registration of transfer of marijuana [Leary v. United States, 395 U.S. 6 (1969)] if compliance would require self-incrimination.

Note: Such cases as *Marchetti* and *Grosso* do not bar conviction for making false statements on the registration form; to avoid incriminating himself, the individual must instead claim the privilege. [United States v. Knox, 396 U.S. 77 (1969)]

D. **METHOD FOR INVOKING THE PRIVILEGE**

How the privilege may be invoked depends upon whether the person seeking to invoke it is a criminal defendant or simply a witness.

1. **Privilege of a Defendant**
    A criminal defendant has a right not to take the witness stand at trial and not to be asked to do so. It is even impermissible to call the jury's attention to the fact that he has chosen not to testify. (*See* G.1., *infra*.)

2. **Privilege of a Witness**
    In any other situation, the privilege does not permit a person to avoid being sworn as a witness or being asked questions. Rather, the person must listen to the questions and specifically invoke the privilege rather than answer the questions.

E. SCOPE OF PROTECTION

1. **Testimonial but Not Physical Evidence**
    The Fifth Amendment privilege protects only testimonial or communicative evidence and not real or physical evidence. Thus, the state may require a person to produce ***blood samples*** [Schmerber v. California, *supra*, VII.C.2.], ***handwriting exemplars*** [Gilbert v. California, *supra*, VII.C.2.], or ***voice samples*** [United States v. Wade, *supra*, V.E.] without violating the Fifth Amendment, even though such evidence may be incriminating. In addition, a court may order a suspect to authorize foreign banks to disclose records of any accounts he may possess. Merely signing an authorization form is not testimonial if it does not require the suspect to acknowledge the existence of any account. For a suspect's communication to be considered testimonial, it must explicitly or implicitly relate a factual assertion or disclose information. [Doe v. United States, 487 U.S. 201 (1988)]

    Likewise, admission into evidence of a defendant's ***refusal to submit to a blood-alcohol test*** does not offend the right against self-incrimination even though he was not warned that his refusal might be introduced against him. [South Dakota v. Neville, 459 U.S. 553 (1983)]

2. **Compulsory Production of Documents**
    A person served with a subpoena requiring the production of documents tending to incriminate him generally has no basis in the privilege to refuse to comply, because the act of producing the documents ***does not involve testimonial self-incrimination***. Note, however, that if the document *is* within the privilege but in the hands of an attorney, the attorney-client privilege would permit the attorney to refuse to comply with the subpoena. [Fisher v. United States, 425 U.S. 391 (1976)]

    a. **Corporate Records**
        A custodian of corporate records may not resist a subpoena for such records on the ground that the production would incriminate him in violation of the Fifth Amendment. The production of the records by the custodian is not considered a personal act, but rather an act of the corporation, which possesses no Fifth Amendment privilege. [Braswell v. United States, 487 U.S. 99 (1988)]

3. **Seizure and Use of Incriminating Documents**
    The Fifth Amendment does not prohibit law enforcement officers from searching for and seizing documents tending to incriminate a person. The privilege protects only against being compelled to communicate information, not against disclosure of communications made in the past. [Andresen v. Maryland, *supra*, III.C.4.c.]

F. RIGHT TO ADVICE CONCERNING PRIVILEGE

A lawyer may not be held in contempt of court for her good faith advice to her client to invoke the privilege and refuse to produce materials demanded by a court order. Because a witness may require the advice of counsel in deciding how to respond to a demand for testimony or evidence, subjecting the lawyer to potential contempt citation for her advice would infringe upon the protection accorded the witness by the Fifth Amendment. [Maness v. Meyers, 419 U.S. 449 (1975)]

G. PROHIBITION AGAINST BURDENS ON ASSERTION OF THE PRIVILEGE

1. Comments on Defendant's Silence

A prosecutor may not comment on a defendant's silence after being arrested and receiving *Miranda* warnings. The warnings carry an implicit assurance that silence will carry no penalty. [Greer v. Miller, 483 U.S. 756 (1987)] Neither may the prosecutor ordinarily comment on the defendant's failure to testify at trial. [Griffin v. California, 380 U.S. 609 (1965)] However, where the defendant does not testify at trial, upon timely motion she is constitutionally entitled to have the trial judge instruct the jury that they are to draw no adverse inference from the defendant's failure to testify. [Carter v. Kentucky, 450 U.S. 288 (1981)] Moreover, a judge may warn the jury not to draw an adverse inference from the defendant's failure to testify, without violating the Fifth Amendment privilege, even where the defendant objects to such an instruction. [Lakeside v. Oregon, 435 U.S. 333 (1978)]

a. Exception

The prosecutor can comment on the defendant's failure to take the stand when the comment is in response to defense counsel's assertion that the defendant was not allowed to explain his side of the story. [United States v. Robinson, 485 U.S. 25 (1988)]

b. Harmless Error Test Applies

When a prosecutor impermissibly comments on a defendant's silence, the harmless error test applies. Thus, the error is not fatal where the judge instructs the jury to disregard a question on the defendant's post-arrest silence. [Greer v. Miller, *supra*] Similarly, the error is not fatal where there is overwhelming evidence against the defendant and the prosecutor comments on the defendant's failure to proffer evidence rebutting the victim's testimony. [United States v. Hasting, 461 U.S. 499 (1987)]

2. Penalties for Failure to Testify Prohibited

The state may not chill the exercise of the Fifth Amendment privilege against compelled self-incrimination by imposing penalties for the failure to testify or cooperate with authorities.

Example: The state may not fire a police officer [Garrity v. New Jersey, 385 U.S. 493 (1967)], take away state contracts [Lefkowitz v. Turley, 414 U.S. 70 (1973)], or prohibit a person from holding party office [Lefkowitz v. Cunningham, 431 U.S. 801 (1977)] for failure to cooperate with investigating authorities.

H. ELIMINATION OF THE PRIVILEGE

1. Grant of Immunity

A witness may be compelled to answer questions if granted adequate immunity from prosecution.

a. **"Use and Derivative Use" Immunity Sufficient**

The Supreme Court has held that a grant of "use and derivative use" immunity is sufficient to extinguish the privilege. [Kastigar v. United States, 406 U.S. 441 (1972)] This type of immunity guarantees that the testimony obtained and evidence located by means of the testimony will not be used against the witness. This type of immunity is not as broad as "transactional" immunity, which guarantees immunity from prosecution for any crimes related to the transaction about which the witness testifies, because the witness may still be prosecuted if the prosecutor can show that her evidence was derived from a *source independent* of the immunized testimony.

b. **Immunized Testimony Involuntary**

Testimony obtained by a *promise of immunity* is, by definition, coerced and therefore involuntary. Thus, immunized testimony may not be used for impeachment of the defendant's testimony at trial. [New Jersey v. Portash, 440 U.S. 450 (1979)] Immunized testimony may be introduced to supply the context for a perjury prosecution. Any immunized statements, whether true or untrue, can be used in a trial for making false statements. [United States v. Apfelbaum, 445 U.S. 115 (1980)]

c. **Use of Testimony by Another Sovereign Prohibited**

The privilege against self-incrimination prohibits a state from compelling incriminating testimony under a grant of immunity unless the testimony and its fruits cannot be used by the prosecution in a federal prosecution. Therefore, federal prosecutors may not use evidence obtained as a result of a state grant of immunity, and vice versa. [Murphy v. Waterfront Commission, 378 U.S. 52 (1964)]

2. **No Possibility of Incrimination**

A person has no privilege against compelled self-incrimination if there is no possibility of incrimination, as, for example, when the statute of limitations has run.

I. WAIVER OF PRIVILEGE

The nature and scope of a waiver depends upon the situation.

1. **Waiver by Criminal Defendant**

A criminal defendant, by taking the witness stand, waives the privilege to the extent necessary to subject her to any cross-examination proper under the rules of evidence.

2. **Waiver by Witness**

A witness waives the privilege only if she discloses incriminating information. Once such disclosure has been made, she can be compelled to disclose any additional information as long as such further disclosure does not increase the risk of conviction or create a risk of conviction on a different offense.

XV. JUVENILE COURT PROCEEDINGS

A. IN GENERAL

Some—but not all—of the rights developed for defendants in criminal prosecutions have also been held applicable to children who are the subjects of proceedings to have them declared "delinquents" and possibly institutionalized.

B. RIGHTS THAT MUST BE AFFORDED

The following rights must be given to a child during the trial of a delinquency proceeding:

(i)   Written *notice* of the charges with sufficient time to prepare a defense;

(ii) The *assistance of counsel* (court-appointed if the child is indigent);

(iii) The *opportunity to confront* and cross-examine witnesses;

(iv) The *right not to testify* (and other aspects of the privilege against self-incrimination); and

(v)   The right to have *"guilt"* (the commission of acts making the child delinquent) established by proof *beyond a reasonable doubt.*

[*In re* Gault, 387 U.S. 1 (1967); *In re* Winship, 397 U.S. 358 (1970)]

C. RIGHTS NOT APPLICABLE

1. Jury Trial

The Supreme Court has held inapplicable to delinquency proceedings the right to trial by jury. In the juvenile court context, jury trial is not necessary to assure "fundamental fairness." [McKeiver v. Pennsylvania, 403 U.S. 528 (1971)]

2. Pretrial Detention Allowable

A finding that a juvenile is a "serious risk" to society and likely to commit a crime before trial is adequate to support pretrial detention of the juvenile, and does not violate the Due Process Clause as long as the detention is for a strictly limited time before trial may be held. [Schall v. Martin, 467 U.S. 253 (1984)]

D. DOUBLE JEOPARDY AND "TRANSFER" OF JUVENILE TO ADULT COURT

In many jurisdictions, a juvenile court may, after inquiry, determine that a child is not an appropriate subject for juvenile court processing and "transfer" the child to adult court for trial as an adult on criminal charges. If the juvenile court adjudicates the child a delinquent, however, jeopardy has attached and the prohibition against double jeopardy prevents him from being tried as an adult for the same behavior. [Breed v. Jones, 421 U.S. 519 (1975)] The transfer issue must be *resolved before the adjudication of delinquency.*

XVI.   FORFEITURE ACTIONS

A. INTRODUCTION

State and federal statutes often provide for the forfeiture of property such as automobiles used in the commission of a crime. Actions for forfeiture are brought directly against the property and are generally regarded as quasi-criminal in nature. Certain constitutional rights may exist for those persons whose interest in the property would be lost by forfeiture.

B. RIGHT TO PRE-SEIZURE NOTICE AND HEARING

The owner of *personal* property (and others with interests in it) is not constitutionally entitled to notice and hearing before the property is seized for purposes of a forfeiture proceeding. [Calero-Toledo v. Pearson Yacht Leasing Co., 416 U.S. 663 (1974)] A hearing is, however, required before final forfeiture of the property. Where *real property* is seized, notice and an opportunity to be heard is required before the seizure unless the government can prove that exigent circumstances justify immediate seizure. [United States v. James Daniel Good Real Property, 510 U.S. 43 (1994)]

C. FORFEITURES MAY BE SUBJECT TO EIGHTH AMENDMENT

The Eighth Amendment provides that excessive fines shall not be imposed. The Supreme Court has held that this Excessive Fines Clause applies only to fines imposed as punishment, *i.e.*, penal fines. The Clause does not apply to civil fines. Thus forfeitures that are penal are subject to the Clause, but forfeitures that are civil are not.

1. Penal Forfeitures

Generally, a forfeiture will be considered penal only if it is provided for in a criminal statute. If it is penal and the Clause applies, a forfeiture will be found to be excessive only if it is *grossly disproportionate to the gravity of the offense.* [United States v. Bajakajian, 524 U.S. 321 (1998)]

Example: The Court held that forfeiture of $357,144 for the crime of merely failing to report that that sum was being transported out of the country was grossly disproportionate since the crime caused little harm (it would have been legal to take the money out of the country; the only harm was that the government was deprived of a piece of information). [United States v. Bajakajian, *supra*]

2. Compare—Nonpenal Forfeitures

a. Civil In Rem Forfeitures

Civil in rem forfeitures treat the property forfeited as a "wrongdoer" under a legal fiction; the action is against the property and not against an individual, and therefore this type of forfeiture is *not* subject to the Excessive Fines Clause.

b. Monetary Forfeitures

Monetary forfeitures (*e.g.*, forfeiture of twice the value of illegally imported goods) have also been found to be remedial in nature where they are brought in civil actions. They are seen as a form of liquidated damages to reimburse the government for losses resulting from the offense. Therefore, they are not subject to the Eighth Amendment. [*See* United States v. Bajakajian, *supra*]

D. PROTECTION FOR "INNOCENT OWNER" NOT REQUIRED

The Due Process Clause does *not* require forfeiture statutes to provide an "innocent owner" defense *e.g.*, a defense that the owner took all reasonable steps to avoid having the property used by another for illegal purposes, at least where the innocent owner *voluntarily entrusted* the property to the wrongdoer. [Bennis v. Michigan, 517 U.S. 292 (1996)—due process not violated by forfeiture of wife's car that husband used while engaging in sexual acts with a prostitute even though wife did not know of use] In justifying its holding in *Bennis*, the Court also noted that the statute was not absolute, since the trial judge had discretion to prevent inequitable application of the statute.

BAR REVIEW

Evidence

celebrating over

30 YEARS

*of preparing
law students
for the bar exam*

EVIDENCE

TABLE OF CONTENTS

I. GENERAL CONSIDERATIONS

A. DEFINING EVIDENCE LAW

The law of evidence is a system of rules and standards by which the admission of proof at the trial of a lawsuit is regulated. The material facts in the controversy are determined by proof that is filtered through the applicable rules of evidence. This proof includes testimony, writings, physical objects, and anything else presented to the senses of the jury.

B. SOURCES OF EVIDENCE LAW

In some states, evidence law is derived from a blend of common law rules and miscellaneous statutes. However, today, most jurisdictions have enacted modern evidence codes, which form a comprehensive set of statutes or rules covering all major areas of evidence law. The most important codification is the Federal Rules of Evidence, which became effective July 1, 1975. The Federal Rules govern on the Multistate Bar Examination.

C. FEDERAL RULES OF EVIDENCE

The Federal Rules of Evidence are applicable in all *civil and criminal* cases in the United States courts of appeal, district courts, Court of Claims, and in proceedings before United States magistrates. [Fed. R. Evid. 101 and 1101] For the most part, the Federal Rules have codified well-established principles of evidence law. Where the Federal Rules depart from the traditional rules of evidence, the adopted Federal Rule is likely to represent an important modern trend, which the states are likely to follow as they revise and codify existing law.

D. THRESHOLD ADMISSIBILITY ISSUES

A shorthand summary of evidence law might be stated in one sentence: *Material* and *relevant* evidence is admissible if *competent*.

1. Materiality: The Proposition to Be Proved

Materiality exists when the proffered evidence relates to one of the substantive legal issues in the case. The key questions to ask regarding materiality are: What issue is the evidence offered to prove? Is that legal issue material to the substantive cause of action or defense in the case? The answer to these questions and the determination of materiality depend upon the substantive legal issues framed by the pleadings. Thus, evidence is immaterial if the proposition for which it is offered as proof is not a legal issue in the case.

Example: In a workers' compensation proceeding, evidence of the claimant's contributory negligence would be immaterial since the workers' compensation statute abrogates it as a defense.

2. Relevance: Probativeness—The Link Between Proof and Proposition

Probativeness embraces the test of materiality and something more. Probative evidence *contributes to proving or disproving* a material issue. Assuming that the issue the evidence is offered to prove is a material one, is the evidence logically probative of that issue? Does the evidence tend to prove that issue? Does the evidence tend to make the material proposition (issue) more probably true or untrue than it would be without the evidence?

Example: Evidence that the defendant drove recklessly on a prior occasion is material because it speaks to the question of his negligence. However, it is not sufficiently probative of the issue of negligence on this particular occasion, and is therefore not relevant.

3. Federal Rules—Materiality and Probativeness Combined

In the Federal Rules of Evidence, as in most modern codes, the requirements of materiality and probativeness are combined into a single definition of relevance. Thus, Federal Rule 401 provides that "relevant evidence" means evidence tending to prove (probativeness) any fact of consequence to the action (materiality). You should watch for both aspects of the relevance problem. Ask yourself (i) whether the fact sought to be proved is itself in issue under the pleadings and the substantive law, and also (ii) whether the evidence helps to prove the fact for which it is offered.

4. Competence

As mentioned above, material and relevant evidence is admissible if competent. Evidence is competent if it ***does not violate an exclusionary rule***. Basically, then, if evidence is material and relevant, the only reason such evidence would not be admitted is if it is prohibited by a special exclusionary rule of evidence. Exclusionary rules that prevent admissibility of relevant and material evidence are founded upon one or more of the following:

a. Policies Related to Truth-Seeking

The need to ensure the reliability and authenticity of evidence is a truth-seeking policy. Examples of exclusionary rules that perform this truth-seeking function are the hearsay rule, the best evidence rule, and Dead Man statutes.

b. Policies External to Litigation

The need to protect extrajudicial interests of society is an external policy goal. Rules granting testimonial privileges, for example, admittedly hamper the in-court search for truth.

E. EVIDENCE CLASSIFICATIONS

1. Direct or Circumstantial

a. Direct Evidence Relies on Actual Knowledge

Direct evidence goes directly to a material issue without intervention of an inferential process. Evidence is direct when the very facts in dispute are communicated by those who have actual knowledge by means of their senses.

Example: On the issue of whether anyone had recently crossed a snow-covered bridge, the testimony of a witness that he saw a man crossing would be direct evidence.

b. Circumstantial Evidence Relies on Inference

Circumstantial evidence is indirect and relies on inference. It is evidence of a subsidiary or collateral fact from which, alone or in conjunction with a cluster of other facts, the existence of the material issue can be inferred.

Example: On the issue of whether anyone had recently crossed a snow-covered bridge, the testimony of a witness that he saw human footprints in the snow on the bridge would be circumstantial evidence.

2. Testimonial, Documentary, or Real

a. *Testimonial* evidence is oral evidence given under oath. The witness responds to the questions of the attorneys.

b.   *Documentary* evidence is evidence in the form of a writing, such as a contract or a confession.

c.   *Real* evidence is the term applied to evidence consisting of things as distinguished from assertions of witnesses about things. Real evidence includes anything conveying a firsthand sense impression to the trier of fact, such as knives, jewelry, maps, or tape recordings.

F.   LIMITED ADMISSIBILITY

1.   Admissible for One Purpose but Not Another
The use of admissible evidence is a frequently encountered problem. It often happens that evidence is admissible for one purpose but is not admissible for another purpose.

Example: At the trial of the accused for assault, defendant's prior conviction for robbery may be shown by the prosecution to impeach the credibility of testimony given by the accused as a witness. The prior conviction is not admissible on the issue of defendant's guilt on the assault charge.

2.   Admissible Against One Party but Not Another
It is also possible that the evidence is admissible against one party but is not admissible against another party.

Example: A post-accident admission of a negligent employee truck driver may be admissible against the truck driver in an action for negligence. However, under certain circumstances it may not be admissible against a defendant employer who owned the truck.

3.   Jury Must Be Properly Instructed
As a general rule, if evidence is admissible for one purpose, it is not excluded merely because of the danger that the jury may also consider it for another incompetent purpose. When evidence that is admissible as to one party or for one purpose but is not admissible as to another party or for another purpose is admitted, the court must, upon request, restrict the evidence to its proper scope and instruct the jury accordingly. [Fed. R. Evid. 105]

II.   RELEVANCE

A.   INTRODUCTION
Relevance, in the sense of probativeness, has to do with the tendency of evidence to *prove or disprove a material issue*, to render it more probably true, or untrue, than it would have been without the particular evidence. Relevance is concerned with the *substance or content* of the evidence, not with the form or manner in which it is offered (*e.g.*, hearsay rule, best evidence rule). It can be stated, as a general proposition, that all relevant evidence is admissible if it is offered in an unobjectionable form and manner. (As usual, there are some exceptions to this generalization, since some perfectly relevant evidence that is in the proper form is excluded for policy reasons.)

B.   DETERMINING RELEVANCE
Relevant evidence is evidence having any tendency to make the existence of any fact that is of

consequence to the determination of an action more probable than it would be without the evidence. [Fed. R. Evid. 401] Note that this definition of relevance includes materiality since it requires that the disputed fact be of consequence to the determination of the action. The basic questions to ask regarding relevancy are: "What proposition is the evidence being used to prove? Is this a material issue in the case? Is the evidence probative of that proposition?" This type of relevance is sometimes called "logical relevance."

1. **General Rule—Must Relate to Time, Event, or Person in Controversy**
    Whenever testimony or exhibit evidence that relates to a time, event, or person other than the time, event, or person directly involved in the controversy being litigated is offered, the relevance of that evidence is suspect and should be examined more carefully. In most cases, a previous similar occurrence proves little or nothing about the one in issue. In addition, the risk of confusion and unfair prejudice usually outweighs the helpfulness of this type of evidence (*see* C., *infra*). Note that when considering the relevance of such evidence, one of the important factors to consider is its proximity in time to the current events. A circumstance that would be relevant had it occurred in close time proximity to the event in question is irrelevant if instead it was very remote.

    Examples: 1) Defendant is alleged to have run a red light and hit a pedestrian in the crosswalk. Proof that defendant ran other red lights in the past has little probative value in proving the occurrence in question. The probative value of such proof is outweighed by the confusion and unfair prejudice that would result from its admission.

                         2) On the issue of the fair market value of property in a condemnation action, the relevance of the sale price of other property depends on how comparable the other property is to the property being condemned, how close it is geographically, and how recent that sale was. Sale of a neighbor's comparable property six months ago is probably relevant, but the sale of the same property five years ago probably is not relevant.

                         3) In a murder prosecution, evidence that the accused had threatened the alleged victim the day before the killing may be very relevant. But compare a threat a week before; a month before; a year before; 10 years before.

2. **Exceptions—Certain Similar Occurrences Are Relevant**
    Despite the above rule, previous similar happenings and transactions of the parties and others similarly situated may be relevant if they are probative of the material issue involved, and if that probative value outweighs the risk that the evidence will confuse the jury or result in unfair prejudice. Of course, whenever a similar occurrence is offered to establish an inference about the subject occurrence, the quality of the inference depends on the similarity between the other happening and the one in issue. The following are examples of relevant similar occurrences.

    a. **Causation**
        Complicated issues of causation may often be established by evidence that concerns other times, events, or persons. For example, evidence that other homes in the same area were damaged by defendant's blasting operations is some evidence that the damage to plaintiff's home was caused by defendant's activities.

b.   Prior False Claims or Same Bodily Injury
Evidence that a person has previously filed similar *tort claims* or has been involved in *prior accidents* is *generally inadmissible* to show the invalidity of the present claim. At best, such evidence indicates plaintiff's tendency toward litigation or accident-proneness. In either case, the probative value is outweighed by the risk of confusion of issues and undue prejudice.

But if evidence is introduced that the party has made previous similar *false* claims, such evidence is usually relevant, under a common scheme or plan theory, to prove that the present claim is likely to be false. Likewise, where the prior claim was for an injury to the *same portion of plaintiff's body* that she claims was injured in the present case, evidence of the prior claim or injury may be relevant to prove that her present claim is false or exaggerated.

c.   Similar Accidents or Injuries Caused by Same Event or Condition
Where similar accidents or injuries were caused by the same event or condition, evidence of those prior accidents or injuries is *admissible to prove*:

(i)   That a defect or dangerous *condition existed*;

(ii)   That the defendant had *knowledge* of the defect or dangerous condition; and

(iii) That the defect or dangerous condition was the *cause* of the present injury.

Example: In an action for dust damage from a mill, it may be proper to introduce evidence that plaintiff's neighbors have previously suffered similar dust damage, in order to prove that the mill created dust, that the mill owners knew of the dust, and that the dust caused plaintiff's damage.

1)   Absence of Similar Accidents
Many courts are reluctant to admit evidence of the absence of similar accidents to show absence of negligence or lack of a defect. However, where a structural condition is involved and that condition is unchanged, the court has discretion to admit evidence of absence of other complaints to show lack of a defect. Evidence of prior safety history and absence of complaints is admissible to show *defendant's lack of knowledge* of any danger.

d.   Previous Similar Acts Admissible to Prove Intent
Similar conduct previously committed by a party may be introduced to prove the party's present motive or intent when such elements are relevant.
Example: In an action against a school board for excluding a black child from school, similar exclusions of black children will be admissible into evidence to show intent.

e.   Rebutting Claim of Impossibility
The requirement that prior occurrences be similar to the litigated act may be relaxed when used to rebut a claim or defense of impossibility. For example, if defendant

denies negligent speeding on the ground that his automobile could never go above 50 m.p.h., plaintiff may rebut by showing that on other occasions, even under different circumstances, the vehicle was traveling at 75 m.p.h.

f. Sales of Similar Property

Evidence of sales of similar personal or real property that are not too remote in time is *admissible to prove value*. However, unlike commonly sold items of personal property, each parcel of real property is considered unique. Thus, the problem of producing evidence of other transactions requires a preliminary finding that the character, usage, proximity, date of sale, etc., are sufficiently similar to the property in issue. Evidence of prices quoted in mere *offers* is *not admissible* because to determine the sincerity of these offers would lead to collateral disputes. However, offers by a party to the present action to buy or sell the property may be admissible as admissions.

g. Habit

Habit describes one's regular response to a specific set of circumstances (*e.g.,* "she always takes a staircase two steps at a time"). In contrast, character describes one's disposition in respect to general traits (*e.g.,* "she's always in a hurry"). Since habits are more specific and particularized, evidence of habit is relevant and can be introduced in circumstances when it is not permissible to introduce evidence of character. Thus, under Federal Rule 406, "evidence of the habit of a person . . . is relevant to prove that the conduct of the person . . . on a particular occasion was in conformity with the habit . . . ."

Example: Evidence could be introduced to show that a driver habitually failed to stop at a certain stop sign as circumstantial evidence that she failed to stop at the time in question. In contrast, evidence cannot be introduced to show that a person is a careless driver since that is closer to character than habit.

Many states either do not admit evidence of habit to show that a particular act occurred, or else limit admissibility to those cases where there are no eyewitnesses. Federal Rule 406 admits habit evidence freely and abandons the "no eyewitness" requirement. Even where admissible, however, the habit must be shown to be a regular response to a repeated specific situation.

h. Industrial or Business Routine

Just as evidence of personal habit is relevant to show conduct, evidence that a business or firm had an established business routine is relevant as tending to show that a particular event occurred.

Example: Evidence of a regular mailing procedure, such as a custom of picking up letters from a certain table and mailing them, would be relevant as evidence to show that a particular letter left on the table was duly mailed.

i. Industrial Custom as Evidence of Standard of Care

1) Industrial Custom Distinguished from Business Routine

Custom of the industry should be distinguished from business routine. In the latter case, the particular conduct and habit of a party are being offered to show that the party acted in the same manner on the occasion in question. Custom of the industry is offered to prove the actions of other persons in the same industry in an attempt to show adherence to or deviance from an industry-wide standard of care.

2) Relevant to Standard of Care but Not Conclusive

When one of the issues in dispute is negligence arising out of inadequate safety devices or precautions, evidence of general custom or usage in the same kind of business under the same circumstances may be introduced by either party as tending to establish a standard by which reasonable or ordinary care may be judged. Although custom of the trade or business is admissible on the standard of care to be exercised, it is not conclusive.

C. DISCRETIONARY EXCLUSION OF RELEVANT EVIDENCE (PRAGMATIC RELEVANCE)

A trial judge has broad discretion to exclude relevant evidence if its probative value is substantially outweighed by the danger of *unfair prejudice*, *confusion of the issues*, or *misleading the jury*, or by considerations of *undue delay*, waste of time, or needless presentation of cumulative evidence. [Fed. R. Evid. 403] *"Unfair surprise"* is listed as an additional basis for exclusion under some state rules, but it was omitted under the Federal Rules on the theory that surprise can be prevented by discovery and pretrial conference or mitigated by granting a continuance.

Certain items of evidence may be directed to a material issue in the case and may be very probative of that issue, but they are excluded because of predictable policies designed to ensure an orderly and efficient proceeding and to encourage certain public policy solutions to legal problems. For example, inflammatory matter, which may be very probative of the issues, will not be admitted because of the potential prejudicial effect on the jury.

D. EXCLUSION OF RELEVANT EVIDENCE FOR PUBLIC POLICY REASONS (POLICY-BASED RELEVANCE)

Certain evidence of questionable relevance is excluded by the Federal Rules because public policy favors the behavior involved. For example, the law encourages the repair of defective premises that cause injury, and consequently, evidence of the subsequent repair may not be admitted to prove antecedent negligence, even though it may be probative of the issue. Evidence excluded for public policy reasons is set forth below.

1. Liability Insurance

a. Inadmissible to Show Negligence or Ability to Pay

Evidence that a person was or was not insured against liability is *not admissible* upon the issue of whether she *acted negligently* or otherwise wrongfully. Nor is it admissible to show *ability to pay* a substantial judgment. [Fed. R. Evid. 411]

b. When Admissible

Proof that a person carried liability insurance may be admissible and relevant for other purposes. Issue identification is important in these cases, since proof of the fact that the defendant maintained insurance *may be used*:

1) To Prove Ownership or Control

Evidence that the defendant maintained insurance may be admitted for the limited purpose of proving the defendant's ownership or control when ownership or control is disputed.

Example: P sues D and alleges that D owned the building in which P fell on a defective staircase, further alleging a cause of action for negligence. D denies all allegations, and thereby puts in issue the question of ownership of the premises. P may show that D had insured the premises as evidence of ownership, but the evidence will only be used for the limited purpose of proving that issue.

2) For Purposes of Impeachment

Evidence that the defendant is insured may be used for the limited purpose of impeaching a witness.

Example: An investigator testifies on behalf of defendant. Plaintiff may demonstrate the bias or interest of this witness by showing that she is employed by defendant's liability insurance company.

3) As Part of Admission

An admission of liability may be so coupled with a reference to insurance coverage that the reference to insurance cannot be severed without lessening its value as an admission of liability.

Example: "Don't worry; my insurance company will pay off."

2. Subsequent Remedial Measures

a. Inadmissible to Prove Negligence or Culpable Conduct

Evidence of repairs or other precautionary measures made following an injury is inadmissible to prove negligence, culpable conduct, a defect in a product or its design, or a need for a warning or instruction. [Fed. R. Evid. 407] The purpose of the rule is to encourage people to make such repairs.

b. When Admissible

Although evidence of subsequent repairs is not admissible to prove negligence, etc., this evidence may still be admissible for other purposes. Some of these purposes are:

1) To Prove Ownership or Control

Evidence of subsequent repairs performed by the defendant may be introduced to prove ownership or control, since a stranger would hardly make repairs.

2) To Rebut Claim that Precaution Was Not Feasible

Evidence of repairs or other precautionary measures made following an accident is admissible to establish the feasibility of precautionary measures when such feasibility is controverted.

3) To Prove Destruction of Evidence

Evidence of subsequent remedial measures may be admitted to prove that the opposing party has destroyed evidence; *e.g.,* repainting a fender to cover up evidence of a collision (spoliation).

3. Settlement Offers—Negotiations Not Admissible
Evidence of compromises or offers to compromise is inadmissible to prove liability for or invalidity of a claim that is disputed as to validity or amount. [Fed. R. Evid. 408] *Rationale:* Public policy favors the settlement of disputes without litigation, and settlement would be discouraged if either side were deterred from making offers by the fear that they would be admitted in evidence.

The Federal Rules also exclude "any conduct or statement" made in the course of negotiating a compromise, as well as the offer to compromise itself; therefore, admissions of fact made during compromise negotiations are inadmissible. This position encourages settlements by allowing complete candor between the parties in negotiations. [Fed. R. Evid. 408] *But note:* Rule 408 does not exclude evidence that would *otherwise be discoverable* because it was presented during compromise negotiations. Thus, if defendant presents a document to plaintiff during compromise negotiations to facilitate a compromise and the document was discoverable by plaintiff, it will be admissible in evidence notwithstanding that it was presented during compromise negotiations.

a. Must Be a Claim
Although the filing of a suit is not a prerequisite for this exclusionary rule, there must be some indication, express or implied, that a party is going to make some kind of claim. Thus, a party's volunteered admission of fact accompanying an offer to settle immediately following the incident is usually admissible because there has not been time for the other party to indicate an intent to make a claim.

b. Claim Must Be Disputed as to Liability or Amount
To trigger the exclusionary feature of Rule 408, the claim must be disputed as to liability or amount. Thus, if a party admits liability and the amount of liability but offers to settle (rather than litigate) for a lesser amount, every statement made in connection with that offer is admissible.

4. Withdrawn Guilty Pleas and Offers to Plead Guilty Not Admissible
Under the Federal Rules neither withdrawn guilty pleas, pleas of nolo contendere, offers to plead guilty, nor evidence of statements made in negotiating such pleas are admissible in any proceeding. [Fed. R. Evid. 410] Most jurisdictions concur. The *evidentiary value* of a withdrawn plea of guilty as an admission is deemed *offset by the prejudicial effect* of the evidence. Moreover, it is felt that the judge who permitted the withdrawal of the guilty plea must have decided that there was a good reason to withdraw it and, under these circumstances, the significance of the initial plea is minimal. Most courts exclude offers to plead guilty on reasoning similar to that advanced for not admitting offers to compromise as proof of liability in civil cases.

a. Waiver
The protection of Rule 410 for plea negotiations may be validly waived unless there is an affirmative indication that the defendant entered the waiver agreement unknowingly or involuntarily. [United States v. Mezzanatto, 513 U.S. 196 (1995)]
Example: Defendant, who was charged with a drug offense, wished to arrange a deal with the government in exchange for his cooperation. As a prerequisite to this discussion, Prosecutor required that Defendant (i) be

completely truthful and (ii) agree that any statements made by him in the course of the plea negotiations could be used to impeach him if he testified in a contrary fashion at trial. Defendant agreed. If at some point thereafter the discussion breaks off and Defendant is tried on the charges, Prosecutor may use statements made in the plea negotiations to impeach Defendant. [United States v. Mezzanatto, *supra*]

5. Payment of Medical Expenses Not Admissible

Similarly, evidence that a party paid (or offered to pay) the injured party's medical expenses is *not admissible to prove liability* for the injury. [Fed. R. Evid. 409] This rule is based upon the concern that such payment might be prompted solely by "humanitarian motives." However, unlike the situation with compromise negotiation (3., *supra*), *admissions of fact* accompanying offers to pay medical expenses *are admissible*.

E. CHARACTER EVIDENCE—A SPECIAL RELEVANCE PROBLEM

The rules regarding use of character evidence are affected by three major concerns. These are: (i) the purpose for which evidence of character is offered; (ii) the method to be used to prove character; and (iii) the kind of case, civil or criminal.

1. Purposes for Offer of Character Evidence

a. To Prove Character When Character Itself Is Ultimate Issue in Case

When a person's character itself is the ultimate issue in the case, character evidence must be admitted. Cases where character is itself one of the material propositions in issue are confined mostly to civil litigation and are rare even among civil actions.

b. To Serve as Circumstantial Evidence of How a Person Probably Acted

It is the use of character as circumstantial evidence of how a person probably acted that raises the most difficult problems of relevance, especially in criminal cases.

c. To Impeach Credibility of Witness

The discussion of the use of character evidence to impeach the credibility of a witness is postponed for later discussion under the heading of "Credibility—Impeachment." (*See* VI.E., *infra*.)

2. Means of Proving Character

Depending upon the jurisdiction, the purpose of the offer, and the nature of the case, the following types of evidence may be used to prove character:

a. Evidence of Specific Acts as Demonstrating Character

Evidence of specific acts of the person in question as demonstrating that person's character is permitted only in a few instances, such as where character is itself one of the ultimate issues in the case.

b. Opinion Testimony

Witnesses who know the person may testify regarding their opinions about the person's character.

c. Testimony as to Person's General Reputation in Community

Testimony by witnesses as to a person's general reputation in the community is in some sense hearsay since reputation is really what people say about a person. On the other hand, because reputation is a general indication of character, and because it involves fewer side issues than either of the above methods, it is the most common means of showing character.

3. **Generally Not Admissible in Civil Cases**

Evidence of character to prove the conduct of a person in the litigated event is generally not admissible in a civil case. The reasons given are that the slight probative value of character is outweighed by the danger of prejudice, the possible distraction of the jury from the main question in issue, and the possible waste of time required by examination of collateral issues.

Examples: 1) Defendant may not introduce evidence that she is generally a cautious driver to prove that she was not negligent on the day in question.

                   2) Plaintiff may not introduce evidence that the defendant is usually a reckless driver to prove that she was negligent on the day in question.

Such circumstantial use of prior behavior patterns for the purpose of drawing the inference that, at the time and place in question, the actor probably acted in accord with her prior behavior pattern is not permitted. A person's *general behavior patterns* (as distinguished from her habits and business routines) are *irrelevant* and inadmissible in evidence.

a. **Exception—When Character Is Directly in Issue**

When a person's character itself is one of the issues in the case, character evidence is not only admissible, but indeed is the best method of proving the issue.

Examples: 1) In a defamation action, when D is being sued for calling P a thief and pleads as an affirmative defense that she spoke the truth (*i.e.*, that P is indeed a thief), P's character is clearly in issue.

                   2) When an employer is charged with negligently retaining an employee "of unstable and violent disposition," the character of the employee is also in issue.

When character is directly in issue, almost all courts will admit evidence of specific acts that show this character (*e.g.*, in Example 1) above, D may offer evidence that on different occasions P has stolen things to show that he is a thief). Under the Federal Rules, any of the types of evidence (*reputation*, *opinion*, *or specific acts*) may be used to prove character when character is directly in issue. [Fed. R. Evid. 405(b)]

4. **Accused in a Criminal Case—Prosecution Cannot Initiate, but Accused Can**

The general rule is that the prosecution cannot initiate evidence of the bad character of the defendant merely to show that she is more likely to have committed the crime of which she is accused. However, the accused may introduce evidence of her good character to show her innocence of the alleged crime.

The rationale is that even though the evidence is of some relevance, the prosecution should not be permitted to show that the defendant is a bad person, since the jury might then decide to convict her regardless of her guilt of the crime charged. However, since the life or liberty of the defendant is at stake, she should be allowed to introduce evidence of her good character since it may have a tendency to show that she did not commit the crime charged.

a. How Defendant Proves Character

1) Reputation and Personal Opinion Testimony

A defendant puts her character in issue by calling a qualified witness to testify to the defendant's good reputation (or that he has heard nothing bad) *for the trait involved* in the case. Under Federal Rule 405, the witness may also give his personal opinion concerning that trait of the defendant. However, the witness may *not* testify to *specific acts of conduct* of the defendant to prove the trait in issue.

2) Testifying Places Defendant's Credibility—Not Character—in Issue

A defendant does not put her character in issue merely by taking the stand and giving testimony on the facts of the controversy. However, if the defendant takes the stand, she puts her credibility in issue and is subject to impeachment. (*See* "Credibility—Impeachment," VI.E., *infra*.)

b. How Prosecution Rebuts Defendant's Character Evidence

If the defendant puts her character in issue by having a character witness testify as to his opinion of the defendant or the defendant's reputation, the prosecution may rebut in the following manner:

1) Cross-Examination

The prosecution may test the character witness by cross-examination regarding the basis for his opinion or knowledge of the reputation that he has testified about. In most jurisdictions, one is allowed to inquire on cross-examination whether the reputation witness has *heard* of particular instances of the defendant's misconduct pertinent to the trait in question. The rationale is that since the reputation witness relates what he has heard, the inquiry tests the accuracy of his hearing and reporting. Since the character witness may now testify in the form of opinion as well as by reputation, it follows that the basis of the opinion can be exposed. Thus, under Federal Rule 405(a), cross-examination inquiry is allowable as to whether the opinion witness *knows* of, as well as whether he has *heard* of, specific instances of misconduct. The distinction in form between "Have you heard" and "Do you know" is eliminated by the statement in Rule 405(a), which provides that "on cross-examination, inquiry is allowable into relevant specific instances of conduct." Note that if the witness denies knowledge of these specific instances of conduct, the prosecutor *may not* prove them by extrinsic evidence; he is limited to inquiry on cross-examination.

2) Testimony of Other Witnesses as to Defendant's Bad Reputation

The prosecution may rebut the defendant's character evidence by calling qualified witnesses to testify to the defendant's bad reputation or their opinion of the defendant's character for the particular trait involved.

5. Victim in Criminal Case

a. Defendant's Initiative

The defendant may introduce reputation or opinion evidence of a bad character trait of the alleged crime victim when it is relevant to show the defendant's innocence. However, by specific exception, this rule does not extend to showing the bad character of rape victims.

Example: In an assault or murder prosecution where the defendant claims self-defense, she may introduce evidence of the victim's violent character as tending to show that the victim was the aggressor.

b. Prosecution Rebuttal

Once the defendant has introduced evidence of a bad character trait of the alleged victim, the prosecution may counter with reputation or opinion evidence of (i) the *victim's good character*, or (ii) the *defendant's bad character* for the *same trait*. [Fed. R. Evid. 404(a)]

Example: Defendant is charged with the murder of Victim. Defendant pleads self-defense and offers evidence that Victim was a violent person. Prosecutor can rebut such evidence with evidence that Victim was a nonviolent person and/or with evidence that Defendant is a violent person.

c. Rape Cases—Victim's Past Behavior Inadmissible

In any civil or criminal proceeding involving alleged sexual misconduct, evidence offered to prove the sexual behavior or sexual disposition of the alleged victim is generally inadmissible. [Fed. R. Evid. 412(a)]

1) Exceptions in Criminal Cases

In a criminal case, evidence of sexual behavior by the victim offered to prove that a person other than the accused was the *source of semen, injury, or other physical evidence* is admissible. Also, specific instances of sexual behavior between the victim and the accused are admissible by the prosecution, or by the defense to prove *consent*. Evidence of a victim's sexual behavior is also admissible when its exclusion would violate the defendant's constitutional rights. [Fed. R. Evid. 412(b)(1)]

2) Exceptions in Civil Cases

In civil cases, evidence offered to prove the sexual disposition or behavior of the alleged victim is admissible if it is otherwise admissible under the Federal Rules and its probative value substantially outweighs the danger of harm to the victim and of unfair prejudice to any party. Evidence of an alleged victim's reputation is admissible only if it has been placed in controversy by the victim. [Fed. R. Evid. 412(b)(2)]

3) Procedure

To offer evidence under the above exceptions, the party must file a motion 14 days before trial describing the evidence and its purpose, and must serve the motion on all parties and notify the victim. Before admitting the evidence, the court must conduct an in camera hearing and afford the victim and the parties a right to be heard. [Fed. R. Evid. 412(c)]

6. Specific Acts of Misconduct Generally Inadmissible

The basic rule is that when a person is charged with one crime, extrinsic evidence of her other crimes or misconduct is inadmissible if such evidence is offered solely to establish a criminal disposition. Thus, this statement of Federal Rule 404(b) is merely another way of saying that the prosecution may not show the accused's bad character to imply criminal disposition. The danger again is that the jury may convict the defendant because of past crimes rather than because of her guilt of the offense charged.

a.   Admissible If Independently Relevant

Evidence of other crimes or misconduct is admissible if these acts are relevant to some issue other than the defendant's character or disposition to commit the crime charged. While acknowledging that prior acts or crimes are not admissible to show conformity or to imply bad character, Federal Rule 404(b) goes on to say that such prior acts or crimes may be admissible for other purposes (*e.g.*, to show motive, opportunity, intent, preparation, plan, knowledge, identity, or absence of mistake) whenever these issues are relevant in either a *criminal or a civil case*. Upon request by the accused, the prosecution in a criminal case must provide reasonable notice prior to trial (or during trial if pretrial notice is excused for good cause shown) of the general nature of any of this type of evidence the prosecution intends to introduce at trial.

Example: Husband is on trial for the alleged shooting murder of Wife. Husband claims an accident occurred as he was cleaning the gun. Prosecution may prove that six months ago Husband tried to stab Wife. This evidence is not offered to show that the defendant is the kind of violent man likely to have murdered his wife (*i.e.*, general bad character or violent disposition); rather, it is offered to show absence of mistake, that the killing was probably not an accident.

1)   Examples of Relevant Misconduct

a)   Motive

The commission of a prior crime may be evidence of a motive to commit the crime for which the defendant is accused.

b)   Intent

In many crimes, such as forgery, passing counterfeit money, larceny by trick, and receiving stolen property, intent is the gravamen of the crime. Evidence that defendant committed prior similar wrongful acts is admissible to establish guilty knowledge and to negate good faith.

c)   Absence of Mistake or Accident

There are cases in which the defense of accident or mistake may be anticipated. In these situations prosecution evidence of similar misconduct by the defendant is admissible to negate the possibility of mistake or accident. (*See* example above.)

d)   Identity

Evidence, including misconduct, that connects this defendant to the crime (*e.g.,* theft of gun used in later crime) is admissible. Similarly, evidence that the accused committed prior criminal acts that are so distinctive as to operate as a "signature" may be introduced to prove that the accused committed the act in question (modus operandi).

e) **Common Plan or Scheme—Preparation**
Evidence that the defendant recently stole some burglar tools is probative of the fact that she committed the burglary for which she is accused.

f) **Other**
Similar acts or related misconduct may be used to prove opportunity, knowledge, or any relevant fact other than the accused's general bad character or criminal disposition.

2) **Quantum of Proof for Independently Relevant Acts of Misconduct**
Under Federal Rule 404(b), independently relevant uncharged misconduct by the defendant will be admissible, without a preliminary ruling, as long as (i) there is *sufficient evidence to support a jury finding* that the defendant committed the prior act (*i.e.,* the standard of Federal Rule 104); and (ii) its probative value on the issue of motive, intent, identity, or other independently relevant proposition is not substantially outweighed by the danger of unfair prejudice (*i.e.,* the test of Federal Rule 403). [Huddleston v. United States, 485 U.S. 681 (1988)]

b. **Prior Acts of Sexual Assault or Child Molestation**
Evidence of a defendant's prior acts of sexual assault or child molestation is admissible in a civil or criminal case where the defendant is accused of committing an act of sexual assault or child molestation. The party who intends to offer this evidence must disclose the evidence to the defendant 15 days before trial (or later with good cause). [Fed. R. Evid. 413-415]

III. JUDICIAL NOTICE

A. **JUDICIAL NOTICE OF FACT**
Judicial notice is the *recognition of a fact as true without formal presentation of evidence*. In most instances the costly, time-consuming, and cumbersome process of formal proof is required to ensure fact-finding accuracy. However, self-evident propositions need not be subjected to this process, but instead may be judicially noticed. Judicial notice, like the presumption, is a judicial shortcut, a substitute for proof. The underlying policy considerations include expediting the trial and avoiding judicial disrepute where the lack of evidence might result in a conclusion contrary to well-known facts. For example, requiring proof that Washington, D.C., is the capital of the United States would require unnecessary time in a situation where a contrary conclusion would be ridiculous.

1. **Facts Appropriate for Judicial Notice**
The Federal Rule conforms to the existing state rules governing judicial notice. Federal Rule 201(b) defines a fact that may be noticed as "one not subject to reasonable dispute in that it is either (i) generally known within the territorial jurisdiction of the trial court" (notorious facts), or (ii) "capable of accurate and ready determination by resort to sources

whose accuracy cannot reasonably be questioned" (manifest facts). Judicial notice may be taken of such facts *at any time*, whether or not requested, and such notice is mandatory if a party requests and supplies the court with the necessary information. A party is entitled to be heard on the propriety of taking judicial notice and the tenor of the matter noted.

a. Matters of Common Knowledge in the Community—Notorious Facts

Judicial notice will be taken of the body of facts that well-informed persons generally know and accept. Though usually facts of common knowledge are known everywhere, it is sufficient for judicial notice if they are known in the community where the court is sitting.

Examples: A court sitting in New York City will take judicial notice that:

1) The streets in Manhattan are numbered east and west from Fifth Avenue and that the odd numbers are on the north side of the street.

2) Many people are subject to low blood pressure and poor circulation.

3) The ordinary period of human gestation is 280 days.

b. Facts Capable of Certain Verification—Manifest Facts

Some facts, while not generally known and accepted, are easily verified by resorting to easily accessible, well-established sources.

Examples: 1) Judicial notice will be taken of the time of the rising or setting of the sun and moon on a particular day since this fact, although not commonly known, can be estimated quickly and accurately by reference to an almanac.

2) The court will accept without proof that February 14, 1999, was a Sunday by reference to a calendar.

c. Judicial Notice of Scientific Principles

1) Judicial Notice of Scientific Basis of Test Results

Trial courts have increasingly taken judicial notice of scientific principles as a type of manifest fact. Once a particular scientific test or principle has become sufficiently well-established (*i.e.*, generally accepted among the scientific community), courts no longer require proof (expert testimony) of the underlying basis of the test. The results of such a test are therefore admissible into evidence.

Example: A trial court will take judicial notice of the reliability of radar speed tests, ballistics tests, and paternity blood tests, and will admit the results of these tests into evidence upon a showing that the tests were properly conducted.

2) Conclusiveness of Test Results

Some scientific tests have achieved such universal acceptance that not only are the test results admissible into evidence, but the results are binding on the finder of fact in civil cases.

> *Example:* Where a blood test indicates that the accused father could not have been the parent of the child, that result is conclusive on the issue of paternity, and other evidence on that issue will be excluded.

d. Judge's Personal Knowledge
What a judge knows personally is not the same as what he may judicially notice. A judge may have to ignore facts that he knows as a private person if those facts are neither commonly known in the community nor capable of certain verification by resort to easily accessible sources of indisputable accuracy.

2. Procedural Aspects of Judicial Notice

a. Requirement of a Request
The general rule is that a party must formally request that notice be taken of a particular fact.

b. Judicial Notice by Appellate Court
Judicial notice may be taken for the first time on appeal. A reviewing court is required to take judicial notice of any matter that the trial court properly noticed or was obliged to notice.

c. Conclusiveness of Judicial Notice
Federal Rule 201(g) provides that a judicially noticed fact is conclusive in a civil case but not in a criminal case. The Federal Rule states that in a civil case, the court shall instruct the jury to accept as conclusive any fact judicially noticed; in a criminal case, on the other hand, the jury is instructed that it may, but is not required to, accept as conclusive any fact judicially noticed.

3. "Adjudicative" and "Legislative" Facts
The Federal Rules govern *only judicial notice of "adjudicative" facts* (*i.e.*, facts that relate to the parties in a particular case) not "legislative" facts (*i.e.*, policy facts that relate to legal reasoning and the lawmaking process). The drafters of Federal Rule 201 reasoned that "legislative" facts are a necessary part of the judicial reasoning process, so that a rule imposing a requirement of indisputability and a formal procedure for taking judicial notice of these matters would destroy the concept of judge-made law. [Advisory Committee Note to Rule 201] Therefore, "legislative" facts need not meet the requirements of Rule 201 that facts must be either of common knowledge or capable of indisputable verification to be judicially noticed.

B. JUDICIAL NOTICE OF LAW—MANDATORY OR PERMISSIVE
The judge's task of finding applicable law is accomplished by informal investigation of legal source materials. This process, unmentioned in the Federal Rules of Evidence, has been traditionally described in terms of the judge taking judicial notice of the law applicable to the case.

1. Classification Depends on Accessibility of Source Materials
Judicial notice of law is mandatory in some instances and permissive in others. This mandatory-permissive classification is explainable in terms of the likely accessibility of source materials for different types of laws. State public law is easily available in reported volumes

and, therefore, it is reasonable to require the court to be aware of and to notice it. Descriptions of foreign law or private acts are usually less available and, therefore, the court is permitted—but not required—to judicially notice such laws. In some cases, the contents of such laws may have to be established by proof to the satisfaction of the judge.

2. Mandatory Judicial Notice

Most courts must take judicial notice without request of:

a. *Federal public law*—the United States Constitution, federal treaties, public acts of Congress, and federal case law.

b. *State public law*—the constitution, public statutes, and common law of the states.

c. *Official regulations*—the official compilation of codes and rules and regulations of the forum state and the federal government, except those relating to internal organization or management of a state agency.

3. Permissive Judicial Notice

Most courts may, upon being supplied with sufficient information, take judicial notice of municipal ordinances and private acts or resolutions of Congress and of the local state legislature. Similarly, the laws of foreign countries may be judicially noticed.

IV. REAL EVIDENCE

A. IN GENERAL

1. Addressed Directly to Trier of Fact

Real or demonstrative evidence is addressed directly to the trier of fact. The object in issue is presented for *inspection by the trier of fact*. Ordinarily the evidence is addressed to the sense of sight (*e.g.*, exhibition of injured arm to jury to demonstrate extent of injury), but it may be directed to other senses as well (*e.g.*, sound recording of factory noise played during a nuisance trial).

2. Special Problems

This form of proof, which allows the triers of fact to reach conclusions based upon their own perceptions rather than relying upon those of witnesses, frequently involves special problems. Often there is concern regarding *proper authentication* of the "object." Additionally, the possibility exists that physical production of the thing may be too *burdensome* or may inspire *prejudicial emotions* outweighing its probative value to the litigation.

B. TYPES OF REAL EVIDENCE

1. Direct

Real evidence may be direct evidence; *i.e.*, it may be offered to prove the facts about the object as an end in itself. For example, in a personal injury case, evidence of a permanent injury could be introduced by an exhibition of the injury itself to the trier of fact.

2. Circumstantial

Real evidence may also be circumstantial; *i.e.*, facts about the object are proved as a basis for an inference that other facts are true. For example, in a paternity case, the trier of fact may be shown the baby for the purpose of comparing its appearance and the appearance of the alleged father. In this case, the trier of fact is being asked to draw an inference that, since the child and alleged father look alike, the paternal relationship exists.

3. Original

Real evidence may be original; *i.e.*, it may have had some connection with the transaction that is in question at the trial. An example of this kind of evidence would be an alleged murder weapon.

4. Prepared

Real evidence may also be prepared; *e.g.*, sketches or models may be made to be shown to the trier of fact. This category of real evidence is called *"demonstrative evidence."*

C. GENERAL CONDITIONS OF ADMISSIBILITY

Real evidence, like all other forms of evidence, must be *relevant* to the proposition in issue. The admissibility of real proof also depends on additional legal requirements, such as those that follow.

1. Authentication

The object must first be identified as being what the proponent claims it to be. Real evidence is commonly authenticated by recognition testimony or by establishing a chain of custody.

a. Recognition Testimony

If the object has significant features that make it identifiable upon inspection, a witness may authenticate the object by testifying that the object is what the proponent claims it is.

Examples: 1) If a prosecutor offers a knife into evidence and claims that the knife is the very weapon used in the murder, the object may be authenticated by a witness who testifies that he can identify the knife as the one found next to the deceased.

2) If a prosecutor offers a knife into evidence and claims that it is *similar* to the knife used in the murder, it may be authenticated by a witness who testifies that the offered knife is indeed similar to the one found next to the deceased.

3) A witness can testify that a photograph is a fair and accurate representation of that which it is purported to depict.

b. Chain of Custody

If the evidence is of a type that is likely to be confused or can be easily tampered with, the proponent of the object must present evidence of chain of custody. The proponent of the evidence must show that the object has been held in a substantially *unbroken chain of possession.* The proponent need not negate all possibilities of substitution or tampering, but must show adherence to some system of identification and custody.

Example: A custodial chain—from the taking, to the testing, to the exhibiting of the sample—must be established before evidence of a blood alcohol test will be admitted.

2. Condition of Object; Useful Probativeness

If the condition of the object is significant, it must be shown to be in substantially the *same condition at the trial.* Moreover, the object must be logically helpful or reliable in tending to prove the proposition in issue.

Example: Would it be helpful in a paternity proceeding to present the baby so that the trier of fact can ascertain physical resemblance to the alleged father?

3. Legal Relevance

Assuming the object has been properly identified and is probative, the discretion of the trial judge is called upon to decide whether some auxiliary policy or principle outweighs the need to admit the real evidence. Such policies limiting the use of real evidence frequently concern:

a. *Physical inconvenience* of bringing the object into the courtroom;

b. *Indecency or impropriety*; or

c. *Undue prejudice* where the probative value of the object or exhibit is outweighed by the danger of unfair prejudice.

D. PARTICULAR TYPES OF REAL PROOF

1. Reproductions and Explanatory Real Evidence

When properly authenticated, relevant photographs, movies, diagrams, maps, sketches, or other *reproductions are admissible* if their value is not outweighed by the danger of unfair prejudice. On the other hand, items used entirely for *explanatory purposes* (such as skeletons, anatomy charts, etc.) are permitted at a trial, but are usually *not admitted into evidence* and are not given to the jury during its deliberations. These items are not represented to be reproductions of the real thing, but are merely used as aids to testimony.

Example: A doctor may use a model of an average male skeleton to explain his testimony. The skeleton may be marked for identification in order to preserve the record, but it is not admitted into evidence.

Compare: If the skeleton was offered as a reproduction of the bone structure of the deceased, assuming there is no undue prejudice, it may be admitted into evidence on a showing that it accurately represents the bone structure of the deceased.

2. Maps, Charts, Models, Etc.

Maps, charts, models, etc., are usually admissible for the purpose of illustrating testimony. Since these are all reproductions, they must be authenticated by testimonial evidence showing that they are *faithful reproductions* of the object or thing depicted. As with other real evidence, introduction of these items is within the discretion of the court, and they may be excluded where they would be wasteful of time or where they would unduly impress the trier of fact with the importance of the material.

3. **Exhibition of Child in Paternity Suits**
Almost all courts permit exhibition of the child for the purpose of showing whether it is of the race of the putative father. The courts are divided with respect to the propriety of exhibiting the child in order to prove physical resemblance to the putative father, but a growing majority of courts refuse to permit exhibition of the child.

4. **Exhibition of Injuries**
The exhibition of injuries in a personal injury or criminal case is generally permitted, but the court has discretion to exclude this evidence if the exhibition would result in unfair prejudice.

5. **Jury View of the Scene**
Closely related to real and demonstrative evidence is the matter of jury views of premises and places at issue in the case. In the trial court's discretion, they are permitted, sparingly, in both civil and criminal cases. The importance of information that could be obtained by a view, and the ease with which photographs, diagrams, or maps could be substituted for such a view, will be pivotal considerations to the trial judge. Any significant changes of condition in the premises that are to be viewed will also affect the decision. The trial judge usually need not be present during a jury view. The parties and their attorneys are usually permitted to attend, but the view will be conducted by a disinterested court attaché and neither counsel nor the parties will be permitted to engage in any commentary.

6. **Demonstrations**
The court, in its discretion, may permit experiments or demonstrations to be performed in the courtroom.

    a. **Demonstrations Showing Effect of Bodily Injury**
    Demonstrations to show the effect of bodily injury are usually excluded where the exhibition would reveal hideous wounds, elicit cries of pain, or otherwise unduly dramatize the injury and inflame the minds of the jurors.

    b. **Demonstrations Under Sole Control of Witness Are Excluded**
    Demonstrations may also be excluded where they are under the sole control of the witness and thus not subject to effective cross-examination. For example, an injured plaintiff might attempt to demonstrate lack of locomotion by showing that he cannot move a limb. The demonstration itself cannot be effectively cross-examined. However, if testimony is given to the same effect, it may be impeached by contradictory evidence.

    c. **Scientific Experiments**
    The judge may permit scientific experiments to be performed in the courtroom provided:

        1) The conditions are ***substantially similar*** to those that attended the original event, and

        2) The experiment will ***not result in undue waste of time or confusion*** of the issues.

V. DOCUMENTARY EVIDENCE

A. IN GENERAL

Documentary evidence, like other kinds of evidence, *must be relevant* in order to be admissible. In the case of writings, the authenticity of the document is one aspect of its relevancy. Of course, documentary evidence, even if fully authenticated and relevant, *may be excluded if it violates a rule of competency* such as the best evidence or hearsay rule. Whenever any problem or question concerns a document, you should consider three separate and distinct possible barriers to admissibility (authentication, best evidence, and hearsay).

B. AUTHENTICATION

Before a writing or any secondary evidence of its content may be received in evidence, the writing must be authenticated by proof showing that the writing is what the proponent claims it is. The writing is usually not self-authenticating. It needs a testimonial sponsor or shepherding angel to prove that the writing was made, signed, or adopted by the particular relevant person. [Fed. R. Evid. 901-903]

1. Quantum of Proof of Authenticity

Authentication of documentary or, for that matter, real evidence requires only enough evidence to support a finding that the matter is what its proponent claims it is. It is not required that the proponent establish its genuineness by a preponderance of the evidence as a condition to admissibility. All that is necessary under Federal Rules 104(b) and 901 is proof *sufficient to support a jury finding* of genuineness.

2. Authentication by Pleadings or Stipulation

The genuineness of a document may be admitted through the discovery process, through stipulation at pretrial conference, or by a failure to deny an allegation in a pleading.

3. Evidence of Authenticity

In general, a writing may be authenticated by any evidence that serves to establish its authenticity. The Federal Rules do not limit the methods of authentication, but rather list several examples of proper authentication. [Fed. R. Evid. 901]

a. Admissions

A writing may be authenticated by evidence that the party against whom the writing is offered has either *admitted* its authenticity or *acted upon* the writing as authentic.

b. Testimony of Eyewitness

A writing may be authenticated by testimony of one who *sees it executed* or *hears it acknowledged*. Modern statutes eliminate the common law necessity of producing a subscribing witness, unless specifically required by statute. [Fed. R. Evid. 903] If testimony of a subscribing witness is required (*e.g.*, in authenticating a will), his denial or failure to recollect the execution of the writing does not preclude authentication by other evidence.

c. Handwriting Verifications

A writing may also be authenticated by evidence of the genuineness of the handwriting of the maker.

1) Nonexpert Opinion

A lay witness who has personal knowledge of the handwriting of the supposed writer may state his opinion as to whether the document is in that person's handwriting. (This is an exception to the opinion rule, *see* VI.C.1., *infra*.) Note, however, that a nonexpert cannot become familiar with the handwriting merely for the purpose of testifying.

2) Comparison of Writings

An expert witness or the trier of fact (*e.g.*, jury) can determine the genuineness of a writing by comparing the questioned writing with another writing proved to be genuine. (Note that authentication by comparison is not limited to handwriting. Fingerprints, blood, hair, clothing fibers, and numerous other things can be authenticated by comparison with authenticated specimens.)

d. Ancient Documents

Under the Federal Rules, a document may be authenticated by evidence that it:

(i) Is at least *20 years old*;

(ii) Is in such condition as to be *free from suspicion* concerning its authenticity; and

(iii) Was *found in a place* where such writing, if authentic, would likely be kept.

1) Federal Rules Distinguished from Majority of Jurisdictions

The Federal Rules apply to *all writings*. However, most jurisdictions limit the ancient documents rule to *dispositive instruments* (*e.g.*, deeds, wills, etc.). In addition, most courts require that such documents be over *30 years old*.

e. Reply Letter Doctrine

A writing may be authenticated by evidence that it was written in response to a communication sent to the claimed author. The content of the letter must make it unlikely that it was written by anyone other than the claimed author of the writing.

f. Circumstantial Evidence in General

The rules for ancient documents and reply letters, above, involve authentication by circumstantial evidence. A complete list of ways to authenticate by circumstantial evidence would be impossible. Any proof tending in reason to *establish genuineness* is sufficient. For example, authentication may be established by the content of the writing and a showing that it contains information known only to the purported author. Alternatively it may be demonstrated that the author had the disputed writing in his custody at a prior time under circumstances evidencing his belief in its genuineness.

g. Photographs

1) Accurate Representation of Facts

As a general rule, photographs are admissible only if identified by a witness as a portrayal of certain facts relevant to the issue and verified by the witness as a correct representation of those facts. It suffices if the witness who identifies the photograph is familiar with the scene or object that is depicted. In general, it is **not necessary to call the photographer** to authenticate the photograph.

2) Unattended Camera—Proper Operation of Camera

In some situations, a photograph will portray an event that was observed by the camera. For example, an unmanned surveillance camera may produce a photograph of a burglar taken at a time when no other person was on the premises. Such a photograph may be admitted upon a showing that the camera was properly operating at the relevant time and that the photograph was developed from film obtained from that camera.

h. X-Ray Pictures, Electrocardiograms, Etc.

Unlike photographs, an X-ray picture cannot be authenticated by testimony of a witness that it is a correct representation of the facts. Therefore, a different procedure of authentication is necessary. First, it must be shown that the **process used is accurate** (as to X-rays, the court will usually take judicial notice of this). Then it must be shown that the **machine itself was in working order** and the **operator was qualified** to operate it. Finally, a **custodial chain** must be established to forestall the danger that the evidence has been substituted or tampered with.

4. Compare—Authentication of Oral Statements

Oral statements often require authentication as to the **identity of the speaker**. Although this is technically a "relevance" topic, the rules are the same as those that apply to the authenticity of documents.

a. When Necessary

Not all oral statements need to be authenticated; only where the identity of the speaker is important (*e.g.,* admission by a party) is authentication required.

b. Methods of Authentication

1) Voice Identification

A voice, whether heard firsthand or through a device (*e.g.,* a tape recording) may be identified by the opinion of anyone who has heard the voice at **any time**. Thus, in contrast to the rule for handwriting verification, a person can become familiar with a voice after litigation has begun and for the sole purpose of testifying.

2) Telephone Conversations

Statements made during a telephone conversation may be authenticated by one of the parties to the call who testifies to one of the following:

a) He recognized the other party's voice.

b) The speaker has knowledge of certain facts that only a particular person would have.

c) He called, for example, Mr. A's telephone number, and a voice answered, "This is Mr. A" or "This is the A residence." This authenticates the conversation as being with Mr. A or his agent.

d) He called the person's business establishment and talked with the person answering the phone about matters relevant to the business. This is sufficient to show that the person answering the phone held a position in the business.

5. Self-Authenticating Documents

Contrary to the general rule, which requires testimonial sponsorship, there are certain writings that are said to "prove themselves" or to be "self-identifying" on their face. Federal Rule 902 specifically provides that extrinsic evidence of authenticity as a condition to admissibility is not required as to the following:

a. Certified copies of *public records*;

b. *Official publications* (*i.e.,* books, pamphlets, or other publications purporting to be issued by a public authority);

c. Printed materials purporting to be *newspapers or periodicals*;

d. *Trade inscriptions,* signs, tags, or labels purporting to have been affixed in the course of business and indicating ownership, control, or origin;

e. *Documents accompanied by a certificate of acknowledgment* executed in the manner provided by law by a notary public or other officer authorized by law to take acknowledgments;

f. *Commercial paper,* signatures thereon, and documents relating thereto, to the extent provided by general commercial law; and

g. *Business records* certified as such by a custodian or other qualified person.

C. BEST EVIDENCE RULE

The best evidence rule is more accurately called the *"original document rule."* It may be stated as follows: In proving the terms of a writing (recording, photograph, or X-ray), where the terms are material, the original writing must be produced. Secondary evidence of the writing, such as oral testimony regarding the writing's contents, is permitted only after it has been shown that the original is unavailable for some reason other than the serious misconduct of the proponent. [Fed. R. Evid. 1002]

1. Rule Expresses Preference for Originals

Simply stated, the rule applies to writings and expresses a preference for originals. It reflects the belief that the exact words of a writing, particularly in the case of operative or dispositive instruments such as contracts, deeds, or wills, should be presented to the court; that there is a hazard of inaccuracy in common methods of approximating the contents of a writing; and that oral testimony based on memory of the terms of the writing presents greater risk of error than oral testimony concerning other situations.

2. Applicability of the Rule

For the most part, the rule applies to two classes of situations: (i) where the writing is a *legally operative or dispositive instrument* such as a contract, deed, will, or divorce decree; or (ii) where the *knowledge of a witness* concerning a fact results from having *read* it in the document.

Examples:

1) Witness may not testify about the content of a written deed unless sufficient reason is given for not producing the original deed.

2) Witness who memorized mileage recorded on car sticker for a certain date, and who had no other source of knowledge on this significant litigated issue, may not testify as to the mileage without establishing a reason for the unavailability of the writing.

3. Nonapplicability of the Rule

a. Fact to Be Proved Exists Independently of Any Writing

Where the fact to be proved has an existence independent of any writing, the best evidence rule does not apply. Therefore, the rule does not apply to all events that happen to have been memorialized by documents. There are many writings that the substantive law does not regard as essential repositories of the facts recorded. These writings happen to record details of essentially nonwritten transactions. As to these, oral testimony may be given without production of, or explanation for the absence of, the original writings.

Examples:

1) Witness may testify orally that he paid for goods received without producing the receipt that was given.

2) Facts such as birth, marriage, age, and death may be proved orally, although certificates evidencing these facts are in existence. However, since a divorce is effective only by a judicial decree, the best evidence rule requires that the fact of divorce be proved by the decree itself.

3) Testimony heard at a prior trial may be testified to in another case without production of the stenographic transcript of the prior testimony. One who heard the prior testimony can repeat it.

4) Admissions or confessions of a party may be testified to orally by anyone who heard them, even though the admissions or confessions were later reduced to writing.

The above examples are in contrast to those writings that are considered as essential repositories of the facts recorded. Written contracts, deeds, wills, and judgments are viewed as such repositories—they are considered written transactions—and as such are within the rule.

b. Writing Is Collateral to Litigated Issue

Any narration by a witness is likely to include references to transactions consisting partly of written communications. The best evidence rule does not apply to writings of minor importance (*i.e.*, ones that are collateral) to the matter in controversy. [Fed. R. Evid. 1004(4)] For example, an expert witness testifying on the value of a car is allowed to establish his status as a car dealer without production of his dealer's license. The test of "collateralness" is likely to take into account:

1) *Centrality* of the writing to the major issues of a litigation;

2) *Complexity* of the relevant features of the writing; and

3) Existence of a *genuine dispute* as to the contents of the writing.

c. Summaries of Voluminous Records

When it would be inconvenient to examine a voluminous collection of writings, recordings, or photographs in court, the proponent may present their contents in the form of a chart, summary, or calculation. [Fed. R. Evid. 1006] However, the originals or duplicates (*see* 4.c., *infra*) must be made available for examination and copying, and the judge may order them to be produced in court.

d. Public Records

The best evidence rule is modified so that a proponent may offer into evidence a copy of an official record or a copy of a document that has been recorded and filed. Such a copy must be *certified as correct* by the custodian of the document or other person authorized to do so, or *testified to be correct* by a person who compared it to the original. [Fed. R. Evid. 1005] The purpose of this exception is to prevent the loss or absence of public documents due to litigation.

4. Definitions of "Writings," "Original," and "Duplicate"

a. Writings, Recordings, and Photographs

The Federal Rules govern writings, recordings, and photographs. Writings and recordings are defined broadly as "letters, words, or numbers, or their equivalent; set down by handwriting, typewriting, printing, photostating, photographing, magnetic impulse, mechanical or electronic recording, or other form of data compilation." Photographs are more narrowly defined as "still photographs, X-ray films, and motion pictures." [Fed. R. Evid. 1001]

b. "Original"

An original is the writing or recording itself or any duplicate intended by the person executing it to have the same effect as an original.

Example: D types a ribbon and one carbon of a letter that is defamatory to P. D sends a ribbon copy to P himself and the carbon to the newspaper. In P's defamation action, the document legally operative to create tort liability was the "published" carbon, not the ribbon copy.

c. Admissibility of Duplicates

The Federal Rules define a duplicate as "a counterpart produced by the same impression as the original, or from the same matrix, or by means of photography . . . or by mechanical or electronic re-recording, or by chemical reproduction, or by other equivalent techniques which accurately reproduce the original." [Fed. R. Evid. 1001(4)] A duplicate is thus an *exact copy of an original*, *e.g.*, a carbon copy or photocopy. Duplicates are *admissible* the same as originals in federal courts, *unless* (i) the authenticity of the original is challenged, or (ii) under the circumstances, it would be unfair to admit the duplicate in place of the original. [Fed. R. Evid. 1003] The rationale for admitting duplicates under such a relaxed standard is that by definition these documents are exact copies of the original, and therefore their introduction into evidence would be objectionable only if some question existed as to the genuineness of the original.

5. Admissibility of Secondary Evidence of Contents

If the proponent cannot produce the original writing or recording in court, he may offer secondary evidence of its contents in the form of copies (*e.g.*, handwritten copies, which would not be considered duplicates because they are not exact copies), notes, or oral testimony about the contents of the original if a satisfactory explanation is given for the nonproduction of the original.

a. Satisfactory Foundation

A valid excuse justifying the admissibility of secondary evidence would include:

1) Loss or Destruction of Original

A proper foundation for the admissibility of secondary evidence is laid by a showing that the original has been lost and cannot be found despite diligent search, or was destroyed in good faith.

2) Original Outside Jurisdiction and Unobtainable

If the document is within the jurisdiction, it must be subpoenaed. If not, some reasonable effort or request to the third party for production must be shown before secondary evidence will be admitted. A proper foundation is laid, however, if it is shown that the original is (i) in the possession of a third party, (ii) outside the jurisdiction, and (iii) unobtainable.

3) Original in Possession of Adversary Who, After Notice, Fails to Produce

If the opponent has custody of the original, a showing of his custody, service of a timely notice to produce, and his failure to produce it in court will justify the admissibility of secondary evidence. Where the pleadings give notice to the opposite party that he will be charged with possession of the writing, service of the notice to produce is unnecessary.

b. No Degrees of Secondary Evidence

The Federal Rules recognize no degrees of secondary evidence. Once a satisfactory explanation for nonproduction of the original is established, the party seeking to prove the contents of a writing, photograph, or recording may do so by any kind of secondary evidence ranging from handwritten copies to oral testimony. This abolition of degrees of secondary evidence is a departure from the rule existing in most American jurisdictions. [Fed. R. Evid. 1004]

c. Testimony or Written Admission of Party

A proponent may prove the contents of a writing, recording, or photograph through the testimony, deposition, or written admission of the party against whom it is offered, and need not account for the nonproduction of the original. [Fed. R. Evid. 1007] However, it is also generally held that the *contents* of a writing, photograph, etc., *cannot be proved simply by out-of-court oral admissions* of the party against whom such evidence is offered (unless of course the original is otherwise accounted for).

Example: Witness testifies, "I heard D say that the telegram he received stated . . . ." D's oral admissions outside court are inadmissible to prove the contents of the telegram. [Fed. R. Evid. 1007]

6. Functions of Court and Jury

Ordinarily, it is for the court to make the determinations of fact that determine the admissibility of duplicates, other copies, and oral testimony as to the contents of an original. However, the Federal Rules specifically reserve three questions of *preliminary fact for the jury*:

(i)   Whether the original ever existed;

(ii)   Whether a writing, recording, or photograph produced at trial is an original; and

(iii)   Whether the evidence offered correctly reflects the contents of the original.

[Fed. R. Evid. 1008]

D. PAROL EVIDENCE RULE

The essence of the parol evidence rule is as follows: If an agreement is reduced to writing, that writing is the agreement and hence constitutes the only evidence of it. All *prior or contemporaneous negotiations* or agreements *are merged* into the written agreement. Parol (extrinsic) evidence is not admissible to add to, detract from, or alter the agreement as written.

1. Substantive and Evidentiary Aspects

This rule, although actually a part of the substantive law of contracts, is also important as an evidentiary principle because of its *impact on materiality*. Prior and contemporary oral agreements are not material when offered to vary the terms of an apparently complete written contract.

2. Nonapplicability of Parol Evidence Rule

From an evidentiary standpoint, counsel invoking the rule is saying, "Here is the agreement. Its terms, having been reduced to writing by the parties, are indisputable; they cannot be put in issue. It follows that no evidence can be received in respect to those terms." This approach helps to explain why the parol evidence rule does not apply to exclude evidence of prior or contemporaneous agreements on the following issues:

a. Completion of Incomplete or Ambiguous Contract

In some situations, the written instrument may be valid but still incomplete or ambiguous. In these cases, parol evidence is admitted not to contradict or vary the writing but to complete the entire agreement of which the writing was only part. In these situations, parol evidence will be admitted if the contract does not appear on its face to be the entire agreement between the parties and the parol evidence is consistent with, and not contradictory of, the written instrument. If there is uncertainty, ambiguity, or reasonable dispute as to the meaning of contract terms, parol evidence is admissible to explain the ambiguity.

b. Reformation of Contract

Where a party alleges facts, such as mistake, entitling him to reformation of the written agreement, the parol evidence rule is inapplicable. This is so because the party is asserting that, despite the apparently unambiguous contract, its terms do not in fact constitute the agreement intended.

c. Challenge to Validity of Contract

The parol evidence rule does not bar admission of parol evidence to show that what appears to be a contractual obligation is, in fact, no obligation at all. Thus, evidence is admissible to show that the *contract was void or voidable* and has been avoided, or was made subject to a valid *condition precedent* that has not been satisfied. Specifically, parol evidence is admissible to establish or disprove a contract attacked on grounds of:

1) Fraud, duress, or undue influence inducing consent;

2) Lack of consideration;

3) Illegality of subject matter;

4) Material alteration;

5) Nondelivery, if the agreement required delivery for the instrument to be effective; or

6) Execution or delivery upon a condition precedent, as long as the parol condition does not contradict the writing. However, proof of an oral condition subsequent allegedly made at or before the time of the written contract would be barred by the rule.

3. Subsequent Modifications of Written Contract

The rule applies only to negotiations or agreements made *prior to, or at the time of,* the execution of the written contract. Parol evidence is admissible to show subsequent modification or discharge of the written contract.

VI. TESTIMONIAL EVIDENCE

A. COMPETENCY OF WITNESSES

Witnesses are not "authenticated" in the same sense as real or documentary evidence. However, they too must pass tests of basic reliability to establish their competence to give testimony. Unlike the authentication situation pertaining to real or documentary proof, witnesses are generally *presumed to be competent* until the contrary is demonstrated.

1. Basic Testimonial Qualifications

There are four basic testimonial attributes that every witness must have to some degree. These are the capacity to observe, to recollect, to communicate, and to appreciate the obligation to speak truthfully. These, along with sincerity, are the qualities at which the cross-examiner directs his skill.

A diminution of any of these capacities usually goes only to the weight of the testimony and serves to make the witness less persuasive. However, a witness can be so deficient in one or more of these basic qualifications that she will be deemed incompetent to testify at all. The problem of infancy is a good example for all aspects of the basic qualifications. A witness may be too young *at the time of the event* to be able to accurately perceive what happened or to be able to remember at the time of the trial. The witness may also be too young *at the time of the trial* to effectively relate or communicate or appreciate the obligation to tell the truth.

a. **Ability to Observe—Perception**
The issue of a witness's ability to observe may arise in the following manner: W testifies on direct to details of how an intersection automobile collision occurred. On cross-examination, W admits that her attention was directed to the intersection by the sound of the crash. The direct testimony regarding details of the accident occurring before the collision will be stricken.

b. **Ability to Remember—Memory**
An example of a witness incompetent for this reason would be one who is suffering from senility or amnesia.

c. **Ability to Relate—Communication**
The ability to relate concerns the ability of the witness to communicate effectively with the trier of fact.

d. **Appreciation of Oath Obligation**
The witness must have sufficient intelligence and character to know and desire to tell the truth. The witness may be sworn by oath or affirmation. However, unsworn testimony may be permissible if the witness (*e.g.*, a child) appreciates the obligation to tell the truth.

2. **Federal Rules of Competency**

a. **Personal Knowledge and Oath Required**
Federal Rule 601 provides that "Every person is competent to be a witness except as otherwise provided in these rules." The rules do not specify any mental or moral qualifications for witness testimony beyond these two limitations:

1) *The witness must have personal knowledge* of the matter he is to testify about. The requirement of "personal knowledge" means that the witness must have observed the matter and must have a present recollection of his observation. [Fed. R. Evid. 602]

2) *The witness must declare he will testify truthfully*, by oath or affirmation. [Fed. R. Evid. 603]

b. **Use of Interpreter**
If a witness requires an interpreter, the interpreter must be qualified and take an oath to make a true translation. [Fed. R. Evid. 604]

c. **Applicability of State Rules in Diversity Cases**
Federal Rule 601 provides that the competency of a witness shall be determined by

state law in civil actions "with respect to an element of a claim or defense as to which state law supplies the rules of decision."

3. Modern Modifications of Common Law Disqualifications

At common law there were several grounds upon which a person could be disqualified from giving testimony. Persons were incompetent to testify if they had a financial interest in the suit, if they were the spouse of a party, if they lacked religious belief, if they had been convicted of a crime, or if they lacked mental capacity. These common law disqualifications have been almost entirely removed under the Federal Rules and in the vast majority of American jurisdictions.

a. Lack of Religious Belief

Lack of religious belief is no longer a basis for excluding a witness. Not only are a person's religious convictions irrelevant in determining the competence of a witness, but they may also not be shown or commented upon for the purpose of affecting the credibility of a witness.

b. Infancy

There is *no precise age* at which an infant is deemed competent or incompetent to testify under oath. The competence of an infant depends on the capacity and intelligence of the particular child. This test is an individual one, to be determined by the trial judge upon preliminary examination.

c. Insanity

An insane person, even one who has been adjudicated incompetent, *may testify*, provided he understands the obligation to speak truthfully and possesses the capacity to give a correct account of what he has perceived in reference to the issue in dispute.

d. Conviction of Crime

The common law disqualification of felons has been removed by statute in most states. However, conviction of a crime may be shown to *affect the credibility* of the competent witness.

e. Interest

The common law disqualification of parties or interested persons has been abolished in most states. The only remaining vestiges of this disqualification are the so-called Dead Man Acts, discussed later.

f. Judge as Witness

Federal Rule 605 provides that the presiding judge *may not testify as a witness*, and that no objection need be made to preserve the point. The basis for this disqualification is that when the judge is called as a witness, her role as a witness is inconsistent with her role as presiding judge which requires her to maintain impartiality.

g. Juror as Witness

Under Federal Rule 606, jurors are *incompetent to testify* before the jury in which they are sitting. The rationale is that a juror-witness cannot impartially weigh his own testimony and cannot be thoroughly cross-examined for fear of creating antagonism.

The Federal Rule also prevents a juror from testifying in post-verdict proceedings as to matters or statements occurring during the course of jury deliberations, except that a juror may testify as to whether "extraneous prejudicial information" or any "outside influence" was brought to bear on any juror.

4. Dead Man Acts

The last remaining vestige of true incompetency of a witness appears in Dead Man Acts. These statutes exist in most jurisdictions and their provisions vary from state to state. Although there is *no Dead Man Act in the Federal Rules of Evidence*, state Dead Man Acts operate to disqualify witnesses in federal cases where state law provides the rule of decision (most diversity cases). For bar examination purposes, only generalized comments are appropriate, and there are common provisions to most Dead Man Acts that could appear in a multistate bar exam question.

a. Rationale

The Dead Man Acts generally provide that a party or person interested in the event, or his predecessor in interest, is incompetent to testify to a *personal transaction or communication with a deceased*, when such testimony is offered against the representative or successors in interest of the deceased. The rationale of the statute is to *protect estates from perjured claims*. The assumption is that the survivor claimant may lie since the deceased cannot talk back. Because death has silenced one party, the statute closes the mouth of the living person who, being interested in the litigation's outcome, wishes to testify on her own behalf against someone who is suing or defending in a representative capacity (*e.g.*, executor, administrator, heir, legatee, devisee).

b. Common Elements

Most Dead Man Acts have the following common elements and applications:

1) Applicable to Civil Cases Only

The bar to competency created by a Dead Man Act applies only to civil cases and has no application in criminal cases.

2) Protected Parties

The statute is designed to protect those who claim directly under the decedent. They usually include an executor, administrator, heir, legatee, and devisee. If a protected party is on either side of the lawsuit (suing or defending), the statute applies to prevent an interested person from testifying on his own behalf.

Examples: 1) Plaintiff sues the executor of the estate for a debt owed by the decedent. The executor is a protected party and the act applies.

2) Executor sues defendant for negligence in causing the death of the decedent. Executor is a protected party and the act applies.

3) Heir sues executor, legatees, and devisees in a will contest. Heir is a protected party, as are the adverse parties. The act applies.

3) Interested Person

A person is "interested in the event" if he stands to gain or lose by the direct and immediate operation of the judgment, or if the judgment may be used for or against him in a subsequent action. Thus, in states where a spouse has an inchoate right in the other spouse's property, both spouses may be interested and incompetent to testify. Similarly, a shareholder of a corporation and the co-maker of a note may be disqualified under the rule.

a)   Predecessor in Interest
Most Dead Man Acts disqualify not only the person interested but also the predecessor in interest.

Example: If A assigns to B a claim against Decedent, and B sues the estate, both A and B are incompetent. B is interested in the event; A is the person from, through, or under whom B derived his interest.

b)   Party Adverse to Protected Party
As a short rule of thumb, a party adverse to the protected party is always an interested person who will be rendered incompetent by the Dead Man Act. For other nonparty witnesses, ask whether the witness has a *pecuniary interest in the outcome of the case* or is a predecessor in interest with the adverse party.

4)   Exceptions and Waiver of the Act
There are numerous situations where the Dead Man Act either will not apply against an interested person or the protected party may waive its effect. Of course, if an exception applies or the statute is waived, the interested person is competent to testify. The following are common to most jurisdictions:

a)   Facts Occurring After Death
An interested person may always testify to facts that occurred *after* the death of the deceased, since the protection of the rule is not needed.

b)   "Door Openers"
The estate representatives and those claiming under the decedent may *waive the protection* of the statute. Common provisions for waiver include:

(1)   If the protected party calls the interested person to testify about the transaction, the interested person may explain all matters about which he is examined.

(2)   Where the testimony of the deceased given at a former trial or at a deposition is read in evidence, the interested person may explain all matters about which he is examined.

(3)   Where there is a failure to make timely and proper objection. Objection is to the incompetency of the witness, not to the incompetency of the testimony.

(4)   If the protected party or an agent of the deceased testifies to a transaction with an interested person, the interested person may testify about the same transaction.

B. FORM OF EXAMINATION OF WITNESS

The judge may exercise reasonable control over the examination of witnesses in order to aid the effective ascertainment of truth, to avoid wasting time, and to protect witnesses from harassment or undue embarrassment. Questions that frequently arise concerning the form of examination of witnesses are: when may leading questions be used, what other types of questions are objectionable, and when and how may a witness use memoranda.

1. Leading Questions

a. Generally Objectionable

A question is leading and generally objectionable on direct examination when it suggests to the witness the fact that the examiner expects and wants to have confirmed. Questions calling for "yes" or "no" answers and questions *framed to suggest the answer desired* are usually leading.

Example: On direct examination plaintiff is asked, "Is it true or not that at the time in question, you were driving well within the speed limit?" The question is leading.

b. When Permitted

Leading questions are permitted on *cross-examination*. Trial judges will usually allow leading questions on *direct examination* in noncrucial areas *if no objection is made:*

(i) If used to elicit *preliminary or introductory matter*;

(ii) When the witness *needs aid to respond* because of loss of memory, immaturity, or physical or mental weakness; or

(iii) When the witness is *hostile* and improperly uncooperative, an *adverse* party, or a person *identified with an adverse party*.

[Fed. R. Evid. 611(c)]

2. Improper Questions

The following types of questions are improper and are not permitted:

a. Misleading

A question is misleading and thus is not permitted if it is one that cannot be answered without making an unintended admission.

Example: "Do you still beat your wife?"

b. Compound

Questions that require a single answer to more than one question are not permitted.

Example: "Did you see and hear the intruder?"

c. Argumentative

Argumentative questions, which are leading questions that reflect the examiner's interpretation of the facts, are improper.

Example: "Why were you driving so recklessly?"

d. Conclusionary

A question that calls for an opinion or conclusion that the witness is not qualified or permitted to make is improper.

Example: "What did your friend think about that?" The witness could not know his friend's thoughts, and is not permitted to give his opinion as to his friend's thoughts.

e. Assuming Facts Not in Evidence

An attorney is not allowed to ask a question that assumes a disputed fact is true when it has not been established in the case.

Example: In a case where there is no evidence that Defendant had been drinking, the following question is improper: "After Defendant finished his fifth beer, he got up and went to his car, didn't he?"

f. Cumulative

An attorney is generally not permitted to ask a question that has already been asked and answered. More repetition is allowed on cross-examination than on direct, but if it is apparent that the cross-examiner is not moving forward, the judge may disallow the question.

g. Harassing or Embarrassing

The trial judge, in her discretion, may disallow cross-examination that is unduly harassing or embarrassing.

3. Use of Memoranda by Witness

A witness cannot read her testimony from a prepared memorandum. However, a memorandum may be used in certain circumstances to refresh the recollection of the witness, to substitute for the witness's forgotten testimony upon authentication of the memorandum, or in cross-examination of the witness.

a. Present Recollection Revived—Refreshing Recollection

A witness may use any writing or thing for the purpose of refreshing her present recollection. She usually may not read from the writing while she actually testifies, since the writing is *not authenticated*, is *not in evidence*, and may be used solely to refresh her recollection. The writing is intended to help her to recall by jogging her memory. The sworn testimony must demonstrate a *present* recollection.

b. Past Recollection Recorded—Recorded Recollection

Where a witness states that she has insufficient recollection of an event to enable her to testify fully and accurately, even after she has consulted a writing given to her on the stand, the *writing itself may be read into evidence* if a proper foundation is laid for its admissibility. This use of a memorandum as evidence of a past recollection is frequently classified as an *exception to the hearsay rule*. The foundation for receipt of the writing into evidence must include proof that:

(i) The witness at one time had *personal knowledge* of the facts recited in the writing;

(ii) The writing was *made by the witness* or made *under her direction* or that it was *adopted by the witness*;

(iii) The writing was *timely made* when the matter was fresh in the mind of the witness;

(iv) The writing is *accurate* (*i.e.,* witness must vouch for the accuracy of the writing); and

(v) The witness has *insufficient recollection* to testify fully and accurately.

Remember that, under the Federal Rule, if admitted, the writing may be read into evidence and heard by the jury, but *the document itself is not received* as an exhibit unless offered by the adverse party. [Fed. R. Evid. 803(5)]

c. Inspection and Use in Cross-Examination
Under Federal Rule 612, whenever a witness has used a writing to refresh her memory on the stand, an adverse party is entitled to have the writing produced at trial, to inspect it, to cross-examine the witness thereon, and to introduce into evidence those portions that relate to the witness's testimony. If the witness has refreshed her memory before trial by looking at the writing, it is within the court's discretion to require production of the document and to permit inspection, cross-examination, and introduction of pertinent excerpts.

As noted above, under Federal Rule 803(5), an adverse party may introduce into evidence a writing that the proponent has read into evidence as past recollection recorded.

C. OPINION TESTIMONY
The word opinion used in this context includes all opinions, inferences, conclusions, and other subjective statements made by a witness. A basic premise of our legal system is that, in general, witnesses should testify as to facts within their personal knowledge and that the trier of fact should draw any conclusions therefrom. Therefore, the general policy of the law is to restrict the admissibility of opinion evidence, except in cases where the courts are sure that it will be necessary or at least helpful. Of course, the difference between "fact" and "opinion" is a matter of degree. Therefore, there cannot be any clear-cut opinion rule.

1. Opinion Testimony by Lay Witnesses

a. General Rule of Inadmissibility
Opinions by lay witnesses are generally inadmissible. However, there are many cases where, from the nature of the subject matter, no better evidence can be obtained. In these cases, where the event is likely to be perceived as a whole impression (*e.g.,* intoxication, speed) rather than as more specific components, opinions by lay witnesses are generally admitted.

b. When Admissible
In most jurisdictions and under the Federal Rules, opinion testimony by lay witnesses is admissible when:

(i) It is rationally *based on the perception of the witness;*

(ii) It is ***helpful to a clear understanding*** of her testimony or to the determination of a fact in issue; and

(iii) It is ***not based on scientific, technical, or other specialized knowledge*** (if so based, the witness's testimony would need to meet the requirements for expert testimony stated in Rule 702, *see* 2.a., *infra*).

[Fed. R. Evid. 701]

Example: Think how much easier and clearer it is for a witness to say someone looked "drunk" than it is to describe her gait, speech, eyes, diction, breath, and manner. All these things can also be brought out, but the term "drunk" may be more meaningful than any of them.

Some jurisdictions are stricter and allow lay opinion testimony only in cases of "necessity" when it is difficult for the witness to express her perception in any form other than opinion.

c. Procedure

Unless waived by a failure to object, a proper foundation must be laid by showing that the witness had the opportunity to observe the event that forms the basis of her opinion. Additionally, the court in its discretion may require a witness to state the facts observed before stating her opinion.

d. Situations Where Opinions of Lay Witnesses Are Admissible

1) General Appearance or Condition of a Person

Testimony that a person was "elderly," "about 60 years old," "strong," "weak," or "ill" would be admissible, but testimony that a person is suffering from specific diseases or specific injuries usually requiring knowledge of an expert would not.

2) State of Emotion

A witness would be permitted to testify that a person appeared "angry" or "was joking" but probably not that two persons were "in love" or appeared to have a strong affection for each other.

3) Matters Involving Sense Recognition

A witness would be permitted to testify that an object was "heavy," "red," "bulky," or that a certain beverage tasted like whiskey.

4) Voice or Handwriting Identification

Lay opinion is permissible and often essential to identify telephone voices and handwriting. In these instances a foundation must first be laid to show familiarity with the voice or handwriting.

5) Speed of Moving Object

A witness may estimate in miles per hour the speed of a moving object but must first show some experience in observing the rate of speed of moving objects. Characterization that a vehicle was going "fast" or "very fast" has been permitted.

6) Value of Own Services

A witness may give her opinion as to the value of her own services.

7) Rational or Irrational Nature of Another's Conduct (Sanity)

In many jurisdictions, a witness is permitted to state her opinion as to the sanity of another person. Some states limit these opinions to testimony describing the acts of a person whose sanity is in question and allow the witness to state only whether those acts impressed her at the time as rational or irrational (*e.g.*, "She acted like a madwoman").

8) Intoxication

A witness who has seen a person and is able to describe that person's actions, words, or conduct, may express an opinion as to whether that person was or was not intoxicated. In many states, the details of the person's appearance must be given as a foundation for the opinion.

Example: In Defendant's trial on a charge of driving while intoxicated, Witness testifies for the prosecution that Defendant "smelled of alcohol, his speech was incoherent, his eyes glassy and bloodshot, he could not stand or walk without assistance, he was slumped over the wheel of his vehicle," and, finally, that he "was intoxicated."

e.   Situations Where Opinions of Lay Witnesses Are Not Admissible

1) Agency or Authorization

When agency or authorization is in issue, the witness generally may not state a conclusion as to her authorization. Rather she must be asked by whom she was employed and the nature, terms, and surrounding circumstances of her employment.

2) Contract or Agreement

When the existence of an express contract is in issue, a witness generally may not state her opinion that an agreement was made. Rather she must be asked about the facts, the existence or nonexistence of which establish whether a contract existed.

2.   Opinion Testimony by Expert Witnesses

a.   Requirements of Expert Testimony

The expert may state an opinion or conclusion, provided the following conditions are satisfied:

1) Subject Matter Must Be Appropriate for Expert Testimony

Under Federal Rule 702, expert opinion testimony is admissible if the subject matter is one where scientific, technical, or other specialized knowledge would assist the trier of fact in understanding the evidence or determining a fact in issue. This test of assistance to the trier of fact subdivides into two requirements:

(i)   The opinion must be *relevant* (*i.e.*, it must "fit" the facts of the case); and

(ii) The methodology underlying the opinion must be *reliable* (*i.e.*, the proponent of the expert testimony must satisfy the trial judge by a preponderance of the evidence that (a) the opinion is based on sufficient facts or data; (b) the opinion is the product of reliable principles and methods; and (c) the expert has reliably applied the principles and methods to the facts of the case).

[Fed. R. Evid. 702; *and see* Kumho Tire Co. v. Carmichael, 526 U.S. 137 (1999); Daubert v. Merrell Dow Pharmaceuticals, Inc., 509 U.S. 579 (1993)]

2) Witness Must Be Qualified as an Expert

To testify as an expert, a person must have special knowledge, skill, experience, training, or education sufficient to qualify him as an expert on the subject to which his testimony relates. [Fed. R. Evid. 702]

3) Expert Must Possess Reasonable Probability Regarding His Opinion

The expert must possess reasonable certainty or probability regarding his opinion. If the opinion of the expert is a mere guess or speculation, it is inadmissible.

Example: It would be error to permit plaintiff's medical expert to testify that plaintiff's symptoms "suggested" diabetes and "indicated" that the disease was caused by the accident.

4) Opinion Must Be Supported by Proper Factual Basis

The expert's opinion may be based upon one or more of these three possible sources of information: (i) facts that the expert knows from his own observation; (ii) facts presented in evidence at the trial and submitted to the expert, usually by hypothetical question; or (iii) facts not in evidence that were supplied to the expert out of court, and which are of a type reasonably relied upon by experts in the particular field in forming opinions on the subject. Note that the expert may give opinion testimony on direct examination without disclosing the basis of the opinion, unless the court orders otherwise. However, the expert may be required to disclose such information on cross-examination. [Fed. R. Evid. 705]

a) Personal Observation

If the expert has examined the person or thing about which he is testifying, he may relate those facts observed by him and upon which he bases his opinion. [Fed. R. Evid. 703]

Example: An expert may testify that he examined plaintiff's leg following the accident, and in his opinion the plaintiff sustained a compound fracture.

b) Facts Made Known to Expert at Trial

The expert's opinion may be based upon the evidence introduced at the trial and related to the expert by counsel in the form of a *hypothetical question*. The hypothetical question may be based on facts derived from any of the three sources of information noted above. Federal Rule 705 adopts the modern trend in providing that the hypothetical question need not be asked.

c) Facts Made Known to Expert Outside Court

Under Federal Rule 703, the expert may base an opinion upon facts not known personally but supplied to him outside the courtroom (*e.g.*, reports of nurses, technicians, or consultants). The Federal Rule further provides that such facts ***need not be in evidence or even of a type admissible*** in evidence, as long as the facts are of a kind ***reasonably relied upon*** by experts in the particular field. However, if the facts are of a type inadmissible in evidence, the proponent of the expert opinion must ***not*** disclose those facts to the jury unless the court determines that their probative value in assisting the jury to evaluate the expert's opinion ***substantially*** outweighs their prejudicial effect.

> *Example:* A physician bases his expert opinion upon (i) a personal examination of the patient, (ii) statements by the patient as to her medical history, and (iii) medically germane statements by the patient's relatives. The results of the personal examination are admissible and may therefore be relied upon by the physician because they are relevant, material, based on personal knowledge, and not subject to any exclusionary rule. The statements of the patient are admissible through an exception to the hearsay rule. The statements by the relatives, though inadmissible hearsay, may properly form a basis for a physician's expert opinion testimony because they are the facts reasonably relied upon by physicians in making a diagnosis; however, these statements should not be disclosed to the jury without the court first finding that their probative value substantially outweighs prejudice.

b. Opinion May Embrace Ultimate Issue

Federal Rule 704(a) and the modern trend repudiate the traditional prohibition on opinions embracing the ultimate issue in the case. The rule provides: "Testimony in the form of an opinion or inference otherwise admissible is not objectionable because it embraces the ultimate issue to be decided by the trier of fact." Note, however, that to be admissible under the Federal Rules, the expert opinion must "assist the trier of fact" to understand the evidence or determine a fact in issue. Thus, an expert's conclusion that "X had testamentary capacity" is still inadmissible because it is not helpful to the jury.

1) Exception—Criminal Defendant's Mental State

The Federal Rules *prohibit* ultimate issue testimony in one situation: In a criminal case in which the defendant's mental state constitutes an element of the crime or defense, an expert may not state an opinion as to whether the accused did or did not have the mental state in issue. [Fed. R. Evid. 704(b)]

c. Authoritative Texts and Treatises

An expert may be cross-examined concerning statements contained in any scientific publication, as long as the publication is established as reliable authority. For example, the witness may be asked, "Doesn't Dr. Killum, in his book on diseases of the pancreas, disagree with your conclusion here?" A publication may be established as reliable by: (i) the direct testimony or cross-examination admission of the expert, (ii) the testimony of another expert, or (iii) judicial notice. Thus, even if the expert refuses to recognize the text as authoritative, it can be used on cross-examination if its reliability is established by one of the other methods.

The Federal Rules have expanded the admissibility of learned texts and treatises beyond impeachment of experts. Statements from an established treatise may be read into the record as substantive evidence, and may even be introduced on direct examination of a party's own expert. [Fed. R. Evid. 803(18)—exception to hearsay rule] There are two important limitations: (i) an expert must be on the stand when a statement from a treatise is read into evidence; and (ii) the relevant portion is read into evidence but is not received as an exhibit (*i.e.,* the jury never sees it).

D. CROSS-EXAMINATION

1. Necessity for Cross-Examination

Cross-examination of adverse witnesses is a matter of right in every trial of a disputed issue of fact. It is recognized as the ***most efficacious truth-discovering device***. The principal basis for excluding hearsay is that the declarant whose testimony is offered cannot be subjected to the test of cross-examination. If adequate cross-examination is prevented by the death, illness, or refusal of a witness to testify on cross-examination, the direct examination is rendered incompetent and will be stricken.

2. Scope of Cross-Examination

Although a party is entitled as of right to some cross-examination, the extent or scope of cross-examination, like the order of calling witnesses, is frequently a matter of judicial discretion. Cross-examination is hedged about by far fewer rules than is direct examination. On cross-examination, leading questions are permissible, as are, obviously, efforts at impeachment. The most significant restriction is that the scope of cross-examination cannot range beyond the subject matter of the direct examination. This restriction does not apply to inquiries directed toward impeachment of the witness.

a. Restrictions on Scope

Under Federal Rule 611(b) and in the majority of American jurisdictions, ***cross-examination is limited to***: (i) matters brought out on ***direct examination*** and the inferences naturally drawn from those matters, and (ii) matters affecting the ***credibility of the witness***.

b. Significance of Restrictions

The question of the proper scope of cross-examination is important since it affects the ***right to use leading questions***. And, in jurisdictions that do not allow a party to impeach his own witness, going beyond the scope of direct examination means that you have made the witness "your own witness" and therefore cannot impeach his testimony. Further, if the party placing a witness on the stand is the holder of a privilege, the court may hold it waived to the extent that the other party may engage in cross-examination; therefore, the scope of cross-examination permitted may determine to what extent the cross-examining party may inquire into privileged material.

c. Collateral Matters

The general rule is that the cross-examiner is ***bound by the answers of the witness*** to questions concerning collateral matters. Thus the cross-examiner cannot refute the response of the witness by producing extrinsic evidence. Indeed some federal courts resolve the matter under Rule 403 by treating the evidence on the collateral matter as being substantially outweighed by time considerations and the danger of confusion of the issues. Certain matters of impeachment, however, are recognized as sufficiently important to merit development by extrinsic evidence (*e.g.*, bias or interest of the witness may be shown by other evidence even if denied by the witness on cross-examination). Other matters of impeachment are limited solely to inquiry on cross-examination (*e.g.*, prior misconduct of the witness not resulting in conviction but affecting the witness's credibility). Once beyond recognized impeachment techniques, the test as to what is "collateral" is sufficiently vague to permit a wide exercise of discretion by the trial judge.

E. CREDIBILITY—IMPEACHMENT

Impeachment means the casting of an adverse reflection on the veracity of the witness. The primary method of impeachment is by cross-examination of the witness under attack, although witnesses are often impeached by extrinsic proof that casts doubt on credibility. In terms of relevance, any matter that tends to prove or disprove the credibility of the witness should be admitted here.

1. Accrediting or Bolstering

a. General Rule—No Bolstering Until Witness Impeached

A party may not bolster or accredit the testimony of his witness until the witness has been impeached.

Example: A prior statement made by W at the time of the event that is consistent with W's in-court testimony would not be admissible to show that W's memory of the event is excellent or that he told the same story twice and therefore is especially worthy of belief.

b. Exceptions

The rule against accrediting is subject to exception where timeliness may raise an inference on the substantive issues of the case.

1) Timely Complaint

In certain cases a party may prove that the witness made a timely complaint, in order to bolster the party's credibility.

Examples: 1) Evidence of a prompt complaint of a rape victim is admissible to bolster the complainant's credibility in a subsequent criminal prosecution.

2) Where a defendant in a criminal trial claims that a confession offered against him was obtained by coercion, he may show that he complained of mistreatment at the first suitable opportunity.

2) Prior Identification

Evidence of any prior statement of identification made by a witness is admissible not only to bolster the witness's testimony but also as substantive evidence that the identification was correct. [Fed. R. Evid. 801(d)(1)(C); *and see* VII.B.1., *infra*]

2. Any Party May Impeach

Contrary to the traditional rule, under which a party could not impeach his own witness, the Federal Rules provide that the credibility of a witness may be attacked by any party, *including the party calling him*. [Fed. R. Evid. 607] Even under the traditional rule, however, a party could impeach his own witness if the witness: (i) was an adverse party, (ii) was hostile, (iii) was one required to be called by law, or (iv) gave damaging surprise testimony.

3. Impeachment Methods—Cross-Examination and Extrinsic Evidence

A witness may be impeached either by cross-examination (by eliciting facts from the witness that discredit his own testimony) or by extrinsic evidence (by putting other witnesses on the stand who will introduce facts discrediting his testimony).

There are certain well-recognized, often-used impeachment methods. These traditional impeachment devices include: the use of prior inconsistent statements; a showing of bias or interest in the litigation; an attack on the character of the witness by showing convictions of crime, prior acts of misconduct, or poor reputation for veracity; and a showing of sensory deficiencies. The basic questions for each of these methods are: Is the examiner limited to impeachment by cross-examination alone or may he produce extrinsic evidence? If extrinsic evidence is permissible, must a foundation first be laid by inquiry on cross-examination?

a. Prior Inconsistent Statements

For the purpose of impeaching the credibility of a witness, a party may show that the witness has, on another occasion, made statements that are inconsistent with some material part of his present testimony. Under the Federal Rules, an inconsistent statement may be proved by either cross-examination or extrinsic evidence. To prove the statement by extrinsic evidence, certain requirements must first be met: (i) a *proper foundation* must be laid; and (ii) the statement must be *relevant* to some issue in the case, *i.e.*, it cannot be a "collateral matter."

1) Laying a Foundation

Extrinsic evidence of the witness's prior inconsistent statement is admissible only if the witness is, at some point, given an *opportunity to explain or deny* the allegedly inconsistent statement. (The opportunity need not come before introduction of the statement under the Federal Rules.) This foundation requirement may be dispensed with, however, where "the interests of justice otherwise require" (as where the witness has left the stand and is not available when his prior inconsistent statement is discovered). [Fed. R. Evid. 613(b)] The courts generally agree that inconsistent statements by a hearsay declarant may be used to impeach the declarant despite the lack of a foundation (obviously, where the declarant is not a witness no foundation could be laid anyway). [Fed. R. Evid. 806]

2) Evidentiary Effect of Prior Inconsistent Statements

In most cases, prior inconsistent statements are hearsay, admissible only to impeach the witness. However, where the statement was made *under oath at a prior trial, hearing, or other proceeding, or in a deposition, it is admissible non-hearsay* (*i.e.*, it may be considered as substantive proof of the facts stated!). (*See* VII.B.1., *infra*.)

b. Bias or Interest

Evidence that a witness is biased or has an interest in the outcome of a suit tends to show that the witness has a *motive to lie*. A witness may always be impeached by extrinsic evidence of bias or interest, provided a proper foundation is laid. Note that evidence that is substantively inadmissible may be admitted for impeachment purposes if relevant to show bias or interest.

Examples: 1) It may be shown that a witness is being paid to testify, that a witness is financing the case, or that he otherwise has a financial interest in the outcome of the litigation.

2) Inferences of bias may be shown by evidence of family or other relationship, business relationship, or by conduct or expressions of the witness demonstrating a friendship toward a party.

3) In a criminal case, it is proper for the defense to ask a prosecution witness whether he has been promised immunity from punishment for testifying, whether an indictment is pending against him, or whether he is on parole. This evidence may show a motive for the witness to curry the favor of the state.

4) Hostility toward a party may be shown by adverse statements against the party, or by the fact that the witness had a fight or quarrel with him or has a lawsuit pending against him.

1) Foundation

Most courts require that before a witness can be impeached by extrinsic evidence of bias or interest, he must first be asked about the facts that show bias or interest on cross-examination. If the witness on cross-examination admits the facts claimed to show bias or interest, it is within the trial judge's discretion to decide whether extrinsic evidence may be introduced as further proof of bias or interest.

2) Justification for Bias

Even though it is shown that a witness is biased, no evidence may be admitted to show that he was justified in his bias. This might make him look more reasonable, but is not very relevant to whether his bias might make him less credible.

c. Conviction of Crime

Under certain circumstances, a witness may be impeached by proof of conviction of a crime. [Fed. R. Evid. 609] The fact that the witness (including a defendant who testifies in a criminal case) has been convicted of a crime may usually be proved by either eliciting an admission on cross-examination or by the record of conviction.

1) Actual Conviction Required

This type of impeachment requires an actual conviction of a crime. The fact that the witness has been arrested or indicted may not be elicited here.

2) Type of Crime

a) Crime Involving Dishonesty

Under the Federal Rules, a witness may be impeached by *any crime* (felony or misdemeanor) ***involving dishonesty*** (deceit) ***or a false statement***. The trial court has no discretion—not even under Federal Rule 403—to disallow impeachment by such crimes.

b)   Felony Not Involving Dishonesty

A witness may also be impeached, under the Federal Rules, by ***any felony*** whether or not it involves dishonesty or a false statement. However, if the felony is one that does not involve dishonesty or false statement, the trial court may exercise discretion to exclude it under one of the following standards.

(1)   Accused in Criminal Case

If, in a criminal case, the witness being impeached is the accused, the felony conviction will be admitted only if the government shows that its probative value as impeachment evidence outweighs its prejudicial effect.

(2)   Witness Other than Accused in Criminal Case

In the case of any witness other than the accused in a criminal case, any felony conviction is admissible, but the court retains discretion under Rule 403 to exclude it if its probative value as impeachment evidence is ***substantially outweighed*** by the danger of unfair prejudice.

(3)   Compare the Balancing Tests

Note that under Federal Rule 609, different balancing tests apply for the exercise of discretion. If the felony conviction is offered to impeach the accused in a criminal case, the discretionary standard (*supra*) favors exclusion since the probative value of the felony (not involving dishonesty or false statement) must outweigh prejudice. In the case of ***all*** other witnesses, the balancing test favors admission since the conviction will be excluded only if the danger of prejudice substantially outweighs its probative value.

3)   Must Not Be Too Remote

Under the ***Federal Rules***, a conviction is usually too remote and inadmissible if ***more than 10 years*** have elapsed since the date of ***conviction*** or the date of ***release*** from the confinement imposed for the conviction, whichever is the later date. In extraordinary circumstances, such convictions can be admitted, but only if the trial judge determines that the probative value of the conviction substantially outweighs its prejudicial effect, and the adverse party is given notice that the conviction is to be used as impeachment. [Fed. R. Evid. 609(b)]

4)   Juvenile Adjudication Generally Not Admissible

Juvenile offenses are generally not admissible for impeachment purposes. However, under the Federal Rules, a judge has the discretion in a criminal case to admit evidence of a juvenile offense committed by a witness other than the accused if the evidence would be admissible to attack the credibility of an adult and if the evidence is necessary to a determination of the accused's guilt or innocence. [Fed. R. Evid. 609(d); Davis v. Alaska, 415 U.S. 308 (1974)]

5) **Effect of Pardon Depends on Basis**

In most states, a conviction may be shown even though the witness has subsequently been pardoned. Under the Federal Rules, however, the conviction may not be shown if the pardon was based on innocence or if the person pardoned has not been convicted of a subsequent crime punishable by death or imprisonment in excess of one year. [Fed. R. Evid. 609(c)]

6) **Pending Appeal Does Not Affect Admissibility**

In most jurisdictions and under the Federal Rules, a conviction may be used to impeach even though an appeal is pending, though the pendency of the appeal may also be shown. [Fed. R. Evid. 609(e)]

7) **Constitutionally Defective Conviction Invalid for All Purposes**

Where the prior felony conviction was obtained in violation of the defendant's Sixth Amendment rights (*e.g.*, to have counsel, to confront witness, etc.), the conviction is generally invalid for all purposes—including impeachment.

8) **Means of Proof—Extrinsic Evidence Permitted**

A prior conviction may be shown either by the *cross-examination* of the witness or by *introducing a record* of the judgment. *No foundation need be laid*. Note, however, that when a witness is being cross-examined about previous convictions, the questions must be asked in good faith (*i.e.*, with a reasonable belief as to the existence of the conviction). Improper questioning may be grounds for a mistrial.

d. **Specific Instances of Misconduct—Bad Acts**

1) **General Rule—Interrogation Permitted**

The traditional majority view is that, subject to discretionary control of the trial judge, a witness may be interrogated upon cross-examination with respect to any immoral, vicious, or criminal act of his life that may *affect his character* and show him to be *unworthy of belief*. Inquiry into "bad acts" is permitted even though the witness was never convicted. Federal Rule 608 permits such inquiry, in the discretion of the court, only if the act of misconduct is *probative of truthfulness* (*i.e.,* is an act of deceit or lying).

2) **Counsel Must Inquire in Good Faith**

The cross-examiner must act in good faith with some reasonable basis for believing that the witness may have committed the "bad act" inquired about.

Example: It would be error for the prosecution to inquire about an act when the prosecutor knows that the witness has been tried for the act and acquitted.

3) **Extrinsic Evidence Not Permitted**

Extrinsic evidence of "bad acts" is not permitted. A specific act of misconduct relevant to impair credibility can be elicited *only on cross-examination* of the witness. If the witness denies the act, the cross-examiner cannot refute the answer by calling other witnesses or producing other evidence. It is not usually improper for the cross-examiner, acting in good faith, to continue the cross-examination after a denial in the hope that the witness will change his answer.

e. **Opinion or Reputation Evidence for Truth**

1) **By Proof of Reputation**

A witness may be impeached by showing that she has a poor reputation for truthfulness. The usual method of impeachment is to ask other witnesses about her general reputation for truth and veracity in the community in which she lives. The modern view is to allow evidence of reputation in business circles as well as in the community in which the witness resides.

2) **By Opinion Evidence**

Most states do not allow the impeaching witness to state her opinion as to the character of a witness for truth and veracity. However, the *Federal Rules allow* an impeaching witness to state her personal opinions, based upon acquaintance, as to the truthfulness of the witness sought to be impeached. [Fed. R. Evid. 608(a)]

f. **Sensory Deficiencies**

A witness may be impeached by showing that he had no knowledge of the facts to which he testified, or that his faculties of perception and recollection were so impaired as to make it doubtful that he could have perceived those facts. Such a showing can be made either *on cross-examination or by the use of extrinsic evidence*.

1) **Defects of Capacity**

a) **Perceptive Disabilities**

It is, of course, proper to show deficiencies of the senses, such as deafness or color blindness, that would have substantially impaired the witness's ability to perceive the facts to which he testifies. It may also be shown that at the time the witness observed the events his perception was temporarily diminished (*e.g.*, that he was sleepy or under the influence of alcohol or drugs).

b) **Lack of Memory**

A witness can be impeached by showing that he has a poor memory of the events about which he testifies. This is usually done on cross-examination by asking the witness about other related matters to suggest the inference that if his memory of related matters is poor, his recollection of the events to which he is testifying is doubtful.

c) **Mental Disorders**

Psychiatric evidence of a mental disorder that would affect a witness's credibility has been admitted by some courts (particularly in sex offense cases).

2) **Lack of Knowledge**

a) **Expert Witnesses**

The credibility of an expert witness may be attacked by cross-examining him as to (i) his general knowledge of the field in which he is claiming to be an expert, and (ii) his particular knowledge of the facts upon which his opinion is based.

b) **Opinion Witnesses**

The credibility of an opinion witness may be attacked by showing lack of knowledge. For example, a witness who gives opinion evidence on the value of land may be cross-examined regarding her knowledge of land values and may be asked about sales of other land.

c) **Character Witnesses**

As discussed earlier, when a character witness testifies to the good character of another (*e.g.*, a defendant), the witness may be cross-examined regarding the basis of his statement that the defendant's character is good. In other words, the testimony of the character witness may be discredited by asking him about specific criminal or immoral acts committed by the defendant, on the theory that if the witness has no knowledge of these acts, he does not really know the defendant's character. [Fed. R. Evid. 405(a)]

In most courts, a character witness may testify only as to *reputation*. Therefore, on cross-examination, the only acceptable form of question is: "Have you *heard* that the defendant . . . ?" However, under the Federal Rules and in modern jurisdictions that permit character witnesses to testify as to their *opinions* of character, questions in the form, "Do you *know* . . . ?" would be proper.

4. **Impeachment on Collateral Matter**

Where a witness makes a statement not directly relevant to the issues in the case, the rule against impeachment (other than by cross-examination) on a collateral matter applies to bar the opponent from proving the statement untrue either by extrinsic contradictory facts or by a prior inconsistent statement. The purpose of the rule is to avoid the possibility of unfair surprise, confusion of issues, and undue consumption of time resulting from the attempt to prove and disprove facts that are not directly relevant.

Example: Plaintiff's witness testifies, "I saw the accident on the way home from church." If it is conceded that the witness saw the accident, it would be a collateral matter for the defendant to show that the witness was on his way home from a pool hall rather than church. It would not be "collateral" to show that the witness was on his way home from a dinner at the plaintiff's house, because that suggests *bias*, which is a separate basis for impeachment (*see* 3.b., *supra*).

5. **Impeachment of Hearsay Declarant**

There are many occasions in which out-of-court statements are admitted into evidence by means of exceptions and limitations to the general rule excluding hearsay. These statements are frequently admitted into evidence even though the person who made the statement (the declarant) does not testify at the trial. The party against whom the statement has been admitted may wish to impeach the credibility of the declarant so that the jury will discount or assign less probative value to the statement. Under Federal Rule 806, the credibility of a declarant may be attacked (and if attacked, may be supported) by evidence that would be admissible if the declarant had testified as a witness. Of course, the declarant need not be given the opportunity to explain or deny prior inconsistent statements. In addition, the party against whom the out-of-court statement was offered may call the declarant as a witness and cross-examine him about the statement.

6. Rehabilitation

A witness who has been impeached may be rehabilitated on redirect examination or by extrinsic evidence.

a. Explanation on Redirect

For purposes of rehabilitation, the witness on redirect examination may explain or clarify facts brought out on cross-examination.

Example: A witness testifying for the prosecution in an organized crime murder trial admitted to making a prior inconsistent statement. On redirect, the witness is permitted to explain that he gave a prior untruthful statement favoring the defendant out of fear of being killed by the defendant's gang.

b. Good Reputation for Truth

When the witness's general character for truth and veracity has been attacked, the party for whom the impeached witness has testified may call other witnesses to testify to the good reputation for truth of the impeached witness or to give their opinion as to the truthfulness of the impeached witness.

c. Prior Consistent Statement

1) Generally Not Permitted

A party may not ordinarily rehabilitate a witness by showing a prior consistent statement. As a general rule this is true even when the witness has been impeached by showing a prior inconsistent statement. The inconsistency is not removed by the fact that the witness made more than one consistent statement.

2) Exceptions

Where the opposing counsel has impeached the credibility of a witness by making an express or an implied charge that the witness is lying or exaggerating because of some motive, counsel may introduce into evidence a prior consistent statement made by the witness before the time of the alleged motive to lie or exaggerate. Under Federal Rule 801(d)(1)(B), this statement not only is used to bolster the witness's testimony, but also is substantive evidence of the truth of its contents. (*See* VII.B.1., *infra.*)

Example: Defense attorney intimated on cross-examination that the prosecution witness was biased against his client because of a fight they recently had. The prosecutor may introduce evidence of a statement the witness made, consistent with his testimony, before the fight occurred.

F. OBJECTIONS, EXCEPTIONS, OFFERS OF PROOF

1. Objections

Unless an objection is made by opposing counsel, almost any kind of evidence will be admitted. Failure to object is deemed a *waiver* of any ground for objection. The trial judge need not raise grounds for objection on her own, but may take notice of plain errors affecting substantial rights (*e.g.*, admission of coerced confession not objected to by defense).

a. Objections to Trial Testimony

Objections should be made after the question, but before the answer, if it is apparent that the question calls for inadmissible matter (*e.g.*, hearsay) or that the question is in improper form (*e.g.*, leading). Otherwise, a motion to strike must be made as soon as the witness's answer emerges as inadmissible (*e.g.*, "Q: What color was the automobile? A: My sister told me it was gray").

b. Objections to Deposition Testimony

Objections to the *form* of a question (*e.g.*, leading) are waived unless made during the deposition, thereby affording counsel an opportunity to correct the form of his question. An objection based on a *testimonial privilege* should also be made then, lest it be deemed waived. However, objections going to the substance of a question or answer (*e.g.*, relevance, hearsay) can be postponed until the deposition is offered in evidence.

c. Specificity of Objections

An objection may be either *general* ("I object") or *specific* ("Object, hearsay"). The importance of whether an objection is general or specific lies in the extent to which each type preserves the evidentiary issue on appeal. The following rules apply:

1) General Objection Sustained

If a general objection is sustained and the evidence excluded, the ruling will be upheld on appeal if there was *any ground* for the objection. In the absence of specificity in the trial court, it will be assumed that the ruling was placed upon the right ground.

2) General Objection Overruled

If a general objection is overruled and the evidence admitted, the objection is not available on appeal unless the evidence was *not admissible under any circumstances* for any purpose.

3) Specific Objection Sustained

If a specific objection is sustained and the evidence is excluded, the ruling will be upheld on appeal only if the ground stated was the correct one, unless the evidence excluded was not competent and could not be made so.

d. "Opening the Door"

One who introduces evidence on a particular subject thereby asserts its relevance and cannot complain, except on grounds other than relevance, if his adversary thereafter offers evidence on the same subject. And counsel need not "stand" on his overruled relevance objection; he can offer counterevidence without thereby abandoning his relevance objection.

e. Effect of Introducing Part of Transaction

Where part of a conversation, act, or writing, etc., is introduced into evidence, the adverse party may require the proponent of the evidence to introduce any other part that ought, in fairness, to be considered contemporaneously with it. [Fed. R. Evid. 106] The party who introduced the original part of the transaction cannot object to the introduction of other parts on the ground of lack of competency or hearsay, etc. The theory is that the party has *waived any objections by introducing the part.*

f. **Motion to Strike—Unresponsive Answers**

Unresponsive answers are subject to a motion to strike by examining counsel, but not by opposing counsel. Examining counsel, in other words, can "adopt" an unresponsive answer if it is not objectionable on some other ground.

2. **Exceptions**

The common law rule requiring a party to "except" from an adverse trial court ruling in order to preserve the issue for appeal has been abolished in most jurisdictions. In some states, however, a written motion for a new trial, specifying the grounds, may be required.

3. **Offers of Proof**

On some occasions, error cannot be based on exclusion of evidence unless there has been an "offer of proof" that discloses the nature, purpose, and admissibility of the rejected evidence. There are three types of "offers of proof."

a. **Witness Offer**

Subsequent to a sustained objection by opposing counsel, the examining counsel proceeds with his examination of a witness on the stand, out of the jury's hearing, thus making his record by the question-and-answer method.

b. **Lawyer Offer**

Counsel himself states, in narrative form, what the witness would have testified had he been permitted to do so. The "witness offer" is generally preferred to the "lawyer offer" and can be required by the trial court, especially if opposing counsel denies that the witness would testify as narrated.

c. **Tangible Offer**

A marked, authenticated, and offered item of tangible evidence is its own offer of proof.

G. TESTIMONIAL PRIVILEGES

Testimonial privileges, which permit one to refuse to disclose and prohibit others from disclosing certain sorts of confidential information in judicial proceedings, have two basic reasons for their existence: (i) *practicality*, and (ii) society's desire to *encourage certain relationships* by ensuring their confidentiality, even at the high price of losing valuable information.

Some of the testimonial privileges are frankly grounded on hardheaded practicality. The particular kind of disclosure could not be obtained, as a practical matter, even if there were no privilege. No priest, even when confronted by a contempt of court citation, would breach the priest-penitent relationship. Society values some relationships sufficiently that it is willing to protect their confidential nature even at the expense of the loss of information relevant to the issues of a lawsuit. These relationships will be encouraged if confidentiality, when desired, is assured. To put it more concretely, persons might forgo needed medical attention or be less than candid with legal counsel were there no guarantee that communications made during the physician-patient and attorney-client relationships would be accorded confidential status in legal proceedings.

1. **Federal Rules—No Specific Privilege Provisions**

The Federal Rules have no specific privilege provisions. Federal Rule 501 provides that the privilege of a witness or person shall be governed by the principles of the common law as they may be interpreted by the courts of the United States in the light of reason and experience. The federal courts currently recognize the attorney-client privilege, the privilege for spousal communications, and the psychotherapist/social worker-client privilege. In civil actions when state law supplies the rule of decision as to an element of a claim or defense, the state law applies with respect to testimonial privileges as well. Thus, in *diversity* cases, the state law of privilege applies.

2. General Considerations

a. Persons Who May Assert a Privilege

A privilege is personal, and may be asserted only by the party whose interest is sought to be protected or by someone authorized to assert it on the holder's behalf (*e.g.,* guardian of incompetent holder). If the privilege is held by more than one person, each of them can claim the privilege. In certain cases, the person with whom the confidence was shared may claim it on the holder's behalf. For example, an attorney may assert his client's privilege in the client's absence.

b. Confidentiality

To be privileged, a communication must be shown to have been made in confidence. Many states, however, recognize a presumption that any disclosures made in the course of a relationship for which a privilege exists were made in confidence.

c. Comment on Privilege Forbidden

No inference should be drawn from the fact that a witness has claimed a privilege. Thus, counsel for the parties and the judge are not permitted to make any comment or argument based on a claim of privilege.

d. Waiver

All types of privileges are waived by the following:

(i) *Failure to claim the privilege* by the holder herself or failure to object when privileged testimony is offered;

(ii) *Voluntary disclosure* of the privileged matter by the holder (or someone else with the holder's consent) unless the disclosure is also privileged; or

(iii) A *contractual provision* waiving in advance the right to claim a privilege.

A privilege is not waived where someone wrongfully disclosed information without the holder's consent. Similarly, a waiver of the privilege by one joint holder does not affect the right of another joint holder to claim the privilege.

e. Eavesdroppers

A privilege based on confidential communications is not abrogated because the communication is overheard by someone whose presence is unknown to the parties; *i.e.,* the privilege still applies to the parties to the confidential communication. There is some question, however, as to whether the eavesdropper may testify. The traditional view is that the eavesdropper may testify to what he has overheard. But a significant number of modern cases and statutes assert that as long as the holder of the privilege was not negligent, there is no waiver of the privilege, and the eavesdropper is also prohibited from testifying.

3. Attorney-Client Privilege

The first testimonial privilege ever established was the attorney-client privilege. It is a common law privilege, although in some jurisdictions it has now been codified by statute. It carries with it fewer exceptions than any other privilege.

Essentially, communications between an attorney and client, made during professional consultation, are privileged from disclosure. In other words, a client has a privilege to refuse to disclose, and to prevent others from disclosing, confidential communications between herself (or her representative) and her attorney (or her attorney's representative). Objects and preexisting documents are not protected.

a. Attorney-Client Relationship

The attorney-client privilege requires that the attorney-client relationship exist at the time of the communications. The client, or his representative, must be seeking the professional services of the attorney at the crucial time. Retainer negotiations, involving disclosures made before the attorney has decided to accept or decline the case, are covered if the other requirements of the privilege are present.

1) Client

A "client," in the context of the typical formulation of the attorney-client privilege, can be an individual private citizen, a public officer, a corporation, or any other organization or entity, public or private, seeking professional legal services.

2) Representative of Client

A "representative of a client" is one having the *authority to obtain legal services or to act on advice* rendered by an attorney, on behalf of the client.

3) Attorney

An "attorney" is any person who is authorized or, in many jurisdictions, who is *reasonably believed* by the client to be authorized, to practice law in any state or nation.

4) Representative of Attorney

A "representative of an attorney" is one employed by the attorney to assist in the rendition of professional services, *e.g.*, a clerk or secretary.

5) Corporation as Client

A corporation, as indicated above, can be a "client" within the meaning of the attorney-client privilege. The statements of *any corporate officials or employees* made to the attorney are protected if they were authorized or directed by the corporation to make such statements.

b. Confidential Communication

A communication is "confidential" if it was not intended to be disclosed to third persons, other than those to whom disclosure would be in furtherance of the rendition of legal services to the client or those who are necessary for the transmission of the communication. Communications made in the known presence and hearing of a stranger are not privileged.

1) Communications Through Agents

Communications made to third persons are confidential, and thus covered by the attorney-client privilege, if necessary to transmit information between the attorney and client. Examples include: communications by the client to the attorney's secretary or messenger; information (not documents) given to the attorney by the client's accountant; communications between the client's liability insurer and the attorney; and communications through an interpreter.

a) Examination by Doctor

When a client is examined by a doctor at the attorney's request, the communications involved between the client and doctor (and the doctor and attorney) are not covered by the physician-patient privilege because no treatment is contemplated. These communications are, however, covered by the attorney-client privilege because the examination is necessary to help the client communicate her condition to the attorney. Note that this privilege would be waived if the doctor were later called as an expert witness by the same client.

Example: P, a pedestrian, was struck by a car driven by D. P employs Attorney to bring a negligence suit against D to recover for the physical injuries P suffered in the accident. Attorney sends P to Dr. Z for an evaluation of the extent and permanence of P's injuries. Attorney does not intend to call Dr. Z as an expert witness at trial. At trial, D's attorney, believing that P may have admitted to some negligence of his own when describing his injury, calls Dr. Z to testify to his examination of P. If P objects claiming attorney-client privilege, he may prevent Dr. Z from testifying.

2) No Privilege Where Attorney Acts for Both Parties

Where an attorney acts for both parties to a transaction, no privilege can be invoked in a lawsuit between the two parties (they obviously did not desire and could not expect confidentiality as between themselves in a joint consultation), but the *privilege can be claimed* in a suit between either or both of the two parties and *third persons* (multiple parties can desire and expect confidentiality as against the outside world).

c. Client as Holder of Privilege

The privilege, if it exists, can be claimed by the client, her guardian or conservator, the personal representative of a deceased client, or the successor, trustee, or similar representative of a corporation, association, etc. The person who was the attorney at the time of the communication can claim the privilege, but only on behalf of the client. The attorney's authority to do this is presumed in the absence of any evidence to the contrary.

d. Duration of Privilege

The attorney-client privilege applies indefinitely. Termination of the attorney-client *relationship* does not terminate the privilege. The privilege even continues to apply after the client's death. *Rationale:* Knowing that communications will remain confidential even after death encourages the client to communicate fully and frankly with her attorney. [Swidler & Berlin v. United States, 524 U.S. 399 (1998)]

e. **Nonapplicability of the Privilege**
There are three significant exceptions to the application of the attorney-client privilege:

1) **Legal Advice in Aid of Future Wrongdoing**
There is no privilege if the services of the attorney were sought or obtained as an aid in the planning or actual commission of something that the *client knew, or should have known, was a crime or a fraud.*

2) **Claimants Through Same Deceased Client**
There is no privilege regarding a communication relevant to an issue between parties, all of whom claim through the same deceased client—regardless of whether the claims are by testate or intestate succession or by inter vivos transaction.

3) **Dispute Between Attorney and Client**
There is no privilege for a communication that is relevant to an issue of *breach of duty* by the attorney to his client (malpractice) or by the client to her attorney (*e.g.*, client's failure to pay her attorney's fee for professional services).

f. **Waiver of the Privilege**
The privilege belongs solely to the client and she alone can waive it. If the client chooses to waive the privilege, her attorney may be compelled to testify.

g. **Attorney's Work Product**
Documents prepared by an attorney for his *own use* in prosecuting his client's case are not protected by the attorney-client privilege. However, they may be protected by the attorney's "work product" rule. In *Hickman v. Taylor*, 329 U.S. 495 (1947), the United States Supreme Court held that the work product of a lawyer—in that case, statements of interviews with potential witnesses—is not subject to discovery except in cases of necessity.

4. **Physician-Patient Privilege**
The physician-patient privilege is a statutory privilege, which has not been adopted in all jurisdictions. However, in a substantial number of jurisdictions, a physician (and, in some jurisdictions, a dentist or nurse) is foreclosed from divulging in judicial proceedings information that he acquired while attending a patient in a professional capacity, which information was necessary to enable the physician to act in his professional capacity.

a. **Elements of Physician-Patient Privilege**

1) **Professional Member of Relationship Must Be Present**
If the professional member of the relationship is not present for purposes of treatment, and that fact is known to the patient, the relationship does not exist and no privilege attaches.

2) **Information Must Be Acquired While Attending Patient**
The information must be acquired while attending the patient in the course of

treatment; the privilege does not apply to information obtained by the professional in some other way.

3) Information Must Be Necessary for Treatment

If information given by the patient deals with a nonmedical matter (*e.g.*, details of an accident), the information is not privileged. Physicians have also been held competent to testify regarding facts that a lay witness might observe which are not induced by the professional relationship, such as the observable fact that the patient was ill, dates of treatment, or description of clothing worn by the patient.

Example: A treating physician who removed clothing of unconscious accident victim will be permitted to testify that a heroin packet fell out of the patient's right sock.

b. Nonapplicability of the Privilege

There are many exceptions and implied waivers of the physician-patient privilege, and the privilege is of little importance as a result. The privilege does not apply (or is impliedly waived) in the following situations:

1) Patient Puts Physical Condition in Issue

The physician-patient privilege is not applicable in those situations creating the largest number of litigated cases, since a person cannot invoke the privilege where he himself has put his physical condition in issue, *e.g.*, where he sues for personal injuries.

2) In Aid of Wrongdoing

Like the attorney-client privilege, there is no privilege if the physician's services were sought or obtained in aid of the planning or commission of a crime or tort, or to escape detection or apprehension after the commission of a crime or tort.

3) Dispute Between Physician and Patient

There is no privilege regarding a communication relevant to an issue of breach, by the physician or by the patient, of a duty arising out of the physician-patient relationship, *e.g.*, malpractice, failure to pay one's bill.

4) Agreement to Waive the Privilege

The patient may agree by contract (*e.g.*, life insurance policy) to waive the privilege.

5) Federal Cases Applying Federal Law of Privilege

In cases where state law does not supply the rule of privilege (*i.e.,* most federal question cases), the federal courts do not recognize any physician-patient privilege. They do, however, recognize a psychotherapist-client privilege (*see* below).

c. Criminal Proceedings

There is a split of authority as to the applicability of the physician-patient privilege in criminal proceedings. In some states, the privilege applies in both civil and criminal cases. In a number of others, it cannot be invoked in criminal cases generally. In still other states, the privilege is denied in felony cases, and in a few states, it is denied only in homicide cases. Note that where a psychiatrist is involved, however, the applicable privilege is the psychotherapist-client privilege (below), which is more widely accepted in all proceedings than the physician-patient privilege.

d. Patient Holds the Privilege
The privilege belongs to the patient, and he may decide to claim or waive it.

5. Psychotherapist/Social Worker-Client Privilege
The United States Supreme Court recognizes a federal privilege for communications between a psychotherapist (psychiatrist or psychologist) or licensed social worker and his client. [Jaffee v. Redmond, 518 U.S. 1 (1996)—confidential communications between police officer and licensed social worker following a shooting were privileged] Thus, the federal courts and virtually all of the states recognize a privilege for this type of confidential communication. In most particulars, this privilege operates in the same manner as the attorney-client privilege (*supra*).

6. Husband-Wife Privilege
Under the early rule, spouses were absolutely incompetent to testify for or against each other during the period of marriage, and this incompetency had the same effect as the Dead Man Acts—neither spouse could speak out in court if the other spouse was a party. The prohibition against spousal testimony in favor of the party-spouse has been abandoned. However, there remains in many states a rule that permits an accused in a criminal case to prevent his spouse from testifying against him. Apart from this rule of spousal immunity, a modern separate privilege exists in most jurisdictions that protects confidential communications during marriage. Thus, there are two separate privileges as follows: (i) the privilege not to testify against a spouse in a criminal case—spousal immunity, and (ii) the privilege for confidential marital communications.

a. Spousal Immunity

1) Privilege Not to Testify in Criminal Cases
In many jurisdictions, a married person whose spouse is the defendant in a criminal case *may not be called as a witness by the prosecution*, and a married person *may not be compelled to testify* against his spouse in *any* criminal proceeding. (This second part of the privilege exists even where the spouse is not a defendant, such as in grand jury proceedings.) The purpose of this immunity is to protect the marital relationship from the disruption that would follow from allowing one spouse to testify against the other.

a) Federal Courts—Privilege Belongs to Witness-Spouse
In federal courts, one spouse *may* testify against the other in criminal cases, with or without the consent of the party-spouse. Thus, the witness-spouse may not be compelled to testify, nor may she be foreclosed from testifying (except as to confidential communications, *infra*). [*See* Trammel v. United States, 445 U.S. 40 (1980)] Some states (*e.g.*, California) follow the federal view.

b) State Courts—Privilege Belongs to Party-Spouse
In most state courts, the privilege belongs to the party-spouse. Thus the

witness-spouse may not be compelled to testify, and she may be foreclosed from testifying if the party-spouse asserts the privilege.

2) Valid Marriage Required

There must be a valid marriage for the privilege to exist. No privilege exists if the marriage is void (*e.g.*, because it is incestuous, bigamous, or a sham).

3) Immunity May Be Asserted Only During Marriage

The privilege lasts only during the marriage and terminates upon divorce or annulment. If a marriage exists, the privilege can be asserted even as to matters that took place *before* the marriage. Remember, however, that in federal court the privilege belongs to the witness. Therefore, an accused cannot use marriage to silence a federal court witness.

b. Privilege for Confidential Marital Communications

In any civil or criminal case, either spouse, whether or not a party, has a privilege to refuse to disclose, and to prevent another from disclosing, a confidential communication made between the spouses while they were husband and wife. The rationale is to encourage open communication and trust and confidence between husband and wife.

1) Both Spouses Hold Privilege

Both spouses jointly hold this privilege, and either can refuse to disclose the communication or prevent any other person from disclosing the confidential communication.

2) Elements of the Privilege

a) Marital Relationship

The communication must be made during a valid marriage. Divorce will *not* terminate the privilege retroactively, but communications after divorce are not privileged.

b) Reliance upon Intimacy

The communication must be made in reliance upon the intimacy of the marital relationship. Routine exchanges of a business nature, abusive language, and misconduct directed to the spouse are not privileged. If the communication was made in the *known* presence of a stranger, it is not privileged. The confidential communication may be by conduct and need not be spoken.

c. Nonapplicability of Privileges

Neither the spousal immunity nor the confidential marital communications privilege applies in actions between the spouses or in cases involving crimes against the testifying spouse or either spouse's children (*e.g.*, assault and battery, incest, bigamy, child abuse, etc.).

7. Privilege Against Self-Incrimination

Under the Fifth Amendment of the United States Constitution, a witness cannot be compelled to testify against himself. (For full discussion, *see* Criminal Procedure outline.) Thus, any witness may refuse to answer any question whose answer might incriminate him, and a criminal defendant may use the privilege to refuse to take the witness stand at all. The privilege belongs to the witness; a party cannot assert it on the witness's behalf.

a. "Incriminating" Defined

Testimony is incriminating if it ties the witness to the commission of a *crime* or would furnish a lead to evidence tying the witness to a crime; the testimony need not prove guilt. [Hoffman v. United States, 341 U.S. 479 (1951)] A witness cannot refuse to answer because of exposure to civil liability; it must be to avoid *criminal* liability.

b. When Privilege Applies

The privilege can be claimed at any state or federal proceeding, whether civil or criminal, at which the witness's appearance and testimony are compelled (*e.g.,* by subpoena). The privilege can be invoked only by natural persons, not corporations or associations.

8. Clergy-Penitent Privilege

A person has a privilege to refuse to disclose, and to prevent others from disclosing, a confidential communication by the person to a member of the clergy in the clergy member's capacity as a spiritual adviser. A member of the clergy can be a minister, priest, rabbi, or other similar functionary of a religious organization, or reasonably believed to be so by the person consulting him. This common law privilege is very similar in its operation to the attorney-client privilege, *supra.*

9. Accountant-Client Privilege

This is a statutory privilege, found in a number of jurisdictions, which is similar to the attorney-client privilege, *supra.*

10. Professional Journalist Privilege

Whether a journalist may be forced to divulge her sources of information has been a much litigated question and the subject of a trend of statutory authority. The Supreme Court has held that there is no constitutional protection for a journalist's source of information, so the existence of the privilege is *limited to individual state statutes* which have been recently growing in number.

Less than half of the states have enacted statutes protecting the journalist's source of information, and the protection ranges from an absolute privilege to one qualified by the need for disclosure in the public interest.

11. Governmental Privileges

a. Identity of Informer

The federal government, or a state or subdivision of a state, generally has a privilege to refuse to disclose the identity of a person who has furnished to a law enforcement officer information purporting to reveal the commission of a crime.

1) Privilege Claimed by Government

The privilege can be claimed by an appropriate representative of the government, such as a prosecutor.

2) No Privilege If Identity Otherwise Voluntarily Disclosed

No privilege exists if the identity of the informer or his interest in the subject matter of his communication has been voluntarily disclosed by a holder of the privilege, such as a prosecutor, or if the informer appears as a witness in the case.

3) Judge May Dismiss If Informer's Testimony Crucial

If the government elects not to disclose the identity of an informer and there is a reasonable probability that the informer could provide testimony necessary to the fair determination of guilt or innocence, the judge on his own motion or that of the accused shall dismiss the proceedings.

b. Official Information

This is a general catch-all privilege that attaches to certain communications made *by or to public officials*. Official information has been defined as information not open to the public, relating to the internal affairs of the government or its subdivisions. It applies to some fairly low-level communications made by or to officials (*e.g.*, a judge's communications to his law clerk).

H. EXCLUSION AND SEQUESTRATION OF WITNESSES

Upon a party's request, the trial judge will order witnesses excluded from the courtroom so they cannot listen to the testimony of other witnesses. [Fed. R. Evid. 615] The trial judge may also do this on his own motion. However, Federal Rule 615 prohibits the exclusion of: (i) a *party* or a designated officer or employee of a party, (ii) a person whose *presence is essential* to the presentation of a party's case, or (iii) a person *statutorily authorized* to be present.

VII. THE HEARSAY RULE

A. STATEMENT OF THE RULE

The Federal Rules define hearsay as "a statement, other than one made by the declarant while testifying at the trial or hearing, offered in evidence to prove the truth of the matter asserted." [Fed. R. Evid. 801(c)] The rule against hearsay is probably the most important exclusionary rule of evidence. If a statement is hearsay, and no exception to the rule is applicable, the evidence must be excluded upon appropriate objection to its admission. [Fed. R. Evid. 802] An out-of-court statement that incorporates other hearsay is known as "hearsay on hearsay." This type of statement is admissible only if each part of the statement falls within an exception to the hearsay rule. If one part of the statement is inadmissible, the entire statement is inadmissible.

1. Reason for Excluding Hearsay

The reason for excluding hearsay is that the adverse party was *denied the opportunity to cross-examine the declarant*; *i.e.*, the party had no chance to test the declarant's perception (how well did she observe the event she purported to describe), her memory (did she really remember the details she related), her sincerity (was she deliberately falsifying), and her ability to relate (did she really mean to say what now appears to be the thrust of her statement).

a. Cross-Examination of Declarant

Note that it is the declarant who made the statement that the adverse party was not able to cross-examine. Of course, the adverse party can cross-examine the witness who repeats the statement, but this does not help much where all the witness does is repeat a statement as to which the party needs to cross-examine the original declarant.

If W (witness on the stand) testifies as to what D (declarant making out-of-court statement) said about an event, and D's statement is *offered for its truth*, then the opportunity to cross-examine W is not enough. The party against whom W testifies has *no opportunity to test* the perception, the memory, the articulateness, or the veracity of D, the very witness whose account of the event the jury is being asked to believe. Of course, W is available for cross-examination, but W is only repeating what D said, and W is of little help in the attempt to question the accuracy of D's version.

b. Cross-Examination at Time Statement Made
Note too that the *declarant and witness can be the same person*. For example, a witness might state, "I don't remember anything about the accident but I do remember that later that day I said to my wife, 'the black car went through the red light.' " Since the adverse party could not cross-examine the witness-declarant as to his perception, memory, sincerity, or ability to relate at the time the statement was made, the statement is hearsay. It is *contemporaneous* cross-examination that is required.

2. "Statement"

For purposes of the hearsay rule, a "statement" is (i) an oral or written assertion, or (ii) nonverbal conduct intended as an assertion. [Fed. R. Evid. 801(a)]

a. Oral Statements
"Statement" includes oral statements (*i.e.,* where the witness testifies that somebody said " . . . ").

b. Writings
Any written document that is offered in evidence constitutes a "statement" for hearsay purposes.

c. Assertive Conduct
Conduct intended by the actor to be a substitute for words (*e.g.*, the nod of the declarant's head indicating yes) is a "statement" within the meaning of the hearsay rule.

d. Nonassertive Conduct
Under the traditional common law definition of hearsay, "statement" included non-assertive conduct—sometimes called "Morgan hearsay." Nonassertive conduct is conduct the declarant *did not intend as an assertion* but which is being offered as an assertion. However, under modern codes and the Federal Rules, evidence of non-assertive conduct is not hearsay. The rationale is that the likelihood of fabrication is less with nonassertive conduct than with assertive or verbal conduct.

Examples: 1) Consider the conduct of a deceased sea captain who, after examining every part of a ship, embarked in it with his family, when his conduct is being introduced on the question of the seaworthiness of the vessel. Although the sea captain did not intend his embarking on the vessel to serve as an assertion of anything, his conduct can be used to imply that he thought the ship was seaworthy and, since he knew his business, that the ship was in fact seaworthy.

2) Similarly, the fact that a doctor treated a person for plague is non-assertive conduct by the doctor that could be used to show that the person had plague.

3. **"Offered to Prove the Truth of the Matter"**
This is the most crucial component of the hearsay rule. The basic reason for rejecting hearsay evidence is that a statement offered to prove that which it asserts is true may not be trustworthy without the guarantees of cross-examination. However, where the out-of-court statement is introduced for any purpose other than to prove the truth of the matter asserted, there is no need to cross-examine the declarant, and so the statement is not hearsay.

Example: The witness on the stand testifies, "On April 2, Decla said to me, 'Yesterday I was in Buffalo.'" If the issue is whether Decla was in Buffalo on April 1, the testimony is hearsay. It is *not* hearsay if the issue is whether on April 2, Decla was capable of talking. On the latter issue, it is enough to cross-examine W.

The following are other examples of out-of-court statements that are not hearsay.

a. **Verbal Acts or Legally Operative Facts**
There are certain utterances to which the law attaches legal significance (*e.g.,* words of contract, defamation, bribery, cancellation, permission). Evidence of such statements (sometimes called "legally operative facts") is not hearsay because the issue is simply whether the statements were made.

Examples: 1) In an action on a *contract*, words that constitute the offer, acceptance, rejection, etc., are not hearsay because they are offered only to prove what was said, and not that it was true.

2) Similarly, in a *defamation* action, the statement alleged to be a slander or libel may be admissible as nonhearsay. Thus if D said, "X is a thief," X will introduce D's statement not to show its truth—that he himself is a thief—but merely to show that the actionable statement was made.

b. **Statements Offered to Show Effect on Hearer or Reader**
A statement that is inadmissible hearsay to prove the truth of the statement may nevertheless be admitted to show the statement's effect on the hearer or reader.

Examples: 1) In a *negligence case* where knowledge of a danger is the issue, a third person's statement of warning is admissible for the limited purpose of showing *knowledge or notice* on the part of a listener. Thus, a statement to the defendant driver, "Your tire is about to burst," is admissible to show that the defendant had notice of the possible danger. Of course, it is inadmissible hearsay to show that the statement was true—*i.e.,* that there was in fact a defect or dangerous condition.

2) H is on trial for the stabbing murder of W. H claims the killing was done by a bushy-haired, one-armed man whom H saw fleeing the scene. Policeman, P, testifies for the prosecution that H was arrested immediately after the killing and that a letter was found in H's possession. The

letter states, "Your wife has been having an affair with your neighbor, Mr. Gigolo, for the last five years. Wise up!" The letter was signed, "A friend." Prosecutor offers this letter to establish H's motive for killing W. Is the letter hearsay? No! True, the letter is an out-of-court statement of "friend." But it is not offered to prove the truth of its contents. The letter is relevant to the issue of *motive* and would still be relevant to motive if, in fact, W had been faithful. The letter, true or not, is offered to show the probable effect it had on H when he read it.

c. **Statements Offered as Circumstantial Evidence of Declarant's State of Mind**
Statements by a declarant that serve as circumstantial evidence of the declarant's state of mind are not hearsay. Such statements are not offered to prove the truth of the matters asserted but only that the declarant *believed* them to be true. The most common examples of this type of nonhearsay are evidence of *insanity* and evidence of *knowledge*.

Examples: 1) In a proceeding where the declarant's sanity is in issue, evidence is offered to show that the declarant had stated out of court, "I am John the Baptist." This statement would not be introduced as proof of its truth, but rather as circumstantial evidence of the declarant's insanity.

2) Evidence that before an accident an automobile driver stated, "My brakes are defective," is not admissible to prove that the brakes were defective, but is admissible to show that the declarant believed the brakes were defective but drove the car anyway.

1) **Compare—State of Mind Exception**
Statements that reflect directly (rather than circumstantially) on the declarant's state of mind are *hearsay but are admissible* under an exception to the hearsay rule (*see* D.1., *infra*). Many courts have used this "state of mind exception" to admit all declarations that reflect on the declarant's state of mind without regard to the fact that many could simply be admitted as nonhearsay. Although the ability to distinguish the two may be helpful for exam purposes, as a practical matter, the distinction makes little difference because the result (admissibility of the statements) is the same.

4. **Nonhuman Declarations**
There is no such thing as animal or machine hearsay. Hearsay involves an out-of-court statement by a *person*. Therefore, a witness who testifies to the time of day (what the clock says) or to radar readings (what the machine says) is not testifying to hearsay. Similarly, the behavior of a drug-sniffing dog in identifying a suspect is not hearsay. The issues presented by these examples are ones of relevance or reliability of the mechanism or animal. For example, a witness may testify to the actions of a drug-sniffing dog in identifying a suspect if there is a foundation showing that the dog was properly trained and is reliable in identifying drug carriers.

5. **Illustrations of Hearsay and Nonhearsay**
The following are specific examples of the application of the hearsay definition.

a. Hearsay

1) On the issue of whether the traffic light was red or green, the witness testifies that he was told by Decla that the light was green. (*Oral* hearsay.)

2) On the issue of whether a glassine envelope contained heroin, the prosecution offers a crime laboratory report that the envelope contained heroin. (*Written* hearsay.)

3) On the issue of whether Spano had been a resident of New York for one year prior to commencing his lawsuit, Spano offers the affidavit of Decla that Spano had lived in Buffalo for 10 years. (*Written* hearsay; under oath, but hearsay nonetheless.)

4) On the issue of whether Yuckl was the child molester, a police officer testifies that when he asked the child-victim whether the perpetrator had a beard, the child nodded his head. (Hearsay by *assertive conduct*; nodding, which translates, "Yes, the man had a beard.")

5) On the issue of whether the painting sold to Harvey was actually a genuine Picasso, there is offered a dealer's bill of sale describing the painting as a Picasso. (*Written* hearsay.)

b. Nonhearsay

1) In a contract action, the written, executed contract is offered. (Although an extrajudicial writing, it is not offered to prove the truth of matters asserted in it; *legally operative fact*.)

2) In an action for fraud, on the issue of defendant's good faith in representing to plaintiff that a painting was a genuine Picasso, defendant offers a bill of sale from his art dealer describing the painting as a Picasso. (Offered to prove *defendant's good faith* in repeating a representation; not offered to prove that the painting was in fact a Picasso. The evidence, in other words, was offered to show the impact of the dealer's representation on the defendant's state of mind, *i.e.,* his belief.)

3) On the issue of whether landlord knew about a defective stair, a witness testifies that he heard Decla say to the landlord, "The stair is broken." (Offered to prove *notice*, not that the stair was in fact broken.)

4) On the issue of whether the complaining witness had a venereal disease, Grutz testifies for the prosecution that the complaining witness had not been placed in the venereal disease ward upon her admission to the girls' reformatory. (Nonhearsay under the Federal Rules, since it is *nonassertive conduct*.)

5) On the issue of whether a transfer of a share of stock from Decla to Bushmat was a sale or a gift, Bushmat testifies that Decla made a statement at the time of the transfer: "I'm giving you this share of stock as a birthday present." (*Legally operative* words of gift.)

6) Action for personal injuries by a guest in an automobile against its owner. On the issues of contributory negligence and assumption of risk, a witness testifies that an hour before the accident a mechanic said to the owner in the presence of the guest, "The tread on that left front tire is paper thin. You're likely to have a blow-out." (***Notice, knowledge***; not offered to establish that in truth the tread was thin.)

7) Action of P against D. Witness No. 1 testifies for P that D's car was going "over 70 miles an hour." To impeach Witness No. 1, D offers the testimony of Witness No. 2 that Witness No. 1 said a day after the accident that D was going "slowly." (Used solely to cast ***doubt on credibility***; not offered to establish the truth of the assertion.)

B. STATEMENTS THAT ARE NONHEARSAY UNDER THE FEDERAL RULES

Federal Rule 801(d) removes from the definition of hearsay certain statements that would be hearsay under the common law definition. Since the following types of statements are not hearsay, when relevant, they are admissible as substantive evidence.

1. Prior Statements by Witness

Certain statements by a person who testifies at the trial or hearing, and is ***subject to cross-examination*** about the statements, are not hearsay.

a. Prior Inconsistent Statement

A witness's prior inconsistent statement is not hearsay if it was made ***under oath*** at a prior proceeding or deposition. [Fed. R. Evid. 801(d)(1)(A)] For example, a statement made by the witness during grand jury testimony, if inconsistent with her in-court testimony, would be admissible not only to impeach her credibility (VI.E.3.a., *supra*) but also as substantive proof.

b. Prior Consistent Statement

A prior consistent statement, regardless of whether made under oath, is not hearsay if it is offered to rebut an express or implied charge that the witness is lying or exaggerating because of some motive. [Fed. R. Evid. 801(d)(1)(B); *see* VI.E.6.c., *supra*] Note that a consistent statement offered for this purpose is admissible only when made ***before*** the alleged motive to lie or exaggerate came into being; *i.e.*, a prior consistent statement made after the motive to lie arose is not admissible. [Tome v. United States, 513 U.S. 150 (1995)]

c. Prior Statement of Identification

A witness's prior statement identifying a person after perceiving him is not hearsay. [Fed. R. Evid. 801(d)(1)(C)] Photo identifications are within the scope of this rule. Note that the prior identification need not have been made at a formal proceeding or under oath, and its admissibility is not limited to rehabilitation of the witness.

2. Admissions by Party-Opponent

Although traditionally an exception to the hearsay rule, an admission by a party-opponent is not hearsay at all under the Federal Rules. [Fed. R. Evid. 801(d)(2)] An admission is a statement made or act done that amounts to a ***prior acknowledgment*** by one of the parties to an action of one of the relevant facts. If the party said or did something that now turns out to be inconsistent with his contentions at trial, the law simply regards him as ***estopped*** from preventing its admission into evidence. The party who made the prior statement can hardly complain about not having had the opportunity to cross-examine himself. He said it. He is stuck with it. Let him explain it if he can.

a. In General

To be an admission, the statement need not have been against interest at the time it was made (compare the statement against interest exception, C.3., *infra*). The statement may even be in the form of an opinion.

1) Personal Knowledge Not Required

Lack of personal knowledge *does not necessarily exclude* a party's admission (*e.g.*, president of defendant company said, "My company has investigated the matter thoroughly and the reports indicate that we were negligent"). In fact, an admission may be predicated on hearsay.

2) Judicial and Extrajudicial Admissions

Formal judicial admissions (in pleadings, responses to requests to admit, stipulations) are *conclusive*; informal judicial admissions made during testimony *can be explained*; extrajudicial (evidentiary) admissions are *not conclusive and can be explained*. A formal judicial admission in one proceeding may become an extrajudicial or evidentiary admission in another proceeding. (Plea of guilty to traffic infraction admissible in civil action on same facts.) A formal judicial admission that is withdrawn may in that same action become an informal admission (statements in original answer admissible though superseded by amendment). A withdrawn plea of guilty in a criminal case is not, however, admissible against a defendant in any civil or criminal proceeding. [Fed. R. Evid. 410]

3) Adoptive Admissions

A party may expressly or impliedly adopt someone else's statement as his own, thus giving rise to an "adoptive admission." [Fed. R. Evid. 801(d)(2)(B)]

Example: Where Plaintiff claims an orthopedic abnormality in a suit against Defendant, Defendant may properly offer against Plaintiff, Plaintiff's prior application for a chauffeur's license which included a doctor's certificate stating that Plaintiff had "no orthopedic abnormality."

a) Silence

If a party fails to respond to accusatory statements where a reasonable person would have spoken up, his silence may be considered an implied admission. For silence to be an admission the following requirements must be met:

(i) The party must have *heard and understood* the statement;

(ii) The party must have been *physically and mentally capable of denying* the statement; and

(iii) A *reasonable person would have denied* the accusation under the same circumstances.

Note that failure to reply to an accusation or statement made by the police in a criminal case can *almost never* be used as an implied admission of a criminal act.

b. Vicarious Admissions

An admission is frequently not the statement or act of the party against whom the admission is offered at trial. The question that remains is—what relationship must exist between the declarant and the party to make the former's statement admissible against the latter?

1) Co-Parties

Admissions of a party are *not receivable against her co-plaintiffs or co-defendants* merely because they happen to be joined as parties to the action. If there are two or more parties, the admission of one is receivable against her but, in the absence of authority, not against her co-party.

2) Principal-Agent

Under the Federal Rules, statements by an agent concerning any matter within the scope of her agency, made *during the existence of the employment relationship*, are not hearsay and are admissible against the principal. [Fed. R. Evid. 801(d)(2)(D)] Therefore, under the Federal Rule, if a truck driver-employee has an accident while on the job and admits that she was negligent, this admission may be introduced against her employer. Under the traditional admission exception to the hearsay rule, an agent's statements were admissible against the principal only if making such statements was within the scope of her authority.

3) Partners

After a partnership is shown to exist, an admission of one partner, relating to matters *within the scope of the partnership business*, is binding upon her co-partners since, as to such matters, each partner is deemed the agent of the others.

4) Co-Conspirators

Admissions of one conspirator, made to a third party *in furtherance of a conspiracy to commit a crime or a civil wrong*, at a time when the declarant was participating in the conspiracy, are admissible against co-conspirators. The thought is that a conspiracy is analogous to a partnership: "partners in crime." The government need not demonstrate the unavailability of a nontestifying co-conspirator as a prerequisite to admission of the co-conspirator's out-of-court statements under Rule 801(d)(2)(E). [United States v. Inadi, 475 U.S. 387 (1986)]

5) Privies in Title and Joint Tenants—State Courts Only

Where one person succeeds to the same property rights formerly enjoyed by another, there is often such privity that the rights of the present owner may be affected by admissions of the former owner made before the owner parted with her interest. In most state courts, admissions of each joint owner are admissible against the other, and admissions of a former owner of real property made at the time she held title are *admissible against those claiming under* her (grantees, heirs, devisees, or otherwise). These statements are not considered admissions under the Federal Rules, although they may be admissible under one of the hearsay exceptions (*e.g.*, as a statement against interest).

6) **Preliminary Determination of Agency or Conspiracy—Court Must Consider Contents of Hearsay Statement**

Before a hearsay statement is admissible as a vicarious admission, the court must make a preliminary determination of the declarant's relationship with the party against whom the statement is being offered. When making a determination of (i) the declarant's authority to make the statement, (ii) the existence and scope of an agency relationship, or (iii) the existence of a conspiracy and participation by the declarant and the party, the *court must consider the contents of the offered statement*, but the statement alone is not sufficient to establish the required relationship or authority. [Fed. R. Evid. 801(d)(2)]

C. HEARSAY EXCEPTIONS—DECLARANT UNAVAILABLE

Certain kinds of hearsay are considered to have special guarantees of trustworthiness and are recognized exceptions to the hearsay exclusion. The Federal Rules treat the exceptions in two groups—those that require the declarant be unavailable, and those under which the declarant's availability is immaterial. This section covers the five important exceptions requiring the declarant's unavailability: (i) former testimony, (ii) statements against interest, (iii) dying declarations, (iv) statements of personal or family history, and (v) statements offered against party procuring declarant's unavailability.

1. **"Unavailability" Defined**

A declarant is unavailable if:

(i)   He is exempted from testifying by court ruling on the ground of *privilege*;

(ii) He persists, despite a court order, in *refusing to testify* concerning the statement;

(iii) He testifies to *lack of memory* of the subject matter of the statement;

(iv) He is unable to be present or testify because of *death or physical or mental illness*; or

(v)   He is absent (*e.g.*, beyond the reach of the trial court's subpoena) and the statement's *proponent* has been *unable to procure* his *attendance or testimony* by process or other reasonable means.

[Fed. R. Evid. 804(a)(1)-(5)] Note that a declarant is not unavailable if his "unavailability" was procured by the proponent of the statement.

2. **Former Testimony**

The testimony of a now unavailable witness given at another hearing or in a deposition taken in accordance with law is admissible in a subsequent trial as long as there is a sufficient similarity of parties and issues so that the opportunity to develop testimony or cross-examine at the prior hearing was meaningful. [Fed. R. Evid. 804(b)(1)] This exception is the clearest example of hearsay with special guarantees of trustworthiness, since the former testimony was given during formal proceedings and under oath by a witness subject to cross-examination.

a. **Identity of Parties**

The requirement of identity of parties does not mean that parties on both sides of the controversies must be identical. It requires only that the party *against whom* the testimony is offered must have been a party, or in privity with a party, in the former action. (Privity includes grantor-grantee, testator-executor, life tenant-remainderman, joint tenants.) The requirement of identity of parties is intended merely to ensure that the party against whom the testimony is offered (or a party in privity with him) had an adequate opportunity and motive to cross-examine the witness.

b. **Identity of Subject Matter**

The former testimony is admissible upon any trial in the same or another action of the same subject matter. Again, the sole purpose of this requirement is to ensure that the party against whom the transcript of testimony is offered had an adequate opportunity to cross-examine the unavailable witness on the relevant issue. Obviously, the "cause of action" in both proceedings need not be identical. It is enough if the "subject matter" of the testimony is the same. In other words, the party against whom the testimony is offered must have had an opportunity and similar motive to develop declarant's testimony at the prior hearing.

c. **Opportunity to Develop Testimony at Prior Hearing**

The party against whom the former testimony is offered (or a predecessor in civil cases) must have had the opportunity to develop the testimony at the prior proceeding by direct, cross, or redirect examination of the declarant. Thus, the *grand jury testimony* of an unavailable declarant is *not admissible* as former testimony against the accused at trial. This is because grand jury proceedings do not provide the opportunity for cross-examination.

d. **Under Oath**

The former testimony must have been given under oath or sworn affirmation.

e. **Use in Criminal Proceedings**

It has been argued that the use in a criminal proceeding of former testimony from some prior trial violates the defendant's constitutional *right to confront and cross-examine* all adverse witnesses. However, the Supreme Court has rejected this argument, holding that there is *no violation* of an accused's right of confrontation, as long as:

1) The accused or his attorney was present and *had the opportunity to cross-examine* at the time the testimony was given (*e.g.*, at a preliminary examination or a former trial for the same offense); *and*

2) The witness, whose former testimony is sought to be used, is now *unavailable*, despite bona fide efforts by the prosecution to produce him. [California v. Green, 399 U.S. 149 (1970)] *Note:* A greater showing of "unavailability" is required in criminal cases than in civil cases. For example, a mere showing that a witness is incarcerated in a prison outside the state has been held insufficient to establish "unavailability" (because no showing that he could not be produced by prosecution). [Barber v. Page, 390 U.S. 719 (1968)]

3. Statements Against Interest
A statement of a person, now unavailable as a witness, against that person's pecuniary, proprietary, or penal interest when made, as well as collateral facts contained in the statement, is admissible under the statement against interest exception to the hearsay rule. [Fed. R. Evid. 804(b)(3)]

The reason for this exception lies in the exigency of the declarant being unavailable and the circumstantial probability of trustworthiness (declarant is unlikely to knowingly make a statement against her interest unless the statement is true). The statement against interest differs most significantly from an admission in that under the statement against interest exception the statement *must be against interest when made* and the declarant whose statement is admitted may be a stranger to the litigation rather than a party.

a. Requirements of the Statement
To qualify as an exception to the hearsay rule, a statement against interest must meet the following requirements:

1) The statement must have been *against pecuniary, proprietary, or penal interest when made*.

2) Declarant must have had *personal knowledge of the facts*.

3) Declarant must have been *aware that the statement is against her interest* and she must have had *no motive to misrepresent* when she made the statement.

4) Declarant must be *unavailable as a witness*.

b. Collateral Facts
In addition to the fact against interest, the statement often contains collateral facts not against interest. These connected collateral facts are also admissible.
Example: A written receipt acknowledging payment and specifying date of payment, the person who made payment, and the nature of the claim paid is admissible in its entirety.

c. Risk of Civil Liability
Under the Federal Rules, statements subjecting the declarant to civil liability are specifically admissible. [Fed. R. Evid. 804(b)(3)]

d. Risk of Criminal Liability
Many courts have been reluctant to admit evidence of statements that subject the declarant to penal liability for fear of opening a door to a flood of perjured testimony. The modern trend and the Federal Rules permit statements against penal interest. However, where a criminal defendant wishes to show her own innocence by introducing statements by another admitting the crime, the Federal Rules require that there be *corroborating circumstances* indicating the trustworthiness of such statements. [Fed. R. Evid. 804(b)(3)]

1) **Third-Party Confession Allowed**
States that do not allow statements against penal interest may not exclude the

confession of a third party where to do so would deprive the accused of a *fair trial*. [Chambers v. Mississippi, 410 U.S. 284 (1973)]

2) Co-Defendant's Confession May Not Be Admissible

The confession of a co-defendant *implicating herself and the accused* may not be admissible because of *confrontation* problems.

e. "Statement" Means Single Remark

A "statement" against interest for purposes of the exception means a single self-inculpatory remark, not an extended declaration. Thus, if a person makes a declaration containing statements that are against his interest and statements that are not, the statements that are not against interest are not admissible, even though they are part of a broader narrative that is on the whole against the declarant's interest. [Williamson v. United States, 512 U.S. 594 (1994)]

Example: X confessed to receiving and transporting drugs, but in so doing implicated Y as the owner of the drugs. The statements implicating Y did not contain any information against X's interest, although the confession as a whole was clearly against X's penal interest. X refused to testify at Y's trial. X's statements implicating Y are not within the scope of the hearsay exception for statements against interest and are thus inadmissible. The exception covers only those remarks that inculpate the declarant, not the extended declaration. [*See* Williamson v. United States, *supra*]

4. Dying Declarations—Statements Under Belief of Impending Death

In a prosecution for *homicide or a civil action*, a declaration made by the now unavailable declarant while *believing his death was imminent* that concerns the *cause or circumstances* of what he believed to be his impending death is admissible. [Fed. R. Evid. 804(b)(2)] The declarant need not actually die, but he must be unavailable (*see* 1., *supra*) at the time the declaration is offered.

Note that under the traditional view, still followed by some states, the declaration was admissible only in homicide prosecutions (not civil actions) and then only if the declarant actually died.

5. Statements of Personal or Family History

Statements concerning birth, marriage, divorce, death, relationship, etc., are admissible under an exception to the hearsay rule. Hearsay statements concerning family history are often necessary to prove the facts of people's everyday lives. For example, most people rely on the hearsay statements of others for the knowledge of where they were born, who their relatives are, etc.

a. Statement Need Not Have Been Made Before Controversy

In most jurisdictions, the statement must have been made at a time when no controversy existed as to the matters stated—to ensure their reliability. However, the Federal Rules have dropped this requirement on the theory that the time at which the statement was made affects its weight rather than its admissibility. [Fed. R. Evid. 804(b)(4)]

b. Usually Declarant Must Be a Family Member
The now unavailable declarant must be a member of the family in question or otherwise intimately associated with the family. Most jurisdictions require that the declarant be related by blood or marriage to the family whose history is involved. Some jurisdictions, and the Federal Rules, have extended this requirement to admit statements by declarants who are so intimately associated with the family that they are likely to have accurate information concerning the matters declared (*e.g.*, the family doctor). [Fed. R. Evid. 804(b)(4)]

c. Personal Knowledge Required
The declarant's statements may be based either on her own personal knowledge of the facts involved or on her knowledge of family reputation.

d. Other Ways to Prove Pedigree
Personal and family history may be proven by use of other exceptions to the hearsay rule. For example, it may be proven by: vital statistics [Fed. R. Evid. 803(9)]; records of religious organizations [Fed. R. Evid. 803(11)]; marriage certificates and other certificates [Fed. R. Evid. 803(12)]; family records [Fed. R. Evid. 803(13)]; statements in property documents [Fed. R. Evid. 803(15)]; reputation [Fed. R. Evid. 803(19)]; and judgments [Fed. R. Evid. 803(23)]. For these exceptions, the declarant's availability is immaterial.

6. Statements Offered Against Party Procuring Declarant's Unavailability
The statements of a person (now unavailable as a witness) *are admissible* when offered against a party who has engaged or acquiesced in wrongdoing that intentionally procured the declarant's unavailability. [Fed. R. Evid. 804(b)(6)] In effect, a party forfeits his right to object on hearsay grounds to the admission of an unavailable declarant's statements when the party's deliberate wrongdoing procured the unavailability of the declarant as a witness.

D. HEARSAY EXCEPTIONS—DECLARANT'S AVAILABILITY IMMATERIAL
The following exceptions do not require that the declarant be unavailable. The admissibility of these declarations proceeds upon the theory that the out-of-court declarations were made under circumstances that make them more reliable and therefore preferable to the actual in-court testimony of the declarant. Included in this group of exceptions are the following:

1. Present State of Mind
A statement of a declarant's then-existing state of mind, emotion, sensation, or physical condition is admissible. [Fed. R. Evid. 803(3)] The exception is based on the need to obtain evidence as to the declarant's internal state of mind or emotion. It must usually be made under circumstances of apparent sincerity. The statement is often offered to establish the *intent* of a person, either as a direct fact to be proved as such (domicile, criminal intent) or as a basis for a circumstantial inference that the intent was probably carried out.

a. Rationale
The rationale is that (i) insofar as the declarant knows her own state of mind, there is no need to check her perception; (ii) since the statement is of present state of mind, there is no need to check her memory; and (iii) since state of mind is in issue, it must be shown some way—and very often, the declarant's own statement is the only way.

b. When Admissible

1) State of Mind Directly in Issue and Material to the Controversy
Declarations of existing state of mind are admissible when the declarant's state of mind is directly in issue and material to the controversy.

Example: In a case where the domicile of Edwina is material, Edwina's statement that "I love living in Colorado" is admissible.

2) Offered to Show Subsequent Acts of Declarant
Declarations of existing state of mind are also admissible when the declarant's state of mind is not directly in issue—if they are declarations of intent offered to show subsequent acts of the declarant; *i.e.,* a declaration of intent to do something in the future is admitted as circumstantial evidence tending to show that the intent was carried out. In *Mutual Life Insurance Co. v. Hillmon*, 145 U.S. 285 (1892), a hearsay written statement was admitted into evidence to prove the declarant did what he said he intended to do.

Examples: 1) The location of X on May 15 is relevant. W may testify that she heard X say on May 8 that "I intend to go to Denver next week."

2) In a prosecution of a husband for murder of his wife, the wife's prior statements that she intended to commit suicide are admissible.

c. Statements of Memory or Belief Generally Not Admissible
The hearsay statement is *not admissible* if it expresses a memory or belief of the declarant, and the statement is offered for the purpose of proving the *truth of the fact remembered or believed.*

Example: Declarant's out-of-court statement, "I think I left the keys in the car," may not be introduced for the purpose of proving that he left the keys in the car.

Statements of memory or belief are *admissible*, however, to prove facts remembered or believed concerning the execution, revocation, identification, or terms of *declarant's will*.

2. Excited Utterances
A declaration made by a declarant during or soon after a startling event is admissible. The declaration must be made under the stress of excitement produced by the startling event. The declaration must concern the immediate facts of the startling occurrence. [Fed. R. Evid. 803(2)] The spontaneousness of such a declaration and the consequent lack of opportunity for reflection and deliberate fabrication provide an adequate guarantee of its trustworthiness.

a. Startling Event Required
There must have been some occurrence startling enough to produce a nervous excitement and thus render the declaration an unreflective and sincere expression of the declarant's impression. The declaration *must relate to the startling event*.

b. Declaration Must Be Made While Under Stress of Excitement
The declaration must have been made while the declarant was under the stress of the

excitement (*i.e.,* **before the declarant had time to reflect** upon it). The time element is the most important factor in determining whether the declaration was made under the stress of the excitement. If a declaration is made while the event is still in progress, it is easy to find that the excitement prompted the utterance. Declarations made shortly after the event have sometimes been excluded as mere narrative of past events. But when the declaration is made so near to the time of the occurrence as to negate any probability of fabrication, it is usually admissible.

3. Present Sense Impressions
A present sense impression is admissible as an exception to the hearsay rule.

a. Comment Made Concurrently with Sense Impression
If a person perceives some event that is not particularly shocking or exciting, and it does not in fact produce excitement in the observer, that person may nevertheless be moved to comment on what she perceived at the time of receipt of the sense impression or immediately thereafter. [Fed. R. Evid. 803(1)]

b. Safeguards
Such a comment regarding a situation then before the declarant, *i.e.,* the statement of a present sense impression, does not have the supposed safeguards of impulse, emotion, or excitement, but there are other safeguards of reliability. Statements of present sense impression are **safe from defects in memory**. There is usually little or **no time for calculated misstatement**. The statement will usually have been made to another person—the very witness who reports it—who would have **equal opportunity to observe** and to contradict or correct a misstatement.

Example: Decla said to N, "Look at that car go." W may testify that Decla made the statement in order to prove that the car was speeding.

4. Declarations of Physical Condition

a. Present Bodily Condition—Admissible
Generally, declarations of present bodily condition are admissible as an exception to the hearsay rule, even though they are not made to a physician. They may be made to a spouse, relative, friend, or any other person. Of course, declarations made to a physician are admissible. [Fed. R. Evid. 803(3)] Such declarations relate to symptoms, including the existence of pain. Because they are contemporaneous with the symptoms, they are more reliable than present testimony based upon recollection.

Example: Victim tells friend, "My ankle hurts so much it must be broken." The statement is admissible as a declaration of present pain, although it is not to be used to prove the ankle was in fact broken.

b. Past Bodily Condition—Admissible If to Assist Diagnosis or Treatment
As a general rule, declarations of past physical condition are excluded, since there is no way to check the memory of the declarant by cross-examination and there is a greater likelihood of falsification where the declarant is describing a past condition. However, the Federal Rules, recognizing that a patient has a strong motive to tell the truth when seeking medical treatment, admit declarations of past physical condition *if made to medical personnel to assist in diagnosing or treating the condition*. [Fed. R. Evid.

803(4)] Furthermore, the Federal Rule allows declarations not only of past symptoms and medical history, but also of the *cause or source of the condition* insofar as reasonably pertinent to diagnosis or treatment. Moreover, contrary to the majority state view, Rule 803(4) permits such declarations even when made to a doctor employed to testify.

5. Business Records

Any writing or record, whether in the form of an entry in a book or otherwise, made as a memorandum or record of any act, transaction, occurrence, or event is admissible in evidence as proof of that act, transaction, occurrence, or event, if made in the regular course of any business; and if it was the regular course of such business to make it at the time of the act, transaction, occurrence, or event or within a reasonable time thereafter.

a. Rationale

The rationale for this exception lies in the belief that special reliability is provided by the *regularity* with which business records are kept, their *use and importance* in the business, and the *incentive* of employees *to keep accurate records* or risk employment penalties. If a record qualifies as a business record, it may be admitted without calling the author of the record or the employee with personal knowledge of the recorded event. It makes no difference that the record is self-serving and offered in evidence by the party whose business made the record.

b. Elements of Business Records Exception

Under the Federal Rules and modern statutes (Commonwealth Fund and Uniform Business Records as Evidence Acts), the main requirements for admissibility of a business record are as follows:

1) "Business"

Under the Federal Rules, "business" includes every "association, profession, occupation, and calling of every kind, whether or not conducted for profit." Thus, the definition would include records made by churches, hospitals, schools, etc. [Fed. R. Evid. 803(6)]

2) Entry Made in Regular Course of Business

It must also appear that the record was made in the course of a regularly conducted business activity, and that it was customary to make the type of entry involved (*i.e.*, that the entrant had a duty to make the entry).

a) Business Activity

The record must have been maintained in conjunction with a business activity.

(1) Example—Hospital Records

Entries in hospital records are generally admissible to the extent that they are *related to the medical diagnosis or treatment* of the patient (the primary business of the hospital). For example, a patient's statement that she was injured on X's property would probably be inadmissible because whether she was injured on X's property or someone else's is unrelated to her medical treatment.

(2) The Rule of *Palmer v. Hoffman*—Records Prepared for Litigation
A similar aspect of the "business activity" requirement was raised in the case of *Palmer v. Hoffman*, 318 U.S. 109 (1943). In that case, railroad personnel, in accordance with their regular practice, prepared a report concerning an accident in which the railroad was involved. The United States Supreme Court held that the report was not admissible at trial because it was prepared in anticipation of litigation, and railroading, not litigating, was the railroad's primary business.

(a) Narrow Interpretation
Many courts have interpreted the rule of *Palmer v. Hoffman* narrowly. These courts have generally *excluded* such a self-serving employee accident report only when the report was prepared *primarily* for litigation and the author of the report had a strong motive to misrepresent.

(b) Federal Rules—Court's Discretion
The Federal Rules have dealt with the problem of *Palmer v. Hoffman* by granting the trial court discretion to exclude any business record if the *source of information* or other circumstances indicate the record lacks trustworthiness. [Fed. R. Evid. 803(6)]

b) Entrant Under Duty to Record
For a record to have been made in the regular course of a business activity, the entrant must have had some duty to make the entry as part of her employment (*i.e.*, records kept as a hobby do not qualify). This duty may be either public (statutory, etc.) or private (contractual—including duties imposed by an employer).

3) Personal Knowledge
The business record must consist of matters within the personal knowledge of the entrant *or* within the personal knowledge of someone with a business duty to transmit such matters to the entrant.

a) Recorder Need Not Have Personal Knowledge of Event
Most business records statutes do not require that the person making the entries have personal knowledge of the event. Indeed, where the one who has personal knowledge of the transaction (informant) and the one making the record (recorder) are both employees of the business, there is no problem. Once established as a business record, it is admissible without calling either the informant or the recorder, even though the recorder lacked personal knowledge. The integrity of the special reliability assumption is maintained because the informant was under a *business duty to report* accurately and the recorder was under a *business duty to properly record* the information.

b) Informant Must Be Under Business Duty to Convey Information
A problem arises, however, when the informant with personal knowledge is

an outsider, having little or no connection with the business whose records are being offered in evidence. The well-known case of *Johnson v. Lutz*, 253 N.Y. 124 (1930), engrafted a limitation on the business records exception. It holds that an entry is admissible as a business record only when the record was made by the employee recorder on information obtained directly by him or imparted to him by an informant who was under a business duty to convey such information. Thus, a police report entry by a police officer was held inadmissible where the informant was a third person who was under no "business" duty to convey information (the "business" being law enforcement). The statutory business records exception, in other words, was not intended to permit receipt in evidence of hearsay statements made by third persons not engaged in the business in question or under any duty in connection with it. Thus, the rationale is that the assumed reliability justifying the hearsay exception cannot be maintained if the information in the record was supplied by an outsider who had no business incentive to report accurately.

c) **Recorded Statement May Be Admissible Under Other Exceptions**
If, as in *Johnson v. Lutz*, the record-maker and the informant are not business related, the recorded statement of the informant may nonetheless be receivable with the help of some other exceptions to the hearsay rule. This involves a two-phase process. The business records exception serves as a vehicle for demonstrating the bare fact that the *statement was made* (*i.e.*, it allows the paper record to substitute for the in-court testimony of the employees who received the information); the second phase involves reference to some *independent ground of admissibility* of the statement to establish the *truth* of assertions contained in it. A police report entry is receivable where the informant was a party and his statement constituted an *admission*. Note too that certain police reports may be admissible under the public records exception (*see* 7.a., *infra*).

4) **Entry Made Near Time of Event**
The entry must have been made at or near the time of the transaction while the entrant's knowledge of the facts was still fresh.

5) **Authentication**
The authenticity of the record must be established. The usual method of authentication is to have the custodian or other qualified witness testify to the identity of the record and the mode of its preparation. However, a foundation witness is not necessary to authenticate the record (*i.e.,* the record will be self-authenticating) if the custodian or other qualified person certifies in writing that the record meets the requirements of the business records exception. [Fed. R. Evid. 803(6), 902(11)]

Normally, the original or first permanent record of the transaction must be introduced, but where the records to be introduced are voluminous, summaries or compilations may be admitted.

6) **Entrant Need Not Be Unavailable**
For the business record to be admissible, the person who made the entry need not be unavailable as a witness.

7) Trustworthiness
The court may exclude an otherwise qualifying business record if the source of information or the method or circumstances of preparation indicate lack of trustworthiness.

c. Use of Business Records as Evidence of No Transaction
At common law, business records were admitted only to prove the facts contained therein. They were not admissible for negative purposes—*i.e.*, to show that no transaction had taken place. However, the modern trend allows business records to be used to prove the nonoccurrence or the nonexistence of a matter if it was the regular practice of the business to record all such matters. [Fed. R. Evid. 803(7)] For example, the lack of any entry showing payment in a business record may be evidence that in fact no payment was made.

6. Past Recollection Recorded
Witnesses are permitted to refresh their memories by looking at almost anything—either before or while testifying. This is called *present recollection revived* (*see* VI.B.3.a., *supra*). However, if the witness's memory cannot be revived, a party may wish to introduce a memorandum that the witness made at or near the time of the event. Use of the writing to prove the facts contained therein raises a hearsay problem; but if a proper foundation can be laid, the contents of the memorandum may be introduced into evidence under the *past recollection recorded* exception to the hearsay rule. The rationale is that a writing made by an observer when the facts were still fresh in her mind is probably more reliable than her testimony on the stand—despite the fact that cross-examination is curtailed. For admissibility requirements, *see* VI.B.3.b., *supra*.

7. Official Records and Other Official Writings

a. Public Records and Reports
The exception for public records and reports is necessary to avoid having public officers leave their jobs constantly to appear in court and testify to acts done in their official capacity, especially since the entrant could probably add nothing to the record. Also, such records are presumed to be trustworthy because officials are under a duty to record properly that which they do.

1) What May Be Admitted
Records, reports, statements, or data compilations, in any form, of a public office or agency are admissible to the extent that they set forth:

(i) The activities of the office or agency;

(ii) Matters observed pursuant to a duty imposed by law (excluding police observations in criminal cases); or

(iii) In civil actions and proceedings and against the government in criminal cases, factual findings (including opinions and conclusions) resulting from an investigation made pursuant to authority granted by law, unless the sources of information or other circumstances indicate lack of trustworthiness.

[Fed. R. Evid. 803(8); Beech Aircraft Corp. v. Rainey, 488 U.S. 153 (1989)]

Examples: 1) A manual prepared by the office that processes Medicare claims explaining which claims are properly payable under Medicare is admissible against the defendant in a Medicare fraud case under Federal Rule 803(8)(A).

2) A police officer arrives at the scene of the accident. Several witnesses tell him that Dan drove through a stop sign and hit Vic, who was riding a bicycle. The police officer has had many years' experience in evaluating accident scenes. From the tire marks, he decides that Dan did indeed run the stop sign. In his report he includes the statements of the witnesses and his evaluation of the scene, including his conclusion that Dan ran the stop sign. Everything except the witnesses' statements can be admitted under Federal Rule 803(8)(C), including the officer's conclusion. The witnesses' statements can be admitted only if they fall within some other exception. Remember that the investigative report is admissible only in civil cases and only *against the government* in criminal cases. The report could not be offered against Dan in a criminal prosecution.

3) An Equal Employment Opportunity Commission investigator's report would be admissible in an action against an employer alleging discriminatory employment practices. As with the officer's report above, any hearsay statements will be excised unless they fall within an exception, but the investigator's conclusions and opinions are admissible.

2)   Requirements for Admissibility

a)   Duty to Record
The writing must have been made by, and within the scope of duty of, the public employee.

b)   Entry Near Time of Event
The writing must have been made at or near the time of the act, condition, or event.

c)   Trustworthiness
The sources of information and other circumstances must be such as to indicate its trustworthiness.

b.   Records of Vital Statistics
Records of births, deaths, and marriages are admissible if the report was made to a public office pursuant to requirements of law. [Fed. R. Evid. 803(9)]

c. **Statement of Absence of Public Record**
A certificate from the custodian of public records that she has diligently searched and failed to find a record is admissible to prove that the matter was not recorded, or, inferentially, that the matter did not occur. [Fed. R. Evid. 803(10)]

d. **Judgments**
A certified copy of a judgment is always admissible proof that such judgment has been entered. The problem is to what extent the facts adjudicated in the former proceeding can be introduced to prove facts in the present case.

1) **Prior Criminal Conviction—Felony Conviction Admissible**
The traditional view, still followed by most state courts, is that a judgment of conviction is inadmissible. First, it is merely the "opinion" of the jury, and second, it is hearsay as proof of the fact asserted, *i.e.*, the guilt of the defendant. Of course, under certain circumstances the conviction may be used for impeachment. The Federal Rules, however, specifically provide that judgments of felony convictions are *admissible in both criminal and civil actions to prove any fact essential to the judgment*. In the Rules, felony convictions are defined as crimes punishable by death or imprisonment in excess of one year. [Fed. R. Evid. 803(22)] The convictions that may be used are limited to felonies because persons may choose not to defend misdemeanor charges (*e.g.*, traffic violations).

   a) **Admissible to Prove Fact Only Against Accused**
   In a criminal case, the government may use a prior conviction for this purpose only against the accused. Against persons *other than the accused*, the government may use prior convictions *only for impeachment*.

2) **Prior Criminal Acquittal—Excluded**
The exclusionary rule is still applied to records of prior acquittals. The reason is that a criminal acquittal may establish only that the state did not prove the defendant guilty beyond a reasonable doubt, whereas the evidentiary standard is lower in civil cases.

3) **Judgment in Former Civil Case**

   a) **Inadmissible in Criminal Proceeding**
   A civil judgment is clearly inadmissible in a subsequent criminal proceeding because of the differing standards of proof.

   b) **Generally Inadmissible in Civil Proceeding**
   The general rule is that civil judgments are also inadmissible in subsequent civil proceedings. However, there are certain statutory *exceptions* to the rule of inadmissibility. For example, under the Federal Rules, a prior civil judgment is admissible as proof of matters of personal, family, or general history, or boundaries of land, if it would be provable by reputation evidence (*e.g.*, X may prove her citizenship by a judgment establishing that X's parents were citizens). [Fed. R. Evid. 803(23)]

8. **Ancient Documents and Documents Affecting Property Interests**
Under the Federal Rules, statements in *any* authenticated document *20 years old or more*

are admissible. [Fed. R. Evid. 803(16)] Moreover, in contrast to the traditional view that only ancient property-disposing documents qualified for the exception, statements in a document affecting an interest in property (*e.g.*, deed, will, etc.) are admissible regardless of the age of the document. [Fed. R. Evid. 803(15)]

9. Learned Treatises

Many courts do not admit statements from standard scientific treatises or authoritative works as substantive proof, limiting admissibility to use as impeachment of the qualifications of the expert witness. The Federal Rules recognize an exception to the hearsay rule for learned treatises. Federal Rule 803(18) provides for the substantive admissibility of a learned treatise if the treatise is:

(i) Called to the attention of the expert witness upon cross-examination or relied upon by her during direct examination; and

(ii) Established as reliable authority by the testimony or admission of the witness, by other expert testimony, or by judicial notice.

Even under the Federal Rules, however, the relevant portion of the treatise is not actually shown to the jury; it is admissible by being read into the record.

10. Reputation

In addition to reputation testimony concerning a person's character [Fed. R. Evid. 803(21)], reputation evidence concerning someone's personal or family history [Fed. R. Evid. 803(19)] or concerning land boundaries or the community's general history [Fed. R. Evid. 803(20)] is admissible hearsay.

11. Family Records

Statements of fact concerning personal or family history contained in family Bibles, genealogies, jewelry engravings, engravings on urns, crypts, or tombstones, or the like are admissible hearsay. [Fed. R. Evid. 803(13)]

12. Market Reports

Market reports and other published compilations (lists, directories, etc.) are admissible if generally used and relied upon by the public or by persons in a particular occupation. [Fed. R. Evid. 803(17)]

E. RESIDUAL "CATCH-ALL" EXCEPTION OF FEDERAL RULES

The Federal Rules provide a general catch-all exception for hearsay statements not covered by specific exceptions. [Fed. R. Evid. 807] There are three requirements for a statement to be admitted under the catch-all exception:

1. "Trustworthiness" Factor

First of all, the statement must have "circumstantial guarantees of trustworthiness" that are equivalent to those of statements admitted under other hearsay exceptions.

2. "Necessity" Factor

The statement must be offered on a *material fact*, and must be *more probative* as to that fact than any other evidence which the proponent can reasonably produce so that the *"interests of justice"* will be served by its admission.

3. Notice to Adversary
Finally, the proponent must give notice in advance of trial to the adverse party as to the nature of the statement (including the name and address of the declarant) so that the adversary has an opportunity to prepare to meet it.

F. CONSTITUTIONAL ISSUES

1. The Confrontation Clause
In criminal cases, it may be argued that the use of hearsay evidence violates the accused's *right to "confront" and cross-examine* the witnesses against him. Supreme Court decisions have veered away from reading the hearsay rule into the Constitution; *i.e.*, the Court has indicated that the requirements of the Confrontation Clause may be met where circumstances indicate the reliability of the hearsay statement. [Dutton v. Evans, 400 U.S. 74 (1970)]

a. Two-Step Analysis for Former Testimony
In a case concerning the admission of a statement given by the declarant at a defendant's preliminary hearing, the United States Supreme Court formulated a two-step analysis for Confrontation Clause issues. [Ohio v. Roberts, 448 U.S. 56 (1980)]

1) Unavailability
First, the prosecution must produce the declarant or demonstrate that the declarant is unavailable.

2) Reliability
If the declarant is unavailable, the prosecution must then show that the hearsay it is offering is reliable. The prosecution may do this by showing either that: (i) the hearsay falls within a firmly rooted hearsay exception; or (ii) there are particularized guarantees of trustworthiness, *i.e.*, that the hearsay statement was made under circumstances that are likely to produce a trustworthy statement.

b. One-Step Analysis for Other Hearsay Exceptions

1) No Unavailability Requirement
Unavailability will not be required when it serves no useful purpose (*i.e.*, a more reliable statement is not possible). For example, in *United States v. Inadi*, 475 U.S. 387 (1986), the Court held that the Confrontation Clause did not require the prosecution either to produce the declarant or to demonstrate her unavailability if the hearsay statement offered was an admission by a co-conspirator. The Court reasoned that such a statement, having been made during and in furtherance of a conspiracy, would be more reliable than the in-court testimony of the declarant. Subsequently, the Court has held that hearsay may be offered under the excited utterance and statements for medical diagnosis or treatment exceptions without having first to produce the declarant or demonstrate unavailability. [White v. Illinois, 502 U.S. 346 (1992)]

2) Reliability
When the hearsay falls within a firmly rooted hearsay exception, the Confrontation

Clause is satisfied. The Court has held admissions by co-conspirators fall within a firmly rooted exception, as co-conspirators' statements have traditionally been admissible. [Bourjaily v. United States, 483 U.S. 171 (1987)] In *White v. Illinois, supra*, the Court found that the excited utterance and statements for medical diagnosis or treatment exceptions were also firmly rooted. However, in *Idaho v. Wright*, 497 U.S. 805 (1990), the Court held that Idaho's residual hearsay exception was not firmly rooted. Therefore, the Court examined the admitted hearsay—an out-of-court accusation of sexual abuse made by a three-year-old to a doctor—to see if there were particularized guarantees of trustworthiness. The Court found that the statements were not made under circumstances that would likely produce trustworthy statements and held that the admission of these statements violated the Confrontation Clause.

c. **The Right to Physically Face Witnesses**

The Sixth Amendment guarantee of confrontation includes not only the right to cross-examine witnesses, but also the right to physically face them at trial. The Supreme Court held that right to be violated at a child sex abuse trial because a screen was erected in court between the defendant and two youthful complainants so they could not see the defendant as they testified. [Coy v. Iowa, 487 U.S. 1012 (1988)] However, the Court has also held that the right of confrontation is not absolute. A child witness in a sexual abuse case may testify via one-way closed circuit television without violating the defendant's confrontation rights *if the trial judge makes individual findings of probable trauma to the child* from testifying in the defendant's presence. [Maryland v. Craig, 497 U.S. 836 (1990)]

2. **The Right to a Fair Trial**

In addition, the Court has held that state hearsay rules and other exclusionary rules cannot be applied where the effect would be to deprive an accused of her Fourteenth Amendment due process right to a *fair trial* [Chambers v. Mississippi, 410 U.S. 284 (1973)], or deny her right to compulsory process [Rock v. Arkansas, 483 U.S. 44 (1987)].

VIII. PROCEDURAL CONSIDERATIONS

A. BURDENS OF PROOF

The term "burden of proof" as used by judges and lawyers at trial encompasses two separate meanings or burdens. Thus, burden of proof can mean:

1. **Burden of Producing or Going Forward with Evidence**

a. **Produce Sufficient Evidence to Raise Fact Question for Jury**

This defines the burden of one party to introduce sufficient evidence to avoid judgment against her as a matter of law. It is the burden of producing sufficient evidence to create a fact question of the issue involved, so that the issue may appropriately reach the jury. The burden of producing evidence is a critical mechanism for judicial control of the trial. Although the burden is usually cast upon the party who has pleaded the existence of the fact, the burden as to this fact may shift to the adversary when the pleader has discharged her initial duty.

b. Prima Facie Case May Shift Burden of Production
Consider *Plaintiff v. Defendant* in a negligence action. Plaintiff offers evidence in her case-in-chief of Defendant's negligence. Defendant's motion for a nonsuit made at the conclusion of Plaintiff's case is denied. This denial reflects a judicial ruling that Plaintiff has made out a prima facie case of Defendant's negligence. Put another way, it means that Plaintiff has met her burden of going forward with evidence on the negligence issue.

Now assume that Defendant rests immediately after Plaintiff's case-in-chief without producing any rebuttal evidence. Plaintiff then moves for a directed verdict in her favor, claiming that Defendant was negligent as a matter of law. If this motion were granted, it would mean that (i) Plaintiff's evidence was sufficiently persuasive, (ii) the burden shifted to Defendant, and (iii) Defendant failed to meet his newly imposed burden of producing evidence of no negligence. If Plaintiff's motion were denied, it would mean only that Plaintiff met her initial burden but that it did not shift to Defendant; and, therefore, the burden of production having dropped out of the case, the matter is now for the jury. Once in the hands of the jury, the question is whether Plaintiff has met her burden of persuasion.

2. Burden of Persuasion (Proof)

a. Determined by Jury After All Evidence Is In
This is what is usually meant when the term "burden of proof" is used. This burden becomes a crucial factor only if the parties have sustained their burdens of production and only when all the evidence is in. When the time of decision comes, the jury must be instructed how to decide the issue if their minds remain in doubt. There are no tie games in the litigation process. Either the plaintiff or the defendant must win. If, after all the proof is in, the issue is equally balanced in the minds of the jury, then the party with the burden of persuasion must lose.

b. Jury Instructed as to Which Party Has Burden of Persuasion
The burden of persuasion does not shift from party to party during the course of the trial simply because it need not be allocated until it is time for a decision by the trier of fact. The jury will be told which party has the burden of persuasion and what the quantum of proof should be. The jury is never told anything about the burden of going forward with evidence because that burden is a matter for the judge alone.

c. Quantum or Measure of Proof
The trier of fact must be persuaded of the truth of disputed facts by one of the following standards, depending upon the nature of the action:

1) Preponderance of the Evidence
The preponderance of the evidence standard applies in most civil cases. This standard has been defined as meaning that the fact finder must be persuaded by the party to whom the burden on the issue has been allocated that the fact is *more probably true than not true.*

2) Clear and Convincing Proof
Some civil cases (an oral contract to make a will or issues of fraud) often require

proof by "clear and convincing evidence." This standard requires the trier of fact to be persuaded that there is a **high probability** that the fact in question exists.

3) Beyond a Reasonable Doubt

This is the **highest standard** and applies to criminal cases. In a criminal prosecution, the guilt of the defendant must be established beyond a reasonable doubt.

B. PRESUMPTIONS

A presumption is a rule that requires that a particular inference be drawn from an ascertained set of facts. It is a form of substitute proof or evidentiary shortcut in that proof of the presumed fact is rendered unnecessary once evidence has been introduced of the basic fact that gives rise to the presumption. Presumptions are established for a wide variety of overlapping policy reasons. In some cases, the presumption serves to correct an imbalance resulting from one party's superior access to the proof on a particular issue. In others, the presumption was created as a time saver to eliminate the need for proof of a fact that is highly probable in any event. In other words, the inference from the basic fact to the presumed fact is so probable and logical that it is sensible to assume the presumed fact upon proof of the basic fact. In still other situations, the presumption serves as a social or economic policy device. It operates to favor one contention by giving it the benefit of a presumption and to correspondingly handicap the disfavored adversary.

Example: A common presumption is that the driver of a vehicle is the owner's agent. When plaintiff has been injured by the negligent operation of a vehicle, the nondriving, owner-defendant will be liable for the negligence of the driver if the driver is the owner's agent. Plaintiff's burden of proving that the driver was the agent of the owner is aided by a presumption of agency that arises upon proof of ownership. The justification of this presumption of agency from ownership may be explained in terms of *fairness* in light of defendant's superior access to the evidence; in terms of *probability* since it is unlikely that defendant's car was stolen by the driver; or in terms of a *social policy* of promoting safety or increasing available compensation for traffic victims by widening the responsibility of owners.

1. Effect—Shift Burden of Production

Federal Rule 301 provides that a presumption imposes on the party against whom it is directed the burden of going forward with evidence to rebut or meet the presumption. A presumption does not, however, shift to such party the burden of proof in the sense of the risk of nonpersuasion, which remains throughout the trial upon the party on whom it was originally cast.

Example: Plaintiff has the burden of going forward and the burden of persuasion on the issue of Edwina's death. Plaintiff introduces evidence sufficient to support the fact that Edwina has been absent without tidings for a period of seven years. The proof of this basic fact causes a presumption of the presumed fact, Edwina's death. Plaintiff has made out a prima facie case on Edwina's death. More than that, if the defendant is silent and fails to offer proof in rebuttal (either of the presumed fact of death, or the basic fact of absence for a period of seven years), the jury will be instructed that they **must** find Edwina is dead if they believe the absence for seven years.

2. Rebutting a Presumption

A presumption is overcome or destroyed when the adversary produces some evidence contradicting the presumed fact. In other words, the *presumption is of no force or effect* when sufficient contrary evidence is admitted. This is the federal view adopted by Federal Rule 301 except where state law provides the rule of decision (*see 6., infra*).

Example: Plaintiff-victim of automobile driver's negligence sues owner. Plaintiff proves ownership, thus giving rise to the presumption that the driver was the agent of the owner. Defendant-owner testifies that the driver was not his agent, and his evidence could justify a jury finding that the driver was without authority from the owner. At this point, plaintiff's presumption is gone. He will have to sustain the burden of proving by a preponderance of the evidence that the driver was the agent of the owner or his case will fail.

a. Amount of Contrary Evidence Necessary

The amount of contrary evidence that must be introduced to overcome the presumption has never been clearly articulated. Some cases require "enough evidence to support a finding of the nonexistence of the presumed fact." Others simply require "substantial evidence."

3. Distinguish True Presumptions from Inferences and Substantive Law

The true presumption with its mandatory rebuttable inference should not be confused with inferences and rules of substantive law.

a. Permissible Inferences

The permissible inference (prima facie case or sometimes erroneously called "presumption of fact") will allow a party to meet the burden of production but *will not shift the burden* to the adversary. Examples of situations giving rise to permissible inferences are:

1) Res Ipsa Loquitur

A permissible inference of negligence arises where the instrumentality causing injury was under the exclusive control of the defendant and the accident would not ordinarily occur without negligence.

2) Spoliation or Withholding Evidence

The intentional destruction or mutilation of relevant evidence may give rise to an inference that the destroyed evidence is unfavorable to the spoliator. An unfavorable inference may also arise when a party fails to produce evidence or witnesses within his control which he is naturally expected to produce.

3) Undue Influence

Where the attorney who drafted a will is its principal beneficiary to the exclusion of the natural objects of the testator's bounty, an inference of undue influence may be found.

b. "Presumptions" in Criminal Cases

1) Accused Is Presumptively Innocent

The accused in a criminal case is presumptively innocent until the prosecution proves every element of the offense beyond a reasonable doubt. Accordingly, it is clear that in criminal cases "presumptions" do not shift to the accused the burden of producing evidence, nor of persuading the fact finder. A "presumption" in a criminal case is truly nothing more than a *permissible inference.*

2) Judge's Instructions on Presumed Facts Against Accused

The trial judge in a criminal case is not free to charge the jury that it *must* find a "presumed" fact against the accused. When the existence of a presumed fact is submitted to the jury, the judge shall instruct the jury that it *may* regard the basic facts as sufficient evidence of the presumed fact but that it is not required by law to do so. If the presumed fact establishes guilt, is an element of the offense, or negates a defense, its existence must be found (proved) beyond a reasonable doubt.

c. Conclusive Presumptions

This form of inference goes beyond the true presumption since it *cannot be rebutted* by contrary evidence. A "conclusive" presumption is really a rule of substantive law.

Example: In some states, it is conclusively presumed that a child under a certain age (*e.g.,* seven years old) cannot commit a crime. No evidence to the contrary can rebut this presumption, and part of the proof of the case requires a showing that the accused is over the minimum age.

4. Specific Presumptions

The following are common rebuttable presumptions:

a. Presumption of Legitimacy

The law presumes that every person is legitimate. The presumption applies to all cases where legitimacy is in dispute. The mere fact of birth gives rise to the presumption. The presumption is destroyed by evidence of illegitimacy that is "clear and convincing." For example, the presumption is overcome by proof of a husband's impotency, proof of lack of access, or the negative result of a properly conducted blood grouping test.

b. Presumption Against Suicide

When the cause of death is in dispute, a presumption arises in *civil* (not criminal) cases that the death was not a suicide.

c. Presumption of Sanity

Every person is presumed sane until the contrary is shown. The presumption of sanity applies in *criminal as well as civil* cases.

d. Presumption of Death from Absence

A person is presumed dead in any action involving the property of such person, the contractual or property right contingent upon his death, or the administration of his estate, if:

1) The person is unexplainably absent for a continuous period of *seven years* (death is deemed to have occurred on the last day of the seven-year period); and

2) He *has not been heard from,* or of, by those with whom he would normally be expected to communicate.

e. Presumption from Ownership of Car—Agent Driver
Proof of ownership of a motor vehicle gives rise to the presumption that the owner was the driver or that the driver was the owner's agent.

f. Presumption of Chastity
There is a presumption that every person is chaste and virtuous.

g. Presumption of Regularity
The general presumption is that no official or person acting under an oath of office will do anything contrary to his official duty, or omit anything that his official duty requires to be done.

h. Presumption of Continuance
Proof of the existence of a person, an object, a condition, or a tendency at a given time raises a presumption that it continued for as long as is usual with things of that nature.

i. Presumption of Mail Delivery
A letter shown to have been properly addressed, stamped, and mailed is presumed to have been delivered in the due course of mail. The presumption is said to be based upon the probability that officers of the government will perform their duty.

j. Presumption of Solvency
A person is presumed solvent, and every debt is presumed collectible.

k. Presumption of Bailee's Negligence
Upon proof of delivery of goods in good condition to a bailee and failure of the bailee to return the goods in the same condition, there is a presumption that the bailee was negligent.

l. Presumption of Marriage
Upon proof that a marriage ceremony was performed, it is presumed to have been legally performed and that the marriage is valid. A presumption of marriage also arises from cohabitation.

5. Conflicting Presumptions
If two or more conflicting presumptions arise, the judge shall apply the presumption that is founded on the weightier considerations of policy and logic. For example, where the validity of a later marriage is attacked by evidence of a prior valid marriage, the presumption of the validity of the later marriage is deemed to prevail over the presumption of the continuance of the first marriage.

6. Choice of Law Regarding Presumptions in Civil Actions
Under the Federal Rules, the effect of a presumption respecting a fact that is an element of a claim or defense as to which the rule of decision is supplied by state law is also governed by state law.

C. RELATIONSHIP OF PARTIES, JUDGE, AND JURY

1. Party Responsibility

Ours is an adversarial adjudicative process and so, the focus is on party responsibility or, perhaps what is more to the point, on lawyer responsibility. Very little happens in the litigation process unless some lawyer makes it happen by filing pleadings and motions, by initiating discovery, by entering into stipulations, by calling witnesses and offering exhibits at trial, or by interposing objections to the admission of evidence. In other words, the parties, through their lawyers, frame the issues in a litigation by making allegations, admissions, and denials in their pleadings, and by entering into binding stipulations. They assume the burden of proving the issues they have raised. And then, by deciding which witnesses to call to the stand and what tangible exhibits to introduce (and by deciding to what they will object), they control the flow of evidence. But the parties and their lawyers are not the only ones to be allocated important responsibilities in the adversary trial process.

2. Court-Jury Responsibility

Under our system, the trial court is more umpire than advocate. The trial judge's primary responsibility is to fairly superintend the trial; the judge is not permitted to become a partisan in it. As a general rule, questions of law are for the trial court to deal with, and questions of fact determination are for the jury, although trial judges frequently encounter the necessity of making preliminary fact determinations in connection with such matters as the admission or exclusion of evidence. (Of course, both types of questions—legal and factual—are for the trial court in a nonjury case.)

3. Preliminary Determination of Admissibility

In most cases, the existence of some preliminary or foundational fact is an essential condition to the admissibility of proffered evidence. Thus, before a written contract may be received in evidence, it must be shown that the contract is genuine; and before testimony as to an alleged dying declaration may be admitted into evidence, it must be shown that the declaration was made under a sense of impending death. In some cases, the existence or nonexistence of the preliminary fact is determined by the jury with the judge merely deciding whether the evidence of the foundational fact is sufficient to allow the jury to find its existence. In other cases, the question of the preliminary fact must be decided by the judge alone—in which case the evidence will not even be heard by the jury unless the judge first finds the preliminary or foundational fact.

a. Preliminary Facts Decided by Jury

The Federal Rules of Evidence distinguish preliminary facts to be decided by the jury from those to be decided by the judge, on the ground that the former questions involve the *relevancy* of the proffered evidence, while the latter questions involve the *competency* of evidence that is relevant. Rule 104(b) of the Federal Rules of Evidence defines preliminary facts to be decided by the jury as those where the answer to the preliminary question determines whether the proffered evidence is relevant at all. For example, if a statement is proffered to show notice to X, the jury must decide whether X heard it. If X did not, the statement is irrelevant for that purpose; but the decision is left ultimately to the jury because if the jury does not believe X heard it, they will not use it anyway.

1) Role of the Judge

Before the judge allows the proffered evidence to go to the jury, she must find that the proponent of the proffered evidence has introduced evidence sufficient to sustain a finding of the existence of the preliminary fact. The court may *instruct the jury* to determine whether the preliminary fact exists and to disregard the proffered evidence if the jury finds that the preliminary fact does not exist. Such an instruction may be desirable if the trier of fact would otherwise be confused, but with most questions of conditional relevancy the instruction will be unnecessary, since a rational jury will disregard these types of evidence anyway unless they believe in the existence of the foundational fact. If the judge allows the introduction of evidence and then subsequently determines that a jury could not reasonably find that the preliminary fact exists, she must instruct the jury to disregard that evidence.

2) Examples of Preliminary Facts Decided by Jury

a) Agency

If plaintiff sues defendant upon an alleged contract, evidence of negotiations with a third party is inadmissible because it is irrelevant unless the third party is shown to be defendant's agent. However, the evidence of the negotiations with the third party is admissible if there is evidence sufficient to sustain a finding of the agency.

b) Authenticity of a Document

If there is a dispute about whether a note was signed by the defendant (as opposed to a forger), the authenticity of the document is to be left for the jury. In a sense this is merely an issue of relevancy, since the note, if forged, is irrelevant to the liability of the defendant.

c) Credibility

When a conviction of a crime is offered to attack the credibility of a witness, the judge must admit the evidence and allow the jury to determine the witness's credibility if there is evidence sufficient to identify the witness as the person convicted.

d) Personal Knowledge

The question of whether a witness had personal knowledge can go to the jury if there is sufficient evidence to sustain a finding that the witness had personal knowledge.

b. Preliminary Facts Decided by Judge

1) Facts Affecting Competency of Evidence

The question of the existence or nonexistence of all preliminary facts other than those of conditional relevance must be determined by the court. In most cases, the questions which must be decided by the judge involve the competency of the evidence or the existence of a privilege. These questions are withheld from the jury because it is felt that once the jury hears the disputed evidence, the damage will have been done and the instruction to disregard the evidence, if the preliminary fact is not found, will be ineffective.

2) Requirements for Privilege

Preliminary facts to establish the existence of a privilege must be determined by the court. This must be so or else a privilege might be ignored merely because there was sufficient evidence (and this might not be a great deal) for a jury to find it did not exist. Whether or not the jury believed that the facts giving rise to the privilege existed, they would still have heard the privileged evidence, subject only perhaps to a most unrealistic instruction to disregard it if they found the privilege to exist.

3) Requirements for Hearsay Exceptions

All preliminary fact questions involving the standards of trustworthiness of alleged exceptions to the hearsay rule must also be determined by the court. For example, the court must decide whether a statement offered as a dying declaration was made under a sense of impending death, or whether a purported business record was made in the regular course of business. The reason for this is that otherwise the jury will hear the hearsay evidence where the judge's finding is not that it fell within an exception to the hearsay rule, but only that there was enough evidence for the jury to so find. The jurors, however, once they have heard the hearsay evidence, might ignore the judge's instruction to disregard it unless they found the preliminary fact.

4) Others

The above two cases are the most important where the judge must first determine the existence of a foundational fact. However, there are several other major categories.

a) The judge must determine whether a witness is disqualified for *lack of mental capacity.*

b) The judge must rule on the qualifications of a witness as *an expert.*

c) If a conviction of a crime is offered to attack credibility and the disputed preliminary fact is whether a *pardon* has been granted to the witness so convicted (the pardon rendering the impeaching conviction inadmissible), the judge must make the determination.

d) The judge must determine whether a witness is sufficiently acquainted with a person whose sanity is in question in order for him to be *qualified to express an opinion* as to that person's sanity.

e) The judge is required to determine the preliminary facts necessary to warrant reception of *secondary evidence of a writing* (*e.g.,* whether original writing was lost or destroyed).

f) The judge is required to determine the *voluntariness of a confession* before he allows the jury to hear it. This is a rule of constitutional law. The theory is that otherwise the jury might hear involuntary confessions but rely on them anyway because the jury felt that they were nonetheless trustworthy.

5) Procedure for Preliminary Fact Determinations by Judge

a) What Evidence May Be Considered
Federal Rule 104(a) permits the trial judge to consider any (nonprivileged) *relevant evidence,* even though not otherwise admissible under the rules of evidence. Thus, the trial judge may consider affidavits or hearsay in ruling on preliminary fact questions. Most state courts, however, hold that the rules of evidence apply in preliminary fact determinations as much as in any other phase of the trial; thus, only admissible evidence may be considered.

b) Presence of Jury
Whether the jury should be excused during the preliminary fact determination is generally within the discretion of the trial judge. However, because of the potential for prejudice to the accused in a criminal trial, the jury *must* be excused during hearings on the "voluntariness" of the accused's confession, or whenever the accused testifies during the preliminary fact hearing and requests that the jury be excused. [Fed. R. Evid. 104(c)]

c. Testimony by Accused Does Not Waive Privilege Against Self-Incrimination
An accused may testify as to any preliminary matter (*e.g.,* circumstances surrounding allegedly illegal search) without subjecting herself to having to testify generally at the trial. Furthermore, while testifying upon a preliminary matter, an accused is not subject to cross-examination on other issues in the case. [Fed. R. Evid. 104(d)]

d. Judicial Power to Comment upon Evidence
The trial judge is expected to marshal or summarize the evidence when necessary. However, in most state courts, the trial judge may not comment upon the weight of the evidence or the credibility of witnesses. In federal court, the trial judge has traditionally been permitted to comment on the weight of the evidence and the credibility of witnesses.

e. Power to Call Witnesses
The judge may call witnesses upon her own initiative and may interrogate any witnesses who testify but may not demonstrate partisanship for one side of the controversy.

f. Rulings
A trial judge has an obligation to rule promptly on counsel's evidentiary objections and, when requested to do so by counsel, to state the grounds for her rulings.

g. Instructions on Limited Admissibility of Evidence
When evidence that is admissible as to one party or for one purpose, but inadmissible as to another party or for another purpose, is admitted, the trial judge, on request, shall restrict the evidence to its proper scope and instruct the jury accordingly, *e.g.,* "Ladies

and gentlemen of the jury, the testimony that you have just heard is receivable against the defendant Bushmat only and will in no way be considered by you as bearing on the guilt or innocence of the co-defendant Lishniss." [Fed. R. Evid. 105]

BAR REVIEW

Trusts

celebrating over

30 YEARS

*of preparing
law students
for the bar exam*

TRUSTS

TABLE OF CONTENTS

I.   INTRODUCTION

A.   TRUST DEFINED

A trust is a fiduciary relationship in which a trustee holds legal title to specific property under a fiduciary duty to manage, invest, safeguard, and administer the trust assets and income for the benefit of designated beneficiaries, who hold equitable title.

B.   TYPES OF TRUSTS

Trusts are classified according to the method of their creation: (i) *express* trusts, which arise from the expressed intention of the owner of property to create the relationship with respect to the property; (ii) *resulting* trusts, which arise from the presumed intention of the owner of property; and (iii) *constructive* trusts, which do not depend on intention but rather constitute a useful equitable remedy in cases involving fraud and unjust enrichment.

C.   CATEGORIES OF EXPRESS TRUSTS

Express trusts fall into two categories: private trusts and charitable trusts. These two categories of trusts are distinguished primarily by the identity of their beneficiaries. A private trust is created for the benefit of certain ascertainable persons; thus, a trust "to T in trust for my husband, and at his death to my children," is a private trust. A charitable trust, on the other hand, is created for the benefit of an indefinite class of persons or the public in general; thus, a trust providing scholarship funds for needy students at a named university is considered a charitable trust.

II.   EXPRESS PRIVATE TRUSTS

A.   CHARACTERISTICS OF AN EXPRESS TRUST

A trust is a fiduciary relationship with respect to property in which one person, the *trustee*, holds the legal title to the trust property, the *res*, subject to enforceable equitable rights in another, the *beneficiary* (cestui que trust). It is basically a device whereby one or more persons manage the property for the benefit of others. The trust must have a valid *trust purpose*. The trustee ordinarily has legal title to the property and the beneficiaries have equitable title. The testator or grantor who creates an express trust is the trustor or *settlor*, who must have had the *intent* to create the trust. Consideration is not required for the creation of a trust; in fact, trusts are usually created gratuitously.

1.   Intention to Create a Trust

a.   Manifested by Words, Writing, or Conduct

The settlor's manifestation of intention to create a trust is essential to the existence of an express trust. Except as limited by requirements of the Statute of Wills or Statute of Frauds (applicable to real property), this intention may be manifested by written or spoken words or by conduct, and it need not be manifested in any particular form of language. An oral trust of personal property is valid in all jurisdictions.

1)   Delivery of Deed May Manifest Intent

Although some external expression of trust intent is required, the failure of the settlor to communicate his intention to the beneficiaries or other persons does not prevent the creation of a trust. Delivery *to the trustee* of the deed creating the trust is sufficient.

a) Problem Where Settlor Is Also Trustee

However, where the settlor is also the trustee and does not notify anyone of the trust, the trust may fail for lack of intent to create a trust. When the beneficiaries are not notified, evidence that the settlor-trustee segregated the property and kept separate account books for it is relevant in establishing that a trust was intended.

b. Must Be Manifested While Settlor Owns Property

The intention to create a trust must have been manifested by the settlor at a time when he owned the trust property and prior to its conveyance to another.

1) Must Manifest Intent Prior to Conveyance

One cannot convey property outright and later execute a trust instrument declaring that the transfer was actually one in trust. The conduct of the transferor and the transferee subsequent to the conveyance, however, may be important as evidence of the intention that existed at the time of the conveyance.

2) Must Intend Trust to Take Effect Immediately

The settlor must have intended the trust to take effect immediately and not at some future time (*e.g.,* a promise by A to create a trust when he collects a debt from B does *not* create a trust now).

a) Future Interest May Be Trust Res

However, a presently declared trust can have as the trust res a future interest in property (*e.g.,* A can convey "to B for life and then to C as trustee for D"; C has present duties to protect D's equitable future interest).

b) Effect of Promise to Create Trust

If the settlor promises gratuitously to create a trust in the future, a trust arises in the future only if, at that time, the settlor manifests anew his intention to create the trust. Often this promise will be to hold property in trust when the property is acquired. On the other hand, if the promise is *supported by consideration*, the trust can arise in the future, when the property is acquired, without any further manifestation of intent.

c. Precatory Expressions

Usually a settlor clearly directs the trustee to carry out the intended terms of the trust, but difficulties arise when the transferor merely expresses a hope, wish, or suggestion that the property be used for a certain purpose. A direction such as "to B with the hope that B will use the property to provide for the support of C" is precatory language. Most courts today infer from such language that *no trust* was intended, but only that the transferor wished his desires to be known so that the transferee could comply with them if willing to do so. This inference may be overcome if:

1) The directions are *definite and precise*, not vague;

2) The directions are addressed by a decedent to his *executor* or *administrator*, or to one who otherwise occupies the position of a fiduciary under the will;

3) Failure to impose a trust results in an *"unnatural" disposition* by a testator (*e.g.*, a close relative takes no interest under the will); or

4) Extrinsic evidence shows that the transferor had been supporting the alleged beneficiary *prior to executing the instrument*, and the "beneficiary" would not have sufficient means of support absent a finding that a trust was created (*e.g.*, A gives property to B with what appears to be precatory directions to use the property for C's benefit, but evidence shows that A had always supported C, suggesting that A intended to impose enforceable trust obligations on B).

2. Trustee

Although a trustee is essential to the operation of a trust, once a trust is established it will not fail merely because of the trustee's death, incapacity, resignation, or removal. Thus, where a will names X as trustee, the trust does not fail merely because X has predeceased the testator. A successor trustee will be appointed in order to carry out the testator's intention, except in the unusual case where it clearly appears that the trust is to continue only as long as the originally designated trustee continues to serve.

a. Absence of Trustee—Testamentary vs. Inter Vivos Trusts

The refusal of a named trustee to accept an appointment or his failure to qualify, or even the complete failure to name a trustee in a will, does not defeat a *testamentary trust* (a trust created by a will). On the other hand, because of the necessity of a present and effective transfer in order to create a *trust by deed* (*see infra*), the absence of a trustee may result in an attempted *inter vivos* trust (a trust created during settlor's lifetime) failing for want of delivery. Such a trust fails because there has been no transfer—not because there was no trustee, for equity would supply the trustee had there been a valid delivery of the deed creating the trust.

Example: O hands $10,000 to X, telling X to invest the $10,000 and pay the income to A for life, remainder to B. X remains silent, but takes the $10,000. The law may presume X's acceptance of the trust from his acceptance of the trust property, although inaction might also be a disclaimer. The particular circumstances and inferences therefrom must be examined. If X accepts delivery of the trust property but refuses to act as trustee, a trust may still have been created if that was O's intent. In such a case, the court will appoint a substitute trustee thereby preventing the failure of the trust.

b. Trustee Must Have Duties

An "active trust" exists when the trustee has duties. A "passive trust," one where the trustee has no duties at all, will fail and the beneficiaries will take legal title immediately. However, in many jurisdictions the duty to convey title to the beneficiaries is enough to make the trust "active." If the duties are not spelled out in the trust instrument, the court will imply the trustee's duties if (i) there is an intention to create a trust; (ii) there is a res; and (iii) the beneficiary is identified.

Example: T bequeaths "$600 to X, as trustee for X's child, A; the trust to terminate when A reaches age 18." Nothing is said about the trustee's duties.

Therefore, the court will imply that the income is to be accumulated and the accumulated income and principal invested and paid to A at age 18, and the trust will not fail.

c. Qualifications of Trustee

1) Capacity to Acquire or Hold Title for One's Own Benefit

In the absence of statute, anyone who has capacity to acquire or hold title to property for his own benefit has capacity to take property as a trustee. Unincorporated associations can be trustees only where they can hold title to property for their own benefit. If a partnership cannot hold title to property, a purported transfer to the partnership in trust may be deemed to be a transfer to the partners individually as trustees.

2) Administrative Capacity

Although a party may have capacity to take and hold property as a trustee, he may not have the capacity to administer it. For example, minors or insane persons may take title to property, but since their contracts or acts are usually voidable, they are generally held to lack capacity to administer the trust. Such a trustee will be removed by the court and replaced with a qualified trustee.

3) Statutory Limitations on Right to Serve as Trustee

Statutes sometimes limit the right of some persons or corporations to serve as trustees. This is particularly common in the case of testamentary trusts. Foreign corporations are often denied the right to conduct trust business in states other than their state of incorporation.

Example: T dies a resident of California. Her will bequeaths $10,000 to the Chicago Northern Bank, an Illinois corporation, in trust for B. By statute, the Chicago bank cannot serve as trustee of a testamentary trust in California, so the court will appoint another trustee.

d. Removal of Trustee

A court has the power to remove a trustee or to refuse judicial confirmation of the appointment of a trustee in a will. (Denial of confirmation will be ordered when the named trustee is incompetent or declines to serve.)

1) Grounds for Removal of Trustee

Basically, a court may remove a trustee if his continuation in office would be detrimental to the trust (taking into consideration both the settlor's intent and the interests of the beneficiaries). There are numerous grounds upon which a trustee may be removed, including the following:

a) Commission of a serious *breach of trust*;

b) Legal or practical *incapacity* to administer the trust;

c) *Unfitness* for the position (*e.g.*, habitual drunkenness, commission of a crime involving dishonesty, permanent or long continued absence from the state, or extreme old age or other practical inability);

d) *Refusal to post bond or to account*;

e) The existence of a *significant conflict of interest*;

f) The *trustee's insolvency* if the court feels that this situation jeopardizes the welfare of the trust; and

g) *Extreme friction or hostility* between the trustee and the beneficiaries, where such hostility is likely to interfere with the proper administration of the trust. However, the mere existence of friction that does not interfere with proper administration is not a ground for removal.

2) **Effect of Settlor's Knowledge of Grounds Prior to Appointment**
Circumstances that might constitute grounds for removal, such as the existence of conflicting interests, need not be acted upon by a court where such circumstances were known to the settlor at the time he created the trust. The existence and knowledge of grounds at the time the trust was created, however, are *not conclusive*, and in extreme cases a court may nevertheless proceed to remove the trustee. The terms of the trust are significant, of course, in this regard.

3) **Beneficiaries Cannot Compel Removal Without Grounds**
Absent grounds for removal, the beneficiaries cannot compel the removal of a trustee, *unless this power is granted* to them by the trust instrument. The power to remove a trustee without grounds *may also be reserved by the settlor.*

e. **Disclaimer or Resignation by Trustee**
A trustee who has not accepted the trust—either expressly, by implication, or by contracting in advance to do so—can disclaim and refuse appointment arbitrarily. However, he cannot accept a trust in part and disclaim it in part. Also, after having accepted the trust, the trustee cannot thereafter disclaim; the problem then becomes one of resignation (*see* below).

1) **Relation Back of Acceptance**
The trustee's acceptance of a testamentary trust "relates back" to the settlor's death, because the trust is treated as having been in existence from that date. Thus, it is possible for the trustee, by accepting, to become personally liable on tort claims arising prior to the time he accepted.

Example: T devises an apartment house to X, in trust for B. P is injured by a defective stairway the day after T's death. X accepts his duties as trustee the following day. By accepting, X becomes personally liable to P on the tort claim (although as discussed *infra,* X is entitled to be reimbursed from the trust estate since he was not personally at fault).

2) **Resignation**
Once a trustee has accepted appointment, he cannot resign without permission of the appropriate court, unless (i) authorized to do so by the terms of the trust, or (ii) consent is given by all of the beneficiaries, all of whom have capacity to give this consent. The acceptance of a trustee's resignation is within the discretion of the court.

f.   Merger of Title Where Sole Trustee Is Also Sole Beneficiary
Where the sole trustee, who holds legal title, and the sole beneficiary, who holds equitable title, are one and the same person, there is a merger of the legal and equitable titles. This defeats and terminates the trust, creating a fee simple absolute in the trustee-beneficiary. If the trustee does not hold precisely the same interests, both legal and equitable, there is no merger and the trust continues. The existence of either multiple trustees or multiple beneficiaries will normally preclude merger.

3.   Trust Property

a.   No Res—No Trust
Where there is no trust property, the trust fails because the trustee has no property to manage.

b.   Property May Be of Any Type
The property may be real or personal, tangible or intangible, legal or equitable, and it may be either a present interest or a future interest, whether vested or contingent.
Example: T devises Blackacre to A for life, then to such of A's children as survive him. B, A's child, transfers his contingent interest to X in trust for the benefit of B's wife. This is a valid trust.

c.   Trust Property Must Be an Existing Interest in Existing Property
An interest that has not yet come into *legal existence* cannot be held in trust (*e.g.,* a son's hope of inheriting his father's property). If there is no trust res when the trust instrument is executed, the trust will not come into effect when the res comes into existence unless the settlor at that time manifests anew an intention to create a trust.

1)   Future Earnings Can Be Trust Res
Future earnings from an *existing contract* or employment can be the res of a trust, but it is doubtful whether earnings from a contract or employment not yet in existence could be the res.

2)   Doctrine of Potential Possession—Future Crops, Unborn Animals
Under the mortgage doctrine of potential possession (which may not be applied to trusts), a person has a present interest in a thing to be produced if he has the means of producing the thing. Thus, future crops or unborn animals might constitute a res if the settlor owns the land or the mother animal.

d.   Property that Settlor Has Power to Convey Can Be Subject of Trust
The trust res must be existing property that the settlor has the power to convey. The res *need not be tangible* property, but the settlor must have an assignable interest. Thus, a promissory note, a contract, a patent or royalty interest, and a future interest can be the subject matter of a trust.

e.   Trust Res Must Be Segregated from Other Property
The requirement that the trust property be identifiable and segregated means that the property is described with such certainty that it can be ascertained from existing facts. A person cannot declare himself trustee of "the bulk of my estate," because the description is too indefinite. But a conveyance of "all of my real property except Blackacre" is

effective, since by inventorying all the settlor's real property on the date of the conveyance and excluding Blackacre, the identity of the trust estate can be established.

1) Res May Include Fractional or Undivided Interests

A trust res may be, or may include, fractional or undivided interests in specific property, and it may include patents, copyrights, choses in action, and an almost limitless variety of other types of property. Because of the possibility of holding undivided interests in trust, it is probable (although the law is not settled and courts are divided) that the requirement of identification and segregation is satisfied where one declares himself trustee or otherwise purports to create a trust of a particular quantum or portion of fungible goods, such as "half the grain in my storehouse" or "$10,000 of the cash in my safe deposit box" (which contains more than that amount at the time).

f. Debtor Cannot Hold Own Debt in Trust

A person cannot be a trustee of his own debt to another. Thus, if A owes money to B, A's declaration (even with B's consent or B's direction to A) that A shall hold the amount owed in trust for B's children would not make A the trustee for B's children. *Rationale:* A, as trustee, cannot sue A, as debtor, to collect the debt. However, A can declare himself trustee of his *particular property* from which the debt is to be paid. Thus, A could declare himself trustee of his bank account for the purpose of paying B. Note also that A's debt can be held in trust by another person. Because A's debt to B is an asset of B, B can transfer the debt to C to hold in trust for B's children.

g. Unenforceable Gratuitous Promise Cannot Be Trust Res

An unenforceable gratuitous promise cannot be the subject of a trust.

Example: A promises to pay B $5,000 and declares that he holds this amount in trust for B. Unless A actually sets aside $5,000, which becomes the trust res, there is no trust res.

4. Beneficiaries

Generally, a trust cannot exist without someone to enforce it. Thus, a beneficiary is *necessary to the validity* of every trust except charitable trusts (which can be enforced by the state attorney general although the beneficiaries are indefinite) and so-called honorary trusts (trusts for animals and to maintain graves). A private trust requires that there be *definite beneficiaries* (or at least that the beneficiaries will be ascertainable within the period when all interests must vest under the Rule Against Perpetuities). Where a trust fails for lack of a beneficiary, a *resulting trust* in favor of the settlor or his successors in interest is presumed (*see infra*).

a. Capacity

Any person, natural or artificial, capable of taking and holding title to property can be a beneficiary of a private trust. An unincorporated association, which has no capacity to take title, cannot be a trustee, and it is doubtful that it can be the beneficiary of a trust, since it is not a legally recognized person.

Example: T bequeaths $100,000 to X in trust for the benefit of the Socialist Labor Party, an unincorporated noncharitable association. The association cannot take equitable title because it is not a legally recognized person, and therefore cannot be the beneficiary of a trust.

b.   Incidental and Indirect Beneficiaries

Not every person who stands to benefit from the operation of a trust is to be regarded as a "beneficiary." If the trust operates only incidentally to benefit a person, that person is not a beneficiary and cannot enforce rights thereunder.

Example: If A conveys "to T in trust to pay the creditors of A," even assuming that this is a trust rather than a mere agency (there is a split of authority), it would probably be considered a trust for the benefit of A and not one enforceable by his creditors (except perhaps as third-party beneficiaries under a contract). It would seem that A could terminate the trust because he is its sole beneficiary.

1)   Named Attorney Not Deemed Beneficiary

Where a trust requires the trustee to employ a named attorney for the trust, the attorney is not deemed a beneficiary and has no right to enforce a provision for his appointment. The trustee can refuse to employ the attorney, and in fact should do so, when he feels that the best interests of the trust will not be served by the appointment. However, the right to have the named person appointed as the attorney is a term of the trust presumably intended for the benefit of the beneficiaries, and the failure to make the appointment would be actionable by the beneficiaries (rather than by the attorney) if it resulted in a loss to the trust.

c.   Notice to and Acceptance by Beneficiary

Notice to the beneficiary that a trust is being created for his benefit is not essential to the validity of the trust. (The failure to give such notice may, however, serve as evidence contesting an alleged present intention to create a trust.) However, the beneficiary must accept his rights under the trust. A *trust cannot be forced* on the beneficiary without his acceptance.

1)   Acceptance May Be Express or Implied

Acceptance may be express or implied, even by silence or inaction, and the acceptance of a beneficial interest is *normally presumed*. The acceptance, whether express or implied, relates back to the date the trust was created.

2)   Beneficiary May Renounce Before Acceptance

Before acceptance, and within a reasonable time after learning of the creation of the trust, the beneficiary may renounce or disclaim his rights thereunder.

d.   Definiteness of Beneficiaries Under Private Trust

To have a private trust, there must be definite beneficiaries. Otherwise, there would be no one to enforce the trust, and the trustee could appropriate the trust property for himself, which is not what the settlor intended.

1)   Unascertained Beneficiaries

Beneficiaries need not be identified at the time a trust is created, but they must be *susceptible* of identification by the time their interests are to come into enjoyment.

a)   Unborn Beneficiaries

An unborn beneficiary may be described in the instrument, and the trust will be valid even as to his interest. Thus, for example, if A conveys to T in trust for B for life, remainder to B's children, the beneficiaries are "definite" even though B had no children at the time of the trust conveyance. It is sufficient that B's children would be susceptible of identification at the time their interests were to come into enjoyment (*i.e.,* on B's death).

b) Determining Identities of Unascertained Beneficiaries

The means by which the unascertained beneficiaries are to be determined must satisfy the formal requirements necessary for the creation of a trust. They must be described in a manner that satisfies the Statute of Wills or the Statute of Frauds, although methods such as incorporation by reference and acts of independent significance may be relied upon in the same fashion that they may be relied upon to complete the terms of a will.

2) Class Gifts

A private trust may exist for the benefit of members of a class, provided the class is one that is sufficiently definite. In fact, as long as the class is a *reasonably definite* one, it is permissible that the members of the class are to be selected by the trustee in his discretion, or that the property is to be held for such members of the class as the trustee finds meet certain requirements. If the class is too broad, however, the trust may be unenforceable; instead the instrument could be construed as an outright gift to the trustee or as a power of appointment.

e. Resulting Trust Remedy Where Express Trust Invalid

If A transfers to B by written deed, will, or declaration of trust that states A's intention to create a trust but fails to identify the intended beneficiary, or if B refuses to act as trustee according to an oral agreement with A naming the beneficiary, B holds upon a resulting trust for A. (*See* VII.B.2., *infra,* concerning resulting trusts.) This is the result because it is clear that B holds in trust, and since the terms of the trust are not provided, the equitable interests are undisposed of and remain in the settlor.

f. Charitable Trusts Need Not Have Definite Beneficiaries

(*See* III.A., *infra,* on charitable trusts.)

5. Trust Purposes

Trusts may be created for any purpose that is not deemed contrary to public policy. An intended trust or a provision in the terms of a trust is *invalid if*:

(i)   It is *illegal*;

(ii) Its performance involves the commission of a *criminal or tortious act* by the trustee; or

(iii) Its enforcement would be *contrary to public policy*, even though not involving criminal or tortious conduct by the trustee.

a. Definition of Acts Contrary to Public Policy

Public policy is violated if the purpose of a trust is to: induce others to engage in criminal or tortious acts; encourage immorality; or induce a person to neglect parental, family, or civic duties.

Example: T bequeaths a sum in trust "for A for life if he divorces B, remainder to A's children; otherwise, to C." This is probably an ***invalid*** trust purpose because it encourages divorce, which is generally against the public policy favoring marriage.

Compare: T bequeaths a sum in trust to pay for the care of minor black children whose fathers or mothers have been imprisoned as a result of conviction of a crime of a political nature. This was upheld as a ***valid*** trust, and not a trust to induce a breach of the criminal law.

b. Effect of Invalidity of Condition
Where a condition is attached to an interest and the condition is held to violate public policy, the consequences of the condition's invalidity depend upon a number of circumstances.

1) Provision by Settlor Controls
If the settlor provides what is to happen in the event a condition is held invalid, that will control.

2) Interest Relieved of Illegal Condition Subsequent
If the settlor has made no alternative provision, and the condition is determined to be a condition subsequent to the interest to which it pertains, the condition is invalidated, but the trust remains valid and the interest is relieved of the condition. Thus, if a person's right to certain benefits would be divested upon a condition subsequent that is invalid, the benefits would continue absolutely and free of the condition.

3) Invalid Condition Precedent Stricken
If the invalid condition is a condition precedent to a certain interest, upon striking out that condition the court may:

(i) Hold that the ***interest fails*** altogether, regardless of whether the condition occurs, ***or***

(ii) Hold that the ***interest is valid*** regardless of what happens in regard to the condition.

The general intent of the settlor will control. Holding the interest valid is the preferred view, unless there is evidence that the settlor's probable intention is to void the beneficiary's interest altogether if the condition is unenforceable.

c. Rule Against Perpetuities
Violations of the Rule Against Perpetuities can arise in creating interests in trust.

B. CREATION OF EXPRESS TRUSTS
A trust is generally created in three ways:

(i) An ***inter vivos trust*** may be created by a ***declaration of trust*** by a property ***owner***, stating that he holds the property as trustee in trust;

(ii)   An *inter vivos trust* (sometimes called a "living trust") is also created by *transfer* of property by the settlor during his lifetime; and

(iii)   A *testamentary trust* is created by *will*.

Trusts can also be created by the exercise of a power of appointment or by a promise enforceable under contract law.

1.   Inter Vivos Trusts

a.   Present Declaration or Present Transfer of Trust Required

1)   Declaration of Trust
A person can create a trust by declaring herself trustee for another (*e.g.*, A declares that she holds 100 shares of GM stock in trust for B). Where there is a declaration of trust, no delivery is required because the settlor is the trustee. When the trustee is another person, the property must be delivered to the trustee in order to transfer it in trust.

2)   Transfer of Property
A trust can be created by the transfer of property to another as trustee. The *trustee takes legal title* upon delivery of a deed or other document of title, or upon actual delivery of manually transferable property.

3)   Delivery Required
Delivery means an act that places *the trust property out of the settlor's control* (unless the settlor is to serve as trustee). A settlor may also deliver to a third person with instructions to that person to deliver to the trustee. As indicated previously, failure to name a trustee or a promise to name one in the future may indicate a lack of present intention and may prevent a delivery of the trust res.

4)   Must Manifest Intent When Trust Res Exists
If a trust is not established because there is no trust res, and the subject matter of the trust later comes into the settlor's hands, a trust arises at the subsequent time if, and only if, the settlor manifests an intention *then* to create a trust.
Example: A tells B she is leaving him $10,000 by will. Before A dies, B declares a trust of this legacy. The trust is invalid because there is no res. However, if after A dies, B in some way manifests an intention to hold the $10,000 in trust, the trust arises at that time.

b.   Formal Requirements—Statute of Frauds

1)   Writing Required for Trusts of Land
Most states *do not require a writing* for a trust of *personal property*. If, however, the subject matter of an inter vivos trust is *land*, *a written instrument* is commonly required under the Statute of Frauds to make the trust effective. The writing must be signed by the person entitled to impress the trust upon the property. Note that, in certain circumstances, an otherwise invalid oral trust of land may be enforced by way of a constructive trust (an equitable remedy). (*See* VII.C.5., *infra*.)

2) Parol Evidence Rule

In most jurisdictions, evidence outside the written agreement is permitted for the purpose of showing the true intent of the parties only where the writing is ***ambiguous on its face***. A few states, however, will allow the parol evidence even if the writing is unambiguous, holding that the necessary ambiguity may be created by the extrinsic evidence itself.

2. Testamentary Trusts

a. Formalities

To create a trust by will, the intention to create a trust and the other essentials of the trust (identification of the beneficiaries, the trust property, and the trust purposes) must be ascertainable in one of the ways permissible under the applicable Statute of Wills. This means that the trust intent and the ***essential terms*** of the trust must be ***ascertained*** from one of the following:

1) The ***terms of the will*** itself.

2) An existing writing properly ***incorporated by reference*** into the will (where incorporation by reference is recognized).

   Example: In a will executed on July 31, 2001, T bequeaths a sum to First National Bank in trust for the purposes set forth in a trust instrument executed by T on June 30, 2001. No trust came into being on June 30, 2001, because no res was put in the trust. T then dies. The June 30, 2001 trust instrument is incorporated by reference, and a testamentary trust by reference to that instrument is established.

   If T had amended the trust on September 14, 2001, the amendment could not have been incorporated by reference because it was ***not in existence*** when the will was executed. Even so, by statute (below) in most states the amendment is given effect under the Uniform Testamentary Additions to Trusts Act or its equivalent.

3) Facts having a substantial, ***independent significance*** apart from their effect on the terms of the will.

   Example: T establishes an inter vivos trust of $100,000 for the benefit of B on June 30, 2001. In a will executed on July 31, 2001, T bequeaths $200,000 in trust to be added to the trust established on June 30, 2001. T amends the trust on October 17, 2001. T then dies. The trust has independent significance (an inter vivos trust of $100,000). The $200,000 is added to the inter vivos trust ***as amended***, and does not become a separate testamentary trust (*see* below).

4) The exercise of a ***power of appointment*** created by the will.

   Example: T bequeaths a sum in trust for the benefit of "such persons as A shall appoint by deed or will." The trustee holds on a resulting trust for T's estate until A exercises his power of appointment, and then he holds in trust for the beneficiaries appointed by A.

b.   "Secret" and "Semi-Secret" Trusts

1)   Absolute Gift But Trust Intended (Secret Trust)—Constructive Trust May Be Imposed

In the case of a secret trust, the will makes a gift, absolute on its face, to a named beneficiary. However, in reality, the gift was made in reliance upon the beneficiary's promise to hold the gift property in trust for another. To prevent the unjust enrichment of the named beneficiary (secret trustee), courts will allow the intended trust beneficiary to present *extrinsic evidence* of the agreement. If the agreement can be proved by *clear and convincing* evidence, a constructive trust will be imposed on the named beneficiary. The *Statute of Frauds* is not a bar because the suit is not to compel enforcement of the trust, but rather to impose a constructive trust to prevent unjust enrichment. The *Statute of Wills* is not a bar because the constructive trust does not operate on the will itself, but rather on the property, once it comes into the hands of the named beneficiary.

Example: T left 14 colleges $1.6 million. Concerned about a statutory restriction on gifts to charities, T executed a codicil giving the residue of his estate to R. The will gave no indication of a trust, or that R was not to have beneficial ownership. On T's death, the gift to the colleges failed and passed to R through the residuary clause. Evidence was offered that R had promised to hold the residuary in trust for the colleges. *Held:* To prevent unjust enrichment, a constructive trust was imposed upon clear and convincing evidence that R agreed to hold the gift in trust. [Trustees of Amherst College v. Ritch, 151 N.Y. 282 (1897)]

a)   Promise Enforceable Whether Made Before or After Will's Execution

Unlike the rule applicable to lifetime conveyances (*see infra*), in the case of wills, relief is given whether the agreement to hold in trust is made before or after the will is executed. In either situation there is *induced reliance*—if the promise is made after the will's execution, the testator is induced not to change her will. Also, it does not matter whether the person intended to perform the agreement at the time he made his promise. All that matters is that the testator executed her will in reliance on the promise.

b)   Compare—Attempted Modification of Gift Outside Will

If a testator executes a will making an absolute devise, then writes a note (opened after the testator's death) telling the legatee that she wants the legatee to hold the property in trust for certain enumerated purposes, the Statute of Wills prevents enforcement of the trust. No constructive trust is raised because there is no induced reliance and no unconscionable conduct on the part of the legatee. He cannot be compelled to execute the trust because no trust was created by the will.

2)   Gift "In Trust" Without Beneficiary (Semi-Secret Trust)—No Trust Created

In the case of a semi-secret trust, the will makes a gift to a person in trust, but *does not name the beneficiary.* The testator may have communicated the terms to the "trustee." The majority of courts have taken the position that the trust is unenforceable because of the Statute of Wills. The will does not identify the intended beneficiary, and it would violate the policy of the wills statute to permit identification by parol testimony. The gift fails for want of identification of the beneficiary. The named trustee holds the property on a resulting trust for the testator's heirs.

3) Different Result in "Secret Trust" and "Semi-Secret Trust" Cases Explained

Why is it that in the secret trust cases (will purports to make absolute disposition) the trust can be proved, but in the semi-secret trust cases it cannot? The answer lies in who the litigants are in the two cases. In the secret trust case, the issue is between the legatee and the beneficiaries of the alleged oral promise; to prohibit proof of the legatee's promise would lead to unjust enrichment. But in the semi-secret situation, the one thing that is clear is that the legatee himself was not intended to take beneficial enjoyment; the disposition to him was "in trust." Thus the dispute is between the intended but unidentified beneficiaries and the heirs; the "induced reliance-unjust enrichment" element is not present.

III. CHARITABLE AND HONORARY TRUSTS

A. DISTINCTIVE RULES APPLY TO CHARITABLE TRUSTS

Charitable trusts, because of their substantial benefit to society, are granted some special exemptions from the rules that apply to private trusts. In general, charitable trusts are liberally construed. The rules governing charitable trusts differ from those applicable to private express trusts in three important particulars.

1. Must Have Indefinite Beneficiaries

To be sustained as a charitable trust, the trust, if not for a specified charitable agency, must be in favor of a reasonably large class of indefinite beneficiaries and cannot be for the benefit of identifiable individuals. By contrast, a private trust must be for definite and ascertainable beneficiaries.

2. Cy Pres Doctrine Applicable

Where it is impossible to give the settlor's intention effect (*e.g.,* the designated charity goes out of existence), the court may redirect the trust to a purpose "as near as possible" to the charitable endeavor initially designated by the settlor.

3. May Be Perpetual

A charitable trust may last forever; it is not subject to the Rule Against Perpetuities. By contrast, all interests in a private trust must "vest" within the period of the Rule Against Perpetuities.

B. TRUST MUST BE FOR CHARITABLE PURPOSES

The purpose of a charitable trust must be one that is considered to **benefit the public**. Charitable purposes include the relief of poverty, the advancement of religion or education, the promotion of health, and the accomplishment of governmental purposes (*e.g.,* parks, museums, playgrounds). A purpose that limits the benefits of the trust to a particular class of the public (*e.g.,* Chicago orphans) may be charitable, but the class may not be so narrowly defined that it designates only a few individuals upon whom the settlor wishes to confer private benefits. A trust for the dissemination of ideas may be charitable even though the ultimate purpose may be to accomplish a change in present law (*e.g.,* a trust to promote the abolition of discrimination against women, tariffs, or capital punishment).

Examples: 1) A trust for disseminating the views of a ***particular political movement*** qualifies as educational and hence charitable, since awareness of political action is deemed to be beneficial to the public. However, a trust for the benefit of a ***political party*** is not charitable. A fine line is drawn here. For example, a trust for the Socialist Labor Party is not charitable, but a trust to advance the doctrines of socialism is charitable.

2) A trust is charitable if its purpose ***benefits the community***, even though some persons not needing charitable assistance will benefit. For example, if the trust is for widows of police officers slain on duty, it is irrelevant that wealthy widows will be entitled to share, since the public as a whole is benefited by such protection for police officers' wives. However, a trust for widows of the presidents of the Elks would not be a charitable trust unless limited to needy widows, as the public as a whole is not benefited by such a trust.

3) A trust is also nonetheless charitable though ***matching funds*** are required (*e.g.,* $1 to Red Cross for every $1 it raises from other sources).

Compare: 1) Where the beneficiary is a ***profit-making entity*** and the profits are not applied to charity, the trust is not charitable (*e.g.,* if the beneficiary is a private school that pays out profits in dividends to investors, it is irrelevant that the gift also promotes education).

2) Where the beneficiary is ***not predominantly devoted to charitable objects***, the trust is not charitable. Thus, where a gift was to a fraternal order (*e.g.,* the Knights of Columbus), it did not qualify as charitable because, even though the group was involved in charitable endeavors, it was primarily devoted to advancing social and fraternal relations among its members (noncharitable objective).

1.   General Terms Acceptable

The charitable purpose may be expressed in very general terms. Thus, a direction to a trustee to apply funds for such "charitable" or "humanitarian" causes as he selects is sufficient. Where the trust was for "benevolent" or "worthy" causes, the English cases and some older cases held the trust void on the theory that "benevolent" meant proceeding from a good motive and did not limit the objects to charitable ones. Many courts now interpret the words "charitable" and "benevolent" to be synonymous, so that a trust for "benevolent purposes" will be limited to charitable objectives and be upheld. Note, however, that if benevolence is not construed to mean charitable, the trust will fail. For example, a trust to provide gifts of money each Christmas to children in the John Kerr School has been held void because it was not limited to charitable causes; had it been for ***needy*** children it would have been valid.

2.   Effect of Gift Controlling Factor

It is the ***effect*** of the gift to the public or a portion thereof, ***not the motive*** of the settlor, that controls. Thus, if S establishes a trust to build public tennis courts on land adjacent to his home, it is irrelevant that his motive was so he could use them. Likewise, it is irrelevant that a school, park, scholarship, etc., created through a trust is required to be named after the donor (*e.g.*, John Jones Memorial Park).

3.   Mixed Trust
Where the beneficiaries of a single trust are both charitable and noncharitable, the trust is a "mixed trust," and the special *rules for charitable trusts do not apply*. However, two separate trusts will be found if there is some indication as to (i) how much of the corpus the settlor intended to be applied towards charitable purposes or (ii) how long the settlor intended the corpus to be applied towards charitable purposes.

Example: T bequeaths $100,000 to trustees to distribute the income "to such educational institutions and worthy individuals as the trustees should select." This is a mixed trust and is not exempt from the Rule Against Perpetuities as charitable trusts are (below). It is void because the trustees' discretionary power to distribute income to worthy individuals can be exercised beyond the period of the rule. (*See* Real Property outline on Rule Against Perpetuities applied to powers of appointment.)

4.   Charitable Trust Implied When Charitable Purpose Clear
A gift "for the needy" implies that a trustee should be appointed to carry out the purpose. A gift "to the Red Cross" implies that the organization takes the property as trustee to apply it to the charitable purposes of the Red Cross. If the charitable organization is an unincorporated association unable to take title, a trustee will be appointed to administer the funds for the benefit of the organization. Of course, the trustee itself need not be a charitable organization (*e.g.*, to Bank of America as trustee for indigent widows).

C.   INDEFINITE BENEFICIARIES
Beneficiaries of a charitable trust must be indefinite. For example, a trust to assist needy migrant farm workers meets this test, because the permissible recipients are an *unnamed and changing class*. But if particular individual farm workers were the designated beneficiaries, even if they were very needy, the trust would not qualify as "charitable," because of the absence of an indefinite or changing group of beneficiaries.

Examples: 1) The indefinite class can be quite small. Thus, a trust to assist needy children of persons convicted for participating in political demonstrations qualifies as charitable. The entire community benefits when any needy group receives necessary sustenance, education, etc.

2) Trusts to aid victims of a certain disaster (*e.g.*, a fire or a hurricane) are charitable even though, in a sense, the beneficiaries are a fixed group.

D.   ENFORCING CHARITABLE TRUSTS

1.   Settlor and Potential Beneficiaries Have No Standing to Sue Charitable Trustee
Since the purpose of a charitable trust is to benefit the community, the courts consider the community at large the beneficiary of a charitable trust rather than the particular individuals who happen to receive benefits from it. The settlor of a charitable trust is deemed to have no greater interest in the performance of a charitable trust than any other member of the community,

and therefore may not maintain an action for its enforcement. Nor may any potential recipients of the charitable trust maintain such an action.

> *Example:*   S creates a trust to provide scholarships for Spanish-speaking residents of Chicago. S has no standing to bring suit against the trustee concerning administration of the trust, nor does Juanita Hernandez, who lives in Chicago and claims that she has been discriminated against in not receiving a scholarship from the trust.

2.   Charitable Trusts Enforceable by State Attorney General
In most states, the duty to enforce charitable trusts is placed upon the state's attorney general. Thus, in the above example, the settlor or Juanita Hernandez would have to persuade the attorney general to look into the matter.

E.   RULE AGAINST PERPETUITIES
Charitable trusts may be perpetual. The Rule Against Perpetuities does not apply to charitable trusts. Also, under the "charity to charity" exception to the Rule, the Rule Against Perpetuities does not apply to transfers where a limitation is used to shift the beneficial interest from one charity to another on the happening of a remote condition. Note carefully, however, that the Rule *will apply to a limitation shifting the interest* from a private use to a charitable use or from a charitable use to a private use.

> *Examples:*   1) "To the Cook County YMCA for so long as the premises are used for YMCA purposes, and if the premises shall ever cease to be so used, then to the Cook County United Fund." The gift is valid under the charity to charity exception.
>
> 2) "To the Cook County YMCA, its successors, and assigns: provided, however, that if the premises ever cease to be used for YMCA purposes, then over to Joan Smith, her heirs, successors, and assigns." The gift over violates the Rule; the invalid interest is stricken, and the Cook County YMCA has a fee simple absolute.
>
> 3) "To Joan Smith, her heirs, successors, and assigns for so long as the land is used for residential purposes; and if the land ever ceases to be used for residential purposes, then over to the Cook County YMCA." The gift over violates the Rule; Joan Smith has a fee simple determinable and the grantor has a possibility of reverter.

F.   CY PRES
Since a trust for charitable purposes may be perpetual, it often happens that the specific charitable purpose indicated by the settlor is accomplished or becomes impractical. In such a case, where the settlor had a general charitable intent, the court will direct that the trust property be applied to another charitable purpose as close as possible to the original one, rather than permit the trust to fail and become a resulting trust (*see* VII.B.2.d., *infra*).

1.   Rationale
The idea underlying cy pres (translated, it means "as near as possible") is this: The settlor had a general charitable intent as reflected by the trust (such as the curing of disease, the dissemination of knowledge, or the promulgation of a particular religious faith). To carry out her general charitable objective, she selected this particular agency as trustee or as the beneficiary. But her general charitable intent should not be frustrated because this secondary

intent (that the named trustee or beneficiary be the agency for carrying out these objectives) can no longer be accomplished. Instead, the court will select another trustee or beneficiary whose work will most closely approximate the general objectives sought by the settlor.

2.   Finding of General Charitable Intent Required

Where the specified charitable use is no longer possible or practical, the court must decide whether the settlor intended the trust to fail or would have wished the property devoted to a similar use. Of course, where the settlor has provided for such a contingency, her direction controls. The fact that a gift is given "on condition" that it be used for a specific charitable purpose has not precluded a finding of general charitable intent. Where a specific intent alone is found, the trust fails and passes as a resulting trust to the settlor's successors in title. The fact that a resulting trust would be impractical because through the passage of time those entitled are numerous and would take small shares often influences a court to find a general charitable intent.

3.   Selecting a Purpose "As Near As Possible"

In formulating an alternative use for the trust property, the court must determine the settlor's primary purpose, although her other purposes should be taken into account.

Example: Where funds were given to a church to build a memorial hospital for tuberculosis patients, in formulating an alternative use it must be decided which of the settlor's purposes she considered most important: the church as recipient, the memorial nature of the building, or the medical nature of the gift.

4.   Compare—Equitable Deviation

Even if the court refuses to apply cy pres—because the purpose of the trust can still be carried out—it can, by exercising its equitable power, authorize equitable deviation from an *administrative term* of the trust.

Example: Assume a trust is created for the benefit of students in Greenville City High School. The city high school district is subsequently consolidated with the county high school district. Equitable deviation may be applied, extending benefits to students in all high schools in the county. (However, there is some judicial disagreement over whether a geographical limitation is an administrative term of the trust.)

G.   HONORARY TRUSTS

An "honorary" trust is a trust that is *not for charitable purposes* and has *no private beneficiaries*. Examples are trusts for maintenance of a cemetery plot and trusts for pets. These are called "honorary" trusts because there is no beneficiary who can enforce the trust by bringing an action against the trustee; the trustee is on her honor to carry out the trust. Even though not enforceable, honorary trusts are upheld in the sense that if the named trustee is willing to carry out the terms of the trust, she will be permitted to do so. If, however, she fails or refuses to do so, a resulting trust will be imposed for the settlor or the testator's estate.

1.   Void If It May Continue Beyond Perpetuities Period

Most courts hold that an honorary trust is void if it may continue beyond lives in being plus 21 years. This creates a problem for most honorary trusts. Since the "measuring lives" that can be used for Rule Against Perpetuities purposes must be human lives (cannot use poodles, turtles, or elephants), absent special drafting to avoid the problem, a trust for the care of the settlor's dog may be held invalid. Under the "what might happen" remote possibilities test of the Rule Against Perpetuities, the dog *might* outlive anyone now alive by more than 21 years. Since the named trustee cannot be compelled to carry out the terms of the trust, she is treated as having a power of appointment, which might be exercisable beyond the period of the Rule Against Perpetuities.

2. Constructional Outs Taken to Avoid Perpetuities Problem
To uphold an honorary trust, some courts have taken these constructional "outs" to save the gift:

a. Trust Was Personal to Named Trustee
In a bequest of $5,000 "to my sister Sue, to be used by her to take care of my dear Bowser for the rest of his days," the court might hold that the trust was personal to Sue, such that Sue and only Sue could serve as trustee; and when Sue dies the trust will terminate. Since the likelihood is that Sue will outlive Bowser, the trust purposes can be accomplished, and Sue can be used as the "measuring life" for purposes of the Rule Against Perpetuities.

b. Fund Will Be Exhausted Within Period of Perpetuities
The court might stretch to find that the $5,000 bequeathed to Sue will likely be exhausted (by expenditures for dog food and veterinary bills) within the period of perpetuities; therefore, the trust will not last beyond the life in being plus 21 years.

IV. BENEFICIARIES' INTERESTS—TRANSFER, MODIFICATION, AND TERMINATION

A. TRANSFER OF BENEFICIARIES' INTERESTS

1. Alienability in General

a. Voluntary Alienation
In the absence of some provision in a statute or trust instrument to the contrary (*e.g.*, restriction on alienation of contingent interest), the equitable interest of a trust beneficiary is freely alienable to the extent the beneficiary can transfer other property. The transferee takes the interest subject to all conditions and limitations that would have applied but for the assignment.

b. Involuntary Alienation
Except as otherwise provided by statute or as validly restricted by the terms of the trust instrument, the interest of an insolvent trust beneficiary can generally be reached in appropriate proceedings (such as a creditor's bill in equity) to satisfy the claims of his creditors. However, unless the debtor is the sole beneficiary and can presently demand conveyance of the trust property, the creditor reaches only the interest of the beneficiary and not the trust property itself. The basic remedy of the creditor is to sell the beneficial interest and have the proceeds applied to his claim, with the buyer at the sale acquiring the exact interest the debtor held as beneficiary. Because of the sacrifice element involved, a court of equity may refuse to order sale of an income interest and

will instead require the trustee to pay the beneficiary's income to the creditor until the debt is satisfied if the creditor will be paid by this method within a reasonable time.

2. Restraints on Alienation—Spendthrift Trusts

A spendthrift trust is one in which, by statute or more often by virtue of the terms of the trust, the beneficiary is *unable voluntarily or involuntarily to transfer his interest* in the trust. In other words, he cannot sell or give away his right to future income or capital, and his creditors are unable to collect or attach such rights. This type of trust is usually created to provide a fund for the maintenance of the beneficiary which will be secure against his own improvidence.

a. Rights of Creditors

What are the rights of the creditors of an income beneficiary of a spendthrift trust? Creditors cannot reach the beneficiary's interest in the sense of selling it as a means of realizing upon and anticipating his future rights. However, the restraint on alienation does not apply to the income after it has been paid out to the beneficiary. Thus, the property in the beneficiary's hands after distribution is no longer protected by the spendthrift clause and is subject to the claims of his creditors. (However, the creditors have to catch the beneficiary before he spends it!)

b. Restraint on Involuntary Alienation Only—Invalid

A restraint that prohibits creditors from reaching a beneficiary's interest, but does not prohibit the beneficiary from voluntarily alienating his interest, *violates public policy.* If the beneficiary could give his interest away, but his creditors could not reach it, it would violate the basic rule that creditors can reach any interest the debtor can alienate. (Nonetheless, in a few cases the restraint on involuntary alienation alone has been upheld.)

c. Attempted Assignment in Violation of Spendthrift Provision

Assume that A, the income beneficiary of a spendthrift trust, has purported to assign his interests to B. An assignee in such a case cannot compel a trustee to pay. Thus, B cannot compel the trustee to pay the income to him, and the trustee may not do so over A's objection. The purported assignment does, however, operate as an authorization to the trustee to pay income to B, and as long as the authorization has not been repudiated by A, the trustee may, without liability, make payments to B. Such an authorization generally does not violate the spendthrift restraint, because the trustee could pay A, who could turn it over to B. But the authorization may be repudiated by A at any time.

d. Exception—Settlor as Beneficiary

An important exception to the validity of spendthrift restraints is that the settlor cannot protect his own retained interests from his creditors by the inclusion of a spendthrift provision. If S transfers to T in trust to pay income to S for life, remainder to B, and the trust includes a spendthrift clause, S's creditors can reach S's right to the income just as if the spendthrift clause had not been included. *Rationale:* If this were not true, debtors could easily avoid their creditors and retain income from their property.

1) Test for Determining Whether Beneficiary Is Also Settlor

Sometimes it is not clear whether the beneficiary is also the settlor. *If a person furnishes the consideration for the creation of a trust, he is the settlor,* even though the trust is created by another person. Thus, if in consideration of the conveyance of Blackacre from A to B, B transfers Whiteacre to T in trust for A for life, remainder to A's children, A is the settlor of the trust. A's life estate can be reached by his creditors and can be assigned by him, even though the trust contains a spendthrift clause.

e.   Exceptions for Special Classes of Creditors
Even where spendthrift restrictions are valid, in a number of states the beneficiary's interest is subject to certain types of claims such as the claims of *dependents*, the *government*, and *persons supplying necessities* (*e.g.*, a divorced wife can usually reach the husband's interest to satisfy a claim for alimony; and the federal government can reach the interest to pay taxes owing it). In a few states, *tort creditors* can reach the trust assets on the theory that they, unlike contract creditors, have no means of protecting themselves against the beneficiary's actions.

3.   Discretionary Trusts
In a discretionary trust, the trustee is given discretion whether to apply or withhold payments of income or principal to a beneficiary. This discretion relates to more than just the time and manner of payment; it actually limits the extent of the beneficiary's rights to the amounts the trustee decides to give him, with the rest going over to others eventually.

a.   Creditors' Rights

1)   Before Trustee Exercises Discretion—Interest Cannot Be Reached
Before the trustee exercises his discretion to make payments to the beneficiary, the beneficiary's interest is not assignable and cannot be reached by his creditors. The theory is that, because the beneficiary has no right to payment that he can enforce against the trustee, there is nothing for the creditors to reach. That is, the creditors' rights cannot rise above those of the beneficiary.

2)   After Trustee Exercises Discretion—Payments Made to Creditors
If the trustee exercises his discretion and elects to make payments to the beneficiary, the trustee must make those payments not to the beneficiary but directly to his creditors or assignees if the trustee has notice of an assignment or attachment by the creditors, *unless the beneficiary's interest is protected by a spendthrift restriction.*

Example: T bequeaths a sum in trust to pay the income and principal to B in the trustee's uncontrolled discretion. B's creditors cannot require the trustee to pay the income or principal to them. However, by giving notice to the trustee, they can prevent the trustee from paying B until their claims are satisfied. Of course, if there is a spendthrift clause, they cannot reach B's interest in any way and the trustee can pay B if he chooses to do so.

3)   Creditors May Reach Discretionary Interest Created for Settlor
The few cases on point seem to establish the principle that where a discretionary interest is created for the settlor himself, his creditors can reach the retained interest.

b. Beneficiary's Rights
The beneficiary cannot interfere with the exercise of the trustee's discretion unless the trustee abuses his power. What constitutes abuse depends upon the extent of discretion conferred upon the trustee. If the trust is a "support trust," there is more room for a court's interference because the trust has a specific purpose, but even if the trustee's discretion is uncontrolled, the court will interfere if the trustee acts in bad faith or dishonestly.

4. Support Trusts
A support trust is one where the trustee is required to pay or apply only so much of the income or principal as is necessary for the support of the beneficiary.

a. All Income for Support
A trust to "pay all the income to A for his support" is not a support trust. When the whole of the income is to be paid to A for his support, the words "for his support" merely state the motive for the transfer. The beneficiary is not limited to amounts necessary for his support.

b. Not Assignable
Even without a spendthrift clause, the character of a beneficiary's interest in a support trust is such that no one but the beneficiary can enjoy it; his interest is not assignable by definition. His creditors cannot reach it; that would defeat the purpose of the trust.

c. Effect of Other Resources Available to Beneficiary
Whether the beneficiary of a support trust who has other income or resources that can be used for his support is entitled to support out of the trust fund without taking into account such other resources is a question of the *settlor's intention*. The cases are fairly evenly divided, some inferring that the beneficiary should receive his support from the trust regardless of other resources, and others inferring the opposite.

Example: T bequeaths a fund in trust to pay such income to B as is necessary to support B. It requires $25,000 a year to support B. B has $5,000 of income from other sources. The cases are split as to whether B gets $25,000 from the trust or only $20,000.

B. MODIFICATION AND TERMINATION OF TRUSTS

1. Power of Settlor to Revoke or Modify

a. Must Reserve Right to Revoke or Modify
In most states, without an *express* reservation by the settlor of a right to revoke or modify the trust, he has no such powers. [*Cf.* Cal. Prob. Code §15400—unless trust is expressly made irrevocable, it is revocable by settlor]

b. Power to Revoke Includes Power to Amend
Where the power to revoke exists, it includes the power to amend. If the method of revocation is specified in the trust instrument, it must be followed. If no method is specified, any instrument showing the settlor's intent will suffice. However, an inter vivos trust usually cannot be revoked by will, unless the trust expressly so provides.

2. **Modification or Termination by Agreement of Beneficiaries**
    Most jurisdictions permit modification or termination *only if*:

    (i) *All beneficiaries consent* (even a remote contingent interest in an unborn beneficiary is sufficient to preclude termination); *and*

    (ii) The modification or termination *will not interfere with a material purpose* of the trust. This is known as the "*Claflin* doctrine."

    a. **Determining Material Purpose**
        The settlor's purpose in creating a trust is not always clear from the trust language. The following examples explore the problem of determining what constitutes a material purpose of the settlor:

        1) **Distribute Principal at Designated Age**
            Where a testator creates a trust to pay the income to A *until he is 30 years old* and then to distribute the remainder to him, A is the sole beneficiary. (Note, however, had the remainder provision been to A if he is living at a stated age, and if not, then to A's issue, A would *not* be the sole beneficiary.) In this case, should A be allowed to terminate the trust before he reaches age 30? Here a court would probably say no. The primary purpose of the trust in this situation must be to keep the principal of the property out of A's hands until he reaches the designated age.

        2) **Preserve Property for Remainderman**
            If a testator left property for life to A, remainder to B, and thereafter B died leaving his remainder interest to A, A could probably terminate the trust because it was not anticipated by the settlor at the outset that A would end up with all of the interests in the property. The purpose of the trust was probably *to preserve the property for B*. To allow A to terminate now will not obstruct a purpose of the original trust.

        3) **Provide for Successive Enjoyment by Life Tenant and Remainderman**
            The most frequent type of case follows: A has a life interest and B has the remainder, and A and B join together to compel a termination of the trust. How does one determine what purpose the testator had in mind in creating the trust, unless clearly indicated on the face of the instrument?

            Of course, the whole of the instrument and its surrounding circumstances may be considered. The general inference seems to be that a trust such as this one was set up merely for the purpose of providing for successive enjoyment by A and B; and therefore, they can terminate the trust if they both agree. If there is no spendthrift provision, A can convey his life estate to B, resulting in B having the equitable fee and being able to terminate the trust. If the parties can terminate the trust by two pieces of paper (A transfers to B; B demands termination), why not let them do it with one piece (A and B demand termination)?

        4) **Protect Beneficiary from Own Poor Management or Judgment**
            However, if the settlor established a trust to protect a beneficiary from his own

mismanagement or mistakes of judgment, the beneficiary would not be allowed to terminate. In the preceding example, if it is found that the settlor established the trust for A for life because he had no confidence in A's management of the property, a court should refuse termination.

Also, the presence of a spendthrift restriction will preclude the termination of a trust, even if all beneficiaries request it, because the spendthrift clause shows the settlor's purpose and manifests his lack of confidence in the judgment and managerial ability of the beneficiaries.

b. Liability of Trustee

If *all beneficiaries consent* and if the trustee is willing to comply with their request for termination, a termination of the trust and a distribution of the corpus in the agreed fashion among the beneficiaries will almost certainly leave the trustee without any liability. This is so even though the termination of the trust violates an essential purpose of the settlor. The reason for this is that there is *no one to hold the trustee liable* for his act, all beneficiaries being estopped to bring an action against him because of their consent. (However, there is slight authority to the effect that the trustee may remain liable to the beneficiaries in such a case if a spendthrift trust were involved.)

c. Role of Settlor in Terminating Inter Vivos Trust

1) Settlor's Objections May Not Preclude Termination

If the beneficiaries have a right to terminate under the above rules, the settlor's objections will not preclude their terminating the trust. Of course, the settlor's objections might be considered relevant in determining what the purposes of the trust are and whether the termination defeats those purposes.

2) Joinder of Settlor Waives Material Purpose

If under the above rules, all beneficiaries request the termination and termination is precluded only by a material purpose of the settlor, the courts generally agree that the joinder of the settlor in the request for termination will have the effect of waiving that purpose and permitting the beneficiaries to compel termination.

3. Termination of Trust by Its Own Terms

A trust terminates when the duration of the trust as specified by the settlor has expired, or if the instrument specifies no termination time, when the settlor's purposes have been accomplished. Thereafter, the trustee must wind up the affairs of the trust with reasonable promptness, retaining only such powers as are necessary to preserve the property and to distribute it to the beneficiaries.

4. Judicial Power to Terminate or Modify Trust

a. Premature Termination

A court may terminate a trust prior to the time fixed in the trust instrument where: (i) the trust purposes are *accomplished early*; or (ii) the trust purposes become *illegal or impossible* to carry out. Trusts are not to continue where such continuation will be pointless.

b. **Doctrine of Changed Circumstances**
A court may authorize or direct a trustee to deviate from the *administrative* terms of a trust (including permitting acts that are not authorized or are even expressly forbidden by trust provisions) if (i) compliance with the terms of the trust would defeat or substantially impair the accomplishment of the trust purposes; and (ii) the settlor did not know or anticipate the new circumstances.

Example: T devised his World-Telegram newspaper stock in trust for his family and directed the trustee not to sell it. The stock has declined in value over many years and the prospects for recovery are slim. A court should approve the trustee's application to sell the stock.

1) **Doctrine Cannot Change Beneficial Rights of Beneficiaries**
The doctrine of changed circumstances cannot be used to change the beneficial rights of beneficiaries. For example, a court cannot permit invasion of principal for the income beneficiary where this has not been provided for expressly or by implication in the terms of the trust instrument—even though the life beneficiary may be in serious need of additional benefits and even though it appears from the circumstances that the settlor would have wished to permit invasion of principal had he anticipated the needs which subsequently arose.

However, a court may strain to find an implied power of invasion in the trust instrument. Recent statutes in many states give the court the power to invade principal for the income beneficiary if the court finds support of the income beneficiary was the *primary purpose* of the trust.

2) **Court Can Accelerate Vested Rights**
Although a court cannot, through the doctrine of changed circumstances, change beneficiaries' beneficial rights, it can accelerate vested rights.

Example: If B is only to receive income until age 25 and then principal at that age, with no requirement of survivorship, principal can be advanced to him earlier if needed.

V. TRUST ADMINISTRATION

A. POWERS OF THE TRUSTEE

1. **Sources of Trustee's Power**
The trustee can properly exercise only such powers as are expressly or impliedly conferred upon her. These include:

a. Powers expressly conferred upon her by the *terms of the trust*;

b. Powers conferred upon her by the *terms of a statute* or by *court decree*; and

c. Those powers that are "*necessary or appropriate to carry out the purposes of the trust* and are not forbidden by the terms of the trust" [Rest. 2d §186].

2.   Joint Powers

Where there are two or more trustees, the traditional position taken by the courts is that all trust powers had to be exercised by *unanimous* agreement. However, both the Uniform Trust Act and the Uniform Trustees' Powers Act provide that any power vested in three or more trustees may be exercised by a *majority* of them. Nearly half the states now apply this rule. Of course, under either rule, if there are only two trustees, they must act unanimously. Note that any action taken in contravention of the jurisdiction's rule is voidable.

3.   Personal Powers

Trustees' powers generally attach to the office of trustee and are not personal to the occupants originally named to that office; *i.e.,* powers usually pass to successor trustees. However, powers may be personal to a particular trustee and therefore may not pass to a successor trustee. This may be implied from the terms of the instrument and the surrounding circumstances, but courts are generally reluctant to imply such a result. The mere fact that a power is discretionary is not a sufficient basis to treat it as one personal to the particular trustee named in the instrument. Courts will consider the purposes of the trust, the nature of the power, possible special qualifications that the originally appointed trustee may have, and any other factors that appear relevant.

4.   Imperative and Discretionary Powers

    a.   Imperative Powers

    A power is "imperative" (sometimes called a "mandatory" power) where the trust terms require the performance of a particular act—*e.g.,* trustee is absolutely required to "sell all my real estate and hold the proceeds in trust for my grandchildren until they reach age 30."

    b.   Discretionary Powers

    Most powers are discretionary in the sense that the trustee may or may not perform a particular act, as she determines in her judgment to be most appropriate. Exercise of a discretionary power is subject to judicial review to prevent abuse of the trustee's discretion. To the extent that the exercise of such a power involves a *business judgment* rather than a question of law or of interpretation, a court will generally refuse to interfere.

        1)   Effect of Giving Trustee Absolute Discretion

        Where the terms of the trust provide that the trustee shall have "sole" or "uncontrolled" discretion, the trustee's power is still not wholly immune from review.

        Example: T bequeaths a large fund in trust for the comfortable support of specified relatives, and on their deaths, to charity. T's will provides that the trustee has "sole discretion to determine what amounts are payable and shall not be accountable to anyone." One of the beneficiaries is living in poverty and the trustee gives her $100 a month and accumulated income. When she asks for more income, the trustee cuts her off completely. The beneficiary can sue and receive more income by court order. The clause purporting to relieve the trustee of the legal duty to account is void, insofar as it attempts to deprive a court of jurisdiction, if a beneficiary can show that the trustee is not acting in good faith, or, in some jurisdictions, that the trustee is acting unreasonably.

2) Limitation—Trustee Must Exercise Some Judgment

A court will also intervene where a trustee has completely *failed to exercise judgment* with regard to a discretionary power.

5. Implied Powers

a. Power of Sale

Where the trust terms neither confer nor withhold the power to sell trust property, a power of sale is generally quite readily inferred by the courts. In deciding whether to infer a power of sale, courts consider the language of the instrument, the character of the property, the purposes of the trust, and whether the property is to be transferred to the remaindermen on termination of the trust. A power of sale may be more readily inferred in cases involving personal property than in cases involving real property.

1) Directive Not to Sell

Note that the settlor can direct the trustee not to sell certain property transferred into the trust. This directive is valid, and the trustee cannot sell the property without a court order permitting the sale on the grounds that circumstances have changed so much that not selling would put the trust corpus in jeopardy.

b. Power to Incur Expenses

1) Necessary and Ordinary Expenses

It is generally implied that a trustee can incur expenses that are appropriate to carry out the trust purposes. She can incur such expenses as are necessary and ordinary in the management of the trust property and in keeping the property in repair, and she can employ agents and advisors where this is prudent or where she cannot reasonably be expected to personally perform certain duties.

2) Improvements on Trust Property

Courts are less willing to infer the power to make improvements on trust property, but generally improvements can be made. Improvements involve some element of investment discretion, and one might consider in relation to the propriety of a particular improvement whether it will have the effect of concentrating investment in a particular type of property so as to be a violation of the trustee's duty to diversify investments (*see infra*).

c. Power to Lease

Normally, a trustee has an implied power to lease trust property on such terms and for such periods as are reasonable under the circumstances.

d. No Implied Power to Borrow Money

Under ordinary circumstances, the trustee has no implied power to borrow money on the credit of the trust estate; nor has she power to mortgage or otherwise encumber the trust property. However, in the well-drafted trust instrument, the trustee is usually given the express power to borrow and mortgage.

B. DUTIES OF THE TRUSTEE

1. Standard of Care Required of Trustee

In administering the trust, the trustee must exercise that degree of care, skill, and caution that would be exercised by a ***reasonably prudent person*** in managing her own property. ***Care*** relates to her diligence and to the efforts she makes. ***Skill*** relates to the trustee's capabilities. ***Caution*** is the element of conservatism in administering the trust.

2. Duty of Loyalty—No Self-Dealing

Absent court approval or contrary trust provision, a trustee cannot enter into any transaction in which she is dealing with the trust in her individual capacity. A trustee cannot "wear two hats," and in the same transaction represent both her personal interest and the interests of the trust estate. The concern addressed by the self-dealing rules is not that the trustee might act improperly or take advantage of the situation. Rather, the concern is that the trustee's personal interest might affect her judgment as to whether, for example, the price is a fair one, or whether the asset should be sold at all. The possible effect on the trustee's judgment as to the wisdom of the action is what makes the self-dealing transaction improper. A trustee owes a ***duty of undivided loyalty*** to the trust and its beneficiaries, and that loyalty might be tainted by her personal interest. No fraud or bad faith need be shown by the beneficiaries, and no excuse can be offered by the trustee to justify the transaction. The self-dealing rules apply to all fiduciaries, including guardians and personal representatives of decedents' estates.

a. Specific Self-Dealing Rules

1) Cannot Buy or Sell Trust Assets

A trustee may not purchase any property owned by the trust even if he pays full value, and may not sell assets to the trust even if the price is a fair one.

Example: The trust's assets include 2,000 shares of IBM common stock. Determining that there is a need to diversify the trust's investments, the trustee purchases 1,000 shares of IBM stock from the trust, paying the market value as determined by the New York Stock Exchange quotes on the day of the purchase. This is improper self-dealing. If the IBM stock later goes up in value, the trust beneficiaries can demand that the trustee return the IBM stock to the trust and take back his purchase price without interest. (If the IBM stock later goes down in value, the beneficiaries would ratify the transaction and waive the breach of trust, in effect telling the trustee, "thanks for getting rid of that lousy investment.")

2) Cannot Sell Assets from One Trust to Another Trust

A trustee of one trust may not sell property to another trust of which it is also trustee. The concern of this rule is not self-dealing, but the possibility of favoring one trust at the expense of another.

Example: Trust A holds 3,000 shares of Acme common stock. Deciding to diversify the trust's investments, the trustee sells 1,000 shares of the stock to Trust B, of which he is also trustee. Even though the sale price is a fair one, this is a breach of trust—and note that the trustee is in an impossible position. If the Acme stock rises in value, the beneficiaries of Trust A can sue for the lost profits. If the stock declines in value, the beneficiaries of Trust B can sue for the resulting loss.

3) Cannot Borrow Trust Funds or Make Loans to Trust
A trustee may not borrow trust funds, no matter how fair the interest rate and how well-secured the loan. A trustee may not loan his personal funds to the trust, and any interest paid on such a loan must be returned to the trust.

4) Cannot Use Trust Assets to Secure Personal Loan
A trustee may not use trust assets to secure a personal loan, and the lender does not obtain a valid security interest if she knew or had reason to know that the assets belonged to a trust.

5) Cannot Personally Gain Through Position as Trustee
A trustee cannot gain any personal advantage from his position (other than compensation for serving as trustee). The trustee is accountable for any profit arising out of administration of the trust, even if the profit did not result from a breach of trust.

6) Corporate Trustee Cannot Invest in Its Own Stock
A corporate trustee cannot invest in its own stock as a trust investment. But it can *retain* its own stock if such stock was a part of the original trust res when the trust was established, provided that retention of the stock meets the prudent investor standard.

7) Self-Employment Can Constitute Form of Prohibited Dealing
Generally, self-employment is a form of prohibited self-dealing. However, extraordinary services to the trust on the part of the trustee may entitle the trustee to additional compensation. This problem may arise if the trustee renders *legal services* to the trust that are outside the normal scope of her duties and for which additional compensation is fair and appropriate.

b. Indirect Self-Dealing—Transactions with Relatives, Business Associates
The above self-dealing rules apply to sales or loans to a trustee's relative or business associate, and to a corporation of which the trustee is a director, officer, or principal shareholder.

c. Duty to Account
The duty to keep and render accounts, and to furnish information to the beneficiary or his agent at the beneficiary's request, is one way of insuring that the trustee is meeting her obligation of loyalty.

d. Good Faith Irrelevant
Good faith on the trustee's part or benefit to the trust is irrelevant. (For example, a trustee, acting in complete good faith and to help the trust, loans money to the trust and takes a second mortgage on trust property. When the first mortgage is foreclosed, it turns out that the trustee has made a profit. That profit must be turned over to the trust.)

The policy reason for this harsh rule is that personal interest on the part of the trustee opens the door to biased judgments and thus to decisions that may not be in the beneficiary's best interests.

e. Beneficiary's Rights in Case of Prohibited Transaction

If a prohibited transaction takes place, the beneficiary may: (i) *set aside* the transaction; (ii) *recover the profit* made by the trustee, reduced by losses arising out of the same transaction (*see infra*); or (iii) *ratify* the transaction (which would occur when the transaction has turned out to be advantageous to the trust). Thus, the trustee bears the risk of subsequent loss, and is also required to turn over any profit where the dealings with the trust were advantageous to her.

f. Duty Extends Equally to All Beneficiaries

The duty of loyalty extends equally to all beneficiaries, unless the trust instrument specifies otherwise. Dealing impartially with the beneficiaries is more difficult when the beneficiaries are entitled to successive benefits; *e.g.*, A receives income for life, B receives the trust corpus at A's death. The trustee has a duty to A to see that the trust property produces income. She violates her duty to A if the property is not income-producing. On the other hand, to carry out her duty to B, the trustee must insure that the trust property will not depreciate in value.

g. Restrictions on Self-Dealing Can Be Waived by Settlor

The settlor of a trust can waive the rules prohibiting self-dealing by expressly conferring upon the trustee the power to act in a dual capacity. If the self-dealing rules are waived by the settlor, the trustee will not be held liable for his conduct unless he has acted dishonestly or in bad faith, or has abused his discretion.

3. Duty to Separate and Earmark Trust Property—No Commingling

Trust assets must be kept physically separate from the trustee's personal assets and from the assets of other trusts. (Statutory exceptions in most states permit a corporate fiduciary to hold property of trusts of which it is a trustee in a common trust fund.) In addition, trust property must be titled in the trustee, as trustee for a specific trust. For example, money deposited in a bank account must be deposited in the name of "T as trustee," and not in the name of T personally. If the trustee commingles trust assets with her own, she faces several "heads I win, tails you lose" presumptions:

a. Property Lost or Destroyed

If the trustee commingles trust property with her own and some of the property is thereafter lost or destroyed (*e.g.*, casualty loss, or failure of a bank), the presumption is that the property lost was the trustee's own, and that the property still on hand belongs to the trust.

b. Assets that Rise or Decline in Value

If a portion of the commingled assets increased in value, it is presumed that those belonging to the trust increased in value; if a portion declined in value, it is presumed that those belonging to the trustee, individually, declined in value.

4. Duty to Perform Personally (Prohibition on Delegation of Trust Duties)

A trustee cannot delegate the entire administration of a trust. On the other hand, she may delegate acts that would be unreasonable to require her to perform personally (*e.g.*, mailing letters). There is no clear-cut standard for judging when delegation is proper. Should you have a question that raises an issue of improper delegation, discuss the facts in light of what a reasonably prudent person would do, the degree of discretion delegated, and whether someone with special skill is needed to do the act.

a. Investment and Management Decisions

Under the traditional rule, investment decisions could not be delegated. Under the Uniform Prudent Investor Act ("UPIA"), however, a trustee may delegate investment and management functions that a prudent trustee of comparable skills could properly delegate under the circumstances. (For an in-depth discussion of delegating investment and management decisions, *see* C., *infra.*)

b. Following Advice of Others

The trustee can seek the advice of attorneys and others on matters that she may not delegate. However, the trustee must make the decisions. If she appears to take advice without exercising her independent judgment, she may be held liable on the theory that she improperly delegated her duties.

c. Remedy

If a trustee improperly limits or surrenders her control over trust property, she becomes a *guarantor* of the fund. Her motives or the fact that the loss was not directly caused by the abdication of control will not be considered by the court. The trustee is held liable for the *amount of the actual loss* to the trust.

5. Duty to Defend Trust from Attack

Except when the trustee's examination reveals that an attack against the trust is well founded, she has a duty to defend the trust.

6. Duty to Preserve Trust Property and Make It Productive

There is a basic duty to preserve and protect the trust corpus. From this basic duty, there normally will be implied the duty to make the trust property productive, which includes the duty to invest. The duty to preserve and protect the corpus requires that the trustee exercise reasonable care to do the following (and if she has held herself out as having special skills or has been selected on account of such special skills, she will be held to exercise such skills):

a. *Collect all claims* due the trust.

b. *Lease land or manage it* so that it is productive; or sell it if it is not productive (but this does not apply if the trust instrument requires the trustee to convey that land to a beneficiary).

c. *Record recordable documents* to protect title; keep securities and funds in safe places; *pay taxes* on trust assets to prevent liens thereon; and *secure insurance* on trust properties. It is proper for the trustee to obtain insurance on trust property—including liability insurance—even though such insurance protects her individually as well as the trust estate.

    d.   ***Invest trust funds*** within a reasonable period of time following receipt thereof (and continuously review such investments and sell and reinvest when required). If the trustee fails to invest trust monies, she is chargeable with the amount of income that would normally accrue from appropriate investments.

C. INVESTMENTS

The majority of states have enacted a version of the Uniform Prudent Investor Act ("UPIA"), which regulates the investment responsibilities of the trustee. A few states continue to use a statutory "legal list" approach, which establishes approved types of investments for a trust.

1. Uniform Act or Legal List Are Default Rules

No matter which approach to investments a state uses, the trust terms can expand or limit a trustee's powers, including investment powers. Thus, the UPIA or legal list provisions apply *only if there is no contrary provision in the trust instrument*.

a. Grant of Discretionary Powers

If the trust instrument provides for investments to be made "in the discretion of the trustee," it is a question of interpretation whether the trustee's investment power is enlarged beyond the powers prescribed by the UPIA or legal list.

1) UPIA Jurisdiction

In a UPIA jurisdiction, the trustee's authority to make investments "in her discretion" usually permits only those investments that satisfy the prudent investor standard.

2) Legal List Jurisdiction

In a "legal list" jurisdiction, such language is likely to free the trustee from the list and probably permits investment in a manner similar to that under the UPIA.

3) Language Strictly Construed

There is a tendency to strictly construe language that purports to enlarge the trustee's investment powers.

2. Uniform Prudent Investor Act

a. Standard of Care

Under the UPIA, a trustee must invest and manage trust assets as a prudent investor would, taking into account the purposes, terms, distribution requirements, and other circumstances of the trust. To satisfy this objective standard of prudence, the trustee must exercise *reasonable care, skill, and caution*. [UPIA §2(a)]

1) Fiduciaries with Special Skills Held to Higher Standard

A trustee with special skills or expertise, or who has represented herself as having such knowledge, has a duty to use those skills or expertise. [UPIA §2(f)]

2) Loyalty and Impartiality

A trustee must act exclusively for the beneficiary when investing and managing trust assets, or she is acting imprudently. [UPIA §5] If there is more than one beneficiary, she must act impartially in investing and managing the trust assets, taking into account the beneficiaries' differing interests. [UPIA §6]

b. **Prudence Evaluated as to Overall Investment Strategy**
The UPIA is based on the modern portfolio theory of investing. Thus, each investment decision must be evaluated, not in isolation, but in the context of the *entire trust portfolio* (corpus) and as part of an *overall investment strategy* that has risk and return objectives reasonably suited to the particular trust. [UPIA §2(b)] Under this approach, an investment that might be imprudent standing alone because it is too risky can become prudent if undertaken in relation to other, more conservative trust investments.

1) **Investment Performance Measured by "Overall Return"**
Under the UPIA, investment returns are measured by the "overall return" concept rather than the production of ordinary income. Historically, trustees invested with the goal of generating income for the trust (*e.g.*, dividends, interest, rental income). In today's investment world, assets that generate a steady income stream (*e.g.*, corporate bonds) may decline in real value due to inflation. In contrast, many investments (*e.g.*, publicly traded common stock, stock in a closely held corporation) generate little or no dividend income, yet produce substantial profits in the form of capital gains. A prudent investor seeks overall return, not merely income. The prudent investor rule recognizes that the most effective way to provide for current income beneficiaries, as well as the trust remaindermen, may be to generate gains through capital appreciation.

2) **Risk/Return Curve**
Modern investment practices reflect sensitivity to the so-called risk/return curve. Returns correlate strongly with risk, but tolerance for risk varies greatly with the purposes of the trust and the relevant circumstances of the beneficiaries. For example, a trust whose main purpose is to provide support for an elderly retiree of modest means will have a lower risk tolerance than a generation-skipping trust designed to build wealth for the settlor's grandchildren. The UPIA requires the trustee to *tailor an investment strategy* that incorporates risk and return objectives *suited to the particular trust.*

3) **Any Type of Investment Permitted**
The UPIA permits a trustee to invest in *any kind of property or any type of investment* "consistent with the standards of this Act"; therefore, no particular type of investment is inherently imprudent. [UPIA §2(e)] The overriding concern is the risk/return objective of the investment, rather than the classification of investments as prudent or imprudent. Depending on the objectives of the trust and the circumstances of the beneficiaries, it may be prudent for a trustee to invest in recently developed investment vehicles such as derivatives, asset-based securities, options, and commodity futures contracts.

4) **Factors Considered in Making Investment Decisions**
The following circumstances are relevant and must be considered by the trustee in making investment decisions:

(i)   General economic conditions;

(ii)   The possible effect of inflation or deflation;

(iii)   The expected tax consequences of investment decisions or strategies;

(iv)   The role that each investment plays within the overall trust portfolio;

(v)   The expected total return from income and appreciation of capital;

(vi)   Needs for liquidity;

(vii)   An asset's special relationship or value to the purposes of the trust or to one of the beneficiaries; and

(viii) Any differing interests of the income beneficiaries and the remaindermen.

[UPIA §2(c)]

a)   Retention and Disposition of Assets

Within a reasonable time after accepting the trusteeship or receiving trust assets, the trustee must review the trust assets and make and implement decisions concerning their retention and disposition, taking into account the factors listed above. [UPIA §4]

b)   Duty to Investigate

A trustee is also required to make a reasonable effort to verify information likely to affect the investment and management of the trust's assets (*e.g.,* review audit reports). [UPIA §2(d)]

5)   Diversification of Investments

A trustee must diversify the investments of the trust unless the trustee reasonably determines that, because of special circumstances, the purposes of the trust are better served without diversification. [UPIA §3]

6)   Reviewing Compliance with Act

Compliance with the UPIA is determined in light of the facts and circumstances existing *at the time of the trustee's decision or action* and not by hindsight. [UPIA §8] A trustee who acts in substantial compliance with the Act is not liable to the beneficiaries even if the trust estate declines in value or produces less income than anticipated.

c.   Delegation of Investment and Management Functions Permitted

A trustee may delegate investment and management functions that a prudent trustee of comparable skills could properly delegate under the circumstances. This provision recognizes that the trustee (especially an individual trustee) may have limited investment expertise, and that even an experienced investor may have limited expertise in sophisticated investment vehicles. The trustee must exercise *reasonable care, skill, and caution* in:

(i) *Selecting an agent*;

(ii) *Establishing the scope and terms of the delegation*, consistent with the purposes of the trust; and

(iii) *Periodically reviewing the agent's actions* to monitor the agent's performance and compliance with the terms of the delegation.

[UPIA §9(a)]

1) Agent's Duty
The agent has the duty to exercise reasonable care in complying with the terms of the delegation. [UPIA §9(b)]

2) Trustee's Liability
If the trustee exercises reasonable care, skill, and caution in selecting, delegating, and reviewing the agent's actions, she is not liable for the decisions or actions of the agent to whom the function was delegated. [UPIA §9(c)]

3. Statutory Legal Lists
A state's statutory legal list sets forth approved investments for trust assets. The list usually includes government bonds, first mortgages, and other conservative investments.

a. Permissive vs. Mandatory Lists
If the list is deemed to be "permissive," the trustee can invest in securities outside the list but incurs a heavier burden of proving the propriety of each investment when she does so. If the list is "mandatory," the trustee probably commits a breach of trust anytime she invests in properties outside the list, although the cases are not altogether consistent in this regard.

b. List May Not Be Followed Blindly
Under either type of statutory list, the trustee cannot blindly follow the list. The fact that a type of investment is permissible does not necessarily mean that the investment is proper. In selecting among permissible investments, the trustee must exercise reasonable care, skill, and caution. All circumstances must be taken into account, including such things as preserving purchasing power in the face of possible inflation, minimizing risks to capital, and the need to obtain a fair return on the investment. The propriety of particular investments is discussed below.

1) Unsecured Loans and Second Mortgages
Except for bank deposits bearing interest, an unsecured loan of trust funds is normally an improper investment. Most states regard an investment in a second mortgage as a breach of trust in the absence of extreme or compelling circumstances.

2) Corporate Stocks
Most statutory lists exclude common and preferred stocks.

3) Land
The courts are divided on whether investment in land is permissible. Acquisition

of land or other property for the purpose of resale at a profit is speculation and therefore a breach of trust.

Example: Trustee buys 1,000 acres of unimproved desert land. This is an improper investment. Not only is it speculative, but it produces no income and the trustee has the duty of making the trust property *productive.* Otherwise, the life tenant would lose his income by investments in unproductive property.

4) Mortgage Participations

Mortgage participations, under which large sums are advanced by several trusts administered by the same trustee as loans to property owners in exchange for mortgages, are increasingly upheld as proper investments—mainly because they permit a greater diversification than would be possible if a single trust fund had to make the loan by itself.

5) Investment in Mutual Funds

Historically, a trustee could not invest in mutual funds because doing so was regarded as an improper delegation of the investment duty. However, a mutual fund is a *permissible investment* under the UPIA, and statutes in several states *expressly authorize* investment in mutual funds because this produces *diversification* of investments in smaller trust estates.

6) Testator's Business

Where a testator is engaged in business at the time of his death and leaves all his property to his executor in trust, the executor cannot properly continue the business unless authorized by the testator. She must dispose of the business and make proper trust investments, and if she fails to do so within a reasonable time, she is liable for any losses that result.

D. SUMMARY—THE FIDUCIARY OBLIGATION

The standards imposed on the trustee are harsh. The policies behind such stringent standards and remedies for their violation are (i) deterrence of wrongful conduct and (ii) easing the burden of proving a breach of the duty, should that become necessary. Do not overlook mentioning policy reasons in your answer. Watch for a bar exam question regarding *self-dealing, diversification, improper investment,* and *offsetting* gain from one breach against loss from another. You should ask the following questions:

1. Was the act one that the trustee was *authorized* to perform under the terms of the trust and applicable law? If not, there is a breach of trust regardless of the good faith, skill, and diligence with which the trustee performed the act.

2. If the act was proper for the trustee to perform, did the trustee perform in a manner that *satisfies the standard of conduct* required of her? Did she act prudently, diligently, and in good faith, exercising the appropriate amount of care, skill, and caution of a reasonably prudent person under the circumstances?

E. LIABILITIES OF TRUSTEE

1. Enforcement by Beneficiaries

The beneficiaries may seek to have the trustee surcharged (pay damages suffered by the trust) or removed from office if the trustee breaches her duties. The settlor may sue if he is also a beneficiary, but third parties may not seek to enforce the trust.

a. Prior to Breach

A court of equity will compel the trustee to perform her duties or will enjoin her from committing the breach.

b. After Breach

The trustee is liable to the trust estate for losses resulting from the breach and for any profit that clearly would have accrued to the trust but for the breach, as well as any profit made by the trustee as a result of her breach. The trustee will also be liable for interest on her liability from the time of the breach.

c. Defenses

Equity may not enforce the trust if the beneficiaries expressly or impliedly *consented* to or *joined in the breach* of trust. The beneficiary must sue within a reasonable time after the breach or he will be barred from enforcing the trust by the doctrine of *laches*. Note that the mere failure to object when the trustee commits a breach of trust does not constitute consent.

2. More than One Breach of Trust—Losses Cannot Be Offset

Where a trustee is liable for losses resulting from one breach of trust, she cannot reduce the amount of this liability by offsetting it against a gain resulting from another breach of trust.

Example: Trustee is required by the trust instrument to invest in bonds. She invests one-half the corpus ($50,000) in Green Co. stock and one-half ($50,000) in Purple Co. stock. Purple Co. stock becomes worthless, but Green Co. stock doubles in value; so there is no net loss. Even so, the trustee has been dealing with *different* portions of the trust property. The gain in Green Co. stock *cannot be offset* against the loss in Purple Co. stock. Therefore, Trustee is personally liable for the $50,000 loss in Purple Co. stock.

3. Trustee's Liability for the Acts of Others

a. Agents

A trustee is *not liable* to the beneficiaries for the acts of her agents *unless* the trustee:

1) Directs, permits, or acquiesces in the act of the agent, or conceals the act, or negligently fails to compel the agent to redress the wrong;

2) Fails to exercise reasonable supervision over the agent;

3) Permits the agent to perform duties that the trustee was not entitled to delegate; or

4) Fails to use reasonable care in the selection or retention of her agents.

b. Co-Trustees

A trustee is *not liable* to the beneficiaries for a breach of trust committed by a co-trustee *unless* the trustee:

1) Improperly delegated her authority to the co-trustee (one trustee cannot delegate to a co-trustee power to manage the property);

2) Participated, approved, or acquiesced in the breach by her co-trustee, or negligently disregarded her own duties of administration so as to facilitate the breach by her co-trustee; or

3) Concealed the breach or failed to take proper steps to compel redress of it by the co-trustee.

c. Predecessor Trustees

A trustee is *not liable* to the beneficiaries for breaches of trust committed by a predecessor trustee *unless* she:

1) Knew or should have known of the breach and failed to take proper steps to prevent further breach or to compel redress of a prior breach; or

2) Negligently failed to determine the amount of property that should have been turned over to her, or otherwise neglected to obtain delivery of the full trust property from the predecessor.

d. Successor Trustees

A successor trustee can maintain the same actions as could be maintained by the original trustee. She can sue third persons for damaging trust property before she became trustee, and she can sue predecessor trustees to redress a breach of trust.

4. Effect of Exculpatory Clauses

An exculpatory clause is one that attempts to relieve the trustee of liability for breach of duty in the administration of the trust or lowers the standard of conduct required of her. Courts tend to frown upon these clauses and will construe them narrowly. An exculpatory clause designed to absolve the trustee of *all liability* will be held *void* as against public policy. Limited exculpatory clauses are valid except insofar as they attempt to relieve the trustee from liability for *bad faith, intentional breach of trust, or recklessness.* [Rest. 2d §222]

Example: The trust agreement authorizes Trustee to continue the settlor's business, and provides that Trustee shall not be personally liable for negligence. A large hole develops in the front steps of the business. Trustee is aware of this and does not remedy it within a reasonable period. Z falls in the hole and is injured. Trustee is liable since his conduct was reckless, not simply negligent.

5. Trustee's Liability to Third Parties

a. Contract Liability

Unless the contrary is explicitly provided in the contract, the trustee is personally liable to third parties on contracts entered into with them in the course of the trust administration.

1) Indemnification Rights
As long as the trustee acted properly in making the contract (*i.e.*, the contract was within her powers, and she acted with reasonable prudence and care), she is entitled to *indemnification*—either by paying the creditor directly from the trust property or by paying the claim herself and obtaining reimbursement from the trust estate.

2) Reimbursement for Legal Fees
The trustee is also entitled to reimbursement for legal fees incurred in defending suits brought against her by third parties, unless the suit arises out of a breach of duty or from some fault of the trustee.

b. Tort Liability
The trustee is personally liable to third parties for torts to the same extent as would be an *ordinary owner.* She is liable for torts committed by herself or her agents.

1) Indemnification
The trustee is entitled to indemnification from the trust if she is not personally at fault or if the tort liability is a risk that is a normal incident of the type of activity in which the trustee was properly engaged.

Example: T holds in trust an apartment house as a proper investment. T does not take out liability insurance, which is a breach of duty. A is injured when a painter negligently leaves a ladder in the hall. T is liable to A in tort. T is not entitled to indemnification from the trust because, though T was not personally at fault, the loss results from T's breach of duty in not insuring.

2) Creditors
If the trustee is entitled to indemnification, tort creditors can reach the trust assets to satisfy their claims.

F. LIABILITY OF THIRD PARTIES TO THE TRUST

1. Property Improperly Transferred to Party Who Is Not Bona Fide Purchaser
The trustee's transactions with third parties that constitute a breach of trust can be set aside by a beneficiary or successor trustee providing it does not result in taking property from a bona fide purchaser. The third party can be compelled to return the trust property improperly transferred to him or to restore the proceeds or product of that property, if it can be traced into his hands.

2. Transfer to Bona Fide Purchaser Cuts Off Beneficiaries' Interests
A third party who acquires the legal title to trust property *for value and without notice of the trust* takes the property free of the equitable interests of the beneficiaries.

a. Third Party Deemed to Have Notice If Knows Facts Requiring Inquiry
The third party will be deemed to have notice of the existence of the trust if he knows of facts requiring an inquiry that, if pursued, would have disclosed the existence of the trust. If the third party knows the property is held in trust (*e.g.*, the existence of the

trust appears on the face of a document representing the property), courts have generally held that he has a duty to inquire into the trustee's authority; therefore, he will be charged with such information as a reasonable inquiry would produce. Some cases and many statutes relieve persons dealing with trustees of the duty to inquire into the propriety of the trustee's actions.

b. Innocent Donee Is Not Liable for Damages

An innocent donee of trust property must restore the property to the trust but cannot be held liable for damages. If the donee has exchanged the trust property for other property, he can either restore the value of the property when received or its substitute, whichever value is lower.

3. Participation in Breach of Trust

Clearly, a third party who *knowingly* participates in a breach of trust by the trustee is liable for the resulting loss to the trust estate. One who *innocently participates* in a breach of trust is generally not liable to the beneficiaries, except to the extent he is obligated to return property transferred to him when not protected as a bona fide purchaser.

4. Direct Suit by Beneficiary

Generally, the beneficiaries of a trust *cannot* bring an action in law or in equity against a third party who damages the trust property or is liable to the trustee on a contract. The trustee is the proper person to sue the third party. However, the beneficiaries can sue the trustee for breach of trust. The *exceptions* to the general prohibition on a direct suit by the beneficiaries are:

a. Trustee Participates in Breach

If the trustee participates with the third party in a breach, the beneficiaries can sue the third party directly. *Rationale:* The third party has directly wronged the beneficiaries by inducing the trustee to commit a breach of trust.

b. Trustee Fails to Sue

If the trustee fails to sue a third party liable in tort or contract, the beneficiaries can bring a suit in equity to compel her to perform her duty. To prevent multiplicity of actions, the third party can be joined in this suit.

c. Trustee Abandons Office

If the trustee has abandoned her office or has left the jurisdiction and a successor trustee has not been appointed, the beneficiaries can sue the third party in equity without joining the trustee.

G. ACCOUNTING—ALLOCATION OF RECEIPTS AND EXPENSES

Assets received by the trustee must be allocated to either principal or income. For example, suppose a trust is created for A for life, remainder to B. A is to receive the income for life; at A's death, B is to receive possession of the principal. The trustee will usually credit the assets received to principal, and credit all income earned to income. However, certain receipts are of a mixed nature (both income and principal), depending upon how they are viewed, and certain expenses are made to protect both income and principal. Thus, allocation problems occur.

1. **Receipts**

    a. **Dividends on Corporate Stock**

        1) **Cash Dividends—Income**
            All cash dividends are treated as income. Dividends payable by the issuer either in cash or in stock at the option of the trustee are treated as cash dividends.

        2) **Stock Dividends—Principal**
            Dividends payable in the stock of the declaring corporation are allocable to trust principal.

    b. **Wasting Assets**
        Many assets, such as lands from which natural resources can be extracted, patent and royalty rights, and rights to annuity payments, are "wasting assets," which lose value in the income-producing process in a more dramatic fashion than is true where ordinary depreciation and obsolescence are involved.

        1) **Duty to Sell Implied**
            It is normally implied that a trustee has a duty to sell wasting assets within a reasonable time in order to preserve the value of property held for the remaindermen. But if she fails or is unable to sell the property, courts have generally held that the trustee has a duty to set aside a portion of the receipts to preserve the value of the original investment.

        2) **Effect of Authorization by Settlor to Retain**
            On the other hand, where the settlor has expressly or impliedly authorized or directed the trustee to retain such property, courts have generally inferred an intention that all receipts from the wasting asset are to be *allocable to the income beneficiary* without a duty to preserve the value of the asset for the remaindermen.

        3) **Open Mines Doctrine**
            Where the *original* trust estate contains mining property, if the mines have been opened *prior* to the creation of the trust, all the receipts therefrom are treated as income payable to the life beneficiary. On the other hand, if the mines are opened *after* the trust is created, the receipts are treated as principal that the trustee must invest, the income thereon being payable to the life beneficiary. If the mining property is purchased by the trustee after the trust is created, the receipts are likewise principal.

    c. **Unproductive or Underproductive Property**
        Property that is unproductive (produces no income), or underproductive (produces substantially less than the average rate of income on trust investments), poses several problems because its retention would be unfair to the income beneficiary. It is generally implied that the trustee is under a duty to sell such property because it would not satisfy the standards of a proper investment under local trust law. The terms of the instrument, however, may require the trustee to retain the property or permit her to do so in her discretion. If the trustee must retain such property for a period of time, the

question is whether the trustee should allocate a portion of the proceeds of sale to the income account in order to eliminate the unfairness to the income beneficiary that results from the retention of underproductive property.

1) Trustee Has No Duty to Sell—Principal

It is generally agreed that as long as the trustee had no duty to sell, but was required or authorized in her discretion to retain the property, the proceeds of sale *belong entirely to the principal account* and none are allocated to income, whether or not a profit was made on the sale.

2) Trustee Has Duty to Sell—Some Portion Allocated to Income

A quite different result is reached, however, where the trustee is under an obligation to sell the property within a reasonable time period. In such cases, it is inferred that the settlor intended the income beneficiary to receive a normal rate of return on the trust property, and the courts have generally required compensation for the lack of income by allocating a portion of the sale proceeds to income when the property is finally disposed of.

Example: Trustee is given unproductive property at the creation of the trust. Nothing is said in the trust instrument about retaining unproductive property; hence, the trustee has a duty to sell. She sells the property after five years for $130,000. Some portion of the $130,000 must be given to the income beneficiary to reimburse him for the income he would have received had the property been productive. Here, assuming a 6% interest rate and interest uncompounded, $30,000 is allocated to the income beneficiary and $100,000 is allocated to principal. The principal sum is ascertained by dividing $130,000 by 1.30. (The divisor 1.30 is reached by multiplying 6% by five (years) and adding to one.) The current sum divided by the divisor will give you the *original* amount of principal invested for five years at 6%. The difference is income. Forget compound interest. In fact, as long as you know a certain portion is allocable to income when unproductive property is sold, the exact mathematical computation should not be very important.

2. Expenses

The income beneficiaries are entitled to the *net* income of the trust. In determining what is "net income," ordinary and recurring expenses of trust administration and expenses related to the production of income are deducted from gross income (said to be "charged to the income account"). Extraordinary and capital expenditures, and those expenses incurred exclusively for the benefit of the remaindermen, are generally payable out of principal. However, improvements by the trustee are initially payable out of principal, but this is gradually recouped from income through amortization (*see* below).

a. Property Taxes

Ordinary property taxes are chargeable against income, but special assessments that result in permanent improvements (*e.g.,* for sewer construction) are chargeable to principal.

b.   **Mortgage Payments**
Interest on a mortgage debt is chargeable to income, but principal payments are chargeable to corpus.

c.   **Repairs and Maintenance**
Current expenses for repairs and maintenance and insurance premiums are chargeable to *income.*

d.   **Improvements by Trustee**
Where the trustee makes improvements that are likely to depreciate in value, the cost of the improvements is payable out of *principal*, but the cost is amortized out of *income* over the expected life of the improvement so that the principal account is paid back.

Example: The trust corpus consists of an apartment building and $100,000 in stocks and bonds. The trustee decides to install air conditioning at a cost of $10,000. She sells stock worth $10,000 to pay for the installation of the system, which is expected to have a useful life of 10 years. Each year for 10 years the trustee must set aside $1,000 from income of the trust and add it to principal so that at the end of 10 years the $10,000 taken from principal will be repaid.

e.   **Trustee's Compensation**
The trustee's compensation is usually charged against both income and corpus in some fractional manner directed either by statute or by custom in the community (*e.g.*, 5% of the income and .5% of the corpus each year).

f.   **Legal Fees**
Suppose the testamentary trust is contested at the testator's death. The trustee incurs $20,000 in legal fees in defending the trust. The legal fees incurred in establishing a trust are ordinarily payable out of principal, although to be sure, if the trust is not established, the income beneficiaries will get nothing. After the trust is established, legal fees will generally be apportioned in accordance with the protected interests.

VI.   WILL SUBSTITUTES

A.   **IN GENERAL**
If a settlor desires to transfer, at the moment of her death, property interests to a trustee and beneficiaries (or merely to a beneficiary), she must do so by a duly executed will. However, it is possible for a settlor to make an *inter vivos transfer* by which economic benefits pass at her death without the formalities of a will. The principal vehicles by which this is done are *revocable inter vivos trusts, life insurance designations,* and *bank arrangements.*

B.   **REVOCABLE INTER VIVOS TRUSTS**
A revocable inter vivos trust avoids the costs and delays of probate and has a number of advantages over a will. The reason why the revocable trust is not a will, and does not have to comply with the Statute of Wills, is that an *interest passes* to the beneficiary *during the settlor's life*; it merely becomes *possessory* on the settlor's death. The interest can be revoked or divested during the settlor's life, but it passes subject to revocation.

1. **Determining Whether an Interest Passes**

   Whether "an interest passes" during the settlor's life is really a conclusion derived from applying the ritual and evidentiary policies of the Statute of Wills. Where a written instrument is delivered to an independent third-party trustee, there is little doubt that these policies are satisfied. Still, certain problems remain with the revocable trust when the court is not satisfied that the policies are met.

   a. **Where Trustee Given Usual Powers**

      If a settlor transfers property to another in a revocable inter vivos trust, and the trustee has normal trustee powers, the trust is valid everywhere.

      Example: S transfers to T a sum in trust to pay the income to S for life, then on S's death to pay the principal as S directs by will, and if S fails to direct, to pay the principal to C. S retains the right to revoke the trust. This is a valid trust.

   b. **Where Administrative Powers Retained**

      If a settlor transfers property in writing to another in a revocable inter vivos trust, but the ***settlor retains administrative and investment control over the trustee,*** it can be argued that the arrangement is no more than an agency that ceases at the settlor-principal's death. However, almost all modern cases ***sustain*** a revocable trust of this kind.

      Rationale: The ritual and evidentiary policies of the Statute of Wills are satisfied by the writing and delivery, even though the trustee is not independent.

   c. **Declaration of Trust**

      If a settlor declares herself the trustee of a revocable inter vivos trust, the trust might fail on the theory that the settlor is still the owner and no interest has passed to a beneficiary. Inasmuch as any act by the settlor-trustee could be deemed a revocation of the trust, it is hard to see how any beneficiary would ever have any enforceable right against the settlor-trustee. Nonetheless, such a trust has been upheld in modern cases where the settlor notified third parties or ***took some action that made clear her intention to create a trust.***

      Example: S declares herself trustee of shares of stock in Bay View Corporation. The income is payable to S; the trust is revocable at any time, but if it remains unrevoked at S's death, the stock is payable to B. S ***notifies the corporation*** that she is holding the stock under a declaration of trust. The trust is valid.

                       If S merely wrote out a declaration of trust, which she kept in her desk drawer, and did not change the name on the corporation's books or notify anyone, probably no trust would be created.

      Comment: The courts want to be sure that S ***intended*** to make a ***binding*** transfer, even though revocable. The ***witnessing*** of a declaration of trust may give that assurance. Note that the Dacey trust forms in *How to Avoid Probate* are both witnessed ***and notarized*** (though the title to the property is not changed). This double ceremony is to convince the court that the settlor really intended to create a trust.

2.   Advantages of Revocable Trust

A revocable inter vivos trust is widely used in estate planning and has the following advantages:

a.   Management of Assets

Harold has retired, and he and his wife, Wanda, do a lot of traveling in their motor home. This makes management and supervision of Harold's investments rather inconvenient, so Harold transfers his investment assets to Central National Bank as trustee of a revocable trust, to pay the income to Harold for life, then to Wanda for her life, then to distribute the principal to their descendants per stirpes. This arrangement provides for effective management of Harold's assets by a bank with investment expertise and provides the other benefits described below.

b.   Planning for Incapacity—Avoidance of Guardianship

Suppose that Harold, in the above example, has a stroke and is incapacitated. If Harold had not established the revocable trust (and if Harold had not given Wanda or some other family member a "durable" power of attorney), it would be necessary to have Harold adjudicated an incompetent and a guardian appointed to manage his assets. But because Harold transferred legal title in his investment assets to the bank as trustee, the trust continues to operate for Harold's benefit without the necessity of a guardianship administration.

c.   Avoidance of Probate

Suppose Harold dies, survived by Wanda and their children. Since legal title to Harold's investment assets is held by the bank as trustee, the assets are not subject to probate administration. The assets continue to be held for the benefit of Wanda (and the children) without the expenses and delays of a probate administration.

d.   Secrecy

A will is a public record, but an inter vivos trust is not recorded anywhere. Secrecy as to assets and beneficiaries is thus available.

e.   Choice of Law

The settlor can select as trustee a person living in another state and provide that the law of that other state shall govern the trust. Local restrictions on testation can thereby be avoided—*e.g.*, by choosing a state that permits spendthrift trusts, or permits a spouse's statutory forced share to be avoided by a revocable trust.

f.   Defeat Spouse's Forced Share?

In almost all common law states, the surviving spouse is given a forced share (usually one-half) in the decedent's estate at death. By putting her assets in a revocable trust and removing them from her estate, a person can in *some* states prevent the spouse from sharing in her property. In most states, however, a revocable trust is deemed an illusory transfer and can be set aside to the extent of the spouse's forced share.

3.   "Pour-Over" Gift from Will to Revocable Trust

Suppose that S has created a revocable trust that will continue after her death for the benefit of her nephews and nieces. By her will, S wants to bequeath her residuary estate in trust for the same nephews and nieces. One approach might be for S's will to create a testamentary trust. However, this would result in two trusts for the same beneficiaries, two sets of trustee's fees, and added complications. Instead, S's will might provide: "I bequeath my residuary estate to the First National Bank, trustee under an instrument of trust executed by me on May 11, 2000, to be added to and administered in accordance with the trust terms, including any amendments thereto." Such a gift to an inter vivos trust (called a *pour-over* gift in practice) is valid under the Uniform Testamentary Additions to Trusts Act, which has been adopted by most states. The statute thus permits the integrated disposition of testamentary assets with a trust created during the settlor's lifetime.

a. Trust Must Be in Existence Before or Executed Concurrently with Will
A pour-over gift from a will to an inter vivos trust is not valid unless the trust was executed prior to, or contemporaneously with, the will. If the testator's will (making a pour-over gift) is executed on a Monday but the trust is established two weeks later, the pour-over gift is invalid and lapses.

b. Trust May Be Amendable and Revocable
A pour-over gift by will is valid even though the inter vivos trust is amendable and revocable. The gift is to the trust as it exists at the testator's death, including amendments to the trust made after the will was executed.

c. Gift Is Valid Even Though Trust Unfunded During Settlor's Lifetime
The statute authorizes pour-over gifts to a trust that is not funded with any assets during the settlor's lifetime and whose sole purpose is to receive such a testamentary gift. The statute eliminates any basis for challenging the gift on the ground that no valid trust was created during the settlor's lifetime because the trust had no res. Such a devise is valid even though the only res of the trust is the possibility of receiving a devise under a will. Another statute authorizes the payment of life insurance proceeds, employee death benefits, and similar benefits to an unfunded trust whose sole purpose is to receive such benefits on the settlor's death.

C. LIFE INSURANCE TRUSTS
Life insurance trusts are usually one of the following kinds:

1. Contingent Beneficiary Trust
W, owner and insured under a life insurance policy, designates the policy beneficiary as her husband, H; and if H does not survive W, to B to hold in trust for W's children. This is a *valid inter vivos trust*, which becomes effective immediately. The contingent right to the proceeds in W's children is a sufficient res. B has *active duties* in that he waits to see if H dies before W and, if he does, collects the proceeds on W's death. This is not a testamentary trust, even though B receives the proceeds, if at all, only on W's death, because the trust came into being during W's life.

2. Assignment of Policies
A, owner and insured under a life insurance policy, assigns the policy to B to hold in trust for A's children. The trust can be funded (*i.e.*, other funds are transferred to B from which B pays the premiums), or unfunded (*i.e.*, the only trust res is the policy and A continues to pay the premiums). In either event, it is valid as an *inter vivos transfer*.

3. Payable to Testamentary Trustee

A, owner and insured under a life insurance policy, designates as beneficiary "the trustee *named in my will*." In A's will, she names her brother B as trustee of her property for the benefit of her children. Some courts have held that this is a testamentary designation that does not comply with the Statute of Wills and, thus, fails. Others (*e.g.*, California) have held that if A has a will executed *prior* to the change in beneficiary designation, an inter vivos trust arises as soon as the beneficiary designation is made, since A so intends. However, if the beneficiary designation is "the trustee *to be named in my future will*," no inter vivos trust would arise at the time of the change of beneficiary, and the attempted designation would fail as a testamentary act. In many states (*e.g.*, California), statutes have been passed *permitting* trustees "to be named in a will" to be designated as insurance beneficiaries without rendering the transaction testamentary.

D. TOTTEN TRUST BANK ACCOUNTS

"Totten trust" is the name given to a bank account in the depositor's name "as trustee" for a named beneficiary (*e.g.*, "A, trustee for B"). Under such a bank account, A, the depositor, retains the passbook and continues to make deposits and withdrawals during her lifetime. B has no beneficial interest in the account during A's lifetime, but succeeds to whatever is on deposit at A's death. It is called a Totten trust because it was first recognized in *In re Totten,* 179 N.Y. 112 (1904).

1. Trustee-Depositor Has Full Rights During Lifetime

A Totten trust is not really a trust because there is no separation of legal and equitable title. The depositor remains the owner of all funds on deposit during her lifetime and can withdraw them at any time.

2. Revocation by Other Lifetime Act

While Totten trusts are revoked by withdrawals, they can also be revoked by any lifetime act that manifests an intent to revoke.

Example: A delivered to her attorney a document expressly revoking "all of my 'in-trust-for' accounts." This is a valid revocation, even though the revoking instrument was not delivered to the various banks. Thus the funds passed under A's will rather than to the designated Totten trust beneficiaries. The fact that A did not comply with the method for changing beneficiaries set out in the bank signature card was irrelevant; that agreement was solely for the protection of the bank and did not limit A's right to revoke.

3. Revocation by Will

If A leaves a will that says, "I bequeath all funds on deposit in my 'in-trust-for' savings accounts to my friend C," this is a valid disposition. C, and not the beneficiaries named in A's Totten trusts, is entitled to the funds on deposit.

a. Compare—Joint Bank Accounts

By contrast, a joint bank account with survivorship provisions *cannot* be bequeathed by a will.

Example: A deposits funds in a savings account, the signature card for which (signed by A and B) provides that A and B hold "as joint tenants with right of survivorship." A leaves a will that purports to bequeath all of her interest in the bank account to C. The gift to C is ineffective since on A's death the fund passed by right of survivorship to B.

4. Gift upon Delivery of Passbook

Most states hold that if depositor A delivers the passbook to beneficiary B, this constitutes a valid gift to B of the amount on deposit.

5. Subject to Creditors' Claims

Since the depositor has complete control over the deposit during his lifetime, he is treated as the owner insofar as his creditors are concerned. His creditors can reach the deposit while he is living, and can reach it as part of his estate on death.

6. Terminates If Beneficiary Predeceases Depositor

If beneficiary B predeceases depositor A, the trust automatically terminates. The funds on deposit belong to A absolutely and do not pass to B's estate. (The beneficiary must survive the depositor-trustee in order to succeed to the amount on deposit under a Totten trust account.)

E. UNIFORM TRANSFERS TO MINORS ACT ("UTMA")

To provide a convenient procedure for making gifts to minors who have no legal capacity to manage or sell property, every state has enacted some version of the UTMA, under which property may be transferred to a person (including the donor) as custodian for the benefit of a minor. The transfer may be made to a custodian by an executor, trustee, or guardian under a governing instrument (*e.g.*, will, power of appointment, or deed, for a minor beneficiary). The transfer is in the form, "To [name of custodian] as custodian for [name of minor] under the [name of state] Uniform Transfers to Minors Act." Under the Uniform Act, custodianship terminates when the donee attains age 21. [UTMA §20]

1. Custodian's Powers and Duties

A custodianship is not a trust. The custodian does not hold legal title to the custodial property; legal title is in the minor, subject to the custodian's statutory power. The custodian has statutory powers: (i) to collect, hold, manage, invest, and reinvest the custodial property; (ii) to pay to or on the minor's behalf so much or all of the custodial property as the custodian deems advisable for the minor's use and benefit; and (iii) to the extent not expended, to pay over the property when the minor attains age 21 (or to the minor's estate should she die before age 21). A custodian is a fiduciary and is subject to the standard of care of a prudent person dealing with property of another.

2. Qualifies for Annual Gift Tax Exclusion

A custodial gift made pursuant to the Uniform Act qualifies for the $11,000 per donee annual federal gift tax exclusion.

VII. TRUSTS ARISING AS A MATTER OF LAW—RESULTING AND CONSTRUCTIVE TRUSTS

A. IN GENERAL

Resulting and constructive trusts do not arise by a settlor's express declaration of trust. They are *implied* by law or *imposed* by the courts. Resulting trusts involve a reversionary interest when the equitable interest in property is not completely disposed of and are based on the presumed intent of the settlor. The doctrine of constructive trusts was developed by equity courts as a means of granting relief where, by a series of events, one person has obtained legal title to property (real or personal) that, the conscience of equity feels, rightfully belongs to another, the purpose being to prevent unjust enrichment by the person who has obtained title. Since resulting and constructive trusts are implied by the courts, the Statute of Frauds is inapplicable; no writing is necessary even where real property is involved.

B. RESULTING TRUSTS—WHEN WILL THEY BE IMPLIED?

Resulting trusts are generally of three types: (i) *purchase money resulting trusts*, (ii) resulting trusts arising on *failure of an express trust*, and (iii) resulting trusts arising from an incomplete disposition of trust assets (*i.e., excess corpus*). In resulting trusts, the person who is declared by equity to be the beneficiary of the resulting trust is the one responsible for supplying the trust property (corpus). He has either directly conveyed the property to the person held to be the trustee, or he has supplied the consideration for a transaction through which the other person, the "trustee," acquired title to the property. Thus, the person who holds title did not give consideration. From this fact, equity presumes that he was not intended to have the benefits of ownership and that he should be a trustee for the person who did furnish the consideration or conveyed title to him.

1. Purchase Money Resulting Trusts

In the typical situation, there is a sale of property—real or personal—in which Y obtains legal title from the seller (*e.g.*, a deed names him as grantee; stock certificates list him as owner). But Y, who takes title, did not supply the consideration; another person, X, paid the consideration. Unless X and Y are close relatives, it is unlikely that X intended a gift. X probably intended to retain some benefit; thus, the courts imply that Y is trustee and X is beneficiary of a resulting trust. ("Resulting" in that it results from X having furnished the consideration.) This resulting trust is dry or passive in that Y, the title holder and trustee, has no management duties. His sole duty is to convey his title to X, the beneficiary. The court's decree that there is a resulting trust will likely order him to do so.

a. Form of Consideration Immaterial

The consideration given by X, the beneficiary, is usually money; but it need not be. The resulting trust will arise if the seller asks for consideration in the form of services and X supplies them, or if X gives consideration by canceling a debt owed to him by the seller. The trust will be implied whether X pays the consideration directly to the seller or deposits it with Y, who in turn passes it to the seller and takes title. *But note:* A resulting trust arises only from consideration *given for actual purchase of the property.* This excludes money furnished by X to pay off a mortgage, to pay taxes on the land, or to build improvements on it.

b. Time When Consideration Furnished

For a resulting trust to arise, the beneficiary, X, must supply the consideration *at or before* the time Y takes title (*e.g.*, in the case of real property, at the time of delivery of the deed to Y). It is also sufficient if X obligates himself, prior to or at the time Y takes title, to pay the consideration (*e.g.*, X gives the seller a promissory note). Payments made by X *after* Y has taken title will not give rise to a resulting trust unless X has bound himself to make such payments.

c. **Burden of Proof on One Claiming as Beneficiary**

The burden is on X, the party claiming to be the beneficiary of a resulting trust, to prove by clear and convincing evidence that he supplied the consideration. He is entitled to bolster his claim by extrinsic evidence (*i.e.*, evidence outside the contract of sale of the property and the deed or other document of title given to Y) that Y had agreed to hold the property solely for his benefit. Of course, if there is an actual trust agreement between X and Y, and if any applicable Statute of Frauds provision is satisfied, the trust would be an express trust, not a resulting trust.

d. **Rebuttable Presumption of Resulting Trust**

Once X proves he supplied the consideration, a resulting trust is presumed. However, Y, the title holder and alleged trustee, may rebut the presumption by submitting evidence that no trust was intended and that, to the contrary, the money used as consideration for the purchase was either: (i) a *gift* from X to Y; (ii) a *loan* from X to Y; or (iii) *payment* by X of a *debt owing* to Y.

1) **Presumption Rebutted by Proof of Loan**

If X loans the money to Y to buy the property, there is no resulting trust, because the money belonged to Y (who had obligated himself to repay the loan) when the consideration was paid. On the other hand, if X lends money to Y to purchase property and title is taken in the name of X, the lender, there is a resulting trust in favor of Y as beneficiary because he supplied the consideration (funds he had borrowed) and yet did not receive title.

2) **Recitals as to Who Paid Consideration Not Conclusive**

A recital in the contract of sale, deed, or other document of title that X (or Y) paid the consideration is not conclusive. Extrinsic evidence will be received to establish not only how much the consideration for a transfer was, but also who paid it.

3) **Effect of Agreement Between Parties as to Nature of Interest**

The alleged trustee, Y, may *partially* rebut the presumption of a trust by showing, for example, that X and Y had agreed that X (who paid the consideration) would have only a life estate or some other interest less than a full fee simple absolute in resulting trust.

e. **Major Exception—No Trust Presumption Where Parties Closely Related**

If X (the person supplying the consideration) is a close relative of Y (the one taking title), *a gift* from X to Y of the funds used for consideration, rather than a resulting trust, is presumed. The close family relationship between X and Y precludes any presumption of a trust.

1) **Relationships Where Gift Is Presumed**

A gift, not a trust, is presumed from the following relationships:

(i) *Parent* supplies consideration, title taken in *child's* name.

(ii) *Grandparent* supplies consideration, title taken in *grandchild's* name.

(iii) *Husband* supplies consideration, title taken in *wife's* name.

Note: Older cases assumed a wife was under her husband's domination and that where she supplied the consideration and he took title, no gift would be presumed. Some recent cases are contra (on the theory that in contemporary marriages wives are not dominated by husbands and are as likely to make gifts to their spouses as are husbands).

2) Relationships Where Trust Is Presumed
The normal presumption of a trust applies where the person furnishing consideration is the *uncle, aunt, brother, sister, child, or grandchild* of the person receiving title.

f. Second Exception—Unlawful Purpose
Equity will usually decline to imply a trust where the arrangement under which title is taken in Y's name is for an unlawful purpose, such as:

(i)   X, who supplied the consideration, is trying to keep property from his creditors.

(ii)   X is trying to avoid a tax liability.

(iii)   Y is eligible for financing (*e.g.*, he is a veteran) that X cannot get.

This exception is often justified on the ground that X cannot invoke the equitable resulting trust doctrine because he has "unclean hands." Under recent decisions, however, illegality of purpose may not always bar relief by way of resulting trust, especially where the gravity of the illegal scheme is slight compared to the unjust enrichment that will occur if Y is permitted to keep the property for which he did not pay.

g. Third Exception—Transferee Obtained Title Wrongfully
For there to be a resulting trust, the placing of title in Y's name must be with the consent of X, the one furnishing consideration. Where Y has taken title without such consent, there is usually fraud or other wrongdoing sufficient to raise a *constructive trust* in favor of X.

h. Pro Rata Resulting Trusts
Where X pays only part of the purchase price, the resulting trust in his favor will be only for a pro rata portion of the title. Thus, if the total price is $8,000 and X paid $2,000 of it, the resulting trust doctrine makes X the equitable owner of an undivided one-fourth interest. He is a co-tenant with the title holder, Y (or perhaps with some other resulting trust beneficiary who paid all or part of the remaining $6,000).

2. Resulting Trusts Arising on Failure of Express Trust
Typically, S, the settlor, creates an express trust and conveys legal title to T, the trustee. A problem arises when the beneficiary of the trust cannot be located or is dead, or the trust is unenforceable or void for some other reason (*e.g.*, it violated the Rule Against Perpetuities), and the settlor, S, in creating the trust, did not provide what should be done with the property in this event. Equity implies the answer: The express trust ends and a resulting trust arises in which S is the beneficiary. This resulting trust is dry or passive—T's duty as trustee of the resulting trust is simply to convey title back to S. If S is dead, his estate is the beneficiary. The property will go to his heirs or to those who took under his will.

52. TRUSTS

a. **Rationale**

The theory of this type of resulting trust is that S must have intended the property to revert to him or his successors if the trust could not be carried out. T was intended only to manage the property and not to have full beneficial ownership. Since the trust has failed, T's duties have ended and he should not be entitled to retain title to the trust property.

b. **No Resulting Trust Where Consideration Paid to Settlor**

There is no resulting trust in favor of S where he received consideration for his conveyance of the property to the trustee. If someone other than T paid the consideration, a trust may result in favor of that person. If T paid it, T keeps title.

c. **On Failure of Charitable Trust**

Where the express trust is charitable and the designated beneficiary ceases to exist (*e.g.*, the XYZ Home for the Blind closes down operation), a resulting trust in favor of the settlor is implied *where no general charitable intent* by S appears (so that the cy pres doctrine is inapplicable).

d. **Limitation—Illegal Purpose**

If the express trust that fails was established by S for an illegal purpose (*e.g.*, to defraud S's creditors), equity may refuse to imply a resulting trust, allowing T to keep title plus the beneficial interest. Recent cases indicate equity will imply a resulting trust despite the illegal scheme if the gravity of S's wrongdoing is slight compared to the unjust enrichment T would obtain if he were permitted to keep the trust property.

3. **Resulting Trust Implied from Excess Corpus**

A resulting trust in favor of the settlor also arises when the trust purpose is fully satisfied and some trust property remains (*e.g.*, trust was to construct a lodge building and the project is completed with funds left over). There could be a resulting trust of part of the corpus even where the trust is not completely terminated, if it is clear that the trust property is in excess of the amount needed to carry out the trust purpose.

C. **CONSTRUCTIVE TRUSTS—WHEN WILL THEY BE IMPLIED?**

A constructive trust is not really a trust at all. Rather, "constructive trust" is the name given to a flexible remedy imposed by a court of equity to prevent an unjust enrichment of one person at the expense of another as the result of *wrongful conduct*, such as fraud, undue influence, or breach of a fiduciary duty. The constructive trustee's *only* duty is to convey the property to the person who would have owned it but for the wrongful conduct. This permits the wronged party to receive the very property of which he was deprived. This remedy is especially important where property has increased in value since it was wrongfully acquired.

Proof of the facts necessary to establish a constructive trust must be by *clear and convincing evidence*.

1. **Constructive Trust Arising from Theft or Conversion**

If Y steals or converts property from X, *title remains in X*, so there is no need to imply a trust to restore title to the owner, X. But if Y uses the proceeds of his theft to buy other property, he takes title to it. X can trace to this new property and have a constructive trust imposed upon it to prevent Y from profiting from his wrong. X is the beneficiary of the constructive trust; Y is the trustee. Y's sole duty is to convey the property to X, for once a constructive trust is declared by a court to exist, it is a dry trust, the trustee having no active management duties.

2. **Constructive Trust Arising from Fraud, Duress, Etc.**
Where Y, by fraudulent misrepresentation or concealment (*see* Torts outline) ***causes X to convey title to property to him,*** X is entitled to a decree that Y holds the property in constructive trust for X's benefit. Moreover, if Y, after defrauding X out of property, sells or exchanges it for other items, the items would be the subject of a constructive trust under the tracing doctrine.

  a. **Property Conveyed to Third Party Who Is Not a Bona Fide Purchaser**
  If Y acquired title from X by fraud and conveyed title to a third party, Z, who is not a bona fide purchaser (*e.g.*, he did not pay value or he knew that Y had acquired title by fraud), the constructive trust could be imposed against Z, requiring him as "trustee" to convey title back to the victim, X.

  Accordingly, where the third party, Z, has given value to Y to acquire X's property and has acquired it with notice of fraud, the victim, X, will have a choice of two possible constructive trusts to pursue (*i.e.*, X can have Z declared constructive trustee of the original property or have Y declared constructive trustee of the proceeds from the sale to Z).

  b. **Circumstances Giving Rise to Constructive Trust**
  As in the case of fraud, a constructive trust will be declared against a party who obtains title to property by ***duress, undue influence, or mistake of fact***. (Under recent decisions, even a unilateral mistake of material fact by the owner of property, causing him to convey it, is a sufficient basis for implying a constructive trust.)

  c. **Where Will Is Concealed or Fraudulent**
  Where Y conceals X's true will and takes property under a prior will or by intestacy, he holds the property as constructive trustee for the aggrieved devisees and legatees. Where a party takes title to property under a forged or fraudulent will, he is a constructive trustee for decedent's aggrieved heirs or devisees, even if he was innocent of wrongdoing.

  d. **Interference with Contract Relations**
  The constructive trust remedy is also available against a party who obtains title to property by committing the tort of interference with contract relations.

3. **Constructive Trust Arising from Breach of Fiduciary Duty**

  a. **Fiduciary Relationship Defined**
  One who stands in a fiduciary relationship to another person owes that person a duty to deal fairly with his property. Examples of the fiduciary relationship are attorney to client, guardian to ward, director to his corporation, trustee to trust beneficiary, executor to estate, etc. The fiduciary's duty prohibits him from taking title to property belonging to the beneficiary (at least not without making full disclosure as to its value,

etc.), and from seizing for himself an opportunity to acquire property that comes to him in his capacity as fiduciary. (*See, e.g.*, the Corporations outline on the duty of a director not to "usurp a corporate opportunity.")

b. Breach of Fiduciary Duty

If the fiduciary violates this duty, he will be required to hold the property he thereby acquires in constructive trust in favor of the person to whom he owes the duty. Under the same principle, if an attorney advising a client on his will permits the client to leave property to the attorney without the attorney's making full disclosure of all he knows concerning its value, the attorney will, on the client's death, hold title to the property in constructive trust for the estate of the client.

4. Constructive Trust Arising from Homicide

If one person kills another and is convicted of murder or manslaughter, he holds any property he acquires from the victim by will or intestacy as constructive trustee in favor of whomever would have taken the property (*e.g.*, a more distant relative of the victim) had the killer predeceased the victim. (*See* Wills outline.)

a. Where Victim and Killer Held Property in Joint Tenancy

Where the victim held property in joint tenancy with the killer, the latter obtains full legal title to the property. However, he holds at least one-half interest therein as constructive trustee for the estate of the victim. In some states, he holds the whole fee in constructive trust for the victim's estate, less his own life estate in one-half.

5. Constructive Trust Arising from Breach of Promise

a. General Rule—No Constructive Trust

Generally, a person's mere breach of a promise is not a sufficient basis for implying a constructive trust. Thus, where A conveys real property to B on B's oral promise either to hold it as trustee for C or to convey it to C, and B later repudiates his promise, the majority rule is that there is no constructive trust. (If the rule were otherwise, the purpose of the Statute of Frauds would be frustrated.) However, A may be able to get a constructive trust imposed in his favor. (A minority of cases and the Restatement (Second) of Trusts say he can.) A can then convey the property directly to C. The theory is that to permit B to keep the property would result in unjust enrichment, which thwarts the purpose of the Statute of Frauds.

1) Consideration for Promise Irrelevant

The general principle that a mere breach of promise will not raise a constructive trust uniformly applies even where there was consideration for the promise. A may recover damages and, in some circumstances, obtain specific performance, but a constructive trust will not be imposed.

b. Exceptions to General Rule

1) Breach of Fraudulent Promise—Fraud in the Inception

If A conveys land to B on his oral promise to hold it for, or convey it to, C, and if *at the time he made the promise B did not intend to keep it*, there is almost certainly fraud (misrepresentation) and a constructive trust will be imposed against B in favor of C (or perhaps in favor of A, who will then be able to convey directly to C).

2)   Breach of Promise by One in Confidential Relationship
Where the grantee who orally promises to hold the property in trust is in a confidential relationship with the grantor (family relation, attorney-client, business partners, etc.), the breach of the grantee's promise is constructively fraudulent and the agreement to hold in trust may be shown for the purpose of imposing a constructive trust for the benefit of the intended beneficiaries. The grantee's promise must be proved by clear and convincing evidence.

This is the big loophole in the Statute of Frauds. Such a confidential relationship exists not only where there is a fiduciary relationship such as attorney-client, but also where the transferor, because of family relationships or otherwise, is accustomed to being guided by the judgment of the transferee. Very seldom will a person give a deed of land to another on an oral trust where a confidential relationship does not exist.

3)   Breach of Promise Concerning a Will or Inheritance
Broken promises to a decedent concerning devolution of his property on death are a major exception to the general rule that a mere breach of promise is an insufficient basis for imposing a constructive trust. This exception appears to stem from the fact that when the promise is broken, the promisee is dead, unable to personally seek enforcement, and thus particularly in need of assistance from equity.

Examples: 1) H wills all his property to W in reliance on her oral promise to leave it to H's children at her death. H dies; W takes the property, but on her death wills it to X. X holds title as constructive trustee for H's children. (*See* Wills outline on will contracts.)

2) A writes his will leaving his property to B (or forgoes changing a prior will in favor of B) in reliance on B's promise to hold the property for C or to convey it to C. A dies, B takes title and does not carry out his promise. The majority rule holds that B is a constructive trustee for C. The same rule applies where A forgoes writing any will and dies intestate in reliance on a promise by his intestate heir, B, to hold for or convey to C. (*See* discussion of secret and semi-secret trusts, II.B.2.b., *supra*.)

In both examples 1) and 2), the required promise of the constructive trustee can be implied, as where the testator asks him if he will dispose of the inheritance or bequest in a certain manner and he remains silent under circumstances, suggesting acquiescence.

3) X renders services to Y in reliance on Y's promise to leave property to X, and Y does not do so. Some courts will find the heir or devisee of Y who has taken title on Y's death to be a constructive trustee for X, particularly ***where X's services are difficult to***

value so that an action for quasi-contract against Y's estate is not an adequate remedy; *or where X would suffer unconscionable injury* because he has been induced to make a detrimental *change of position* in reliance on the oral agreement. Other jurisdictions hold that the Statute of Wills or the Statute of Frauds bars the constructive trust remedy in this context.

4) Promise Causing Debtor to Forgo Bidding at Foreclosure Sale

Some jurisdictions will impose a constructive trust on the promisor where his promise to buy and convey land to the debtor causes the debtor to forgo bidding at the foreclosure sale.

Example: A's land is to be sold in a foreclosure sale. B promises to buy the land for A's benefit; and, in reliance, A does not bid at the sale. B buys the land but breaks his promise to hold for A or convey to A. A number of jurisdictions will hold B a constructive trustee for A, on condition A repay B's expenses, particularly where B's actual damages are hard to value. Other jurisdictions hold that the Statute of Frauds bars the constructive trust remedy under such facts.

c. Standard of Proof—Clear and Convincing Evidence

The party seeking to have a constructive trust imposed must prove the facts he relies on (*e.g.*, fraud, breach of confidence, theft, etc.) by clear and convincing evidence (*i.e.*, more than a mere preponderance).

D. OBLIGATIONS OF TRUSTEE OF CONSTRUCTIVE OR RESULTING TRUST

1. Duty to Convey Title

From the time the court declares a constructive or resulting trust to exist, *the sole duty of the trustee is to convey legal title to the beneficiary.* If he does not do so, he is responsible for the profits the beneficiary would have earned. This problem is usually avoided by the court decreeing title to be in the beneficiary at the time it finds an implied trust to have arisen.

2. Other Trustee Duties and Liabilities—Constructive Trusts

When a court declares a constructive trust to exist, such a trust is retroactive to the later of (i) the date the trustee took title or (ii) the time of the fraud, breach of promise, or other wrongful conduct on which the trust is based.

a. All Profits Taken from Property

From that date, the trustee is accountable to the beneficiary for all profits he has taken from the property and, if he has used it himself, its fair rental value.

b. Profits on Transactions in Breach of Fiduciary Duty

Also, from that date, the trustee owes a fiduciary duty to the beneficiary to deal fairly with the property and to make full disclosure, and he will be accountable for profits made on transactions where he breached this duty.

c. Liability for Damage to Property

During this period of time and prior to conveying title to the beneficiary, the trustee will be held liable for damages to the property that he willfully or negligently causes.

d. **No Duty to Invest**
   The trustee has no duty to invest the trust property.

3. **Other Trustee Duties and Liabilities—Resulting Trusts**
   The rules above are also applicable to trustees of resulting trusts from the date on which they arise:

   a. In the case of a resulting trust on failure of express trust, from the date the express trust becomes void, or from the date it becomes inoperable for lack of a beneficiary;

   b. In the case of excess corpus, from the date the trust purpose is completed; and

   c. In the case of a purchase money resulting trust, from the date the trustee takes title to the property.

4. **Tracing Assets**
   The doctrine of tracing trust assets is fully applicable to dealings by the trustee of a constructive or resulting trust with trust property and the profits from trust property.

E. **APPLICATION OF EQUITABLE PRINCIPLES**
   Actions in which a party seeks a declaration imposing a resulting or constructive trust were historically actions in equity. Thus, most equitable principles are applicable.

1. **Party Claiming as Beneficiary Must Not Have "Unclean Hands"**
   The party claiming to be the beneficiary of such a trust may be denied relief if he has "unclean hands" (*i.e.*, his conduct regarding the matter at issue has been unlawful or inequitable, *e.g.*, if he has made misrepresentations to other parties).

2. **Party Claiming as Beneficiary Must Be Willing to "Do Equity"**
   The party claiming to be the beneficiary of such a trust and seeking relief in equity must himself "do equity." For example, if the alleged trustee has in good faith paid taxes on the property, paid for sewer liens and the like, or constructed improvements on the land, the beneficiary must agree to make reasonable reimbursement to the trustee.

3. **Exception—Adequate Remedy at Law Does Not Preclude Relief**
   While most equitable principles apply to actions seeking to impose a resulting or constructive trust, there is one important exception: These remedies are generally available even though the one claiming to be the beneficiary has an adequate remedy at law (*e.g.*, a suit for damages). In answering a question on constructive or resulting trusts, you should expressly state that an adequate remedy at law ordinarily does not preclude such type of equitable relief. However, as noted above, an adequate remedy in damages at law may preclude a constructive trust in two particular instances: (i) breach of oral promise to make a will; and (ii) breach of oral promise to hold property purchased at foreclosure sale for the benefit of the promisee.

BAR REVIEW

Wills

celebrating over

30 YEARS

of preparing law students for the bar exam

WILLS

TABLE OF CONTENTS

I. INTRODUCTION

A. HISTORICAL BACKGROUND

Historically, real property and personal property were treated differently (the law relating to real property originated with the common law courts, while the law relating to personal property originated with the ecclesiastical courts). The modern trend is to eliminate any differences in the treatment of real and personal property, but some distinctions still exist in many jurisdictions. The vocabulary of intestate succession and wills also has a historical basis.

B. TERMINOLOGY

Although the distinctions between many of these terms have now been blurred (*e.g.,* any dispository clause in a will may be termed a "devise"), the following list of terms is helpful in understanding any discussion of the passing of property at death.

1. When property passes by *intestate succession:*

    a.   The decedent is the "intestate";

    b.   The person entitled to property is the "heir" (who takes by "descent");

    c.   "Issue" and "descendants" are synonymous, both referring to all *lineal descendants* and including adopted offspring; and

    d.   The personal representative is the "administrator."

2. When property passes by *will:*

    a.   The decedent is the "testator";

    b.   The clause directing disposition of land is the "devise";

    c.   The person entitled to land is the "devisee";

    d.   The clause directing disposition of personal property is a "legacy" as to money and a "bequest" as to other personal property;

    e.   The person entitled to personal property is the "legatee"; and

    f.   The personal representative is the "executor," where named in the will (otherwise, the "administrator cum testamento annexo," *i.e.,* administrator with the will annexed).

II. INTESTATE SUCCESSION

A. IN GENERAL

Intestate succession is the statutory method of distributing assets that are not disposed of by will. Property may pass by intestate succession where:

(i)   The decedent dies without having made a will;

(ii) The decedent's will is denied probate (*e.g.,* due to improper execution or successful will contest);

(iii) The decedent's will does not dispose of all his property (resulting in "partial intestacy") either because a gift has failed or because the will contains no residuary clause; or

(iv) The decedent's will specifies that his property should pass according to the laws of intestate succession.

At common law, all real property passing by intestate succession went to the decedent's children (the surviving spouse was entitled only to dower or curtesy). Personal property went one-third to the surviving spouse and two-thirds to the surviving children. Today, the distribution of an intestate decedent's property is governed by state statute.

B.   INTESTATE SHARE OF SURVIVING SPOUSE

1.   Descendants Also Survive
If the decedent is survived by a spouse and by descendants, in most states the surviving spouse takes ***one-third or one-half of the estate***. Some states give the surviving spouse a specific dollar amount plus the one-third or one-half of the estate. In some states (*e.g.,* states adopting the Uniform Probate Code ("UPC")), however, the surviving spouse takes the entire estate if the decedent is survived by descendants who are all descendants of the surviving spouse.

2.   No Descendants Survive
If the decedent is survived by a spouse, but no descendants, in most states the surviving spouse takes the entire estate. In UPC states, the spouse takes the entire estate only if the decedent is not survived by descendants or parents.
Example: W dies, survived by her husband H and her parents, M and D. In most states, H would inherit the entire estate.

C.   INTESTATE SHARE OF CHILDREN AND OTHER DESCENDANTS
The portion of the estate that does not pass to the surviving spouse, or the entire estate if there is no surviving spouse, passes to the decedent's children and descendants of deceased children. Parents and collateral kin never inherit if the decedent is survived by children or more remote descendants.

1.   Majority Rule—Per Capita with Representation
In most states, the decedent's issue take their shares per capita with representation. Under this pattern of distribution, the property is divided into equal shares at the first generational level at which there are living takers. Each living person at that level takes a share, and the share of each deceased person at that level passes to his issue by right of representation.
Examples: 1) D, a widow, dies intestate survived by: (i) child A, who has a son, W; (ii) X and Y, grandchildren by D's deceased child B; and (iii) grandchild Z, the daughter of D's deceased child C.

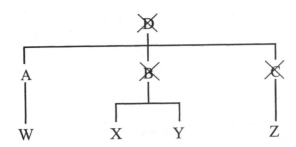

Since there is a living heir at the first generational level, D's estate is divided into three equal shares at that level. A takes one-third. The one-third that B would have inherited had he survived D passes by right of representation to his children, X and Y (one-sixth each). Similarly, Z takes a one-third share. W takes nothing even though he is D's issue because his mother A is alive to inherit.

2) Same family tree as above, except that A also predeceased D. Since there are no living takers at the first generational level, the shares are determined at the second generational level. Each grandchild takes a one-fourth share.

This type of distribution is often called a "per stirpes" distribution. Note, however, that this is different from a "strict per stirpes" distribution (followed by only a few states), under which the stirpital shares are determined at the first generational level beyond the decedent even if there are no living takers.

2. Modern Trend—Per Capita at Each Generational Level

The modern trend is to replace the above scheme with a rule under which the distribution is per capita at each generation. Under this scheme, the initial division of shares is made at the first generational level at which there are living takers, but the shares of deceased persons at that level are combined and then divided equally among the takers at the next generational level. Thus, persons in the same degree of kinship to the decedent always take equal shares.

Examples: 1) W, a widow, dies intestate survived by: (i) her son, A; (ii) by grandchild Q (the child of her deceased son B); and (iii) grandchildren X, Y, and Z (the children of her deceased daughter C).

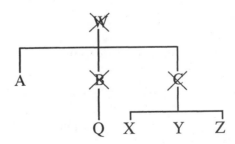

Under a *per capita with representation distribution*, A would take one-third; Q would take one-third; and X, Y, and Z would take one-ninth each, taking by representation the share of their deceased parent. In effect X, Y, and Z were penalized because they came from a larger family than their cousin Q.

Under the ***per capita at each generational level*** scheme, A takes one-third (because there are three lines of issue). The other two one-third shares are combined into a single share (amounting to two-thirds of the estate) and distributed in equal shares at the next generational level. Q, X, Y, and Z take one-sixth each.

2) Same facts as above, except that A also predeceased W, leaving no issue.

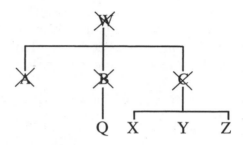

Here, the first generational level at which there are living takers is the grand-child level. The grandchildren take per capita, one-fourth each.

D. SHARES OF OTHER HEIRS

1. Parents
If the decedent is not survived by a spouse or descendants, in most jurisdictions the estate passes to the decedent's parents (one-half each) or surviving parent (who takes all).

2. Descendants of Parents
If the decedent is not survived by a spouse, descendants, or parents, the estate passes to the descendants of the decedent's parents, *i.e.,* the decedent's brothers and sisters and the issue of deceased brothers and sisters.

3. Grandparents
In most states, if the decedent left no spouse, descendants, parents, or descendants of parents, one-half of the estate passes to the decedent's maternal grandparents or their descendants and one-half passes to the paternal grandparents or their descendants.

4. Nearest Kin
If the decedent is not survived by any of the above, most states divide the estate into maternal and paternal shares. One-half goes to the nearest kin on each side of the family, no matter how remotely related to the decedent. Some states, however, have enacted "laughing heir" statutes, which cut off inheritance by persons so remotely related to the decedent that they suffer no sense of loss, only gain, at the news of the death. These statutes usually cut off inheritance rights of persons related to the decedent beyond the descendant-of-the-grandparents level.

5. Escheat
If the decedent does not leave any relative capable of taking the estate, the estate passes to the state. This is called escheat.

E. SPECIAL CASES INVOLVING CHILDREN

1. Adopted Children

a. As to Adopting Family—Adopted Child Treated Same as Natural Child

For purposes of intestate succession, an adopted person is treated the same as a natural child of his adopting parents. The adopted child can inherit from and through his adopting parents, and the adopting parents and their kin can inherit from and through the adopted child. A child adopted after the execution of a will is considered to be a pretermitted child within the meaning of a pretermitted child statute (*see* IX.B., *infra*). Similarly, an adopted child is considered to be a lineal descendant within the meaning of an anti-lapse statute (*see* VIII.A., *infra*).

b. As to Natural Parents—All Inheritance Rights Cut Off

Where a child is adopted by a new family, the adopted child and his kin have no inheritance rights from or through the adopted child's natural parents, and the natural parents and their kin have no inheritance rights from or through the natural child who has been put up for adoption.

1) Exception—Adoption by Spouse of Natural Parent

Adoption of a child by the spouse of a natural parent has no effect on inheritance rights between the child and that natural parent or his family. Inheritance rights concerning the other natural parent, however, are severed. Under the UPC, such an adoption has no effect on inheritance rights from or through *either* natural parent. Therefore, under the UPC, an adopted child may inherit from or through both natural parents as well as the adopting parent, whether the marriage of the natural parents was ended by divorce or death.

Example: Wanda and Harry have a child (Art). Wanda divorces Harry. Some years later, Wanda marries Sam; Sam adopts Art. For purposes of inheritance, Art is a child of his natural mother Wanda, and is a child of his adoptive father Sam and any inheritance rights concerning Harry have been severed. Under the UPC, however, Art has three lines from which he can inherit: Wanda and her family, Sam and his family, and Harry and his family.

2) Exception—Death of Natural Parent

Adoption of a child by the spouse of a natural parent who married the natural parent after the death of the other natural parent has no effect on inheritance rights between the child and the family of the deceased natural parent. Also, adoption of a child by a close relative has no effect on the relationship between the child and the families of the deceased natural parents.

Example: Suppose in the above example, Art's natural father (Harry) died, and Art's natural mother subsequently married Sam, who adopted Art. This second exception simply means that Art continues to have inheritance rights through his deceased natural father (*e.g.,* his natural grandparents—Harry's parents) notwithstanding his adoption by a new father.

2. Stepchildren

a. General Rule—No Inheritance Rights

Generally, stepchildren have no inheritance rights. Suppose W, a widow, has a daughter D. W marries H. Thereafter, the three live as a family unit, **but** H does not adopt D. There is no legal relationship between H and D. If D dies intestate, H is not a "parent" for inheritance purposes. If H dies intestate, D is not a "child" for inheritance purposes.

b. Exception—Adoption by Estoppel

However, under the right facts, in the above example D might be able to establish adoption by estoppel. This equity-type doctrine permits a stepchild or foster child to inherit from or through his stepparents or foster parents as though legally adopted. The doctrine is invoked where stepparents or foster parents gain custody of a child under an *agreement with the natural parent* that they will adopt the child. Just as the stepparent or foster parent would be estopped from denying the existence of a valid adoption, so also are those claiming under him on his intestate death.

3. Posthumous Children

Generally, one cannot claim as an heir of another person unless he was alive at the other person's death, but an exception is made for a posthumous child. A child in gestation at the decedent's death inherits as if born during the decedent's lifetime.

Example: Sam and his brother Bill die in the crash of a private plane. Bill's wife is three months pregnant, and six months later Bill Jr. is born. For the purposes of distributing **Bill's** estate, Bill Jr. is an heir. However, for purposes of distributing **Sam's** estate, Bill Jr. is not an heir because he was not alive at his uncle's death and he was not Sam's issue.

4. Nonmarital Children

At common law, a nonmarital child could not inherit from either parent, but only from his own issue. Today, all states permit inheritance from the mother, and the modern trend permits inheritance from the father as well, provided paternity is established. In fact, as a result of constitutional litigation expanding rights of nonmarital children, in most states these children can inherit from the natural father if:

a. The father married the mother after the child's birth ("legitimated by marriage");

b. The man was adjudicated to be the father in a paternity suit; or

c. After the man's death, he is proved (usually by "clear and convincing evidence") to have been the father of the child in the probate proceedings.

5. No Distinction Between Half Bloods and Whole Bloods

Half bloods are brothers and sisters who have only one common parent. Most jurisdictions have abolished all distinctions between siblings of the half blood and those of the whole blood. Thus, they inherit equally.

Example: H and W have a daughter A. H dies; W marries H-2, and has two daughters (B and C) by that marriage. H-2 does not adopt A. Then H-2 and W die. A and C are sisters of the half blood: They have only one common parent. By contrast, B and C are siblings of the whole blood: They share two common parents.

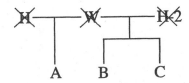

Suppose C dies intestate, unmarried, and without descendants. Her nearest kin are her half sister A and her full sister B. A and B each would take one-half of C's estate.

III. SUBSIDIARY PROBLEMS COMMON TO INTESTACY AND WILLS

A. SIMULTANEOUS DEATH

A person cannot take as an heir or will beneficiary unless he survives the decedent because property cannot pass to a dead person. (*See* discussion of lapse, VIII.A., *infra*.) Because it is often difficult to determine whether a person survived the decedent (*e.g.*, both are fatally injured in same car accident), nearly all states have enacted a statute to deal with simultaneous deaths or deaths in quick succession.

1. Uniform Simultaneous Death Act—Property Passes as Though Owner Survived

Most states have enacted a version of the Uniform Simultaneous Death Act ("USDA"), which provides that when the title to property or its devolution depends on priority of death and there is insufficient evidence that the persons have died otherwise than simultaneously, the property of each person is disposed of as if he had survived. [USDA §1] In other words, the property passes as though the beneficiary or heir predeceased the other decedent.

The purpose of the Act is to prevent the property of one person from passing to a second person (and then to the second person's beneficiaries), resulting in double administration and possibly double taxation of the same assets in quick succession, even though the second person did not survive long enough to enjoy ownership of the property.

2. Simultaneous Death Act Applies to All Types of Transfers

The Act applies to distributions of property *by any means* (intestacy, will, joint tenancy with right of survivorship, life insurance contract, etc.).

Examples: 1) A is the insured under a life insurance policy that names "B, if he survives the insured," as the primary beneficiary and C as the contingent beneficiary. A has a will that devises Blackacre to B and her residuary estate to the Red Cross. B has no will. A and B die simultaneously in a plane crash.

The life insurance proceeds are distributed as though A, the insured, survived B, the beneficiary. Thus, the proceeds are paid to C. For purposes of construing A's will, A, the testator, is deemed to have survived B, the beneficiary. Thus, the devise to B lapses and (assuming the anti-lapse statute does not apply) Blackacre passes under the residuary clause as undisposed-of property. For purposes of distributing B's intestate estate, B, the property owner, is deemed to have survived A.

2) H and W own real estate as tenants by the entirety. H and W die simultaneously in an automobile accident. "When there is insufficient evidence that two joint tenants or tenants by the entirety died otherwise than simultaneously, the property so held shall be distributed one-half as if one had survived and one-half as if the other had survived." Thus one-half passes through W's estate as though W survived H, and the other half passes through H's estate as though H survived W. (The point: There is no evidence to trigger the right of survivorship.)

3. Simultaneous Death Act Applies Unless Instrument Provides Otherwise

No one is compelled to have the statute's presumption apply to her estate. Thus, the presumption raised by the Simultaneous Death Act does not apply if the decedent's will or other instrument makes a different provision regarding survival.

Example: W has a $1 million estate; her husband H has little property of his own. W's will provides: "I devise one-half of my estate to my husband H. I devise the remaining one-half of my estate (or my entire estate if H does not survive me) to my descendants per stirpes." If W dies survived by H, the $500,000 given to H will qualify for the federal estate tax marital deduction, and will save substantial taxes in W's estate. But if W and H die simultaneously, and if the Simultaneous Death Act presumption applies to her estate, nothing will be deemed to pass to H. W's estate will not qualify for a marital deduction.

In this case, it is common to include a *marital deduction reverse presumption* clause: "If my husband and I die under such circumstances that the order of our deaths cannot be established by sufficient evidence, for purposes of this marital deduction gift my husband shall be deemed to have survived me." Now, if W and H die simultaneously, H will be deemed to have survived W. The $500,000 will pass to H (and then through his estate to the couple's descendants). W's estate will qualify for a $500,000 marital deduction, saving taxes in her estate. This "reverse presumption" is valid.

4. Evidence of Simultaneous Death

The Simultaneous Death Act applies only if there is "no sufficient evidence" of survival.

Example: Sue has a will that devises her entire estate "to my sister Mary if she survives me; otherwise to my brother Bill." Mary has a will that devises her estate to her husband, Horace. Sue and Mary are in a terrible automobile accident. Sue is pronounced dead at the scene of the accident. Mary, alive but unconscious, is taken to a local hospital where she dies two hours later. Here, there is sufficient evidence that Mary survived Sue. Thus, Sue's entire estate passes under her will to Mary, and then passes under Mary's will to Horace.

a. 120-Hour Rule

To cover the above situation, many states require that a person survive the decedent by 120 hours in order to take as a will beneficiary, intestate heir, life insurance beneficiary, or surviving joint tenant (absent a contrary provision). This is the position of the

Uniform Probate Code and the revised version of the Uniform Simultaneous Death Act.

b. Time-of-Survival Clause
In drafting wills, the technique most commonly used to cover the contingency of simultaneous deaths, or deaths in quick succession, is to make all gifts (other than marital deduction gifts) contingent on surviving the testator by, for example, 60 days.

B. DISCLAIMERS

1. Disclaimed Interest Passes as Though Disclaimant Predeceased Decedent
No one can be compelled to receive a gift. Therefore, a beneficiary or heir may disclaim any interest that otherwise would pass to the person from the decedent or the decedent's estate, with the consequence that the interest passes as though the disclaiming party predeceased the decedent. Disclaimers are made primarily for tax reasons.

Example: M, who is 75 years old, dies leaving a will that devises her entire estate to her descendants per stirpes. M is survived by her daughter D and her son S, each of whom has several children in college. D is a doctor and has a substantial estate and a substantial income in her own right. The effect of the inheritance will be to aggravate D's own income tax and estate planning problems. If D accepts the inheritance and then makes gifts to her children, there will be gift tax consequences. *Solution:* D disclaims all or a part of her inheritance. (Partial disclaimers are valid under federal tax law.) The result is that the disclaimed interest passes from the decedent to D's children, per stirpes, with no gift tax consequences.

In contrast, S is a law professor whose only outside source of income is from fees for giving bar review lectures. Under these economic circumstances, the idea of disclaiming his inheritance does not even cross his mind.

2. Must Be in Writing, Irrevocable, and Filed Within Nine Months
To be effective for federal estate and gift tax purposes, the disclaimer of a gift by will, an intestate share, or life insurance or death benefit proceeds must be (i) in writing; (ii) irrevocable; and (iii) filed within nine months *of the decedent's death*. [I.R.C. §2518] Although some state disclaimer statutes impose additional procedural requirements, most state statutes have been drafted to conform to the federal statute.

a. Beneficiary Under Age Twenty-One
A beneficiary who is under age 21 has until nine months after her 21st birthday to make a disclaimer under the federal statute.

b. Joint Tenants and Future Interests
A surviving joint tenant may disclaim only within nine months after the interest was *created* (*i.e.,* when the joint tenancy property was acquired). The same rule applies to future interests under federal law. While some states allow disclaimer of a future interest within nine months of its vesting in possession, to avoid federal gift tax, the interest must be disclaimed within nine months of its creation.

3. Disclaimer May Be Made on Behalf of Infant, Incompetent, or Decedent
A disclaimer may be made by a guardian or personal representative on behalf of an infant,

incompetent, or decedent, but the court having jurisdiction of the estate of the incapacitated person or decedent must find that it is in the ***best interests*** of those interested in the estate of the beneficiary and is not detrimental to the best interests of the beneficiary.

Example: H dies leaving a will that devises "all my property" to his wife W "if she survives me; otherwise to our children." W survives H, but dies four months later. The result is that (because of the unlimited federal estate tax marital deduction) the property is not taxed in H's estate, but the entire property is taxed in W's estate with no marital deduction available. *Solution:* W's executor could disclaim, on behalf of W's estate, one-half of the gift from H, thus eliminating the estate tax on the disclaimed gift, and the property would go directly to the children.

4. Estoppel If Any Benefits Accepted

An interest cannot be disclaimed if the heir or beneficiary has accepted the property or any of its benefits. In other words, a person who, for example, transfers or encumbers the property or enters into a contract for its sale is estopped from disclaiming the property.

5. Creditors' Claims

In most states, a disclaimer can be used to defeat creditors' claims. Since the effect of the disclaimer is that the property passes as though the disclaimant predeceased the decedent, the disclaimant has no interest that can be reached by creditors.

6. Disclaimer of Life Estate Accelerates Remainder

Since the disclaimed interest passes as though the disclaimant predeceased the decedent, upon disclaimer of a life estate the remainder is accelerated.

Example: T's will devises property in trust: "Income to A for life, and on A's death, principal to her descendants then living, per stirpes." A makes a timely and valid disclaimer for tax reasons. The will is read as though the disclaimant predeceased the testator, and thus the remainder is accelerated. A's "descendants then living per stirpes" are determined at T's death (not at A's death), and the property is distributed outright to them.

C. DECEDENT'S DEATH CAUSED BY HEIR OR BENEFICIARY

Most courts hold that one who feloniously and intentionally brings about the death of a decedent forfeits any interest in the decedent's estate. The property passes as though the killer predeceased the victim. This result is usually accomplished either through the operation of a specific statute or the imposition of a constructive trust.

1. Rule Applies to All Forms of Transfer and Benefits

The typical statute disqualifies the killer from taking under a will, by intestacy, or as beneficiary of a life insurance policy on the decedent's life. The killer is also disqualified from taking an elective share, a homestead life estate, an exempt personal property set-aside, a family allowance, or as a pretermitted spouse.

Example: Frank's will devises Blackacre "to my son Sam." Sam murders Frank. Frank is survived by Sam (now serving 20 years in the penitentiary) and by Sam's son Gordon. Since the gift of Blackacre passes as though Sam predeceased Frank, Gordon takes Blackacre under most anti-lapse statutes (discussed VIII.A., *infra*).

2. **Joint Ownership—Right of Survivorship Severed**

If one joint owner in a joint tenancy, tenancy by the entirety, or joint bank account kills the other, the killer loses the benefits of the right of survivorship.

Example: H and W own Whiteacre as tenants by the entirety. W kills H. The right of survivorship is severed; in effect, the estate is treated as a tenancy in common. H's one-half interest passes under his will (or by intestacy) as though W predeceased him. W continues to own her undivided one-half interest in Whiteacre.

Note: W does not forfeit *her* interest in the property because of the killing. The purpose of the statute is to prevent W from benefiting from her wrongful act by taking H's interest by right of survivorship.

3. **Proof of Killing—Evidentiary Standard**

A final judgment of conviction of murder in any degree is conclusive for purposes of this type of statute. However, in the absence of a conviction of murder in any degree, the court may determine by a *preponderance* of the evidence whether the killing was unlawful or intentional.

Example: M dies under suspicious circumstances. Her daughter D is charged with murder in the first degree, but she is acquitted. Notwithstanding the acquittal, under the typical slayer statute the court could find that D unlawfully and intentionally brought about M's death, and that D forfeited all interests in M's estate. This is because the evidentiary test would be the "preponderance of the evidence," not the "beyond a reasonable doubt" standard of the criminal action.

D. ADVANCEMENT OF INTESTATE SHARE

An advancement is a gift made to a next of kin with the intent that the gift be applied against any share which the next of kin inherits from the donor's estate.

1. **Common Law—Lifetime Gift to Child Presumptively an Advancement**

At common law, it was presumed that an intestate desired to treat all of his children equally. Consequently, when an intestate made a substantial gift to one child and not to others during his lifetime, the gift was held to be an "advancement" (*i.e.,* an advance payment) of the child's intestate share upon the parent's death.

2. **Modern Law—Common Law Presumption Reversed**

Most states hold that the advancement doctrine can apply to any heir but reverse the presumption by providing that a lifetime gift is presumptively *not* an advancement unless shown to be intended as such. States that have adopted the UPC approach are even more stringent, requiring a writing to prove an advancement. In those states, no lifetime gift is considered an advancement unless it is: (i) declared as such in a contemporaneous writing by the donor, or (ii) acknowledged as such in writing by the donee. (The donee's writing need not be contemporaneous.) [*See* UPC §2-109]

3. **Procedure If Advancement Found**

Once it has been determined that an advancement was made, the amount advanced is computed with the net value of the estate for purposes of distribution; or, as the courts say, the amount advanced is brought back into ***hotchpot***. Thus, an heir who has received an advancement has his share reduced by the amount of the advancement. However, if the advancement is greater than the heir's intestate share, he is not responsible for returning the excess.

Examples: 1) In a state that applies the common law doctrine of advancements, Hortense, a widow, gives land worth $50,000 to her son Seth. Several years later, Hortense dies intestate survived by Seth and her daughter Debbie as her nearest kin. Hortense leaves an estate valued at $200,000. The land given to Seth is worth $80,000 at Hortense's death. The gift to Seth is treated as an advancement, *i.e.,* a partial satisfaction of Seth's share of his mother's estate. If Seth wishes to take a share of the estate as heir, he must allow the ***date of gift value*** to be brought into hotchpot:

$200,000	actual intestate estate
+ 50,000	date of gift value of advancement
$250,000	

Seth's share of the estate is $125,000, of which he is deemed already to have received $50,000. Thus, Seth takes $75,000 of Hortense's estate, and Debbie takes $125,000.

2) Same facts, except that the UPC applies. The gift is ***not treated as an advancement*** unless Hortense so indicated in a writing made at the time the gift was made, or unless Seth made a written declaration that he understood that the gift was intended as an advancement. (The writing by the donor must be ***contemporaneous*** with the gift, but the writing by the donee can be made at any time after the gift.) If there is no such writing, the gift to Seth is ignored, and the $200,000 estate is divided equally between Seth and Debbie.

4.   Advancee Predeceases Intestate
Generally, an advancement is binding upon those who succeed to the estate of the advancee in the event the advancee predeceases the intestate. In states following the UPC approach, however, an advancement is ***not binding*** on a predeceased heir's successors ***unless*** the required writing or acknowledgment specifically provides otherwise.

5.   Advancement Valued at Time of Gift
The value of an advancement is determined as of the time the gift was made, and any fluctuations in the value of the advanced property will not affect the position of the next of kin.

E.   SATISFACTION OF LEGACIES
The same rules apply to lifetime gifts to will beneficiaries as to intestate heirs. Under modern law, a testamentary gift may be satisfied in whole or in part by an inter vivos transfer from the testator to the beneficiary subsequent to the execution of the will, if the testator intends the transfer to have that effect. For obvious reasons, this doctrine does not apply to gifts made prior to execution of the will. In states following the UPC approach, the doctrine does not apply unless the testator provides for satisfaction in the will or a contemporaneous writing or the devisee acknowledges, in writing, the gift as one in satisfaction. [*See* UPC §2-609]

Example: T's will bequeaths $10,000 to A. After executing the will, T transfers $10,000 to A along with a written statement that this is in satisfaction of the bequest in T's will. The bequest to A is satisfied; A takes nothing under T's will.

1. **Value of Gifts in Satisfaction**
    Generally, if a gift is found to be in satisfaction of a testamentary provision, the value of the gift must be determined as of the time that gift was made. In states following the UPC approach, gifts in satisfaction are valued at the time the devisee comes into possession or enjoyment or at the death of the testator, whichever occurs first.

2. **Gift of Specifically Bequeathed Property to the Beneficiary**
    There is one situation in which satisfaction of a bequest can occur even if not proved to have been so intended. If the testator gives the specifically described property to the beneficiary, there is both a satisfaction of the legacy and an ademption (*see* VIII.B., *infra*).

IV. FORMAL REQUISITES AND EXECUTION OF WILLS

A. WHAT CONSTITUTES A WILL
A will is an instrument executed with certain formalities, that usually directs the disposition of a person's property at death. A will is revocable during the lifetime of the testator and only operative at his death. Thus, an instrument that is operative during the testator's lifetime (as by presently transferring an interest in property) cannot be a will.

1. **Codicil**
    A codicil is a *supplement* to a will that alters, amends, or modifies the will.

2. **Instrument Need Not Dispose of Property to Be a Will**
    Although most wills dispose of property at death, the disposition of property is not a legal requisite of a will. The term "will" includes an instrument that merely appoints a personal representative or revokes or revises another will.

3. **Will Has No Legal Effect Until Testator's Death**
    A will takes effect only upon the death of the testator. Until that time, the will may be revoked or amended, and the beneficiaries have only an *expectancy* (*i.e.,* they acquire no property rights under the will). Because of the ambulatory nature of a will, it operates upon circumstances and properties as they exist at the time of the testator's death ("a will speaks at the time of death"). In construing the will, however, the circumstances that existed at the time the will was executed are considered to discern what the testator meant by the words he used.

B. TESTAMENTARY INTENT
For a will to be valid, the testator must intend that the particular instrument operate as his will. In the case of a well-drafted will, this issue is rarely in doubt. Testamentary intent is established by the document itself (*e.g.,* "I, Hobie Gates, do hereby declare this instrument to be my Last Will"). The problem cases have involved instruments that contain no such recital and are ambiguous as to whether they were intended to be testamentary in effect. In these cases, testamentary intent will be found only if it is shown that the testator: (i) intended to dispose of the property; (ii) intended the disposition to occur only upon his death; and (iii) intended that the instrument in question accomplish the disposition.

1. **Present Intent Required**
    The intention required is a present testamentary intent. A signed and witnessed statement of an

intent to make a will in the future (*e.g.*, "I am going to make a will leaving all my property to you") is not a will, for it shows that the instrument itself was not intended to be a will.

2. Sham Wills

An instrument containing a recital that "this is my Last Will" raises a presumption of testamentary intent, but the presumption is rebuttable. Evidence is admissible to show, for example, that a person made a will naming his girlfriend as beneficiary to induce her to sleep with him [Fleming v. Morrison, 72 N.E. 499 (Mass. 1904)], or that the instrument was executed as part of a ceremonial initiation into a secret order.

3. Ineffective Deed Cannot Be a Will

If a deed fails as an inter vivos conveyance (*e.g.*, for want of delivery), it cannot be probated as a will even though it was signed and attested by the required number of witnesses. If the grantor intended the deed to be operative during his lifetime, it cannot be a will.

4. Conditional Wills

A conditional will is one that expressly provides that it shall be operative only if some condition stated in the will is satisfied. However, language that reads like a condition may be interpreted by the court as merely expressing the testator's ***motive or inducement*** for making the will.

a. Condition Must Be Expressed in Will

Parol evidence is not admissible to show that a will absolute on its face was intended to be conditional. Parol evidence may be admitted to show that the instrument was not meant to have any effect at all (*e.g.,* a sham will), but not to show conditions.

b. Condition vs. Motive

Suppose Mary signs a duly attested instrument that reads, "I am going on a safari to Africa. If anything happens to me on the trip, here is how I want my property disposed of. . . ." Mary returns safely from the trip, but dies five years later. Should her will be admitted to probate? This question has no clear answer, and in your answer you should ***argue both ways***. Many courts have held that this language merely reflects that Mary was thinking generally about the possibility of death and the need for a will, which at that moment took the specific shape of not returning from Africa. [Eaton v. Brown, 193 U.S. 411 (1904)] However, on very similar facts, a number of cases have held the will to be conditional on not returning from the particular trip, and have denied probate. [*In re* Pascal's Estate, 2 Misc. 2d 337 (N.Y. 1956)] The following factors have been cited by the courts in favor of holding that the will was unconditional:

1) The fact that the testator executed a will is an indication that she ***did not intend to die intestate***.

2) The fact that the testator ***preserved the document*** after returning from the trip is another indication that the will's operation was not intended to be limited.

C. TESTAMENTARY CAPACITY—MUST BE EIGHTEEN AND OF SOUND MIND

In nearly all states, a person who has attained age 18 has the right and power to make a will. If a 16-year-old executes a will and dies 20 years later, the will is not valid because the testator did not have capacity at the time the will was executed. In addition, the testator must be of sound mind. The requirements for establishing testamentary capacity are discussed in Chapter X., Will Contests.

D. EXECUTION OF ATTESTED WILLS

For a will to be valid and admissible to probate, the testator must meet the formal requirements of due execution imposed by the statutes of the appropriate state. These statutes are often referred to as a state's Statute of Wills. If the statutory requirements are not met, the will is void (not merely voidable), and cannot be admitted to probate even if there is no objection. The formalities required for execution of a will vary from state to state. Most states require the following formalities:

(i)   The will or codicil must be *signed by the testator*, or by another person at the testator's direction and in her presence.

(ii) There must be *two attesting witnesses* (a few states require three).

(iii) The testator must sign the will (or acknowledge her previous signature or acknowledge the will) *in each of the witnesses' presence*.

(iv) The witnesses must sign in the *testator's presence*.

Some states impose one or more of the following additional requirements:

(v)   The testator must *sign at the end* of the will.

(vi) The testator must *"publish" the will*, *i.e.*, declare to the witnesses that the instrument is her will or otherwise communicate this fact so that the witnesses know they are witnessing a will rather than some other legal document.

(vii) The *witnesses must sign in the presence of each other*.

1. Signature Requirement

a. What Constitutes a Signature

Any mark affixed by the testator, with the intent that the mark operate as the testator's signature, satisfies the signature requirement. "Betty," "Mom," "J.R.," and the X of an illiterate person, and even the testator's fingerprint are all valid signatures. In addition, the testator's signature may be made by another person at the testator's direction and in the testator's presence. In fact, if that person writes the testator's name and then writes his own name, the person can be counted as one of the two needed attesting witnesses.

Example: Goldie, who is illiterate, has a will prepared. In the presence of Herb Miller, Goldie asks Ollie Pinkston to sign her name for her. The will has signature lines for the testator and for only one witness. On the signature line for the testator, Ollie writes "Goldie Lomineck, by Ollie Pinkston." Herb then signs on the witness line. "Ollie Pinkston" counts as the signature of an attesting witness, and the will has been validly executed.

b. Contemporaneous Transaction Doctrine—Order of Signing Not Critical

Suppose that one or more of the witnesses sign the will before the testator signs it (or that the testator and the witnesses sign on the wrong lines). The exact order of signing is not material, as long as all of the signings occurred as a part of a single, contemporaneous transaction.

c. Placement of Signature

In most states, a will is valid as long as the testator signs somewhere on the instrument (*e.g.*, on the margin, or in the first clause). In a substantial minority of states, however, a will must be *subscribed* (*i.e.*, signed at the end). In states with this requirement, what happens if additional materials (*e.g.*, clause naming an executor) follow the testator's signature? In many states with this requirement, if anything other than the attestation clause follows the testator's signature, the entire will is void. However, by statute or case decision in several states, everything appearing above the testator's signature is given effect, but any matter following her signature is not considered a part of the will and is disregarded.

1) Compare—Words Added After Will Executed

Suppose that, after the will is signed and witnessed, T adds several clauses, making a new gift and naming an executor, underneath her signature. This case does *not* involve the "signature at the end" requirement. Here the added clauses are not given effect for another reason: They are *unattested words*. Only the words present on the will at the time it was executed are part of the duly executed will.

2. "Presence" Requirement

Signing in someone's presence is required under many statutes, although the requirement takes various forms. In most states, each witness must sign in the testator's presence, but not necessarily in each other's presence. In other states, the witnesses must sign in the testator's presence and in the presence of each other. In most states, the testator must sign or acknowledge the will or signature in the presence of each witness, but not necessarily at the same time. Courts have applied various tests to determine when a person is in another's presence.

a. Majority View—"Conscious Presence" Test

A majority of courts apply the more liberal "conscious presence" test: The presence requirement is satisfied if each party was conscious of where the other parties were and what they were doing, and the act of signing took place nearby, within the general awareness and cognizance of the other parties.

Examples: 1) The will is signed in a hospital room. T, lying in bed behind a heavy screen, cannot see the witnesses (and vice versa) because they are standing in the doorway, 20 feet away. Nevertheless, the parties have signed in each other's conscious presence. [Nichols v. Rowan, 422 S.W.2d 21 (Tex. 1967)]

2) T and one witness sign the will in Attorney's office. Attorney then excuses himself and takes the will into the office two doors down the hall, where the second witness signs. Here the conscious presence test was *not* satisfied. Merely being in the same suite of offices does not constitute "presence." [Morris v. West's Estate, 643 S.W.2d 204 (Tex. 1982)]

b.   Minority View—"Scope of Vision" Test

Some courts take the view that the parties must be in each other's scope of vision when they sign. Under this test, a person is present only if he could have seen the signing. (An exception is made for blind persons.) This does not mean that the signing must actually have been observed, but only that the person was in such close proximity that he could have seen the signing had he looked.

3.   Witnesses

Most states require that a will be attested by two competent witnesses.

a.   Competency In General

All jurisdictions require that witnesses be competent. Competency for this purpose generally means that, at the time the will is executed, the witness is mature enough and of sufficient mental capacity to understand and appreciate the nature of the act she is witnessing and her attestation, so that she could testify in court on these matters if necessary. Most states do not impose a minimum age requirement for witnesses.

b.   Interested Witnesses

At common law, an attesting witness who was also a beneficiary under the will was not a competent witness, and was barred from testifying as to the will's execution. If one of the two necessary, attesting witnesses was a beneficiary, the will could not be probated. This harsh rule has been abolished in every state.

1)   Majority Rule—Will Valid, But Bequest to Interested Witness Is Void

In most states, statutes solve the interested witness problem by eliminating the interest: The will is valid, but the gift to the witness-beneficiary is void. These are called *"purging statutes,"* since they operate to purge the bequest to the witness.

a)   Exception—Supernumerary Rule

An exception is made if the witness-beneficiary was a supernumerary witness, *i.e.,* if there were three witnesses, two of whom were disinterested, and the will can be proved by the disinterested witnesses.

b)   Exception—Witness-Beneficiary Would Take If Will Had Not Been Admitted to Probate

The statutes also carve out an exception if the interested witness would have taken if the will were not admitted to probate, *i.e.,* if the beneficiary would have been an heir if there were no will, or if the beneficiary was also given a bequest in an earlier will that he did not witness. In such a case, the witness-beneficiary takes the lesser of: (i) the legacy; or (ii) his intestate share (or gift under earlier will).

2)   Uniform Probate Code—Interested Witness Rule Abolished

Under the UPC, a will or codicil, or any part thereof, is not invalid because the will or codicil is signed by an interested witness. [UPC §2-505]

Example: T's will bequeaths $25,000 to Harry, and devises his residuary estate to Sue. Harry signs the will as an attesting witness. In most states the bequest to Harry would be purged unless (i) Harry was one of three attesting witnesses or (ii) Harry would be an heir (or legatee under an earlier will) if the will had not been executed. Under the UPC, Harry takes the $25,000 legacy in any case since the UPC has abolished the interested witness rule.

4. Attestation Clause

A well-drafted will invariably contains an attestation clause. This clause, which appears immediately below the signature line for the testator and above the witnesses' signature lines, recites the elements of due execution.

Example: "On the above date, the testator declared to us, the undersigned, that the foregoing instrument was her last will. She then signed the will in our presence, we being present at the same time. We then signed the will in the testator's presence and in the presence of each other, we and each of us believing the testator to be of sound mind on the date hereof."

An attestation clause is prima facie evidence of the facts recited therein. Unlike a self-proving affidavit (*see* 5., *infra*), however, an attestation clause does not constitute sworn testimony and cannot serve as a substitute for the courtroom testimony of the attesting witnesses. Attestation clauses can be useful in two situations:

a. Witness with No Memory

Suppose witness A testifies that, although he recognizes his signature on the will, he has no recollection of signing it and thus does not recall whether he signed in the testator's presence. The courts have uniformly held that probate of a will does not turn upon the memory of the attesting witnesses. The void created by the witness's memory lapse is filled by the attestation clause, which is prima facie evidence that the facts as recited therein actually occurred.

b. Witness with Faulty Memory

Suppose witness B testifies that she remembers the execution ceremony very well even though it occurred 10 years before, and that the one thing she especially "remembers" is that the testator was not in the room when she signed the will. A number of cases have upheld probate of the will after a jury finding that the attestation clause, and not the witness on the witness stand, is telling the truth.

5. Self-Proving Affidavit

Many states permit a will to be made self-proved at the time it is executed. The testator and the attesting witnesses sign the will, and then sign a sworn affidavit before a notary public reciting that the testator declared to the witnesses that the instrument was her will, and that the testator and the witnesses all signed in the presence of each other. (The affidavit can be executed at any time subsequent to the will's execution, but standard practice is to execute both the will and the self-proving affidavit in one ceremony.)

a. Substitutes for Court Testimony of Attesting Witnesses

The self-proving affidavit serves the same function as a deposition or interrogatory. It is a method by which the witnesses' sworn testimony can be secured at the time the will is executed, eliminating the need to track down the witnesses and arrange for their testimony in probate court after the testator's death. Self-proved wills may be admitted to probate without further proof.

b. Signatures on Affidavit Can Be Counted as Signatures Needed on Will
Signatures on the affidavit usually can be counted as the signatures needed on the will itself, since there is generally no requirement that the witnesses sign at any particular place on the will.

Example: T signs the will, and then T and the witnesses sign the self-proving affidavit (on a separate page stapled to the will) before a notary public. However, neither witness signs the will itself underneath the attestation clause. Has the will been validly executed? A few courts have said no, ruling that the signatures on the affidavit cannot be counted because the affidavit, a procedural document designed to facilitate probate, was not executed with testamentary intent. Under the majority and better view, however, the will is validly executed. Since there is generally no requirement that witnesses sign in a particular place, the signatures on the affidavit are sufficient for execution.

6. Attorney Liability for Negligence in Preparation of Will
A growing number of states have discarded the "privity of contract" defense and have held that the attorney owes a duty, not just to the client who contracted for his services, but to the beneficiaries named in the will. Thus, the beneficiaries can sue the attorney for negligence in the preparation of a will or for negligence in supervising its execution. The amount of the recovery can be substantial (*e.g.*, the amount the beneficiaries would have received had the will been admitted to probate).

E. HOLOGRAPHIC WILLS

The UPC and about one-half of the states recognize holographic wills and codicils. [*See* UPC §2-502] A holographic will is one *that is entirely in the testator's handwriting and has no attesting witnesses.* Where recognized, a holographic will usually may be made by any testator with capacity, but a few states limit them to persons serving in the armed forces or mariners at sea.

1. Testator's Handwriting
Generally, to be valid, a holographic will must be *entirely* in the testator's handwriting. However, most states that recognize holographic wills accept a will that contains some typewritten text as long as the portion not in the testator's handwriting is not *material* (*i.e.*, the typewritten portion may be disregarded without violating the testator's intent). Note that most states do not require that a holographic will be dated.

2. Testator's Signature
A holographic will must be signed by the testator, but there is no requirement that it be signed at the end of the will. The signature can even be found in the opening caption (*e.g.*, "I, Jane Jones, do hereby declare . . ."). Courts also take a liberal view of what constitutes a signature; most will allow initials, a first name only, or a nickname.

3. Testamentary Intent
A question often arises with respect to documents offered as holographic wills as to whether the document was really intended to be a will. Often a letter or informal memorandum is offered for probate as a holographic will, and the court must make the determination of

whether the document was so intended. ***The test is whether some future writing was contemplated.*** Extrinsic evidence is admissible to establish that an ambiguous document was intended to be a will.

Examples: 1) T's attorney received the following handwritten letter:

> Dear Attorney:
>
> I have decided to change my will as follows: I wish my daughter A to receive $10,000, rather than $20,000. My son B should receive $30,000, instead of the $20,000 as the will presently reads. Also, the downtown condominium should pass one-half to A and one-half to B, instead of passing to C. Please make these changes, and I will sign the necessary papers next week.
>
>   /s/T

T died before signing the new will drafted by the attorney. B seeks to offer T's letter into probate as a holographic will because it is entirely in T's handwriting and is signed by T. The court will refuse to admit the letter as a holographic will because it clearly lacks testamentary intent. Obviously another writing was contemplated by T when she wrote the letter, and she did not intend the letter itself to be her will.

2) A hospital patient gives a nurse a note, saying, "Take care of this. It is my will." The note reads, "Everything I own should go to my sister Sharon. /s/ Testator." The nurse may testify as to what the testator said, and this, along with the circumstances of the writing, will probably be sufficient evidence of testamentary intent to admit the note as a holographic will.

4. Interlineations
Most states that recognize holographic wills give effect to handwritten changes, such as substituting beneficiaries, made by the testator after the holographic will is completed. By contrast, these types of interlineations are generally not given effect if made to an attested will (unless the changes themselves are sufficient to constitute a holographic codicil and the jurisdiction recognizes such codicils).

F. ORAL WILLS
Most states that recognize oral wills do so only for the disposition of personal property and only if made by: (i) soldiers or sailors (only during a time of armed conflict in some states); or (ii) any person during his last sickness or in contemplation of immediate death. Generally, there must be at least two witnesses to such a will.

G. CONFLICT OF LAWS ISSUES

1. Real Property
To the extent that a will disposes of real property, its validity and effect are determined by the law of the state where the ***property is located***.

2. **Personal Property**
   With respect to dispositions of personal property, the law of the testator's *domicile at the time of her death* controls the validity and effect of the will.

3. **Foreign Wills**
   Under the law of many states and the UPC, a will is admissible to probate in a jurisdiction if it has been executed in accordance with:

   (i)   The law of that jurisdiction;

   (ii) The law of the state where the will was executed;

   (iii) The law of the testator's domicile at the time the will was executed; *or*

   (iv) The law of the testator's domicile at death.

   [*See* UPC §2-506]

V. COMPONENTS OF A WILL

A. INTEGRATION
A will often consists of more than one sheet of paper, yet the testator and the witnesses sign and attest on only one sheet: the last page of the will. The rarely litigated doctrine of "integration" concerns the following question: What sheets were present at the time of will execution and thus comprise the decedent's last will? If an integration question is raised, the will proponent must show that the pages were present when the will was executed and were intended by the testator to be a part of the will. The requirements of intent and presence are presumed when there is a physical connection of the pages (staple, paper clip, etc.), or when there is an internal coherence by provisions running from one page to the next. These requirements also can be established by the testimony of witnesses or other extrinsic evidence.

Example: A will was prepared in haste for T, who was hospitalized. By oversight, page 4 (which named an executor) of the five-page will was left out when the will was stapled. Thus only pages 1 through 3 and 5 (which contained the dispositive provisions) were part of the will that was signed and witnessed. On these facts, pages 1 through 3 and 5 should be admitted to probate. Page 4 cannot be admitted to probate because it was not part of the duly executed will. However, the other four pages should be admitted if they embrace the substance of T's dispositive plan.

B. CODICIL
A codicil is a later testamentary instrument that amends, alters, or modifies a previously executed will. A codicil must be executed with the same testamentary formalities as a will. In some cases, it may be important to establish the date on which a will is deemed to have been executed. Under the doctrine of *republication by codicil*, a will is treated as having been executed on the date of the last validly executed codicil thereto.

Example: T executes a will that bequeaths one-half of her estate to her husband, H, and the other one-half to her child, C. Two years later, T has another child, D. T then executes a codicil that changes the executor named in the original will. T dies without having otherwise modified the original will. Under the doctrine of republication by codicil, the will is deemed to have been executed when the codicil was executed. Therefore, D is not an afterborn child, and gets no protection from the pretermitted child statute. (*See* IX.B., *infra*.)

C. INCORPORATION BY REFERENCE

In most states, an extrinsic document (not present at the time the will was executed) may be incorporated into the will by reference so that it is considered a part of the will. To incorporate a document by reference, three requirements must be met:

(i) The document must be *in existence* at the time the will was executed;

(ii) The language of the will must *sufficiently describe* the writing to permit its identification; and

(iii) The will must *manifest an intent to incorporate* the document.

1. Document Must Be in Existence at Time of Execution of Will

The requirement for incorporation most strictly adhered to by courts is that the document must be in existence at the time the will is executed. The courts are fearful that if this requirement is not adhered to, a testator could incorporate "a paper to be written which will be placed in my desk drawer," and could later name new beneficiaries by an unattested writing. Obviously, the safeguards of the Statute of Wills would be in serious danger if that were given effect.

Examples: 1) If the will executed and attested to on May 1, 2001, provides "$1,000 to each of the persons named in a letter that I have written and dated March 1, 2000, which will be found in my safe deposit box at the Acme Bank," and if the letter was in existence at the time the will was executed, the letter is incorporated by reference and the gifts are valid.

2) If the will provides "$1,000 to each of the persons named in a letter that will be found in my safe deposit box at the Acme Bank," but it can be shown that the letter was written *after the will's execution*, the letter is *not* incorporated by reference and the intended gifts will fail.

a. Exception for List Disposing of Items of Tangible Personal Property

Sometimes clients seem more concerned about making gifts of personal items of sentimental value (crystal bowls, Winchester rifles, etc.) than about disposing of their intangible wealth or real estate holdings. Also, division of personal and household effects among the surviving family members can lead to arguments unless the testator has given clear directions as to how these items are to be divided. To provide a convenient mechanism for making gifts of such items, many states have enacted statutes carving out an exception to the rule that, to be incorporated by reference, the document must be in existence at the time the will is executed. In those states, a will may refer to a written statement or list to dispose of items of *tangible personal property* (not money, intangible property, or property used in a trade or business) not otherwise specifically disposed of by the will. The writing must be signed by the testator and must describe the items and the devisees with reasonable certainty. The writing may be referred to as one in existence at the time of the testator's death. It may be prepared before or after the execution of the will, and it may be altered by the testator after its initial preparation. Note that unless a state has a specific statute addressing this issue, such lists prepared after the execution of the will are invalid.

2. Identification of Extrinsic Document

The language of the will must refer to the extrinsic document in such a way as it may be reasonably identified, and the document must correspond to the description given in the will.

Example: M purchased a will form at a stationery store. In the space for naming the beneficiaries of his estate, M wrote: "Attached dated June 7, 2001." After M's death, the will (which was duly executed) was found in an envelope along with a handwritten and signed (but unwitnessed) memorandum dated June 7, 2001. The memo, which was paper-clipped to the will, designated the beneficiaries of M's estate. The will's reference to the date of the memo and its being "attached" were sufficient to incorporate the memo by reference.

D. ACTS OF INDEPENDENT SIGNIFICANCE

Under the "acts of independent significance" doctrine (sometimes called the doctrine of "non-testamentary acts"), a will may dispose of property by reference to acts and events that have significance apart from their effect on the dispositions made by the will. Even though the identification of a beneficiary or the amount of a bequest will be determined by some future unattested act, the bequest is nonetheless valid if the act has some lifetime significance other than providing for the testamentary gift.

1. Identification of Beneficiaries

The future act may relate to the identification of the beneficiaries.

Example: T's will provides "a legacy of $1,000 to each person who is in my employ at the time of my death." Thereafter, T hires three new employees and fires two longtime employees. Under this doctrine, it is assumed that T would not make employment decisions simply to make or unmake legacies in his will. The act of employment has independent significance apart from its effect on T's will. The gifts are valid.

2. Identification of Property

This doctrine also permits identification of the property that is to be the subject matter of a bequest.

Examples: 1) T's will bequeaths "my house and its contents to my sister Sarah." Thereafter, T buys new furniture and several valuable paintings, totally redecorating her house. The gift is valid and includes all items of furniture and furnishings that are in T's house at her death, *i.e.,* "those items of tangible personal property that convert an empty building into an inhabitable dwelling." The gift *does not include intangible property* that happened to be stored in the house (stock certificates worth $377,000; savings account passbook covering deposits of $124,000).

2) T's will bequeaths "the oil paintings in my den to the persons whose names I plan to write on the back of each painting." Thereafter, T writes various names on post-its and sticks them on the back of several paintings in his den. The gifts are ineffective since the tagging has no significance except as a testamentary act.

3. Acts of Third Persons

The doctrine of independent significance has been used with regard to acts of third persons as well as to acts of the testator. The usual situation is where a testator directs that his property be distributed in accordance with the will of another person. If the will is executed, and the other requirements of incorporation are met, the other person's will can be incorporated by reference. The more difficult case is where the testator provides that his property shall be disposed of as provided in the future will of another person.

Example: T executes his will devising the residue of his estate to any charitable trust established by the last will and testament of his brother, Barney Robles. Barney is alive and has no will. Subsequently, Barney executes a will devising all his property to the Robles Trust for Mental Health, a testamentary trust established by his will. Then Barney dies. Then T dies. It is generally held that the doctrine of independent significance applies, and the gift is valid.

E. POUR-OVER GIFT TO INTER VIVOS TRUST

The usual fact situation is like this: T established a revocable inter vivos trust. T then executed his will devising the residue of his estate to the trustees of the inter vivos trust to hold under the terms of the trust instrument as amended on the date of T's death. Subsequently, T amended the trust and then died. Can the residue be poured over into the trust as amended? The amendment could not be incorporated by reference because it was not in existence when the will was executed. Some courts, however, held the amendment had independent significance if the inter vivos trust had a significant amount of property and was set up for lifetime motives. The problem was solved by legislation permitting this very useful estate planning device.

In most states, the Uniform Testamentary Additions to Trusts Act, or its equivalent, has been enacted. A devise or bequest made to a trustee of an inter vivos trust is valid, notwithstanding the fact that the testator has reserved the power to amend or revoke the trust or has actually amended the trust after executing his will, and further notwithstanding the fact that the trust instrument or any amendment was not executed in accordance with the Statute of Wills. [Uniform Testamentary Additions to Trusts Act §1]

F. NONPROBATE ASSETS CANNOT BE DISPOSED OF BY WILL

Only property owned by the decedent at death can be disposed of by will. A will cannot make a gift of "nonprobate assets"—interests that pass at death other than by will or intestacy. Also, nonprobate assets are not subject to the personal representative's possession for purposes of administering the decedent's estate. There are three principal categories of nonprobate assets.

1. Property Passing by Contract—Life Insurance Proceeds and Employee Benefits

Life insurance proceeds (and death benefits under an employee retirement plan) are payable to the beneficiary designated by the insured (or employee) in his contract with the life insurance company (or retirement plan carrier).

Example: Tom is the insured under a $50,000 Prudential life insurance policy that names Mary as primary beneficiary. Tom dies leaving a will that provides: "I direct that the $50,000 proceeds under my Prudential life insurance policy be paid to my brother Bill rather than to Mary." This will provision is ineffective. Payment of the insurance proceeds is governed by the contract between Tom and Prudential, and the beneficiary can be changed only by complying with the terms of the policy governing beneficiary designations. Mary takes the $50,000 proceeds.

2. **Property Passing by Right of Survivorship**
   Property held by the decedent and another person as joint tenants with right of survivorship, and property held by the decedent and his spouse as tenants by the entirety, pass directly to the survivor outside of the probate process.

   Example: H and W owned a house as tenants by the entirety. W filed for divorce, and the parties tentatively agreed upon a property settlement under which the house would be awarded to W. In anticipation of this, W executed a will that devised the house to C. However, W died before the hearing on the divorce petition was held. *Held:* W's will was ineffective as to the house since the parties were married at W's death. Title to the house passed to H by right of survivorship. Moreover, there is no basis for impressing a constructive trust in C's favor since no wrongful conduct or unjust enrichment was involved. [Miller v. Miller, 487 A.2d 1156 (D.C. 1985)]

3. **Property Held in Trust**
   When an inter vivos trust is established, legal title to the settlor's assets is transferred to the trustee, and if the trust continues in operation after the settlor's death, legal title remains in the trustee.

   Example: Sam establishes a revocable self-declaration of trust that names himself as trustee. The trust provides that all income is to be paid to Sam for life. Upon Sam's death or incapacity, Miami National Bank is to become successor trustee. After Sam's death, all trust income is to be paid to Sam's wife Wilma for life. On the death of the survivor of Sam and Wilma, the trust principal is to be distributed to Sam's descendants. Sam dies; the trust continues in operation free of the probate process.

VI. REVOCATION OF WILLS

A. IN GENERAL

1. **Must Have Capacity to Revoke Will**
   A person who has testamentary capacity (must be of sound mind, must have the capacity to know the nature of the act he is doing, etc.) may revoke his will at any time prior to death.

2. **Contractual Will May Be Revoked**
   Even a testator who has validly contracted not to revoke a will (*see* VII.C., *infra*) may do so, and the will must be denied probate. In this case, however, there may be an action for breach of contract against the decedent's estate, and the remedy may be the imposition of a constructive trust upon the beneficiaries under the will. (*See* Trusts outline.)

3. **Methods of Revocation**
   Once validly executed, a will may be revoked only by the methods prescribed by statute or permitted by case law. These methods include revocation by operation of law, by subsequent instrument, and by physical act.

B. REVOCATION BY OPERATION OF LAW

In many states, a will may be partially or totally revoked by operation of law in the event of subsequent marriage, divorce, or birth or adoption of children. The theory of the rules providing for such revocation is that it is assumed the testator would not want the will (or the will provision) to operate in view of the changed family situation.

1. Marriage Following Execution of Will—Pretermitted Spouse

In most states, marriage following execution of a will has *no effect* on the earlier will, even though it makes no provision for the new spouse, on the theory that the new spouse is given adequate protection by the state's elective share statute (or, in community property states, by the community property system). However, in a minority of states, if a person marries after executing a will and the spouse survives the testator, the new spouse takes an intestate share of the testator's estate as a "pretermitted spouse." In most of these states, the will is only partially revoked, *i.e.,* only to the extent necessary to provide the spouse with an intestate share. In making up the pretermitted spouse's intestate share, the usual abatement rules (discussed XI.E., *infra*) apply. Property passing by partial intestacy (if any) is first used, then the residuary estate, then general legacies, demonstrative legacies, and finally, specific devises and bequests.

Note that even in states with pretermitted spouse statutes, no revocation occurs and the spouse does not receive the intestate share if: (i) the will makes provision for the new spouse; (ii) the will provides that the spouse's omission was intentional; or (iii) it appears that the will was made in contemplation of the marriage.

2. Divorce Revokes All Provisions in Will or Revocable Trust in Favor of Former Spouse

In most states, by statute, divorce following execution of a will revokes all gifts and administrative appointments in favor of the former spouse. The rest of the will remains valid, and is read as though the ex-spouse predeceased the testator.

Example: Mary's will provides: "I leave all my property to my husband Horace if he survives me, and if Horace does not survive me I leave it all to my sister Sue. I name my husband Horace as executor if he survives me; otherwise I name my brother Bill executor." Thereafter Mary divorces Horace; then Mary dies without having changed her will. Even though Horace survived Mary, the statute revokes the provisions in his favor. Sue takes Mary's estate under the will, and Bill is appointed as executor.

a. Statutes Do Not Apply to Life Insurance Policies

The statutes apply only to wills and revocable trusts, not to insurance policies.

Example: Suppose, in the foregoing example, Mary had a $25,000 life insurance policy that named Horace as primary beneficiary "if he survives me" and Sue as contingent beneficiary. After the divorce, Mary does not change the beneficiary designation. Horace takes the $25,000 policy proceeds.

b. Statutes Apply Only to Divorce by Testator or Settlor

The only divorce relevant under the statutes is the testator's or settlor's.

Example: T's will bequeaths property "to my brother's wife, Louise Ellstrom." Thereafter, T's brother divorces Louise, and Louise changes her name back to Smith, her maiden name. Louise takes the gift under T's will. The designation of "my brother's wife" was not a condition to the gift, but merely described which Louise T had in mind.

3. Pretermitted Children

Most states have pretermitted child statutes. (*See* IX.B., *infra.*) Under these statutes, if the testator fails to provide in his will for any of his children born or adopted after the will is executed, the child is entitled to a share of the estate equal in value to what he would have received if the testator had died intestate. In making up the child's share, the general rules of abatement apply. Thus, in the ordinary case, the pretermitted child's share comes out of the residuary estate, and the will is revoked to that extent.

C. REVOCATION BY WRITTEN INSTRUMENT

1. Instrument of Revocation Must Be Executed with Testamentary Formalities

A will or any part thereof may be revoked or altered by a subsequently written will, codicil, or other writing declaring such revocation, as long as there is a present intent to revoke and the instrument is executed with the same formalities as are required for the execution of a will. In states that recognize holographic wills, a valid holographic will may revoke a typewritten, attested will.

Example: A revocation can be by a writing that says nothing more than "I revoke my will," provided such writing is executed and attested with proper formalities. However, the usual method of revoking a will is to execute a new will that states: "This is my last will and testament, and I hereby revoke all earlier wills and codicils thereto."

2. Revocation by Implication—Inconsistent Provisions

Suppose that a testator executes a second testamentary instrument that does not contain any express language of revocation of an earlier will. To the extent possible, the two instruments are read together; *i.e.,* the second instrument is treated as a codicil to the will. However, the second instrument revokes the first to the extent of any inconsistent provisions.

Examples: 1) T executes a will that leaves all her property to John. Later, T executes a second will that leaves all her property to Dolly, but the will does not contain an express clause revoking the first will. When T dies, Dolly takes T's entire estate, the first will having been revoked completely by the inconsistent provision of the second will.

2) By his first will, T bequeaths his stamp collection to Art and his residuary estate to Ruth. By a later instrument executed with proper formalities, T bequeaths his stamp collection to Jack, his Studebaker convertible to Susan, and $5,000 to Tom. This second instrument contains no words of revocation. The second instrument is treated as a codicil, and revokes the first will only to the extent of inconsistent provisions. Thus Jack (not Art) takes the stamp collection, Susan takes the Studebaker, Tom takes $5,000, and Ruth takes T's residuary estate.

D. REVOCATION BY PHYSICAL ACT

1. Requirements

a. Physical Act

The statutes of each state specifically prescribe the acts sufficient to revoke a will. Typically, these acts are burning, tearing, obliterating, or canceling a material portion of the will. The act must be shown to have had an actual effect on the will or its language.

Example: T writes "Void. Isadore Berman" at the bottom of each page of a three-page will, not intersecting or coming into contact with any portion of the will. *Held:* The will was not revoked because the writing was: (i) not a revocation by subsequent instrument since it was not signed by attesting witnesses, and this jurisdiction does not recognize holographic wills; and (ii) not a revocation by physical act because no portion of the will was canceled, defaced, or obliterated.

1) Burning

Burning a material portion of the will's language is sufficient to revoke the will, but merely burning the will's outside cover or singeing the corners is insufficient.

2) Tearing

Tearing or cutting is sufficient if a material part, such as a dispositive provision or the testator's signature, is cut or torn.

Example: T cuts her signature off the will with scissors. *Held:* This is a valid revocation by physical act, as this act of canceling or defacing shows a clear intent that T intended to revoke the will in its entirety.

3) Obliteration

Revocation by obliteration (*e.g.*, inking out or erasing) requires damage to a material part of the will.

4) Cancellation

Lining out or writing an "X" or the word "void" across a will is sufficient to revoke if the lines touch the words of the will. Thus, writing words of cancellation on the back or in the margin of the will are ineffective to revoke the instrument.

Example: T's act of writing "Not Valid" across the *face* of each page of a three-page will constitutes a sufficient canceling, defacing, or obliterating to revoke the will.

b. Intent to Revoke

The intention to revoke must be present *at the time of the physical act* for revocation to be effective.

Example: Tom's house is badly damaged by a fire. When advised that his will was among the items destroyed by the fire, Tom states: "That's all right; I wanted to revoke it anyhow." The will has not been revoked since the intent to revoke did not accompany the physical act of destruction.

2. Revocation by Proxy Permitted

In most states, a will may be revoked by physical act by a person other than the testator, provided that the revocation is: (i) *at the testator's direction*, and (ii) in the testator's *presence*.

3. Partial Revocation

Most statutes authorize partial, as well as total, revocation by physical act. The problem is in determining whether the testator intended a partial or full revocation. Extrinsic evidence is admissible to make that determination.

a. Only Residuary Gifts May Be Increased

Courts are reluctant to give effect to nontestamentary actions that operate to increase the size of a general or specific bequest, but the testator can always increase the size of a residuary gift by canceling or obliterating a general or specific bequest.

Examples: 1) T's will provides: "I devise Blackacre to A for life, remainder to B. The rest and residue of my estate to C." If T attempts to strike the words "for life, remainder to B," thus giving a fee simple absolute to A, the change will not be given effect. Increasing the gift from a life estate to a fee simple is like making a new gift without complying with testamentary formalities.

2) If, in the above example, T struck the entire devise of Blackacre, the change would be valid and the residue would be increased. C would take Blackacre along with the rest of the residue of the estate.

4. Presumptions as to Revocation

a. Will Not Found After Testator's Death

Where a will that was last seen in the testator's possession or control cannot be found after the testator's death, a presumption arises that the will was revoked (*i.e.,* the reason the will cannot be located is that the testator destroyed it with the intent to revoke). However, if the will was last seen in the possession of a third person or if a person adversely affected by its contents (*e.g.,* an heir, or a legatee under an earlier will) had access to the will, no presumption of revocation arises.

b. Will Found After Death in Mutilated Condition

Where a will last seen in the testator's possession or control is found after his death in a mutilated condition (*e.g.,* torn in two, or crossed out with felt-tip pen), a presumption arises that the testator did the mutilating with the intent to revoke the will.

c. Evidence to Overcome Presumption of Revocation

To overcome the presumption of revocation raised in the foregoing situations, extrinsic evidence is admissible to show the testator's intention.

5. Effect of Revocation on Other Testamentary Instruments

a. Revocation of Will

The revocation of a will revokes all codicils to that will.

b. Destruction of Duplicate Will

Where a will has been executed in duplicate (both original and duplicate are signed and witnessed), an act of revocation performed by the testator upon *either* copy revokes the will. Both signed copies of the will are of the same legal stature.

However, the destruction of an ***unexecuted*** copy of the will, accompanied by an intent to revoke, does ***not revoke*** the will. The act of obliteration, destruction, etc., must be done on the will itself.

c. **Revocation of Codicil**

A physical act of revocation performed on a codicil ***revokes only the codicil***, not the prior will. In the absence of evidence to the contrary, it is presumed that in revoking the codicil the testator intended to reinstate the will provisions changed by the codicil as though the codicil had never been executed.

Example: T executed a will, and later executed three separate codicils to the will. Thereafter, T revoked the third and then the second codicil; then T died. *Held:* Read the will and first codicil as though the second and third codicils had never been made.

6. **Lost or Destroyed Will—Contents Must Be Clearly and Distinctly Proved**

Suppose that a will is accidentally destroyed in a fire, or that the will cannot be located after the testator's death, but the presumption of revocation that is raised by such facts is overcome by proof that the testator did not intend to revoke the will. All states permit probate of a lost or destroyed will provided that the following three elements can be proved: (i) valid execution; (ii) the cause of nonproduction (*i.e.,* that revocation is not the reason for nonproduction); and (iii) the contents of the will. The contents are usually proved by the testimony of at least two witnesses or by production of a carbon or photocopy of the will.

E. REVIVAL OF REVOKED WILLS

In most states, a will, once revoked, is not revived unless it is reexecuted or republished by codicil. Thus, a will revoked by a subsequent instrument is not automatically revived when the revoking instrument is itself revoked.

Example: T executes Will-1. Sometime later, T executes Will-2, which expressly or impliedly revokes all (or part) of Will-1. T keeps Will-1. If T later revokes Will-2, Will-1 is not revived. Will-1 was revoked immediately upon the execution of Will-2. Thus, Will-1 had no legal existence after that point and could not be resurrected merely by revoking Will-2.

Note that the UPC and a minority of states hold that destruction of the revoking instrument may revive the revoked document depending on the testator's intent as established by the testator's statements and the circumstances surrounding the case.

1. **Reexecution**

A will can be reexecuted with full testamentary formalities or by the testator acknowledging her signature on the will or acknowledging the will and having this attested to by two witnesses.

2. **Republication by Codicil**

Provided the first will is still in physical existence, it may be revived by the valid execution of a codicil that expressly refers to it.

F. DEPENDENT RELATIVE REVOCATION

1. **Mistake of Law as to Validity of Another Disposition**

Dependent relative revocation ("DRR") is an equity-type doctrine under which a ***court may disregard a revocation*** if it determines that the act of revocation was premised on a mistake of law and would not have occurred but for the testator's mistaken belief that another disposition of her property was valid. If the other disposition is ineffective for some reason, the revocation accompanying the attempted disposition also fails and the will remains in force. Necessary to application of DRR is that the disposition that results from disregarding the revocation comes closer to effectuating what the testator tried (but failed) to do than would an intestate distribution.

Examples: 1) Tillie validly executes a will that devises her entire estate to her sister Ann. Later, Tillie executes a second instrument that bequeaths $10,000 to her friend Fred and the remainder of her estate to Ann. However, the instrument is signed by only one attesting witness. Tillie, erroneously believing that the second instrument has been validly executed, tears up the first will. Tillie dies, survived by her sister Ann and her brother Bob as her nearest kin. The second instrument is not admitted to probate because it was not properly attested. On these facts, DRR would be applied so as to disregard the revocation of the first will, which would be admitted to probate upon compliance with the proof of lost wills statute. *Rationale:* Although Tillie revoked the first will by physical act, her act of revocation was based on her mistaken assumption that the second instrument was a valid will. Had Tillie known that the second will was invalid, she would not have revoked the first will. (Of course, if Tillie had known the true situation, she would have properly executed the second will! It's too late for that now, however.) Since Ann was the principal beneficiary under both instruments, disregarding the revocation of the first will comes closer to what Tillie tried (but failed) to do than would an intestate distribution, under which Bob would take one-half of Tillie's estate.

2) Trevor executes a will that devises one-half of his estate to his sister Sue and the other one-half to his son (and sole heir) Steve. Later, Trevor executes a second will that, after expressly revoking the first will, devises one-third of his estate to Sue and two-thirds to Steve. Trevor does not destroy the first will. Trevor then changes his mind once again. He destroys the second will, intending to revoke it and to revive the first will. Under the no-revival rule, the first will is not revived. Now it appears that both wills have been revoked! Here, DRR would be applied to disregard the revocation of the second will. Trevor's act of revoking the second will was based on the mistaken belief (a mistake of law) that, by doing so, he could revive the first will. The courts reason that Trevor would prefer that one-third of his estate pass to Sue under the second will than to have Trevor's entire estate pass to his son by intestacy. Disregarding the revocation comes closer to what Trevor tried but failed to do than would an intestate distribution.

If the second will said "one-third to my friend Hobie Gates and two-thirds to Steve" and the other facts were the same, DRR would ***not*** be applied. Trevor's revocation of the second will (in effect, "I do not want Hobie Gates to take anything") would be ***independent*** of his intent to revive the earlier will that made a gift to Sue. To disregard the revocation of the second will would defeat Trevor's intent. On these facts, the conventional rules would be applied and an intestacy would result.

3) Tim's validly executed will includes a bequest of "$2,000 to my niece Nellie." Thereafter, Tim crosses out the "$2,000" and writes in "$5,000" above it, intending thereby to revoke the gift of $2,000 and replace it with a gift of $5,000. The attempt to increase the gift to Nellie is ineffective as an unattested writing. Although Tim's striking of "$2,000" was an effective partial revocation by physical act, DRR will be applied so as to disregard the revocation. Tim would not have revoked the $2,000 bequest but for the erroneous belief that the $5,000 bequest was valid. (But if Tim had attempted to reduce the $2,000 bequest to $500, DRR would not be applied. In this situation, by striking the $2,000 Tim in effect said, "I do not want Nellie to take $2,000." It cannot be assumed that Tim would prefer Nellie to take $2,000 rather than zero.)

4) Same facts as in *Example* 3), except that Tim strikes the entire "$2,000 to my niece Nellie," and writes in above it "$5,000 to my sister Sue." Here, DRR should not be applied. Tim's revocation of the gift to Nellie (in effect, "I do not want Nellie to take anything") would be *independent* of his ineffective attempt to make a gift to Sue. To disregard the revocation would defeat Tim's intent. On these facts, the conventional rules would be applied, and the bequest to Nellie would be revoked.

VII. CONTRACTS RELATING TO WILLS; JOINT WILLS

A. CONTRACT TO MAKE A GIFT BY WILL

1. Contract Law Governs

Assuming the usual requirements of a valid contract are met, a contract to make, not to make, or not to revoke a will is valid. Problems in this area are controlled by contract law and not by the law of wills. The contract is not a will; it does not have to be executed with testamentary formalities; it cannot be probated. Likewise, the contract cannot be used to oppose the probate of a properly executed will that is inconsistent with the terms of the agreement. Such a will must be probated. There may be an action for damages or a suit in quasi-contract for the consideration provided, but the usual remedy is for a court of equity to impose a *constructive trust* upon the appropriate beneficiaries under the will.

2. Consideration

The promisee does not have any enforceable contract rights unless she provided some consideration for the testator's promise to name her as a will beneficiary. Without consideration, the testator's promise is merely a promise to make a gift in the future and is not enforceable. But note that in a contract to make a gift by will in exchange for a promise by the beneficiary to provide care to the testator, the mere fact that the testator died before the promisee could provide much in the way of care does not render the contract unenforceable— the promise to provide the care was sufficient consideration.

3. Formalities

As a general rule, a contract to make a will or a gift by will need not be in writing unless land is involved. Many states have, however, enacted statutes requiring all such contracts to be in writing. Many follow the lead of the UPC, which states that a contract to make a will or not to revoke a will can be established only by:

(i) *Provisions in the will* stating the material provisions of the contract;

(ii) An *express reference* in a will to the contract and extrinsic evidence proving the terms of the contract; or

(iii) A *writing signed by the decedent* evidencing the contract.

[UPC §2-514]

4. Remedies for Breach

a. During Testator's Life

Generally, there is no remedy during the testator's life because there is no way of knowing whether the testator will carry out his promise until his death. If the testator repudiates the contract after substantial performance by the promisee, however, the promisee may seek damages, quantum meruit (value of services rendered), or equitable relief.

b. After Testator's Death

If the promisor fails to make the promised testamentary gift, the promisee can seek damages equaling the value of the property promised. If the promise was to devise specific property, however, the usual remedy is for the court to impose a constructive trust on the property for the promisee's benefit.

B. JOINT AND RECIPROCAL WILLS

1. Introduction

a. Joint Will

A joint will is the will of two or more persons executed on the same piece of paper and intended to serve as the will of each. Thus, a joint will is a single instrument executed by two or more testators. A joint will is admissible to probate on the death of each testator; it is as if there were separate pieces of paper. If one of the joint testators should revoke his joint will, the document would still serve and be admissible to probate as the will of the other(s).

b. Reciprocal Wills

Reciprocal wills are separate wills executed by two or more testators that contain substantially similar or "reciprocal" provisions. Thus, a reciprocal will is an instrument executed by only one person but which is similar in its provisions to the terms of another testator's will. A "***mutual will***" may refer to a reciprocal will ***or*** it may refer to a joint will or a reciprocal will executed in accordance with a ***contract*** ("mutuality" referring to a contract).

Example: H makes a will leaving everything to W if she survives H, and if W does not survive H, everything is to go one-half to W's heirs and one-half to H's heirs. W makes a will leaving everything to H if he survives W, and if H does not survive W, everything is to go one-half to W's heirs and one-half to H's heirs. H and W have reciprocal wills.

2. Revocability

Joint wills or reciprocal wills are revocable at any time during a testator's life in the same manner as any other will. This is true even if the wills are executed pursuant to a contract which provides that the wills shall not be revoked (although such revocation may give rise to a cause of action for breach of contract; *see* below).

3. No Presumption of Contract

The stated majority rule is that the mere execution of joint wills does not raise a presumption that the wills are contractual (*i.e.,* that they were executed pursuant to a promise by each party not to revoke). However, many courts do in fact find that joint wills are contractual. By contrast, an overwhelming majority of courts find that mere execution of reciprocal wills (even when drafted by the same attorney and executed on the same day) does not constitute evidence that the wills are contractual.

C. CONTRACTS NOT TO REVOKE

Just as parties can enter into a contract to make a will or a gift by will, a testator may enter into a contract not to revoke her will. Most of these cases involve a joint will or reciprocal wills (*see* above).

1. Contractual Will Revocable During Both Parties' Lifetimes

Either party may revoke a contractual will provided she gives notice to the other party to the contract, so that the other party will have a chance to change his will.

2. Relief Denied If First Party Dies in Breach

If one party secretly revokes her will (*i.e.,* does not give notice to the other party to the contract) and predeceases the other party, the survivor has no remedy because he has not been damaged. The survivor is alive and able to change his will so as to avoid sustaining any damage.

3. Constructive Trust Remedy If Survivor Dies in Breach

If the surviving party to a contractual will revokes her will and executes a new one, the new will is admissible to probate. However, since this is a breach of contract, the beneficiaries of the contractual will have a cause of action against the estate. The usual remedy is to impose a constructive trust on the property. The beneficiaries under the new will, which was executed in breach of contract, hold on constructive trust for the benefit of the contract beneficiaries; *i.e.,* their duty as trustee is to convey the property to the contract beneficiaries.

Example: H and W execute a joint will that expressly provides that the will is contractual and that the survivor cannot revoke it after the first party's death. H dies and W probates the will and accepts its benefits. W then executes a new will that revokes the joint will and devises her estate to other beneficiaries. After W's death, both wills are offered for probate.

The joint will cannot be probated because W revoked it by a later will. The second will is admissible to probate because it was W's last will and it was validly executed. (Wills law controls to this extent.) However, the beneficiaries of the joint will can now bring an action to impress a constructive trust against the beneficiaries of the second will, since execution of that will was in breach of W's contract with H.

a. Compare—Remedy for Breach During Survivor's Lifetime
If the surviving party to a contractual will attempts to dispose of property covered by the agreement (*e.g.*, property received from the other contracting party) during his lifetime, the contract beneficiaries may be able to impress a constructive trust upon the property. In contrast, if the surviving party merely revokes his will (no inter vivos transfer or other act of clear repudiation) in breach of the contract, the contract beneficiaries have no cause of action until that party's death.

VIII. CHANGES IN BENEFICIARIES AND PROPERTY AFTER WILL'S EXECUTION

A. LAPSED GIFTS AND ANTI-LAPSE STATUTES

1. Gift Lapses If Beneficiary Predeceases Testator
If a will beneficiary dies during the testator's lifetime, the gift to him lapses; *i.e.,* it fails. A will cannot make a gift to a dead person.
Example: T's will provides: "I bequeath all of my IBM stock to my good friend Jim Brown; and I bequeath my residuary estate to my sister Sarah Goode." Jim Brown predeceases T. The gift to Jim Brown lapses, and the IBM stock falls into the residuary estate as undisposed-of property.

2. Anti-Lapse Statutes
Nearly all states have anti-lapse statutes that operate to save the gift if the predeceasing beneficiary (i) was in a *specified degree of relationship* to the testator, *and* (ii) *left descendants* who survived the testator. The beneficiary's descendants take by substitution under the anti-lapse statute. The anti-lapse statutes vary as to the scope of beneficiaries covered by them. In many states, the anti-lapse statute applies only when the predeceasing beneficiary is a *descendant of the testator*. Several states and the UPC extend the application of the statute to any predeceasing beneficiary who is *the testator's grandparent or a descendant of the testator's grandparent*. [UPC §2-603] There are a few states with very broad statutes that apply to any relative of the testator or any beneficiary at all.
Examples: 1) T's will provides: "I devise Blackacre to my brother William Baxter; and I devise my residuary estate to my husband John." William predeceases T, leaving a will that bequeaths "all my property to my wife Wanda"; William is survived by Wanda and by a child Billy, both of whom also survive T. Under the most restrictive statute, the anti-lapse statute would not apply because

William was not T's descendant. Under a UPC-type statute, however, the anti-lapse statute would apply because brother William was a descendant of T's grandparents. Billy would take Blackacre by substitution under the statute.

Note: Blackacre does ***not*** pass to Wanda under William's will. The anti-lapse statute does not save the gift for the predeceasing beneficiary's estate. Instead, it provides substitute takers—here, William's descendant Billy. William, having predeceased T, had no interest in T's estate that he could devise by will.

2) Same facts, except that William was not survived by any descendants. Although William (T's brother) was within the scope of the UPC-type anti-lapse statute, the statute does not apply because William left no descendants. The gift of Blackacre lapses; Blackacre falls into the residuary estate and passes to T's husband John.

3. Anti-Lapse Statute Does Not Apply If Contrary Provision in Will

The anti-lapse statute does not apply if there is a contrary will provision; *i.e.*, the gift is contingent on the beneficiary's surviving the testator.

Example: T's will provides: "I bequeath $25,000 to my daughter Mary if she survives me." Mary dies during T's lifetime, leaving a child (Monica) who survives T. The anti-lapse statute does ***not*** operate in Monica's favor because the will shows a contrary intention. The gift to Mary was, by its terms, contingent on Mary's surviving T. Since Mary predeceased T, the condition to the gift was not satisfied. The gift fails according to its own terms.

4. Statute Applies Only to Gifts by Will

The anti-lapse statute applies only to testamentary gifts. It does not apply to inter vivos trusts, life insurance beneficiary designations, or other nonprobate transfers.

5. Lapse in the Residuary Gift

a. Common Law—"No Residue of a Residue"

Suppose that a testator devises her residuary estate to two or more beneficiaries, one of the beneficiaries predeceases the testator, and the anti-lapse statute does not apply. At common law, and in some states today, the share devised to that beneficiary does ***not*** pass to the remaining beneficiaries (unless the will so provides). Instead, the lapsed residuary gift "falls out of the will" and passes under the intestacy statutes to the testator's heirs. This was called the "no residue of a residue" rule.

Example: T's will devises "all the rest, residue, and remainder of my estate in equal shares to my friend Alan Adams, my Uncle Bill, and my sister Carrie." Alan Adams predeceases T, leaving a child (Alice) who survives T. Under the common law rule, the one-third share devised to Alan lapses; it falls out of the will and passes by intestacy to T's heirs. Bill and Carrie each take one-third of the residuary estate as provided in the will.

b. Majority Rule—Surviving Residuary Beneficiaries Take
Most states have replaced the "no residue of a residue" rule with a statutory rule under which the residuary beneficiaries who survive the testator take the deceased beneficiary's share of the residuary estate. If the residue is devised to two or more persons and the share of one of them fails for any reason, absent a contrary will provision, his share passes to the other residuary beneficiaries in proportion to their interests in the residue.

Example: Consider the example immediately above, except that the majority rule applies. Again, Alan Adams predeceases the testator. Since Alan was not related to T, the anti-lapse statute does not apply. Under the "surviving residuary beneficiaries rule," the one-third share devised to Alan passes to the other residuary devisees. Bill and Carrie each take one-half of the residuary estate.

1) Exception If Anti-Lapse Statute Applies
If the predeceasing residuary beneficiary was within the scope of the anti-lapse statute and left descendants, the anti-lapse statute takes precedence over the rule that the surviving residuary beneficiaries take.

Example: Suppose in the previous example that T's Uncle Bill predeceases T, leaving a child (Willette) who survives T. Suppose further that this occurs in a jurisdiction that has adopted a UPC-type anti-lapse statute. Since Bill was a descendant of a grandparent of the testator, the anti-lapse statute applies, and Willette takes the one-third share of the residuary estate that was devised to Bill. The "surviving residuary beneficiaries rule" gives way to the anti-lapse statute when the predeceasing residuary beneficiary is within the scope of the statute *and* leaves descendants who survive the testator.

6. Class Gifts

a. Class Gift Rule—Class Members Who Survive Testator Take Gift
If a will makes a gift to a class of persons ("children," "brothers and sisters," etc.) and a class member dies during the testator's lifetime, those class members who survive the testator take the gift (absent a contrary will provision). The rationale for the class gift rule is that the testator did not want anyone other than members of the designated class to share in the gift. Another explanation for the rule is that the will is read and the takers are determined as of the testator's death, and only those who meet the class description at that time share in the gift. The best way to understand the class gift rule is to contrast it with the courts' treatment of gifts to individually named beneficiaries.

Example: Tom's will bequeaths 600 shares of Xerox stock "to the children of my good friend Homer Hanson," and devises his residuary estate to his sister. At the time the will is executed, Homer has three children: Dan, Fran, and Stan. Dan predeceases Tom, leaving two children who survive Tom. The anti-lapse statute does not apply because Dan was not related to Tom. Since the bequest of the Xerox stock was made to a class, Dan's share of the gift does not fall into the residuary estate. Instead, the class gift rule applies, and the class members who survived the testator share the gift. Thus, Fran and Stan each take 300 shares of Xerox stock.

Compare: Tammy's will devises Blackacre "in equal shares to my good friends, Al Anson, Bill Bryce, and Carol Carter," and bequeaths her residuary estate to her husband, Fred. Al Anson dies leaving two children; then Tammy dies. The anti-lapse statute does not apply because Anson was not related to Tammy. Since this was a gift of one-third shares to the three named beneficiaries, the share devised to Anson lapses and falls into the residuary estate. Tammy's husband Fred owns one-third of Blackacre along with Bill Bryce and Carol Carter.

b. **Exception If Anti-Lapse Statute Applies**
As with the "surviving residuary beneficiaries rule," the "class gift rule" gives way to the anti-lapse statute when the predeceasing class member was within the scope of that statute *and* left descendants who survive the testator.
Example: Consider the same facts as in the previous example, except that the gift of Xerox stock was "to the children of my *son* Homer Hanson." Again, Dan predeceases Tom, leaving two children who survive Tom. Since Dan was Tom's descendant, his two children take by substitution under the anti-lapse statute. (This is true under any anti-lapse statute.) They take 100 shares each; Fran and Stan take 200 shares each.

7. **Beneficiary Dead When Will Executed—Void Gift**
If a will makes a gift to a beneficiary who was dead at the time the will was executed, the gift is void. In most states, the rules that apply to lapsed gifts (anti-lapse statute; "surviving residuary beneficiaries rule") also apply to void gifts.

B. ADEMPTION

Under the doctrine of ademption, when specifically bequeathed property is not in the testator's estate at death (*e.g.*, it was destroyed, sold, given away, or lost), the bequest is adeemed; *i.e.*, it fails. Ademption applies because the property that was to have satisfied the bequest is not in the estate.

1. **Applies to Specific Devises and Bequests**
Ademption applies *only* to specific devises and bequests. A specific legacy is a gift of property that is particularly designated and is to be satisfied only by the receipt of the particular property described.
Examples: 1) T's will bequeaths "my Rolex watch to my sister Sue." After the will is executed, T sells her Rolex watch and uses the sale proceeds to purchase a Seiko watch. Ademption operates since the testamentary disposition was of a Rolex watch, not a Seiko, and T did not own a Rolex watch at her death.

2) T's will devises Blackacre to his brother Bill. Thereafter, T sells Blackacre for $30,000 and deposits the sale proceeds in a savings account. Unless evidence of T's intent is admissible (*see* below), ademption applies and Bill takes nothing. Neither the proceeds of the sold item nor similar items purchased with the proceeds go to the beneficiary.

a. **May Not Apply to Gift of Sale Proceeds**
Suppose, in the second example above, that T's will provides: "I direct that my executor sell Blackacre and distribute the sale proceeds to my brother Bill." Most courts hold

that ademption does not apply, and that Bill takes the sale proceeds—to the extent that they can be traced. *Rationale:* Since the gift was of the proceeds from the sale, it should not matter whether Blackacre was sold by T during his lifetime or by the executor after T's death. T's intent can still be effectuated by giving the sale proceeds to Bill. (But if the sale proceeds cannot be traced—if, for example, T has spent the proceeds—ademption applies.)

b.   May Not Apply to Gift of Testator's Interest in Property
If the bequest is of the testator's interest in the property, rather than of the property itself, the gift may not be adeemed.

Example: T's will devises "all of my right, title, and interest in Blackacre to my brother Bill." T sells Blackacre on an installment contract under which the vendee promises to pay T $10,000 per year for 10 years. The contract gives T a vendor's lien. Since the gift was not of Blackacre itself but of T's *interest* in Blackacre, Bill takes T's interest as it exists at T's death. Bill takes the remaining installment payments and T's security interest (the vendor's lien).

2.   Testator's Intent

a.   Testator's Intent Irrelevant
Most courts apply the "identity" theory of the common law, under which the ademption issue is decided solely on the basis of an objective test: whether the specifically bequeathed property is a part of the testator's estate at her death. Under this approach, the testator's intent is irrelevant. The courts do not speculate on the reasons why the property was not in the estate or what the testator might have intended.

b.   Statutory Modifications
Many states have enacted statutes that soften the ademption rule in certain circumstances:

1)   Where *casualty insurance proceeds* for the loss of the specifically bequeathed property are paid after the testator's death, the beneficiary is entitled to the proceeds.

2)   The beneficiary is entitled to the *condemnation award* in cases where the specifically devised property is taken by eminent domain before the testator's death, but the award is paid after the testator's death.

3)   Where specifically devised property is subject to an *executory contract* at the testator's death, the beneficiary is entitled to all of the testator's rights under the contract, including the right to the remaining payments and any security interest retained by the testator.

4)   Where a will makes a specific bequest of *securities* in one entity, the beneficiary is entitled to securities in another entity owned by the testator as a result of merger, consolidation, reorganization, or other similar action initiated by the entity.

5) If a testator becomes *incompetent* and the specifically devised property is *sold by a guardian* or a condemnation award or insurance proceeds are paid to the guardian for the property, the devisee is entitled to a general pecuniary legacy equal to the amount of the proceeds.

3. Partial Ademption

Partial ademption applies when, for example, the testator devises a large tract of land, then sells a portion of the tract. Ademption applies to the portion of the property not in the estate, but the remaining portion in the estate at death passes to the beneficiary.

4. Ademption Does Not Apply to General or Demonstrative Legacies

Ademption applies only to specific devises and bequests. It does not apply to general or demonstrative legacies.

a. General Legacy

A general legacy is a bequest of a dollar amount that is payable out of the general assets of the estate without a claim on any particular source of payment.

Example: "I bequeath the sum of $5,000 to my nephew, Ringo." At T's death there is not that much cash in his estate. It does not matter. Ademption does not apply to general legacies. Other property in T's estate must be sold, if necessary, to satisfy Ringo's general legacy. Alternatively, the personal representative could make a "distribution in kind" (*i.e.,* a distribution of assets worth $5,000) in satisfaction of the legacy.

b. Demonstrative Legacy

A demonstrative legacy is a gift of a general amount that identifies a particular asset as the primary source of payment.

Example: "I bequeath $10,000 to my niece Nancy, to be paid out of the proceeds of my IBM stock." Before his death, T sells all of his IBM stock, and there is no such stock in his estate at his death. The $10,000 legacy is not adeemed; the $10,000 must be raised by the sale of other property in T's estate. Ademption does not apply to demonstrative legacies.

c. Bequests of Securities—Special Rules Apply

The courts will construe a bequest of securities as a general legacy, if it is possible to do so, in order to avoid application of the ademption doctrine. The cases turn on whether testator made a gift of "200 shares" or "*my* 200 shares."

Examples: 1) Tom's will bequeaths "my 200 shares of Acme common stock to my cousin Bill." Thereafter, Tom sells the Acme stock, and does not own any such stock at his death. Since the bequest is of "*my* 200 shares" of Acme stock, this is a *specific bequest* of the shares that Tom owned at the time the will was executed. Ademption applies, and Bill takes nothing.

2) Tom's will also bequeaths "200 shares of Baker common stock to my niece Nora." Thereafter, Tom sells the Baker stock, and does not own any such stock at his death. Here the courts seize on the absence of a possessive pronoun (he did not say "*my* 200 shares") and conclude that Tom did not intend to make a gift of the 200 shares of Baker stock that

he owned. Rather, Tom's will made a *general legacy* of the *value* of 200 shares of Baker stock. Since ademption does not apply to general legacies, Nora is entitled to the date-of-death value of 200 shares of Baker stock. (The courts would reach this result even if Tom owned exactly 200 shares of Baker stock at the time the will was executed!) The only way this strained "reasoning" can be explained is that the courts want to avoid application of the ademption doctrine in cases such as this.

C. INCREASES TO PROPERTY AFTER EXECUTION OF WILL

1. Increases Occurring Before Testator's Death

Increases to specific gifts occurring during the testator's lifetime are distributed as follows: income on property (*e.g.*, rents and profits) goes into the general estate, but improvements to real property go to the specific devisee. (*See* below for rules regarding stock splits and dividends.)

2. Increases Occurring After Testator's Death

Any increase to specific gifts occurring after the testator's death passes to the specific beneficiary because the beneficiary is deemed to own the property from the time of the testator's death.

3. Stock Splits and Stock Dividends

Suppose that the testator's will makes a specific bequest of shares of stock, and the corporation thereafter declares a stock split or a stock dividend. Most states follow the common law rule: A specific bequest of stock includes any additional shares produced by a stock split, but does not include shares produced by a stock dividend.

Examples: 1) T's will includes a bequest of "my 100 shares of IBM stock to my daughter Carol." Thereafter, IBM declares a two-for-one stock split, and a stock certificate for an additional 100 shares is issued to T. On T's death, Carol takes all 200 shares of IBM stock. *Rationale:* T's 200 shares of IBM stock after the split represented the same proportionate share of ownership in IBM as the 100 shares before the split. Carol is entitled to the ownership interest that T held when he wrote his will.

2) Same facts, except that T's will bequeathed "100 shares [not "*my* 100 shares"] of IBM stock to my daughter Carol." Thereafter, IBM declares a two-for-one stock split. Despite the absence of a possessive pronoun, this was a specific bequest of IBM stock, and Carol takes the additional 100 shares produced by the stock split. Wait a minute! In *Example* 2) under c., above, when the issue was ademption, a bequest of "200 shares of Baker stock" was classified as a general legacy! How can the same form of bequest be classified as specific when a stock split has occurred? Because, say the courts, different issues are involved. A bequest of stock can be classified as general for one purpose (ademption) and specific for another purpose (stock split).

3) T's will bequeaths "my 200 shares of Acme common stock to my sister Ruth." Thereafter, Acme declares a 10% stock dividend, and a certificate for

an additional 20 shares of Acme stock is issued to T. On T's death, Ruth takes only the 200 shares of Acme stock. The courts treat stock dividends the same as cash dividends, and a legatee of stock is not entitled to stock (or cash) dividends declared during the testator's lifetime.

IX. RESTRICTIONS ON POWER OF TESTATION— PROTECTION OF THE FAMILY

A. PROTECTION OF THE SURVIVING SPOUSE—ELECTIVE SHARE STATUTES

Nearly all states have enacted elective share statutes designed to protect a surviving spouse from disinheritance. These statutes give the spouse an election to take a statutory share (usually one-third or one-half) of the decedent's estate *in lieu of* taking under the decedent's will.

1. Amount of Elective Share

The elective share amount varies from state to state. In most states, the amount is one-third of the net probate estate if the decedent is survived by issue and one-half if the decedent is not survived by issue.

2. Property Subject to Election

In most states, the share is calculated from the decedent's net estate, which is the probate estate minus the payment of expenses and creditors' claims. In some states, however, the share fraction is applied to the decedent's "augmented estate," which includes certain lifetime transfers (*see* 6., *infra*).

3. Notice Must Be Filed

The right to an elective share is not automatic; the surviving spouse must file a notice of election within a specified period (usually within six months after the will is admitted to probate).

4. Right to Election Is Personal to Spouse

Generally, only the surviving spouse may make the election to take against the will. Election can be made, however, on behalf of a legally incapacitated spouse by a guardian, with court approval, upon a showing that an election is necessary to provide adequate support for the spouse during his or her life expectancy. In contrast, if the spouse dies before the election is made, the election *cannot be made by the spouse's personal representative*. The reason for this is that the statute is intended to protect the surviving spouse against disinheritance, not to provide benefits to the spouse's heirs.

5. Effect of Election on Testamentary Plan

The elective share is paid in the manner causing the least disruption to the testator's testamentary plan. Thus, the elective share is first paid in cash or kind from the assets passing under the will that, but for the election, would have passed to the spouse outright. (Life estates are treated as though the spouse predeceased the testator, and the remainder is accelerated.) To the extent that these assets are insufficient to satisfy the share, the excess is paid pursuant to the abatement rules that apply to creditors' claims (*see* XI.E., *infra*).

6. Lifetime Transfers to Defeat Elective Share

In most states that have addressed this issue by statute, lifetime transfers by the decedent are subject to the elective share if the grantor-spouse retained the power to *revoke or to invade, consume, or dispose of the principal*. Thus, in these states, revocable trusts may not be used to defeat a spouse's right of election. If it were otherwise, the policy underlying the elective share statute could easily be defeated by these types of transfers. The UPC states, which are included in the above discussion, also include other lifetime transfers in which the decedent retained an interest (*e.g.*, retained life estates, right of survivorship estates) in their concept of the "*augmented estate*" used for purposes of calculating the elective share. [*See* UPC §2-205]

7. Compare—Dower and Curtesy

At common law, a surviving wife's dower right entitled her to a life estate in an undivided one-third of all lands of which her husband was seised during marriage. Dower was *inchoate* during the husband's lifetime and became a possessory estate on the husband's death. Dower applied not only to lands owned by the husband at death, but also to lands conveyed by the husband during his lifetime without the wife's joinder on the deed. A surviving husband's right of curtesy gave him a life estate in all (not just one-third) of his wife's lands *if* issue were born of the marriage. Dower and curtesy took precedence over claims by creditors of the deceased spouse. Most states have abolished dower and curtesy in favor of the statutory substitutes discussed, *supra*.

B. PROTECTION OF CHILDREN—PRETERMITTED CHILD STATUTES

A testator may disinherit her children; *i.e.*, a parent need not bequeath anything to her children. Pretermitted child statutes are not intended to address that issue, but are designed to protect children from being *accidentally omitted* from the will.

1. Omitted Child Entitled to Intestate Share

In most states, the statute operates so that a child born or adopted *after the will was executed* takes an intestate share of the decedent's estate (*i.e.*, the share he would have taken had the decedent died intestate), provided none of the exceptions below apply. In making up the child's share, the normal abatement rules apply.

2. Exceptions

Under most statutes, the pretermitted child will not take a share if:

a. It appears from the will that the *omission was intentional*;

b. At the time the will was executed, the testator had other children and devised substantially all of his estate to the *other parent* of the omitted child; or

c. The testator provided for the omitted child by a *transfer outside of the will* with the intent that it was in lieu of a testamentary gift.

3. Protects Children of Testator Only

In most states, the pretermitted child statute operates only in favor of the testator's children; the testator's grandchildren are not covered.

C. HOMESTEAD, FAMILY ALLOWANCE, AND EXEMPT PERSONAL PROPERTY

1. Homestead

Most states have statutes that protect the family residence or farm from creditors' claims. These statutes usually exempt a certain amount of land from the claims of the decedent's creditors. The amount of land exempted depends on whether the residence is urban or rural. These homestead laws often include a provision that the surviving spouse or minor/dependent children are entitled to occupy the homestead as a residence for as long as they so choose despite the disposition of the residence in the decedent's will.

2. Family Allowance

Nearly all states authorize the payment of a family allowance to the decedent's surviving spouse or minor children. Some states limit the allowance to a specific dollar amount (*e.g.*, $10,000), while others authorize payment of an amount needed to maintain the spouse and children for one year or a "reasonable amount" to be fixed by the court. The purpose of the allowance is to provide funds for support of the spouse and children during the period the decedent's assets are tied up in probate administration. The family allowance, which usually takes precedence over all claims other than funeral and administration expenses, is in addition to the amount passing to the spouse (or children) by will, intestacy, or elective share.

3. Exempt Personal Property

In addition to homestead rights and a family allowance, the surviving spouse of a decedent usually is entitled to petition to set aside certain items of tangible personal property listed in the statute. Typically, this exemption applies to household furnishings, appliances, personal effects, farm equipment, and sometimes automobiles. These items are in addition to amounts passing to the spouse under the decedent's will, by intestate succession, or under the elective share. If there is no surviving spouse, these items may be set aside for the decedent's minor children. The items are exempt from all claims against the estate except perfected security interests thereon.

D. TESTAMENTARY GIFTS TO CHARITY

Most states do not place any restrictions on charitable devises and bequests. A few do, however, still have mortmain statutes that restrict charitable bequests by voiding all charitable bequests made in wills executed within a short time before death or by limiting the gifts made within that time to a fixed percentage of the estate. These mortmain statutes may be unconstitutional. Several courts have found them to violate state and federal Equal Protection Clauses.

X. WILL CONTESTS

A. GROUNDS FOR CONTEST—IN GENERAL

A will contest challenges whether the document offered for probate is a valid will. The contestant may raise any matter tending to show that the will is not valid and should be denied probate. A will may be contested on any of the following grounds:

(i) *Defective execution* (*e.g.*, only one witness when two are required);

(ii)   The will offered has been validly *revoked*;

(iii) The testator *lacked testamentary capacity*;

(iv)   The testator *lacked testamentary intent*;

(v)   The will or a gift therein is a product of *undue influence*;

(vi)   The will or a gift therein was procured by *fraud*; or

(vii) The document was executed or a gift was made as the result of a *mistake*.

Note that most wills are challenged on the grounds of lack of testamentary capacity or undue influence.

B. PROCEDURAL ASPECTS

1. Time for Contest
Although the statutory period varies from state to state, in most states, a will contest must be filed within *six months* after the will is admitted to probate.

2. Proper Contestants
Only *interested parties* have standing to contest a will. To be an interested party, the person must have a direct interest in the estate that would be adversely affected by the admission of the will to probate. Examples of interested parties are intestate heirs and legatees under earlier wills. Creditors do not have standing to contest a will, and neither do executors or testamentary trustees named in earlier wills.

3. Necessary Parties
In most states, *all legatees under the will and all heirs* are necessary parties to a will contest and must be given notice.

4. Burden of Proof
The burden of proof is on the will contestant to establish the grounds.

5. Will May Fail Either Partially or Entirely
A will is void if its execution is procured by undue influence, fraud, duress, or mistake. If only a part of the will was so procured, only that part is void, and the remainder of the will is given effect.

C. TESTAMENTARY CAPACITY

1. Must Be Age Eighteen to Make a Will
In most states, a person must be 18 years of age or older to make a will. The requirement is applied as of the *date of execution* of the will, not as of the date of death.

2. Mental Capacity
The capacity required for making a will is a different and lower standard of capacity than that required to make a contract. To have mental capacity to make a will, the testator must have sufficient capacity to be able to understand:

(i) The nature of her *act*; *i.e.*, she must actually know she is executing a will;

(ii) The *nature and extent of her property*;

(iii) The persons who are the *natural objects of her bounty*; and

(iv) The *nature of the disposition* she is making, *i.e.*, "a general understanding of the practical effect of the will as executed."

a. Testator's Capacity Determined at Time of Will Execution

It is at the making of the will, not at death, that the mental capacity must exist. This being so, all circumstances existing at the time of execution are admissible on the capacity issue, as well as evidence relating to the testator's state of mind shortly before and after the execution of the will. Generally, the more distant in time from the will's execution a particular fact might be, the less significance will be attached to that fact in determining the testator's capacity at the time of execution.

b. Testator with Physical Ailments or Drug Addiction

The fact that the testator was very old, physically frail or ill, that she possessed a failing memory, or was a habitual drinker or addicted to drugs does *not* mean that she lacked the requisite mental capacity and was unable to comprehend the nature of her act.

c. Testator Adjudicated Insane

A person who has been adjudicated insane or for whom a guardian or conservator has been appointed does not necessarily lack testamentary capacity. While such an adjudication is *evidence* of a lack of the required mental capacity, it is *not conclusive* and can be overcome by showing that the testator still met the specific standards set out above.

3. Insane Delusion

"Insane delusion" is a distinct form of incapacity. A person may have sufficient mental capacity to conduct his affairs and to make a will, but may be suffering from an insane delusion so as to require a particular provision in a will to fail on the ground of testamentary incapacity. An insane delusion may invalidate the entire will or only a particular gift.

a. Causation Requirement

A will can be set aside on the ground of insane delusion only if and to the extent it can be shown that the delusion *caused* the testamentary disposition. The contestant must show that the testator would not have made the disposition in question *but for* the insane delusion.

b. "Insane Delusion" Defined

An insane delusion is a legal, not a psychiatric, concept. Such a delusion is a belief in facts that do not exist and that no rational person would believe existed.

Example: A belief that all children are spies for Communist China is an insane delusion. A belief that all children are cruel and mean, however, may not be an insane delusion if the testator's life experiences are such that a sane person could come to that conclusion.

1) Unusual Religious Beliefs

Unusual and bizarre religious beliefs ordinarily do not constitute insane delusions, and if they do, it is usually difficult to prove they caused the devise. On the other hand, a belief that Henry Hart, to whom the testator's estate is devised, is God is probably an insane delusion.

2) False Beliefs

False beliefs or groundless prejudices of testators with respect to members of their families give rise to difficult cases. Since courts generally do not give relief for mistake in the inducement (*see* F.2., *infra*), disinherited heirs often claim the testator was suffering from an insane delusion. A groundless belief that the testator's wife is sleeping with other men or that his children are not his has been held to be an insane delusion, but there are cases contra. In these "false beliefs about family members" cases, it is very difficult to predict whether a court will hold that testator was merely mistaken (and no relief can be granted) or was suffering from an insane delusion. These cases tend to be resolved on their own facts.

4. Burden of Proof as to Mental Capacity on Contestant

Whether the testamentary disposition is rational or irrational, many states recognize a presumption that the testator was competent. The burden of introducing evidence to the contrary is on the contestant. If the contestant introduces evidence sufficient, if believed, to warrant a finding of mental incapacity, the presumption drops and the proponent must now introduce evidence of capacity.

D. UNDUE INFLUENCE

A will (or a gift in a will) is invalid if it is obtained through the exercise of undue influence. However, mere pleading, cajoling, nagging, or threatening the testator does not constitute undue influence. Influence is not undue unless the free will of the testator is destroyed and the resulting testamentary disposition reflects the desires not of the testator but of the party exerting undue influence.

1. Requirements

To establish undue influence, the contestants, who have the burden of proof, must establish that:

a.   *Influence* was exerted on the testator;

b.   The *effect* of the influence was to overpower the mind and free will of the testator; and

c.   The *product* of the influence was a will that would not have been executed but for the influence.

2. Circumstantial Evidence Does Not, By Itself, Establish Undue Influence

Over half of the appellate cases in which the jury finds undue influence are reversed on appeal because the court finds only circumstantial evidence, and no direct evidence, that influence was exerted. These factors, by themselves, are insufficient to establish undue influence:

a. Mere Opportunity to Exert Influence

A will cannot be set aside on proof of facts that, at most, merely show that a party had ample opportunity to exert influence (*e.g.*, she lived next door to her mother, had a key to her mother's house, held a power of attorney to act on her mother's behalf, took care of her mother's financial affairs, etc.).

b. **Mere Susceptibility to Influence Due to Age or Physical Condition**
The fact that the testator was elderly, in poor health, had memory lapses, took Valium, etc., does no more than indicate that the testator was susceptible to undue influence. This evidence does not establish that the testator's mind was in fact subverted and overpowered at the time the will was executed.

c. **"Unnatural Disposition" that Favors Some Relatives Over Others**
The mere fact that the will makes an unnatural disposition that favors some relatives over others (*e.g.*, two-thirds of the testator's estate to her daughter, one-third to her church, and nothing to her son) is not sufficient to establish undue influence. It is only when all reasonable explanation for the bequests is lacking that the trier of fact may take this as a circumstance showing undue influence.

3. **Presumption of Undue Influence**
A presumption of undue influence may be created by the following facts:

(i) That a *confidential relationship* existed between the testator and the beneficiary who was alleged to have exercised undue influence;

(ii) That the *beneficiary participated* in some way in procuring or drafting the will or in some other significant activity relating to the execution of the will; and

(iii) That the provisions of the will appear to be *unnatural* and favor the person who allegedly exercised undue influence.

Once these elements appear, the *burden shifts* to the proponent of the will to prove that it was not induced by his undue influence.

a. **Confidential Relationship**
A presumption of undue influence arises when a confidential relationship exists and the beneficiary participated in drafting the will. A "confidential relationship" includes a relationship between an attorney and client, doctor and patient, and husband and wife. Other relationships in which it is shown that one person relied heavily upon and placed more than a normal amount of confidence in another may also suffice to show a confidential relationship.
Example: Granddaughter G, who took care of her 90-year-old blind and bedridden grandmother, cashed her social security checks, and paid her bills, was in a confidential relationship. Since G was active in procuring the will (which was written by a notary public who was G's close friend) and there were suspicious circumstances (other relations who were in the house at the time were unaware that the will was being signed by the testator and witnessed by two of G's friends), a presumption of undue influence arose.

b. **Procurement of Will**
The criteria for determining whether the beneficiary was active in procuring the will

can include one or more of the following: (i) the beneficiary's presence when the testator expressed the desire to make a will, (ii) the beneficiary's recommending an attorney to prepare the will, (iii) the beneficiary's giving an attorney instructions as to what the will should contain, (iv) the beneficiary's knowledge of the will's contents prior to its execution, (v) the beneficiary's securing witnesses for the will, (vi) the beneficiary's being present when the will is executed, and (vii) the beneficiary's safe-guarding the will after its execution.

c. Unnatural Disposition

A presumption of undue influence may arise, despite the absence of a confidential relationship between the testator and beneficiary, when the execution of a will is surrounded by suspicious circumstances, as where the testator disinherits her children in favor of a stranger. However, the mere fact that a will is unnatural in preferring a stranger over blood kindred is not sufficient to give rise to a presumption of undue influence unless there are other suspicious circumstances.

E. FRAUD

Where the execution of a will or the inclusion therein of a particular gift is the result of fraud, the will or the particular gift is invalid. A finding of fraud requires that the testator has been willfully deceived as to the character or the content of an instrument, or as to the extrinsic facts that would induce the will or a particular disposition, or with respect to facts material to a disposition. (Innocent misrepresentation does not constitute fraud, although relief might possibly be available on the ground of mistake.)

1. Causation

Fraud invalidates a will only if the testator was *in fact* deceived by and acted in reliance on the misrepresentation. In other words, a gift is invalid only if the testator would not have made it had she known the true facts.

2. Fraud in the Execution (Fraud in the Factum)

In the case of fraud in the execution, there is a misrepresentation as to the nature of the contents of the instrument.

Examples: 1) Upon hearing a statement by A that the instrument presented to T gives A a power of attorney to pay T's bills while T is in the hospital, T signs it. In fact, the instrument contains provisions devising all T's property to A.

2) A tells T the instrument is T's will, but in fact A has substituted a will containing different provisions.

3. Fraud in the Inducement

In the case of fraud in the inducement, the testator intends to execute the instrument as her will and to include the particular contents of that instrument, but she is fraudulently induced into making this will or some particular gift therein by misrepresentations as to facts which influence her motivation. The will or the particular gifts affected by the fraud must be set aside.

Example: Where Lilly tells T that his son, Isaac, is dead, it may be uncertain whether the new will, leaving everything to Lilly, was induced by the belief that Isaac was dead or whether the will would have been made in the same fashion had T known Isaac was still alive. T might wish to exclude Isaac, from whom he had not heard in many years, in favor of Lilly, who had remained a dutiful daughter.

Such situations are resolved by inferences drawn from the family circumstances and other extrinsic evidence (excluding T's oral declarations) as to what T's probable intent was.

4. Fraudulent Prevention of Will

Cases occasionally involve a fraudulent prevention of the execution of a will by one or more of the persons who would take by intestate succession. The cases are split as to whether any relief is available.

a. Intestate Succession Laws Apply

Some courts conclude there is no way of granting relief because a court "cannot write a will on behalf of a decedent"; hence, the intestate succession laws apply.

b. Better View Is to Impose Constructive Trust

The better view is that a constructive trust may be imposed against the intestate successors, for the benefit of those who would have been beneficiaries of the will that the decedent was fraudulently prevented from executing. Some courts have even imposed constructive trusts in these cases on innocent heirs who were not themselves wrongdoers but who would be unjustly enriched.

F. MISTAKE

1. Mistake in Execution of Will

a. Mistake as to Nature of Instrument—Extrinsic Evidence Admissible

Extrinsic evidence is admissible to show that the testator was unaware of the nature of the instrument she signed (*e.g.*, she believed it to be a power of attorney). Such a mistake relates to the issue of whether the testator had the requisite testamentary intent, without which the will would be invalid.

b. Wrong Will Signed—Courts Divided on Relief Question

In cases where the testator has signed the wrong will, the courts are divided on the question of whether relief should be granted. Suppose that reciprocal wills are prepared for H and W, under which each devises his or her estate to the other. By mistake, H signs the will prepared for W, and W signs the will prepared for H. Thus, the will signed by H reads, "I, Rose Snide, leave all my property to my husband, Harvey Snide." Some courts have denied relief on the ground that H lacked testamentary intent because he did not intend to execute the document that he signed. [*In re* Pavlinko's Estate, 148 A.2d 528 (Pa. 1959)] However, the better and modern view is that the court should grant relief since both the existence and the nature of the mistake are very obvious. The court should insert "Harvey" for "Rose" and "husband" for "wife" (and vice versa), as appropriate. [Matter of Snide, 418 N.E.2d 656 (N.Y. 1981)]

2. Mistake in Inducement—No Relief Granted

If the alleged mistake involves the reasons that led the testator to make the will (or the reasons for making or not making a particular gift therein), and the mistake was not fraudulently induced, no relief is granted. *Rationale:* To allow evidence as to the alleged mistake would open the door to fraudulent testimony, since the testator is dead and cannot contradict the testimony as to the supposed mistake. Moreover, even if the alleged mistake were shown, this would not establish that the testator would have made a different disposition had the true facts been known.

Example: T's son Ron is a prisoner of war. Assuming that Ron is dead, T revokes a will that left everything in equal shares to Ron and T's other son, Don, and executes a new will leaving everything to Don. After T's death, Ron returns alive. Evidence of the mistake is not admissible, and Don takes T's estate under the second will.

a. .Exception If Mistake Appears on Face of Will

The courts have recognized (more often in dictum than in actual holdings) that if the mistaken inducement appears on the face of the will, relief will be granted.

Example: Same facts as above, except that T's new will says, "Since my son Ron is dead, I revoke my earlier will and leave all my property to my son Don." Several courts have stated in dicta that since the mistake is shown on the face of the will and extrinsic evidence need not be relied on to show the mistake, the court should deny probate of the second will and instead probate the will that benefits Ron.

3. Mistake as to Contents of Will

a. Mistaken Omission—No Relief Granted

Extrinsic evidence is not admissible to show that a provision was mistakenly omitted from a will, or that a provision contained in the will is not what the testator intended. Absent evidence of fraud, duress, or suspicious circumstances, it is conclusively presumed that the testator understood and approved the terms of the new will when she signed it. *Rationale:* The courts are reluctant to have property pass, not pursuant to the terms of a duly executed will, but on the basis of oral testimony.

Example: T executes a will that makes only minor changes from an earlier will (which was revoked by the new will). Unlike the earlier will, the new will does not contain a residuary clause. The attorney who prepared the new will makes a sworn affidavit stating that the omission was inadvertent and was contrary to T's instructions. The affidavit is not admissible, and the new will must be probated. Since the will is clear as to its meaning and is not ambiguous, extrinsic evidence as to T's intent is inadmissible. Correction would require the addition of a new provision, and *the courts cannot reform a decedent's will.*

b. Plain Meaning Rule—Evidence Not Admissible to Contradict Plain Language

If the language of a will is unambiguous, evidence is not admissible to show that the testator made a mistake in describing a beneficiary or the property that was to be the subject of the gift. *Rationale:* The testator signed the will and is conclusively presumed to have read, understood, and intended its contents. To allow oral testimony to contradict the will's plain meaning would open the door to fraud.

Examples: 1) T's will bequeaths "200 shares of IBM stock" to B. Evidence, no matter how compelling, is *not* admissible to show that T actually owned 300 shares of IBM stock and intended to bequeath all 300 shares to B.

2) T's will bequeaths property "to my cousin, John Smith." T had a cousin John Smith whom he had not seen in 10 years. T also had a

nephew John Smith of whom he was particularly fond, and T had told third parties that he had made a gift to the nephew in his will. Evidence is **not** admissible to show that T intended to make a gift to his nephew and not to his cousin.

4. Latent or Patent Ambiguity—Extrinsic Evidence Admissible to Cure Ambiguity

a. Latent Ambiguity

A latent ambiguity exists when the language of the will, although clear on its face in describing a beneficiary or property, results in a misdescription when applied to the facts to which it refers. Extrinsic evidence is admissible to cure the ambiguity. *Rationale:* Reliance on parol evidence does not have the effect of "rewriting" the will or adding to its terms. Instead, the evidence is being received to give meaning to the words the testator actually used. *But note:* If the extrinsic evidence does not resolve the ambiguity, the gift fails.

Examples:

1) T's will devises Blackacre "to my niece Nellie." T has two nieces named Nellie. Parol evidence is admissible to show which niece T intended to benefit.

2) Same facts as above, except that T does not have a niece named Nellie. He does, however, have a niece named Norrie and a cousin named Nellie. Parol evidence is admissible to show whether T intended to make a gift to cousin Nellie or to niece Norrie. But if the evidence does not establish which one T had in mind, the gift fails.

3) A devise of "Lot #6, Square #403," which T did not own, could be shown by extrinsic evidence to pass Lot #3, Square #406, which T did own. [Patch v. White, 117 U.S. 210 (1886)]

4) T's will bequeathed her residuary estate "to Apollo Medical Center as a memorial to my late husband." Apollo was acquired by another corporation, and the hospital's name was changed to Humana Hospital. Thereafter, T executed a new will that repeated the gift to the Apollo Medical Center. Evidence was admitted to show that T intended the gift for the hospital at which her husband was treated before his death, and that the name change did not defeat the gift. "The misnomer of a devisee will not cause the devise to fail where the identity of the devisee can be identified with certainty."

b. Patent Ambiguity

A patent ambiguity exists when the uncertainty appears on the face of the will (*e.g.,* where the will mentions two cousins, Mary Jones and Mary Smith, and then makes a gift "to my cousin Mary"). The traditional view is that extrinsic evidence is not admissible to correct a patent ambiguity, and that the gift fails because of the misdescription. However, the modern and better view is that such evidence is admissible.

Example:

T's will bequeathed one-third of his business to A and B, but the will was unclear as to whether A and B were to receive one-third each or whether, instead, the one-third share was to be divided between A and B (giving them one-sixth each). *Held:* This was a patent ambiguity, and extrinsic evidence should be admitted to cure the ambiguity.

G. NO-CONTEST CLAUSES

A no-contest clause (sometimes called an *in terrorem* clause) provides that a beneficiary who contests the will forfeits his interest under the will. In most states, a no-contest clause is *enforceable*, and the beneficiary forfeits his legacy *unless he had probable cause* for bringing the contest (*i.e.,* it was not a strike suit whose sole purpose was to provoke a settlement). Whether the beneficiary had probable cause is a question of fact. Note that suits objecting to the court's jurisdiction, challenging the appointment of an executor, and asking the court to construe the will are not will contests within the meaning of most no-contest clauses.

Example: Tom dies leaving a will that bequeaths $10,000 to his son Roy, and the rest of his substantial estate to his friend Ruby. The will contains a no-contest clause that reads: "Should any beneficiary named herein contest this will or any of its provisions, he shall forfeit all interests given to him by my will." Roy brings a will contest on grounds of undue influence and lack of capacity. Roy loses the will contest, and Tom's will is admitted to probate. In most states, Roy forfeits the $10,000 bequest.

XI. PROBATE AND ESTATE ADMINISTRATION

A. TERMINOLOGY AND OVERVIEW

"Probate" refers to the proceeding in which an instrument is judicially determined to be the duly executed last will of the decedent (or, if there is no will, the proceeding in which the decedent's heirs are judicially determined). At the probate proceeding, a *personal representative* is appointed to carry out the estate administration. In most states, the personal representative is called an *executor* if named in the decedent's will, and an *administrator* if named by the court.

Testate estates must go through some form of administration. Intestate estates need not be administered if the heirs are able to agree as to the distribution of property; however, they often are administered in order to cut off creditors' claims and to ensure clear title in the heirs.

B. SUMMARY OF RULES AND PROCEDURE

The following is a summary of probate rules and procedure:

1.   Any interested person may *file* a petition for probate.

2.   The custodian of a will *must produce it within a certain time* (*e.g.,* 30 days) after the death of the testator.

3.   The *testator's domicile at the time of death*, not the place of death, determines the place of "primary" administration of the estate (but "ancillary" administration, including probate, is also necessary wherever property to be administered is located).

4.   A will *must be offered for probate within a specified number of years*. For example, the UPC requires that a will be probated within three years or the decedent is deemed to have died intestate.

5. A will must be *probated* in order for a person to *take* under its terms.

6. A probated will *cannot be collaterally attacked* (*e.g.*, in a later will contest) when a specified short statute of limitations after probate has run.

7. A *lost or destroyed will* may be probated, provided its contents can be proved.

8. In a probate proceeding, the *following facts must be proved*:

   a. That the testator is dead (this fact is jurisdictional);

   b. That the formalities of execution were observed; and

   c. That the notice requirements for probate have been complied with.

C. PERSONAL REPRESENTATIVE

1. Appointment of Personal Representative
Any person who has *capacity to contract* may serve as personal representative. Thus, an incompetent or a minor cannot serve.

a. How Executor or Administrator Is Appointed
If an "executor" is named in the will, he will be appointed as personal representative unless subject to a particular disqualification. If no executor is named in the will or if the executor named cannot serve, an "administrator cum testamento annexo" will be appointed as personal representative. If the decedent died intestate, an "administrator" will be appointed as personal representative.

b. Preference of Appointment
A typical statutory order of preference for appointment of a personal representative would be: (i) the person named as executor in the will; (ii) the surviving spouse, if a will beneficiary; (iii) any will beneficiary; (iv) the surviving spouse; (v) any other heir, and (vi) after 45 days, a creditor.

c. Authority of Representative
The authority of the personal representative is derived from his court appointment, and he serves as an officer of the court.

d. Bond Required for Issuance of Letters Testamentary
The personal representative must file a bond for the faithful performance of his duties, unless the testator has provided in his will that no bond shall be required. When the personal representative has filed the required bond, "letters testamentary" (for an executor or administrator cum testamento annexo) or "letters of administration" (for an administrator) are issued certifying his authority to act on behalf of the estate.

2. Powers and Duties of the Personal Representative
The personal representative has functions generally analogous to those of a receiver of a

defunct corporation or a trustee in bankruptcy, and must take whatever steps are necessary to wind up the decedent's affairs. In that respect, the primary functions of the personal representative are to:

(i) *Give notice* to devisees, heirs, and claimants against the estate;

(ii) *Discover and collect the decedent's assets* and file an inventory;

(iii) *Manage* the assets of the estate during administration;

(iv) *Pay expenses* of administration, claims against the estate, and taxes; and

(v) *Distribute* the property.

Like the trustee, the personal representative serves in a fiduciary capacity. (*See* Trusts outline.) Unlike the trustee, however, the personal representative is primarily a liquidator, rather than a manager, and generally must have court approval for such activities as borrowing money, operating a business, or selling property.

3. **Compensation of Personal Representative**
The personal representative is entitled to compensation for his services rendered on behalf of the estate. Rates of compensation may be governed by statute, *e.g.*, based on the estate's value. If there is no controlling statute, the court has discretionary authority to award reasonable compensation. Factors a court might consider in determining reasonable compensation include the amount of time spent performing appropriate services, the degree of difficulty involved, and a reasonable hourly rate.

    a. **May Be Provided for by Will**
    The testator may provide compensation for the personal representative by means of a gift in the will. However, the personal representative may renounce such a testamentary gift, and take whatever compensation to which he would otherwise be entitled.

    b. **May Be Denied for Wrongful Conduct**
    The court may deny compensation where the personal representative has engaged in dishonest or fraudulent conduct, or has otherwise acted in bad faith or willful neglect of his duties.

D. CREDITORS' CLAIMS

1. **Notice**
One of the personal representative's first tasks is to give notice to the creditors of the estate, advising them of the pendency of the administration and when and where claims must be filed. Notice may be accomplished by publication, but the personal representative must mail or personally deliver the notice to creditors who are known or are reasonably ascertainable.

2. **Nonclaim Statutes**
In most states, creditors' claims must be filed within a specified period of time (*e.g.*, three months after notice) or they are barred. These statutes apply to all claims: liquidated and nonliquidated, matured and contingent, contract and tort.

a. Exception—Failure to Give Notice

If notice is not given to creditors in accordance with the statute, claims are barred only after a specified number of *years* have passed since the decedent's death.

3. Priority of Claims

Typically, statutes provide that claims are to be paid in the following order:

a. Administration expenses;

b. Funeral expenses and expenses of the last illness (up to specific dollar amount);

c. Family allowance;

d. Debts given preference under federal law (*e.g.*, tax claims);

e. Secured claims (up to the value of the security interest);

f. Judgments entered against the decedent during his lifetime; and

g. All other claims.

E. ABATEMENT

Abatement is the process of reducing testamentary gifts in cases where the estate assets are not sufficient to pay all claims against the estate and satisfy all bequests and devises. The testator may set out an order of abatement in the will. If there are no contrary provisions in the will, estates in most jurisdictions abate in the following order:

(i) Real or personal property passing by intestacy;

(ii) The residuary estate;

(iii) General legacies, which abate pro rata;

(iv) Specific devises and bequests.

1. Abatement Within Categories

Within each category, some states provide that personal property abates before real property.

2. Demonstrative Legacies

To the extent that the property from which the gift was to be satisfied is in the estate at death, demonstrative legacies are treated as specific legacies for abatement purposes. To the extent the fund is insufficient, however, the demonstrative legacy is treated as a general legacy.

F. EXONERATION OF LIENS

At common law and in many states today, if specifically devised property is, at the testator's death, subject to a lien that secures a note on which the testator was personally liable, the beneficiary is entitled to have the lien exonerated (unless there is a contrary will provision). Thus, the beneficiary is entitled to demand payment of the debt out of the residuary estate so that the property passes to him free of any encumbrance. A growing number of states, however, are enacting statutes that provide that liens on specifically devised property are not exonerated unless the will so directs. In these states, a specific devise passes subject to a security interest even if the will contains a general (rather than specific) provision to pay all debts.

G. GUIDELINES WHEN WILL AMBIGUOUS

It is commonly stated that where the language of a will is clear and unambiguous, there is no need for either interpretation or construction. The directions in the will must be followed. Where there is some ambiguity, the court will interpret the will and consider any admissible extrinsic evidence to determine the testator's intent. Only where there is no evidence of the testator's intent is it necessary to use a rule of construction as a presumption concerning that intent. Of course, inevitably the existence of rules of construction will influence a court when it sets out to interpret a will.

1. Interpretation—Testator's Actual Intent

a. Will Clear—Extrinsic Evidence Inadmissible
If the will clearly specifies a particular disposition, it must be carried out, and extrinsic evidence of a contrary intent of the testator, no matter how persuasive, is inadmissible.

b. Will Ambiguous—Extrinsic Evidence Admissible
If a provision in the will is ambiguous, the court should attempt to find the testator's intent within the "four corners" of the instrument. Only if that attempt fails should the court admit certain extrinsic evidence that is probative on the issue of intent. Extrinsic evidence may be used only to explain the meaning of what is written in the will and cannot subtract from the will, add missing provisions, or show some entirely different meaning.

1) Testimony Regarding Surrounding Circumstances Permitted
Testimony regarding the testator's surrounding circumstances at the time of execution is permitted, *e.g.*, the amount and character of his property, the natural objects of his bounty, his relations with his relatives, and their situations and circumstances.

2) Declarations of Testator Not Admissible
What would seem the most probative evidence of the testator's intent—his declaration as to what he meant to do—is generally **not** admissible because of the high chance of perjured testimony.

a) Exception—Equivocation
The only exception to this rule concerns a so-called latent ambiguity (*see* X.F.4.a., *supra*) known as "equivocation." An equivocation is where the description of a beneficiary or of the property describes more than one person or more than one item of property. In such cases, and in those only, testimony of the declarations of the testator is admissible.
Example: T bequeaths $10,000 to "my cousin Bill," but unknown to T he had two cousins named Bill. Testimony that he knew only

one of them would be admissible as "surrounding circumstances." In addition, testimony by T's lawyer that T said, "I want $10,000 to go to my cousin Bill Smith of Chicago" is admissible.

c. Intent as of Time of Execution
The intention of the testator should be sought as of *the time of execution* of the will (or of a later codicil that republishes it).

Example: T leaves his estate to his "heirs." Thereafter the statute of descent and distribution is amended. The estate should pass to those who would have been T's heirs under the statute in force at the time the will was executed.

2. Rules of Construction
When there is no evidence of the actual intent of the testator, the court must resort to rules of construction such as those noted below:

a. Favor those who *would take intestate*.

b. Favor the construction *that avoids intestacy*.

c. Favor the construction that is *consistent with the perceived "plan"* of disposition.

d. *Every portion* of the will should be given effect if possible.

e. Between totally inconsistent clauses, the *latter is most likely the final intent*.

3. Beware of Finding Gifts by Implication
As much as the court wants to find that the will disposes of all the property, however, sometimes there will be a situation that the will does not cover. Do not invent or imply what the testator would have done.

XII. WILL SUBSTITUTES

A. IN GENERAL
Individuals wishing to avoid taxes and to eliminate the cost and inconvenience of probate often turn to various "will substitutes" to transfer their property upon death. Frequently, the decedent's testate or intestate takers argue (usually unsuccessfully) that these forms of transfer constitute "testamentary" transfers and are, therefore, invalid for failure to comply with the required formalities for execution of a will. The following are examples of will substitutes:

1. Life insurance;

2. Joint tenancies or tenancies by the entirety (*see* Real Property outline);

3. Inter vivos trusts (*i.e.,* trusts created during the settlor's lifetime);

4. Bank arrangements;

5. Deeds;

6. Contracts; and

7. Inter vivos gifts, including gifts causa mortis (*i.e.*, gifts made in contemplation of death).

B. LIFE INSURANCE

Life insurance is probably the most widely used will substitute. Assume H takes out a life insurance policy on his life, payable to W. H owns the policy and can cash it in or change the beneficiary. The life insurance contract clearly has testamentary effect in the sense that at H's death an economic interest will pass from H to W. Nevertheless, it is not a "will," and the designation of W as beneficiary does not have to be attested by witnesses. Rather, the courts have held that a life insurance policy is a contract, and the disposition is governed by the terms of the contract. (Note that most life insurance policies provide that a change of beneficiaries can be effected by the owner only by notification to the company during the owner's life. Thus, a will cannot change the beneficiary designation, unless the terms of the contract permit this.)

C. BANK ARRANGEMENTS

1. Totten Trusts

A "Totten trust" (named after an early case) is a deposit of money in the depositor's own bank account in trust for another person. The majority rule is that such a transfer creates a valid revocable trust, even though the depositor retains complete control over the account during her lifetime and the transfer is complete only upon her death. The trust is revoked to the extent of withdrawals made by the depositor before her death, and may also be revoked by the depositor's will. Creditors of the depositor can reach the funds in the account during her life.

2. Joint or Survivor Accounts

The deposit of money in a bank in the names of two persons "with right of survivorship" is generally held effective to give the survivor the absolute right to all the money. However, in many states, extrinsic evidence is admissible to show that the dead depositor did not intend a gift to the survivor, and that the account was only a convenience for paying the depositor's bills. Where the survivor is not the spouse but someone else, this issue has been frequently litigated.

3. Payable on Death Designations

Most courts have held a payable on death ("P-O-D") designation on a bank account ineffective, on the rationale that no interest of any type is transferred to the designated beneficiary during the depositor's lifetime, and hence the unattested designation violates the Statute of Wills. This result has been criticized by many authorities on the ground that a Totten trust is distinguishable from a P-O-D designation only by the fact that the depositor has recited that he holds the deposit "in trust," and yet the Totten trust device is upheld.

D. DEEDS

A deed deposited in escrow, with delivery conditioned upon the grantor's death, may be a valid nontestamentary transfer (*see* Real Property outline). Similarly, if a deed that is by its terms effective only upon the grantor's death has actually been delivered to the grantee, a court may sustain the transfer as nontestamentary by construing the deed as a present transfer of a future interest, subject to a life estate reserved in the grantor.

E. CONTRACTS

A contract that purports to dispose of property upon death is testamentary in nature and must comply with the formalities required for a will in order to be enforceable.

XIII. POWERS OF APPOINTMENT

A. THE TERMINOLOGY OF POWERS—BASIC DEFINITIONS

1. Power of Appointment Defined

A power of appointment is an authority created in or reserved by a person enabling that person (called the *donee* of the power) to designate, within the limits prescribed by the creator of the power (called the *donor*), the persons who shall take certain property and the manner in which they shall take it. When a person reserves a power in herself, she is both donor and donee of the power. Other important terms include the following:

a. The *objects* of the power are the persons in whose favor a power is exercisable.

b. The *appointees* are the persons in whose favor the power is actually exercised.

c. The *appointive property* is the property that is the subject of the power.

d. The *takers in default of appointment* are the persons designated to take the property if the donee fails to effectively exercise his power of appointment.

2. General vs. Special Power of Appointment

While the concept of and distinction between general and special powers derive from the common law, the only definition of importance today is the one set forth in section 2041 of the Internal Revenue Code, which applies the federal estate tax to assets over which the decedent held a general power, but not to assets over which she held a special power.

a. General Power

A general power of appointment is one exercisable in favor of the donee herself, her estate, her creditors, *or* the creditors of her estate.

b. Special Power

A special power of appointment is one exercisable in favor of a specified class of persons, which does *not* include the donee, her estate, her creditors, or the creditors of her estate.

3. Presently Exercisable vs. Testamentary Power

A presently exercisable power of appointment is one exercisable by the donee during her lifetime. A testamentary power is one that is exercisable only by the donee's will.

Examples: 1) T's will devises property "to A for life, and on A's death to such persons as A shall appoint by will; in default of appointment to B." T is the donor of the power of appointment. A is the donee of a ***general testamentary power.*** It is a general power because the objects of the power ("such persons") include A's estate or the creditors of A's estate. It is testamentary because it is exercisable only by will. B is the taker in default of appointment; B holds a vested remainder subject to total divestment. For purposes of classifying B's interest, the power of appointment is treated as a divesting condition subsequent since B takes ***unless*** A exercises the power of appointment.

2) T's will devises property "to A for life, and on A's death to such of A's issue as she shall appoint during her lifetime or by will; in default of appointment, to A's issue then living, per stirpes." A is the donee of a ***special power of appointment*** that is exercisable during A's lifetime or by will. It is a special power because A is limited to appointing among her issue. "A's issue then living" are the takers in default of appointment; there is a contingent remainder in A's issue.

In most states, a presently exercisable power of appointment is also exercisable by the donee's will unless the donor has expressly limited exercise of the power to the donee's lifetime.

B. GENERAL POWERS OF APPOINTMENT

1. Donee Acts as Donor's Agent
The basic theory of powers of appointment (whether general or special) is that the donee is the donor's agent in designating the beneficiaries of the appointive property; she is not the owner of the property. When the donee exercises the power, it is treated as though the donee is "filling in the blanks" in the donor's will or trust. An appointment is deemed to relate back to the donor's will so that the appointee takes title directly from the donor of the power rather than from the donee. This is referred to as the ***doctrine of relation back.***

2. Power of Appointment Is Personal to Donee
A power of appointment is personal to the donee. If she dies without having exercised the power, it terminates; she cannot devise the power by her will. The donee cannot delegate the power to another; nor can she assign it. (She can, however, exercise the power by creating another power in the appointee. This is true in all cases if it is a general power; it is true of a special power in some cases—this is discussed in C., *infra*).

3. Appointive Property Not Subject to Dower or Elective Share Statute
Dower does not attach to real property over which the husband holds a power of appointment, because the husband did not own the property. Also, a surviving spouse's elective share does not apply to assets over which the deceased spouse held a power of appointment.

4. Generally Creditors Cannot Reach Appointive Assets
Under the theory that the donee does not own the appointive property, if the donee does not exercise her general power (whether presently exercisable or testamentary), her creditors cannot reach the property.

a. If Donee Exercises Power—Creditors Can Reach Those Assets

If the donee exercises the general power, the courts have abandoned the agency theory in favor of a fiction that enables the donee's creditors to reach the property. This is true whether the donee appoints to herself or to some other person. The theory is that the donee, in making the appointment, is exercising a dominion that is practically identical to that exercised by her over her own property, and so her creditors can reach the appointive property as though she were the owner. *Minority Rule:* By statute in several states (*e.g.,* California, Michigan), creditors of the donee of a general power can reach the appointive property regardless of whether the power is exercised.

b. If Donee Is Also Donor—Creditors Can Reach Appointive Assets

If the donee of a general power is also the donor, her creditors can reach the appointive assets whether or not she exercises the power. A general power of appointment cannot be used to squirrel away one's assets from her creditors. (This is analogous to the rule that a spendthrift clause in favor of the settlor of a trust is invalid.)

5. Failure to Exercise General Power of Appointment

If the donee of a general power fails to exercise the power and the donor's instrument creating the general power contains no gift in default of appointment, the appointive property reverts to the *donor's estate* and passes according to the residuary clause of the donor's will or by intestacy to the donor's heirs.

C. SPECIAL POWERS OF APPOINTMENT

1. Exclusive vs. Nonexclusive Special Powers

A special power of appointment is *exclusive* if it may be exercised in favor of some objects of the power to the exclusion of others; *i.e.,* the donee can exclude some objects and can appoint unequal shares. A special power is *nonexclusive* if it must be exercised in favor of all the appointees.

a. Strong Presumption that Special Powers Are Exclusive

Special powers are presumed to be exclusive unless the donor expressly provides otherwise.

Examples: 1) On A's death the trustee shall distribute the corpus *among* A's children as A shall appoint by will." By traditional analysis, use of the word "among," without any other qualifying words, makes the power *nonexclusive*. However, it is not likely that you will ever see a nonexclusive power, for invariably there is qualifying language, along the lines of the examples that follow, that leads to a finding of "exclusive."

2) "Among *such* of A's children as he shall appoint by will." Although the word "among" has been used, the reference to "such of" A's children clearly indicates that the power is exclusive.

3) "Among A's children as A shall appoint by will, *in such shares and proportions* as A shall determine." The power is exclusive.

b. Nonexclusive Powers—Illusory Appointment Doctrine

Suppose A has a special power to appoint *among* his children. He has three children and the special power is deemed to be nonexclusive, meaning that he cannot exclude any of the children in exercising the power. What prevents A from appointing $10 to one child and the rest of the property to the other two children? To resolve this problem, the common law courts developed the "illusory appointment" doctrine.

When a special power is nonexclusive, the donee may not favor some of the appointees by making an "illusory" appointment to the other appointees. He must appoint a "substantial" share to *all* appointees. Most courts have recognized and applied this doctrine despite the difficulties involved in determining what is a "substantial" share.

2. Implied Gift in Default of Appointment

If the donee of a special power of appointment does not exercise the power *and* there is no gift in default of appointment, a gift to the objects of the special power is implied.

Example: Property is devised to S for life, with a testamentary power to appoint "among his children, if he should have any; and in case he should die not leaving any children, I give and devise the same to the children of my daughter." S is survived by children but he did not appoint to them by will. The court will imply a gift in default of appointment and direct a distribution among S's children.

3. Absent Fraud, Creditor of Donee Can Never Reach Appointive Assets

Under the agency theory of powers of appointment, the creditor of the donee of a special power cannot reach the property *even if the donee exercises the power*. This is true even if the donee of the special power is also the donor, unless the transfer was in fraud of the donor-donee's creditors. This is an extension of the principle that any irrevocable disposition, not made with the intent to defeat creditors' claims, is not subject to challenge by the transferor's creditors.

D. EXERCISE OF POWERS OF APPOINTMENT

1. Any Instrument Can Exercise Power Unless Donor Directs Otherwise

Unless the donor directs otherwise, a power of appointment can be exercised by any instrument that is effective to transfer title to property. The donee must have legal capacity to execute an effective instrument of transfer. Of course, if it is a testamentary power, it must be exercised by a will that is validly executed under the laws of the particular jurisdiction.

If, however, the donor calls for the power's exercise "by an instrument specifically referring to this power," this mandate must be complied with to effectively exercise the power.

2. Residuary Clause Does Not by Itself Exercise Testamentary Power

The majority rule is that a residuary clause, by itself, does not exercise any power of appointment held by the testator as donee.

Example: A, holding a general testamentary power of appointment, dies leaving a will that does not in its terms refer to the power, but contains a residuary clause that devises "all the rest, residue, and remainder of my property, of whatever kind or nature and wherever located" to various persons. Under the majority rule, A's will does not exercise the power of appointment, and the appointive assets pass to the takers in default of appointment named in the donor's will.

3. Exception—Exercise by Implication

The courts will find that a power of appointment (whether general or special) was exercised by implication (i) when the donee purports to dispose of the property as though it were her own, meaning that the disposition can be given effect only if it is treated as an exercise of the power; or (ii) when the disposition cannot be given its intended meaning or any effective meaning unless the donee is treated as having exercised the power. An exercise by implication can be found *unless* the donor called for appointment "by an instrument expressly referring to this power."

Example: B holds a life estate and a general testamentary power over a group of assets that includes Blackacre. B dies leaving a will that provides: "I devise Blackacre to my son, B Jr." B's general power is exercised with respect to Blackacre (but not as to the other appointive assets), for this is the only way the disposition in B's will can be given effect.

This will be the result *unless* the donor in creating the power called for its exercise by specific reference to the power. In this situation, since B made no explicit reference to the power, it is not exercised. Blackacre (along with the other appointive assets) passes to the takers in default of appointment.

4. "Blanket" Exercise of Power Is Permissible

If a person holding a testamentary power executes a will that devises "all the rest, residue, and remainder of my property, *including any property over which I may have a power of appointment*," this "blanket" exercise of any power of appointment will be given effect *unless* the donor called for an appointment by an instrument that specifically refers to the power.

5. Scope of Power

Many states hold that a donee of a power of appointment, even a special power, may exercise the power by creating a trust for the benefit of an object of the power rather than appointing the property outright. [*See* Restatement (Second) of Property §19.3] Other states reject this view. There is a similar split of authority as to whether a donee of a special power can grant an object of this power a broader special power than the donee had. Since the donee could appoint the property outright, the better view seems to be that he can create a power in the object broader than his own power.

E. APPLICATION OF RULE AGAINST PERPETUITIES

The common law Rule Against Perpetuities, which requires that an interest vest or fail within a life in being plus 21 years, applies to powers of appointment. (For a detailed discussion of the Rule Against Perpetuities, *see* Multistate Real Property outline.) Generally, a power of appointment raises the following perpetuities issues: the validity of the power itself, the validity of its exercise, and the validity of the gift in default of appointment.

1. Presently Exercisable General Powers

A presently exercisable general power is treated the same as fee simple ownership; thus, if it is certain the power will become *exercisable* or fail within the perpetuities period, it is valid. The fact that the donee might not actually exercise the power until after the perpetuities period is irrelevant. Note that when a presently exercisable general power is exercised, the perpetuities period begins to run from the date of exercise; therefore, the interests created must vest or fail within 21 years after the death of a life in being on the date of exercise.

a. Gifts in Default of Appointment
Gifts in default of a presently exercisable general power are rarely invalid under the Rule. The perpetuities period begins to run only when the power ceases.

2. Special and Testamentary Powers
If a special or testamentary power *may* be exercised beyond the perpetuities period, which begins to run from the creation of the power, it is void. Thus, unless expressly limited to the perpetuities period, any special or testamentary power given to an unborn person is invalid.

a. Relation-Back Doctrine
Interests created by the exercise of a special or testamentary power are read back into the original instrument creating the power, and the perpetuities period begins at the date that power was created.

b. Second Look Doctrine
Even though the exercise of the power is read back into the donor's instrument, facts and circumstances existing on the date of exercise are taken into account in determining the validity of the interests created by the exercise.

Example: Testator devises property "to Don for life, then as Don appoints by will." Don appoints by his will "to Ed for life, remainder to Ed's children." This is construed as though Testator's will read "to Don for life, then to Ed for life, then to Ed's children." If Ed was alive at Testator's death, the remainder to Ed's children is valid. If Ed was not alive at Testator's death, the remainder to Ed's children is void.

c. Gifts in Default of Appointment
Gifts in default of appointment are subject to the Rule Against Perpetuities, but the second look doctrine also applies to them.

3. Effect of Invalid Appointment
If a donee makes an invalid appointment, the property passes to the taker in default of appointment, if any. If none, the property reverts back to the donor's estate. However, if the donee of a *general power* manifests an intent to take the property out of the creating instrument and "capture" it for the donee's estate, the property will pass to the donee's estate.

F. CONTRACTS TO APPOINT

1. Testamentary Powers—Contract to Appoint Is Invalid
The donee of a testamentary power cannot contract to make an appointment. Such a contract, if made, cannot be the basis of an action for specific performance or damages. However, the promisee can obtain restitution of the value given by her for the promise unless the donee actually exercised the power pursuant to the contract.

a. Basis of Rule—Power to Be Exercised by Will Only
Where the donee is given a testamentary power, the donor's intent was that the donee

should retain the opportunity to make a judgment as to the power's appropriate exercise until his death. To permit the donee to contract for the power's exercise would defeat this purpose of the donor, and would transform a power that was intended to be testamentary into a presently exercisable power. This applies *whether the testamentary power is special or general.*

2. Presently Exercisable Powers—Contract to Appoint Is Valid

The donee of a presently exercisable power can contract to make an appointment. If, however, it is a presently exercisable *special* power, the contract or promised appointment cannot confer a benefit on a nonobject of the power.

a. Basis of Rule—Donee Can Appoint to Himself

Recognition of the right to contract is simply a recognition that the power is presently exercisable. If the donee has a presently exercisable general power, he could appoint to himself and then give the property in the indicated manner. If he has a presently exercisable special power, he can contract to exercise in favor of an object of the power just as he could directly appoint to the object.

b. Contract to Exercise Special Power Cannot Benefit a Nonobject

In *In re Carroll's Will*, 8 N.E.2d 864 (N.Y. 1937) (a leading case), A had a presently exercisable power to appoint $250,000 "to and among her children or any other kindred in such shares and manner as she thinks proper." A promised that she would appoint the $250,000 to child C if C would agree to pay $100,000 to A's husband, not a permissible appointee. The court held that the resulting exercise of the power in C's favor was entirely void.

XIV. ADVANCE HEALTH-CARE DIRECTIVES: LIVING WILLS AND DURABLE HEALTH-CARE POWERS

A. INTRODUCTION

The majority of states have enacted legislation governing the use of advance health-care directives, which are instructions concerning what to do regarding an individual's health if he becomes unable to make health-care decisions in the future. The two most common types of advance health-care directives are *living wills* and *durable health-care powers.*

1. Living Will

A living will states an individual's desires, if he becomes *terminally ill* or is in a *persistent vegetative state*, regarding: (i) whether to administer, withhold, or withdraw *life-sustaining procedures*; (ii) whether to provide, withhold, or withdraw *artificial nutrition or hydration*; and (iii) whether to provide treatment to *alleviate pain*.

2. Durable Health-Care Power

A durable health-care power (sometimes called a "durable power of attorney for health-care") appoints an agent to make health-care decisions on behalf of the principal. Unlike an ordinary power of attorney, which normally terminates on the incapacity of the principal, a durable health-care power does not become effective *until the principal becomes incapacitated* and it remains effective despite the incapacity. Unless expressly limited, a durable health-care power may extend to any and all health-care decisions that might arise.

3.   **Scope of Advance Directives**
Generally, a living will is a very limited instrument, dealing only with a terminally ill person and pertaining only to life-prolonging or pain relieving measures. A durable health-care power usually is much broader, covering all health-care decisions. However, an individual can define the scope of a living will or health-care power as broadly or as narrowly as he chooses.

B.   **CREATION AND EXECUTION**
Living wills and durable health-care powers must be (i) in *writing*, (ii) *signed* by the testator or principal or another at his direction, and (iii) *witnessed* by two adults. The testator or principal must be an adult, and most states require that he be of sound mind.

1.   **Capacity Is Presumed**
An individual is presumed to have capacity to execute a living will or durable health-care power. Thus, if capacity is challenged, the burden of proof is on the challenger to show that the testator or principal lacked capacity or was unduly influenced.

C.   **REVOCATION**

1.   **Living Will**
A living will can be revoked by: (i) obliterating, burning, tearing, or destroying the will; (ii) a written revocation of the will; or (iii) an oral expression of intent to revoke the will. The majority of states allow a living will to be revoked at any time regardless of the individual's mental or physical condition.

   a.   **When Effective**
   The revocation is effective when communicated to the testator's primary physician.

2.   **Durable Health-Care Power**
Generally, a durable health-care power can be revoked by notifying either the agent or the principal's health-care provider, and the revocation can be either *oral* or *written*. Some states also allow revocation in the same manner as that for living wills, *supra*.

   a.   **Revocation of Prior Powers**
   Unless otherwise provided, the execution of a valid durable health-care power revokes any prior durable health-care powers.

   b.   **Former Spouse as Agent**
   The designation of a principal's spouse as his agent is *automatically revoked* if the marriage is annulled or dissolved. Some states also revoke the designation upon legal separation.

D.   **INDIVIDUALS ELIGIBLE TO ACT AS AGENT UNDER DURABLE HEALTH-CARE POWER**
A principal can appoint as agent anyone *except* an owner, operator, or employee of a health-care facility at which the principal is receiving care (and that individual may be an agent if she is related to the principal).

E. AUTHORITY OF AGENT UNDER DURABLE HEALTH-CARE POWER

The agent has the authority to make any health-care decisions on the principal's behalf that the principal could have made for himself while having capacity. The authority of the agent is within the discretion of the principal and must be stated in the instrument creating the durable health-care power. The agent must act in accordance with the principal's expressed instructions and wishes. If specific powers are not expressed or stated in the instrument creating the durable health-care power, the agent must act in the principal's *best interest*, as determined by the principal's personal values and by weighing the factors likely to be of importance to him.

1. Powers

Some of the powers that the agent has are: (i) the power to consent to or refuse any type of medical care; (ii) the power to admit or discharge the principal from a health-care facility; and (iii) the power to access the principal's medical records.

2. Agent's Liability

The agent is not subject to civil or criminal liability or to discipline for unprofessional conduct relating to health-care decisions provided she acted in *good faith*.